D0051166

A PLUME BOOK

WHAT EVERY AMERICAN SHOULD KNOW ABOUT THE MIDDLE EAST

MELISSA ROSSI is an award-winning journalist who has written articles for *Newsweek, National Geographic Traveler, Newsday, Esquire, George*, MSNBC, and the *New York Observer.* She has written extensively about Europe, Asia, and the Middle East and has lived abroad for many years.

WHAT EVERY ★ AMERICAN SHOULD KNOW ABOUT

THE MIDDLE EAST

Melissa Rossi

A PLUME BOOK

PLUME
Published by the Penguin Group
Penguin Group (USA) Inc., 375 Hudson Street, New York, New York 10014, U.S.A. • Penguin Group (Canada), 90 Eglinton Avenue East, Suite 700, Toronto, Ontario, Canada M4P 2Y3 (a division of Pearson Penguin Canada Inc.) • Penguin Books Ltd., 80 Strand, London WC2R 0RL, England • Penguin Ireland, 25 St. Stephen's Green, Dublin 2, Ireland (a division of Penguin Books Ltd.) • Penguin Group (Australia), 250 Camberwell Road, Camberwell, Victoria 3124, Australia (a division of Pearson Australia Group Pty. Ltd.) • Penguin Books India Pvt. Ltd., 11 Community Centre, Panchsheel Park, New Delhi – 110 017, India • Penguin Group (NZ), 67 Apollo Drive, Rosedale, North Shore 0632, New Zealand (a division of Pearson New Zealand Ltd.) • Penguin Books (South Africa) (Pty.) Ltd., 24 Sturdee Avenue, Rosebank, Johannesburg 2196, South Africa

Penguin Books Ltd., Registered Offices: 80 Strand, London WC2R 0RL, England

First published by Plume, a member of Penguin Group (USA) Inc.

℗ REGISTERED TRADEMARK—MARCA REGISTRADA

ISBN-13: 978-0-452-28959-8

Printed in the United States of America
Set in Helvetica

To the future tourism minister of Egypt,
Mohammed Yehia Zakaria, and
to the angel next door, Lorenzo Dell'Aiuto

Acknowledgments

This was the most difficult book I've ever written, and the most surprising: not only was the Middle East delightful in the months I traveled across it, but unexpected help came from all corners. A number of fabulous photographers in particular aided the cause immensely not only by sharing their gorgeous images, but by sharing their insights. I am forever indebted to Matthew Thistle, Fabien Dany, Eric Lafforgue, Andrew McLoughlin, Ahmad Al-Roomi, Hussain al Baluchi, Simon Chauvin, the Otrakji family, Jeremy and Bridget Palmer, the assorted photographers whose works are posted on Mideastimage.com, Muhammad Mahdi Karim, and Saudi Aramco, which donated amazing photos that had been shot for Saudi Aramco World. American ambassadors, including ambassadors Charles Stuart Kennedy and Andrew Killgore, were a wealth of information. I felt like I had spent a great deal of time with them and a host of other diplomats formerly posted in the Middle East after reading the interviews conducted by Charles Stuart Kennedy and Dayton Mak for the Association for Diplomatic Studies and Training. These "oral histories" are now posted on the Library of Congress site and they are gems. Journalists, authors, and other Middle East observers also provided invaluable information. Jean Sasson, author of *Princess*, not only provided great insight into Saudi Arabia, where she'd previously lived, she even called her contacts around the country to update me on the latest. Oliver Hargreave, Youssef Ibrahim, and Andrew Burke were fonts of insight. I was fortunate enough to meet journalist Pat Lancaster and democracy promoter Steve Pier when I was a monitor for elections in Oman—both were incredibly knowledgeable about Middle Eastern affairs, and I was honored that Abdalla Bashir of the Oman embassy arranged the trip. I could spend months hanging out talking about the Middle East with Yanal Abaza, and I'm still wowed by the kindness shown to me around every bend, particularly that of Mohammed Yehia Zakaria—who traveled across Egypt to get a camera to my photographer. As usual, my amazing editor, Emily Haynes, was my savior on numerous occasions, as was Nadia Kashper, and copy editor Ted Gachot was a true godsend. Plume's brightly guiding light, Cherise Fisher, and production editor Lavina Lee and production queen Norina Frabotta were also lifesavers. Utmost thanks, too, to sharp-eyed intern Heidi Blauvelt. Oliver Benjamin and Dave Nicolai were oh-so-helpful in the graphics department. My agent, Bill Gladstone, my family, Katherine Dunn, Gayle Newhouse, and Muriel Hastings got to hear more than their fair share of my rantings and ravings, and I'm amazed they didn't hang up the phone. And Steve Warner got me out of my darkest funks. The Egyptian Tourism Authority, the Jordanian Tourism Board, and Dubai's DTCM's Virginia Goff were extremely helpful, as were a number of hotels who ensured we had an incredible view into local happenings. Four Seasons Cairo and Four Seasons Damascus, Banyan Tree al-Areen in Bahrain, Qatar's Sharq Village, Park Hyatt Dubai, One&Only Royal Mirage, Fairmont Dubai, Ritz-Carlton in Doha and Sharm el-Sheikh, Syria's Beit al Mamlouka, Al Moudira in Luxor, and Movenpick's Royal Lotus Nile cruise liner were just a few places we stayed that knocked our socks off with their hospitality. Special thanks to Bryan Kresie, Dalia Nadim, Randy Shimabuku, Naram Omran, Leila Arbouz, Rhoda Adams, Katherine Kaczynska, Peter Collins, and Lauren Finocchiaro for all their help. To all, and so many more, I am deeply grateful.

Contents

----

x   Contents

WHAT EVERY AMERICAN
SHOULD KNOW ABOUT
THE MIDDLE EAST

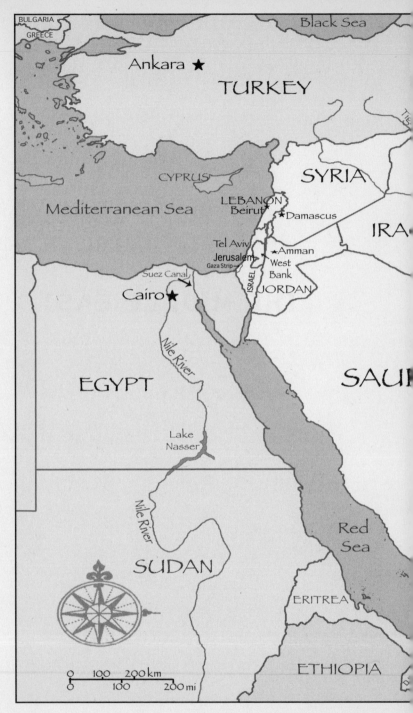

Despite all the attention given to the Middle East, nobody is quite sure exactly which countries it includes. For our purposes, the Middle East covers the land from Egypt to Iran, from Yemen to Syria. What's not obvious on maps is that there are actually two Middle Easts: the eastern half is rich in oil and

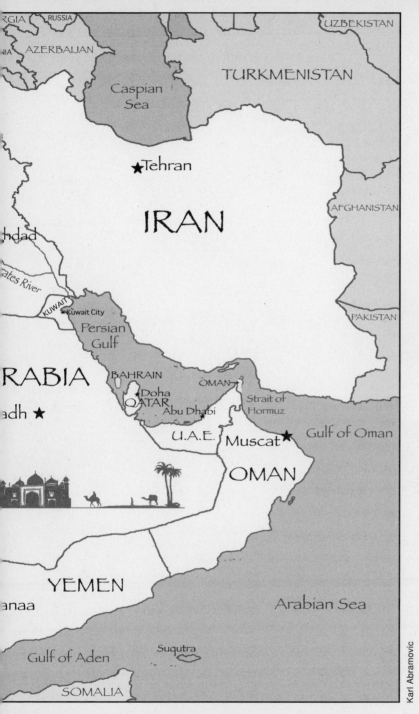

mostly ruled by monarchs. The western half is oil poor and obsessed with
Israel, by far the richest, and, lately, the most aggressive country in the
neighborhood.

Introduction

Last year, when I told American friends about my upcoming travels across the Middle East, the response was nearly universal: "Oh no." I was cautioned, warned, urged to take out more life insurance. Nobody mentioned, as they usually do, that they were jealous; not one person asked to come along, although a few asked if I would be wearing a burka.

But they clearly didn't understand the Middle East. They didn't understand that this land brimming with history and ancient architecture is also thick with culture and over-the-top luxury. They didn't know what I'd already learned on a previous visit: the Middle East, beyond being exotic and gorgeous, is always intellectually stimulating and often downright fun. It is utterly fascinating, from the call of the muezzin from slender minarets five times a day—a call I came to adore—to the souks where one can find everything from soft shawls to nuggets of frankincense. They didn't know about Arab hospitality. They didn't know about geological wonders like the wadis, dried up riverbeds among mountains, or the thrill of camping with bedouins in the desert. They didn't know about dining in Syrian courtyards or sailing on wooden dhows off Oman, where forts are chiseled into the cliffs. They didn't know the calm of cruising the Nile or the hopping nightlife of Dubai. They didn't know the sheer luxury of the hotels across the Gulf: the stunning sleepery designed like an old pearling village in Qatar, the double villas with a swimming pool canopy in Bahrain, the Cairo hotels filled with such priceless finery they felt like museums. They didn't know about the food, although they must have guessed after I left skinny and returned smiling and roly-poly.

That's one of the themes of this book: the Middle East isn't necessarily what we're told it is. It isn't a land of 132 million Osama bin Ladens; it's not traversed by camel much these days; and car bombs aren't blowing up around every bend. There are indeed a few parts you couldn't pay me to step into at the moment—Iraq being one, and the Gaza Strip another. In fact, during interviews about those places and while reading reports about them I often found myself crying—a lot. There were other places where I couldn't get in, such as Iran and Saudi Arabia. But every stop on the four-month tour was eye-opening, and the people I met were full of kindness and hospitality. I didn't have one frightening, or even dodgy, moment, although I left part of my stomach in the desert of the UAE after a dune ride the mere thought of which still makes me dizzy.

Granted, this isn't a tour book, and I'm not in the PR business. What I hope this book does is provide a context for better understanding the Middle East, what's great and what's not so great about it. As is my wont, when I find matters offensive, I don't sugarcoat them. When I find U.S. policy questionable, I question it. Most important, the Middle East poses some of the most divisive cultural and political questions of the day, and in researching and writing this book my point of view often fell on one or the other side of those divides.

U.S. foreign policy in the region is a particular sticking point for me. I'm upset that the U.S. economy is so dependent on the sale of arms. I think we need to get out of that business, which makes the world a more hazardous place. Weapons have become currency—they buy oil, they buy power, they buy votes. Heck, they even buy peace. The United States gives over three billion dollars a year, mostly in freebie arms, to support the Egyptian-Israeli peace treaty, a practice I find absurd and wish we would cease.

I'm appalled that the United States is so quick to go to war—a means that no longer seems to solve anything and that the Bush administration peddled with lies. I'm equally stunned that until recently the media didn't have the nerve to question it much. And I'm angry that American schools don't teach us about this region, about its history and social issues and the arms-for-oil wheels that spin there.

The former administration contributed greatly to the political quagmire in the Middle East, and a few of its members deserve mention. I have no respect for Dick Cheney. In the situations I found most objectionable or controversial—those points where I felt a wrong step had been taken—Dick Cheney was almost invariably there, often initiating that step. I believe he is the very face of the military-industrial complex that Eisenhower warned about five decades ago, and I think he and Donald Rumsfeld and George Bush have made the world a far more unstable and hateful place.

I'm disgusted by the neocons and the dangerous actions DC has taken at their behest. If I ruled the world, Paul Wolfowitz, Richard Perle, Douglas Feith, Michael Ledeen, and the rest of the bunch would be permanently barred from the political arena—even from advisory positions. Their words drip with deception, and I urge the incoming administration to keep the hands of them and their ilk out of government dealings.

I'm really sickened by DC's practice of painting two horns and a tail on countries it finds threatening. I'm appalled that the Bush administration had the nerve to wheel out its "axis of evil"—and that the American media and public didn't hurl that term right back at them. And I hope the incoming administration buries it and sticks a stake through its heart.

My anger and distress isn't directed simply at certain actors within and actions by the U.S. government. There are also a number of leaders in the Middle East that I find alarming. A few of them are thankfully out of the picture: the late PLO chairman Yasir Arafat, the departed Saddam Hussein, and the former Israeli prime minister Ariel Sharon, who has been in a coma for two years. I find Iran's President Ahmadinejad annoying—I just want to slap him—and Yemen's President Saleh alarmingly two-faced. Syria's government strikes me as a mafia ring, and Israel's current leadership is far too aggressive for my taste. There are some leaders I like—Qatar's Sheik Hamad, Oman's Sultan Qaboos, and Dubai's Sheik Mohammed among them—and I'd love to see Iran's Mohammad Khatami and Israel's Shimon Peres return to the presidential seat.

I don't agree with the recent cold-shoulder approach to diplomacy—it creates anger and hatred. I don't think any country or leader or militia that's acting up should be diplomatically isolated. The only way to muddle through the problems of the Middle East is to sit down at the table and talk. And you can be sure I'd be inviting Osama bin Laden, Hamas, Moqtada Sadr, and Hezbollah's Hassan Nasrallah to sit down at the table, just to figure out what is really on their minds.

The Middle East is more than politics and militia and oil and wars. There are so many topics that one may delve into and this is only one book.

I hope this book will help open up a whole new world and provide the insights needed to get beyond the stereotypes and the war images and to get a better handle on the real Middle East, a most mesmerizing and misunderstood place. The region is rapidly changing and I've tried to keep readers up to date with additions at chapter ends—called "Last Word."

I urge those who want to explore the unknown to take a trip here—even if it's armchair travel. Tourism to the region is booming—you can't open up a British magazine without finding articles raving about the place. Try it yourself, and you will see why. And you will also, like me, find yourself scratching your head wondering why this treasure chest of architecture, history, and culture doesn't match the world beamed to us from our TV screens. One warning: you may return home, not only with eyes wide open, but a bit roly-poly.

Chapter One

Misunderstanding the Middle East

The most ubiquitous symbol of the Middle East, where Islam was born, is the mosque, which can range from spartan domes in the desert to lavish affairs dripping with Swarovski crystals. Pictured here: a mosque in Jeddah, Saudi Arabia.

At the mere mention of the Middle East, a feeling of unease sets in as years' worth of mental newsreels start rolling: bombs dropping over Baghdad, smoke billowing from Lebanon, Israeli tanks shelling villages, Palestinian teens blowing themselves up, soaring oil prices, blackened shells of cars, a tumbling statue of Saddam Hussein, George W. Bush declaring victory over the same from an aircraft carrier, villagers dancing in celebration of 9/11, the long-bearded face of Osama bin Laden threatening to destroy the West, the even longer-bearded face of the Ayatollah Khomeini wagging his gnarled finger at the Great Satan—and horrifying us even further at his funeral procession, when his scantily clothed corpse slipped out from its casket. Along with the images, we mentally replay the headlines: more Americans dead from Iraq than from 9/11; dead Iraqi civilians number over 151,000;[1] Iran defies nuclear warnings; al Qaeda targets Saudi oil refineries; Hamas wins Palestinian elections; Hezbollah kidnaps Israeli soldiers; Israel invades Lebanon; Iran and Syria behind Iraqi insurgency, Bush claims; Israeli spy plane fires on Syrian mystery facility; sectarian violence rips Iraq apart; oil prices hit new highs—one hundred dollars a barrel; peace talks stall.

Few Americans may understand exactly what those headlines imply or what's behind them, and bewilderment only makes the situation appear more alarming. The Middle East is no longer just a region where the United States keeps snatching up oil, jumping into wars, buying friendships, propping up questionable regimes, and unleashing chaos: it's now a volatile state of mind, a panic-filled expression hurled by politicians and thundered from the pulpit: THE MIDDLE EAST! The anxiety-provoking buzzword is shorthand for militant Islam, crazed Arabs, WMD-seeking Iranians, overpriced oil, endless wars, oppression of women, suicide bombers, insurgents, and religious fanatics run amok. THE MIDDLE EAST! A land of nothing but terrorism, decapitations, flying limbs, hostages, and suicide bombers. THE MIDDLE EAST! A term now synonymous with *dismal* and *grave*, *powder keg* and *ticking time bomb*. The way American politicians and headline writers paint the picture (with a shockingly unimaginative vocabulary), you'd think the whole place is ready to blow any second and is held together only by divine providence and U.S. military intervention.

Given the image stamped in our brains by the American media, it's funny that you can travel the region—drinking in the dazzling pink stone city of Petra in Jordan, wandering through the souks of Aleppo in Syria, cruising past crumbling ruins on Egypt's famous Nile, sipping fine wines at chic bars in Dubai (the United Arab Emirates' answer to Las Vegas)—and never encounter a problem. Given all the bad press, it's interesting to find that you can float in the mineral-rich waters of the Dead Sea, feast on seafood along the blue waters of the Red Sea, or witness the late-night arrival of turtles laying eggs on Oman's coasts and feel total bliss. Strange how we hear so little about the education revolution under way, with universities like MIT and Georgetown starting up Middle Eastern branches in "carbonless villages" and "education cities," and how we've ignored the high-tech million-volume libraries opening in places like Alexandria, Egypt, and Doha, Qatar. Weird how Americans persist in thinking that all Middle Eastern women must be veiled and that we have entirely missed the recent changes that have given nearly all females the rights to drive and vote—not to mention the rise of women in high government offices. Odd how we imagine that travel is still predominantly by camel, in a region that is pushing the envelope in engineering know-how with dazzling mega-projects including colleges, hospitals, and experimental villages powered by solar energy, as well as designer island chains shaped like palms, oyster shells, and Arabic poems. How is it that we know almost nothing about the applause-worthy developments under way in the Middle East, where a new generation of young, progressive rulers is sitting down at the control board and revamping their lands by empowering women, giving grassroots businesses a hand, boosting literacy, and promoting economies that don't rely solely on oil? British magazines are brimming with articles about touring the region, but American publications mostly skip the ritzy luxury hotels that have opened from Bahrain to Israel and the deluxe new airlines that are taking off. We're not told how cities from Cairo to Damascus are abuzz with culture and vibrant nightlife: wine bars, chill-out lounges, chichi restaurants and glitzy fashion, luxurious spas and six-story malls, as well as the colleges, galleries, and museums that are popping up—even a branch of the Louvre.

These realities exist right alongside the ones displayed on our evening news. Hopefully, this book will enable Americans to begin to understand the region's many identities, conflicts, and agendas and to see that the Middle East is not all doom and gloom but in fact a vital and intriguing part of the world. Hopefully, this book will provide a more thorough understanding of the effects of U.S. foreign policy—particularly during the Bush years—and why so many in the region are now vociferously angry at the acts of the United States, and of how clueless Americans remain.

THE CLUELESS AMERICAN

Residents in the Middle East are bewildered by Americans' lack of understanding of the region—including that not all in the region are Arab and that many are not Muslim, or that there are two very different branches of Islam (Shia and Sunni) and that historically the two haven't gotten along. Americans often miss what DC's actions are doing—from creating refugees to churning up unrest that compels countries to acquire U.S.-made arms. DC has a hand in numerous pots, and many escape media scrutiny. A few to keep an eye on:

Resource wars wrapped in misleading packages: Since 1990, under the guise of taking down Saddam Hussein and battling terrorism, the United States has tremendously boosted its military presence in the Persian Gulf. Guarding oil transport routes with its string of new military bases, the United States has its eye not just on access to oil, but also on protecting access to natural gas. Iran happens to hold the second biggest reserves of both, and access to it is one possible bonus in any U.S. military action there.

The nuclearization of the Middle East: The fact that Israel has nukes has long made Middle East leaders nervous, but Iran's previous moves toward nuclear weapons has many regional leaders jumping head first into nuclear energy, even though their motives are peaceful of course. Who's pushing this move into nuclear: the United States and France, both making megabucks out of nuclear reactor sales.

A new cold war: Russia works behind the scenes in Iran and Syria, selling Iran commercial nuclear technology and missiles and reportedly setting up at least one military base in Syria, which it also arms. We may soon see a new cold war as Russia and the United States fight for dominance.

Assorted religious wars: Shia and Sunni Muslims are fighting in Iraq—the first time in centuries that these two branches have directly taken each other on in the name of religion. This is forging new alliances—Shia Iran, Syria, and

Hezbollah on the one hand, Shia-anxious Sunni countries such as Saudi Arabia, Egypt, and Jordan on the other. The two groups are also dangerously bristling in Lebanon. A second religious war is also afoot, although it's not billed as a religious war: Zionism and Christian Zionism versus Islam. Although battled under the name of fighting terrorism, most of the recent wars launched by Israel (and supported by DC) have also had the idea of territorial expansion woven through them—which some believe harks back to the idea of claiming all land that Jews believe was promised to them by God. Christian Zionists in the United States—some within the Bush administration—embrace this idea. Most believe that Israel must extend over all of its ancient kingdom for Christ to return. Most Christian Zionists want to see Israel extending over all of Palestine, for starters, and their beliefs appear to deeply sway DC's actions.

The portrayal of the Middle East as an endless battlefield of tanks, smoldering cities, masked militias, and self-exploding militants simply isn't the reality in most of the region. The scenes that are so disturbing to Westerners are just as disturbing to those who live in the Middle East, who see the same pictures on television in their apartments and suburban homes, who read the newspapers in their offices and hear the headlines when they're stuck in traffic jams—and the images portrayed may seem nearly as far away to them as they do to us. However, while most of the Middle East is peaceful, much of it gorgeous, and in many parts the quality of life is improving (by Western standards at least), it's certainly not a rosy picture through and through. As anyone with a pulse can point out, there are problems, big problems, particularly in certain countries, and they loom even larger since we can't understand them. The media, for all its efforts, often doesn't spell out what's really happening, treating events as if they unfolded in a vacuum and not seeing the cause-and-effect links in the chain.

VERY HOT SPOTS

Iraq: Though no fun when Saddam Hussein was dictator, at least then Iraq was stable, the electricity worked, people had homes and jobs, and car bombs weren't exploding right and left. Anticipating the U.S. invasion, Saddam set up a smashing welcome, inviting in Sunni extremists to make life hell for American forces. With Sunni radicals such as Abu Musab al-Zarqawi in Iraq and ready to fight,[2] the U.S. invasion of 2003 was never going to be the cakewalk that Ahmed Chalabi's group of dissidents—the fib-telling Iraqi National Congress—had promised. However, DC worsened the situation by firing Iraq's army, police, and government officials and trying to sell off Iraqi factories instead of repairing or reopening them. Those moves put millions out of work, who were then hired by militias. The United States delayed elections and appointed a puppet government loyal to Chalabi and other dissidents who'd

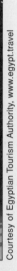

Courtesy of Egyptian Tourism Authority, www.egypt.travel

Courtesy of Dubai DTCM

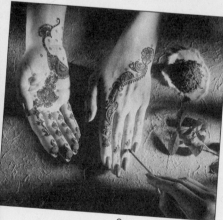

Courtesy of Dubai DTCM

The Middle East mixes tradition and modernity. Here (clockwise from top left) a falconer, Luxor tourists, henna hands, and luxury on the Red Sea in Jordan.

Courtesy of Jordanian Tourism Board, www.visitjordan.com

been out of the country for decades. When locals, including Shia cleric Mo-qtada Sadr, asked to be appointed, the United States denied the requests. Sidelined Sadr threatened to create a shadow government and unleashed his Mahdi Army—until then a do-gooder group. When the Shia Mahdi Army met up with Zarqawi's Sunni boys in 2004, all hell broke loose: religious gangs launched turf wars, shoving residents out of their homes and creating all-Sunni or all-Shia neighborhoods, while imposing Taliban-like rule—beheading barbers who shaved beards and chopping off the fingers of smokers. The government—top-heavy with former CIA informants—is still weak, electricity still falters, civil war still rages, gangs still control neighborhoods, but the United States is getting its oil, which was the main reason we went into Iraq in the first place, even though some in DC have the gall to deny it.[3]

Palestinian territories: Better known as the West Bank and Gaza, the territories are home to many of the Arabs (Palestinians) made homeless by the expansion of Israel as the result of several Arab-Israeli wars. The people are well educated, but their leaders are hopelessly inept. The local government, the Palestinian Authority, created after the 1993 Oslo Accords peace treaty with Israel, is notoriously corrupt—billions have disappeared. Often lacking electricity and running water—their availability is largely controlled by Israel—most Palestinians are broke and over one-third are unemployed. The increasingly lawless land of permanent refugee camps (now apartment high-rises) is a rich recruitment ground for militants and uprisings against Israelis, including suicide bombers. What we're missing in our view of the territories is that while Palestinians have been noted for their acts of violence, Israel also has been very aggressive. Palestinian areas have drastically shrunk as a result of Israeli settlers, highways, and walls—methods used by Israel to annex more Palestinian land. Israel now has Gaza entirely walled off, with sealed checkpoints and halted trade. Israel uses 95 percent of the water available to Palestinians, who aren't allowed to dig wells or build on Palestinian land,[4] and while Palestinian suicide bombers in Israel rate headlines, we don't get much news about Israel's frequent attacks, killing thousands of Palestinians in retaliation for the hundreds killed with suicide bombs. What's more, the United States demanded that free-and-fair elections be held in 2006, and when those elections brought the anti-Israel militia Hamas in to power, the United States and Israel shut them down (see below), which only added to the anger and sense of injustice already roiling there.

Lebanon: The gorgeous land of deeply folded wine country, where Christians, Sunni, and Shia share power, Lebanon fell apart in a bloody civil war from 1975 to 1990. Syria and Israel both stepped into the action and stayed put for decades. Syria used Lebanon as a money-cleaning machine and sucked from its economy, while Israel parked in southern Lebanon from 1982 to 2000, sucking its water.[5] Prime Minister Rafiq Hariri rebuilt the devastated country but was nudged out by the Syrian government, which is now widely accused of snuffing him out with a car bomb in 2005. The country erupted in the U.S.-backed Cedar Revolution and ran Syria's thugs and military out, but chaos now reigns. Dozens of leaders and media stars have been killed since 2005, and the weakly ruled country is floundering. Above all, it hasn't recovered from the 2006 U.S.-backed attack by Israel—prompted by the kidnapping of an Israeli soldier by Hezbollah—which aimed to take Shia militia Hezbollah down, but instead pounded the whole country, inflicting billions in damages and weakening the wimpy government further. Hezbollah meanwhile emerged barely scathed and with renewed popularity: it now unofficially rules the southern third of the country and is fighting for control of the capital, Beirut, threatening to launch a civil war. Foreign Sunni jihadists have entered the picture: some believe their arrival is part of a plan to diminish Hezbollah and Shia power, and that the United States is funding them.[6]

Yemen: Where did all the armed, trained, and pent-up Arab-Afghans who fought in the Soviet-Afghanistan War go when it ended in 1988? To one of the poorest, most gorgeous, lost-in-time countries of the world: Yemen. There they were welcomed and employed by the government to tame rebellions. Responsible for the 2000 attack on the USS *Cole*, the fervently Sunni, violent Arab-Afghans also spread the extremist values of Wahhabism (Salafism, see above) far and wide in Yemen and are gunning to take down Saudi Arabia's oil infrastructure. Saudi Arabia is hastily erecting a wall at the Saudi-Yemeni border.

American solutions in the region have been simplistic: bring in democracy, we say, ignoring the fact that the most organized parties are those of Islamists who don't want democracy; they want Islamic rule. We ravage entire countries to eject one man, to go after one group, and then seem surprised at the mayhem and rage that follows. Even though the trouble spots make frequent headlines, we all too often miss the big picture, the underlying dynamics and causes, the reality on the ground.

Take, for instance, Iraq. While Americans are now clear on the fact that the WMDs we charged in to yank out weren't actually there, and while most regard the war as a fiasco costing U.S. taxpayers more than one trillion dollars so far, it's harder to discern just how successful the operation was in achieving the Bush administration's apparent goals. The 2003 invasion rooted the United States in the Middle East, with permanent military bases in Iraq. The resulting instability has helped to sell billions of American arms across the Gulf. American reconstruction companies made multibillions from Iraqi funds handed out by the occupying U.S. government, and, even though U.S. companies bungled their jobs, Iraq can't get the money back since the United States gave those companies immunity. The United States illegally tried to sell off state-owned factories, and even though the Iraqi people are opposed and the U.S.-favoring national oil bill hasn't passed, American oil companies are still moving into the very fields

Wars have made refugees of millions in the Middle East—four million from the 2003 Iraq War alone. Homeless and unhappy, refugees may live for decades in camps, which are recruitment grounds for millitants.

Saddam had barred them from. This should come as little surprise, given that many leading Iraqi officials were dropped into power by the United States, were on the U.S. payroll for a decade, and continued to receive Uncle Sam's paychecks even after they were part of Iraq's government.

Just as you might never guess that the United States helped create the Iraqi insurgency by turning potential leaders into dangerous enemies by initially blocking them from the government and by causing mass unemployment—with the jobless joining the paying militias—what's also missing from the headlines is that the faux democracy the United States inflicted on Iraq instead created a theocracy where Islamist gangs control the streets and women are now for the first time forced to wear veils and told not to work, wear lipstick, or talk on the phone. Likewise often overlooked, indeed rarely even mentioned by President George W. Bush, are the four million homeless that his adventure in Iraq created.

REFUGEES

Refugees are an issue frequently overlooked in the United States, one might even say ignored. Surprising, since refugeeism is perhaps the biggest problem in the Middle East. Over eight million have lost their homes because of a war. Four million have been made homeless as a result of the 2003 Bush-led war on Iraq. Another four million or more Palestinians who lost their land during the Arab-Israeli wars have been living in camps for over forty years. Refugee camps typically start as tent camps and slowly become cheaply walled slums. They are breeding grounds for discontent: militants recruit in them, and militias hide in them. And they are often under attack: camps in Gaza and the West Bank are frequently bombed by Israel, and a refugee camp in Lebanon was the site of a summerlong urban war between a Sunni guerrilla group and the army in 2007. Beyond the problem of how to get people out of them—since they have no home to return to and are often restricted from getting jobs—the biggest question is how to stop creating situations that create millions of permanent refugees.

The acts of the Bush administration in the Middle East made only one thing quite clear: war isn't working as a means to fight terror. As illustrated in Iraq and Afghanistan as well as in Israel's 2006 war against Hezbollah in Lebanon (which the United States supported, armed, and helped plan), we can knock out a government and slam in a new flag, but we can't make it stick. Wars are fine testing grounds for new weapons and new strategies—they certainly give development companies such as Bechtel and Halliburton new projects—they create "free market economies" by using our armed forces to open up resources put out of our reach by foreign governments, even though such actions defy the idea of free markets. However, they wreak havoc on societies and set countries back billions for reconstruction. Yet they leave terrorists little harmed: bin Laden is still running about; the Taliban's back, inflicting Islamic rule along with warlords in Afghanistan; in Iraq, guerrillas have more power than the government; and Hezbollah emerged as apparent victor in Lebanon when, after a month of furious attacks, Israel couldn't diminish its strength. It should be obvious by now: these wars have simply created more violent enemies out of people who are ticked off that they have nowhere to live and furious at the civilian deaths that number into the hundreds of thousands and by some estimates well over a million. In fact, given that one of the defining parameters of terrorists is that they don't distinguish between military targets and civilians, it's hard to tell who is the terrorist anymore. The "collateral damage"—that is, civilian deaths—caused by the United States' war on terror numbers well into the hundreds of thousands, far more than the civilian deaths racked up by all known terrorist groups added together.

Our heartfelt desire to plant democracy throughout the region is an equally misguided and dangerous exercise: beyond creating phony democracies such as that in Iraq, the United States continually demands that Middle Eastern governments hold free elections. But as we've been shown repeatedly in recent years, the big winners in these elections are typically Islamists, who don't want democracy: they want to put an Islamic theocracy in place. When Hamas, an Islamist, anti-Israel militia infamous for its suicide bombers, won the 2006 parliamentary elections in the Palestinian territories—elections the Bush team insisted take place—DC shut the Hamas government down, freezing its money and backing its opponents,

Fatah, which suddenly looked preferable. Those actions very much gave the impression that democracy is only valid when the preferred party wins. The same thing happened in Egypt when the United States forced free-and-fair parliamentary elections there in 2005: the Islamist Muslim Brotherhood scored a major victory, with over 20 percent of the seats, even after the Egyptian military barred many voters in Muslim Brotherhood strongholds from getting to the polls. The Bush government didn't comment when the Egyptian government began rounding up thousands from the Muslim Brotherhood and throwing them into prison, holding many without charges, and then rewrote election laws to bar them from running.

> *Another irony: many of the Middle East's so-called republics, such as Egypt and Syria, where leaders are theoretically voted in, are actually dictatorships; while the most progressive governments are monarchies such as those in Qatar, the United Arab Emirates, Oman, and Jordan, where votes have nothing to do with the leadership. What's more, in the monarchies, the ruled can often meet face-to-face with the rulers and tell them what's on their mind.*

The Bush administration has lambasted Iran for its nuclear energy program, which the United States and Israel insist is a cover for making nuclear weapons, but what we're not told (besides the fact that Iran holds the world's second-largest supplies of oil and natural gas) is that the United States and France have been hard-peddling nuclear energy setups (sending in the secretary of energy to officially advise that nuclear is the correct choice) to most Middle Eastern countries, including countries that reportedly have pursued nuclear weapons programs in the past, such as Egypt and Saudi Arabia.[7] Bush lauded nuclear desalination as a nifty idea during his 2008 trip to the Mideast, although this is a land drenched in sun, making it ideal for solar desalination like that used in Australia. While the radioactive waste from nuclear energy isn't weapons-ready, it can provide the raw materials for nuclear arms and, at the very least, dirty bombs. What's more, nuclear reactors and waste storage areas are ideal targets for guerrillas, who frequently strike at power plants, and terrorists. But just like the arms deals that the United States keeps making in the Middle East (assuming that its friends won't lose power and the next regime won't use those weapons against us), the nuclear plants that the Bush administration blindly assumes will be safe in the Mideast carry hefty price tags and bolster the American (and French) economy.

> *Among those who have signed on for nuclear energy since 2007: Egypt, Saudi Arabia, Jordan, United Arab Emirates, Qatar, Algeria, Morocco, and Turkey. Israel is considering nuclear plants as well.*

Perhaps the biggest irony, however, is that while the United States lashes out at Iran's supposed nuclear weapons program—which a December 2007 U.S. intelligence report said was frozen in 2003—there is indeed a true nuclear threat in the region: Israel, which has hundreds of nuclear weapons on land and sea. Israel is the sole country in the Middle East to possess nuclear weapons. Ever since that fact became widely known in the 1970s, it's created a regional imbalance, and Israel does not want to see the playing field leveled out and other countries possessing nuclear arms.

"If there is a nuclear program in Israel, then we can blame nobody and no country if they want to acquire the same . . . this is an invitation to an arms race—a very, very serious and dangerous policy."
—Egyptian foreign minister Amre Mousa at a 1996 press conference[8]

AMERICA'S FIFTY-FIRST STATE?

The American alliance with Israel is a peculiar and delicate matter that until recently rarely received any scrutiny from the press. If one peers closely into this can of worms, questions arise, such as why Israel for decades has received the bulk of the foreign aid budget (over sixty billion dollars since 1975)? Is it because Israel is the most well-developed democracy in the Middle East? Is it because the United States and Israel are testing out new weapons in wars against Arabs, and are partners in missile shield defense? Does the strong bond with Israel reflect the weighty Israeli lobbies such as AIPAC, regarded as the second-most powerful working Congress (outside of the seniors group AARP)? Is it risky to have appointed so many neocons, who have deep bonds with Israel and have worked for Israeli prime ministers and parties, to the highest levels of the U.S. government? Why has the United States vetoed thirty-two United Nations resolutions concerning Israel, from calls for cease-fires to demands to return occupied territories? Why does the United States consistently support Israel's aggressive moves against its neighbors—be it Lebanon, Syria, or the Palestinian territories—while lambasting any of the neighbors' aggressive moves or words against Israel? Why does the United States try to negotiate Palestinian peace on behalf of Israel, when recently it appears that Israel simply wants that Palestinian land? And how have powerful evangelical Christians—specifically Christian Zionists who believe that Jews must occupy all of Palestine (by some definitions including Jordan and beyond) before Christ will return—influenced U.S. actions regarding Israel and the Middle East? Such questions are worthy of answers, though they aren't forthcoming, and even raising them, as renowned scholars John Mearsheimer and Stephen Walt did in their book *The Israel Lobby and U.S. Foreign Policy*, creates a furor.

Jimmy Carter, who negotiated the 1979 Israeli-Egyptian peace treaty, also caused a flap with his book *Palestine: Peace Not Apartheid*, which likened Israeli actions in the Palestinian territories to South Africa's apartheid, noting that Israel occupies "territory deep within the West Bank, and connects 200-or-so settlements . . . with a road, and then prohibits the Palestinians from using that road, or in many cases even crossing the road. This perpetrates even worse instances of apartness, or apartheid, than we witnessed in South Africa." To bring up these issues raises red flags of anti-Semitism, but the issue isn't treatment of Jews, it is U.S. relations with Israel—often called America's "fifty-first state"—and it needs to be aired for public debate, all the more since Israel now appears to be gunning to strike Iran—with U.S. support.

Each year for the past twenty, American taxpayers have handed at least $2 billion to Israel and $1.3 billion to Egypt mostly to buy U.S. arms or in the case of Israel to develop its own. Under the program, which started in 1979 as part of the Camp David Accords and the Israeli-Egyptian peace treaty that resulted, the United States has thus far shucked over $150 billion for war toys—and there's no end in sight. In fact, in 2007 the U.S. State Department announced that annual gift giving to Israel would be increased to around $3 billion a year[9] with Egypt's share close to $2 billion.

This is where we get into another area that often gets buried in the hysterical reportage on the Middle East. While most everyone knows that the United States depends on a few Middle Eastern countries (mostly Saudi Arabia, Kuwait, and Iraq) for oil, the United States also brokers deals for American companies that usually make up for the billions spent on petroleum. How? Through arms sales. To whom do we sell arms? These days, to pretty much everybody except to Syria as well as Iran, a steady customer a few decades ago. And between the war on terror, the war on Iraq, and a possible upcoming war on Iran, the U.S. government is peddling harder than ever.

A formidable forty-three billion dollars' worth of shiny U.S.-made arms went shooting toward the Arabian Peninsula between 1997 and 2004 alone.[10] In summer 2007, Secretary of State Condoleezza Rice and Defense Secretary Robert Gates drove the arms sleigh through the Gulf, handing out (and taking orders for) another thirty billion dollars plus more giveaways to Israel and Egypt. The reason that Gulf countries in particular needed to stock up, said Rice: Iran and Syria.

Since the 1991 Persian Gulf War, with added incentive since 2001 from the war on terror, the United States has been doing more than hawking billions upon billions in sophisticated weapons to these countries (arms, by the way, that many of the local armies don't know how to use). The Defense Department is also selling security by building up a whole slew of military bases, particularly on the Persian Gulf, known as the Arabian Gulf in most Arab countries. The necklace of Gulf bases stretches from Iraq and Kuwait through Bahrain and Qatar and into the UAE and Oman. Hundreds of thousands of U.S. military men are deployed there, a bigger presence than anywhere else in the world, including the United States. Just as the media isn't pointing out that the United States has moved in for geostrategic control of the Persian Gulf, our pundits have missed what appears to be an emerging turf war, which might be the beginnings of a new cold war. Russia is very much involved in the Middle East: Moscow is building Iran's nuclear plants and making ballistic missile deals with Iran as well as pushing for a natural gas cartel à la OPEC with Iran and Venezuela. Russia is also moving in as an arms supplier to Egypt and is reportedly building at least one naval base in Syria, on the Mediterranean, close to the Lebanese border, where the United States is also rumored to be building a base. The French too have gotten into the action, with a new base going in on the Gulf, off the United Arab Emirates (now a French nuclear energy customer). How this will all play out isn't yet clear, but given that the region is already overarmed, and too many warships are already plying Gulf waters, it adds to a sense of volatility even though outside Iraq the Persian Gulf has been peaceful for decades.

Our views on terror are also naive: we need to stop looking at militants and guerrillas as big bad bogeymen and see them as the gangs and mafia networks that they are. While many have religious goals—for example, building an Islamic empire—they use the same techniques as mafiosos: smuggling drugs and arms, protection rackets, money laundering, and, more recently, kidnapping are all the trademarks of these groups. Also, most are not united. We lump them all under the heading "terrorist" despite the feuding and rivalries between them as well as their own inherent flaws. Al Qaeda, which is hard-core Sunni, hates Shia militia Hezbollah, while Zarqawi, a Sunni who led the insurgency in Iraq, loathed Osama bin Laden, refusing to vow allegiance to him until 2004. One might wonder as well if al Qaeda's heads are dipping into the opium and heroin they are moving: Osama's right-hand man, Ayman al-Zawahiri, has released videotapes where he seems to be seriously on the nod. And despite the initial question after 9/11, "Why do they hate us?" (Bush's ludicrous answer was that they are jealous of our democracy), few listen to what the terrorists' beefs are. Lately, many of their complaints mirror those of nonmilitant residents of the Middle East, who have become furious at the United States—particularly the Bush administration—for their bombed-out backyards, the millions of refugees, and military bases that are popping up faster than mushrooms in a cow patch. Not that long ago, the U.S. government was often applauded or at least tolerated; now it can scarcely be mentioned without other terms like *arrogant, disruptive, bully,* and, often enough, *backing Israel.*

A FEW ISSUES WITH THE UNITED STATES

- The Iraq War was unjustified; it unleashed chaos and resulted in the killing of hundreds of thousands of innocent citizens.
- The United States is exploiting the Middle East's resources and using its military to pry them loose.
- The United States tortured prisoners in Abu Ghraib and unlawfully detains prisoners in Guantánamo Bay, allegedly torturing them there too; it also kidnaps suspects in CIA "renditions" and drops them off in countries such as Egypt, Jordan, and Syria for torture.
- The United States always backs and extensively arms Israel while ignoring the Palestinian problem and the way Israel is taking their land.
- The Pentagon is turning the Middle East into an extended U.S. military base and creating an arms race in the region.
- DC makes unfair accusations and actively cultivates an enemy list, applying double standards as it demonizes leaders, countries, and groups.

But before we get into all these gripes, before we look at the region's weighty problems or examine the Middle East's awe-inspiring history, before we point out what's great and what's screwy in the individual countries, and before we consider the dramatic and indelible effects that Americans (as well as Brits and French) have had on the region (including turning it into an overarmed fortress), it's best to begin with a basic framework for how to look at the Middle East and American interests in it. As mentioned, and explained in more detail later, there are actually two Middle Easts.

Middle East I, or the eastern branch, is the oil-rich region that sits near the Persian Gulf. Its countries, except Iran and Iraq, are ruled almost exclusively by royal families. Many younger rulers in the eastern branch are progressive and are modernizing and opening up their countries, giving new rights to citizens; yet the eastern branch also grapples with the role religion plays in its governments, and there are tensions between conservatives and reformers. This is the region where Shia-Sunni conflicts play out: most of the rulers are Sunni, and since 1979, when Ayatollah Khomeini created a Shia Islamic government in Iran, they've been worried about the rise of both the Shia and Iran—as was made evident in the Iran-Iraq War, which began in 1980 and ended eight years later with over a million dead. Perhaps more important, the region's riches make eastern-branch countries vulnerable to attacks, so they all have mighty arsenals and most have security agreements with the United States. What's more, they are magnets for criminal sorts, be they Russian mobsters or religious mafia like al Qaeda, which reportedly squeezes them financially to prevent attacks.

The other region, Middle East II, or the western branch, lies closer to the Mediterranean and is short on petroleum, tight on money, and slower on development. The only affluent exception is Israel, with whom they are obsessed and have all fought in three, and in some cases more, wars. The obsession stultifies their progress as well as trade in the region, draining resources into their militaries. It also produces powerful militant groups that have taking down Israel as their goal.

Arab-Israeli Wars and Treaties

1948: The local Arab welcome wagon greeted Israel with a war within twenty-four hours of the country's creation. Pushing back Egypt, Syria, Lebanon, and Iraq, victorious Israel, which started with 55 percent of Palestine, ended the war with 78 percent of it. The rest was taken by Jordan and Egypt. War dead: over 8,000.

1956: When Egyptian president Nasser nationalized the Suez Canal, Israel, Britain, and France attacked to get the canal back under British control. The United States shooed them away. War dead: 4,000.

1967: Believing that Arab countries would attack, Israel launched a preemptive strike, decimating Egypt's air force on the ground, for starters. At the war's end, six days later, Israel had taken all Palestinian land as well as claiming new lands in Egypt and Syria and taking Jerusalem as its new capital. Fighting continued sporadically for another three years. War dead: 75,000.

1973: Egypt and Syria, wanting their land back, launched a war on the Jewish holiday Yom Kippur. Israeli prime minister Golda Meir demanded (and got), pronto, a $2.2 billion arms delivery from the United States. This prompted Arab OPEC countries to shut off the oil pipeline to the United States. At the war's end, Israel held on to most territory, losing a sliver of what it occupied in Syria. War dead: over 16,000.

1975–89: Civil war in Lebanon. Syria (1975–2005) and Israel (1982–2000) swooped into the mess and wouldn't leave. The Israeli army drove out the PLO, which made frequent murderous raids into Israel. However, Israeli occupation of southern Lebanon created a new enemy: the Shia militia Hezbollah. War dead: over 131,000.

1979: Egyptians and Israelis signed peace treaty negotiated by President Jimmy Carter.

1987: First Palestinian uprising: when an Israeli military truck killed four Palestinians, riots erupted in the occupied territories. A former Islamic study group transformed into a militia, Hamas—the first to introduce suicide bombers into the picture—in 1993. Dead: 409—specifically 401 Palestinians and 8 Israelis.

1993: Oslo Accords signed between PLO and Israel: this created limited self-government in the Palestinian territories.

1994: Israeli-Jordanian peace treaty signed.

2000–present: The al-Aqsa intifada: When Israel's Likud candidate Ariel Sharon, escorted by a thousand guards, strolled around the the Dome of the Rock, a holy Islamic site in Jerusalem, it triggered another uprising, this one characterized by Palestinian suicide bombers exploding in Israel. Israel responded by building a security wall and erecting hundreds of checkpoints, closing off trade. Dead: over 6,000.

2006:   An Israeli invasion of Gaza, prompted by Hamas kidnapping an Israeli soldier, left hundreds dead. An Israeli invasion of Lebanon, after Iran-backed Hezbollah kidnapped two Israelis, killed over a thousand Lebanese civilians and devastated airports, electrical infrastructure, bridges, and homes, but Hezbollah was barely harmed.

Most Arab leaders in both the western and eastern branches are trying to mitigate the militias' desires to take down Israel by wheeling out peace proposals that call for Israel to pull back to the borders established after the War of 1948, when Israel held over three-quarters of the land that was originally meant to be divided almost equally with the Palestinians. These dreams, however, seem unlikely to manifest; in fact, since the intifada of 2000, Israel has used highways and walls to annex more land. The question is shifting from the basic right of Israel to exist to the right of Israel to expand.

Against this backdrop, the Bush war on Iraq in 2003, which uprooted millions, killed hundreds of thousands, and triggered civil war, unleashed even more problems, and more dislike of the United States, which has become self-appointed ruler of the region, manipulating governments with money and with threats, stonewalling some while boosting others. With American military bases and with American arms sales, with threats and cajoling, what the United States is doing is simple: protecting trade and trade routes. And the resource that is key, of course, is oil. Part of the equation that rarely emerges is that if the United States were entirely cut off from its oil imports, it wouldn't have enough oil to last three years.

With such matters in mind, let us proceed more deeply into the exotic, intriguing, and often baffling world called the Middle East.

Last Word

As of June 2008, all eyes are focused on Iran and Israel. The question is whether Israel will strike Iran's nuclear facilities while it still has the unflagging support of the outgoing Bush administration, which has promised to protect Israel should Iran attack—a promise that might not stick with the next DC administration. A flurry of negotiations is under way between Israel and Iran's allies: Israel is exchanging prisoners with Hezbollah in Lebanon, Egypt helped hammer out a truce between Israel and Hamas, and Israel is even talking with Syria. While we wholeheartedly support these diplomatic efforts, we're sure hoping that Israel (and the United States) take the same diplomatic tact with Tehran, and sidestep any need for attacking Iran.

CHEAT SHEET 1
Basic Concepts and Building Blocks

Hussain Al-Baluchi

The Middle East is often portrayed as a deeply complicated affair best left to the experts to understand and analyze. It's really not all that complex, but you need to hammer down some basic ideas and vocabulary. For those who feel clueless about who's who and what's what, here is the first of three "Cheat Sheets" that outline the key ideas, background concepts, and vocabulary that will appear in this book.

Trillions of U.S. tax dollars go to fight wars in the Middle East—over two trillion dollars for the Iraq War alone—hundreds of billions of American consumer dollars are spent on oil bought there, and billions of dollars' worth of Saudi riyals, Egyptian pounds, Emirati dirhams, and Bahraini dinars flow from the Middle East to buy American goods. Even though it is central to our lives, Americans are entirely baffled by this region, its countries, its people—and our misconceptions are vast and deeply embedded.

> *When looking at money spent by governments, particularly wealthy governments, a rule of thumb is that a government is serious when it's spending at least one billion dollars on a project or program. Millions may mean a lot to individuals, but when the United States gives a few million to a project, it's for show. When it's spending a billion or more, it's a priority. Biggest expense for the United States: military spending, which now consumes more of the federal budget than anything else, including Social Security.*

There are reasons why we are clueless about the Middle East. We don't study the region much in schools, even though it plays a major role in the global economy, and more American money goes there than anywhere else in the world. All major U.S. military action in the past two decades—and most of the minor action—has played out there. Even though humankind's most dramatic evolutionary leaps took place there, we often forget that civilization was born in the Middle East, as were the three major world religions, and that this region gave us many of our most commonly used items, from the wheel to advanced math to the measurement of time in days and hours.

> *Written language, numbers, banking, the calendar, irrigation, farming, organized trade, glass, astronomy, algebra, trigonometry, chemistry, cataract surgery, poetry, libraries, long-distance navigation, medicine, the compass, the Old Testament, the New Testament, the Koran, pyramids, oranges, and tulips are just a few things that grew out of this region.*

Media reports jump around, looking at one situation in one country—the nuclear-enrichment program in Iran, the refugees in Jordan, the Saudi rape victim who was sentenced to jail time, the latest fighting here and there—but not offering an understanding of the entire region or showing how much of it is peaceful and progressive and inspiring. Ten-billion-dollar education programs, million-volume libraries, women leaders, and new science universities just don't grab the headlines like suicide bombers and threats from bin Laden do. What's more, new vocabulary suddenly appears in everyday news reports. Strange names and terms—such as Mahdi Army, Kurd, *jihadi*, and sectarian violence—are suddenly bandied about, often without an explanation of what they mean.

GENERAL TERMS

Jihadi: A fighter in a religious war. This term is often used to describe the troublemakers in Iraq. Usually applied to Sunnis of the Salafi variety.

Mahdi Army: This is the Shia militia in Iraq headed by cleric Muqtada Sadr.

Kurd: An ethnic group in northern Iraq, Iran, Syria, and eastern Lebanon, the Kurds speak their own language, Kurdish, and are often Sunni. They descend from the Medes, an ancient people in what is now Iran, and they were promised their own country, Kurdistan, after World War I, but that promise was not fulfilled. Many still want it. The magi who came to Bethlehem long ago were Kurds.

Sectarian violence: This refers to conflicts between religious sects, whether Sunni Muslim versus Shia Muslim or Catholic versus Protestant.

Secular: Nonreligious. Egypt and Syria, for example, are secular governments theoretically uninfluenced by religion. The socialist Baath Party, once the only party in Iraq, is a secular party.

Baath: A socialist political party that supposedly ignores religion and emphasizes Arab nationalism. The government of Saddam Hussein's Iraq was Baath, as is the current government of Syria. Baathism has mostly become a hierarchical means of keeping a military dictatorship in place.

Islamist: A Muslim in favor of religious government; i.e., an Islamic theocracy.

Most Americans don't even understand what is meant by the term *neocon*. Though the names of "neoconservatives" in the Bush administration such as Paul Wolfowitz, Douglas Feith, and John Bolton are well known and now well sullied, the umbrella ideas that motivated these officials who are responsible for nearly every questionable U.S. act in the Middle East are not often explained. The neocons, in fact, have greatly contributed to our misunderstanding of the Middle East by manipulating the media—sometimes by helping to plant false stories—and pummeling us with inventions like the "axis of evil" that misguidedly frame the Middle East.

NEOCON GOALS

A bright but radical bunch, neoconservatives—many of whom were part of the militaristic and powerful Project for the New American Century—have several common goals:

- They want to establish the United States as world hegemon—from outer space to cyberspace—with wars in major arenas such as the Middle East.
- They want to revamp the military with high-tech weapons and fewer soldiers.
- They want to protect Israel—and many have previously worked for Israel and for the think tank the American Enterprise Institute.

- They do not like international forums like the UN.
- They do not like arms agreements.
- They believe it is fine if the United States is engaged in several wars simultaneously for the foreseeable future.
- They believe the United States has the right to make a first strike and take unilateral action. Many endorse the idea of a U.S. government that is mostly about war and collecting taxes to fund it.

Before getting into the misconceptions that plague us, let's first look at the neocons, this group of self-proclaimed intellectuals that has been so influential in the United States, and thus in the Middle East, and that in fact is responsible for some of those misperceptions. Neocon editorials in the pages of the *Wall Street Journal* and *New York Times*, their TV appearances on CNN and *Meet the Press*, their think tanks (such as the American Enterprise Institute), and their reports for groups such as the Project for the New American Century and the Middle East Forum laid out the blueprints for the actions taken by the Bush administration. The neocons took the United States into Iraq, wheeling out tall tales that dissident Ahmed Chalabi and his Iraqi National Congress spun about Saddam's weapons of mass destruction, which weren't there. The neocons linked Saddam to al Qaeda when no such link existed and made up stories about yellowcake bought in Africa. The neocons tried to take the United States into Iran. And they got the United States involved in Israel's controversial 2006 war against Lebanon and for over a month blocked the United Nations' daily calls for a cease-fire, while Israel did billions in damage and killed over a thousand civilians. A bad PR move, and one that turned the local militant group Hezbollah into heroes because the most formidable army in the Middle East couldn't root them out. The neocons came up with the black or white Bush doctrine: "Either you are with us or with the terrorists"—a heavy-handed ultimatum and another PR blunder.

Helped along by neocon branding and an often unquestioning media, Americans hold a number of major misconceptions about the Middle East.

Misconception 1:   "All residents of the Middle East are Arab." Two-thirds of the population of the Middle East is Arab, but as noted below the region is also home to millions of Persians, Kurds, Jews, Azeris, and Turks, for starters.

ETHNIC DIVISIONS IN THE MIDDLE EAST

The Middle East, as defined in chapter 1, holds about 250 million official citizens; over 10 million are foreign workers, most from India, Pakistan, Sri

Lanka, and the Philippines. Other Arab groups, such as most Palestinians and wandering tribes such as the bidun (distinct from the bedouins), are often officially stateless, so numbers get screwy. However, here are rough breakdowns and definitions of the major ethnicities.

Arab: About 170 million citizens of Middle East are grouped under the umbrella Arab, which, like the concept Middle East, is not well defined. Generally, a local who speaks Arabic is considered an Arab; historically, many Arabs originally descended from tribes in Yemen or the Arabian Peninsula. The biggest Arab population is in Egypt, which holds about 80 million. Most Arabs are Sunni Muslim; however, some are Shia, Druze, Ibadhi, or belong to other Islamic sects. Fourteen million or so are Christian: over 8 million Egyptian Arabs are Copts, for example. Some Arabs are Jewish: they typically live in or near Israel.

Persian: More than thirty-four million citizens of Middle Eastern countries are Persian, and most are in Iran, where they make up over half the population. Persians typically speak Farsi and are ethnically different from Arabs. While many are Muslim, they are typically Shia of the Twelver variety. Persian history is linked with Zoroastrianism, a monotheistic religion that involved fire worship, and Persian culture celebrates many Zoroastrian holidays.

Kurds: Approximately twenty million Kurds live in the Middle East: over five million in Iraq, about the same in Iran, and Kurds are also found in Syria, Lebanon, and the eastern part of Turkey. Ethnically close to Persians, but distinct, they have a strong individualistic identity. After World War I they were promised their own land, Kurdistan. Instead they got lumped into Iraq.

Jewish: Believed to be descendants of the twelve Hebrew tribes that lived in the area of today's Israel in prehistoric times. Most were run out in AD 135 by Romans.

Misconception 2: "All residents of the Middle East are Muslim." Millions of Christians (over fourteen million) and Jews (around six million) live in the Middle East. While the majority of people in the Middle East are Muslim, the religion is practiced in different ways, depending on the country, the sect, and the individual. Like Christianity, Islam is not one tight belief system: it includes variations that are even more striking than those in Christianity. Some are mystical; some are hard-core; some are very laid-back. Saudi Arabia, where the state religion is strict Wahhabism, is extremely religious: women can't go out without veils, and religious police push people toward the mosques five times a day. This, however, is an exception: in most of the Middle East the muezzin calls followers to pray five times a day, but many are not heading toward the mosque or dropping to the floor to pray. Friday is the holy day when many, although not all, stores and markets close and when many Muslims engage most devoutly in worship.

Misconception 3: "Most of the world's Muslims are found in the Middle East." Many of the world's one billion Muslims are found farther to the east; indeed, Indonesia, India, Pakistan, and Malaysia are where the bulk of Muslims reside.

RELIGIOUS DIVISIONS OF THE MIDDLE EAST

Islam: Born on the Arabian Peninsula, the monotheistic religion revealed to the prophet Mohammed in the seventh century is one of the most demanding of faiths. Muslims—the name applies to all who practice Islam, in any of its forms—are called to prayer five times a day, are required to fast during daylight hours during the holy month of Ramadan, must give at least 2.5 percent of their earnings to charity, and are asked to make at least one pilgrimage to Mecca in Saudi Arabia. Islam embraces many ideas held by Jews and Christians, and the Koran calls members of those faiths People of the Book.

Sunni Muslims: 150 million

Shia Muslims: 95 million

Druze Muslims: Less than one million

Ibadhi Muslims: 2 million

Christians: 14 million

Jews: 6 million

Misconception 4: "Women in the Middle East have to veil and cover up." The only country in the Middle East where a woman is forced to cover her face and wear a black cloak is Saudi Arabia, where the state religion, Wahhabism, is traditionally Sunni to the point of being repressive. In Iran, there's big pressure for women to wear head scarves and to slip the *abaya* cloak over their clothes. However, in no other Middle East countries are there religious police or are women forced to adopt Islamic dress; in some countries, such as Egypt and Syria, wearing traditional dress is discouraged and those who do are viewed as flipping off the secular governments. Husbands and brothers may push women to wear head scarves, and the Koran calls for modest dress. In most Middle East countries, however, there is a real mix of fashion: at the malls, which are popular, you can see women in Western attire—though some might add head scarves—as well as cloaked women and some covering their faces. One of the problems in war-torn areas, such as Iraq and Gaza, is that hard-core religious militias call the shots, and many of them are forcing extreme Islam—making women wear a veil and even forbidding modernities such as ice. However, the problem for many women, such as those in Saudi Arabia, isn't that they have to don veils, it is that women don't have many rights and that domestic abuse is common.

Misconception 5: "Women in the Middle East can't drive and can't vote." There is only one country where this is true: Saudi Arabia, the most restrictive country in the region. In the United Arab Emirates, neither women nor men can vote, although that may be changing.

Misconception 6: "Muslim men take four wives." This practice, originally meant to address a shortage of men (lost in wars) and to take care of widows, is falling out of practice: only the very wealthy can afford four wives. Many Middle Eastern women have a fit if their hubby takes a second wife, and some prenuptial agreements make it grounds for divorce, with the woman getting the real estate. In fact, a bigger problem is that many young men can't afford to take even one wife: in most countries the groom must have an apartment or house, give the bride-to-be lots of gold, and shower her family with riches—perhaps buying her father a car, for example. Unless they come from wealthy families, most young men can't afford it, so they live at home, trying to save up.

Camels made trade in the Middle East possible; now they're revered at the race tracks.

Misconception 7: "The Middle East needs the United States to keep peace." With the destruction, arms, military bases, and favoritism DC has recently brought to the region, this premise needs to be examined. Regional leaders such as Qatar's Sheik Hamad, Oman's Sultan Qaboos, Jordan's King Abdullah, Saudi King Abdullah, and Egypt's Hosni Mubarak have all been pushing a number of peace deals lately, some more successful than others. Perhaps it's time for the United States to back down from its role of international policeman, especially since under the Bush administration the United States appeared to be less impartial order-keeper and more lying crook.

Misconception 8: "The Middle East can be portrayed in blacks and whites." This is a region where there are tons of grays—social agencies that also have military arms, autocrats that serve their people, and elected officials who don't being just a few examples. There are few pure "goods" or pure "evils" around here, and when DC politicians paint them that way, be sure to cock an eyebrow, because it's rarely true.

GEOPOLITICAL CONSIDERATIONS

It's crucial to understand that until the twentieth century, when the British and French blew in making maps, the Middle East wasn't made up of countries. It was a bunch of territories, locally ruled by tribal chiefs, sheiks, sultans, and emirs (tribal princes). These tribes were often pulled together in umbrella empires and kingdoms and were forced to pay taxes and give food and goods to emperors, kings, and Islamic rulers (caliphs). As will be explained in upcoming chapters, the Persian Empire roped together much of the region starting in the sixth century BC, then came the Greek Empire (along with its offshoot, the Seleucid Empire), then the Roman Empire. In the seventh century AD, these lands were unified under Arabs in the Islamic Caliphate, which linked them with a new religion, Islam. The caliphate began fracturing around the tenth century, when assorted Islamic leaders ruled over various chunks, and the Mongols ultimately fractured it further when they disastrously took over part of it in the fourteenth century as part of the Mongol Empire.

The region was again lassoed into one empire under the sixteenth-century Ottomans, whose Islamic rulers were Turks based in today's Istanbul (Turkey), but as had always been the case, local rulers (as well as Ottoman administrators) called the shots locally. When the Ottoman Empire crumbled in 1919 as a result of World War I, the people living in the Middle East expected independence. Instead the British and French shoved in to officially carve up the former Ottoman Empire in 1920, finding several broad regions:

Greater Syria: This included land west of Iraq to the Mediterranean—today's Syria, Lebanon, and Palestine (which until 1920 included the land that is today's Jordan as well as Israel and the Palestinian territories).

Mesopotamia: Essentially the land that is today's Iraq, but broken into three "city states"—Basra, Baghdad, and Mosul.

Egypt: It was the closest thing to a country when it broke off from the Ottoman Empire in the early nineteenth century, and later annexed Sudan to its south, but it was for long centuries ruled directly and indirectly by foreigners, including the British, who ran it as a colony.

Persia: Not part of the Ottoman Empire, it extended north into territories around the Caspian Sea, west into Mesopotamia at points, and east into Afghanistan, but wars had shrunk it to what is essentially today's Iran.

Chapter Two

Jogging Through the Millennia

Andrew McLoughlin

The Middle East is thick with relics of ancient civilizations. These are found in San Simeon, Syria.

Maybe it was the meteorites that made this place special: more fall in the Middle East than anywhere outside the poles. Perhaps the chunks of asteroids ionized the land. Perhaps it was geography—as the land bridge between Asia, Africa, and Europe the region was destined to become a trading hot spot that attracted novel ideas. Maybe it was the richness of the soil or the frequent earthquakes or the fact that these cultures tinkered with magic: doctors and

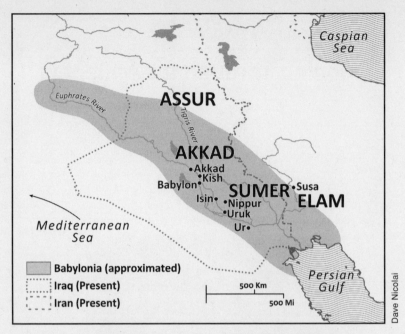

The settlements that sprang up between the Tigris and Euphrates rivers—in Sumer, Babylonia, and Assyria—beginning around 3500 BC, kicked off civilization with farming and the rise of cities complete with libraries, laws, calendars, and banks. Fond of math, they measured distances using the right-angle system usually credited to the Greek philosopher Pythagoras (sixth century BC) millennia before Pythagoras even learned to count. Circle-obsessed Sumerians living around 2500 BC gave us not only our sixty-minute hour, twenty-four-hour day, and twelve-month year[1] but also used the wheel.

exorcists were VIPs in ancient Middle Eastern civilizations. However you put the pieces together, whatever tools you use, whichever era you start in, and whatever chunk of land you look at, you can't escape the reality that the Middle East has always been a bizarre place. Whatever the reason—scorching heat, space dust, fault lines, or a potent genetic brew—something electrified the people, causing the region's civilizations to soar into new orbits. Humanity's biggest leaps occurred in this thick belt of land that stretches from the Mediterranean Sea to what today is India: water was directed to crops, farming took off, cities were born, the wheel began rolling, writing began, numbers were counted, bronze was concocted, glass was created, trade brought distant goods near, money traded hands, banks came into being, measures were standardized, distances were calculated, and legal codes penned—all in ancient times, over five thousand years ago.

DECIPHERING MESOPOTAMIA

Ancient Greece was long and mistakenly believed to be the birthplace of advanced civilization—where legal codes emerged, math was invented, and humanity fully evolved. The secrets held in the ground in Mesopotamia, buried in mounds and engraved into walls, changed that thinking. Nineteenth-century Europeans ventured to ancient Mesopotamian sites in search of artifacts for their museums, but what they found triggered a revolution in the way history was written. The layers of earth they sifted through revealed several highly developed civilizations, with mathematicians and writers who wanted their worlds to be remembered. These digs provided surprising insights into ancient minds and lifestyles: not only were these early humans well versed in geometry, but they also dabbled in chemistry and practiced medicine.

Sumer: Best known for its ziggurat-happy city Ur, and also famous for burial tombs and the walled city of Uruk where fifty thousand lived within four square miles, the kingdom of Sumer is widely regarded as the birthplace, not only of civilization, but also writing, irrigation, and the wheel. A major trade center, its cities were connected by canals, and each had its own god, ranging from the moon goddess to the lord of the ghost land.

Babylonia: This southern kingdom, most famous for the tiered Hanging Gardens of Babylon, was obsessed with stars and time. The Babylonians are believed to have invented the zodiac and to have used water clocks and calendars with seven-day weeks.

Assyria: The warriors of the north were brainy too. In the city of Nineveh, twenty-six thousand clay tablets were uncovered in the library of King Sennacherib (seventh century BC), which included early dictionaries, epic poems, and books on medicine "which give good, honest, practical prescriptions for every ill under the sun—from earache to childbirth and the restoration of the apparently drowned—showing a knowledge of some five hundred drugs . . ."[2]

THE POWER OF THE STYLUS

What were humans writing about five thousand years ago? The first scribes were accountants, bureaucrats, and royal publicists who pressed wedge-shaped cuneiform symbols into tablets of wet clay around 3400 BC to record land deals, rulers' decrees, and payments collected and due. Writers soon picked up the stylus to record riddles, poems, proverbs, and zesty tales; diarists pondered the meaning of life and lamented the behavior of youth, and the tablets also served as letters—sent in clay envelopes. *The*

Epic of Gilgamesh, a twelve-tablet lyrical poem about the bawdy, fantastical adventures of a third-millennium-BC king and his sidekick Enkidu, battling monsters and romping about the underworld, was a popular item found in early private libraries, along with spells and incantations, detailed weather reports, dream-symbol dictionaries, recipes for medicinal potions, and astrological forecasts. Thanks to the written word, rulers could also hammer down detailed legal codes: Babylonian king Hammurabi did so in 1760 BC, spelling out laws about marriage, inheritance, and interest rates on loans and even setting down minimum wages. Law 109 reads like an ancient USA Patriot Act: "If conspirators meet in the house of a tavern keeper, and these conspirators are not captured and delivered to the court, the tavern keeper shall be put to death."

Mesopotamia, however, wasn't alone in blazing new trails. Ancient Egyptians pulled off engineering miracles, from the creation of property-marking obelisks (they didn't wash away with the flooding Nile) to the building of pyramids. The question of exactly how they pulled off these feats continues to confound us. Their magical rites and burial rituals, such as mummification, still mystify today, while magicians and Egyptologists still whisper the message written in *The Emerald Tablet*: "As above, so below." Ancient Persians, living in what is now Iran, may have developed cities even before the Mesopotamians. They built intricate underground water tunnels used for irrigation, were the inventors of chess, and introduced gold coins and the world's first long-distance postal system.

Beyond inventions that spurred leaps in civilization, the early inhabitants of the Middle East were skilled in getting their fineries to the market. As cities swelled and local industries grew, traders hauled off the goods to international markets. A two-day sail from Mesopotamia, the islands of Bahrain were a major trade stop in the Persian Gulf, where copper from Oman, textiles from Persia, and glass from Mesopotamia were bought and sold. Around 3000 BC, trade exploded far beyond the Gulf, and boats, rafts, ships, and camel caravans began delivering goods to Africa, Europe, and the Far East. What powered that explosion was an aromatic found in southern Arabia, where winged serpents and monsters were said to hover about guarding its treasure.

Boswellia sacra, a squat tree found in today's Oman and Yemen, isn't much to look at it, but the milky sap it bears, which quickly hardens into nuggets of frankincense, triggered a revolution about five thousand years ago.[3] Used in every rite from marriage to mummification, its white smoke was believed to be the wings that delivered prayers to heaven, its blackened ashes used as eye-lining kohl, its essence blended in holy waters by Moses, its scent captured in perfumes concocted for kings, and its value so priceless that it made the perfect gift for certain special babies wrapped in swaddling clothes. Frankincense was so adored by

The frankincense tree brought riches to southern Arabia and launched a trade revolution.

the ancients that the crystallized resin did far more than bestow magnificent wealth upon those who prepared it: the price fetched for this aromatic inspired early traders to create a distribution network as complex as FedEx's. Frankincense and myrrh, which is also found in the monsoon-soaked southern lands, were hauled by camel caravans across Arabia's barren empty quarter by numbers of traders so vast they seemed to the ancient Greek geographer Strabo to be an army crossing the sands. They trekked for two months, each trip involving sixty-five stops, to get to Gaza, where boats laden with the aromatics sailed off to Mediterranean ports and beyond. Frankincense was traded for spices, gems, and fabrics in today's India and beyond. Across southern Arabia and along the

Mediterranean coast, trade towns sprang up, complete with camel hotels, or caravansaries, to accommodate the swelling number of traders.

THE PHOENICIANS

The Phoenicians' Greek-given name means "purple," and was bestowed for the brilliant dyes they extracted from a mollusk gland. The amazing Phoenicians, who around the fifth century BC lived in settlements around the Mediterranean (most on what is today Lebanon's coast), were whizzes at more than creating colors that made their textiles hot sellers. Skilled navigators, they stand out for the distances they traveled to get goods to market: the entire Mediterranean was a pond for these guys, who for centuries monopolized most Middle Eastern trade, including frankincense and myrrh. They regularly showed up in Portugal (like the Lebanese, some Portuguese say they're descendants) and are believed to have sailed to the Far East to trade for spices and gems and to England to buy tin. But even that feat wasn't what made the Phoenicians most memorable: it was the alphabet they devised and taught to those along their trade routes, leaving trade partners with written materials in the form of receipts, orders, and bills. The stick letters they introduced to the world became the basis for Hebrew, Latin, and Greek. But while they gave the gift of written memory to the masses, the progressive Phoenicians left few clues about themselves: they scrawled their history and insights on papyrus, which crumbled with time.

As the network expanded, so did the variety of goods hauled along the Frankincense Trail, a route used by far more traders (carrying goods that yielded far more money) than even the well-trodden Silk Road that connected Syria with China. Skin bags were stuffed with gold powder, cinnamon, ivory, ambergris, textiles, and pearls; boats heaved with brightly colored wool, pepper, rubies, sapphires, coffee, and alabaster. But the commodity with a price more dear than today's caviar, oil, or gold was frankincense, and its popularity held up for millennia: it's still used today in some of the world's priciest perfumes.

THE MYSTERIOUS NABATEANS

Their story still hasn't been told, and the Nabateans apparently wanted it that way. This shadowy tribe, which dominated trade beginning around the fourth century BC, dealt in luxury goods and slaves as well as prostitution services. Notorious tellers of tall tales, this paranoid bunch often disguised themselves, hid water supplies on their routes to avoid talking to locals, and apparently refused to write anything down out of fear that their secrets would be uncovered. They even went so far as to hide their cities. Pink-stone Petra is deeply carved into the sides of a tucked-away canyon, visible only when one stumbles around a bend and comes directly upon it. Although its existence was rumored, moderns didn't lay eyes on the stone city until 1812. Since then, the city of the mysterious salesmen has starred as a movie setting and in 2007 was voted one of the New Seven Wonders of the World. Yet Petra has yielded little insight into the lost history of its creators.

The reason why the incense trade went up in smoke remains hazy: whether due to the collapsing Roman Empire or raiding Persians who destroyed the resin-bearing trees, the incense market and network it had created dried up by the fifth century AD. As a result, until the advent of Islam in the seventh century, there wasn't much reason to cross the desert—unless, of course, unseen voices compelled one to do so. More than a world of markets, math, astronomy, and engineering breakthroughs such as irrigation canals and ancient dams,

Courtesy of Jordan Tourism Board

Petra, an ancient city carved into a pink sandstone gorge in Jordan, is one of the Middle East's many touristic draws. It was also a hideaway for the Nabateans.

the Middle East was a land of magic and amulets, visions and astrology, a world where a plethora of deities was worshipped and hearing voices was apparently rather common. And it was there that the gods turned singular and monotheism was born. The first to hear the "one God" call was Abraham, or Abram as he was known until his self-inflicted circumcision, a resident of Mesopotamia who had a gorgeous wife, a good heart, and a burning desire to breed.

MYSTERIOUS ABRAHAM: FATHER OF THREE RELIGIONS

For a guy considered the patriarch of over half the world's population—being an ancestor of the Jews, Christians, and Muslims alike—Abraham is sure hard to pin down. Historians and archaeologists have tried to find a record of the man, but their search thus far ends with a shrug. And that is appropriate, perhaps, since the story of Abraham/Abram is really all about faith. Abram, the biblical story goes, started out a typical third-millennium-BC guy from Ur: he got married, settled down, and wanted kids. Years later, Abram and his missus, Sarai, were still childless. Saddened, Abram hears a promising voice: that of God, who introduces himself as Yahweh. If Abram sticks by him and is faithful, Yahweh promises to "make thy seed as the dust of the earth so that if a man can number the dust of the earth, then shall thy seed also be numbered." Encouraged, Abram makes a vow to honor and follow one God, Yahweh, who promises further that "thou shalt be a father of many nations . . . And I will establish my covenant between me and thee and thy seed after thee in their generations for an everlasting covenant."[4]

Yahweh puts Abram through numerous tests to prove that his faith is real. Problems start almost immediately: Abram's "one God" speeches, and his tendency to smash displays of idols, get him run out of Ur. With Sarai and nephew Lot, he heads to the Mediterranean coast and jumps through Yahweh's hoops. Abram thought he'd found the correct land and erected an altar there—but no kids. He moved elsewhere, constructed another altar. No kids. He endured famine, moving to Egypt with the clan, where Sarai was plucked by the pharaoh for his harem; she didn't produce any baby pharaohs either. Yahweh inflicted plagues on the pharaoh, and they all escaped back to the north, where Abram tried to save the lewd and libidinous inhabitants of Sodom and Gomorrah from Yahweh's wrath, but only Lot (who'd moved there) was righteous enough to be rescued. And still, despite Abram's altar building and sacrificing left and right, no kids. Turns out Sarai's infertile; feeling guilty, she hands over her Egyptian maid, Hagar, to be Abram's "wife." He finally gets his long-prayed-for kid, Ishmael. But Yahweh informs Abram that this wasn't the kid he was talking about that would produce a nation. Barren Sarai is so jealous that she kicks out Hagar and Ishmael, shooing them off into the desert with but a jug of water and loaf of bread. But as soon as the water runs out, an angel shows Hagar where there's a fresh spring of water, a moment now ritualized in the annual Muslim pilgrimage to Mecca.

Yahweh dangles another carrot: if Abram will undergo circumcision, and promise that his descendants will too, then Yahweh will accept the role as Abram's creator and find him better land. Oh, and Sarai will get pregnant (even though according to modern scholars Sarai is already about ninety years old). Abram (himself a sprightly ninety-nine or so) agrees and, postcircumcision, becomes Abraham; Sarai become Sarah and, against all odds, she conceives, bearing Isaac. But then Yahweh tells Abraham to kill Isaac. Abraham trudges up a mountain with Isaac, who keeps asking why they aren't bringing an animal to sacrifice. Atop the mountain—believed to be the Temple Mount in Jerusalem—Isaac discovers that *he* is to be the sacrificial lamb, but in the nick of time an angel prevents the sacrifice, showing up with a ram. Some religious scholars have questioned the accuracy of this test of faith, pointing out that Abraham would have been over 125 years old, and Isaac at least 25, and that Isaac probably would have put up quite a fight—though it sure seems a little late to start questioning a story that has been out of the ordinary from the start. It remains a foundation of three major world religions: Judaism, Christianity, and Islam.

The point of the tale is this: Abraham's chosen son, Isaac, who has twin sons, Jacob and Esau, is considered father of the Jews, who because of the vow Abraham made consider themselves the chosen people. Christians consider him crucial to their story as well, since Jesus was a Jew. Meanwhile, Ishmael produced the other major branch in the Holy Land: the Arabs. According to the Koran, Ishmael was father, not only of the Arabs, but of Mohammed, which is to say, father of the Muslims as well. So in fact, Yahweh came through on his promises about Abraham's seed, and between Jews, Christians, and Muslims, Abraham is ancestor to about 3.4 billion (see p. 316).

Abraham wasn't the only one hearing voices, nor was he alone in spreading the word on monotheism. Zoroaster, a Persian prophet, poet, seer, sage, magi, and miracle worker living around the sixth century BC,[5] also tuned into the same "one God" message. In Zoroaster's religion, Zoroastrianism, God's name is Ahura Mazda; creator of the universe, he represents truth, order, and light in a world where humans must battle lies, chaos, and darkness. Zoroaster and his followers worshipped at fire temples—established at gas seeps over petroleum deposits—where the eternal flames prompted ecstasy, visions, and philosophical discussion as well as also providing outdoor heating and a place for barbecues.[6] Around 559 BC, young King Cyrus II fell under his sway and, legend has it, linked arms with the holy man to forge the Persian Empire,[7] the ancient world's first superpower.

CYRUS THE GREAT

Cyrus took his Zoroastrianism seriously, particularly its calls for a just leader. As he set out on his empire-creating campaign, taking village by village, city-state by city-state, kingdom by kingdom, Cyrus was remarkably kind to the vanquished inhabitants, giving them the right to move elsewhere, according to Herodotus, the Greek historian who rode along as frontline reporter for much of the campaign. In Babylon, when ruler Nebuchadnezzar was tricked out of town, the townspeople welcomed Cyrus right in as their new leader, and his enlightened behavior resulted in long-lasting good press. He freed all slaves, including captured Jews, who hated Babylon and most of all its leader because he had destroyed not only Jerusalem but their temple there. Returning the riches stolen by Nebuchadnezzar, Cyrus gave them his own gold and instructed the Jews to return to Jerusalem and to build another house for their God. (See p. 39.)

By 530 BC, when Cyrus died in battle, the Persian Empire stretched from Turkey to India. His son-in-law, Darius, expanded the empire further, constructing a two-thousand-mile highway system still used today, setting up a sophisticated postal system manned by spies, and building spectacular cities such as Persepolis. He also inadvertently invited the Greeks to stomp into these parts.

Visionary in many ways, Darius took the reins in an era when subjects were rebelling from Egypt to Mesopotamia, and he didn't tolerate plots to overthrow him. When spies informed him that Greeks living in Persia were planning a rebellion, he went after not only the Greeks in his land but also the Greek isles. By 513, wars and battles between Persia and Greece were going full steam—Herodotus's *Histories* captures but a fraction in thirteen volumes—and the fighting raged off and on for nearly two centuries. Finally, Macedonian king Philip II pushed in as uninvited leader of Greece, consolidating support from rivalrous Greek city-states with the promise that together they could take back land lost to Persia. Philip's "take back the land" campaign was going quite well, until he was assassinated. His twenty-year-old son, Alexander, soon to be known as Alexander the Great (356–323 BC), continued the battle. And that's how Greeks ended up running Egypt, Mesopotamia, Syria, and Persia. And that's also, indirectly, how North Africa became a magnet for the world's accumulated knowledge and the empire's finest minds. The first European to stomp so far east, Alexander rearranged the region for centuries to come.

ALEXANDER THE GREAT: MIXING UP THE MIDDLE EAST

Perhaps it was his tutelage under Aristotle, or maybe it was sheer bravery, but young Alexander never once lost a campaign—and he conducted many of them, from Hungary to Pakistan. Nobody did more for expanding Hellenism than the king, and nobody destroyed more great cities. He so ravaged stunning Persepolis that all that remained were denuded columns. In avenging the death of his father, which he blamed on the Persians, Alexander had three strengths: strategy, military skill, and an odd sort of diplomacy. He tried to marry Greek culture with those of his conquered lands, for example, taking a Persian wife after conquering the empire and instructing his ten thousand soldiers to do the same. He didn't live long enough to grab all the lands on his "to take" list, among them Arabia and Europe. Forewarned by a fortune-teller not to enter Babylon, Alexander for once ignored the advice, and no doubt died regretting it: indeed, Nebuchadnezzar's Babylon palace was the last place he laid his head, having grown ill after chugging a huge flask of wine. Some said the wine had been poisoned with toxins smuggled in via a mule's hoof; others theorized that it set off a fatal bout of the malaria he'd picked up a few years before. Alexander bequeathed his vast empire to his generals (actually, several just seized the land). By his death it included Egypt and Persia, and weaved together so many cultures that the lands he conquered continued to be not only prosperous but also hotbeds of intellectual pursuits. Not the least of which was Alexandria, soon to be a repository of world wisdom.

Alexander left his most profound mark in Egypt. Embraced as liberator for chasing out the hated Persians, before sailing off, he drew the blueprint for a new town in the north, Alexandria. Leaving his general Ptolemy I to oversee the rise of the new city, Alexander himself never set foot in it again while alive. But return to Egypt Alexander did. Upon word of the warrior's death, in 323 BC, Ptolemy sailed to Babylon and kidnapped the royal corpse, bringing it back to Alexandria, where it laid for centuries in a handsome gold sarcophagus. Ptolemy did this to reinforce the idea among Egyptians that the man they welcomed was still among them, while he figured out how to gracefully take his place.

> Lands claimed by Alexander the Great stayed in the hands of Greek generals: Ptolemy claimed Egypt and Seleucus I Nicator laid claim to Persia, setting up a rivalry between the kingdoms that would last for centuries.

To ensure that he, a Greek, would be accepted in the land that hated foreigners, Ptolemy I (who ruled Egypt from 323 to 283 BC) murdered Alexandria's governor and stepped up to the plate, promising to return greatness to Egypt, which in fact he did: bringing in new business, developing trade, and inviting in wealthy and influential foreigners. To guarantee his acceptance, however, he consulted with Egyptian priests and started his own religious cult, "discovering" a new Egyptian god: kindly Serapis, the healer. When the famous Greek statesman Demetrius of

Phalerum moved to Egypt, news swept the land that he had suddenly gone blind. Days later, fresh news spread: Demetrius had been cured after visiting the temple of Serapis,[8] which quickly became one of Alexandria's most popular.

PR stunts aside, Ptolemy I adopted Egyptian fashion and made Alexandria Egypt's most cosmopolitan city. Palaces shot up alongside temples, theaters, mausoleums, and sprawling markets, and to lure more ships to its shores he erected the lighthouse of Pharos, in which a huge flame blazed, its brightness amplified by reflecting glass. He also built a library complex including a well-endowed museum filled with temples, gardens, a zoo, study halls, courtyards, housing for visiting scholars, and the library, where hundreds of scholars pored over scrolls from across Europe and Asia.

With Demetrius as head librarian, the library at Alexandria was more like an academy: the era's brainiest thinkers—the mathematician Euclid, the poet Apollonius, Archimedes (who proposed that the world was heliocentric), and circumference-calculating Eratosthenes—held court among the columns, reconceptualizing the framework of the universe and the best ways to measure it. Egyptian scholars as well joined in on the debates, and the city drew Phoenicians, Jews, Indians, and Syrians with its flowering intellectualism. The library's collection kept growing: Ptolemy requested that all rulers of the world loan their most important books to the library, where copyists duplicated them. Foreign rulers often discovered that the originals had been kept and copies returned, and they didn't always read like the originals: the library's copyists had a habit of editing even the works of the most famous Greek scribes. To keep the collection up to date, Ptolemy required that all vessels in Alexandria's busy port be searched for reading materials and any of interest copied, usually, before the vessel set back out.

Forever competing with his former colleague General Seleucus, now ruling Persia, Ptolemy was enraged to discover that Seleucus was setting up libraries there. To thwart Seleucus, Ptolemy prohibited sales of papyrus, parchment, and all writing materials to Persia, and since Egypt was the leading papyrus producer, the embargo hurt. Nevertheless, Persia managed to build up its libraries by buying papyrus through intermediaries. The Egyptian king was likewise distressed to learn that Seleucus had war elephants in his arsenal, having inherited those captured by Alexander during battles in India. Determined to integrate them into his army, Ptolemy demanded that his advisers find some; alas, they informed him, elephants resided deep in the south. Ptolemy was so insistent that the pachyderms were indeed shipped up, although doing so required the construction of numerous Red Sea ports along the way, and the elephants didn't arrive for years. Even then, they were disappointing: African elephants, while bigger, are shier than their Indian counterparts, and when finally used in battle, most fled from their Asian cousins.

But it wasn't the library or the war elephants, or Eratosthenes' incredibly close calculation of the circumference of the earth (his calculations were off by only three hundred miles) that made the rule of the Ptolemies memorable for the rest of time. It was Ptolemy's great-great-great-great-great- (or so) granddaughter, Cleopatra, who ensured the era would not be forgotten. Known for her international dalliances, Cleopatra presided over the country during two of Egypt's darkest moments: first the Great Fire of 48 BC, which spread through the city after Julius Caesar set the Egyptian fleet ablaze (he claimed it was an accident) and sent many of the library's seven hundred thousand scrolls up in smoke; then, worse, Cleopatra brought about the end of the Ptolemies' rule.

THE BABE OF THE NILE

Cleopatra (69–30 BC), the last of Alexandria's pharaohs, had a zesty social life. Married to her brother (her rival), she got rid of him (suspected of having him snuffed out) when Roman general (later emperor) Julius Caesar visited her city in 48 BC. Caesar was impressed with Alexandrian hospitality: he was welcomed with a beautiful rolled carpet, with nineteen-year-old Cleopatra inside. The two traveled the Nile for months, and before long the pharaoh was pregnant with the Caesar's child. Cleopatra then married her younger brother while continuing her fling with Caesar until he was murdered in 44 BC. The seductress then honed in on his successor, Mark Antony (part of Rome's ruling triumvirate), who handed her Crete, Cyprus, and Palestine as gifts; he also gave her a collection of two hundred thousand scrolls from a library he'd emptied just for her. It wasn't simply generosity on his part or the fact that she'd borne him twins: Cleopatra was financially backing his battles for power in Rome, and a number of his campaigns, including his attempt to grab Persia, proved disastrous. In 33 BC, while visiting Alexandria, he did the unthinkable: Antony named his son and Cleopatra his successors in Rome and began handing his children the lands he'd won. His Roman coruler Octavian launched a smear campaign against Antony, and the triumvirate fell apart, resulting in civil war. Octavian's forces, after beating Antony's at sea, further humiliated him by winning a brief battle at Alexandria. The shamed Roman killed himself, and Octavian declared war on Cleopatra. Upon winning, he threatened her with death. Rather than chance whatever method he would devise, Cleopatra came up with her own and died from the poison of an asp bite, as befitted the seductress who had a toxic effect.

Octavian's victory in 30 BC ended the Greek Empire. Egypt, Syria, and Palestine fell to the powerful Romans. Persia, however, lay forever out of their grasp, and the Romans' attempt to conquer Arabia turned into a desert fiasco. In fact, the Roman Empire's Middle Eastern holdings proved their most difficult, particularly the land that stretched out to the north of Egypt—an already holy land that was about to turn holier than ever. Sometime around 3 BC, the stars augured such a major occurrence that three Zoroastrian magi set out from Persia to investigate, stopping for presents of frankincense and myrrh on the way.

JESUS THE RADICAL JEW

The teachings of Jesus to follow the tenets set down by God created a new monotheistic religion: Christianity. Jesus apparently didn't intend to start a religion, but his beliefs were found threatening to so many Jews that he was no longer embraced by Judaism. His followers spread his word after his death, but it got its biggest boost from a fourth-century Roman emperor, Constantine.

The crucifixion of Jesus of Nazareth only led to more civil unrest and mayhem, posing continuous threat to the Romans' rule, which had always been rocky at best. Jews didn't want the Romans occupying the land that had once been ruled by the Jews. Christians now loathed the Romans who'd killed their savior. Radical groups formed; one of the era's first terrorist groups, the Zealots, violently ousted the Romans in AD 66. The Romans were back four years later and spent the rest of that century trying to squelch dissent, which never died down. Attempts by the emperor Hadrian, starting in 130, to erect a shrine to Jupiter in the place where their beloved First Temple once stood so outraged the Jews that they rebelled in 132, managing to run the Romans out. Three years later, the Romans were back and ran out the Jews. Violence continued for the next two centuries, until the Roman emperor Constantine had a vision that would have repercussions for the entire empire. While preparing for battle in AD 312, he looked up at the night sky and saw a cross.

The vision so deeply moved Constantine that he proclaimed Christianity as the official religion of the Roman Empire, pushing subjects in Roman-held lands to convert. His mother acceded to the request and while in Jerusalem founded the Church of the Holy Sepulchre near the site where Jesus was crucified.

In AD 330, the Roman Empire split: the western part remained Rome-dominated, but the eastern branch became the Byzantine Empire, and the grand city of Constantinople (Istanbul in today's Turkey) lay at its center.

It was the queen of cities, the richest in Christendom, filled with palaces, markets, zoos, and the most beautiful churches, including the mosaic-thick, silver-rich Hagia Sophia, or Church of Holy Wisdom. Constantinople rose up along the peninsula formed by the meeting of the Bosporus and the azure Sea of Marmara. The capital of the eastern Roman Empire, Constantinople was a city where, like Constantine himself, most spoke Greek and many vestiges of Greek culture lived on. Surrounded by forty-foot-high walls that were sixteen feet thick and spiked with hundreds of high towers, it was Christendom's most secure fortress. And there were indeed enemies about: most threatening were marauding warrior tribes such as the Vandals and the Visigoths, who began swooping into Roman territories. By the fifth century AD, they'd clobbered the western half of the Roman Empire, which was in an irreparable state of decline. The Byzantine Empire took on even greater importance.

By the sixth century AD, most of the Middle East was sucked of vitality. Frequent wars tapped the treasuries, conflict within and without drained life. Most of the rulers across its lands were weak, and once-great civilizations seemed to devolve. But a whole new world was about to be born, one that would reshape that part of the globe for the next fourteen centuries and is still going strong: Islam.

A FEW KEY MOMENTS IN EARLY JUDAISM

As we will see later, one of the sticking points in the Middle East is the belief that the former kingdom of Israel must be restored (in its entirety say some) before the Jewish Messiah returns, although Christians (at least the Zionist variety and those obsessed with the end days) equate the Messiah with the second coming of Christ. Herewith a short summary of relevant dates in Jewish history.

Circa third millennium BC: Abraham makes covenent with God. According to the Old Testament, God promises that Abraham's seed will sire a nation that will be led to the promised land.

Circa twelfth century BC: Moses leads Jews from slavery in Egypt. En route, the Ten Commandments are passed down to Moses from God on Mount Sinai.

Circa 1000 BC: David starts a kingdom for Jews with the capital in Jerusalem.

957 BC: David's son, Solomon, builds the first temple for Jews, believed to be located on the Mount of the Temple in Jerusalem. One room is called the Holy of Holies because it houses the tablets holding the Ten Commandments.

586 BC: First temple destroyed by Babylonians. Jews taken captive and made Babylonian slaves.

539 BC: Persian king Cyrus conquers Babylon, frees Jews, gives them money to rebuild a second temple.

516 BC: Jews build second temple

AD 33: Romans charge Jesus, born a Jew, with not paying taxes to Roman government. Sentenced to death, Jesus is given a possible reprieve when Pontius Pilate says that one man shall be freed. The crowd calls for another man to be let off instead of Jesus.

AD 70: Second temple destroyed by Romans.

AD 135: Romans evict Jews from Palestine.

Chapter Three

Pulling the Pieces Together

Muhammad Mahdi Karim

Now a centerpiece of Islam, the black stone wedged in the eastern corner of the Kaaba—the sixty-foot cube that sits at the heart of Mecca—was mystical to early pagans too. Mohammed claimed the Kaaba for Islam in 630, tossing out the pantheon of nature gods and dedicating the shrine to Allah. The Kaaba drew millions of Muslims for the annual hajj, or pilgrimage, which embraces prehistoric rituals including kissing the black stone (if you can get to it). During a siege in 950, the black stone was pried out of the Kaaba and held hostage in Bahrain for two decades, by a utopian Shia group that apparently wanted to boost tourism. Sunnis reclaimed it, but along the way it shattered: the black stone came back to Mecca in pieces, and its fragments were wedged into cement before being reinserted in the southeastern corner of the Kaaba, which now faces the Grand Mosque.

The rise of Islam is tied in part to a boulder that dropped out of the sky ages ago: some say the white-hot rock fell at the feet of Adam. If the date of its encounter with gravity is murky, one thing is clear: this mysterious meteorite ended up in Mecca, in today's Saudi Arabia, thousands of years ago. And it was revered as magical, so otherworldly and powerful that it made Mecca the peninsula's first tourist spot: pagans trekked here to kiss the black stone, communicate with the dead, and perform elaborate rituals, including circling around it counterclockwise seven times.

The black stone, a foot wide, was eventually built into a shrine—originally an eight-foot-high imperfect cube known as the Kaaba and also filled with 360 pagan idols. The Kaaba grew even more famous in the seventh century, a strange time in the Middle East. The Roman Empire had fizzled out, taking with it an extensive trade network. Persians and Byzantines kept fighting, their battles blocking camel caravan routes; the bubonic plague was ravaging cities; and civilization appeared to be on the decline. Caravans still traveled the Arabian sands—although they were fewer and more fearful of frequent raids—and in Mecca, despite the opening of new copper mines, the number of the impoverished kept growing. Nevertheless, tourists continued to pour into Mecca to see the black stone in the Kaaba.

The prestige the Kaaba and its black stone brought to seventh-century Meccans, and the money incoming pilgrims brought to the town, had everything to do with why many were alarmed when a dark-eyed trader named Mohammed began yelling about the pagan shrine and threatening to destroy the idols within it. Fearful that any change would diminish the touristic draw, Meccans—particularly the wealthy—did not applaud the speeches of this merchant turned mystic who trashed the local polytheism and condemned the hoarding of material riches. Wealth should be shared with the community, he preached, and the poor should be fed. Once a respected member of the Quraysh tribe—keepers of the keys to the Kaaba—Mohammed, around AD 613, began bellowing that there was only one God and that he was His prophet—becoming, as it turned out, the first prophet of the Arab world.

MOHAMMED'S ACCIDENTAL REVOLUTION

He'd gone bonkers. He wanted to jump off a cliff. So Mohammed, a trader turned sheep herder, confided to his wife in 610. What had convinced him of his madness was a weekend campout in a nearby cave. On his most recent retreat there, he'd heard a voice, a voice that told him that there was one god. And, added the voice, it was Mohammed's calling to warn his people that they were going astray. His wife, Khadiya, called in her cousin Waraqah who was Christian. Waraqah believed that Mohammed was hearing an angel. When Mohammed returned to the cave, he heard the voice again. For three years, Mohammed kept returning to the cave, and for three years he heard the voice, which identified itself as the angel Gabriel, and he absorbed the angel's teachings. Finally, Mohammed came out of the cave and started preaching the words that he had heard. Perched on a rock, calling out to both merchants and slaves, he beckoned them back into a world that took care of the poor and the weak, a community devoted to one God. He didn't realize at the time—about the year 613—that he was publicizing a new religion, Islam; he believed he was merely guiding the flock back to the same God who'd talked to Adam and Noah, Abraham and Moses, John the Baptist and Jesus—all of whom he regarded as prophets like himself.

He wasn't boring. When Mohammed was preaching, he shook, shuddered, flailed, and his eyes sometimes rolled back in his head;[1] some modern scholars believe he was having epileptic seizures.[2] But if his body twitched jerkily in spasms, the lyrical words from his mouth flowed like honeyed wine, and the force and meaning of those words melted critics—at least some of them. His wife was the first to convert, soon his nephew Ali and friend Abu Bakr gathered with him to partake in rituals that demanded submission, starting with putting one's head to the ground as one prayed. Within a few years, seventy stood behind him, and their numbers soon grew. The faithful, he initially instructed, must announce there was only one God, Allah, and pray to him every day. The needy must be tended to, the poor housed and clothed, the starving fed. Men and women alike should dress modestly, avoid wine, and stop killing girl babies, a common practice. Husbands could have multiple wives—a practice begun because wars and raids had killed so many men—but no more than four, a controversial demand in an era when they often had more; women could inherit property; and material wealth should be shunned along with praying to idols like the ones that sullied the Kaaba.

At first shrugging off the once respected Mohammed as a lunatic, the city's VIPs, whether Christian or pagan, grew more anxious as his following grew and he continually threatened to clean up Mecca and throw the idols out of the shrine that made the city famous. Meccans tried to beat the religion out of their slaves; they discriminated against Mohammed's followers; they forbade anybody from selling them food.[3] The more Mohammed preached of this one God, Allah—the same worshipped by Christians and Jews—the more he recited poetic verse, and the more he stressed social welfare of the community over private wealth, the more Meccans wanted him to go. After nine years of threats and harassment, Mohammed and his believers trekked to nearby Medina. That hike, called the Hijra, marked the true beginning of Islam, and its importance is reflected in the Islamic calendar, which begins with that year, 622 in Gregorian time.

VOCABULARY

Caliphate: Islamic empire.

Caliph: Successor to Mohammed, leader of the caliphate.

Mosque: Islam's place of prayer, now typically domed and with at least one slender tower (minaret) from which the muezzin calls Muslims to prayer five times a day.

Zakat: The 2.5 percent tax paid by Muslims to the caliphate.

Jizya: The substantially higher tax paid by non-Muslims living in territories claimed by the caliphate.

Arab: Technically defined as anybody who speaks Arabic, ethnically it includes tribes that came out of today's Yemen and western Arabia.

Persian: Originating from central-Asian tribes, Persians are the dominant ethnic group in today's Iran; the common language today is Farsi, previously it was Pahlavi. Even when under Arab rule, Persians kept their culture and language distinct.

Imam: A generic term for the prayer leader of a Sunni mosque, it usually means one of seven or twelve divine leaders when used by the Shia.

In Medina, the widower Mohammed built a small mosque from mud and reeds, subdividing the rooms to house several new wives. In the new locale, where he was regarded as a wise man, two significant changes unfolded that deeply affected the shape of Islam, both as a faith and as a future empire. The first was his relationship with local Jews. The second was his followers' means of survival.

ISLAM AND THE PEOPLE OF THE BOOK

Jews and Christians—the descendants, it was believed, of Abraham's son Isaac—were rolling in prophets, thousands of them. Until the seventh century, however, Arabs (descendants of Isaac's half brother Ishmael) hadn't been called on by God. When Mohammed was tapped, it was a source of relief and ushered in an individualistic Arab take on faith. Arabic, the script and language of the Koran, evolved as the only true language of Islam, and the representation of the script's flowing curves and dots soared as an Islamic art form. While Muslims thought Jews and Christians were worshipping the right God—the same one Muslims worshipped—they believed the initial message of staunch monotheism and total submission to God had been tarnished, and that Islam was bringing it back: the very posture of a praying Muslim shows that submission. While embracing the original ideas of Judaism and Christianity, and adopting many of the Bible's tales and beliefs as their own, Muslims believed that only Islam was, by renewing those ideals, the way to live by the will of God; thus they frequently invited Jews and Christians to convert. Forced conversion, however, was forbidden, which is why in later years, when Islam became the fuel that drove an empire, non-Muslims were allowed to retain their beliefs. Besides, non-Muslims were taxed at a higher rate, funds the government needed; occasional conversion campaigns sorely depleted the treasury.

Matson Collection, Library of Congress

Once a slab altar, the Kaaba is now a perfect cube—sixty feet high and sixty feet wide. Muslims face toward it when praying. Mideast hotels show the direction with an arrow in a drawer—the qibla—*that points toward Mecca.*

Mohammed's sermons and practices embraced many Jewish beliefs: stressing the importance of Abraham, he often spoke of Moses and referred respectfully to both Jews and Christians, calling them "People of the Book." And initially Islam resembled Judaism more closely: as directed by Mohammed, early Muslims, like Jews, prayed three times a day in the direction of the Jewish holy city, Jerusalem, and adopted Jewish holidays such as Passover. The Prophet was shocked by the reception he got by the Jews: he invited them to partake in Islamic rituals and to join his burgeoning community. The Jews passed on the offer; many laughed at him and pooh-poohed his new ways of worship. The days of prophets were long gone, he was informed—an assessment that diminished him to the level of a charlatan in their eyes. As for his religion, as the chosen people, the Jews preferred to celebrate their holidays and their religion only with other Jews. The rejection stung, and Mohammed quickly modified Islam: Muslims redirected their prayers, facing not in the direction of Jerusalem, but toward Mecca, specifically in the direction of the Kaaba that held the black rock. The Passover holiday was deleted from Islamic practice and replaced by Ramadan, an entire month of fasting during the day followed by feasting at night.

Sixty feet high and sixty feet wide, the Kaaba, with the foot-wide black meteorite embedded in its southeast corner, is the object toward which Muslims pray. Muslims traveling in the Middle East know which direction to face simply by looking in the desk drawer of any hotel room, where an arrow points toward the shrine's home, Mecca. In the early days, however, determining the qibla, *the precise direction to the Kaaba, prompted speculations into spherical trigonometry and new uses for astrolabes. Although the Koran holds that the Kaaba was built by the original mono- theist, Abraham, and his son Ishmael, idol-worshipping pagans were among the earliest pilgrims to the Kaaba, believing that the black rock, alongside 360 nature gods assembled with the structure, enabled them to speak to the dead.*

The second innovation that occurred in Medina provided a new source of income and ultimately the basis for an Islamic empire. Most who'd followed Mohammed to Medina no longer had work. Mohammed adopted the survival techniques of the bedouins, nomads who attacked settled towns and traveling caravans, not to kill or to acquire land, but for food and supplies. He endorsed raiding caravans, including those of his tribesman the Quraysh, en route to Mecca. The raids turned into tribal battles, some against Meccans or Jewish tribes in Medina who'd

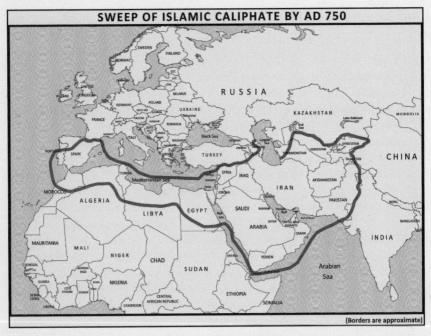

SWEEP OF ISLAMIC CALIPHATE BY AD 750

(Borders are approximate)

Oliver Benjamin

The caliphate rapidly expanded into Christian lands formerly held by the Byzantine Empire. Sieges and raids weren't the only means of conquest. Some cities and settlements were simply notified that they were a target of Muslim armies and given three options: (1) peacefully submit, convert, and pay the zakat, *a tithe; (2) continue practicing as before, but acknowledge Muslim rule and pay the higher tax; (3) resist and be violently conquered, with riches plundered and lands taken—and then, once conquered, pay the higher tax.[4] With the exception of Spain and Portugal, the lands taken by the caliphate have remained Muslim.*

warned Meccans about the plans of the Muslims. Known as just and wise, and still regarded by Muslims as the perfect man, Mohammed displayed a brutal side on the battlefield. Over the next decade, as the Muslims took Mecca and territories beyond, western Arabia's sands were soaked with blood.

Spread by word of mouth, and blade of spear, Islam soon held all of the Arabian Peninsula within its sway, and it didn't stop there. Even though Islamic fighters (estimated at forty thousand) were outnumbered five to one by Byzantine Christians, Islamic warriors won battle after battle, seizing Jerusalem then all of Palestine, Syria, Mesopotamia, Egypt to the south, Persia to the northeast, Armenia, and even Turkmenistan. In total, Islamic forces—on horse, on camel, and on foot, sometimes fighting with bare hands and praying even in the midst of battle—captured an area over twice the size of the Arabian Peninsula within a decade of the Hijra in 622. By the eighth century, the territories ruled by Islamic caliphs stretched from India to Spain.

Muslims were forbidden to attack Muslims, so one way to avoid being raided was to convert. In just a few years, most of Arabia had done so. As part of that conversion, practitioners and towns alike paid the *zakat,* a tithe of 2.5 percent of a person's worth (income plus possessions), theoretically as alms for the poor, but also a means of keeping the new religion and associated government running. The conquered were not forced to convert; the Koran was explicit in its calls to allow People of the Book to retain their own faith. But to remain protected in Muslim communities, the *dhimmi* (non-Muslims) had to cough up a poll tax, the *jizya,* which was considerably more than the *zakat* paid by Muslims.

THE FIVE PILLARS OF ISLAM

The five most important acts of worship in Islam are:

1. Shahada: The profession of faith: "There is no god but God, and Mohammed is a messenger of God."

2. Salah: Muslims must pray five times a day while facing in the direction of Mecca (in Saudi Arabia) and recite the above credo.

3. Zakat: Muslims must give to charity.

4. Sawm: Muslims must fast during the daylight hours of the holy month of Ramadan.

5. Hajj: Muslims must try to make a pilgrimage to Mecca at least once.

Islam was the rage until 632, when Mohammed died leaving no successor. At least that's how many interpreted the events. There were some, however, who believed that Mohammed had spelled out who should follow him: Ali, his cousin and son-in-law. On Mohammed's final pilgrimage to Mecca, he had said, "To whomever I am their leader, then Ali is their leader." Some interpreted this as a general recommendation; others said it meant that Ali should be next to carry the torch.

The death of Mohammed was the first test of the new religion; it dealt such a blow that it's surprising Islam survived. The passing of the power baton went

to Mohammed's friend Abu Bakr in 632, without struggle in the inner circle, although Ali was late to sign on in support. But across the peninsula, the death of
Mohammed meant to many the death of the religion and the cancellation of any
zakat. As the new caliph, Abu Bakr's first task was to convince them otherwise.
In his battles to recapture the lost followers, he solidified the religion, banning
the variations that had already sprung up and bringing the strayers back into
the zakat-paying core. Thanks to his fighters, his efforts were surprisingly successful.

THE TEACHINGS OF ISLAM

Mohammed's successor Abu Bakr ordered the compilation of notes from
Mohammed's lectures into the Koran. Calling believers back to the basics of
monotheism while also endorsing the concept of community, the Koran spells
out everything from religious practices to legal codes and public health measures. The first book written in Arabic—then a language more often spoken
than penned—the Koran is believed by Muslims to be the direct, literal word of
God transmitted by Mohammed, his prophet. How literally Muslims should interpret it has been the subject of violent debate since the first copies circulated.
While the Koran is the main holy book, two other books are also drawn from:
the Sunnah records the acts of Mohammed's life; the Hadith is a collection of
secondhand reports of his actions and stated opinions. While most recognize
the Sunnah, the Hadith, because of its secondhand nature, is more controversial; some scholars reject a number of accounts in the Hadith, while some
sects, such as the more hard-core Salafi/Wahhabi, embrace the Hadith.

Dying two years later from illness, Abu Bakr was followed by Umar, who, during his ten-year reign as the second caliph, continued Islam's geographical expansion, moving into North Africa and Persia. Killed by an unhappy Persian,
Umar was followed by Uthman, who solidified Islam: he rounded up variant copies of the Koran, ensuring that there was but one official version, and built five
thousand new mosques. He created a navy, which soon moved the faith into Cyprus and Sicily, and he boosted trade: he issued Islam's first coins, encouraged
the founding of hotels for traveling merchants, and initiated loans for entrepreneurs. Known to free slaves, he ensured care of the poor, widowed, and or-
phaned and initiated public forums to address grievances. He even improved
water systems empire-wide.

Uthman sent off Islam's first ambassador via the seas. Arriving in China in
650, the ambassador unsuccessfully tried to convert the emperor to
Islam, but he did convince him to build the first mosque in China.[5]

Some of Uthman's other acts were more controversial: he increased the amount of the zakat, and he appointed his relatives as governors in the outlying territories. In 656, he was killed by Ali-supporting rebels.

Finally, it was Ali's turn to sit in the hot seat, and he made a huge PR blunder: he didn't avenge Uthman's death, committed by his devoted followers. By not punishing Uthman's killers, however, he divided his power base. Mohammed's third wife, Aisha, was among those calling for Ali to step down. Uthman's cousin Mu'awiyah, the governor in Syria, demanded the same. It all erupted into a civil war. Battle-wise Ali was victorious, but chronic fighting weakened his leadership. Five years after he walked in as caliph, Ali was struck down—fatally stabbed with a poisoned sword by a member of the Kharijites, a rebel sect he had alienated. To avoid further bloodshed, Ali's eldest son, Hasan, next in line from the Prophet's house, signed an agreement handing over the caliphate to Mu'awiyah. Years later however, when Hasan died, the people of Kufa (today's Iraq) invited

Islam's main religious text, the Koran, which means "recitation," is actually a collection of notes from speeches Mohammed gave—neither Mohammed nor most of his followers could read. But those who could write took notes during these lectures, which Muslims believe to be the words of God revealed to Mohammed via the angel Gabriel. Other parts of the Koran's 114 chapters were originally recited as rhyming poems.

Husayn, Hasan's younger brother, to rule from their city as the next caliph. Mu'awiyah's son Yazid sent troops to Kufa and made sure they changed their minds, retracting the invitation. But Husayn was convinced that the sight of Mohammed's descendants, arriving to rightfully restore Islam, would change the minds of those in Kufa. In 680, outside the city of Karbala (also in Iraq), Yazid's warriors slew Husayn's entourage, killing all seventy-two family members. Husayn's head was chopped off and paraded back to the caliph in Damascus, and his body left dumped on the battlefield. This was the last straw for Ali's supporters.

SUNNI/SHIA: WHAT'S THE DIFF?

In the same way that Christians don't all share the exact same faith—Baptists, Catholics, Lutherans, and Presbyterians differ on numerous issues—not all

Muslims practice Islam identically. And no two groups disagree on more issues than Sunni Muslims (about 85 percent of Muslims worldwide) and Shia Muslims (about 15 percent). The basic issue separating them goes back to the question of who should have succeeded Mohammed in leading the faith: the Sunni believed that successors could be "elected"; the Shia believed successors should be a blood relative of Mohammed. That initial split evolved into more disagreements and even geographic and ethnic distinctions. The Shia, who revere Mohammed's cousin Ali as well as his son Husayn (both assassinated by Sunnis) have martyrdom thickly layered into their beliefs, and their take on Islam is more mystical, including, for instance, deciphering the symbols in the letters of the Koran. Shia typically put more faith in their religious leaders, imams, than in leaders of government, and some dead imams are considered divine. Sunnis, whose leaders dominated the rise of Islam as its rulers, are more focused on mundane matters in how they interpret the Koran as a legal code. With centuries of bloody battles and mutual discrimination behind them, the rift is now nearly embedded in the genes and could be drawn out on a map: most Sunni are Arab; most Shia are Persian (Iranian), and the majority of the world's Shia lives in Iran and Iraq. In fact, for nearly a thousand years there have been no Arab countries headed by Shia—until the recent change of guard in Iraq.

That battle at Karbala marks the point where Islam dramatically divided: the supporters of Ali and Husayn formed a breakaway sect, Shia, for Shiat Ali, meaning "the followers of Ali." Those who followed the Islamic caliphs were called Sunni, short for Ahl as-Sunnah, "People of the Sunnah, the way of the Prophet." After 680, Shia no longer respected caliphate rule, looking to Shia imams as spiritual advisers and chafing under demands to pay the zakat to caliphs, most of whom were Sunni.

The Rashidun, or the Rightly Guided, is the name given by Sunnis to the first four caliphs, from Abu Bakr to Ali, who ruled from 632 through 661. On the one hand, the title reflects the early leaders' relative piousness (later, caliphs lived lives of luxury) and closeness to Mohammed. On the other hand, it's a way of flipping off the Shia, who recognize only Ali, the fourth caliph, as legitimate.

THE RISE OF SECTS

The Shia weren't the only Muslims who disagreed with the paths the first four caliphs had blazed. Others, such as the Ibadhi, the Kharijite, and the Sufi, also developed paths separate from the Sunni. Their ideas were threatening to Sunni rulers, and at times forced them to meet in caves, their words kept secret, and their beliefs sometimes evident only in symbolic gestures and codes. But these dissident sects often sniffed at each other, and even within the sects, particularly the Shia, divisions soon arose, further subdividing any opposition to Sunni dominance. Among the Shia divisions: the Twelvers (who believe that their twelfth religious leader went into hiding and will return at the end of the world); the Fivers (who believe there were only five true imams), and the most mystical Ismailis (who believe there were only seven true imams), tried to establish utopian communities on earth and now regard the Aga Khan as their leader. The Sunni also subdivided into sects divided by legal interpretations of the Koran and the importance placed on supplemental writings such as the secondhand reports in the Hadith.

While sects secretly practiced their faiths, or moved to mountains and far-off lands where they could practice without fear, the dominant Sunni leapt into fantastical new realms of power and riches, the empire swelling across even larger expanses of the map. Like the trade revolution earlier kicked off by frankincense, the rise of Islam still astounds for its remarkable geographic advances, spreading so quickly not only as a new faith but as a reigning religious power complete with its own government, to which the ruled paid taxes. While Muslims took their successes as a sign that such was the will of God, other onlookers, including those in Christian Byzantium (the remaining eastern vestige of the Roman Empire, centered in Constantinople) were mystified at the Muslims' progress—and all the more since they had conquered the great empire of Persia with relative ease.

> *"How could naked men, riding without armour or shield . . . bring low the proud spirit of the Persians? . . . [O]nly a short period passed before the entire world was handed over to the Arabs; they subdued all fortified cities, taking control from sea to sea, and from east to west."*
> —John Bar Penkaye, a Byzantine monk, writing in the late seventh century[6]

THE CALIPHATES

After the first four caliphs—Abu Bakr to Ali—the caliphate changed. It became bigger, spawned dynasties, moved out of Arabia, and several coexisted at the same time. Among the standouts:

Umayyad (660–750): Started by Mu'awiyah, this dynasty based in Damascus was known for building the most commanding architecture of its day, including the Dome of the Rock in Jerusalem, promoted as a new pilgrimage site during a period when rebels seized Mecca. Calligraphy was developed as an art form, but the most amazing advances of the Umayyad's occurred in Spain.

Umayyad Spain (756–1031):   The caliphate in Spain, actually started by an Umayyad ruler who escaped a takeover in Damascus, was home to brilliant cities of learning. In Córdoba, Toledo, and Granada, advanced agricultural practices coaxed forth new crops: the perfume of orange blossoms wafted through courtyards, and outlying hills burst with almonds, dates, lemons, and limes alongside fields thick with rice and sugarcane.

Abbasid (750–1258):   Based in Baghdad, this dynasty was boozy and licentious, but the libraries and hospitals of the era were legendary.

Fatimid (909–1171):   The first Shia dynasty built Cairo and the first Islamic university, al-Azhar, which still stands in Egypt but is now an important Sunni institution.

During the early years of Islam's rise, many Muslims became prosperous: the growing empire brought new markets and novel goods to trade. Few, however, including the rulers, flaunted their wealth. The early caliphs were based in the religious centers of Mecca and Medina, but in later centuries, as Islam stretched across the map, the caliphs lived grandly, and the capitals sparkled as the urban jewels of their day, boasting the most eye-grabbing architecture and drawing the finest minds to their libraries and royal courts. The expansion of the caliphate did more than increase the tax base: it wove together foreign cultures, new ideas, and novel inventions, creating a dynamic intellectual climate that profoundly shaped the Renaissance that would follow in Europe seven hundred years later. Some inventions and ideals that we associate with the age of da Vinci and Michelangelo were in fact the fruits of this wildly brilliant era, when studies of stars, numbers, chemicals, words, and the writings of the ancients catapulted thinking into new realms.

INVENTIONS OF THE EARLY ISLAMIC EMPIRE

Forget the idea that science was born during the Renaissance in Europe. Bringing together ideas and observations from Egyptians, Persians, Mesopotamians, and Greeks before them, Muslim thinkers jumped into new realms, starting in the ninth century, with a surprising list of inventions often credited to later eras:

Algebra and algorithms: These numerical abstractions are credited to ninth-century mathematician Mohammed al-Khwarizmi.

Glass: Introduced in Spain by ninth-century scientist Abbas ibn Firnas.

Glider: Abbas ibn Firnas tried out what is believed to be the first attempt to fly.

Surgery: A tenth-century court physician in Córdoba, Abu al-Qasim al-Zahrawi, is considered the father of modern surgery.

Medicine: A tenth-century Persian, Avicenna, is considered the father of modern medicine for his advances in clinical drug studies and the fight against infectious disease and STDs.

Dictionaries: The first known complete dictionary was penned in ninth-century Baghdad, along with historic encyclopedias such as the *History of the World* and *History of Conquests*.

Pharmacies: Baghdad is where they first showed up, along with books on pharmacology and hospitals.

Scientific method: Scientist/historian/astronomer/geographer/geologist al-Biruni, the inventor of scientific method, wrote over 140 books and is now considered one of the brightest minds of all time.

Compasses: The Chinese had the magnetic needle, but the Arabs are believed to have first put it to use as a navigational device.

Paper factories: The Chinese knew the formula, but the Muslims made it a ninth-century industry in the wider world.

Windmills: First used in Persia in the seventh century.

Kerosene: First distilled in ninth-century Baghdad.

Insane asylums: Where we suspect a few of Baghdad's drunken poets ended up.

A succession of Islamic caliphs and their warriors brought the religion to new corners of the world—as far east as the Spice Islands (Moluccas) and as far west as Portugal. Some caliphates coexisted simultaneously with others, but some were replaced—as is the case of the Umayyads, who were taken down in a bloody rebellion by the Abbasids. The Abbasid rulers launched one of Islam's finest eras with their caliphate headquartered in today's Iraq. Enlisting scholars from Persia, Palestine, India, and Egypt, and bringing together Muslims, Christians, and Jews, the empire produced not only libraries and bookstores—thousands of them open to the public, some three hundred in Baghdad alone—but hundreds of thousands of books. There were translations of works by ancient Greeks, from Hippocrates to Euclid; observations of stars and distant lands; encyclopedias and atlases; original medical treatises and papers on optics; and many broke new ground in fields from zoology to math. Language schools made translations possible, skilled copyists churned out upward of fifty thousand books every year, and Baghdad's paper factory became the world's first.[7] Indeed, the epicenter of this intellectual earthquake—which would result in unprecedented progress in the arts, science, and everything in between—was Baghdad, where the Abbasid ruler opened the doors to the House of Wisdom, a think tank for the region's finest minds.

BAGHDAD AND THE HOUSE OF WISDOM

From the eighth century through the thirteenth, the Abbasid capital, Baghdad, was a center of learning, art, and luxury, where medicine and sciences flourished, and *The Thousand and One Nights* was penned, along with histories of the world, travelogues, and dictionaries. Alchemists and astronomers, philosophers and mathematicians, physicians and scientists flocked to the city, as did architects, artisans, and linguists. While medieval Europe languished in the Dark Ages, Baghdad glittered with gaslit streets. Apothecaries dispensed potions brewed up at the city's medical schools. Scholars debated interpretations of Islamic law so complex they divided Sunni Muslims into four schools and numerous sects. New literary genres appeared, such as bawdy "wine poetry,"[8] odes to the drink favored by the caliph and his court of scholars, eunuchs, and boozy poets. A magnet for inventions, treasures, and intelligence about the goings-on in the far reaches of the empire, Baghdad boasted marble palaces filled with tapestries, furnishings from China, and elaborate mosques of striped arches. The city was thick with gardens and public parks; water was brought to homes via aqueducts; streets were wide and paved; markets boasted the finest silks, gleaming swords, and delicate sculptures in porcelain; hospitals performed surgeries for hemorrhoids and cataracts; and students learned Latin, botany, algebra, and trigonometry. Observatories tracked celestial bodies, while astrolabes, early sextants, and star charts guided ships on trade routes to Africa and the Far East. Baghdad, along with Islamic cities such as Córdoba, initiated what five centuries later would become the European Renaissance, which their translations of the ancient Greeks helped spur.

The rise of Islam was terrifying to some, especially as the conquests kept moving closer to Christian turf. As Islamic fighters moved to the west, the Christian emperor in Constantinople sent out an SOS to the Catholic pope. Pope Urban II worked it into a publicity stunt. The Muslims were slashing open the stomachs of Christians, ripping out their guts as they dragged them through the streets, he announced.[9] They had defiled the altars of Christendom's holiest sites. It was best to not even say what the savages were doing to the chaste Christian women, he declared.

Filled with lies and propaganda, the speech the pope passionately delivered that day in November 1095 to a crowd in southern France so stirred up the Christians—with its call to every good Christian, whether robber or knight, to take down the Muslims—that the Crusaders didn't even wait for an organized attack. Forty thousand or more headed off on their own—followed months later by twenty-five thousand princes and knights—to defeat the horned Arab. Beyond reviving belief in Catholicism, which had suffered a downturn, besides mending recent bad relations between Rome and Constantinople by lending a hand, beyond adding new territory to the Catholic holdings, he kicked off a nightmarish fad that would continue for centuries. That one speech unleashed havoc for

Andrew MacLoughlin

Saladin ran out Crusaders from Jerusalem, but could never take their fortress, Krak des Chevaliers in Syria (pictured). A fierce warrior, he was also a pragmatic diplomat, cautioning, "Spilled blood never sleeps."[10]

years to come, not only in the Middle East, but in the cities along the way. As the Crusaders set off, sometimes with little more than a hoe for a weapon, they demanded free food and lodging in every city they passed through, unleashing violence on those who didn't wish to comply, particularly those who were Jews.

On July 15, 1099, when this motley crew of wealthy princes and tattered peasant warriors traveling on foot breached the wall of their main destination, Jerusalem, the violence was even worse: the Crusaders slaughtered almost every resident of the town; so much blood filled the streets that the mild accounts have it flowing above their ankles. And they kept Jerusalem for almost two centuries, setting up "Crusader states" and garrison towns along the Mediterranean coast and throughout present-day Lebanon and Syria, fighting off frequent attacks until a fierce fighting Kurd, Saladin, became sultan of the Ayyubid dynasty that ran in Egypt and Syria. Saladin led his fighters in vicious battles that took back Jerusalem in 1187, releasing many Crusaders in exchange for ransom. Two years later, the Crusaders returned for a rematch that was an embarrassing failure.

But in 1198, Pope Innocent III renewed the cry for a run on Jerusalem. In 1202, when the Crusaders returned to Constantinople en route to try to claim the holy city, pretty much everybody loathed these self-proclaimed holy fighters, including the Byzantines. In 1204, the Christian warriors took Constantinople—the very Christian city they were supposed to protect—sacking it; denuding the hundreds of churches of their gold, silver, and finery; smashing icons; destroying holy books; and having drunken orgies in the holiest church, the Hagia Sophia. And they remained in power in Constantinople for the next fifty-seven years.

Over in Baghdad, the Abbasid Empire came crashing down in 1255, in a cloud of dust from the East. The wealth and knowledge accumulated in Baghdad through the centuries rose up in a thick black cloud in 1255 when the Mongols showed up

Upon capturing Christian Constantinople in 1453, the Ottomans quickly built mosques. The Blue Mosque (shown above) was once surrounded by schools, baths, and hospitals.

with an arsenal of weapons never before seen in these parts. Blasting through city walls with explosives, hurling fire bombs and grenades—by some accounts they even used napalm—the horsemen from northern Asia torched books, decimated buildings, destroyed water systems, and looted treasures, killing thirty thousand in Baghdad alone. Their rule—from 1255 to 1335—was the nadir of the empire. The caliphate stagnated from lack of ideas, and the only things that sparkled were jewels plundered from cities abroad. At least the Mongols converted to Islam: Sunni Islam.

By the sixteenth century, infighting, battles over succession, and invasions had taken their toll: empires were crumbling, dynasties had disappeared. But in the mountain villages of today's Turkey, a new fire was roaring. The Ottomans—Turkish warrior tribes who, like the Mongols, had charged in from the East and converted to Islam—wrangled away the former caliphates' lands during the early 1500s. As they roped in new territories across the Middle East, they accomplished what no other Islamic army had succeeded in doing: they took Constantinople, and with the crashing of this last eastern vestige of Christendom, a whole new era began: the Ottoman Empire, the most powerful the Middle East had yet seen.

It was the cruelest day in all history, a Tuesday in 1453 when the blessed Christian city of Constantinople fell to the Ottoman Turks who had besieged it for weeks and ultimately walked in because somebody forgot to close a gate in the wall.

Or so it appeared to the West. The Turks had just pried away the last Christian foothold in the Near East, killing and driving out many of the inhabitants, turning churches into mosques, and renaming the beloved city Istanbul, city of Islam. And they didn't stop there: they took Turkey, the Balkans, and twice laid siege to Vienna unsuccessfully. But no Muslims had ever moved so close into Europe's heartland, and for Christians they were the "evil empire" of the day.

In the West, the Turks were portrayed as barbarians, an image reinforced by practices such as the sultan's immediate slaying of all his brothers upon taking the scepter or the janissaries' tendency to impale the heads of victims on poles. Their military men were drafted as boys, and one tax imposed on the Balkans was that a fifth of the young males would be turned over to the state. Converted to Islam and trained as fighters, they remained warrior slaves—janissaries—their whole lives.

To some, however, the pragmatic Ottomans were kind: they invited Jews into Istanbul as merchants, in some cases waiving the jizya tax, rescuing them along with Muslims from the Spanish, who had run out the Muslim rulers in 1492 and were now driving out Jews.

SULEYMAN THE MAGNIFICENT

Twenty-five when he took the throne, and a goldsmith by training, Suleyman spent his youth studying the war strategies of Alexander the Great. It showed on the battlefield, where his forces took Belgrade, most of Hungary, parts of Persia, and North Africa. He eased draconian laws, making them more just and easing the tax burden for many, while closing down the shops of unscrupulous vendors. A patron of the arts, he showcased Istanbul as one of the most creatively vibrant and stunning cities of the day and a headquarters of fashion. But if that's not enough for which to remember Suleyman, Europeans owe him at least a nod when they wake up in the morning. Suleyman's troops, lightening their load after the battle of Vienna, left behind their supplies of coffee, which became the rage across Europe.

The Ottoman Empire was more than a military force. It was a remarkably efficient machine. The Ottomans weren't thinkers. They weren't innovators, they were administrators: Islamic bureaucrats who ran their government with a precision that's more typically confined to the military, with every duty delegated to a different department. The military had its own elaborate system: corps to bake, corps to set up camps, corps to ensure that roads ahead were usable. Given the size of the empire, Ottomans divided the territory into districts with governors, pashas, assigned to see that all remained orderly and that taxes were paid to Istanbul.

The Ottomans also had style, ushering in one of the most luxurious, eye-catching, flashy, unforgettable eras in human history. Predictably, there was even government control of creativity, with departments of textiles, departments of fashion design, departments of architecture, and even departments of book illustrators. Yet it didn't stop the flow of gorgeous creations.

What's believed to be the world's first coffeehouse opened its doors in Istanbul in 1555, but the kafke, *drunk over games of backgammon, was only part of the draw: storytellers, musicians, incoming sailors, and poets made it a hotbed of entertainment and news, and coffeehouses spread through the city, often located outside of mosques.*

Velvet caftans lined with fur, robes of intricate silk brocade, wrapped turbans punctuated with rubies the size of plums. Sumptuous *was a word invented for the Ottoman Empire, with its taste for rich tapestries hung from walls, fine carpets covering floors, and the favorite chair being satin pillows. For centuries, rank was announced by fashion: janissaries wore chimney-stack hats, wealthy women wore bubbles of silk atop their heads, and sultans wore a new robe every day. The Ottomans even had laws about who could wear what, and some sultans doubled as unofficial fashion police, chastising those who dressed sloppily or out of rank.*

Flashy textiles woven with threads of gold were more than just part of the lifestyle, they were a huge element of trade: not only the biggest import—from Russian furs to Persian silks—but the biggest export of the Ottoman Empire. Every house had a loom and a spinning wheel, every woman, rich or poor, knew how to embroider, and state-owned factories produced cottons, woolens, rugs, hats, and silks. For centuries, at least half of the labor force was employed in some aspect of textile making. Hundreds of thousands alone were employed in raising silkworms and their valuable cocoons.

Taxes and tributes made the Ottoman government tick: the empire, based in Istanbul, collected duties and imposed this fee and that fee on everything that crossed Ottoman-controlled land, which included most of the Middle East. And when they began imposing taxes and duties and fees on spices coming from the East, boosting prices and cutting profits for spice merchants in the Mediterranean, the Europeans—who really wanted those spices—opted for another plan. Forget the Muslim middlemen. They would go get the spices themselves. There was only one problem: the early European navigators couldn't figure out how to get to the Spice Islands until an Arab navigator helped them out.

MUSLIM NAVIGATION

Given their long history of maritime trade, as well as their contact with Chinese seafarers who shared technological advances from the rudder to the compass, it should come as no shock that the Arabs and Persians were leagues ahead in the navigation department. Europeans often sailed easily maneuvered rivers; Arabs and Persians sailed oceans and seas, learning how to take advantage of the monsoon winds, drawing detailed maps, and developing new means to calculate distances. Using elaborate compasses, ornate astrolabes, simple sextants made out of knots, and advanced mathematical calculations, these Muslim navigators mastered the seas, sailing to China and Indonesia, around Africa and into Europe, centuries before Europeans began showing up in those parts. Indeed, Arabs crossed the Atlantic in the ninth century. In the Middle East, thirteenth-century almanacs already gave details of star positions, predicted sunrises and sunsets, and ran schedules of three-masted ships sailing to international destinations, while Europeans clung to entirely misguided, outdated maps and grappled with fears about the world being flat.

Arab sailors were often hired as guides by fifteenth-century Europeans, who gritted their teeth as they headed out on the oceans, fearing they would fall off the edge of the world. Arab guides were, for example, on board Columbus's transatlantic voyages, but they never helped Europeans go east. Fear that the world was flat kept the Europeans out of most waters until, in 1498, Portuguese captain Vasco da Gama picked up a pilot on Africa's east coast, believed to be the famous Omani navigator Ahmad ibn Majid. The guide not only led da Gama around Africa to the south of India, thus opening up the spice route, but he also opened the door to the Persian Gulf, a fateful error that would result in genocide and deprivation for the next 150 years.

At the dawn of the sixteenth century, the Ottomans looked up to see two very big problems that quickly rearranged the Middle Eastern playing board: one problem came from the West, the other from the East. The Portuguese, having finally gotten over their hang-up that the world was flat, were blasting into Ottoman territory, literally: they wanted to control the spice trade from the Spice Islands to Europe, and to monopolize trade in the Persian Gulf. Fired up by the Inquisition, the Portuguese were perhaps the most savage fighters ever to show up in those parts.

THE PORTUGUESE

The late fifteenth-century Portuguese, who barreled into the Gulf with their galleons and cannons, not only changed the nature of the warring game, they rearranged life along the coast of Arabia and beyond. Conquering trading centers along the peninsula's eastern shores, snatching up forts in Oman and islands such as Bahrain, they also conquered Persian ports including Hormuz, until then one of the world's richest. And they weren't leaving: the Portuguese, who at that point were the only Europeans who had figured out how to get to the Spice Islands and the Persian Gulf, stayed for the next century and a half. The Inquisition-happy Portuguese so savagely massacred their Muslim victims that they imparted a hatred for all Europeans and Christians—as the British, French, and Dutch who later appeared in these waters would discover. Burning, beheading, and crucifying victims, torching and routinely sinking locals' boats, the Portuguese not only destroyed the region's economic livelihood, they monopolized and effectively blockaded the waters for all trying to leave. They also imposed heavy duties on the goods of those sailing in, ushering in economic deprivation and unintentionally encouraging piracy, as unemployed, hungry sailors tried to fight back. The Gulf waters only grew more treacherous as other Europeans wandered in (en route to India), making them into a floating battlefield and further strangling trade.

Between the Portuguese and the pirates, Persian Gulf waters became so treacherous that many traders dropped anchor at Aden (in today's Yemen), refusing to haul their goods any farther. As trade plummeted further due to the dangers of the Pirate Coast (the name given to what today is the United Arab Emirates and Oman), violence and piracy only increased, since former traders turned to looting as the sole means to get their goods.

While the Portuguese were controlling local water routes, the other problem for the Ottomans appeared to the east: Persia. A religious brotherhood of Islamic mystics who lived hidden away in the Zagros Mountains, studied the stars in hidden observatories, and kept secret books in clandestine libraries, had come out of hiding. They took over Persia in 1501 and then took over Mesopotamia (Iraq). What's more, they were turning their empire into a strict Islamic theocracy that allowed only their own religion. But these Persians, who called themselves Safavids, weren't Sunni. They were Shia, and they made Shiism part of Persia's new identity: those who didn't convert were killed or run out. In fact, denouncing the Sunni became a government function: the Safavid government created a department to lead public chants against the first three caliphs, nurturing the long-held Shia wound that Ali, the fourth caliph, should have been the first.

> *Forced conversion in the Safavid Empire made Persia for the first time dominantly Shia and left a lasting mark: Persia, now Iran, has been dominantly Shia ever since, and for centuries the only country to have a ruling Shia majority.*

THE SAFAVID EMPIRE: 1501–1722

Having grown up in an underground Sufi sect, the Grand Masters of the Safaviyeh, Shah Ismail I launched the Safavid Empire in 1501. He was full of contradictions: using his Sufi colleagues to help take Persia, he then forced them to convert—or die. He persecuted all who weren't Shia—Twelver Shia at that—killing Sunnis, Sufis, Christians, Jews, and driving the Zoroasters to India. If one overlooks that, the Safavid Empire he started stands out for its refined taste. Miniature paintings that require a magnifying glass to drink in their detail, ornamental gardens with pools and mazes, the finest silks studded with jewels, and intricately patterned Persian rugs are but a few of the Safavid Empire's legacies. As with the Ottomans, textiles became the jewel of the economy under future leader Shah Abbas I (1571–1629), who opened state factories for carpets, clothes, and silk. Despising the Ottomans, his competitors in textiles and for territory in the Middle East, he devised means to screw them with trade, locking in exclusive agreements with Europe and cutting off sales of Persian silks so the Ottomans couldn't resell them. Before long, the Shia Safavids of Persia and the Sunni Ottomans were meeting head-on in war. And the territory they fought over was Mesopotamia (Iraq), which held the most important Shia holy sites, the tombs of Ali and Husayn. For the Ottomans, Mesopotamia was an important source of tributes the territory was forced to pay and taxes collected from overland travel. Another reason that Ottomans wanted Mesopotamia: it held back Safavid expansion.

From the early sixteenth into the eighteenth century, the Sunni Ottomans and Shia Persians duked it out, and, in a preview of coming attractions, the favorite battlefield was Mesopotamia, particularly Baghdad. The Persians took Baghdad in 1509; then the Ottomans nabbed it in 1534; the Persians yanked it back in 1623; and the Ottomans took it again in 1638, this time keeping a tight hold. The next year, boundaries were drawn between Iran and Ottoman-held Iraq—boundaries that still hold today.

The Middle East was suddenly getting very crowded. The Ottomans were going at it against Persia, while Portugal was trying to control all trade. And into this strange dynamic sailed the British, who'd gotten hold of Portuguese maps to these parts, and were interested in the spice trade the Portuguese were monopolizing—and in controlling the Persian Gulf.

The Persians were still scheming ways to stick it to the Ottomans. During the reign of Shah Abbas I, who came to power in 1588, two English adventurers who'd trained as soldiers helped Persia regain its former might. Revamping the military, they introduced the use of gunpowder weapons, and soon Abbas had blasted the Portuguese out of Bahrain. Then with the aid of the British navy they ripped the Portuguese from their Persian treasure chest, Hormuz, which is how the Persians and Brits became so buddy-buddy—and how the British came to dominate the Gulf.

THE ARRIVAL OF THE BRITISH

Despite the dangers of the Gulf—then dominated by the Portuguese and thick with pirates—the British East India Company kept pushing into its waters with hopes of making inroads into the trade in textiles and spices. Wanting to control Gulf trade themselves, they helped locals uproot the Portuguese—at the moment not quite so high and mighty since Spain had just annexed their kingdom—and by the 1660s the troublesome occupiers, who had set local economies back centuries, finally shoved off back to Lisbon. Still, these were hazardous waters: the plundering continued and the cannons the Portuguese left behind were now aimed at trader ships. Some Arab tribes converted to infidel-despising Wahhabism and now slaughtered Christians of any nationality with the same bloodthirstiness with which Arabs had been murdered by the Portuguese.

Establishing a stronghold first in Persia and later in the Arabian seaport Aden, the British launched a charm offensive, making treaties with the Gulf's emirs. Offering protection against all attackers (be they Arab, Persian, or European), the British encouraged trade to resume (as long as they were the only Europeans traded with). In exchange, the Brits demanded safe ports, unhampered passage through the waters, and control over the foreign affairs of their new "protectorates." The Gulf shores once called the Pirate Coast were unpoetically renamed the Trucial Coast; local villages and boats hoisted flags showing white to indicate friendly status. The Queen's men also amped up the economy as trade in the oyster's prize, shut down during Portuguese rule, was again pried open. Europeans adored pearls.

The British have a bad reputation for sucking all vitality out of their colonies and protectorates and leaving them economically and socially devastated. Their initial effect on the Gulf countries, which they "adopted" as protectorates, was—surprisingly—generally positive: they dampened (if not extinguished) fiery disputes and didn't exploit the local resources, if only because for most of the 150 years during which they "guarded the Gulf" there weren't many resources to exploit. The British kept attackers at bay; solved conflicts; mediated border disputes; bolstered local trade; and, admirably, supplied food when there was none to be had. However, they hampered the "survival of the fittest": they changed the normal evolution of the Middle East by protecting favored kingdoms and ensuring the survival of those that weren't necessarily fit. Furthermore, the British imposed foreign ideas on these parts, including the concepts of states and borders, reflecting their own desires over the better interests of the protectorates. While espousing parliaments and representation, they propped up the Gulf rulers whom they could most easily manipulate, showering them with money and turning some into autocrats. They sometimes threw support behind "the enemy of their enemy," not because he deserved to be backed, but simply because he diluted the power of the Ottomans. The effects of this unofficial British rule are still playing out. The general map they imposed on the peninsula surprisingly still remains; against the odds, the countries they protected—Kuwait and Bahrain being two prime examples—while still weak and needy have somehow survived.

The British control of the Gulf that began in the 1700s and continued for centuries—slamming the Ottoman economy—wasn't the only headache for the Ottomans. Their armed forces kept rising up in revolt. And the governors they'd placed in far corners of the empire weren't content with relative autonomy and a financial tribute to Istanbul. Everywhere from the Balkans to Egypt, they started sawing off these territories and proclaiming them independent.

THE FATHER OF MODERN EGYPT

Mohammed Ali Pasha (1769–1849)—an Albanian by birth, an Ottoman officer by training, and considered the father of modern Egypt—was sent to the land of the Nile in 1802 to push out Napoléon's troops, who'd grabbed the country from the ruling Mamluks, Egyptian soldiers who'd taken over the government. Made vizier (a government official) by the Ottomans, he notoriously wiped out the Mamluks by inviting them to a feast in Cairo, and then slaughtering everyone shortly after dessert. Without an official okay from Istanbul, with whom he was increasingly at odds, he set his sights to the north, taking Syria (which he gave to his son) and the Hejaz, the region of Arabia that contains Mecca and Medina, and battling the Wahhabi, a newly risen group of fanatical Muslim warriors, to do so. He soon told the government in Istanbul to take a hike and handed Egypt down to his family, many of whom were deranged. Another legacy: militarily and economically, he got all tangled up with the British, who would soon come to run Egypt like a colony.

Thanks to loss of territory, continuing battles and wars, plots by the Persians, and a flood of Mexican silver on the market that caused their currency to plummet in value, the Ottoman Empire faced economic collapse. Meanwhile, the armed forces, militarily out of date, keep rising up in rebellions or serving as militias for revolting workers. In 1826, Sultan Mahmud II abolished janissaries and tried to initiate reforms, Westernizing the country in every way from banking to arms. In an attempt to strip the military and powerful bureaucrats of power, he mandated a fashion change. Forget the chimney hats and puffed turbans that designated rank and power. From then on, everybody would don the fez.

The tasseled hat quickly caught on. But his reforms were a failure. Among his biggest boo-boos: attaching the empire's banking system to Europe's, which wasn't all that stable itself. Down in Egypt, the ruler Ismail—who bore the title khedive—could relate: his dealings with European banks were bankrupting the country. But in Ismail's case, the problem was loans. He'd borrowed the equivalent of billions, at a very bad rate, and could hardly keep up with the interest. And

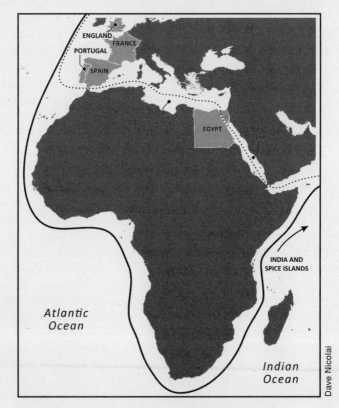

The Suez Canal shaves days of travel and some five thousand miles from ships' journeys by creating a direct route between the Middle East and Europe, as shown by the dotted line.

the reason he'd gone into debt was itself a European idea, a project that linked the Red Sea to the Mediterranean and that was way over budget: the Suez Canal.

When it opened in 1869, the Suez Canal revolutionized trade, cutting weeks off the journey between European markets and the Indian Ocean. But the project cost Egypt plenty: tens of thousands of Egyptians died in the construction, and the loans needed to finance it broke the country's back. In fact, Ismail had to sell most of Egypt's shares to the British. Even the money from the sale didn't keep the country afloat for long. By 1882, Egypt was so in the red that the unpaid military rebelled. Britain rushed in to put out the fire—and ended up running the country as a colony.

The British obsession with the Middle East wasn't simply a fascination with the region's artifacts or its silks and fine pearls, and initially it had nothing to do with oil. It was originally all about India, the subcontinent that the British had netted as a colony and squeezed for raw materials from cotton to rubber and luxury goods such as tea, spices, and brocades—not to mention the hugely lucrative trade in opium, which the Brits produced in India and smuggled to China. The prize of the colonial crown, India was so important that the British grabbed pieces of central Asia (including Persia) to help maintain their grip. To ensure ease of trade, the British dominated the waters from India to the West, including the Persian Gulf (dubbed the "British lake") and the Suez Canal.

But its control of the Suez Canal and Egypt was only one aspect of Britain's grip on the Middle East. It ruled the waters—holding ports in Yemen, Persia, Kuwait, and Bahrain—and Britain's many protectorates on the Gulf couldn't engage in trade with anyone else unless London approved. At the end of the nineteenth century, the British discovered oil in Persia and promptly clamped on to it with agreements that gave them most of the profits. And while the Brits smiled politely while wheeling and dealing with Ottomans, London was dreaming up ways to take the weakened empire down. Within two decades, the Ottoman Empire indeed crashed, just one of the tumultuous events of the twentieth century, which would witness countless revolutions, the rise of Arab nationalism, the transformation of the Gulf into an oil boomtown, the birth of a Jewish nation, and the arrival of militant Islam. All of which the British and the Americans had very much to do with.

Chapter Four

European Designs:
Hacking Up the Middle East

The twentieth century sent the Middle East spinning in a new direction—especially after the Europeans moved in looking for a new way to power war. Pictured: Sufi dancers swirling in Egypt.

Blame Churchill. If you want to know why the Middle East is so screwy today, pasty-faced British prime minister Winston Churchill is a good place to start. The man best known for keeping Britain together when the Nazis bombed the bejeezus out of it had quite the opposite effect in the Middle East. He hacked it apart. When Churchill decided to upgrade the British navy in 1913, he dramatically rearranged the whole region—economically, politically, and geographically—all to best serve Britain's military needs. He simply wanted a lighter warship, one that got more bang for the buck. But when the navy switched to oil instead of much heavier coal—and every major navy in the world soon followed suit—it shifted the weight of the world. Who cared about the lovely pearls found in the British-controlled Persian Gulf when it was rolling in petroleum? No longer was the British-controlled Suez Canal simply a key route for the British ships hauling

Library of Congress

When Churchill switched battleship fuels, he knew that Persia had oil because the British Anglo-Persian Oil Company was already pumping there (the British navy would soon become its biggest investor). So did Iraq, Kuwait, and Bahrain, all of which Britain had or would soon have under its wing.

back riches from India: it was to become a crucial link in the oil transport route, so crucial that should control of it be threatened the British would launch a war. Britain's meddling in Persia (Iran) was no longer about protecting access to India: it was about the oil that sat under the ground. Who cared about lofty principles such as self-determination—that groups of people could put together their own countries based on language and ethnicity? Fine idea for Europe perhaps, but the British weren't about to let such notions interfere with their future access to oil.

With his signature on the dotted ship-order line, Churchill would soon make rich countries out of poor ones and poor ones out of rich ones, as petroleum alone would define their future status in the world. Regions that had functioned as one, such as Greater Syria, were fractured; regions that had always been separate were smashed together, such as Iraq. And the British obsession with map drawing took on new meaning: move the line a hair one way or the other and it meant billions of barrels in oil reserves lost or gained. These map lines, drawn without thought of religion, tribe, or history, suddenly shaped identities, which had traditionally been tribal in the Middle East where the concept of country had not sunk in. Whether Jordan or Palestine, Syria or Kuwait—and whether Churchill or his associates made the political and geographic alignments—the whole region was shaped by his weighty decision to change fuels. And it still hasn't recovered.

Brown-Suarez, Courtesy of Harry S. Truman Library

Chaim Weizmann successfully pitched the idea of a Jewish national homeland to leaders in the East and West, from Syria's King Faisal to President Harry S. Truman. Meeting with the British in the years before World War I, he persuaded them to issue the Balfour Declaration of 1917, which paved the way for the creation of Israel. His 1948 meeting with Truman sealed the deal for U.S. backing of a future Israel.

The changes that would rearrange the Middle East during the twentieth century were not, however, all Churchill's doing. A Russian[1] in London by the name of Chaim Weizmann also deeply influenced the transformation of the region. Weizmann, a chemist who'd made discoveries helpful to the British arms industry, was the salesman of an idea for a new country, a national homeland for the Jews. It was a concept he was ardent about and skillfully lobbied for—starting with the British. Should the British help him establish a national Jewish homeland, he would gather fighters for World War I, promised Weizmann. What's more, if Jews were given Palestine as a national homeland, they could help protect the Suez Canal, which the British worried might be wrested from their control. "England will have a secure barrier," said Weizmann, "and we will have a country."[2] Weizmann brought in money from the Rothschild banking family; he raised money for a national fund to buy land; he met with the leaders of the West and the Middle East to set a whole new direction in motion.

So did Sharif Hussein, ruler of the Hejaz region, jewel of the Arabian Desert, encompassing the two most blessed sites for Islam. Profitable though guardianship of Mecca and Medina were, thanks to money made from annual pilgrimages, any income was siphoned off by tributes to the Ottomans. Hussein, a Hashemite (a clan descended from the prophet Mohammed), believed his clan deserved more power in the region. He signed on to battle the Ottomans with the British, believing that soon the whole Middle East would be independent of foreign domination, and not realizing that his prodigy would be puppets under colonial rule.

The British installed Sharif Hussein's son Faisal (pictured) on the throne in Iraq and began negotiating oil deals that weren't profitable for the kingdom.

All these agendas and more, including those of the French, would all play out against the most dismal era in Middle East history. The late nineteenth century saw a flowering in the region. The engineering marvel of the era, the Suez Canal, was completed. Prosperous Cairo was redone à la Paris, complete with rococo palaces, gay gardens, wide boulevards, and an opera house. Istanbul was connected to London by rail in 1883 and became home to the world's second subway system. Damascus was brimming with courtyard-filled mansions and tourists who meandered through its serpentine souks. But as the world rounded the corner into the 1900s, the Middle East was bucked off the progress horse. One reason was the foreign loans behind all this development—from the Suez Canal to Turkey's subways—which broke rulers' banks. But foreign interference wasn't the only cause for the regional doldrums: progress had been stultified.

Maybe it was because of the press: Gutenberg's 1450 invention was designed for the block letters of Latin roman type, not the flowing calligraphic scripts of dots and squiggles that formed the alphabet of Arabic, Persian, and Ottoman-era Turkish (Napoléon lugged the first press to Egypt when he dropped anchor in 1798). Maybe it was that the British controlled much of the trade, keeping traveling merchants from bringing in news and novelties. Inventions were not only lagging in the region, they had been forgotten. Once a center of innovation and learning, the Middle East was out to lunch. The Ottoman dislike of machines, the roaring industrialization of Europe, and the British tendency to stifle development abroad worked together to keep the region technologically Neanderthal. Raw goods like cotton, silk thread, dates, and pearls were the cash commodities; outside of soap, little was manufactured locally, save for the occasional state-run fez factory or European-owned silk enterprise. Even coffee, which previously brought great wealth to Yemen, was no longer exclusive to the region: it was cheaper to get it from Mexico or islands in the Dutch East Indies such as Sumatra or Java. Many Arabs still lived in the countryside as goat shepherds or subsistence farmers, employing techniques more primitive than those used by the ancients. The elaborate irrigation systems had long since crumbled, and nobody was fixing them. Many plucked cotton or raised caterpillars whose cocoons are the basis of silk; others wove carpets or spun yarn. But these were only sold locally. The silk tapestries and fine textiles that had once brought riches to these lands were no longer able to command high prices in the face of European factories that did the same work, churning out more at lower costs.

Most homes lacked the indoor water that sultans' palaces had boasted a thousand years before;[3] many wouldn't have electricity until the 1970s or later. A small urban elite prospered, but many early twentieth-century locals were tribals living in stone houses, mud huts, grass shacks, or even caves; sometimes dozens of families crammed into dilapidated palaces. Cairo, Istanbul, Damascus, and Jerusalem, while architecturally dazzling, were breeding grounds for disease, from typhus to cholera. Half of Egyptian children died before age five,[4] and most country dwellers had intestinal worms. Bands of raiders (often unemployed traders) and disbanded militias (soldiers that the government could no longer afford) roved like mafia on horses, extorting what they could from villagers and stripping travelers of possessions right down to their skivvies.

Outside of the elite, few Muslims—whether Arab, Turk, or Persian—were educated: fewer than one out of ten could read. And most who could read were Christians or Jews, especially those coming in from Russia and Europe or tied to Western missionaries and traders.

THE RISE OF THE NON-MUSLIM ELITE

Under Ottoman rule, non-Muslims were left to their own devices regarding education: Jews and Christians set up their own schools, missionaries from Europe and the United States founded universities in Beirut and Cairo. Meanwhile, Ottoman finances were such a mess that they'd shut down many schools, which taught little outside of the Koran anyway. The British closed up Egypt's secular schools (in the nineteenth century they'd had thousands[5]), deciding that government revenue was better spent repaying European debts. The result: by the twentieth century, Christians and Jews (including those coming into Palestine from Europe and Russia) were often better educated than Muslims. Thanks to the missionaries, they were also better connected to trade in the West, boosting their chance to thrive in an environment where it was growing tough to survive.

By the very beginning of the twentieth century, the region was nose-diving: Europeans tsk-tsked the Ottoman Empire, calling it "the Sick Man," and areas outside Ottoman hold, such as Persia, Egypt, and the kingdoms along the Persian Gulf, weren't doing any better. Trade was controlled by Europeans. Middle Eastern economies tanked. Corruption was as common as sand. Rulers sucked treasuries dry with lavish lifestyles. Modernization burned money. Development was in foreign hands, and developers demanded financing from European banks, which gave their loans at painfully high rates, often snatching one-third in interest. High prices for cotton (triggered by the cotton shortage during the American Civil War) came crashing down, devastating Egypt's economy and wounding the Ottoman Empire's too. Overland trade dried up as goods were shipped via sea, and thus land-transport duties, a huge source of revenue, also evaporated.

And the more the British moved in, the more markets and money dried up: England's industrial revolution favored cheap raw materials over finished goods, and the British monopolized long-distance trade, cutting locals out of jobs. The British, in control of Egypt's treasury, collected fees from the Suez Canal, and the British governor, Lord Compton, closed down hospitals and schools to pay off debt from the construction of the canal, which most benefited British ships. Without cash or incentive to build modern factories, local economies couldn't compete and kept spiraling downward; attempts to boost incomes by militarily annexing lands brought showdowns that the region's tired armies couldn't win. The Ottomans' wars only further drained the coffers. Over the previous 150 years, they had been clobbered in nine wars; besides losing face, they'd lost so much land and money from tributes that they could no longer afford a large, well-trained army and instead pulled peasants from the fields to fight their battles, while harvests were left to rot.

Money wasn't the only migraine. People in the Mideast were unhappy with their rulers. As nationalism soared across the region, discontent spread like a virus among Ottoman subjects, many of them Arabs sick of being ruled by Turks off in Istanbul who demanded increasingly hefty tributes and did little for them. Ottoman leaders became more nationalistic too: once encouraging multiethnic communities, the Turkish sultans began running out non-Turks and Christians in bloody massacres of Armenians, Greeks, and Assyrians that took down entire towns and ultimately wiped out millions. Subjects who didn't live in the Ottoman Empire were ticked too. The Egyptians bristled under British rule, which had lowered their standard of living, and Persian rulers of the Qajar dynasty hawked Persia's (Iran's) natural resources to foreigners for pennies.

PERSIA FOR SALE: COME ON DOWN

Once dripping in wealth, Persia was seriously hurting by the nineteenth and twentieth centuries: wars with Russia, during which it lost valuable regions along the Caspian Sea, had substantially shrunk the empire, caus- ing revenue to disappear. Persia's agricultural lands, where irrigation sys- tems no longer worked, were in such a sorry state that Persians suffered food shortages. The era was marked by a string of greedy leaders who cared more about tending to their seventeen-hundred-head harems of wives, slaves, and eunuchs[6] than fretting over such frivolous matters as their people, economy, or state. Nasir ed-Din Shah, who ruled between 1848 and 1896, inherited an empty piggy bank; his philosophy was "let's make a deal" as he hawked anything in the country that couldn't run away. He signed decades-long concessions to the British (specifically to Baron Paul Julius von Reuter, who later started the Reuters wire service) for min- ing, railroads, and banks, for a pittance. He even sold off all the country's tobacco for a piddling twenty-five thousand dollars a year, although a peasant revolt and a religious fatwa (edict) from land-owning clerics forced him to torch the sale of the smoke. His crooked son Muzaffar ed-Din bank- rupted the country by taking loans from the Russians to finance pricey jaunts to Europe. He signed an additional seventy-year concession to the British agent William Knox D'Arcy, selling off rights to all minerals except for gold, silver, and gems. Meanwhile, his people were starving: a short- age of bread caused by the dismal state of the farms erupted into calls for a constitution, which was finally written in 1906. But despite moves toward reform, the country was such a weakling that the British (who wanted to protect their mineral rights) and Russians (who wanted access to the sea and repayment of their loans) easily rolled in the next year. For the next decade, the Russians ran the northern third of Persia as their "sphere of influence," the Persians got to keep the middle third, and the British moved into the southern third, where they struck oil. Since the Qajar shah was such a joke, they negotiated the sale with the tribal leader upon whose land the oil gushed. And most of the profits went straight to the Anglo pockets of the Anglo-Persian Oil company, of which the British govern- ment was majority shareholder.

Lust for oil, desire for independence, and promises of power weren't the only forces at work in the Middle East during the early twentieth century. Zionism—Jewish nationalism and the desire for Jews to have their own homeland—was also a major influence. Kicked out of Palestine in the second century AD, the Jews had been a people without a country ever since, forming the world's biggest diaspora by the early twentieth century. Hungarian journal- ist Theodor Herzl launched the movement with his book *The Jewish State,* published in 1896, which became the guiding light for a Zionist revival and calls for a country where Jews could live without persecution. The question was, where? Herzl, who'd never been to Palestine, considered starting up a

Jewish homeland in Argentina or even Cyprus. The British suggested Uganda. There was talk of starting a Jewish state in Alaska and Long Island. But by the beginning of the twentieth century, most Zionists embraced a return to Palestine.

A Zionist is someone who supports the existence of a country for Jews, although not all Zionists are Jews, nor are all Jews Zionists. There are plenty of Christian Zionists who believe the Jews should have a homeland in all of Palestine because such is necessary, according to their interpretation of the Bible, before Jesus will return. In fact, the strongest American backers of U.S. support for Israel are evangelical Protestants.[7]

A HOMELAND FOR JEWS

Subject to expulsions, persecution, and pogroms for millennia, the Jewish Diaspora spread across the world by the nineteenth century. As Zionism took form during several international conferences, many Zionists pushed for a return of Jews to the place where they had last lived as a nation, two thousand years before, and where their religious history unfolded: Palestine. Some Jews were already there, having fled from Russian pogroms in the late 1800s, and more would flee there as anti-Semitism spread across Europe. Many bought land for a national homeland with money raised through the Jewish National Fund, founded in 1901, that mandated that no non-Jew could work or live on Jewish-owned land. Trickling in at first, by the 1920s their numbers had jumped to some two hundred thousand. Initially accepted by the Arabs who lived in the region, the Palestinians, the increasing Jewish population, and land purchases were soon viewed with alarm, particularly as rumors swirled about the Jews taking Palestine as a homeland. But it wasn't until the 1917 Balfour Declaration, which came on the heels of news of the Sykes-Picot Agreement deciding the British would be moving in too, that Palestinians and Arabs in general began to panic (see p. 77).

Across the Middle East, the influence of foreigners would only grow as Westerners following Churchill's lead switched to oil to power their warships and, soon enough, the entire war machine. Before long, the paradox emerged that wars couldn't be fought without oil, but it often took wars to get it. And the war that opened up the Middle East for Western oil exploitation was World War I. Often thought of solely in a European context, the Great War was also fought here, and its effects were dramatic. The war gave Westerners the chance to move in on oil-rich lands held by the Ottoman Empire. And World War I provided Britain as well as France, Russia, and the United States with a reason to dismantle the Istanbul-based empire that blocked their access to the Middle East.

Millions died in the Middle East during World War I, but not all the deaths were military. Many British fell from diseases such as cholera. Despite high fatalities, the British managed to vanquish the Ottomans with help from Arabs and from Indians whom the British marched in to fight for Iraq.

The Ottomans held land known to hold oil, including Iraq (then a collection of separate city-states: Mosul, Baghdad, and Basra), and the Ottomans controlled Palestine, the region Jews wanted to turn into their national home. These factors alone might have been enough to prompt a war, but the Ottomans brought it on by hopping into bed with the Germans, whose private investments jolted the lagging Ottoman economy. The Germans also built railways: the new lines from Europe to Turkey and the Middle East bolstered trade and seriously raised British eyebrows. Generally wary of the Turks, whom they sometimes helped out and sometimes battled, the Brits eyed the rapidly industrializing Germans with deep woe, particularly as Germans were building a fancy military machine, including a fearsome navy that rivaled Her Majesty's fleet. And the British *really* didn't like the new railroad route into oil-rich country that was nearing completion by 1914: even if it took three weeks to get from Istanbul to its final destination in the Middle East, the Berlin–Baghdad line was getting a wee bit too close to the British-controlled Gulf and to oil-holding lands the British had their eyes on. It all came to a head in a big showdown that summer.

The map of Kuwait is a physical illustration of the fears Brits had about the Ottomans and their German railroad-building buddies: the Brits drew the boundaries of Kuwait to create a buffer between Iraq and the Gulf, blocking the Ottomans, who then held the regions of Baghdad and Basra (now Iraq), from easy access to water. Decades later, Saddam tried to negate that bane by invading Kuwait.

Contempt for the Ottoman rulers was universal, even in Istanbul. A 1908 coup had brought to power a secret society, the Young Turks, who shoved out the sultan and put a timid puppet in his place. The Young Turks' most momentous decision was pushing the Ottomans into World War I, which kicked off in 1914: the

Ottomans sided with the Germans, facing off against Britain, France, Russia, and later the United States. The British were determined, not only to win the war, but to give the Ottomans a final push off the cliff. And to weaken the empire's hold in the Middle East, the British turned to the Arabs.

BRITS IN THE SANDS

For all the selfish and imperialist moves the British government made in Middle East, the British people *were* seriously intrigued by the region's culture, and archaeologists and adventurers started flocking there in the nineteenth century. By the early twentieth century, three names stood out, all of them British explorers-writers-spies, and two of them women. Gertrude Bell (1868–1926) and Freya Stark (1893–1993) spoke Arabic and Persian, mingled with the locals, and were fellows of London's Royal Geographical Society, which held the world's largest collection of maps and volunteered services to the British military. Stark was drawn by a love of languages and a search for lost desert cities; at heart a writer, her books about Yemen and Persia still dazzle today. So do those of Bell, a wealthy, brilliant overachiever. Extremely powerful, holding many government posts, she literally drew the doomed boundaries of Iraq; in 1921 she convinced Churchill—then colonial secretary—to renege on promises to make Kurdistan a separate country in what is now northern Iraq. And Bell advised Iraq's first puppet leader, the Hashemite king Faisal, to keep the Shia down and out of power. The third of the trio, T. E. Lawrence, better known as Lawrence of Arabia, promised independence for the Arabs if they fought with him against the Ottoman Turks. In short, they all had tremendous effects on the region, whether by keeping its past alive, drawing boundaries that would cause grief for a century to come, or by offering forked-tongue promises that made the West loathed.

As World War I spilled into the Middle East, the British led the attack on the Ottomans, wresting control of their lands. One subplot that stands out is the 1916 Arab Revolt, which provided the frame through which the West is now viewed. Working with T. E. Lawrence, the Brits hatched a plan with the powerful Hashemite clan that ruled over the Hejaz in Arabia. Lawrence and Sir Henry McMahon (the British high commissioner in Cairo) promised that if the Arabs helped Brits push the Ottomans out of Syria, (a) the Arabs would be independent of foreign rule, and (b) the Hashemites would rule the land from Syria in the north to Yemen in the south.[8] Sharif Hussein, leader of the Hashemites, sent sons Faisal and Abdullah through the region to secure the backing of Arabs, eliciting support and a nod from Syrian secret societies in support of a war against the Ottoman Turks who had laid claim to this land for four centuries. In 1916, the Hashemite-led

Arabs and Brits charged into Damascus, taking the city in 1918. While the Arabs held true to their part of the deal, the British didn't, or couldn't fully, hold up their promises. The British had been talking out of three sides of their mouths, making a few other deals that compromised their promise of Arab independence and Hashemite rule.

BACKROOM DEALS

The complexity of the political arrangements that would unfold over the next three decades is hinted at in an unruly bundle of World War I documents, often contradictory, that were to somehow guide the creation of the modern Middle East. A few of the most important:

Hussein-McMahon letters: The ten letters exchanged in 1915 and 1916 between Hashemite Sharif Hussein and Sir Henry McMahon (the British high commissioner in Cairo), discussed what was on the table if the Hashemites fought with the British to reclaim Ottoman-ruled territory. Though Sharif Hussein was initially promised that the whole Middle East would be ruled by the Hashemites, later letters question what land should be included (see p. 79).

Sykes-Picot Agreement: A secret 1915 agreement signed by British lieutenant-colonel Mark Sykes and French diplomat François Georges-Picot delineating how the British and French would divide the Middle East if the Ottoman Empire fell. Given that the biggest motivation in moving into the region was oil, it's hilarious that neither bothered with central Arabia—the part that would become Saudi Arabia—which holds the biggest oil reserves in the world. British geologists believed it didn't have a drop.

Balfour Declaration: A result of the persuasive abilities of Chaim Weizmann, British banker Lord Rothschild, and other Zionists, this 1917 declaration stated that the British favored a homeland for Jews as long as it didn't harm the rights of the Palestinians. The British support was bolstered by promises that residents of the Jewish homeland would help protect the Suez Canal, a crucial transport link for Britain (see below).

Foreign Office
November 2nd, 1917

Dear Lord Rothschild,
I have much pleasure in conveying to you, on behalf of His Majesty's Government, the following declaration of sympathy with Jewish Zionist aspirations, which has been submitted to, and approved by, the Cabinet.
"His Majesty's Government view with favour the establishment in Palestine of a national home for the Jewish people, and will use their best endeavours to

facilitate the achievement of this object, it being clearly understood that nothing shall be done which may prejudice the civil and religious rights of existing non-Jewish communities in Palestine, or the rights and political status enjoyed by Jews in any other country."
I should be grateful if you would bring this declaration to the knowledge of the Zionist Federation.

Yours sincerely,
Arthur James Balfour

The Brits' seemingly contradictory agreements were made when the outcome of the war wasn't clear. But in 1918, when the four-year "war to end all wars" drew to a close after killing over 25 million[9]—about five million in the Middle East—the Europeans clamped on, and the knives started officially carving up the region. The war had only underscored their need for oil, which powered an expanding arsenal of new vehicles such as tanks, cars, trucks, and planes. Securing control of oil-rich countries was a stated imperative, ordered by the British military and necessitated by a petroleum-fueled military machine. Through treaties, agreements, actions, and the League of Nations (precursor to the United Nations) a new design was imposed on the region, one that would eventually change even more. By 1920, however, several things were clear:

- The Ottoman Empire would no longer exist; all its Middle Eastern holdings were lost.
- The Ottoman Empire's capital, Istanbul, and about a third of the empire's land would become an independent, secular republic: Turkey.
- The French and British were divvying up most the empire's other holdings in the Middle East among themselves.

World War I also brought down the Austro-Hungarian Empire. At the 1919 Paris Peace Conference, where postwar territories were remapped, President Woodrow Wilson unveiled his heady Fourteen Points plan, which included "self-determination" of nations. This ideal guided the creation of new European countries, such as Czechoslovakia and Yugoslavia, formed from former Austro-Hungarian holdings. Desirable Ottoman territories, however, were blocked from independence by the British and French, who had long been licking their lips at the thoughts of the untapped petroleum in the Middle East.

CARVING TURKEY

As the five-century-old Ottoman Empire centered in Istanbul fell, Turkey slid out of the Middle East's main arena. Taken over by Turkish nationalist Kemal Atatürk, the country rapidly modernized and changed everything, starting with fashion and government views on religion. Atatürk insisted that Western dress be adopted—it was illegal to wear fezzes or face veils. And Islam was ditched as the state religion in this new secular country. Even the language was reworked: Atatürk demanded that Turkish be written in the Latin alphabet, and he opened numerous secular schools, which boosted literacy dramatically, from about 9 percent at the end of World War I to about 90 percent today. From the 1920s on, Turkey became more European than Middle Eastern, and many of today's Turks insist that Turkey is not part of the Middle East. It's not yet part of the European Union, but it is expected to enter the union eventually. The politically incorrect holdup is that the EU is a Christian club, and there are fears about allowing in a country that, while secular, is populated mostly by Muslims. In 2007, Turkey militarily entered the Middle East, launching an attack in northern Iraq on the PKK, a group of militant Kurds who want to form Kurdistan. Turkey has always been deeply opposed to this idea. One reason: Turkey would lose much of its eastern flank.

Across the Middle East, one's ethnicity, language, and religion assumed weightier importance as nationalism and demand for self-rule became the defining issues of the day. But while such concepts were fine for determining the future of Europe, the British and French shot them down here. In the opinion of the British and French, who were itching to tap the Middle East resources, Arabs weren't fit to rule themselves. Of course, that assessment had everything to do with oil. As a result of the Brits' mealymouthed triple talk, including clandestine deals with the French, the Arabs discovered that most Middle Eastern territories would not be granted true independence—it would elude them for decades—and the Hashemites discovered that they would not rule over much.

- Syria would be "temporarily" ruled by the French who (for starters) ejected Syria's new king Faisal, a Hashemite, from his throne. The French had plans to water down Arab nationalism by dividing Greater Syria into four sections by religion: Christian, Sunni, Alawite (sort of Shia), and Druze (a different sort of Shia).
- Coastal Arabia, including Kuwait, Oman, Qatar, Bahrain, and assorted emirates would remain British protectorates, with their same rulers.
- Egypt, where rioting against British control had become severe, was granted independence in 1922, but the British continued to control it.

- The British would temporarily rule Palestine, which was the site of a planned Jewish national homeland.
- The British would temporarily "oversee" Mesopotamia, which they rearranged and made into one country, Iraq, simply to better control oil. Hashemite king Faisal would wear the crown, ruling this riot-wracked country that brought together Shia Muslims (who wanted an Islamic theocracy) and Sunni Muslims (who didn't) with the ethnic group called the Kurds (whom the British had promised their own country but had reneged on that promise as well).
- As a consolation prize, the Hashemite emir Abdullah (whom the parliament of the Sunnis in Iraq had voted in as their ruler) *would* get to rule over part of Palestine, 80 percent of which was lopped off to form a kingdom for him (today's Jordan).
- Persia, which would soon be renamed Iran, would continue to be a monarchy, in theory, but often subject to British economic control and occasional occupation by the British (and Russia).

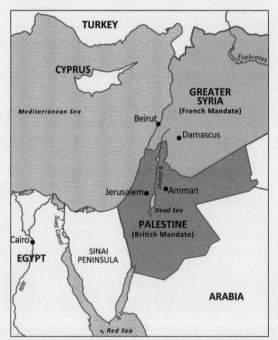

The Middle East of the early twentieth century didn't have "countries" but rather loosely defined territories such as Arabia and Greater Syria. It underwent a vast redesign after the French and British picked up their pens. The map above shows two of the initial chops in 1920, which created the French Mandate of Greater Syria and the British Mandate of Palestine.

POSTWAR AGREEMENTS

Treaty of Sevres (1920):   The tool for the initial dismemberment of the Ottoman Empire, this treaty called for chopping off two-thirds of Ottoman territory and leaving what was left as an independent Turkey. Along with the concurrently signed Tripartite Agreement, it allowed British oil businesses to run in the Middle East and called for an autonomous country of Kurdish lands, Kurdistan, to be formed that would include Mosul (in today's Iraq). Kurdistan, however, was never created, much to the disappointment of the Kurds. The treaty was nullified in 1923, with many key clauses rewritten into the new Treaty of Lausanne (see below).

San Remo Conference: This formalized the Sykes-Picot Agreement: the British and French would divide up the Middle East. However, all the details weren't hammered down, and for the next few years they were trading properties like Monopoly cards: "I'll give you the Litani River (in Lebanon) for Mosul (in Iraq)."

Treaty of Lausanne (1923):   Among other things, this treaty formally recognized the British and French "mandates" in the Middle East. A gussied-up means to disguise the colonial pursuit, the mandates were essentially supervisory babysitting jobs to aid the affected lands in establishing constitutions and governments "until such time as they are able to stand alone." In reality, many already had constitutions, parliaments, and/or working governments in place, but the British and France had the right, via the mandates, to do as they pleased, including dividing the territories and tapping their resources as they saw fit.

British Mandate: After World War I, the League of Nations gave Britain two "mandates," internationally approved assignments to babysit territories. The first mandate was for the territories in today's Iraq; the second was the mandate for Palestine, which included today's Israel, Palestinian territories, Jerusalem, and Jordan. A main thrust of the British Mandate for Palestine was to create a national homeland for Jews.

French Mandate: The territory that the League of Nations assigned the French to babysit after World War I includes today's Syria, Lebanon, and part of eastern Turkey.

One omission on the "mandate" maps is central Arabia, which neither Britain nor France wanted. (Britain already had the coastal areas as its protectorates.) It wasn't that they thought the Arabs in the heart of the peninsula were more advanced and capable of self-rule—between its vast deserts, raiders, bedouin warriors and numerous tribes, these were the rugged backwaters. The reason the Europeans didn't pounce on Arabia is because their geologists had assured them there wasn't an amoeba-sized speck of oil to be found in the whole wasteland.[10] *One suspects that those geologists soon got other jobs, since the central part of Arabia (today's Saudi Arabia) holds a quarter of the world's known oil. And American oil companies Standard Oil of California and Gulf, which would shortly muscle into these lands, instead hit the jackpot.*

The Arabs weren't at all pleased that, despite the promises and the pretensions, foreigners would still be running most of the region. When the French and British began arriving to supervise the creation of the new Middle East, there were no marching bands to greet them, no pretty girls tossing flowers, no showers of confetti.[11] Few cared that their papers were in order, that the League of Nations had issued the Europeans official rights to do whatever they saw fit in setting up new countries, including whittling them away. The Westerners were neither welcomed nor wanted as overseers. The Arabs had made that very clear. They'd expressed it in editorials sent to papers in London, Paris, and New York. They'd expressed it to public opinion pollsters such as the U.S.-led King-Crane Commission that came through in 1919 to take the pulse of the masses and accurately forecasted that what was about to unfold would be one huge ugly mess. The Arabs expressed their feelings at conferences, such as the 1919 Paris Peace Conference where the heady Wilsonian principles of self-determination were bandied about in reference to Europe but forgotten when the conversation turned to the Middle East. Representatives of the Middle East were mostly ignored at the conference. And the King-Crane Commission report, delivered there, was effectively binned.

A FEW FANS

Most Arabs were furious at the turn of events: they'd been used as pawns in World War I, some felt, to take down one foreign regime, the Ottomans, only to have it replaced by more foreign rulers. And for decades the foreign rulers, in most cases, didn't give Arabs a voice in government or in parliament, most of which were shut down. However, there were two small groups who were happy to see the Europeans. Maronite Christians in the mountains of Lebanon welcomed the arrival of the French in 1920: the French that very year came through on a previous promise to give Maronites their own country—Lebanon, carved out of Syria—where they would play first fiddle in a society of Christians and Muslims of assorted sects. The British also found a small group of fans: the Zionists—including Chaim Weizmann, who that year became president of the World Zionist Organization—applauded the British arrival in Palestine, sure that they would help them form the long-sought-after Jewish national homeland. Even among this group, however, some soon began trashing the British. In 1922, Winston Churchill cut off 80 percent of Palestine and gave it to Arab emir Abdullah to become the Hashemite Kingdom of Jordan, which was Arab and mostly Muslim. Many Zionists were aghast. "Revisionists," some of whom would later make up Israel's Likud Party, believed that *all* Palestine had been meant for them as part of a biblical promise made between God and Abraham four thousand years ago. Another upsetting change: in the last-minute property swapping between the British and French, the British had traded part of what was then Greater Syria for an oil-soaked property, Mosul, in Iraq. And the land that the British traded, which ended up in southern Lebanon, included the Litani River that Chaim Weizmann and other Zionists believed from the start would be crucial for the Jewish national homeland. And these issues—the creation of Jordan, where many Palestinians would later flee, and the loss of the Litani River from territory set aside for Jews—would lead to wars and bitterness for many decades to come. In fact, both issues are still thorns.

Despite the reverse-rolling red carpets, the British and the French stomped on in. Arriving in 1920, and greeted with riots, the French blasted their way into power in Syria, killing thousands. The Syrian parliament voted that Greater Syria was independent, accepted King Faisal as its leader, and refused to accept the French Mandate. The French ejected Faisal and disbanded the parliament. The British tried to shoot down dissent in Iraq, as the British called their amalgamated oil dreamland. Shia and Sunni fought together against the Westerners, and the Kurds in the north were the angriest of all, killing any Brit that came near their land. British pilots gunned down Iraqi protesters and pounded villages with chemical bombs, killing over ten thousand Iraqis in the first year—and still the protests continued. Egypt wasn't any better. Prohibited from attending the 1919 Paris Peace Conference, the Egyptians, under British rule for almost four decades, revolted: their protests were so unceasing and violent (even policemen joined in) that finally the British agreed to "independence" in 1922—but it was nothing more than a word on a piece of paper. The British lords and governors and military stayed, exerting backroom control, running the Suez Canal, and collecting the revenue from it. Despite Egypt's "independence," anti-British riots and protests continued.

Arab ire wasn't only directed at the British. Big problems between Arabs and Zionists were brewing up in Palestine. Everywhere across the Middle East there was clamor about the Zionists: Arabs demanded to know what the Balfour Declaration really meant and what exactly the British plans were for a Jewish homeland in Palestine. This idea that—like the French who had immediately created a country for Christians, Lebanon, out of what had been Syria—the Brits might now give Arab land to foreign Jews came to emblematize the traitorous acts of the West.

TROUBLE IN PALESTINE

The Zionist movement to create a Jewish national homeland in Palestine had a catchy slogan: "A land without people for a people without a land." The problem was, only half of the slogan was true. There were people in Palestine, many of them Arab peasant farmers. Their families had been living in these parts, often in the same small stone homes, for centuries. All they had were their homes and their land thick with orange trees and, especially, olive groves, considered an investment and a gift for all future generations since the hearty trees could grow for thousands of years and olive oil never went out of style. Initially, the Arabs welcomed the incoming Jews when they began arriving in the late 1800s. But the dynamics changed in the following decades as the Arabs realized that the Zionists, many of whom regarded this as their promised land, wanted the Arab farmlands, without the Arabs on them, as a Jewish-only national homeland. By 1919, when the poll results in the King-Crane Report rolled in, the positions had become extreme. The Zionists wanted to take over all of Palestine (which then included Jordan), and the Palestinians wanted all of them out.

The British, and to a lesser extent the French, sliced up territory and rearranged boundaries in the Middle East in a manner that behooved only themselves. They violently inflicted their will over loud choruses of dissent and in the process instilled a deep loathing of colonialism and the West that still lives on. The inane map lines the British and French drew, their outright dismissal of the wishes of the occupants, their unabashed exploitation of oil, their violent attempts to suppress the revolting masses, and the subsequent hatred of the West they created is in large part why the Middle East is still so volatile today.

HACKING UP THE OTTOMAN EMPIRE

During their rule of the Middle East, which officially began in 1920, the British and French unveiled a rare talent for creating maps that ensured discord. The region once known as Greater Syria was first to be divided. The British territorially sawed off the southern chunk that hugged the eastern Mediterranean, calling it Palestine: soon it was subdivided, at British hands, into Jordan (initially called Transjordan), and in 1947, at the hands of the United Nations, divided into Israel, Palestinian territories, and Jerusalem (see map, p. 91).

The French grabbed the remaining part of Greater Syria and redivided it into five subsections and sliced off the beloved west coast as Lebanon, a gift to the Maronite Christians, where they could live alongside Shia, Sunni, and the Druze Muslims. Great idea: Lebanon has spent a third of its existence in civil war.

The British also scored a mandate in Mesopotamia, which under the Ottomans held three distinct and separated provinces that had nothing to do with each other: Baghdad, the biggest city of Mesopotamia, which was mostly Sunni; Basra, a Shia province rolling in oil; and Mosul, an oil-rich area in the north, which was home to Kurds. The Brits wanted access to both oil regions and, to make life easier administratively, they molded together all three into one country, Iraq, that had little chance of ever being functional. Beyond merely fomenting dissent within, their map lines ensured problems outside as well: despite being oil-rich, Iraq had scanty access to the Persian Gulf to ship oil out, since the previous British creation of Kuwait was blocking the way, forcing Iraq to share the 120-mile-long river, Shatt al Arab, with Iranians. The British geographical arrangement not only portended future showdowns, it helped create them, including the nasty eight-year Iran-Iraq War that began in 1980 partly over access to the waterway; and, after numerous attempts to annex Kuwait, Iraq invaded and forcefully roped it in 1990.

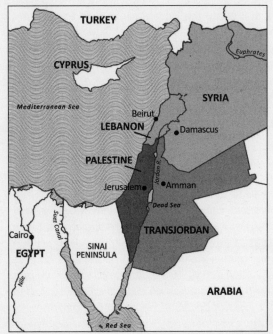

Second cuts: by 1922, the region was already taking on a new look with the British creation of Transjordan (Jordan), a kingdom drawn in the sands for Hashemite emir Abdullah, and the French creation of Lebanon, out of part of Syria, as a country for Christians.

Persia (soon known as Iran) hadn't been part of the Ottoman Empire—it had been an independent monarchy for four centuries—thus it wasn't part of the British Mandate, but the British monopolized oil production there and wanted more control. The 1919 Anglo-Persian Agreement, signed in secret with heavy palm greasing, essentially handed over Persia's economy to the Brits. When news of it leaked out, Persians had a fit: intellectuals roared that the country was now Britain's slave, and some left the country in protest; the French satirized the agreement, saying Persia had been sold off for ten cents. The uproar it caused ultimately led to a 1921 coup that ended the Qajar dynasty: with a behind-the-scenes boost from the Brits, who believed he wouldn't threaten their oil interests, military man Reza Pahlavi appointed himself shah in 1925.

Despite the chaos their arrival had unleashed, the Europeans rolled up their sleeves and got down to the business at hand: oil. Placing Hashemite king Faisal on the throne in Iraq (after he'd been run out of the Syrian palace by the French), the British hastily started up the British-owned Iraqi Petroleum Company, shoving out Turkey (which laid claims to the former Ottoman land's oil) and renegotiating previous contracts. Oil was soon gushing through pipelines to Palestine, where it was loaded onto Europe-bound ships. The British also continued poking around in the Gulf for more oil, signing up concessions in protectorates such as Bahrain and Kuwait.

The search for oil was often couched in terms of a search for water. Western powers convinced Arab leaders that geologists could find the resource that was so scarce it was often delivered in skin bags via boats. Bahrain was the first winner: surveyors tapped sweet water in 1924; eight years later, they struck oil. The next year geologists discovered petroleum off Saudi Arabia. As news of the finds, and the sound of ka-ching, ka-ching echoed across the Gulf, geologists became local leaders' most popular guests. Even if drills didn't turn up oil, there were barrels of money to be had: oil companies shucked over hundreds of thousands of dollars—and millions of dollars in loans—to be granted exclusive rights to search. The money was needed. Reeling from the worldwide economic tsunami unleashed by the Great Depression, the small Gulf kingdoms, dependent on pearling, were hit with a double whammy: in the 1930s Japan introduced synthetic pearls created by placing sand in cultivated oysters, and the natural pearl market snapped shut. Money for oil exploration offset that sting.

Before you could say "fill 'er up," the Americans were swooping in, reminding the Brits that they'd help them win World War I, and wanting to be dealt into the game. Demanding a redline agreement that allowed them stakes in the Iraqi Petroleum Company and to bid on local oil concessions, Standard Oil of California and Gulf Oil barreled in, outbidding the British and the French and gaining the prize concessions, among them Saudi Arabia, which held more oil than anyplace else in the world. One problem: it also held Islam's holiest sites and was the most rigidly Muslim country in the Middle East, practicing the most conservative form of Islam anywhere on the planet. Another snag: the religious leaders did not want to open the desert kingdom to infidel Westerners. And the schism between religion and oil would play out for many decades to come, culminating a half century later in the creation of al Qaeda.

Competition from Yanks was only one British woe of that era. Iran's Shah Reza Pahlavi kept harping about Iran's take of the oil profits, and in 1932 he actually cancelled the British oil concession that was supposed to continue until 1961. The Brits cajoled him back into it, but he wasn't happy with the chintzy terms they offered, 16 percent of profits, and he became adamantly anti-British, sidling up to the Germans. Meanwhile rebellions against the foreigners were breaking out in all corners.

Anti-French rebellions in Syria were going on nonstop, fueled by the fact that France had stifled the press, disbanded the parliament, refused to allow a constitution, and subdivided what was left of Syria into segregated states to diffuse Syrian nationalism. Intellectuals balked and wrote letters, while the Druze, confined to their mountain dwellings, led a bloody rampage on the French in Damascus, causing such anarchy that the French let loose on the capital, killing at least five thousand in a month. In Egypt, Muslim intellectuals were upset that Islam was disappearing: the British didn't encourage it, the king didn't care about it, and there was talk of tearing down mosques as part of urban renovation. Wanting to keep Islam alive, schoolteacher Hassan al-Banna formed an Islamic study group in 1928. The Muslim Brotherhood, as it was called, morphed into a tool of protest against the British and Western customs, including movies, viewed as corrupting. Before long, a militant arm of the Muslim Brotherhood began blasting bombs in cinemas and stores owned by Europeans and Jews.

THE ARAB LEAGUE

Formed in 1945, specifically in response to the Palestinian question, this political, economic, and defense organization of Arab-speaking countries took a united stand against the potential formation of Israel. It has never yet recognized Israel and has taken numerous actions against it, including economic boycotts and creating the Palestine Liberation Organization (PLO) in 1964 specifically to take down the nation of Jews. The league booted out founding member Egypt when President Sadat made peace with Israel in 1979 but let Egypt rejoin a decade later. It was a major to-do when the Arab League accepted the Saudi Peace Plan in March 2002 and offered to recognize Israel's right to exist if the latter pulled back to pre-1967 boundaries; the proposal was rekindled in 2007, and, shockingly, members of the Arab League made an appearance on the floor of Israel's parliament to try to get the measure accepted. Despite the show, few Israelis endorse the plan.

The situation was also out of control in Palestine: furious that they had no representation in government and upset by the swelling wave of Jewish immigrants, which had grown to four hundred thousand, the local Arabs, the Palestinians, refused to pay taxes and frequently rioted. Arab militias such as the Black Hand terrorized Zionist settlers, and Zionist militias terrorized Arabs. The British brought in a group of London officials, the Peel Commission, who in 1937 recommended splitting Palestine into a land for Jews and another for Arabs, and forcefully relocating Arabs to their corner. The protests turned into the three-year Arab revolt. Hurling grenades, throwing stones through windows, and blasting crude explosives, the Arabs—many of them peasants—destroyed the budding Arab-Jewish economy, refusing to sell or buy from Jews. Raids on Jewish farms were answered by counter-raids on Palestinian peasant villages. The Arab revolt had little effect: five thousand Arabs died along with several hundred Brits and Jews. Attempting to quell the violence, the British issued a white paper in 1939 that capped immigration of Jews to seventy-five thousand over the next five years, and the British infamously began turning back ships of Jews escaping from the Nazis. This prompted the Zionists to turn on the British. Illegal immigration via land and sea continued to boost the Jewish population. The British rounded up illegal immigrants and shipped them out or confined them to detention camps. In 1942, one ship denied entry, the battered *Struma*, sunk not far from Palestine, and the 768 on board drowned, sparking more outrage.

Against the backdrop of this mayhem, the war drums began pounding as World War II started up in Europe and, like the First World War, spilled into the Middle East.

MIDDLE EAST ARENAS

Cairo, under British-imposed martial law, became the Allies' command center for the region during World War II, its streets thick with spies. Syria was suddenly under quasi-Nazi rule, since the Nazi-controlled Vichy government in France took over the French Mandate, and Axis powers moved into Syria's ports. A rebellion in Iraq ran out the British and was only somewhat quelled when the British returned in 1944. In Iran, which Shah Reza Pahlavi insisted the world now call Persia, Pahlavi wouldn't allow Allied troops to cross his land, blocking the so-called Persian Corridor to central Asia and substantially lengthening the time needed for Russians to arrive on the battle scene. In 1941, Brits and Russians teamed up to blast into Iran again, killing thousands. Pahlavi, forced to abdicate and to go into exile, was replaced by a ruler the British found more friendly: his son, Shah Mohammed Reza Pahlavi.

World War II underscored two ideas: (1) the Middle East was more crucial than ever to the Western war machine, and (2) the Jews needed protection. These two issues became cornerstones of U.S. policy even though they seemed, and often are, contradictory. This was made clear to President Franklin Delano Roosevelt: In February 1945, on his way back from deciding the fate of post–World War II Europe at the Yalta Conference, Roosevelt made a point of meeting with Saudi Arabia's leader Ibn Saud, whose oil had helped to fuel World War II. One factor in ending the war was that the Allies, thanks to Saudi Arabia, still had oil to burn, while the Axis powers were running seriously low. To guarantee access to future wars, Roosevelt and Ibn Saud struck a deal still in action today: oil for security. The Saudis would provide oil as long as the United States would protect them—and arm them. But there was one other issue that Ibn Saud raised during the meeting: he was worried about the Zionists in Palestine. He was opposed to the idea of the Jewish state. FDR promised Ibn Saud that the United States wouldn't back the creation of a state without Saudi approval. But only a few months later FDR was slammed by realpolitik. The New York Times headline told the story: "FDR backs creation of Jewish state."

When WWII finally gasped to a halt, the search for Middle East oil started up again, this time with a fury. The Arabian Peninsula was transformed into a flurry of dynamite and drills, contracts and lawyers, planes swooping down and oil rigs shooting up. The press tagged along, keeping readers up to date with this lost-in-time world where rulers lived in mud shacks, there was no running water, and falcons were used to find food. At least there were new things to look at—the airplanes flying in, and the oil tankers going out—as the oil bonanza got under way. And while the United States became entrenched in the oil activities of the Persian Gulf, it also became deeply involved in another Middle Eastern matter: the creation of Israel. And Chaim Weizmann helped bring the United States in by lobbying FDR's successor, President Harry S. Truman.

The end of the war in 1945 brought the spotlight back to Palestine. A safe refuge for Jews was obviously needed: among the many atrocities against Jews during the war, some six million had died in Nazi concentration camps. Zionists were more determined than ever to get their homeland in Palestine, whatever it took. Their relations with the British, whom they believed were

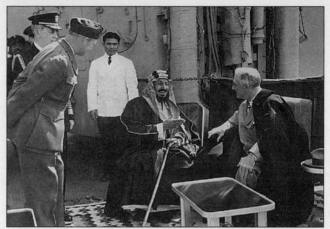

National Archives

On February 11, 1945, President Roosevelt welcomed Saudi Arabia's king Ibn Saud and his entourage of tent carriers, sheep, and goats onto the USS Quincy anchored off Egypt's Suez Canal. During their meeting, they hammered out the formula that dictates Saudi-American relations to this day: American protection in exchange for access to Saudi oil.

unduly influenced by their lust for oil, only worsened as tens of thousands of Jews who'd survived the concentration camps and illegally immigrated to Palestine found themselves rounded up and shut into British detention camps. Zionists blasted the British oil pipeline that ran from Kirkuk in Iraq to Haifa in Palestine. And in 1946, Irgun, a guerrilla Zionist group led by future prime minister Menachem Begin, blew up a wing of Jerusalem's King David Hotel, where the British were meeting, killing ninety-one, Brits, Arabs, and Jews among them. Once cocky and assured, the British were now distraught and overwhelmed with trying to figure out what to do. They finally tossed the hot potato at the UN, and made plans to move out.

A United Nations investigating commission visited Palestine in 1947 and was distressed to see that some fifty thousand Jews who'd entered Palestine illegally were being detained in British camps. The commission recommended a "two-state" solution: a country for Jews and a separate country for Palestinians. With confusion, anger, contradiction, and politicking all along the way, the United Nations finally adopted Resolution 181 in November 1947: it called for the partitioning of Palestine. A little more than half was set aside as a land for Jews, parcels of land in between were allocated for the Palestinians, and the holy city of Jerusalem was to be an independent UN-monitored city, owned by neither, open to both.

Most Zionists accepted the plan, although some, such as revisionist Vladimir Jabotinsky, believed Israel should include all of Palestine and Jordan. The Arabs out-and-out rejected that idea. Protests erupted across the Middle East. At U.S. embassies across the region, relations with Arabs turned icy overnight.

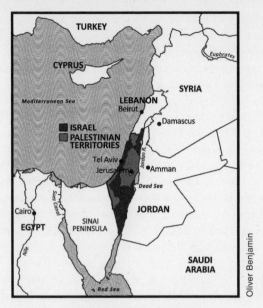

The United Nations 1947 partition of
Palestine allocated lands for two states: one
for Jews and another for Palestinians

FIGHTING POINTS

The hundreds of thousands of Jews who'd come from all over the world to start this new country, the first homeland for Jews in nearly two millennia, didn't much care what the Palestinians thought about the 1947 UN Partition Plan. Traumatized from the horrors of the Nazi holocaust (on the heels of pogroms in Russia), Jews wanted their own turf. Given their history of living in this land under King David in the tenth century BC, they also believed they had a rightful claim to "the promised land," which they believed had in fact been promised to them by God when Abraham made a covenant with him in the second millennium BC. The Arabs didn't see things that way. They had been living in the land for thousands of years, often alongside Jews and Christians; while they didn't deny the Jews' traumas, those horrors had been inflicted by Westerners—not Arabs, not Muslims. Why, they asked, did Arabs have to pay for the sins of the West? The problem wasn't even entirely that the Zionists were not Muslim. The main issue was land: Palestinians would be forced to move from their farms to create the new Jewish homeland. By then Zionists had killed thousands of Palestinians (who had also killed Zionists, though not in the same proportions), and they symbolized all that was wrong about the West and the Westerners who had encroached on Arab lands, remapped Arab territory in ways that suited Westerners, inflicted Western rule (and Western-controlled puppets), and were squeezing Arab land for its resources.

In the morning hours of May 14, 1948, the British hightailed it out of Palestine, cutting loose the land that had brought them nothing but woes since the moment that they'd naively pushed into it nearly three decades before. At midnight, the prime minister David Ben-Gurion proclaimed the birth of the new state of Israel. On May 15, 1948, Israel woke up to explosions and gunfire. The welcome wagon it wasn't: armies from Egypt, Syria, and Jordan marched in to reclaim the land and take down the fledgling country.

The 1948 Arab-Israeli war raged for the next eleven months, ultimately involving Lebanon and Iraq as well. Even though Israel did not even have an army, the Zionist militias led the war effort to keep their land. That the Arabs miserably failed in their mission to take back the land, and that Israel in fact expanded its territory to cover 78 percent of the former Palestine, pushing out hundreds of thousands more Palestinians in the process, only further fueled Arab rage. Despite a 1949 armistice, Arabs refused to accept Israel's "right to exist," a phrase that would come up again and again in the years that followed. Another phrase that would keep popping up was "the right to return." Specifically, the right of Palestinians to return to the lands they were pushed out of in 1948 and would be again nineteen years later. But Israelis weren't the only ones who'd taken Palestinian land in that war. Egypt snagged the Gaza Strip, and Jordan claimed much of the land west of the Jordan River as well as East Jerusalem. The Palestinians were screwed.

In the decades following World War II, Arabia turned into an oil casino, with the petroleum companies playing the slots, and the rulers looking on from behind, holding their breath with every yank of the lever and every drilling of new wells. The destiny of the people of Arabia was being decided in a bizarre petroleum lottery, as if by location alone they had been handed three of the six winning numbers, and nature would determine if they would come up with the rest. Every sheik's future, as well as that of those he ruled, lay under the sands. With so much money to be had, you could almost hear the rulers yelling, "Keep blasting, keep drilling, keep digging, and don't stop!" What was found under the ground (and what wasn't) became the sole element defining a territory's evolution: score big like Kuwait, which by 1962 was the biggest oil exporter of the Middle East, and you could tell the British to shove off, declare independence, build fine hospitals and schools, and buy off your enemies (at least for a time). Lose out, and you could end up like once mighty emirate Fujairah—forgotten.

THE OIL WINNERS AND HOW THEY SPENT THE SPOILS

Within fifteen years of post–World War II exploration, the earth was pocked with holes, but oil was gurgling up all over Arabia—and Western salesmen were rushing in. The reason: the three richest men in the world now lived here. Here's a summary of which kingdoms first struck oil and what their leaders did with the newfound gold:

Bahrain (discovered 1932):   The first winner of the Gulf oil bonanza, Bahrain's sheik Hamad ibn Isa Al-Khalifa, knowing his kingdom held only modest deposits, developed infrastructure, built the most modern city in the region, and diversified the economy. Britain controlled it, though, including running torture prisons.

Saudi Arabia (discovered 1933):   King Abdul Aziz (aka Ibn Saud) didn't drive, but succumbed to the temptations of salesmen showing up from everywhere and offering novelties: he snatched up cars by the dozens, built palaces by the handful, and demanded all payments in cash: oil company Aramco delivered truckloads of silver. His son Saud, the world's richest man by 1957, was worse: while less than 5 percent of his people could read and most were malnourished, he blew through three hundred million dollars a year just taking care of the kin, building boatloads of fifty-million-dollar palaces for his four wives, ninety courtesans, and one hundred kids; somewhere along the line he finally built a hospital, a university, and a concrete plant. Not until Faisal took over in 1964 were public works put into action. Still holds a quarter of known world reserves.

Kuwait (discovered 1938):   Sheik Abdullah al-Sabah, the world's second-richest man in 1957, had one wife, one modest house, and two kids. Within five years of winning the oil lottery, he'd built six hospitals, fifty-one schools, twelve hundred housing units, a desalination plant, and earmarked one-third of all future income for projects to serve his people. Holds 10 percent of world reserves.

Qatar (discovered 1940):   Though finds weren't huge, by the mid-1950s Sheik Ali bin Abdullah was pulling in fifty million dollars a year. Known as kind and kind of goofy, he sat on the front steps of his palace every day, peeling off bills for any of his forty thousand subjects who hit him up for some dough, but also blew through millions on luxury items like Cadillacs that never came out of the crate. Upon building a garish palace that blinked with Las Vegas–style red lights, he missed his previous abode in a fishing village; so decorators added mud walls. Little oil left, but sitting on the third-biggest reserves of natural gas.

Abu Dhabi (discovered 1962):   Sheik Shakhbut (who like Saudi Abdul Aziz demanded payment in cash) kept the emirate's treasury, it's said, stored under his bed and wouldn't spend it on public works or modernization. Deposed in 1965 by his brother Zayed, who built schools, roads, and hospitals, including some in neighboring emirates. Holds 10 percent of world reserves.

Dubai (discovered 1967):   Sheik Rashid invested big money into education and modernization, including building the biggest commercial port in the Gulf, now one of the world's busiest; in later years he launched Dubai's tourism extravaganza. (Will be dry within a decade.)

Oman (discovered 1967):   Inheriting a sultanate that was broke, Sultan Said, one of the few rulers who was educated, had spent years battling imams and bedouin warriors and wearily watching the neighbors grow richer. By the time it was his turn to cash in, he apparently didn't believe it; after several years of doing little in a kingdom that had few roads and little electricity, his son demanded the ruling seat and launched countrywide modernization.

Yemen (discovered 1984):   The only country in the region that isn't a monarchy, guerrilla-ridden Yemen finally hit oil in 1984, but the little there didn't do much; most of it is smuggled to Africa, and outside of the modern capital it's still a poverty-ridden backwater. Scant amount left.

While the oil-rich Gulf countries celebrated their newfound wealth and welcomed the West (particularly the United States), the rest of the Middle East more than ever wanted to boot the West out. Especially after what happened in Iran: when the democratically elected prime minister Mohammed Mosaddeq announced that he was nationalizing the Anglo-Persian Oil Company in 1953, the British and Americans toppled him—a matter that's now part of the public record.

THE CIA IN IRAN

Rarely has the Middle East seen a more colorful, impassioned character than parliamentary leader and theatrical nationalist Mohammed Mosaddeq, an Iranian prone to weep, faint, and show up for summits in silk pajamas. Democratically elected to parliament as leader of the powerful National Front, and appointed prime minister in 1951, his first move rattled the West: he nationalized Iran's oil, ending the oil contract with the British. Furious, the Brits promised legal action but rejected the recommendation of the International Court of Justice to split the profits fifty-fifty with Iran, which was then getting about 16 percent. Instead the British went the covert route: assuring the United States that Mosaddeq would turn Iran commie, the British pulled the Americans into a ploy to oust him. Headed by Kermit Roosevelt, Theodore Roosevelt's grandson and agent of the new CIA, the plot involved payoffs to imams, the shah, and numerous others who were hired as actors, and nearly caused the government to entirely crumble. The CIA forced the shah to can Mosaddeq in 1953, a dismissal that the prime minister did not accept. The military finally pried Mosaddeq from office, and protests blew up everywhere, against pretty much everything and everyone, from the shah to Mosaddeq himself, who escaped the mobs by sneaking out and running over rooftops (in silk pajamas, of course). Alarmed, the shah fled the country, and the riots turned nuttier, but somehow in the mayhem the pro-shah, anti-Mosaddeq forces got the upper hand, and the still-jittery shah was compelled by the CIA to return to his throne and toss Mosaddeq in prison, where he remained for three years. As for the oil, the Anglo-Persian Oil Company was bought out by an international consortium, with most British shares split between Iran and the United States.

Returned to the throne by the CIA, the shah became U.S. ally number one in the Middle East, rising as unquestioned policeman of the Gulf and able to access unlimited amounts of American-made weaponry to help guard American oil. And his power would soon soar even further, thanks to the Cold War. The United States was obsessed by the fear that the Soviets would reach out and grab the Mideast, starting with Iran. There were reasons to worry: long desirous of Iran's long coastline, which would give it a way into waters that took forever to reach from its northern post, Russia had stomped in before. For decades the United States heavily armed Iran, which became its "first pillar" of defense against the Soviets. Saudi Arabia, the second pillar, was heavily armed as well, and arms were further provided to other countries, including Turkey and Lebanon, that signed on the anti-Communist line, beginning a reliance on the United States for arms that still hasn't let up.

Meanwhile, the calls across the region for the British and French to shove off became even louder. A violent two-year uprising in Syria finally prompted the French to disengage in 1946; six years later, the Free Officers in Egypt finally marched the British out the door, and an Egyptian became the country's leader for the first time in two thousand years. A 1958 revolution in Iraq tossed the Hashemites— the king and his family were killed—and pushed out the British as well. Against this backdrop, Egyptian officer Gamal Abdel Nasser charged in as a hero, and not only in Egypt where he led the Free Officers' coup in 1952 that ejected King Farouk from the ruling chair, dismantled the monarchy, replaced it with a republic, and shoved out the British. Premier in 1954, Nasser grabbed the presidency in 1956, ruling with an iron fist until his death in 1970. Dynamic, gutsy, well-read, and outspoken, he rose as the charismatic leader of the entire Arab world, spawning a nationalistic pan-Arabic movement that would instill pride, trigger anti-West revolutions from Yemen to Iraq, and lead to yet more wars.

Although Muslim, his was a secular government, and he ended up steamrolling the Islamic movements, such as the Muslim Brotherhood, even though they had helped him come to power. When the Islamists rose in protest of his nonreligious

Egyptian goverment photo via Wikipedia

Mightiest Arab leader of the twentieth century and president of Egypt (1956–70), Gamal Abdel Nasser rekindled Arab pride, stirred up further anticolonial sentiments, and inflamed the West, particularly when his desire for new weaponry caused him to cozy up to the Soviets. Nasser's rule revamped the Middle East playing board, unleashing American Cold War paranoia and creating a power dynamic with the United States and its Middle Eastern "client states" that still plays out today.

government, and were allegedly behind an assassination attempt, he stomped them out—or tried to—with sweeps of thousands that ultimately led to concentration camps, and for a while drove the Muslim Brotherhood underground, although they would soon reemerge.

The ascent of Egypt's dashing Nasser wasn't applauded by all. Egypt's religious establishment didn't adore him, since he kept diluting the role of Islam in Egypt and forced muftis who opposed him to step down. Nasser was so keen on modernizing Egypt that now women were discouraged from appearing *with* a veil—another factor that blackened his image with the religious community. Saudi Arabia's inept King Saud, who'd taken over the monarchy upon the death of his father, didn't care for him at all: Nasser's fearlessness, economic improvements, and rise as Arab leader showed Saud for the selfish, inarticulate, unlikable wimp that he was. Saud is believed to have been behind several assassination attempts against Nasser, and the Egyptian leader's emphasis on Arab nationalism drove the Sauds to try to trump them by playing the Islamic card as a means of solidifying regional support. Furthermore, Saud's hatred of Nasser prompted Saud to embrace the United States, which was offering arms to allies to fight the Communist threat, thus establishing Saudi Arabia as a "pillar of defense" and a top arms buyer, a role it maintains even today.

THE NEARLY DOOMED DAM

The United States recognized Nasser's government, though the Eisenhower administration from the start had its doubts, since Nasser refused to be a pawn in the Cold War, insisting (like Nehru in India) on a third way. When the West refused to sell him arms and he turned to the Soviet Union to revamp his military, the United States and Britain dropped promised funding for his pet project to revive Egypt's agriculture: the Aswân High Dam. In return, he grabbed the Suez Canal from the British and nationalized it in 1956, to use the revenues to finance his dam. In response, Israel, Britain, and France invaded. The United States forced them out, but the war only pushed Nasser further into the arms of Soviets. Fear of Soviet expansion in the Mideast tapped American Cold War paranoia, and a host of U.S. plots were hatched to battle the commie threat, from heavily arming Iran and Saudi Arabia as "columns of defense" to covert plans to bomb oil installations sky high (see p. 97).

The Suez Crisis—the 1956 attack on Egypt by Israel, Britain, and France—was a turning point. It melted any distinction between the West and Israel, which had been quick to take up arms with the colonial forces. The showdown illustrated how important oil had become: the bulk of Suez traffic was oil tankers. It also marked a low tide in U.S.-Anglo relations: the British had kept Eisenhower entirely in the dark, deceiving him about their plans for attack and leaving him to learn of it from the news. Ike didn't take it well and squeezed Britain where it hurt: he vowed to block a needed World Bank loan for Britain. In response, the British slunk off, taking France and Israel with them, and the United Nations' first peace-keeping mission was deployed to keep the area safe and the canal navigable. The United States had shown itself to be a superpower not afraid to go it alone if need be. And more than ever, the British reputation in the Middle East was mud: even in the Gulf states, where kingdoms were dependent on Brits for protection, commoners so disliked the British that rulers worried about attacks on British-operated oil rigs and refining plants. In fact, there were far greater reasons to worry about the safety of oil fields. Unbeknownst to rulers, they'd been lined with explosives. By the United States, with British help.

EXPLODING BABYSITTER

During World War II, the Americans worried that the Nazis would grab the Middle East, but after the war the professional handwringers in DC had a new reason to fret: what if the Soviets sailed in and lassoed the Gulf's oil-oozing lands, strangling the economies of "the Free World"? Besides giving away billions in free arms to countries to battle back Communists, the U.S. government took other drastic precautions during the 1950s to ensure that Russians could never claim these resources as their own. With a green light from President Truman (and later Eisenhower), the United States secretly planted explosives near Gulf oil installations; if the Soviets tried to seize these wells, the United States would blast the region's oil resources sky-high.[12] While the British were in on the scheme, the local governments were clueless about the nice ways the United States was looking after them from afar—and remained in the dark until Steve Everly, a reporter from the *Kansas City Star*, uncovered the declassified documents in 1996.

Another even more outrageous idea was floating around: the National Security Council considered using radiological booby traps if the Soviets invaded. The pragmatic CIA, however, shot down that idea in NSC 26/3, of June 1950, noting that the United States wouldn't want the oil to be radioactively ruined when we retook the area and that plans should stress "preservation of the resources for our own use after our reoccupation."[13]

The United States, like the Western Europeans, viewed Nasser "as the Saddam Hussein of his day,"[14] seeing him as socialist leaning and Soviet supported. In 1958, at the behest of Syrian leaders, he politically linked Egypt with Syria (a mere four hundred miles away) in one grand nationalistic Arab experiment: the

United Arab Republic. Nasser was subsequently viewed by the West as even more of a menace, since there were plans to also bring in Iraq, Sudan, and other countries under the pan-Arab flag. The United Arab Republic ultimately flopped—the union was officially severed in 1961.

> In 1961, just hours after oil-loaded Kuwait declared independence from the British, Iraq tried to grab its small neighbor. The Kuwaiti emir did what he'd always done in times of deep stress: he rang up Britain. Before you could say "preview of coming attractions," the Queen's ships showed up and Iraq backed down, but the recently created Arab League sent in peacekeeping troops just in case; besides, the Arabs wanted to show Britain that it was no longer needed. Even though Iraq's planned annexation didn't succeed—that time—it spelled out even more clearly what was on everybody's mind. Never mind Nasser's pan-Arabic movement, forget calls for a new caliphate that would bond all Muslims as brothers; despite all the new groups like the Arab League, it was in fact Arab against Arab, Muslim against Muslim, neighbor against neighbor—particularly in the vicious world of "new oil."

Meanwhile, the shah of Iran was basking in the American limelight. His White Revolution of 1963 revamped the country, at least on paper: he gave women the right to vote; he redistributed agricultural holdings, making Iran's serfs landowners; he modernized everything from water systems to schools, making education free and compulsory and creating the Literacy Corp, whereby young men could escape the draft by instead teaching the rural population to read. Widely applauded by the United States, and popular with many in Iran, the White Revolution was loathed by the Shia clerics, many of whom were the landed gentry whose farmlands were given to the peasants. They also abhorred moves to give women the right to vote and to allow non-Muslims to be judges, not to mention the pro-modernization-à-la-the-West theme of the program. What wasn't highlighted in the glowing Western reports was that many of the grand plans never came to fruition: the shah's government was corrupt, and furthermore the shah was spending some 40 percent of his country's GDP on weaponry—a move applauded by the United States, his main supplier, which looked to Iran to battle Communism in the Gulf.

Despite Nasser's reputation as a commie—one reason the United States was trying to overthrow him—the Arab leader had in fact repressed Communists in Egypt while leaning on Soviets for arms. They didn't much care for him either, finding his positions unacceptable, his ideas far-fetched, and even though they loaded him up with aircraft, tanks, rifles, and cannons through the 1960s, they were soon thinking that arming Nasser and other Arab countries obsessed with obliterating Israel was a waste of their resources. Especially after the fiasco of 1967.

THE LEAD-UP TO THE SIX DAYS' WAR

It started with water. In 1964, Israel began drawing water from the Jordan River, which flows south between Israel and Jordan. The Palestine Liberation Organization (PLO), having been recently formed by the Arab League as a tool to eradicate Israel, began raiding Israel's water diversion works. In 1965, Syria decided to dam its source, diverting much of the water into dams that would supply Syria and Jordan, and reducing the flow of water available to Israel. The Israelis attacked the Syrian water project, and meanwhile the PLO continued attacks on the Israeli system. In 1966, an Israeli tank ran over a land mine—believed to have been planted by the PLO—which killed three. In retaliation, Israelis attacked a village in what was then Jordan, which they believed was a PLO base: over three thousand Israeli fighters destroyed 125 houses, a clinic, and a school and killed at least fourteen. Everybody was up in arms about the brutality of the attack: the United States lectured that it was overkill, Jordan's King Hussein was livid at the military action with no warning, and Jordanians were furious with Hussein that he hadn't known about it and fought back. Meanwhile the Baathist government came into power in Syria, and border skirmishes increased; the Syrians captured and killed an Israeli spy, adding more tension. The Soviets upped the ante: they reported in May 1967 that Israel was planning an attack, and Syria, Egypt, and Jordan signed a military-protection pact. Then on June 5 a war broke out that would become *the* defining moment of Arab-Israeli relations.

Being as he was outspoken leader of the Arabs, there was no way Nasser could avoid a showdown with Israel. And Nasser apparently thought he was ready. After all, thanks to the Soviets he had a shiny new air force ready to soar into the skies and bomb Israel into oblivion. A shiny new air force that Israel, in a preemptive strike, bombed into oblivion while it was still on the ground, crippling Egypt before the war ever began. Besides, by all estimates Egypt was not prepared for the war—the Soviets were quick to point that out.

According to a review by the Soviets of the Arabs' battle performance in 1967, the United Arab Republic (of Egypt and Syria) lacked a "command system, the military forces have not mastered modern techniques, it is not properly organized, it does not have fighting capability . . . How the Syrians fought is illustrated by the fact that in the battlefield 120 soldiers fell, but they lost twelve thousand of our automatic rifles . . ."[15]

OPEC

The 1967 war threatened to play out in another arena as well: oil. The Organization of Petroleum Exporting Countries was founded by Iran, Iraq, Kuwait, Saudi Arabia, and Venezuela in 1960 as a means to control price and supply—after the United States devastated the Venezuelan economy by suddenly drastically reducing oil orders from that country. Believing that the United States had helped Israel in its stunning 1967 victory, Arab members tried to enact an embargo on oil shipments to the United States. It wasn't terribly effective at the time, but six years later membership had grown substantially, by then including Arab countries Qatar, Bahrain, Algeria, the UAE, Egypt, and Syria. When Arab OPEC members (and Iran) announced an embargo on oil sales to the United States, it hurt. Imports of Middle East oil dropped to a trickle—plunging from more than a million barrels a day to less than twenty thousand. The price quadrupled to near twelve dollars a barrel—hitting fifty-five cents a gallon in the United States, when you could get it. Shortages caused rationing and mile-long gas lines. And OPEC by then had found its muscle.

The war lasted six days. And during that time, Israel not only held its ground, it nearly doubled in size. Israel took *all* of Jerusalem and the West Bank and Gaza, and seized the Golan Heights in Syria and the large strip of southern land, the Sinai, previously held by Egypt. And now an additional four hundred thousand Palestinians were without a home.

Nasser's career was pretty much over by the time the headlines rolled off the press. The news rocked the Arab world. Anger mingled with embarrassment and disbelief that Nasser, the most powerful Arab of the century, couldn't take out Israel: his failure to do so spelled the death of the pan-Arab movement. The date 1967 became the way to spell shame, all the more when Six Days' War was added to it. At news of the defeat, the "father of modern Syria" Shukri al Quwatli suffered a fatal stroke, which was emblematic of the general reaction. Even the Soviets were taken aback: how could "two million Israelis defeat so many Arabs, equipped with our weapons?" they pondered in conferences. Nasser resigned, which prompted riots regionwide. He came back, and that too prompted riots.

As the pan-Arab idea withered and slithered out the door, other groups rallied to fill in the void. Islamists wanted to install religion-based governments, and clerics interpreted it as a sign: the Middle East had strayed from Islam, under whose banner previous warriors had known centuries of victories. Others took it to mean that an organized army wasn't the best vehicle for attack: what was needed was guerrilla action and terrorism, and the PLO sprang onto the stage—Kalashnikovs in hand.

THE RISE OF THE PLO

Initially, they were more thugs than militants. Founded in 1964 by the Arab League, which kept it well-funded, the Palestinian Liberation Organization made raids into Israel from outlying areas—damaging a water project here, killing a villager or two there, and prompting the wrath of Israel in the process. But the initially inept group soon yanked international headlines for the most heinous attacks of the era, hijacking planes and blowing up a Swiss Air jet in midflight in 1970. After the PLO hijacked three planes on one day in September 1970, Jordan's King Hussein ran them out of his country, in a nasty showdown called Black September that killed at least four thousand PLO members and three thousand Jordanians. Although the group scattered—many going initially to Lebanon, Syria, and Tunis—it kept outraging the world. In 1972, it infamously kidnapped Israeli athletes at the Munich Olympics, holding them hostage for Palestinian prisoners, and killing eleven. And PLO members were behind the 1985 capture of the Italian cruise ship *Achille Lauro*, during which they shoved wheelchair-bound American Leon Klinghoffer into the sea. Despite its constant militant attacks, the PLO nevertheless managed to gain UN observer status in 1974. PLO leader Yasir Arafat swaggered into the General Assembly wearing a holster (he wasn't allowed to take in his gun) and announced, "Today I have come bearing an olive branch and a freedom fighter's gun. Do not let the olive branch fall from my hand." By the 1980s, he'd managed to jockey the PLO, or rather his faction of it, Fatah, into the political leadership of the Palestinian territories, where his ineffective and corrupt government sucked up foreign nations' donations and did next to nothing to further the Palestinian cause. He was nevertheless awarded the Nobel Peace Prize for signing the 1993 Oslo Peace Accords, a secret peace agreement with Israel that marked the beginning of a Palestinian state but these days looks like it's going pretty much nowhere.

Britain, long the superpower of the Middle East, never regained its former status after the 1956 Suez invasion, and it kept losing territories. In 1967, even Aden in Yemen finally shook loose of the British. And the next year, almost three centuries after its boats had first appeared in the Gulf, the British made a startling announcement. They would be shoving off from the Gulf in 1971. Although that news brought joy to many, it brought shivers to some Gulf rulers, who realized that without the British to protect them their newly rich kingdoms were sitting ducks. The small oil kingdoms rightfully fretted that one of the nearby giants would clamp hold, be it Iraq or Iran (both of which claimed historical bonds to Gulf lands) or even Saudi Arabia, making good on Abdul Aziz's original plans to sew up all of Arabia into his kingdom. And indeed, all three lunged toward these long-lusted-after morsels the minute British ships were out of sight. All three were heavily armed. Saudi Arabia's and Iran's arms chests were overflowing thanks to sales from the United States, which viewed the duo as its pillars of defense in the region. Besides, the megabuck sales from the regional arms race helped to balance out all the petrodollars that U.S. companies were throwing into the region's piggy banks.

Despite mutual suspicions, the seven emirates on the eastern shores of the peninsula, including Abu Dhabi and Dubai, banded together in 1971, forming one country, the United Arab Emirates (UAE). Bahrain snuggled up to Saudi Arabia—bigger, richer, and theoretically stronger. Qatar, which didn't have much oil, and where gas reserves hadn't yet been discovered, risked going it alone. Oman, engaged in a civil war, hired the Brits to stick around and provide additional security.

Meanwhile, the new ruler of Saudi Arabia, King Faisal, saw an opportunity to boost his country to the forefront of the Arab world. His first move was to fill the void created by the crash of pan-Arab nationalism as a unifier by bolstering the role of Islam, particularly Wahhabi Islam, the strict interpretation of the religion practiced in Saudi Arabia. Faisal began massive funding for opening Wahhabi religious schools, madrassas, around the Arab world, and beyond—from Sudan to Pakistan, Turkey to Afghanistan. He also saw a new way to make his point to the United States: lobbying—via the American-Saudi oil company Aramco. Before long, oil execs were not only meeting with top officials of the Nixon administration, corporations such as Mobil were taking out full-page ads urging the United States to change its policy and stop favoring Israel, which itself had a powerful lobby in DC (so powerful that their representative had a desk in the State Department). The war of the lobbyists was on.

When Nasser died of a heart attack in 1970, his sidekick Anwar Sadat took control. Faisal helped to convince him that the Soviet connection should be cut, and that if he did so, the United States would pressure Israel to retreat back to the Green Line (the pre-1967 territories). Sadat cut ties with Moscow and in 1971 announced that if Israel would toss back Sinai and Gaza (two of its 1967 territorial expansions), Egypt would be happy to make a peace deal. Israel's response: no deal. The next year Sadat announced that if Israel wouldn't give back the territories, Egypt would invade and forcefully yank them back. Israel's response: whatever. In fact, Sadat's continual threats over the next year and a half certainly should have taken any surprise out of the so-called surprise attack by Egypt and Syria on October 6, while Israel was celebrating Yom Kippur.

Israel also had gotten the news from several other sources: Sadat's chief of staff Ashraf Marwan (married to Nasser's daughter) also happened to be an informant for Mossad (Israel's CIA) and had reportedly told them of the attack. Others say that Jordan's King Hussein tipped off Israel's prime minister Golda Meir, whom the United States counseled not to make a preemptive strike this time. So when Egypt and Syria rolled into Israel in October 1973, Israel should not have been shocked. But she was: not only did Israel misread the signs, they didn't have enough arms to withstand the attack. On the third day of fighting, Israel called up DC demanding that the United States rush over more arms. And this time Israel had a weapon to use against the United States: if the United States didn't come through, Israel was prepared to use its nuclear arms. Nixon promptly flew over $2.2 billion in arms—from fighter planes to missiles.

In the Yom Kippur War, Egyptian forces were better trained, better equipped, and better commanded than in previous conflicts. Initially, they took back the Sinai snatched by Israel eight years before. But their victories were soon reversed. It took longer than six days this time—nearly three months—but Israel drove the invaders out. Israel had managed to win yet again, thanks to the United States. And from that point on, every victory, ever war, every action of Israel was seen by the Arab world as a move fronted and supported by the United States.

The fact that despite the warnings, despite the frantic meetings with oilmen, and despite all the advertisements that had been taken out pleading with it to change its foreign policy, the United States was backing Israel yet again, and this did not please Saudi king Faisal at all. The news didn't play well at the next OPEC meeting either. Sheik Zayed, the president of the United Arab Emirates, demanded an embargo on Gulf oil supplies to the United States (and to the Netherlands, which had also sold arms to Israel). King Faisal seconded the move.

FAMOUS LAST WORDS

Setting: Situation Room, October 17, 1973; approximately 3:15 p.m.
Henry Kissinger briefing staff: "We don't expect an oil cutoff. . . . Did you see the Saudi Foreign Minister come out [of meetings with Kissinger] like a good boy and say they had very fruitful talks with us?"[16]

Setting: Situation Room, October 17, 1973; approximately 3:55 p.m.
News arrives of an OPEC embargo, cutting sales no less than 5 percent and an additional 5 percent every month until Israel withdraws to the 1967 borders. Within a few days, all Arab OPEC countries had shut off oil imports to the United States entirely.

And shortly after OPEC shut off the spigot, gas lines in the United States wrapped around several blocks, then backed up for miles, and finally resulted in gas rationing. Prices worldwide shot to new highs. From five dollars a barrel in September 1973, they'd soared to over eleven dollars with the price increases initiated by the shah. Arab OPEC countries had their first taste of the oil weapon. But the United States had a weapon of its own that it was considering unleashing on the countries that were cutting off its precious petroleum: invade Saudi Arabia, the UAE, and Kuwait, and seize their oil supplies. Five months later, Faisal unilaterally lifted the embargo, and the other OPEC countries soon followed suit. By then, Saudi Arabia had more money than it had ever seen before. And the United States had plenty of ideas about how it should spend it. First, by modernizing the country—using American developers such as Bechtel. Second, by protecting the country—by buying American weapons.

Against this backdrop, with new dynamics in play, the modern Middle East emerged, one where oil became an economic weapon that the United States would go to war over, Islam turned political, peace brought danger, and American actions to battle Soviet dangers created the most dangerous enemy the United States has ever known. It all came to a full boil in one year: 1979.

CHEAT SHEET 2
1979 and Beyond: A Quick Look at Issues

The United States and Israel commonly use drones for spying and for assassinations in the Middle East.

In the previous chapters, we've looked at the historical context for understanding the Middle East, presenting the rise of Islam, the division between Sunni and Shia, the colonial hacking up of the region, and the creation of Israel as a few key moments in its history. As we delve into the era from 1979 to the present, let us quickly point out a few major shifts as well as standout trends, themes, and issues that help to frame the present. Keep your eyes on these bouncing balls.

The year 1979 in many ways marked the beginning of the modern Middle East. That year several major and dramatic events unfolded that still rattle the region today and that brought the United States (and its arms) much more closely into its affairs. Namely:

- The overthrow of the shah in Iran: Islamic revolutionaries in Shia Iran booted out the shah and set up an Islamic government, a theocracy headed by Ayatollah Khomeini. This new government was entirely threatening to Arab leaders, all of whom were Sunni and many of whom played down religion. The Iranian Islamic republic was a Shia regime headed by Persians, and it was the first true

Islamic theocracy to be installed in over five centuries. The new republic became more ominous when revolutionaries in Iran took U.S. diplomats hostage in November 1979 and held them for 444 days. What made the Arab rulers, particularly the Sauds, positively knock-kneed and tongue-tied were the ayatollah's hostile words upon taking control: all of the Arabian Peninsula, Khomeini vowed, would soon be Iran. And all the Sunni would be converted to Shiism. The words couldn't have been more frightening if they'd been uttered by Satan.

- The rise of Saddam Hussein: Previously vice president of Iraq, Saddam took full power in 1979, turned the government into an even more vicious dictatorship, and shortly thereafter attacked Iran, hoping to kick the ayatollah out of power. Instead, the war went on for eight years, killed over a million, and put Saddam fifty billion dollars in debt—events that would lead to the 1990 invasion of Kuwait.

- Islamic radicals in Saudi Arabia seized the Grand Mosque in Mecca, an event that nearly cost the House of Saud its rule. The two-week takeover of the mosque in the Muslim holy place, by those who wanted a theocracy for Saudi Arabia and for Western influences to be erased from the kingdom, forced the Sauds to show they were legitimate Muslim rulers. Among the ways they did so: tossing more money at the Saudi religious establishment to spread their strict sect, Wahhabism, around the world via religious schools and by sending fighters to Afghanistan.

- The Soviets invaded Afghanistan, fighting Muslims in that country. DC cooked up a plan to resist them: the Sauds would recruit Arab fighters, the United States would arm them, and Pakistan would train them. That plan beat back the Soviets but unintentionally led to al Qaeda and the other militants fighting across the Middle East today.

- The U.S.-negotiated Israeli-Egyptian peace. In peace talks held by Jimmy Carter, Egypt and Israel worked out a plan: Israel would return former Egyptian land and Egypt would recognize Israel's right to exist. There were other inducements to sign the Camp David Agreement in 1979—rewards that cost the United States plenty. The United States would give $1.3 billion to Egypt each year, and $2 billion to Israel, most in the form of credits to buy U.S. arms. In a related agreement, the United States guaranteed that it would provide Israel with oil even if doing so caused shortages at home. The West lauded the agreement, but in the Middle East the move was upsetting. Without Egypt, which had the biggest army, Arab countries would not be able to militarily check, or invade, Israel again (see "Cheat Sheet 3," p. 314).

Together, these events triggered a geopolitical earthquake that rated eleven on the Richter scale. Islam turned militant, with new guerrilla groups that wanted to fight holy wars and that saw the infidel West as an enemy. Islam became a political force, with new parties that had turning governments into theocracies as their goal. The Shia-Sunni divide rose up as a major issue and a cause for war, such as that between Iran and Iraq. The West's oil was now at risk, since Islamic militants wanted to sell it only to Muslims. Governments were under pressure to show that they were religious enough.

Significantly, the events that began in 1979 further boosted American arms sales to the region, adding hundreds of billions to the GDP and allowing weapons to be used as a negotiating tool. The biggest sales of U.S. war toys are still to the Middle East, which, along with the wars that the United States keeps jumping into around there, are what saved the American arms industry, poised to crumple up and die when the Cold War ended with the dismantlement of the Soviet Union in 1991. The events of the past three decades reinforced a formula that still holds today: the United States tosses money into the oil pot and then through arms sales takes the money away.

The events of 1979 highlighted another related theme: as noted in the Carter Doctrine proclaimed in January 1980, the United States saw protection of Middle Eastern oil as a reason to declare war. And it further shifted the focus of U.S. attention on the region: Arab-Israeli wars were no longer the issue; much more important were the countries along the Persian Gulf—the oil boys. The Middle East seemed to divide into two: the oil boys—the Gulf countries to the east—and the western countries along the Mediterranean where the central issue was and still is the Arab-Israeli conflict (see "Cheat Sheet 3," p. 314).

More than ever, oil defined which Middle Eastern countries were rich and which weren't—changing the face of the region as much as the religion that sprang up there centuries before. While the countries closest to the Mediterranean have scanty amounts, the lands that ring the Gulf are rolling in black gold, holding some two-thirds of world supplies, which kicks billions of dollars into the regional piggy bank. These countries might be the money bags of the Middle East, but that doesn't mean the citizens necessarily see it.

> *Whereas Qatar's citizens are among the world's richest people—like Kuwaitis and Emiratis, well off and well cared for, with ample state support for education, housing, and health care—those in more populous countries such as Iran and Saudi Arabia aren't doing so well, although certain families in both are fabulously wealthy. Even though Iraq holds nearly 10 percent of the planet's known oil reserves, at the moment oil isn't as important as survival: a mess economically, the place, as we well know, is falling apart. And the 2003 invasion also created the worst refugee problem of the century. Yemenis have even less money, and about three tablespoons of oil, but at least they're politically more-or-less stable. Well, for the moment. They've spent more time in civil war, however, than as a glued-together country.*

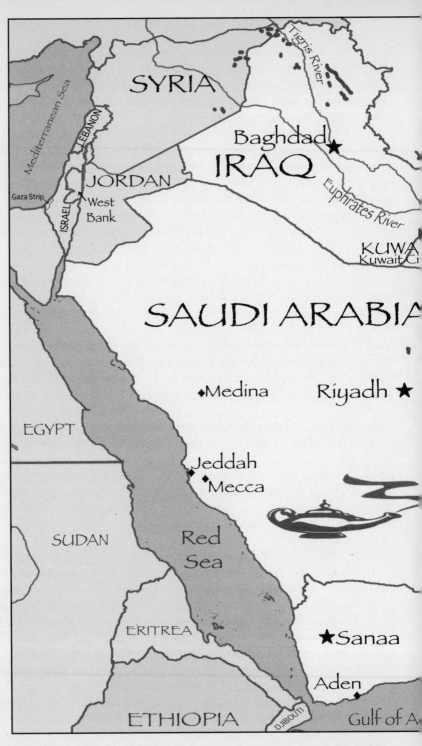

The eastern half of the Middle East is swimming in oil: over half the world's petroleum is found here.

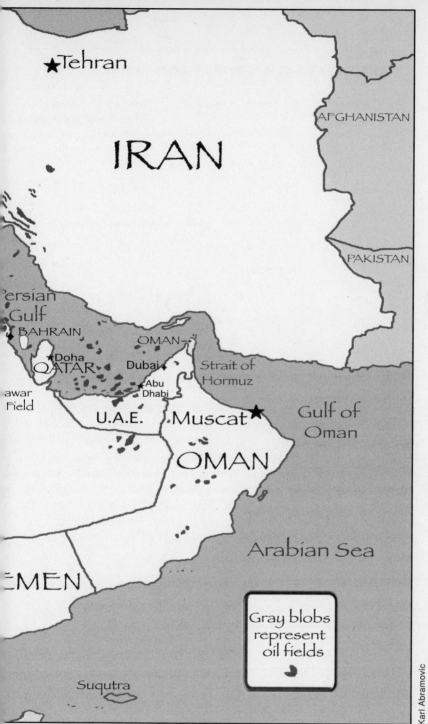

★Tehran

IRAN

AFGHANISTAN

PAKISTAN

Persian
Gulf

BAHRAIN

OMAN→

Strait of
Hormuz

◆Doha
QATAR

Dubai◆

★Abu
Dhabi

awar
Field

U.A.E.

Muscat★

Gulf of
Oman

OMAN

EMEN

Arabian Sea

Gray blobs
represent
oil fields

Suqutra

Karl Abramovic

THE OIL BOYS: A COMPARISON CHART

Country	Sunni/Shia[17] (estimated)	Oil[18]/World	Pop.[19] Mil.	GDP per Capita[20]	Literacy/ Women[21] (%)
Saudi Arabia	90/10	262b/25	27.6[22]	$15,400	79 (71)
Iran	10/90	136b/10	66	$4,200	84 (70)
Kuwait	59/26	96b/10	2.5[23]	$33,500	94 (91)
UAE	81/15	98b/10	4.5[24]	$43,000	78 (82)
Qatar	93/7	15b/2	0.907	$73,000	89 (89)
Bahrain	24/56	negligible	0.708	$26,000	87 (84)
Iraq	32/65	115b/10	28.3	$2,000 (CIA)	74 (64)
Oman	N/A	4.7b	3.2[25]	$16,000	82 (74)
Yemen	N/A	3.7b	22.2	$972	50 (30)

The geographical giants of the region, Saudi Arabia and Iran, are also the Middle East's most fervent Muslims; religion entirely defines life in those countries. While Saudi Arabia is Sunni (the oppressive Wahhabi variety at that), Iran is Shia (more dramatic and prone to martyrdom), but they have similarities: in recent years both governments have encouraged their youth to volunteer as martyrs and partake in religious war. (Nobody has to encourage it in Iraq, however: the Sunni-Shia divide in the post-Saddam era makes that land incendiary.) In these oil-rich countries, the Arab-Israeli issue literally isn't as close to home: instead, the biggest issue is the split between those two Islamic sects.

> Known to toss over handfuls of cash both to Israeli-hostile governments and groups, the richer countries to the east don't send their own troops into battle over that affair on the other side of the Arabian Peninsula.

AYATOLLAH KHOMEINI (RULED 1979–89)

Ayatollah Khomeini, the Shia cleric who led Iran's revolution and transformation from a secular monarchy to an Islamic theocracy, has been six feet under for nearly two decades, but he kicked up issues that are still flapping around. Khomeini and his followers politicized Islam in a way unseen for many centuries, prompting not only the "rise of the Shia" but the rise of Sunni extremism to counter it. By "exporting" the revolution and calling on the oppressed Shia Muslims to overthrow their oppressors (and nonreligious leaders), they also triggered and popularized both Shia and Sunni radicalism, making religious war, suicide bombing, martyrdom, hijacking, kidnapping, and terrorism positively trendy.

The oil-rich countries are also where Islamists—Muslims who want to install religious governments complete with undiluted shariah law—first gained political power. Their influence is now spreading across the region, thanks to increasing measures of democracy. Typically wanting to replace the governments of the countries where they live, Islamists are making great gains by being voted into the legislature. This may be a result of several factors:

- Islamists usually provide social services such as clinics, schools, loans, and housing and take better care of the people than the government does—acts that motivate voters.
- Islamists are organized, getting the votes of entire blocs, such as unions.
- They often run the schools, shaping young minds more likely to later vote for them.
- In many countries where the introduction of a parliament is new, a good percentage of potential voters doesn't head to the polls.
- A vote for Islamists is a vote of dissatisfaction with the way things are.

THE TRAVELS OF THE MUSLIM BROTHERHOOD

The original twentieth-century Islamists, the Muslim Brotherhood, which started in Egypt but has had its most pronounced effect in other countries, works in a number of ways to pursue its goal of installing Islamic governments. Running youth groups and heading unions, it also runs social services, providing ambulances, food, clinics, scholarships, and loans to the needy. Pushed underground in Egypt starting in the 1950s, many of its members left for other Arab countries, becoming an integral part of the education system, right down to writing the textbooks. Lately they've been entering politics and can often be found in the legislatures of the Middle East. While not inherently militant—they're considered moderates as far as Islamists go—they do provide inspiration and are affiliated with the most hard-core guerrilla groups, from Hamas to al Qaeda.

> *While the Muslim Brotherhood has been instrumental in transporting the Islamist idea around the region via education, the Saudis have exported an even more extreme form, Wahhabism, around the world. This rigid, austere, and jihad-applauding school of Islamic thought—a sect of Sunni Islam—was born in today's Saudi Arabia, and the Saudis have spread it far in madrassas, schools for the poor. The Taliban and Osama bin Laden are but a few high-profile devotees of this sect that demands full covering of women and endorses honor killings as well as religious war. Many Arabs who fought in the 1980s Soviet Afghan War also fell under its spell—since many of them were indoctrinated by Saudis.*

The countries of the Middle East all have a convoluted relationship with the United States that intertwines security, arms sales, oil, and wars (including the war on terror) into one complicated tapestry. A few threads in that crazy quilt:

Arms for oil: While politicians bellow about all the money the United States pours into Middle Eastern oil, they neglect to note that most of those petrodollars are poured back into the U.S. economy via arms sales. The United States is the leading arms pusher in the Middle East: using the U.S. State and Defense departments as agents, American arms makers such as Lockheed Martin, Boeing, and Raytheon sell war toys to whomever wants them, unless their name is Syria, Yemen, or Iran (though, until his 1979 ejection, the shah of Iran was also a frequent shopper). With eight billion dollars of fighter planes for the UAE here, and a thirty-billion-dollar variety pack for Saudi Arabia there, it all adds up to one loud *ka-ching*, since the wealthy Gulf countries are America's biggest arms client.

Choosing new enemies: With the Soviet Union gone, the United States draws its enemy list from the region: handing the first two points on the "axis of evil" to Iraq and Iran (North Korea came in at number three) and later updating the list with Syria, Venezuela, and Cuba at the number four, five, and six spots. With Saddam Hussein dead and gone, the Bush administration began looking at Iran, which is building up its nuclear energy program, planning, they said, to make nuclear bombs, and headed by the loudmouthed, hotheaded President Ahmadinejad. Iran also happens to have oodles of oil and natural gas. And the United States helped create its worst enemy, al Qaeda, which grew out of the 1980s Soviet-Afghan War. Dreamed up by DC, militant Muslim men were given arms, funded, and trained (all with U.S. and Saudi money) to fight Soviets, without considering that the same guerrillas might one day turn their ire on the United States.

The expansion of U.S. military bases: The United States now has a dozen bases in the Middle East, most of them built over the past fifteen years, especially in the Gulf, where a necklace of them dangles from Kuwait to Oman. And there are those who might suggest that the United States sometimes manipulates events to create wars (or the fear of them) that spur both arms sales and the building of military bases—as well as multibillion-dollar contracts for American firms during postwar reconstruction.

The effects of U.S. defense budgets: The strangest things seem to happen whenever the Pentagon's budget is about to get slashed, particularly if Dick Cheney is anywhere nearby. In 1990, when Cheney was secretary of defense, his $263 billion war budget, which included huge expenditures funding for the Stealth bomber, the Patriot missile defense system, and a national missile defense program (then known as Star Wars) was about to get hacked to heck. Reason: the Soviet Union was falling and suddenly the United States didn't have a big bad enemy. Until, that is, Saddam Hussein rolled into Iraq that very year. Oddly enough, Cheney (and Rumsfeld) were pushing for a major expansion of the latest-generation missile defense program, funding for which was about to get shot down, when 9/11 occurred. It's not that the United States makes these tragedies unfold. But Cheney, Rumsfeld, and the neocons decided to respond to both Saddam's invasion of Iraq and the 9/11 attacks in ways that ensured that their arms budgets would get funded.

Hypocrisy: When Saddam used skin-melting white phosphorus bombs, they're chemical weapons. When the United States uses them, they're not. When Israel has several hundred nuclear weapons (and the United States has tens of thousands) it's acceptable. When Iran wants to build a nuclear reactor, it's not. When Middle Eastern leaders torture, it's inhumane. When the United States tortures, it's denied. The contradictions are not missed by those living in the Middle East.

Aid: While on paper it may look like the United States is doling out lots of economic aid, when it comes to this region the aid is almost all military—a credit card of sorts, used for buying U.S.-made arms. To wit: the United States gave and loaned $145 billion in aid to Middle Eastern countries between 1971 and 2001.[26] The bulk of that, $131 billion, was gifts to Israel and Egypt; and over half of that amount, $71 billion, was military aid.[27] Between 2002 and 2005, the United States provided over $50 billion in aid, of which $26 billion went to Iraq reconstruction, and the rest mostly to Israel, Egypt, and about $2 billion to Jordan.[28]

Strategic cruelty: Demolishing power plants, airports, and highways may be brilliant military tactics, but they merely cause hardship for civilians and set governments back billions in repairs. Handily, a lot of that reconstruction money goes back to the United States via American contractors.

Karl Abramovic

Iraq is the central stud in the petroleum "black belt" stretching from Saudi Arabia to Iran. It holds the world's third-largest cache of proven oil reserves but must rely on the narrow Shatt al Arab River to get oil to the Gulf. Two-thirds of Iraqi oil lies near the predominately Shia port city Basra. There's loads more oil in the north, where the Kurds have been living semi-autonomously for decades. Theirs is the only part of Iraq that didn't fully implode after the 2003 war. With numerous fields that haven't been tapped or mapped, Iraq may hold more oil than anywhere else on the planet.[1] That sounds mighty appealing in the United States, where wells will run dry within twelve years.

Chapter Five

Iraq: Pardon Our Mess

In the name of bringing democracy, the United States inadvertently unleashed street-level theocracy: Iraqi women, for the first time, are now forced by local militias to cover up (though the soldier pictured here is an American boy just being polite). Guerrillas are now beheading women for such anti-Islamic behavior as wearing lipstick or donning brightly colored scarves.[2]

Iraq is not simply a country. It's a symbol: of the American war machine that can conquer but can't control and of Western oil-sucking imperialism gussied up as missions to spread freedom and vanquish terror.[3] It's yet another illustration that know-it-all neocons, who led the United States into this nightmare (pitching the operation as quick-'n'-breezy), defy statistical probability by almost *always* being wrong.[4] Bomb-battered, bullet-pocked, post-invasion Iraq, where chaos rules and 90 percent say life was better under Saddam,[5] is now a religious-ethnic soap

opera of insurgents and counterinsurgents so twisted it's hard to unwind. However, it's hard not to note the megabucks wrought in creating this mess: the billions paid to American companies to rebuild the smashed country, the scent of
trillions from an oil stash that might make OPEC irrelevant, the billions spent on
arms, and the billions more sold to the panicked neighbors. Keep your eyes on
the bouncing dollar signs and oil barrels, and it's easy to see why the Bush administration waged a propaganda campaign to bring the U.S. military swooping in
here.[6] Short answer: Saddam was about to crack open virgin oil fields and wasn't
inviting American companies to the orgy. An Iraqi dissident with a dream of ruling
over the riches, Ahmed Chalabi, slipped neocons the bogus reason to justify the
United States charging in. Good luck getting Uncle Sam out.

FAST FACTS:
Al Jumhuriyah al-Iraqiyah

Government:	Parliamentary democracy
Formed:	October 3, 1932 (from British Mandate); June 28, 2004 (sovereignty transferred to Iraqi interim government)
Leaders:	President Jalal Talabani; Prime Minister Nouri al-Maliki
GDP 2007:	$55.4 billion (exchange rate); (no listing IMF)
Per-capita GDP:	$1,900
Population:	28.3 million (July 2008 estimate)
Unemployment:	30–40 percent
Literacy rate:	84 percent men, 64 percent women
Ethnicity:	75–80 percent Arab, 15–20 percent Kurd, 5 percent other (Turkoman, Assyrian)
Religion:	97 percent Muslim (60–65 percent Shia; 32–37 percent Sunni), 3 percent Christian and other

---

Leader's Corner

It's ironic that Prime Minister Nouri al-Maliki heads a country plagued by suicide bombers who alone have killed tens of thousands of Iraqis. Maliki's party,
Islamic Dawa, perfected the tactic decades ago, the first to employ suicide
truck bombs in between hijacking planes and taking shots at Saddam, who
eventually chased the shadowy Shia group out of Iraq. Fleeing to Syria in
1979, Maliki reportedly directed the party's "Jihad Office"[7] during an era when
Dawa bombs made big headlines: Iraq's embassy in Beirut was blown to bits in
1982; the next year, weeks after an explosive-laden truck killed seventeen
U.S. servicemen in the unsolved Beirut barracks bombings, a Dawa truck
bomb blasted the U.S. embassy in Kuwait, killing five.[8] Given Dawa's dicey past,

Curt Cashour, U.S. Army, Department of Defense via pingnews

Prime Minister Nouri al-Maliki has a weak grasp on the violence-wracked country. Handy for him that Iraq's parliament is set up in the heavily fortified, U.S.-controlled district called the Green Zone, where he also lives. Iraqis are furious that he can't get the situation under control—or the lights and water back on.

it's also ironic that Maliki, who returned to Iraq in 2003, is applauded by Bush.

Then again, Maliki's been helpful to the United States. Even though Iraq's controversial national oil bill, which proposes selling off development of petroleum fields to foreign firms, hasn't been approved by parliament, Maliki's government has already put new oil fields on the block, showing preferential treatment to American companies.[9] Even though most Iraqis, including many parliamentarians, demand an end to the U.S. occupation, he acted alone to extend it, *and* he gave the green light for permanent American military bases in Iraq. His nods to Bush's wishes should come as no surprise considering his history. Maliki, whose appointment Condoleezza Rice helped secure, was affiliated with the Iraqi National Congress (INC),[10] a dissident group cobbled together by the CIA in the nineties and handsomely funded by the U.S. government for over a decade before being dropped into power in Iraq by the United States in 2003. Even then, after INC members sat on Iraq's governing council well into 2004, the United States continued to pay the group $355,000 a month for its fine intelligence work, which by then had been proven to be dubious.[11] If Iraqis feel betrayed that Maliki and others involved with the CIA-created group, such as President Jalal Talabani, are selling them out, Americans can relate: these were the liars who sold the 2003 invasion, snookering the American people into believing Saddam possessed WMDs.

WHAT MATTERS

Energy matters: Iraq's known oil reserves total 115 billion barrels, the world's third-biggest stash,[12] but it may hold twice that; there's natural gas too. Some 2 million barrels of oil were pumped each day in 2007; a fourth went to the United States.[13] Billions of dollars are being lost due to smuggling and broken oil meters that Halliburton didn't fix (see p. 128). A lingering question: what to do about previous oil agreements with Russia, China, and France made by Saddam? DC says ditch them, the others disagree.

Electricity matters: Blackouts are routine. Most Iraqis have power for only a few hours a day thanks to attacks on plants and the ineptitude of the U.S. companies hired to get the juice running. Ahmed Chalabi is among those hired by the Maliki government to get the electricity back on: that's not reassuring.

Arms matter: The United States has spent more than five billion dollars arming police and military, dipping into money meant for reconstruction. The arms have a way of disappearing, however. Thus far, DC has ignored Maliki's requests for big-boy war toys such as tanks and fighter planes.

Military/security matters: After firing Iraq's army and police forces—many of whom became insurgents—the United States helped to put together a new army. It tends to run away when put into action, however. Permanent U.S. bases are being built: handily, one sits atop an oil export facility. The United States has 140,000 troops committed; over 4,000 have died. The only place that's sort of safe is the Green Zone, the U.S.-controlled, walled district of Saddam's former villas and palaces that is now a self-contained garrison including hotel, hospital, restaurants, shops, and the new U.S. embassy. It ain't terror-free: guerrillas get in occasionally. They blasted a hotel in 2003, a suicide bomber killed eight in the parliament building in April 2007, and as of spring 2008, Shia militias are shooting in rockets.

Militants/insurgents matter: Armed militias kill, kidnap, rob, burn, hijack neighborhoods, torture—and fight each other. Some are anti-America. Some are anti-Shia or anti-Sunni. Some want to establish theocracies. Some are unemployed Iraqis. Some are mafia thugs. They number about 70,000 and strike over 150 times on a typical day.

Religion/ethnicity matters: Many Sunni Arabs fled Iraq when the United States showed up and placed Shia and Kurds in the power seats. Nearly two-thirds of Iraqis are Shia, now the dominant power group; Grand Ayatollah Ali Sistani is the highest Shia cleric in Iraq, but powerful Shia families, like the Sadr family and their foes the Hakim, take more cues from clerics in Iran. Kurds are eyed suspiciously: they're ethnically non-Arab, and have long wanted to secede.

Money matters: The International Monetary Fund (IMF) loaned Iraq a few million dollars but demanded that parliament pass the controversial oil bill before it would lend more. Some former debts racked up by Saddam have been forgiven—including twelve billion dollars owed Russia, a sign that Putin wants Iraq to honor previous oil contracts signed with Saddam.

Politics matter: Iraq's leaders and parliamentarians—many of them former members of dissident groups paid multimillions by the CIA and State Department, and many originally DC-appointed to their government seats—show a bent toward U.S.-favored policies. With many government officials and parliamentarians known to have engaged in criminal and nefarious acts—convicted and alleged embezzlers, smugglers, spies, thieves, and killers aren't hard to find sitting in government chairs—this ineffective administration isn't winning any Good Housekeeping Awards. Many Iraqis are calling for new elections. Likely winner: Moqtada Sadr of Mahdi Army fame.

Unity matters: One issue bouncing around in this mess is how closely Iraq should be united. Those in oil-rich areas, the Kurds and southern Shia, tend to think it should operate as three different powerful regions; some even support turning Iraq into three different countries. However, the Sunni are opposed to this, as are Shia who live around Baghdad. The reason: there's no oil in the middle—if Iraq splits, they'll be shut out of the riches.

Theocracy matters: What's often missed by the U.S. press is that a theocracy is coming into effect. The Iraqi government isn't outwardly religious, but strict Islamic religious rule is now in force in parts of Iraq: it's being introduced and enforced by militias, both Sunni and Shia. And the world they're creating is as repressive as that of Afghanistan under the Taliban; some are so hard-core they even forbid ice, regarding it as too modern.

Interest matters: So much for that fifty-billion-dollar war the neocons pitched. The Iraq occupation is costing about that every three months, and it's being financed with loans. By the time the debts are paid off, around 2017, it will by some economists' estimates have rung in at three trillion dollars.[14]

On the first of May 2003, when President George W. Bush stood aboard the USS *Abraham Lincoln* and declared victory against Saddam Hussein, it was yet another bit of stage magic. Even though he'd gone to all the trouble of putting on a jumpsuit and having Air Force One land on a warship, Bush wasn't anywhere near the smoldering land that U.S. forces had just "freed." The aircraft carrier, where a banner declaring "Mission Accomplished" was draped in the background, was cruising just off the Californian coast. No need for viewers to be distracted from the sweet joy of success by the smoking dump of Iraq, where its tyrant was hunkering down in a hidey-hole, and the doors of hell were about to swing open. The fact that DC had orchestrated the appearance of Bush being near the battle scene was just one of the deceptions involved in the war on Iraq: in pitching this war the Bush administration is on the record for telling nearly one thousand lies.[15] Among them, that Saddam had WMDs and that the adventure had nothing to do with oil. One thing is for sure: this misadventure, which has killed over 4,000 U.S. soldiers and

Cherie A. Thurlby, Soldiers Media Center on flickr.com, Department of Defense

A mural in Baghdad, where over 45,000 civilians have been killed since 2003, celebrates the freedom and democracy that the Bush regime brought. Polls show that many Iraqis, while happy to get rid of Saddam, didn't want the government that replaced him. Among Shia, 40 percent want a theocracy, and among Sunni, 58 percent would prefer a dictator to what they have now.[16] Kurds are more supportive—only 34 percent are opposed to democracy.

over 150,000 Iraqi civilians, is costing U.S. taxpayers over two trillion dollars, has created four million homeless, and has kicked the country back into the Dark Ages.

NUMBERS

One illustration of the messiness of Iraq is the shortage of hard numbers coming out of there. At least 100,000 civilians have died since 2003, although some studies put the figure at over a million, and lord knows how many militants have perished along with them. According to the Special Inspector General for Iraq Reconstruction (SIGIR), by April 2008 over forty-six billion U.S. tax dollars have gone to reconstruct Iraq, but billions of that weren't accounted for; of the nineteen billion dollars earmarked for security, the *New York Times* reported that 190,000 assault rifles and pistols went missing,[17] and the GAO says nearly one-third of money for arms was lost. SIGIR says Iraq may make eighty billion dollars from oil in 2008, but that doesn't include the billions lost to smuggling; nobody is sure how much oil is even going out legally since oil meters are broken, and oil volume is "guesstimated" by how low tankers sink in the water. Nobody even seems clear on exactly how much the new U.S. embassy will cost, and good luck trying to figure out how many U.S. bases will be permanent. It's all a guessing game around here.

From the dazzling fields of flowers in the deeply folded north to the southern swamplands where Marsh Arabs paddle canoes to their homes made of bent reeds, ancient kingdoms soared to new heights here: the wheel was invented, written language was born, and irrigated farmlands allowed former nomads to put down roots. Civilization in modern Iraq, where the Maliki government is as sturdy as Jell-O, has plummeted to new lows. Since April 2003, when Saddam Hussein was toppled and democracy was shoved down Iraqi throats, everybody who can has left or is leaving. The mementos of civilization hidden in the ground for millennia have been looted; now the only subterranean secrets left are bodies thrown into mass graves and warheads leeching depleted uranium. As their society crumbles, Iraqis are witnessing things never seen before: in a country where previously most identified themselves as Iraqis, sectarian wars have broken out that pit not only Shia against Sunni but Shia against Shia and Sunni against Sunni. Gangs and militias have moved in to many areas, inflicting their harsh take on Islamic rule: women are being forced to don *abayas* (cloaks) and veils and are warned not to wear makeup, not to work, and not to talk on the phone. Those who ignore the threats end up on the street, dead.

THAT WAS THEN

Saddam was sadistic, corrupt, and delusional, but life was at least orderly: electricity worked, water came out of the tap, most who survived his bloody purges had jobs, factories produced everything from buses to concrete, and at 90 percent the literacy rate was far above that of most neighbors. In fact, Iraq was outwardly progressive: its health care was the most modern and its economy was the most diverse in the region. Women worked as doctors and lawyers: universities were filled with hundreds of thousands studying science and engineering. Modern architecture glistened; Baghdad, with fancy restaurants, garden districts, and theaters, was the Paris of the Persian Gulf. Under Saddam, Islamic leaders and clerics took a backseat, and the veil wasn't common—especially in Baghdad, where most neighborhoods were religiously mixed. Shia and Sunni worked together on the staff of dashing Saddam Hussein, who, as vice president until 1979, inspired national pride and seemed destined to lead the country to greatness. Instead, as president, a post yanked from his uncle who was about to deal him out in an alliance with Syria, Saddam grabbed on with a white-knuckled grip, obliterating threats—Syrian allies, Sunni merchants, Shia clerics, or Kurds who wanted to secede. Soon thick with paranoia, filled with Baath Party spies, and utterly corrupt, Iraq under Saddam became a land of torture, where enemies had a way of disappearing (many assassinated). The egoist led his people into a virtually nonstop war, transforming the wealthy country to an indebted one handcuffed with sanctions, and driving it over the cliff—although the Bush family helped.

In post-Saddam Iraq, roving Sunni jihadists behead barbers for shaving beards and chop off the fingers of smokers;[18] masked Shia militias torture with drills. Kidnappers demand ransoms of a hundred thousand dollars, delivering bags of loved ones' chopped-up body parts to those who couldn't pay. Over a hundred a day are abducted. Judges, doctors, and teachers keep getting gunned down by the thousands in an attempt to run out professionals. Who lives where is now decided by Shia militias and Sunni jihadis marking their turf, creating neighborhoods defined solely by religion. Militias purge Sunnis from areas deemed Shia; jihadis shove Shia out of areas they've tagged as Sunni. Iraqis live in fear of the "eviction notices," the blood-spattered death threat or the red mark on the door that means "Leave, now!" Once occupants flee their house, militants sell it. There's apparently not a thing anybody—government, military, or police—can, or will, do about it, except wall the problems off. Baghdad is now an ugly checkerboard of newly segregated neighborhoods blocked off by razor wire and ten-foot-high concrete "blast walls," controversially erected by the United States to keep fighting down and the neighborhoods divided, in the process trapping the residents, who can only leave by passing through checkpoints. Driving a few miles now takes hours.

> Of the 26 million Iraqis who lived here when the United States first dropped in, at least 4 million have been run out of their homes or have fled. The 2003 war triggered a mass exodus on a magnitude not seen since World War II. Iraqis are fleeing at the rate of 40,000 a month. Around 1.5 million live in Syria. Another 700,000 or more headed to Jordan, while others left for Egypt, Iran, and Lebanon; others are camping at the borders. Prohibited from working, most of those in foreign countries are using up savings. While Iraqis are coming back, to the tune of 700 each day, it's not a matter of choice. They are returning because they're out of money. While they come in, every day nearly 1,200 others are fleeing.[19] But they're running out of places to go: outside of Syria and Iran, most countries won't let any more in. Those unable to leave, however, are in the most dire straits: the 2 million run out of their homes by bombs and militias have typically moved in with kin; often 20 or more hole up in houses with three rooms—dreading another note slipped under the door that forces them to run yet again.

THE PATCHWORK OF IRAQ

Iraq wasn't always a wasteland of car bombs and rooftop snipers, neighborhoods where the stench of death never leaves, and staccato gunfire asks and answers in armed conversations day and night. The groups that the British smashed together in 1920 to form a new country called Iraq—the name taken from Uruk—historically didn't get along, but they typically didn't fight each other; in fact, at times they linked arms in a concerted attempt to throw out the British, who ran the place in one form or another until 1958.

Kurdistan: The rugged and chilly north is home to Kurds, originally a hard-fighting mountain clan whose most famous warrior was Crusader-slaying Saladin. They have a well-defined culture and a semi-independent territory that was the only place that didn't fall apart during the 2003 war, which Kurds supported. Few battles were fought in the region, outside of Mosul, at least. Speaking their own language, and ethnically different from other Iraqis, they want to form their own country, Kurdistan, with Kurds in Iran, Syria, and Turkey. Turkey is so opposed to the idea that it recently rolled in, ostensibly aiming at the separatist PKK but making a point to the rest. An area to watch.

Central Iraq: Called the Sunni Triangle, running from Baghdad to Tikrit to Fallujah, this area holds the bulk of Iraq's Sunni population. Baghdad is ethnically mixed: it previously had a modern cosmopolitan population, although many have fled. Outside the city center is the worst slum in Iraq: now called Sadr City, it holds two million Shia. Farther out, especially near Fallujah, many Iraqis are tribal.

The south: Residence of the Marsh Arabs, an anachronistic tribe of fishermen whose houses straddle swamps, the south is also home to Shia holy cities Najaf and Karbala. The port city Basra, first secured by the British, has been a mess since they pulled out in 2007: dozens of militias are battling it out, and many want to install a theocracy. Over a hundred women have been killed there since late 2007 for such sins as having a boyfriend.

The cheery claims of the Bush administration and the media reports about the ameliorating effects of the 2007 "surge," when the United States sent in twenty-one thousand additional troops, don't reflect the reality in Iraq, where hundreds of thousands of civilians have died, and fighting and violence have only barely let up. Tanks still roll in, planes still swoop down, and full-fledged U.S. attacks still flatten towns to rid them of insurgents. Once pushed out of one town, the insurgents always appear somewhere else. Military sieges, rooftop snipers, roadside bombs, militia attacks, police purges, guerrillas, and gangs together kill some seventy civilians a day,[20] an improvement over 2006 when an average day snuffed out a hundred or so.[21] And those numbers don't reflect the deaths of police, militants, and insurgents. Street life, it's happily reported in the American media, is returning in Baghdad, though word on the street has it that the United States is paying store owners to reopen. There's little to return to in Fallujah: fancy new American thermobaric weapons left the insurgent stronghold a pile of rocks, disintegrating thirty-five thousand homes.

MEET THE FIGHTERS

When the United States invaded in 2003, militants from all corners of Iraq and the nearby countries entered into the fighting. Some of the fighting was planned: when the invasion appeared imminent, Saddam even invited some Sunni guerrillas into Iraq to ensure future headaches for coalition forces. While the coalition was the original target for most, militias and guerrillas soon began fighting each other in bloody Sunni-Shia attacks. This too was planned, being the strategy of Jordan-born Abu Musab al-Zarqawi, a hard-core Sunni who headed al Qaeda in Iraq: he rightly reckoned that religious infighting would foil DC's attempt to establish order, and sent his Sunni boys out to attack Shia and kick off sectarian violence in Shia areas, often using car bombs, which have killed over fourteen thousand Iraqis. Like most Sunni guerrillas in Iraq, many of whom are foreigners, Zarqawi also wanted to establish a strict Taliban-like theocracy. Religious showdowns, however, aren't just Shia versus Sunni. The two biggest Shia militias, the Mahdi Army and the Badr Brigade, are rivals, battling over control of Shia holy cities for starters. Sunni also fight Sunni: the Anbar Awakening tribes are now fighting al Qaeda in Iraq. Many fighters are unemployed Iraqis who simply needed a job and were hired, first by the likes of al Qaeda, and now by the United States.

Al Qaeda in Iraq / Mujahideen al Shura: Abu Musab al-Zarqawi wasn't initially affiliated with al Qaeda, but he held the same anti-West, anti-Shia, pro-theocracy views. Setting up in northern Iraq prior to the invasion—it's not clear if he too was invited by Saddam to "party crash" the U.S.-led war—he ordered what have been the most high-profile acts of violence, including the August 2003 bombing of the Jordanian embassy in Iraq and the UN headquarters, and an attack on a Shia shrine in Najaf killing 181, including the leader of the Badr Brigade. That got the Sunni-Shia war under way, and since then it has never really let up. His many deeds include killing hostage Nick Berg and blowing up the golden dome of the Al-Askari Mosque in the Shia city Samarra.

Mahdi Army: The black-clad Shia militia of popular cleric Moqtada Sadr began as a charity group of Shia students giving out food in poor Shia areas during the 2003 war. Its numbers rocketed to ten thousand when Sadr, sidelined by the United States, declared his own shadow government. He's launched two major uprisings against coalition forces in battles that lasted for weeks. He's called cease-fires, but his boys don't always listen. The Mahdi Army is active in deciding which neighborhoods are to be Shia, selling off houses taken from Sunnis, and are accused of torturing and killing "un-Islamic" women. In March 2008, after a six-month Mahdi Army cease-fire (cited as an effect of "the surge" in reducing Iraqi violence) had expired, Sadr organized demonstrations against the Iraqi government, even though his political bloc is part of the government. He wants new elections; major violence looms on the horizon. Certainly a formidable force, Sadr may be the next Iraqi leader.

Badr Brigade: The well-trained and well-equipped paramilitary arm of cleric/parliamentarian Abdul Aziz Hakim of the Supreme Islamic Iraqi Council, the Badr Brigade, believed to be twenty thousand strong, often fights its fellow Shia militia, the Mahdi Army, as well as al Qaeda in Iraq, after the latter killed their supreme leader in 2003. Another specialty: smuggling Iraq's oil.

Anbar Awakening / Sunni Awakening: These tribal groups that live near Fallujah initially sided with al Qaeda and fought against the U.S.-led coalition, but they later turned on al Qaeda, who ticked them off by installing theocracies. Another reason they turned: the United States began paying them.

Ansar al-Islam: Hard-core Sunni Kurds who have set up a Taliban-like regime in parts of the north, these guys don't allow music, torch girls' schools, and are real party poopers, known to kill those who attend them. Like Zarqawi's al Qaeda, with whom they sometimes work, they want to establish an Islamic state.

Peshmerga: The fierce Kurdish militia was created along with the early twentieth-century Kurdish independence movement, first fighting the Brits who first promised them independence and then took it away in 1922. They ran guerrilla actions against Saddam and were perhaps the only Iraqi militia that was never run out or obliterated. Now the United States is bringing them in as security in Baghdad and the south—a bad move, since the Kurds, who are not Arab, are already eyed suspiciously because they're sitting on vast oil wealth, and plenty suspect they want to secede with it.

Saddamists: Saddam's former security forces mostly take aim at coalition forces but have showdowns with the Mahdi Army too.

Criminal thugs: Kidnapping, oil smuggling, and looting are lucrative biz for these guys, and they don't take kindly to militants moving into their turf. They are believed to be behind oil-pipeline attacks—they run the tankers called in to haul off the oil when the pipeline is busted.

Storming in as a liberator, the United States is now loathed and condemned for strong-arm tactics, lawless mercenaries (like Blackwater USA), and controversial weapons such as the white phosphorus bombs used in attacks in Fallujah. The torture of prisoners at Abu Ghraib, only one incident of many reported acts of torture and abuse, stirred up hatred, as did early sweeps of thousands of Iraqis rounded up simply to clear the streets of young men, many still held without charge. Within months of occupation—sanctioned by the UN even if the invasion wasn't—and particularly after the uncovering of Abu Ghraib, Iraqis stopped talking to Americans: working for them, helping them, being seen with them. Having anything to do with them spelled death by insurgents, as those who ignored warnings soon learned. More to the point, they rebelled in an insurgency that continues and has spun into a full-on civil war.

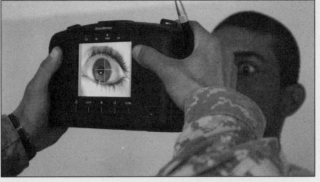

Staff Sgt. Dennis J. Henry, DoD via
Soldiersmediacenter on flickr.com

As part of the neocons' plans to modernize the military, novel
weapons and high-tech equipment are being tested out in
Iraq. Here, iris imaging—part of new bioidentification
systems put in place to keep tabs on Iraqi security and
residents of high-tension cities, such as Fallujah.

DANGEROUS IDEA: CONTRACTING OUT THE WAR

At first, they crept into the war machine with little notice from the public, and they've slipped into the Pentagon's budget to the tune of an estimated hundred billion dollars a year.[22] Halliburton, paid some sixteen billion dollars from 2003 to 2006, is but one high-profile example of a so-called PMC (private military contractor) to whom the U.S. Defense Department tosses many of its biggest and sometimes shadiest jobs. Some PMC work is rather mundane—installing air conditioners and electricity generators, for instance. But some of it is seriously dirty: private mercenaries may be hired to spy, trigger riots, stomp out labor disputes, or guard prisoners. They are regularly headline news, really helping to screw things up in Iraq. Paid as much as a thousand dollars a day—an army private, in comparison, pulls down about fifty—private military contractors such as CACI (whose guards tortured prisoners at Abu Ghraib) and Blackwater (which in September 2007 shot down seventeen civilians) are increasingly controversial not only because the mercenaries tend to be thugs, but because they're not held responsible for their actions in foreign countries, and sometimes in the United States as well. Predictably, increasing the use of PMCs in the U.S. military was another neocon idea, which is to say, one that looks good on the drawing board and goes to hell in practice.

Compounding the problem, despite billions spent in reconstruction projects, clean tap water is rare: two-thirds of Iraqis are now forced to drink polluted water from rivers; cholera and hepatitis are raging. Power plants kick out less than half the electricity that's needed. Sewage systems don't work, much of the oil network is still down, and numerous reconstruction projects in fact make the situation worse. Very few Iraqi companies, or Iraqis, got work out of the handsome reconstruction deals, and half of workers are unemployed—both factors in the insurgency. Landing a job as policeman or soldier often entails hefty bribes, and now to work for American firms is to risk murder, as gruesome videos of what happened to those who did so attest.

While protests and polls show Iraqis want the Yanks out, Bush said they'll be hunkering down for a decade at least. U.S. bases, he said, are permanent. And meanwhile, DC is pressuring Baghdad to get the government out of the oil business and hand over development of oil fields to multinational corporations.

In 2007, 88 percent of Iraqis said the electricity still didn't work; 70 percent reported shortages of drinking water.

Staff Sgt. Bennie Corbett, U.S. Army, Department of Defense

"Iraq is now in almost total chaos," wrote Professor Isam al-Khafaji in the Guardian *four months after the 2003 invasion, explaining why he quit the U.S.-appointed Iraqi Reconstruction Council, an exercise that made him feel like a collaborator. "People cannot understand why a superpower that can amass all that military might can't get the electricity back on. Iraqis are now contrasting Saddam's ability to bring back power after the war in 1991 to the apparent inability of the U.S. to do so now." Five years after the invasion, the electricity still doesn't function properly much of anywhere except in the U.S.-controlled Green Zone and streets frequently flood, as shown here. The infamous "blast walls" can be seen in the background.*

RECONSTRUCTION RIP-OFF

Granted, working in a wartime environment isn't easy. But still, what happened in Iraq makes a mockery of American know-how and is a waste of the Iraqi money used to fund the hundreds of projects with little to show for them. The country that before Desert Storm boasted the best hospitals and health care in the Middle East is so short on medical facilities that wounded police often go untreated. Along with the poor water, hospital scarcity is held responsible for the thousands of Iraqi children who died and are dying each year. It's not like money wasn't put into fixing and building health-care centers. Parsons Corporation of Pasadena, California, was paid $253 million to build 150 clinics across Iraq, starting the task in 2004. By 2006, when it was finally relieved of its duties, only five clinics were finished and it'd already blown through $186 million. Bechtel, commissioned to build the Basra Children's Hospital for $50 million, ran some $100 million over budget then shrugged and ditched the project. The hospital elevator in Hillah that Parsons was paid $660,000 to fix, crashed several weeks later, killing three.[23] Halliburton, tossed $2.4 billion to renovate the oil system, botched a number of projects: repairing pumps at one refinery, it installed the most powerful models, neglecting to replace old pipes, which burst, costing millions in damage and shutting the refinery down. When a bridge that carried a crucial pipeline over the Tigris was destroyed, Halliburton subsidiary KBR was called in but opted to replace the bridge with a much pricier tunnel, and when initial studies showed that it was geologically unfeasible, they pushed ahead anyway. Some $75 million later, the bulldozer is still embedded in the bank, and the pipeline is inoperable.[24]

Twelve billion U.S. taxpayer dollars and twenty billion dollars of Iraq's were paid to seven U.S. companies (Halliburton, KBR, Bechtel, Fluor, and Parsons among them) to fix up the place, but there's not much to show for it. Companies blame insurgents; audits show that bilking, scamming, and overbilling are also factors. One thing is for sure: the Iraqis can't get back their money—one of the U.S. government's first acts was to free Americans of any accountability or responsibility for their acts.

Iraq is falling apart, physically and societally, but one might wonder if societies deemed more cohesive wouldn't fragment as well if put under similar stress. What would happen in the United States if the leader was run out, the government closed down, the military and police disbanded? How would American society hold up if electricity was cut, the spigots ran dry, it took days of waiting in line to get gas, and most workers were suddenly out of jobs? All while a foreign power, say China, bombed the bejeezus out of cities and pounded on doors,

For five years and counting, Iraqis have lived under a reign of terror with a plot they can't even follow. But the nonstop violence is taking its toll: 70 percent of Iraqi children are suffering stress disorders, according to UNICEF; 68 percent of refugees surveyed by the UNHCR said they'd been threatened by militias and insurgents; and 16 percent said they were tortured.

screaming questions in a language not understood, and simultaneously sold off American assets to foreign bidders. That's what happened in Iraq at the hands of the Coalition Provisional Authority, the temporary ruling government set up by the United States just weeks after Iraq was liberated in 2003. The actions of the authority's headman, Paul Bremer, following orders from the Bush neocon schemers, knocked both legs out from under Iraq, which subsequently fell on its face.

THE NEOCON PLAN

The problems shaking Iraq are not merely fallout from a needless, unjustified, and poorly conceived war. They are the results of a neocon plan that had been brewing for years: a quick-'n'-tidy military operation to invade Iraq, a plan that had been finessed by a group of Iraqi dissidents headed by former banker Ahmed Chalabi. Called the Iraqi National Congress (INC), and started in 1991 by the CIA, it was at various points funded by the State Department and Department of Defense, being given twenty-seven million dollars from 2000 to 2003 alone. This group of Shia and Kurds who hated Saddam had made numerous attempts to toss him, being paid many millions of U.S. tax dollars to stage these abortive coups. By 1996, the CIA, which had initially championed Chalabi, had withdrawn its support of Chalabi at least, finding his intel and activities suspicious. But by then Chalabi had hooked up with the neocons, and the war plan had snowballed. Called Eclipse II, this plan hammered together around 1998 embraced numerous neocon ideals for a new military strategy using high-tech weapons and few soldiers to invade and oust Saddam Hussein. Promoting the idea of democracy, the United States would tap Ahmed Chalabi as head of government, appointing other INC members to support his policies. With DC-friendly Chalabi guiding the country, U.S. oil companies could easily get at those virgin oil fields that Saddam had kept foreign hands from touching (especially the United States). Given attractive deals, American businesses would move in and control the economy, and after the war American companies would fix up the country, getting billions for their efforts. The U.S. military would set up permanent bases that would allow DC to safeguard oil and effectively control the region, further protecting the hegemony that was a neocon ideal. And, using Chalabi's intelligence and his knowledge of the country he'd left in 1958, the neocons were assured it would be a piece of cake: within months the bulk of American troops would be out, the oil would be flowing, and any money the United States had put into the venture would, thanks to Chalabi, be quickly paid back. But things just didn't work out that way.

According to former U.S. ambassador to Saudi Arabia James Akins, the plan had Chalabi denationalizing production of Iraq's oil, "and then parceling Iraqi oil out to American oil companies,"[25] But according to writer Robert Dreyfuss, who closely followed Chalabi, the plan wouldn't stop there. Wrote Dreyfuss in 2002, "Even more broadly, once an occupying U.S. army seizes Baghdad, Chalabi's INC and its American backers are spinning scenarios about dismantling Saudi Arabia, seizing its oil and collapsing the Organization of the Petroleum Exporting Countries (OPEC)."[26]

Since the Mongols arrived in the thirteenth century and torched the wealth and knowledge accumulated in Baghdad, ending the Islamic golden era, nobody, not even Saddam, has done more to screw up Iraq than one L. Paul Bremer III. The Bush appointee showed up in May 2003 to set up the bureaucratic-sounding Coalition Provisional Authority, which served as the official DC bullhorn. On the day he arrived, just four weeks after Saddam had been toppled, Baghdad was choked with smoke, much of the city on fire. Since the army, despite repeated warnings from archaeologists, wasn't guarding the museums, archaeological sites, or any ministry except oil, looting was well under way—as was the robbing of tombs and ancient cities, all of which have now been thoroughly cleaned out. Iraq would be robbed even further under Bremer's reign.

Lisa M. Zunzanyika, USAF, Department of
Defense via pingnews

*Head of the Coalition Provisional Authority, Paul Bremer is
a former counterterrorism expert with the State Department who'd headed a project at the Heritage Foundation,
which produced what became the blueprint for the U.S.
Homeland Security plan. From his first week in Iraq, he
sucked any remaining life out of the country, stripping jobs
from hundreds of thousands and creating ripe conditions
for the formation of militias. By the time he left in June
2004, just on the heels of Abu Ghraib, the insurgency
was in full swing.*

Setting up in Saddam's former Republican Palace in the Green Zone, where
life ran relatively normally behind thickly fortified walls wrapped with razor wire
and guarded by heavily armed U.S. forces, Bremer, the temporary leader of Iraq,
wrote out hundreds of orders of highly dubious legality. He granted legal immunity to U.S. forces and soldiers of fortune, which allowed them to do as they wish
without any penalties for bad behavior or shoddy work. He coordinated and oversaw the work of the American companies and paid some twenty billion dollars
(with Iraq's oil money)[27] to get the place running again, although many paid-for
projects weren't finished, weren't done well, or were abandoned.

One of Bremer's first acts was to change the currency used for Iraq oil deals
back to dollars. Since 2000, Saddam had negotiated oil deals in euros: that act
not only challenged the supremacy of the dollar on the world market, it also guaranteed a crappy rate to American buyers, since the euro is strong, and the dollar
keeps sliding in value against it. Saddam's switcheroo was so alarming that some
believe it was a factor in the 2003 invasion of Iraq. As former British assistant
secretary of civil service John Chapman wrote in an article, "The Real Reasons
Bush Went to War," the Bush administration wanted to nip that trend in the bud.
"Worldwide switches out of the dollar, on top of the already huge deficit, would
have led to a plummeting dollar, a runaway from US markets and dramatic up-
heavals in the US," he wrote.[28]

Unemployment was already at 40 percent, and it soared higher by the time
Bremer was done. Refusing to rescue salvageable state-owned factories that had

Master Sgt. Andy Dunaway, DoD

Bremer believed that Iraq should put together a whole new army and police force, but the rebuilding of the Shia-dominant military and security hasn't been easy. In battles, many troops defect, and the police forces have been infiltrated by militias, who not only get free guns but notify fellow militants of upcoming busts. Now police are sent out on the streets without phones. Theirs is a hazardous job: police and soldiers are militia targets, hundreds are killed every month, and the wounded are abandoned by the ailing government.

employed a hundred thousand people, he put nearly the whole country on the block, selling off almost all state-owned companies, lowering tax rates, and allowing foreign firms to pocket all the money made in Iraq. It was such a tantalizing array of perks that the *Economist* described it as a capitalist dream come true. Few investors, however, were snatching up properties in the war-ridden country, so the plants just sat there empty and unfixed, while the unemployed marched outside and wives wrote letters begging him to reopen the factories. But he didn't.

Bremer's most devastating moves, however, blasted the foundations of the society. In what was termed "de-Baathification," Bremer outlawed the Arab socialist Baath Party and barred most Baath Party members from employment. This action, proposed and supervised by Ahmed Chalabi, effectively dismantled the government, since all government ministers as well as most employees, including doctors and teachers, belonged to Saddam's party, not always out of choice. And then Bremer canned the entire security apparatus—military, police, and guards—firing over three hundred thousand. Armed and furious, many of Iraq's former soldiers and security men returned as insurgents.

THROWING THE COUNTRY OUT WITH THE BAATH WATER

Conceived of in the 1940s when the British and the French, who'd taken over most Middle Eastern territories in 1920, still hadn't given up lands across the Middle East and were trying to clamp on more fiercely, the Baath Party was heavy on Arab nationalism while downplaying religion. Drawing on socialist principles, and thus encouraging state-owned economies, it was a popular intellectual concept in Iraq and Syria, though in both it was originally outlawed as a radical movement. Baathism finally took hold in Iraq in 1968 after Saddam's uncle grabbed the presidential seat in a coup that year (and appointed Saddam VP). It took hold two years later in Syria via another coup. Baathism was initially the great equalizer, bringing new opportunity to the underlings of Iraqi society and putting the Shia and Kurds on equal standing with the Sunni. Baath membership was not mandatory: only 10 percent of Iraqis signed on. However, Iraqis couldn't advance far professionally without joining, and only members who climbed to the highest levels of the party ladder were part of the Iraqi elite. When Saddam took over in 1979 and started killing off many of the government's top advisers and officers in his first weeks, things soon turned paranoid. He suspected overthrow from even his closest friends. Baathists spied on nonparty members as well as fellow Baathists, and the party became the emblem of Saddam's militarily enforced dictatorship and white-knuckled regime. A pleasant organization it wasn't; however, without it, the country was instantly crippled.

Bremer had a multibillion-dollar U.S. budget for reconstruction at his disposal, but he instead plowed through most of the money in the Iraqi Development Fund left over from the food-for-oil program. To accomplish his goals, he requested piles of cash that were flown in on military planes. With billions to literally play with—his youthful employees tossed around blocks of hundred-dollar bills as footballs[29]—the money was stashed here and there, vaults left open, keys left on top of desks, and billions doled out, nobody seems sure for what, with little accounting. And there's still a big mystery surrounding the money. Billions of Iraq's money slipped out of the Coalition Provisional Authority's hands in a silent, untraceable poof.

MISSING MONEY

The Coalition Provisional Authority (CPA) was supposed to have an accounting firm oversee its work. Instead, Bremer brought in a small-time bookkeeper, who was soon overwhelmed. Over a year later, when accountants had a look at Bremer's books, they were stunned to discover that $8.8 billion of Iraq's money couldn't be traced.[30] When the Special Inspector General for Iraq Reconstruction—set up by Congress to look through CPA records—conducted a thorough audit in 2004, it discovered tens of thousands of "ghost employees" who'd been paid although they didn't exist, numerous cases of the same work being paid for two or three times, and that a hefty proportion of the services paid for were never delivered. One audit released in April 2005 noted that there was no evidence that goods or services were delivered on 154 of 198 contracts.[31] The Bush administration and Republican legislators took swift action: they tried to shut the auditor down.[32]

> *The lack of government structures and the missing money were only two factors that put postwar Iraq on treacherous footing. Bremer, a notorious control freak, hadn't brought any experts with him to set up Iraq's government because he didn't like to be challenged. His inexperienced staff—American twentysomethings whose only commonality was that they were Bush loyalists who'd applied for a job at the right-wing "think tank" the Heritage Foundation[33]—was given difficult tasks such as opening up the stock market, developing economic policy, and even writing the Iraqi constitution.*

Bremer's dictates made him unpopular from the start, even with Americans working in Iraq, some of whom quit their jobs in protest of what he was doing and how he was mismanaging funds. But beyond angering Iraqis, beyond losing their money, beyond granting immunity to all Americans, Bremer set up a new country that was destined to fail. By dismantling the government, canning security, firing hundreds of thousands while not rebuilding plants, refusing to hold even temporary elections, and not prioritizing the return of lights and water, he put the country into a desperate state. The question is whether that was the goal. Author Naomi Klein says his behavior was "shock therapy" meant to wreak havoc: the idea, she says, was to keep the society reeling so that in the chaos, few would notice that the country's assets were being auctioned off. But the Iraqis did notice what was going on.

Ayatollah Ali Sistani, Iraq's highest Shia cleric, questioned and confronted Bremer from the start. He continually demanded elections, at least for cities and towns—to keep them from collapsing. Bremer continually ignored him. Bremer soon had another force to contend with, a much younger Shia leader who was harder to blow off. The son of Ayatollah Mohammed Sadr, who had been Iraq's most revered cleric, chubby and grubby Moqtada Sadr was already rising in Shia circles, but his showdowns with Bremer would cause his power to soar.

His father had died in 1999 in an assassination believed to be the handiwork of Saddam's Mukhabarat (his CIA), and his uncle was sentenced to death the next year. Sadr, while young, had stepped into their shoes. During the 2003 invasion, Sadr and his followers in Najaf ran a charity on wheels, traveling to the worst slum in Baghdad, Saddam City, to distribute food to the poor, who were so grateful that they renamed their district Sadr City in memory of his pa. His rising popularity in fact had prompted his name to be among those suggested to Bremer as a possible appointee to the Iraqi Governing Council, a committee in charge of putting together a draft constitution and recommending Iraqis to fill the government ministries. Bremer shot the recommendation down. He already had a few people in mind: the members of the Iraqi National Congress (INC) who had been waiting for this very moment since 1992.

Now considered the most powerful man in Iraq, Moqtada Sadr commands the ten-thousand-man Mahdi Army. The most threatening in the country, it was created specifically in protest of Bremer's actions and his appointments to the Iraqi Governing Council.

The Rise of Chalabi and the INC

The first American attack on Iraq, Desert Storm, in 1991 didn't, to the surprise of George H. W. Bush, put an end to Saddam. Neither did two uprisings, one in the Shia south and one in the Kurdish north. The fearless Kurds in the north, whom Saddam had gassed three years before, believing the United States would back them, liberated their historic capital Kirkuk. The Shia in the south, even the tribes that lived hidden in marshes, also demanded liberation. Saddam sent his soldiers to stomp out the rebellions, pushing the Kurds out of Kirkuk and draining southern swamps: three hundred thousand were dead by the end of that ordeal. Without official UN approval, the United States and Britain drew lines in Saddam's sand to protect the Shia and Kurds: no-fly zones, which was to say, Saddam couldn't fly there, but the United States and Britain could. They kept Saddam more contained in his box in the center of the country, but the tyrant was still there. The UN saddled him with sanctions, essentially cutting Iraq off from international trade. But Saddam survived.

Shortly thereafter, Bush directed the CIA to scout out dissidents to devise another means to take Saddam down from within. The CIA approached two Kurdish leaders, Massoud Barzani and Jalal Talabani, who'd led the uprisings. Even though they were rivals, they agreed to sign up for this intelligence-gathering group. In London, agents found a former high-ranking Baathist, Iyad Allawi, whose limp alone spoke of Saddam's response when he'd defected. The CIA rounded up more dissidents—from engineers working in Syria to clerics hiding from Saddam in Iran—and in 1992 the CIA flew some two hundred of these exiles to Vienna for a conference organized by media manipulator James Rendon, who gave the group its name—the Iraqi National Congress. Put on the CIA payroll, the motley crew would publish a dissident newspaper in Iraq, launch a radio station mocking Saddam, they'd recruit, they'd train, they'd help stage rebellions—and, most important, they'd gather dirt on Saddam. Well, supposedly.

The most charismatic of the bunch was a slickly dressed, smooth-talking banker from Jordan, who was chosen to head the group: Ahmed Chalabi. His prosperous family had left Iraq during the revolution of 1958—the year the military killed the king, with whom Chalabi's father was close—and they'd headed to Jordan, where they'd been embraced by the Iraqi king's cousin and ruler of Jordan, King Hussein. A mathematician by training, Chalabi studied at the University of Chicago, growing close to political science professor and nuclear strategist Albert Wohlstetter, a man who would greatly shape the future of some of his students, foremost among them Paul Wolfowitz. The professor did more than impress his ideas about the role of the United States as hegemon on Wolfowitz: he also introduced him to Chalabi, who would be the vehicle to help put those theories into motion on the world stage, alas.

In 1977, Chalabi opened Petra Bank in Jordan but was apparently involved in dodgy practices, including moving money through banks in Lebanon. In the late 1980s, when the Jordanian government realized that he didn't have the reserves he'd claimed to have—some thirty million dollars were missing—he was tried in absentia for embezzlement. Found guilty, he was sentenced to twenty-two years in prison.

Active in rebellions in the Kurdish north, which thanks to the no-fly zones was an autonomous region, Chalabi's star was fading by the mid-nineties: he had power struggles with the Kurds, who were also members of the INC, and he was getting heat from the CIA for his ties with Iran—he'd brought in a few Revolutionary Guard members and had housed them using U.S. tax dollars. Around 1996, the CIA cut off his paycheck.

But Chalabi soon found means to get another. By the mid-nineties, the economic sanctions the UN had heaped on Saddam in punishment for his 1990 invasion of Kuwait, were strangling the country. Without oil money, the economy had nose-dived. Iraqis were working two or three jobs and still couldn't survive. Food was scarce. Medicine was gone. The value of the currency plummeted, and the typical Iraqi went from making three thousand dollars a year in 1980 to thirty dollars a year. Children were dying and many had birth defects—mangled limbs, missing eyes—believed to be the result of the depleted uranium used by the coalition during the war. The UN devised a plan to replenish the economy while keeping Saddam from buying weapons of mass destruction. The food-for-oil program launched in 1996 specified how much oil Iraq could sell, and payments came in a lump sum twice a year. The "food" of the food-for-oil program didn't much make it to the people, but the oil did help out the Baathist elite in Baghdad, which boasted fancy art galleries, designer boutiques, and stores filled with pricey perfume. Shiny Mercedes filled the streets, and Internet cafés began opening. Most of the money was black: oil was snuck off on tankers to Yemen and pumped through pipelines to Syria; it went off on trucks to Jordan—and those who were supposed to be monitoring it turned a blind eye. Smuggling—of oil, stolen cars, and drugs—became a full-time occupation for those who could muscle into it, and those who didn't hocked heirlooms and worked two or three jobs that still barely kept them afloat.

By 1998, some countries were pushing the UN Security Council to drop the sanctions. Namely, Russia, China, and France—three of the permanent members of the council that had inflicted the sanctions in the first place. The reason: oil. Saddam had negotiated deals with all three to develop several of Iraq's untapped fields. But the restrictive sanctions prevented Saddam from opening new fields. Russia, China, and France began demanding that the UN cut the chains. And in the meantime, Saddam made it clear to the United States and Britain that when he opened up these new fields, they would not be included in any deals; after all, the United States and Britain had led the Desert Storm coalition against Iraq.

A series of letters from distinguished Republicans—and a few Democrats—began flying at President Clinton and Congress demanding that the sanctions stay in place. The United States, directed one from the Project for the New American Century (PNAC), should not only keep the sanctions cuffed on, it should lead a war against Iraq—alone if need be—to unseat Saddam, who posed a very real "hazard" to "a significant portion of the world's supply of oil." This was soon followed up with another from PNAC urging Clinton to "establish and maintain a strong U.S. military presence in the region, and be prepared to use that force to protect [U.S.] vital interests in the Gulf—and, if necessary, to help remove Saddam from power." The Committee for Peace and Security, like PNAC, also published a letter to Clinton that summarized a nine-point "comprehensive political and military strategy for bringing down Saddam and his regime." The signatories of the letters were former government officials, now in the private world and holding lofty positions at universities and think tanks: Donald Rumsfeld, Paul Wolfowitz, Dick Cheney, Richard Perle, Douglas Feith, Elliott Abrams, David Wurmser—and the dozens of others who made up the core of the neocons.

By then, Ahmed Chalabi was their pal, promising a pipeline from Iraq to Israel and to open Iraqi oil to the United States—well, if he was in power. Neocons pushed through a bill in Congress, the Iraq Liberation Act, which declared Saddam U.S. Enemy Number One and instructed Clinton to pay $150 million to Iraqi opposition groups for military equipment and information-collection activities. The information collection picked up steam as the Bush campaign took off.

By the time President George W. Bush was in the chair, Chalabi was bringing in dissidents who described firsthand Saddam's lethal arsenal, and after 9/11 he brought more, with details about the chemicals bubbling away in secret labs, the missiles ordered, the nuclear weapons in place. Not to be outdone, Iyad Allawi, who couldn't stand Chalabi, his cousin, and had formed a breakaway group in London, produced his own insiders as well to British prime minister Tony Blair. Chalabi duped the U.S. press: after Judith Miller of the *New York Times* reported that Saddam had weapons of mass destruction it was simply an unquestioned fact that could be repeated by the Bush administration. And Blair shortly thereafter announced to the shocked British parliament that Saddam had weapons that could target London, which, once that button had been hit, was only forty-five minutes away from causing annihilation.

A few months later, in March 2003, the bombs began dropping on Baghdad. The army airlifted Ahmed Chalabi and five hundred fighters to Iraq, where the man whom the neocons dubbed the George Washington of Iraq began his conquest of Saddam country with an eye to sitting in the presidential palace.

Bremer had fulfilled the first part of the plan: in June 2003 he set up the Iraqi Governing Council, tapping Chalabi and other members of INC as well as Allawi and members of his breakaway group, which was also being funded by the U.S. government. Chalabi would serve as rotating president with nine others, including Barzani, Talabani, and Allawi, all of them previously beneficiaries of U.S. largesse. But promise-filled, charming Chalabi was the favorite. Along with Nouri al-Maliki, Chalabi headed the committee concerned with a process that he had conceived of himself, right down to the word: de-Baathification, or firing the Baathists from their jobs.

Like de-Baathication itself, the Iraq Governing Council, which Chalabi had helped conceive, did away with any notions of Arab nationalism. Instead, it highlighted faith and played up factionalism, its members selected to fill a quota: thirteen Shia, five Sunni Arabs, five Sunni Kurds, one Assyrian, and one Turk. The American media applauded the diversity of religions and ethnicity, neglecting to realize that most Iraqis didn't define themselves by their faiths, and not seeing that in the name of fair representation a seed had been planted in bringing the country together that would tear it apart.

Drunk with visions of sugarplums planted in their heads by Ahmed Chalabi, neocon war dreamers assured Americans that U.S. troops would be greeted as liberators, cheered by Iraqis, and welcomed with flowers. While most Iraqis were jubilant that Saddam fell, the applauding masses bearing bouquets never arrived: the country fell in three weeks but once it had, rebel fighters, the so-called insurgents, showed up to run coalition fighters right out. Some were actually "welcoming gifts" from Saddam, who had invited in hard-core Sunni fundamentalists from Yemen weeks before the coalition forces arrived; others were his few remaining loyalists. Among the early arrivals was Abu Musab al-Zarqawi, who traipsed in with hundreds, perhaps thousands, of jihadis. These young firebrand Sunnis had one goal in mind: turn Iraq into an Islamic state. And when Bremer named a puppet council that was heavy on the Shia, Zarqawi's force was bolstered as yet more jihadis of the Wahhabi mold flocked in, determined to run out the infidel who was empowering their enemy, the Shia.

ZARQAWI: A SUNNI THORN

Despite his early linkage in the media with al Qaeda, Jordan-born Abu Musab al-Zarqawi, a Sunni of the Wahhabi model, didn't care for the wealthy Saudi, Osama bin Laden, who headed it, doling out money to those who pledged allegiance. Although they were both fundamentalist Sunni who hated Shia and shared the same goals—ridding the Arab world of Western influences and installing theocracies à la the Taliban across the Middle East—they weren't aligned, at least not back when the United States was marrying them as cohorts in crime. In many ways, Zarqawi was more extreme: launching the first major attacks in Iraq—the bombing of the Jordanian embassy and UN offices in August 2003—he went on to attack Shia mosques, something bin Laden was unlikely to do. He finally signed on with the latter's group in 2005.

When Moqtada Sadr learned that he wouldn't be part of the Iraqi Governing Council, he began to loudly trash it. As an Iraqi who had been in the country his whole life, he claimed more legitimacy than the exiles that Bremer was placing on the council. He was starting a shadow government, he announced. Before long, Sadr had his own newspaper, *Hawza*, and he had his own militia in training. The articles in *Hawza* lashed out at the United States and lashed out at Bremer, whom the paper portrayed as purposefully creating food shortages so that, while the people were struggling to get bread, he could rearrange the economy and the government. But the article in March 2004 that praised 9/11 was what did it for Bremer. He shut down *Hawza*, and shortly thereafter arrested Sadr's assistant. He declared Sadr an outlaw, and pushed the army to take him down.

In April 2004, *60 Minutes* aired a program about the torture at Abu Ghraib outside Baghdad, the prison where American private military contractors from CACI had inflicted grisly abuses, taking photos for amusement. The image of a black-hooded prisoner with arms attached to electrical wires symbolized the United States to many Iraqis. In response, Sadr unleashed his militia—in Najaf, in Basra, in Sadr City, where they attacked coalition troops in weeks of fighting that killed scores. In Fallujah, a local mob pulled four Blackwater employees out of an SUV, and then dragged them through the streets for a mass lynching, the mutilated corpses left to hang from a bridge.

The insurgency had begun.

Iraqis stopped talking to Americans: working for them, helping them, being seen with them, or having anything to do with them spelled death. Protests broke out with women screaming, "No, no, America, no." The tribal clans picked up their guns and joined the foreign jihadi who were now streaming in to rid the country of George Bush. In June 2004, Bremer handed over full authority to the Iraqi Governing Council, renamed the Iraqi Transitional Government, and flew back to the States, leaving behind a country that was exploding with rage.

> *"Since we last met in this chamber, combat forces of the United States, Great Britain, Australia, Poland, and other countries enforced the demands of the United Nations, ended the rule of Saddam Hussein, and the people of Iraq are free. (applause) Having broken the Baathist regime, we face a remnant of violent Saddam supporters. Men who ran away from our troops in battle are now dispersed and attack from the shadows. We are dealing with these thugs in Iraq, just as surely as we dealt with Saddam Hussein's evil regime. (applause)*
>
> *"The work of building a new Iraq is hard, and it is right. And America has always been willing to do what it takes for what is right. Last January, Iraq's only law was the whim of one brutal man. Today our coalition is working with the Iraqi Governing Council to draft a basic law, with a bill of rights. As democracy takes hold in Iraq, the enemies of freedom will do all in their power to spread violence and fear. They are trying to shake the will of our country and our friends, but the United States of America will never be intimidated by thugs and assassins. (applause) The killers will fail, and the Iraqi people will live in freedom."*
> —President George W. Bush, State of the Union, 2004

It didn't turn out as planned, in most every respect. Starting with what happened to the council that took over ruling the country when Bremer left: Chalabi didn't make it to the prime minister's spot. His cousin-in-law Iyad Allawi did. Chalabi, however, did land the spot as deputy prime minister and, most important, he nabbed the post as oil minister. Two months later, however, his office and house were searched—a move apparently requested by the United States, where the neocons were now calling Chalabi a spy for Iran. They charged that he'd passed on top-secret information to Tehran: namely that the United States had broken Iran's secret code. An arrest warrant was issued: during the search, agents had found counterfeit money. Chalabi said the cash was merely a sample he was going to show the finance ministry. He evaded the arrest, but his name was tainted. As elections loomed—the first time any Iraqi leaders would be voted in—most Shia united in a bloc, the United Iraqi Alliance. Chalabi dropped out, since they would not promise him the role of prime minister. Running as an independent candidate, he lost.

While Chalabi was going down, Sadr was rising. Starting his own political party, he aligned with the Shia National Alliance, which won enough votes for six ministers in parliament; one was appointed to the cabinet, landing the health ministry. Hospitals across Iraq soon bore new artwork: photos of Iraq's Ayatollah Ali Sistani alongside Iran's Ayatollah Ali Khomeini.

And therein lies one of the great ironies of the 2003 Iraq War, a war Iran protested against and lobbied the United States to forget. While Bush continually proclaimed that the United States had won the war, later going on to say it *would* win the war and absurdly claiming that "The world is better, and the United States of America is safer" as a result of his boondoggle, the United States has in fact lost quite a lot: thousands of Americans have died, and the U.S. budget and the economy are in shambles. More federal money now goes to the wars Bush started, his defense budget and military operations, than anything else. The chaos the war caused has helped to boost oil prices and the recession has made buying gasoline harder for most. DC has lost face in the world. The Bush administration looks like a pack of liars, and it brought Americans' faith in the country's political system to new lows.

Who has benefited most from the war? Iran. Now Iran has strong religious ties with nearly all Iraq's power boys, from Moqtada Sadr to the prime minister, Maliki. The holy sites in Karbala and Najaf, once closed to Shia pilgrims under Saddam, are now open, and millions of Iranians have flooded in. The two countries have bonded like never before in their history, though the Bush administration continually accused Iran of funding, arming, and training Shia militias in Iraq to attack the United States. What this all spells for the future isn't quite clear. But there's a distinct possibility that Iraq, like Iran, will turn into a theocracy: that ground-level theocracy is unofficially already in place, being the creation of the militias set loose by this war and the blunders the Bush administration made in fighting it.

The irony comes full circle. Saddam, the former vice president, who in 1979 grabbed the presidential seat from his uncle, was plagued by exactly that fear: that Iran would empower Iraq's Shia and help them set up a religious government that would topple his. And it was that fear of a riled-up Shia population installing a Shia theocracy—a fear also shared by the Saudis and the Kuwaitis—that put Saddam in a downward spiral from which he would never pull out. Initially financed by the Sauds and the Sabah family in Kuwait, and helped along by the United States, Saddam launched a war against the radical Iranian Islamic republic in 1980—a showdown he believed he could win in three weeks. Eight years, fifty billion dollars, and a million deaths later, his once-wealthy country was so in debt that he invaded Kuwait in 1990. And that lethal move would bring the Bush administration, led by its secretary of defense, Dick Cheney, into Baghdad and launch an era as chaotic and destructive as that unleashed by the Mongols eight centuries before. And the mayhem, even the electrical problem, assuredly won't be sorted out anytime soon: Prime Minister Maliki recently handed the job of Mr. Fix-it to Ahmed Chalabi, the high-ranking appointed official who now has eight ministries under his control. His mission: to get Iraq working again.

Another group that's benefited from the 2003 war: the Kurds. Sidelined for most of Iraq's history, the Kurds have emerged as a powerful force—with a Kurd holding the presidential post and an autonomous region in the north that's remained relatively calm. Whether they stay put in Iraq or secede to form Kurdistan remains to be seen.

Hotshots

Saddam Hussein: Saddam would do anything to keep hold of his power. He gassed Kurds and massacred Shia, and his government was so corrupt it ran an auto theft operation to bring in extra money. He killed many of his closest friends, one for agreeing with Saddam's own suggestion that he should temporarily step down to halt the Iran-Iraq War. But such qualities didn't bother the United States for quite a while: in the 1950s the CIA hired him to assassinate President Qassim, believed threatening to U.S. oil supplies, and just days after Saddam had "gassed his own people" in 1984, special government envoy Donald Rumsfeld flew to Baghdad with gifts to strike up business deals. Saddam might never have become DC's enemy except for one thing: the Soviet Union that had long topped the enemy charts was crumbling in 1990, right when the secretary of defense was trying to revolutionize the U.S. Army. Cheney's $300 billion budget was in the process of being shot down when Saddam rolled into Kuwait, inadvertently casting himself in a role the George H. W. Bush administration needed filled immediately to keep the defense program afloat: U.S. Enemy Number One.

Moqtada Sadr: Young and mighty, Sadr—who has a political party, a militia, a media machine, and the support of millions—is one of the few Iraqi politicians who wasn't aligned with the INC. He is typically viewed as a foe of the United States, which targeted the Shia cleric as a threat when he questioned Bremer's appointment of exiles who'd been out of the country for decades. And he became more threatening when he unleashed his ten-thousand-man-strong Mahdi Army, turning a do-gooder group into warriors. Whenever the United States lashes out at him, he lashes back with formidable strength. He's shown that he's capable of restraint: the cease-fire he called in 2007 is considered as important as, if not more than, the "surge" in the relative cooling of violence in Iraq. The cease-fire ended and battles against the United States, however, resumed after U.S. forces targeted Mahdi Army centers in March 2008; within hours rockets were hurling into the Green Zone and daily death rates were heading up to pre-surge levels. Given his immense popularity and leadership abilities, perhaps the United States should switch tactics and support him instead of trying to shoot him down. Lily-white he ain't—hard to find hands that aren't dirty around here—but he does back a unified Iraq and is working with Sunni to form a new alliance. There is one group that doesn't like him much: the Kurds, whose autonomy and predilection to secede he publicly questions.

Iyad Allawi: A neurologist and secular Shia who was once a Saddam in-sider, Allawi left Iraq and the Baath Party and spent 1978 recuperating in a British hospital after Saddam's thugs attacked him in London with an ax. Turned informer for British intel, he started the dissident group Iraqi National Accord and worked with the CIA starting in the 1990s. He received millions in U.S. funds for his London-based group. Like his cousin by marriage Ahmed Chalabi, he told whoppers: he's responsible for British prime minister Tony Blair's claim that Saddam's WMDs could hit London in forty-five minutes (which Allawi later admitted was a lie). He returned to Iraq in 2003 and was interim prime minister from June 2004 to April 2005; his rule, some said, was more brutal than Saddam's.

Abdul Aziz Hakim: Descendant of a powerful Shia family that runs the holy city Najaf, Hakim heads the powerful Supreme Islamic Iraqi Council, a political party with a rough-and-tumble paramilitary arm, the Badr Brigade. Hakim spent decades in Iran and is still tight with the power elite in Tehran; nevertheless, the United States backs him—his group was also affiliated with the INC—supporting his militia's battles with Moqtada Sadr.

THE KURDS

Descended from an ancient mountain tribe, the Medea, the Kurds speak a language close to Iranian and have long inhabited their own world in the mountains. They were supposed to get their own country in 1919, Kurdistan, but the oil held in their land resulted, instead, in their being roped into Iraq. They rose up against the Brits in the 1920s, and on several occasions staged major uprisings against the government in Iraq, which on occasion granted them limited autonomy. When President George H. W. Bush urged the Kurds to rebel in 1991, the rebellion was brutally stomped out by Sadd-am's force, but it did result in the Kurds' greatest autonomy in ages: the United States imposed a no-fly zone in the north, where Saddam troops couldn't enter, well, unless they were invited. Infamous for fighting among themselves, the Kurds' most dramatic rivalry was between the Kurdistan Democratic Party (headed by Massoud Barzani, current president of the Autonomous Kurdish Government) and the Patriotic Union of Kurdistan (headed by current president of Iraq Jalal Talabani). Both leaders were tapped back in the early 1990s by the CIA as part of the INC, and they worked together to plot uprisings against Saddam. Plans blew up several times, most famously in 1995 when Barzani requested that Saddam send fighters into the Kurdish city of Arbil to run out Talabani's Patriotic Union of Kurdistan. Relations are better since that bloody time, and the two groups essentially share power in the Kurdish north. There are other forces to con-tend with now, including Islamist hard-core Ansar al Islam, which claims turf of its own. And the separatist group PKK, which hides out in the farthest northern reaches, is seen as such a threat by Turkey that for months in early 2008 Turkish fighters battled the rebels in the mountains. The message, however, was meant for all Kurds: give up the dream of Kurdistan—a dream that would take land from Turkey's east.

While most Kurds are Sunni, one branch, the Yazidi, is Christian.

KING FAISAL

Poor Hashemite king Faisal: he wanted to rule Syria but was ousted by the French and instead sat on the throne in problematic Iraq. Seen as a puppet, he wasn't popular with anybody but the Brits, who forced him to turn over Iraq's oil for pitiful profits. The monarchy ended with a bloody overthrow in 1958.

Hot Spots

Shatt al Arab: The thin waterway shared with Iran is the main oil transport to the Gulf, and it's littered with nearly a hundred sunken ships and other navigation hazards. A new danger along this river where oil smuggling is centered: piracy.

Sadr City: This Baghdad suburb of beige buildings and sewage-flooded streets houses two million of the poorest Shia. Site of frequent violence—car bombs and coalition attacks—it's the heart of Sadr's support system.

Basra: With palm-lined canals, Basra, a former *vilayet* (county seat) in the Ottoman Empire, used to be one of Iraq's most calm and lovely cities—and the only one with a major port. Since the war and the subsequent British pullout in fall 2008, Basra's been swept by a rash of murder—scientists, professors, and unveiled women are among those who have died by the hundreds in recent months—as militias and mafia gangs fight for control. The reason: the port makes it a major smuggling hotbed.

Mosul: The first city where oil was struck back in 1920, Mosul is still oil rich, but it's dangerously violent. The problem: Saddam wanted to depopulate the local Kurds and move Arab Sunni and Shia there in the 1980s in a paid relocation plan; now it's a dangerously mixed city, a magnet for militias who want to turn it all Shia or all Sunni. Complicating matters, the Kurds want back the city that was their historic capital.

Kirkuk: Also historically in Kurd territory, Kirkuk is believed to hold many of the biggest untapped oil finds. Kurds want to annex it into their autonomous region; other Iraqis are balking, and the whole matter is supposed to go to a vote.

Michael Spencer, courtesy of Saudi Aramco/ASC

Marsh Arabs still live among the reeds in southern Iraq, but TVs and refrigerators have arrived too.

Fallujah: West of Baghdad, Fallujah was overlooked when U.S. troops first stormed in. It quickly became a haven for insurgents, some of whom grabbed four Blackwater contractors in 2004 and hung their mutilated corpses from a bridge. Major coalition attacks left it mostly rubble thanks to thermobaric bombs.

Kuwaiti islands: If only Kuwait had leased one of them to Saddam, it may have prevented the 1990 invasion. Now the government of Iraq wants to rent some, to finally give Iraq much-needed Gulf access.

U.S. embassy: The biggest and priciest U.S. embassy anywhere this side of the moon, the massive edifice going up in the Green Zone holds over six hundred apartments as well as its own power plant and water-treatment center. How much it cost to build isn't clear: somewhere between $600 million and $1.3 billion, and it will, absurdly, cost over a billion a year to keep up. Kuwaitis landed the construction contract, and a brouhaha broke out in 2008 over the accusation that they'd used slave labor.

Samarra: The swirling mosque of Samarra is only one of the city's wonders. The Shia's twelfth imam, the Mahdi, was last seen here. When Sunnis blasted the golden dome of the Mahdi's shrine in 2006, Sunni-Shia fighting went on for months.

Stretching along a thousand miles of the Persian Gulf, the Islamic Republic of Iran hasn't stirred up waves in that strategic waterway—through which 20 percent of the world's oil travels[1]—for decades. During the 1980s, however, Iran targeted the Gulf's oil-hauling ships during the nerve-racking Tanker War, an extension of the Iran-Iraq War (1980–88). During that four-year tanker saga, over five hundred ships were damaged and hundreds were killed. Friction with Baghdad had started over the shared Shatt al Arab, the river that is Iraq's only outlet to the Gulf; Iran relies on it to transport oil from its refinery at Abadan. DC now frets that Iran will shut down the seven-mile-wide Strait of Hormuz, where small boats approached a U.S. warship in early 2008; DC claimed they threatened to attack, but that was subsequently questioned. Iran has its worries too, currently being sandwiched by the United States, which has armed forces in Iraq and Afghanistan.

Chapter Six

Iran: Isn't the Party Over *Yet*?

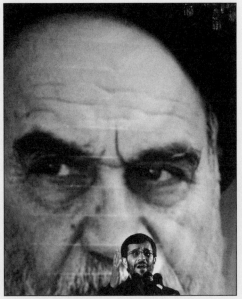

An image of Ayatollah Khomeini, who led the Iranian revolution that brought in an Islamic government three decades ago, looms over cocky President Ahmadinejad, who has rekindled Iran's hatred of the West and is infamous for threats to "the regime that occupies Jerusalem"—i.e., Israel.

Hassan Ammar, Getty Images

For ten years, Khomeini *was* Iran: like a dark wizard, the grizzled cleric held American hostages and hissed about the Great Satan, his nickname for the United States. Harsh words softened under President Mohammad Khatami (1997–2005), whose failure to get DC to sign a peace-and-security treaty (his offers were yawned at by neocons) brought the hardliners' return in the form of the annoying President Ahmadinejad.[2]

The modern mouth of Iran, Ahmadinejad loves to taunt. Especially grating are his brag fests about Iran's nuclear projects followed by an unspoken, "Nah-nah-nah—and ain't nothin' you can do." However, in 2007, it looked like there was: the DC–Tel Aviv war drum was pounding like Dick Cheney's heart after an arms show. But that December a shocking U.S. intelligence report stating that Iran had frozen nuclear arms plans in 2003 made Bush slink off with another WMD tale between his legs. Fuming Israel still may strike Iran's nuclear sites alone: Bush vowed that the United States will protect Israel if Iran ever attacks. While plenty of Iranians wanna smack Ahmie too, and almost everybody is sick of the theocracy, an invasion from outside will only stir up loyalty to the country. Here's hoping the United States and Israel bury that boner of an idea that promises global upheaval.

FAST FACTS:
Jomhuri-ye Eslami-ye Iran

Government:	Theocratic republic, Shia Islam
Formed:	April Fool's Day 1979
Ruler:	Supreme leader Ali Khamenei
GDP 2006:	$294.5 billion (IMF, 2007)
Per capita GDP:	$4,200 (IMF, 2007)
Population:	66 million, nearly half are not Persian (July 2008 estimate)
Unemployment:	15 percent (government stat, many say higher)
Literacy rate:	84 percent men, 70 percent women
Ethnicity:	51 percent Persian, 24 percent Azeri, 8 percent Gilaki and Mazandarani, 7 percent Kurd, 3 percent Arab, 2 percent Lur, 2 percent Baluchi, 2 percent Turkomen, 1 percent other
Religion:	89 percent Shia Muslim; 9 percent Sunni Muslim; 2 percent other (Zoroastrian, Jewish, Christian, Baha'i)

Population stat: Iranians are different. Ethnically they're mostly Persian (and Azeri), not Arab; most Iranians speak Farsi, not Arabic; and the state religion is Shia not Sunni, although Islam long played a secondary role in Iran (until Khomeini came along). Khomeini dropped the legal marriage age to nine, and the Iranian population boomed, growing from thirty-five million in 1979 to sixty million by 1996, when successor Khamenei made birth control and vasectomies legal again.[3] Now the average woman has two kids instead of six. Given Iran's rash of economic ailments, mouths fell open when Ahmadinejad urged families to start expanding at the Khomeini rate, saying the country could easily hold another twenty or so million. Already nearly one in five lives in poverty.

Ayatollah Ali Khamenei, religious leader since 1989, has never commanded the adoration of his predecessor Ayatollah Khomeini, but he is a pragmatist and more of a quiet, moderating force. Ahmie bugs him too.

Leader's Corner

Never mind the picture painted by the media that President Mahmoud Ahmadinejad is running the show. Most power is actually held offstage by the religious elite, with Supreme Leader Ayatollah Khamenei at the top. As commander in chief, he is the sole person who can unleash the warriors. The cleric maintains that Iran's nuclear program is solely for electricity, and in 2005 he wrote a fatwa condemning possessing nuclear weapons in Iran; his decree *should* hold weight. After trying to diplomatically engage the United States, Khamenei has returned to condemnations of U.S. activities, including the U.S. military presence surrounding Iran. However, he's rarely as bellicose as President Ahmadinejad, whom he has tried to rein in.

WHAT MATTERS

Energy matters: OPEC's second-largest producer, Iran sits in second place in conventional world oil reserves, after Saudi Arabia.[4] It also holds the planet's second-biggest reserve of natural gas, much coming from the Gulf field shared with Qatar.[5] Iran heavily subsidizes energy prices at home, eating up 12 percent of its GDP doing so.[6] Short on refineries, it imports half of its gasoline, which lately has been rationed.

Electricity matter: Iran is flickering and prone to blackouts; the place needs new power plants. Too bad they're so keen on the atom.

Arms matter: Theoretically cut off from U.S. arms since 1980—although the Reagan administration's arms-for-hostages Iran-Contra affair made a mockery of that—Iran buys many goodies from Russia. Iran also has a homegrown arms-making industry, recently unveiling high-tech subs and missiles that can't be detected by radar. Unmanned aerial vehicles are also in the arsenal: Iran gave some to Hezbollah, along with long-range rockets.

Military matters: Iran has some 350,000 in its regular armed forces, and the Islamic Revolutionary Guard Corps (Pasdaran) is estimated to have

125,000 under arms, including thousands in its paramilitary arm Al Qods and the 90,000 volunteer forces in the Basij, which serves as religious police.[7] The mafia-like Guard helped bring in Ahmadinejad and is reaping financial paybacks—so many it's now the economic backbone in Iran;[8] Ahmie's handing it big-buck construction projects from subways to pipelines.[9] Some say the economic incentives are necessary since only the Guard keeps the increasingly unpopular theocracy in place. The United States designates the Revolutionary Guard terrorists.

Religion matters: Most Iranians are Twelver Shia, which officially holds that the twelfth imam, the Mahdi, will return at the end of the world. Despite being a theocracy, Islam is more laid-back in Iran. The devout only head to the mosque three times a day, and many don't even go then. Even the holy day, Friday, is fairly relaxed, religion being seen as mostly a personal affair. The culture still celebrates festive Zoroastrian holidays, though the first religion of Persia is no longer practiced. The Zoroastrians fled to India, where they are famous as the well-to-do Parsi.

Ethnicity matters: A little more than half of the country is Persian, the ethnicity of the elite.

Government matters: Columbia University president Lee Bollinger introduced Ahmadinejad in 2007 as "a petty and cruel dictator," a nasty welcome to an invited speaker and erroneous at that. Iran has *some* democratic elements: the president is elected as are parliamentarians and the Assembly of Experts, which selects the supreme leader. However, the Council of Guardians, an appointed twelve-member board of clerics and lawyers, restricts who can run. Over one thousand presidential hopefuls, including all reformists, were nixed as the council whittled the number of approved candidates for the 2005 elections to six.

Money/economy matters: Money stays in the hands of the religious elite, the Revolutionary Guard, and the merchants who work in bazaars, the *bazaaris*. Few flaunt their wealth—the richest bazaaris may dress like paupers. The rest of the people feel like paupers: inflation is soaring, employment is around 25 percent, and energy shortages in this oil- and gas-rich country are making Iranians blow fuses. The government is apparently leaving economic tinkering to the Mahdi: infrastructure is falling apart and the petroleum industry needs a major revamp, as does the entire economy. And the state of the economy is one reason why many want to see the theocracy take a bow.

Militants matter: The Mujahideen-E-Khalq (MEK) remains a thorn, spying on Tehran's nuclear plants and blabbing loudly to the Western press, which should be looking at this bunch with raised eyebrow.

Drugs matter: Gateway to Afghanistan's poppy fields, Iran has a serious jones for opium and smack; addiction, says the government, is Iran's "thorniest" problem, but Khamenei is said to take a toke of opium every so often. The poppy's prize is like aspirin around here.

IRANIAN PLOT

The boys in Tehran love to make Westerners squirm and sputter, a condition that occurs even when we try to refer to the leaders. No wonder DC preferred the shah (Mohammad Reza Pahlavi, who headed Iran from 1941 to early 1979): at least we can pronounce his name.

Khomeini (hoe-men-NEE):   First supreme leader of the country (1979–89), casting himself in the role he created: mortal fill-in until the twelfth imam returns.

Khamenei (ha-men-NAY):   Second supreme leader of the country (1989–present), who stays in the shadows, every so often whispering via well-placed editorials in his own newspaper, "Ahmie, shut up!"

Khatami (ha-ta-MEE):   President (1997–2005) and reformist cleric, who called for "a dialogue between nations," Khatami opened some foreign doors but had them slammed in his face at home and was rebuffed in his efforts to secure "a grand bargain" with DC.

Ahmadinejad (ah-maw-DEE-nah-jawd):   Former Tehran mayor and self-proclaimed professor, the world champion of jabberwocky makes DC and Tel Aviv go ballistic whenever he talks atomic.

Simon Chauvin

Set against a mountain range, Iran's capital, Tehran, is bustling, modern, and congested—filled with markets, businesses, and apartment high-rises. Its symbol is this all-marble Freedom Monument, erected in 1971 for the shah's celebration of Persian culture. The design incorporates features from the Sassanid period.

Last spring, inside the ritzy mansions of north Tehran, where women untie their head scarves and casually sip cocktails, and inside the desert houses made of mud, where a piece of plastic spread on the floor serves as a table, the people of Iran were talking of one thing: tomatoes. In previous months tomatoes had quadrupled in price, so had potatoes, cheese, and milk—the basics Iranians expected to find on their tables, even if it took working two jobs to get them there, *before* the price hikes. Something else was missing from the table, its absence infuriating them even more than the missing tomatoes and spuds. Money. Specifically, the oil money President Mahmoud Ahmadinejad had promised he'd "put on the dinner table" of every Iranian. That was how the former mayor of Tehran, a religious conservative who'd once mandated that elevators be segregated by gender, had won the 2005 presidential election: with the promise of a revamped economy, the promise of change, and the promise that he'd funnel the country's oil riches back to the people. But that money had not shown up—on the table or anywhere else.[10]

Besides his "money on the table" promise, Ahmadinejad's victory was helped along by his mystical beliefs. Some Iranians roll their eyes at the story of the twelfth imam, but Ahmadinejad is a big believer in the return of the Mahdi. He's building hotels for the tourists that will flood here when the Mahdi shows up,[11] which Ahmie believes will be during his reign; he claims to have a special bond with the twelfth imam, whom he credits with helping him win the presidential election.[12] The Mahdi did play a role: Ahmie's devotion to the twelfth imam appealed to the poor, whom he also promised to financially aid.

Instead of delivering on his campaign promise, Ahmadinejad did just the opposite: he slashed government subsidies for gasoline imports, boosting prices at the pump by 25 percent. Overnight, the government slapped on rations: drivers were capped at twenty-six gallons a month, and Iranians abruptly discovered that they'd have to get by on less than a gallon a day. That gallon wouldn't get them far, especially in Tehran's coiled traffic. The response was swift: that May tens of thousands took to the streets, torching gas stations, looting banks, some demanding Ahmadinejad's removal, others calling for his death—and three dying in the mayhem. There hadn't been anything this out of control since the early days of the 1979 revolution, one sign of the increasing displeasure with the regime. Ever since the overthrow of the shah, when the country's identity shifted from a secular monarchy to an Islamic republic, the economy (now the number-one concern of Iranians) has gone to hell.

The gasoline price hike was only from thirty-four to forty-two cents a gallon—prices Americans haven't seen for decades. Prices, in fact, that are the lowest in the world, since the Iranian government heavily subsidizes them. But even that jump was painful in a country where the middle class often works two jobs, many even as unofficial cabbies offering lifts to strangers just to make a few bucks on the side.

Iranians are the Middle East's "drama kings." Theatrics show up during street demonstrations, parliamentary displays, and Shia holidays, which embrace martyrdom in the face of injustice. The Shia remain ticked that in the seventh century Ali was not the first Islamic leader after Mohammed but instead the fourth. The tragedy of Ali's assassination is surpassed only by that of his son Husayn, who was massacred while holding his son, in Karbala in AD 680—the event that created the original Shia-Sunni split. Husayn's death is commemorated each year during Ashura, the climax of the drama-filled ten-day holiday Muharram, when the hard-core get cracking with self-flagellation (now shirts soften the blows) and white-robed pilgrims beat their chests in mock war, while others reenact the bloody death in plays. Women wail over Husayn's demise, and the sadness is so gripping and pervasive that Iranian desk clerks may be prone to lay their heads on the counter in the middle of check-ins, in deep sobs. The Shias' two holiest places, Najaf and Karbala, where Ali and Husayn were slayed, are both in Iraq, until recently a country run by Sunni and off-limits to Shia pilgrims. When the United States invaded Iraq in 2003—and forgot to secure the eastern border with Iran—hundreds of thousands of Iranians flooded in to see firsthand the long-lost holy sites.

REVOLUTIONARY RUST

Iranians don't have a rep for being super-devout Muslims, and the Persian culture dictates national identity as much as Shia Islam, which was shunted aside for most of the twentieth century. The Iranian revolution that culminated in 1979 with the return of Ayatollah Khomeini was much more a reflection of deep unhappiness with the shah and his oppressive, corrupt regime than of a desire to install the Islamic theocracy that Khomeini wrought. Although during his thirty-eight-year rule the shah paved roads, built modern business boxes, and brought big money to some, the middle class and the poor didn't see many benefits: the economy was plagued by inflation, the shah was siphoning off billions for U.S.-made arms, and most Iranians had nowhere to vent grievances in a society that was more fearful and plagued by spies than the Soviet Union (where at least dissidents spoke up). The shah's secret service, known for torture, maiming, kidnapping, and killing upward of fifteen thousand, knocked off most opposition; exiled Khomeini, who'd been lashing out at the shah's Islam-ignoring ways since 1963, was among the few who survived.

Khomeini's anti-shah message elicited wide applause from students to merchants, oil workers to rural farmers, ethnic minorities to intellectuals, many of whom partook in the work shutdown, market closures, and protests that finally unplugged the shah. When Khomeini arrived in February 1979, he soon turned on many of those who had supported him, stomping out intellectuals and ethnic minorities and calling for the death of those who didn't want an Islamic government (with him as its leader). The regime he established was as brutal as the shah's. And nearly a million died during the Iran-Iraq War, which Saddam Hussein started but Khomeini refused to stop. Under the Islamic republic, the economy went kaput: soon plenty were longing for the return of the days of the shah. Few Iranians are happy with the way things are now, as evidenced in the 1997 and 2001 votes for reformist president Khatami, whose efforts to open Iran were blocked by religious bodies in the government. And now the military, particularly the thuggish Revolutionary Guard, has everything to gain by maintaining the theocracy, since it is the big boy in the regime's economic system, which rewards few. The result: it's hard to slam on the brakes on this corroded regime, even though many in the country want to do so.

A telling sign of recent unrest: the anniversary of the death of Khomeini on June 3, 1979, is a holy day. For years millions poured into the street, sobbing as hysterically as they do during Ashura. One recent visitor to Iran, photographer Fabien Dany, was shocked to see only a few hundred turn out for the 2007 Khomeini cry-a-thon in one western city of a million.

But even if the economy is in a downward spiral, with inflation exploding and the cost of everything, including housing, blasting into previously unseen realms, there's still one cause that many Iranians rally around: nuclear power. A symbol of Iranian ingenuity, advanced technology, and a refusal to be bullied around, nuclear power is the touchstone issue for the country today, no matter what side of the debate, or the world, you are on. Bush and Cheney may have launched nuclear power's global renaissance—they have been cheering it on for years as the savior of the planet, giving it a financial boost unseen since Eisenhower's day—but Iran sure as heck wasn't getting invited to *their* nuclear ball.

The problem with Iran's nuclear program isn't simply the nuclear plants, which are very slowly coming online, with none yet in operation, while Iran's electrical supplies are dwindling. The problem is that Iran built a uranium-enrichment

Back in 1976, Iran and the word nuclear *were considered a happy union, as illustrated in this ad campaign that ran in East Coast papers, hailing the shah's wise embrace of nuclear energy. The United States signed up Iran for Eisenhower's peaceful use of atomic energy program; in 1967 it presented the proud monarch with a research reactor that was powered by enriched uranium. By the 1970s, the shah was forking over billions for the full package, from reactors to training. According to those who worked on his nuclear program, those atoms weren't always swirling for peaceful uses: the shah had plans for an atomic arsenal to boot.*

facility without telling the International Atomic Energy Agency (IAEA), which it was supposed to do as part of the Nuclear Non-Proliferation Treaty signed in 1968. It maintains that the enrichment facility, which it claims will supply fuel for upcoming plants, would have been shut if it had told the IAEA about its plans to build it. And that enrichment plant, which indeed can supply fuel for certain types of reactors, can also provide the makings for nuclear bombs. And that was apparently what Iran intended to do. At least until 2003, when the United States moved in next door. And that year, according to the National Intelligence Estimate issued in 2007, Iran froze the program, and it also reached out to the West like never before. The reason was simple: the government could see that it was the next target on the Bush list.

What it didn't know was that the bull's-eye was apparently drawn in India ink, because no matter how hard Iran has tried, it can't get it off. And the reason Iran appears to be permanently on the rogue list has every bit as much to do with the agendas and fears of others as with the actual plans of Tehran.

WHO'S GOT IT OUT FOR IRAN (AND VICE VERSA)

It's a motley group but a powerful, volatile one when they sing together in one loud chant, "Take down Iran!" They all have their reasons.

Israel: Once enjoying a cuddly relationship with the shah, who provided oil to them, and at least a working one with the Islamic republic with whom it supplied arms for oil, Israel now sees Iran as Enemy Numero Uno for three reasons:

1. In the Mideast, only Israel has nuclear weapons. If Iran acquires them, it will throw off Israel's power in the region, where it reigns as king of the arms mountain.
2. Particularly since 2005, with the election of hard-liner president Ahmadinejad, Iran has been tormenting Israel: calling for a reexamination of the Holocaust (which he has denied), Ahmadinejad said "the regime that occupies Jerusalem must vanish from the pages of time" and added that Hamas and Hezbollah had "pressed the countdown button for the destruction of the Zionist regime." Furthermore, Iran's military boasts that it has missiles that could carry nuclear payloads as far as Tel Aviv.
3. Iran arms and trains anti-Israel groups, including Lebanon's Hezbollah (against whom Israel launched a war in June 2006) and Palestinian militants/political party Hamas (now running Gaza in Israel's backyard). Israel worries that they'll give them the makings for dirty bombs or far worse.

Dissident groups: A number of groups may want to take over Iran, but almost all the news about Iran's supposedly nefarious dealings—some of which is correct and some highly dubious—originates with one shady and odd group: the National Council of Resistance of Iran. Now working out of Europe and DC, this group of Iranian dissidents, founded by a married couple, is a front group for the Mujahideen-E-Khalq (MEK), and they loathe the theocratic government in Tehran. The issue: they helped toss out the shah and bring in Khomeini, but then he turned on them in 1979, regarding them as too leftist since this unique cult blends Marxist beliefs with Islam. Ever since the ayatollah unleashed the Revolutionary Guard on them, Maryam Rajavi, who hopes to become the first president of Iran, and her husband, Massoud Rajavi, who heads the military group's wing, have been a nightmare for Iran. Apparently acting out their marital traumas (demanding that followers practice celibacy or divorce), they'd be amusing if it weren't for the assassinations and torture. MEK subcontracted with Saddam to fight its fellow Iranians in the Iran-Iraq War, and Tehran says it has knocked off lots of Iranian political leaders to boot. Both MEK and the National Council of Resistance are now on the U.S. State Department's terrorist list, but that hasn't shut up their mouthpiece Alireza Jafarzadeh, now a Middle East expert for Fox News (see p. 159).

The neocons: Pro-Israel (a number have been paid by Israel's political parties, and several, including advisor Richard Perle, were believed by the FBI to be Israeli spies), the neocons (some in their Bush administration posts, others advisers) who led the United States into Baghdad always had Iran as a target as much (perhaps more) than Iraq; some say the 2003 invasion was simply a step to Tehran, where dwelleth the world's most loathsome "terror masters"—and biggest threat to Israel. Beyond notions of democracy, they may see in Iran, particularly a bombed-to-hell one, a world of opportunity in reconstruction contracts as well as the opportunity to kill OPEC (one of their long-avowed goals) by taking the government hands out of the energy pots. Not to mention Iran's prime real estate and vast oil and gas.

The Sunnis: Never mind the warm smiles and hand-holding, which Saudi king Abdullah and President Ahmadinejad were doing at a recent Gulf Cooperation Council (GCC) summit. Never mind the water being pumped into their arid lands from Iran, the Sunnis don't like the rising Shia crescent, a term they brought to DC's ear: they've armed themselves to the hilt and they've transformed their kingdoms into American bases partly in fear of what the rise of the Shia could do to their Sunni-dominant countries. Then again, while they don't fully trust Iran, they don't want to see an all-out war.

Evangelical Christians: Some born-again, prophecy-believing Americans are lobbying for the United States to take the regime-change idea to Iran because, should Tehran get nuclear weapons and wipe Israel off the map, Bible prophecies wouldn't hold water: Jesus wouldn't be able to come back and there goes their stairway to heaven.

The Bush administration: If Iraq was really about oil, it sure wouldn't be hard to sniff out that petroleum next door, where there's even more, as well as oodles of natural gas—not to mention a key piece on the Gulf chess board.

These background players have worked together to make a case for taking down the regime in Iran, and in most cases are not at all adverse to launching an all-out war to do it. But before Iran is tried, convicted, and blown to smithereens—along with much of the Gulf—it's crucial to note that the Islamic republic not long ago attempted to reach out like never before; although that golden moment for diplomacy was missed, it may come again.

The United States slapped sanctions on Iran beginning in 1980 when Ayatollah Khomeini wouldn't release the fifty-two American hostages that had been kept in Iran since November 1979. Other sanctions have since been applied, including recent ones that affect Iran's biggest banks. The Bush administration bolstered the unilateral sanctions by bringing in the UN Security Council, which began squeezing Iran in fall 2006 with two additional rounds of sanctions to ban trade and freeze assets of nuclear entities and prevent arms transfers out of Iran. The United States had been aiming for a third series of UN Security Council sanctions, but Russia and China were holding out. They looked likely to cave in, however, until the National Intelligence Estimate published in early December 2007 put more questions into the formula.

In the shock of September 11, Iran stopped its anti-West chanting. The country tensed, waiting to see the response; under Khomeini it would have been applause. President Khatami did what had the day before been unthinkable in the land where the national hobby is demonizing the United States. Within eleven hours, as the morning of September 12 awoke Tehran, Khatami condemned the act. Shortly thereafter, Ayatollah Khamenei condemned it as well. At prayers that Friday, the call of "Death to America" didn't echo through the mosque. In the first visit from an Iranian head of state in two decades, President Khatami visited the United States that fall, talking before the UN, speaking on CNN, and spreading a new phrase: "a dialogue of nations."

Something had changed, the first semblance of a breakthrough in twenty-two years. And Jack Straw, Britain's foreign minister, saw how to work it. When DC linked arms with London to go after Osama bin Laden in Afghanistan, Straw checked in with Tehran and asked its advice—in this case the Straw that broke the ice. The Iranians then did something that hadn't been done since the days of the Shah. Tehran actually helped, being happy to see the toppling of the Shia-hating Taliban, their enemy as well, particularly after eleven Iranian diplomats were killed while visiting Afghanistan a few months before. Specifically, in November 2001 Iran asked the Northern Alliance to aid the U.S.-led coalition in taking down the Taliban; without that request, claim the Iranians, American troops would have stumbled into a situation like the war in Afghanistan that embroiled the Russians for eight years.

Believing that a new era of friendship was within its grasp, Iran reached out even further. Learning that the DC team was eyeing Saddam Hussein, who had been loathed by Iran since the Iran-Iraq War, Tehran proffered advice for any upcoming Iraqi invasion: there were tricky ethnic divides, the Iranians explained, that would come popping out once Saddam's rock was turned over. The United States would be looking at chaos, the Iranians warned. Unless, that is, DC let them play on the team—the thinking, apparently, being that if they helped out yet again, the United States would be less likely to unleash its war machine on their country.[13] A new era of alliance was beginning, it seemed.

So as the powers in Tehran settled down to watch President Bush's State of the Union speech on January 29, 2002, they were startled to hear him introduce yet another term into the post-9/11 vocabulary: "the axis of evil." And Bush appointed Iran a position on his axis of evil: number two, just after Iraq.

"Our second goal is to prevent regimes that sponsor terror from threatening America or our friends and allies with weapons of mass destruction. Iran aggressively pursues these weapons and exports terror, while an unelected few repress the Iranian people's hope for freedom. States like these and their terrorist allies constitute an axis of evil, arming to threaten the peace of the world."
—President George W. Bush, State of the Union, January 29, 2002

"We know Iran is actively sending terrorists [to attack Israel and] we also know that they have a very active weapons-of-mass-destruction program."
—Secretary of Defense Donald Rumsfeld explaining how Iran got a starring role on the axis.[14]

What had happened between the attack on Afghanistan and the State of the Union address was this: a ship bearing arms had been picked up by the Israelis en route, Tel Aviv said, to the Palestinian Authority. And it had come, said Tel Aviv, from Iran. Bush would later tell Bob Woodward that Iran's placement on the axis was meant "to inspire those who love freedom in the country." It certainly didn't inspire friendship in Tehran. As former vice president Mohammad Ali Abtahi would later tell *Frontline,* "The very least expectation we had, at the height of our struggles for real reform, was not to be branded like this. Politically, it was an odd thing to do. We helped overthrow the Taliban. Instead of opening a path for even greater cooperation, they turned to this slogan, the 'axis of evil.' That was Mr. Bush's biggest strategic and political blunder."

Tehran also didn't much care for the news that came out of DC on August 14, 2002. As the mic system was checked, the coffee brewed, and the press sheets laid out on the table, a dapper Iranian—with a mustache, piercing eyes, and arched brows, he resembled a modern Hercule Poirot—was about to continue the revenge mission that had started twenty-three years before when Ayatollah Khomeini sent his minions out to attack the MEK, a group that until then had supported the cleric, a group who'd help bring him into power.

"Good day, ladies and gentlemen," he began, as the room filled with reporters and the cameras began rolling. "What I am going to reveal today is the result of

extensive research and investigation . . ." And then Alireza Jafarzadeh, spokesman for the National Council of Resistance of Iran, spilled the beans—bringing
yet another new word into the vocabulary: Natanz. A top-secret uranium enrichment lab was being built in that town in the desert, a hundred miles north of Isfahan.
A lab where workers, wearing gloves and masks, would spin uranium in fast-
twirling centrifuges in a clandestine operation that would be used, it would soon
be decided by DC and Tel Aviv, to make nuclear bombs.

The *New York Times* didn't touch that first "leak," but Natanz danced across
the pages of the *Wall Street Journal,* in Associated Press and Agence France-
Presse stories, not to mention on Al Jazeera. Most important, the item ran
prominently on Fox News. Thus began the media campaign on the "nuclear
threat in Iran" and the career of Alireza Jafarzadeh as a Middle East expert who
would soon make startling revelation upon startling revelation at the National
Press Club. Even though his office was soon raided and shut down by the FBI,
and the State Department put his group on the terrorist list, Jafarzadeh had
turned trashing Iran into a new career.

When the propaganda machine revved up to move in on Saddam Hussein, Iran
started screaming not to do it, fearing that Iraq was but a back door to axis-of-evil
target number two. Even though they loathed Saddam, whose invasion had kicked
off the Iran-Iraq War, he was looking much more preferable to having Uncle Sam
hanging around. Of all the unlikely defenders, Iran piped up in its enemy's defense.
Around the time it became obvious that the United States was coming anyway,
and was simultaneously encircling Iran from almost all sides, including securing
new military bases in Uzbekistan and Kyrgyzstan, Iran cleaned up its act, tucking
away and mothballing any reasons it might appear to have for inviting an attack.
According to the report, it was then, in 2003, that Iran froze (not be confused with
permanently halting) its weapon-making program. And it was around then that a
fax came in from the Swiss embassy—a fax that could have marked an evolutionary leap in diplomacy, but didn't.

At first, Karl Rove didn't believe the two-paged facsimile was authentic.[15] It
said that Iran wanted to make a grand bargain: it would shut down its nuclear
program, stop backing anti-Israeli groups, stop hampering Middle East peace. In
return, Iran wanted two things: a promise that the United States would not invade
and topple the regime, and for the United States to stop protecting the MEK.[16]
Verifying it was the real deal with the Swiss embassy, whom Iran used as the official channel for communications with the United States, Rove was interested.
So was Bush. But shortly after Vice President Cheney and Defense Secretary
Rumsfeld had a peek, the fax was effectively en route to the Dumpster. Nope, uh-
uh, no way—was the unofficial response. The official response was silence. Not
only was Tehran rebuffed, DC didn't even send a response. Cheney and friends
instead told off the Swiss envoy for taking Iran seriously.

Tehran nevertheless succeeded in grabbing the ear of Europe, although its
offers weren't as sweeping. In exchange for economic and technological aid, Iran
would stop its uranium-enrichment facility. In 2004 the International Atomic Energy Agency made the agreement official, sealing the doors of the facility.

But that wasn't the word Jafarzadeh was putting out: Iran was digging new tunnels, funneling hundreds of millions—no, make that sixteen billion—into its nuclear program that was being run by an elite group of the Revolutionary Guard. Iran was smuggling deuterium from Russia, constructing a laser-enrichment center, buying long-range missiles; Iran had opened a heavy-water plant, was trying to smuggle tritium from Korea, and had previously met with Pakistan's infamous nuclear bomb maker A. Q. Khan. Between numerous press conferences, and often under the auspices of the hawkish, Israel-leaning pressure group, the Iran Policy Committee, Jafarzadeh was hired on as a Middle East analyst for Fox, and he also wrote a book, *The Iran Threat: Ahmadinejad and the Coming Nuclear Crisis.* Beyond the nuclear expansion that he frantically updated, Jafarzadeh began making another claim that fit in nicely with any needed attack rationale: Iran was arming Shia militants, who were attacking Americans in Iraq.

PINNING IRAN

The Islamic republic of Iran isn't lily-white in any respect: the theocratic government kills nearly as many prisoners as China—even more than the United States. Tehran's leaders inhibit the press, shutting down reformist papers by the hundreds, though unable to fully keep them quiet. The government machine the ayatollah cobbled together is not only remarkably inefficient, it's corrupt—one factor in why the oil money never seems to get to the people. The Iranian government launches propaganda campaigns such as recently painting American flags on the roads along with the Great Satan moniker—moves that annoy most of the people. When a former revolutionary conducted a survey and published the results showing that a majority of Iranians favored better relations with the United States, he was imprisoned. Canadian broadcast journalist Zahra Kazemi died in 2003 after she was thrown in jail and fatally roughed up, her crime being that she'd filmed outside an Iranian prison. American-Iranian scholars and journalists have been tossed in prison for allegedly trying to start soft revolutions while visiting. Iran heavily funds several militant groups (including Hezbollah, Hamas, and Islamic Jihad) that have as their stated goals the downfall of Israel, and Iran has verbally threatened Israel. Ayatollah Khomeini wouldn't stop fighting the Iran-Iraq War, even when Iraq tried to call it off, and Iran sent out nine-year-olds to serve as cannon fodder. Iran has struck out at the United States in the past, attacking two ships during the Tanker War in the 1980s, and kidnapping fifty-two Americans in 1979 and holding them hostage for 444 days.

However, there are a few things that Iran gets pinned for that it probably didn't do. It hasn't attacked the United States for decades and was falsely accused (it appears) for the Khobar Towers explosion in Saudi Arabia that killed nineteen U.S. servicemen in 1996: that act was most likely pulled off by the precursor of al Qaeda, with whom Iran is not linked. And its government probably did *not* have much to do with the insurgents in Iraq, which Iran has every interest in seeing calmed down.

In summer 2005, when the war in Iraq was growing worse, and Iran was being blamed, President Khatami ended his second four-year term. His ideas for a partnership with the United States had failed, his attempts at reform in Iran were overturned by the Supreme Council. The economy hadn't improved, and as the accusations hurled at it grew louder, it appeared that Iran was damned whatever it did. As Iranians poured into the voting booth, pundits had already predicted the winner would be Akbar Hashemi Rafsanjani—a two-time former president, one of Iran's richest men, a cleric, and a powerful insider who, while not reformist, could manage diplomacy. Instead, Mahmoud Ahmadinejad took the election, and within weeks the seals were ripped off and the uranium-enrichment program began anew.

Widely loathed by the West, Ahmadinejad and his economic failures had, by 2007, made him every bit as unpopular with his own people. He mouthed off in the direction of the United Nations Security Council when it slapped on sanctions, which was admittedly hypocritical since all five permanent members of the Security Council have nuclear weapons. But his cockiness and his dramatic ripping up of UN notices made most everybody, including many Iranians, want to boot him. Worse, his "come on, I dare ya" style of playground behavior made many Iranians nervous that the dare would be taken up. While Iranians defend their right to have nuclear energy—and even nuclear bombs, like Pakistan and Israel—his mouthiness brought loud criticisms at home, including from officials. Even Ayatollah Khamenei was sending messages to the president in the press, suggesting he tone down the brash belligerence, and when other government VIPs, including cleric and big-shot Akbar Hashemi Rafsanjani, cautioned that Ahmie's loud mouth was endangering the country, he defensively lashed out, calling them all traitors. From mothers' groups that wrote letters to student unions that burned his photo (unions he then shut down and replaced with his fans), Ahmie was in the spotlight and under the gun, looking likely to be yanked off the stage, although whether that yank would be from the ayatollah's hook, public uprisings, or bombs wasn't clear.

"The Iranians said they were embarrassed by Ahmadinejad—especially when he made international appearances. They hated the attention the media gave him, complaining, 'He makes us look like we're crazy.' They

> *all wanted to leave—and were trying to get to Australia or Canada. But when I asked the guy who'd been most outspoken in his criticism what he would do if the U.S. or Israel attacked, he said 'I'll be the first one to fight for my country.'"*
> —Journalist Andrew Burke, in 2007 interview with author

In the United States, the propaganda machine was running full-steam. The State Department's National Security Strategy released in March 2006 listed Iran as the United States' biggest threat. The United States, it said, "may face no greater challenge from a single country than Iran."[17] The Congressional Research Service issued a report for the legislature collecting all of Ahmadinejad's quotes against Israel, against the United States, against anybody who told him what to do—a report of a type it had *never* published before. Editorials began popping up about how the United States should have taken out Tehran instead of Baghdad. The president, in that year's State of the Union address, emphasized that Iran was providing "material support" to the insurgents killing American troops in Iraq. U.S. undersecretary of state Nicholas Burns told CNN there was "irrefutable evidence" that Iran was arming the fighters in Iraq. Every time anything happened anywhere, Iran was suddenly behind it.

And from the first of those claims, overseas allies, the American press, and certain factions within the U.S. government began to balk. The British refuted the idea that arms were coming from Iran. The American press, from the *Washington Post* to the *Los Angeles Times*, reported that evidence ranged from nonexistent to scanty. But the claims linking Iran (and its cohort Syria) to the problems in Iraq kept coming, as did a flurry of books that warned of the looming nuclear threat from Iran. Michael Ledeen, adviser to Cheney, came out that September with his new tome *The Iranian Time Bomb*, which took it all a step further, into the deepest levels of absurdity. "When you hear 'Al Qaeda,'" wrote Ledeen, "it's probably wise to think 'Iran.'" And as noted in the *New York Times* review, Ledeen blamed Iran for 9/11. The *New Yorker*'s Seymour Hersh kept reporting the evolving war plans: the shift to a new target, the Shia crescent; the sharpening focus of Iran in the crosshairs. Columnists such as Charles Krauthammer and the *Weekly Standard*'s William Kristol encouraged the United States to take out Iran's nuclear plants while there was still time. The drum machine was a-pumping. Condoleezza Rice, along with Secretary of Defense Robert Gates, toured the Middle East in July, peddling over thirty billion dollars in arms to Gulf countries to defend themselves against Iran and Syria. From the pages of the *Jerusalem Post* to those of the *Washington Post* and the *Wall Street Journal*, the neocon voices were rising up in a chorus of, "Come on, while we're in the neighborhood, let's have at them." That fall of 2007, Bush sent three aircraft carrier groups to the Gulf, a buildup not seen since the Iraq invasion of 2003. Countries from Bahrain to Kuwait, where the United States has bases, developed contingency plans for how to react if the United States struck Iran and Iran struck back.

> "Iran's active pursuit of technology that could lead to nuclear weapons
> threatens to put a region already known for instability and violence under
> the shadow of a nuclear holocaust."
>   —President George W. Bush, August 28, 2007

But somebody, somewhere, in the United States government was having none of
it. The intelligence community gathered together and issued the National Intelligence Estimate on December 3, 2007. And their findings, some asserted, weren't
new at all: Bush, said Seymour Hersh and a chorus of others, had known all
along that Iran had frozen its nuclear arms program.

In fact, the nuclear enrichment facility that Ahmie is so excited about is actually
thirty years late showing up. It had been ordered long ago, by the shah. As early as
1965, the United States had set up the shah with his first mini nuclear reactor that
required enriched uranium as fuel; he liked it so much that he wanted to set up a
full-scale uranium-enrichment program in Iran. And his goal wasn't simply to en-
rich the atoms for peace; those working on the project say he had his eyes set on
nuclear bombs. The project, however, along with a reactor being built at Bushehr
by Germans, didn't fully get off the ground before the shah fell off the pedestal.
And when the Islamic republic showed up, they didn't want nukes. At first.

ATTEMPTING TO REPLUG NUCLEAR

Upon settling down in the power seat once occupied by the shah, Khomeini
pulled the plug on the nuclear energy program and its military corollaries—
programs shrugged off as too expensive, too Western, too high-tech and un-
needed. Not long after the new Islamic regime had shooed away the nuclear
scientists—who flocked to the West in a loud, sucking brain drain—Iran had
reason to rethink its decision. The Iran-Iraq War, during which nearly the
whole world sided with Iraq, brought new appeal to the idea of nuclear weapons. Had Iran had them, Saddam no doubt would not have been so quick to
attack. By the mid-1980s, Tehran seriously wanted to get the program switched
back on. They approached the Germans who'd been building the plant at
Bushehr but were rebuffed with a *nein*. The French, with whom Iran had previous contracts and a half-billion in down payments, gave a *non*. The Chinese
whispered yes, but the United States, after hearing the whisper, thwarted the
sale of reactors to Iran. Finally, in the late 1990s the Russians gave a loud *da*,
and over the past few years have been working to complete a plant at Bushehr
and build other facilities, although Russia has delayed efforts due to lack of
payments. And in the meantime, Tehran, which has been training thousands
in prestigious nuclear engineering programs, began building its own facilities
and experimenting, it says, with different forms of fuel to power them—hence,

it says, the need for the nuclear-enrichment facilities. The rationale *is* fishy: the Russians, after all, are supplying the fuel for the Russian-built reactors; the other plants that Iran is building are many years away from completion— which all leads to the question: Why indeed do they need that enriched fuel years ahead of their nuclear plants?

Nuclear energy, built in defiance of the West, has now become a source of national pride for Iranians, who insist they have every right to build nuclear energy plants, which indeed they do; that is, if they want to follow the bumpy path of this energy source that produces radioactive waste that still cannot be safely disposed of and poses inherent dangers, such as meltdowns, and security problems, such as becoming a terrorist target. Beyond energy, however, many Iranians, and their government, also view nuclear weapons as the only means to guarantee Iran's security; if they have nukes, the United States, Israel, Russia, and anybody else that wanted to attack would be less willing to do so. So *nuclear* has become synonymous, for some at least, with the very survival of the Islamic republic, which has never in its entire existence been more threatened from all sides.

That the Bush administration wants to get rid of the regime, and may still militarily take on Iran, shouldn't be shocking. Beyond strategic location and dominance of the Persian Gulf, Iran is sitting on a mountain of resources, being the world's number two in conventional oil and natural gas, which the United States now craves. Iran is also switching how oil deals are conducted, no longer using the dollar, which since 1945 has been the currency for international business deals, but the euro—a move that could flood the U.S. economy with billions of barrels of even more devalued cash. On an equal one-to-one footing with the dollar when the euro was launched in 1999, the euro is now so much stronger than the dollar that the change could make prices for the U.S. consumer rise to new highs. Some economists believe it was precisely the move from petrodollars to petroeuros by Saddam Hussein in 2000 that prompted the 2003 American takeover, noting that upon wresting control the first thing the Americans did was change the oil-business currency back to the dollar.[18] And besides, Iran remains the face of evil to most Americans, who still equate the country with the rise of Khomeini, the leader who booted the shah and hated all that had made the shah's reign possible, which is to say the United States. Since his emergence in 1979, relations between the two countries, as well as global geopolitics, have never been the same.

The events that in 1979 would rearrange the Middle East and the world order, have their roots in 1953. That was the year Iran's prime minister Mohammed Mosaddeq nationalized Iran's oil company—then held by the British—who were giving Iran a raw deal, doling out a mere 16 percent of profits. The British lured in the United States to help them topple Mosaddeq, warning that he was probably a Communist. It was then that Uncle Sam (and his G-men) became intrigued with the Middle East and its possibilities, resource-wise and strategically. How Iran might be used as a listening post to monitor the Soviets. How Middle Eastern oil was needed, and how they had to keep the Soviets from getting it. Eisenhower gave away plenty of arms to fight Commies, as well as atomic starter kits (including to Iran), but he was also the first to publicly warn of a rising military-industrial complex, which his actions seemed to create.

The United States began cultivating the shah as anti-Communist policeman of the Gulf and cultivating his country as a fine place for investment. DC even gave economic advice on how to transition from a black-market economy reliant on opium to one that was more industrialized. As the Middle Eastern country closest to the Soviet Union, Iran was a fine place to set up listening posts and to establish a bulwark against any Soviet advance, and in return the United States initially supplied free arms to the shah. The shah's deep love of war toys made him susceptible to manipulation, however. President John F. Kennedy nixed any arms increases to the shah until the Iranian leader made serious reforms. The shah took the bait and launched the White Revolution: his economic, political, and social reform plan looked good on paper, at least, and was enough to garner him more freebie arms. But outside of the changes in fashion—now women who wore the veil risked having it ripped off by the police, who two decades later would be doing just the opposite—many changes were superficial and some wreaked havoc, including those for agricultural reform.

Under the shah's plan, the clerics, who until the White Revolution held the farmlands, were forced to hand them over to the peasants, who had served as sharecroppers, being paid with a proportion of the food they grew. The problem wasn't simply that the clerics, as feudal overlords, had provided the seeds—something the government neglected to do—and since peasants didn't have the money to buy them, many walked off the land and moved to the city. Just as important was the fact that the clerics didn't like this move or many other aspects of the shah's White Revolution, including giving women the right to vote. One cleric in particular, a holy man in the city of Qom, was so furious with the changes that he began to write fatwas against them and to slam them in his preaching. So loudly did Ayatollah Ruhollah Khomeini condemn the shah, he was arrested numerous times in 1963. Each arrest of the popular preacher was met with loud protests among clerics and students. And whenever Khomeini was let out, after a few weeks or months, with promises that he'd shut up, within a few days his voice was rising again, his gnarled finger pointing at the corruption and weakness of that sellout the shah and the corrupting influence of the power that pulled his strings: the United States.

By the 1960s, Iran was like a boomtown for arms makers and fifty thousand or so Americans were living there. The American government wanted to ensure that they wouldn't have to deal with Iranian law and the justice system, which by then was getting a nasty rep, helped along by the shah's secret service, SAVAK.

So the next time the shah hit up the United States for some arms, the president, then Lyndon B. Johnson, hemmed and hawed. The situation in the Gulf, said LBJ, didn't look dangerous enough to warrant more arms—be they the fighter planes or the missiles the shah requested. The shah pointed to the growing power of Nasser, the instability in Yemen, and the influence of Soviets and their weapons from Syria to Egypt. LBJ said he'd think on it—if the shah would grant immunity to all Americans accused of crimes in Iran. But LBJ didn't realize that by insisting on that no-mea-culpa clause he was hitting a national sore spot. For centuries, foreigners had been allowed to interfere with business and laws, and it ticked off the Iranians so much that they had a word for it: *capitulations.*

Nevertheless, the shah shoved that law through the parliament. When it passed, Khomeini so bitingly chewed out the government that the secret police didn't throw him in jail. Instead, they sent him out of the country. And from that point on, Khomeini was an illegal topic, a forgotten name that the press dared not print and radio dared not utter.

If there was one thing Ayatollah Khomeini excelled at (besides the intricacies of Islamic law, for which he was a renowned scholar), it was holding a grudge. And he'd have fifteen years to simmer about the humiliation of being the highest religious figure in Iran but nevertheless kicked out and banned from his land. Fifteen years to stoke his hatred of the shah and the American superpower that had built him up. Fifteen years to loathe the way the shah had stripped religion from Iran, shoving the clerics into the city of Qom, where their preaching was heard by few. Fifteen years to plot his return.

Khomeini settled down in Iraq, in the holy town of Najaf, where Ali was buried, and his seventh-century death is commemorated with a grand gold-domed tomb. But the cantankerous cleric never shut up: recording his condemnations of the shah into a cassette tape recorder, he sent his missives over the border and found a very receptive audience.

In the meantime, the shah continued to weaken the clergy, playing up Persian culture over Islam. In 1972, the shah celebrated the twenty-five-hundredth anniversary of the start of the Persian Empire by holding a shindig amid the ancient ruins of Persepolis. He outraged his people when he invited hundreds of world dignitaries to the bash that cost at least forty million dollars—some said three times that. And even when the United States cut him off from freebies, the shah's appetite for arms continued to grow. Iran was making more money thanks to the shah's manipulation of OPEC prices—oil revenue had nearly tripled—but a large chunk of it was going toward more war toys. More Americans were moving to Iran, most of them working for defense industries or related ones like Brown & Root (an arm of Halliburton), which had wrangled a multibillion-dollar contract to build new ports. And if Iranians didn't like the link to the West or the Americans who were showing up, and had little respect for their culture, they weren't allowed to say so.

Popular from the start, the hissing tapes of Khomeini became by the mid-1970s the only voice of reason. SAVAK was routinely rounding up anyone it suspected of not being loyal and adding their names to the thousands of the already dead. Professors whispered that their students, rounded up for questioning, never came back. Visitors to the embassy were increasingly paranoid, asking, "How well do you know your cook? Are you sure they're not listening in? What's in that cage besides the bird?" Meanwhile, the ayatollah's muffled voice promised hope, as he vowed that "freedom and liberation from the bonds of imperialism" would soon be forthcoming.

The shah unveiled a grand industrialization scheme, but his stabs at reform faltered, and his boasts that Iran's economy would soon compete with that of Germany and Japan deflated as inflation grew and the agricultural changes he'd tried to implement resulted in a mass exodus to the cities. Fearing the rise of opponents in political parties, he outlawed them all, creating one party, his party, Rastakhiz, to which all Iranians were forced to belong, for which all Iranians were forced to vote, and to which all Iranians—most of whom were already crushed financially—were forced to pay dues. The religious establishment, fueled by Khomeini tapes, was growing stronger, and when SAVAK began killing clerics, it threw another log on the fire.

During the 1970s, the shah hired a New York PR firm to keep his profile in the American eye, casting him as proud, wise, and invincible, with his puffed-up chest dripping with regalia—images that were displayed in everything from Sunday Times *articles to nuclear energy ads.*

In 1977, Ali Shariati, a popular cleric who happened to be the shah's loudest voice of opposition in Iran, was allegedly killed by the shah's secret police. By then, SAVAK—trained by the CIA—was running amok. The shah, always a control freak, clamped down even further, trying to prevent any information about what was happening from leaking to the West. As had been the case for years, the monarch's picture appeared on the front right corner of the newspaper every morning, and he so controlled every aspect of the news that even the U.S. State Department was prevented from talking to the opposition, or anyone else for that matter: entire reports about Iran sent back to the head of the State Department in DC consisted solely of how that day's meeting with the shah had gone.[19] No political assessment was encouraged, or even allowed, by the embassy—a rule dictated by the State Department itself, much to the bafflement of its employees. So the diplomats and even, probably, the CIA—which got all its tips from SAVAK and was more intrigued by the information it was getting from its listening posts eavesdropping on Russia—didn't see what was happening to the shah. They didn't know about the tinny voice bellowing from the tape recorders.

But the shah knew that with Shariati's death, Khomeini's son, Mostafa, who remained in Iran, was growing in popularity. In October 1977, when Mostafa Khomeini happened to die—from heart problems, it was said—the masses blamed his death on SAVAK. The massive outpouring of emotion at the son's funeral merely boosted the popularity of his father, who by then was one of the few opposition leaders who had survived. That fall, the shah called up the Iraqi government next door, where Saddam Hussein, theoretically the vice president, was calling the military and security shots. The shah asked the Iraqi government (i.e.,

Saddam) to boot the ayatollah out of Iraq or make him shut up. Khomeini's house was surrounded by Iraqi security, who demanded that the ayatollah cease his tape making. The ayatollah agreed but continued making the tapes. Finally, the Iraqis escorted him to the airport and shoved him onto the next flight, which took him to Kuwait. The Kuwaiti authorities would not let him in. Khomeini, the ultimate grudge keeper, never forgot this humiliation, or the one from Saddam, whom he blamed for his forced exodus from Iraq. When Khomeini finally showed up in a village outside of Paris, his tapes grew even more incendiary.

Jimmy Carter apparently didn't know about the rise of Khomeini. Initially pressuring the shah to address human rights in Iran, he slashed international arms shipments to the shah. Carter then did an about-face, the reasons for which still aren't clear. But it probably had everything to do with oil, supplies of which were looking shaky again, prompting another "energy crisis" and Carter's request that Americans turn the thermostat to sixty-eight. Iran was stable at least, and in 1977, the first year of Carter's administration, Uncle Sam was more reliant on the shah's oil than ever before: it kicked in over 9 percent of oil consumed in the United States that year—a record.

"Iran, under the great leadership of the shah, is an island of stability in one of the more troubled areas of the world. This is a great tribute to you, Your Majesty, and to your leadership and to the respect, admiration, and love which your people give you."
   —President Jimmy Carter's New Year's toast to his host, the shah,
      December 31, 1977

Days after Carter's endorsement and coos, Americans living in Iran first began hearing hissings of "Yankee go home." And then some Iranians began throwing rocks at Americans, pushing them out of the markets. Before long, there were letters on their doors, explaining the reasons why the people of Iran wanted them to leave. Only if the Americans left, notes explained, would the power of the shah be weakened; only then would the U.S. government pull back its support of the mad monarch. Only then would they be free.

Shortly after Air Force One soared off, the shah was struck by an idea, a very feeble idea, about how to counter the growing popularity of Ayatollah Khomeini and the growing anti-shah fervor that his secret service men could neither prevent, quash, or kill off. The shah penned an article, a report supposedly about Ayatollah Khomeini, calling the cleric a coward, a traitor, a Communist, and insinuating that he'd partaken in particularly lascivious deeds. On January 7, 1978, when the shah had that article published (under a nom de plume), it was the first time the cleric's name had seen the ink of Iran's printing presses since 1964. It also marked the last time the shah's people were going to put up with his crap.

Iranians knew it was a fake. The article that condemned Khomeini, calling him decadent and a Communist spy, proved to be the noose the shah drew around his own neck. When religious students in Qom read the article, they kicked off a protest that would snowball into a revolution. Marching from the house of one theologian to another asking them to condemn the shah, their numbers grew from a few dozen to thousands, as angry townspeople joined in.[20] Windows were smashed, the crowd chanted "Down with the shah," and several marchers threw stones at police manning a roadblock. The police shot into the crowd, killing five. Or maybe seven or twenty or thirty, although probably not the hundreds that the rumor mill reported had died. Across the country, memorial services were scheduled, and those emotional protests spawned more run-ins with the security and more deaths. Religious students continued protesting so loudly that SAVAK and the military broke up the protests. At least seven students were killed. Riots broke out. Hundreds, then thousands, were killed. The oil workers went on strike, cutting off revenue and domestic supplies. The blackouts began. Even the palace, where the court had disbanded and the sycophants had stopped showing up, was often without lights, and fuel deliveries were done by the dark of night to minimize attacks and hijacking of the hard-to-get heating oil on the trucks. The shah had more than losing his country on his mind. He was losing his life: cancer, lymphoma, was declaring war on his body.

In August, a theater in the oil town Abadan burned down, killing four hundred. Although cinemas were often the target of Islamists, the striking oil workers blamed it on SAVAK. In September, the shah imposed martial law. Iranians were allowed out only between 8:00 a.m. and 5:00 p.m. Those out at other hours were shot. All public meetings were banned, and even two constituted a crowd.

Khomeini's tapes urged followers to rebel. On September 8, 1978, thousands convened in Tehran, centering on Zhaleh Square. In response to a low-key demonstration, the military rolled in—by some accounts with tanks—while helicopters fired down at the crowd. At least eighty were killed on Black Friday, though it may have been hundreds. It marked the shah's darkest hour.

The shah tried deal making with his people. He promised to call off SAVAK. He tossed in a new prime minister—a nationalist. But it had all gone too far. By now the revolution had the full support of the bazaaris, the powerful and religious-leaning merchant class whose networks stem from traders to the countryside, where many are employed in tiny micro-factories making textiles and shoes. Like that in the cities, the rural population backed an overthrow of the shah's regime and backed Khomeini, whose anti-shah message was also embraced by ethnic minorities such as Azeris, Kurds, and Turkomen, and militant dissidents, including the Islamic Marxists known as the Mujahideen-E-Khalq, or MEK.

The situation kept deteriorating, and the Carter team fretted about Communists taking over, not to mention all the arms the United States had sold to the shah, wondering if they could ask for them back. But it soon became clear that the shah had lost his grip. Asked to leave by the prime minister, on the night of January 16, the shah, his wife, and his family secretly hurried from the palace and boarded the royal plane. The shah, a trained pilot, soared off from his land, not shedding a tear, until they'd successfully made it out of Iranian airspace. For the first few months he made a home in Egypt, watching in horror the news of what had happened since he left.

On February 1, 1979, Khomeini returned to Iran, taking charge the minute he descended from the plane: he assembled fighters, creating what would become the Revolutionary Guard, and sent his religious warriors to fight the army, which backed down within a day, refusing to protect the remaining shreds of the shah's government. With absolutely no authority to do so, Khomeini named a new prime minister: Mehdi Bazargan. He announced that Iran would come under religious rule, its top branches headed by clerics—a move that was backed up in a referendum that March.

On the first of April 1979, Ayatollah Khomeini—now the country's supreme leader—declared that this country was no longer a monarchy but the Islamic Republic of Iran. And that day, he declared, was the "first day of God's government." And God's government began its holy reign with an enemy, an enemy that Khomeini hailed as responsible for the decades of misery under the shah: the Great Satan, aka the United States.

Khomeini's arrival brought massive social changes, including forced veiling in public. While Iran has secret clubs, they're not legal. More wholesome meeting places: parks—popular for picnics.

> *The goal of his government, explained Khomeini, was "to eliminate Western influence" and "to break the holds of Western domination, in all its forms"*[21]

God's government burned books in great pyres. Universities were closed. The nuclear devices were shut off. Women were informed that they must now don the chador and hide their hair under a scarf; men were told to grow beards. The opposition was identified and eliminated: the heads of the military; the professors and intelligentsia who didn't want a religious government; the ethnic groups that threatened to rise up; the radical dissidents, including those in the Mujahideen-E-Khalq. And anybody else who didn't want to play Khomeini's game. Before long, it had become a bloody reign of terror in which thousands died.

Despite the housecleaning, despite the referendum, despite the new government, the ayatollah's hold was not firm. Devastated by the previous year's strike, the treasury didn't hold much, and the economy wasn't in top shape to begin with. Leaders across the Gulf, all of whom were Sunni, many of them ruling over Shia who were restive and discriminated against, were uneasy at the appearance of this Shia cleric who called his flock to rise up against the Sunni leaders who oppressed them: some governments, including that of Iraq, were sending in Sunni agitators. There was still debate over the religious constitution he was trying to get passed. Two things would solidify his grasp: a group of radical students and Saddam.

> *The shah's illness was at this point worsening, requiring state-of-the-art medical care, and Carter allowed the shah entry to the United States, a move that infuriated Tehran. Angry students—and the ayatollah—demanded that the United States ship the shah back so he could stand trial in Iran.*

Although the ayatollah continually railed about the Great Satan, lambasting Carter for allowing the shah to come to the United States on October 22, 1979, the truth was the Islamic republic was still in business with the United States. Iran was still selling oil; the United States was still making good on its contracts and delivering arms. And when the prime minister, Mehdi Bazargan, flew to Algiers for a secret meeting with Carter adviser Zbigniew Brzezinski, it somehow ended up on Iranian TV. Even though the ayatollah knew about the meeting, he feigned shock, denouncing the Great Satan's manipulations and firing Bazargan. His condemnations against DC were so strong that a group of students barged into the U.S. embassy the next day and took fifty-two hostages. The ayatollah supported the move, and, from that point on, Iran became America's enemy.

The 1979 hostage-taking incident prompted anti-Iranian
protests across the United States.

Jimmy Carter tried negotiations to free the hostages. When that didn't work,
he embargoed all oil from Iran. He slapped on sanctions. In April 1980, he sent
out the air force for a secret rescue mission: Operation Eagle Claw. A mission
that not only failed but killed eight in a crash. The reason Carter couldn't get the
hostages out may have had everything to do with George H. W. Bush. Already
tapped as Ronald Reagan's vice presidential running mate, he reportedly negotiated an agreement with the regime not to release the hostages to Jimmy Carter,
thus assuring Carter's defeat.[22] Within a day of the inauguration of President
Ronald Reagan and Vice President George H. W. Bush, the hostages, as if by
magic, were released—444 days after they were seized. The odd dance between
the Reagan administration and the Islamic republic didn't stop there. Within a few
years it would be spinning out in a whole different arena, namely arms. Ayatollah
Khomeini would soon be needing lots of them. Because on September 22, 1980,
Saddam Hussein sent out his military in what he thought would be a three-week
war, at most. It lasted eight years.

The Iran-Contra affair, an audacious and intricately wrapped scheme that
emerged in 1987, had the neocons at its heart, apparently starting with
Michael Ledeen. During the 1980s, American hostages had been taken in
Lebanon, allegedly by Hezbollah (which Iran was believed to control), and
Iran needed arms. Ledeen approached Israeli prime minister Shimon
Peres with a plan for Israel to deliver U.S.-made arms to Iran, which would
persuade Hezbollah to release the hostages. Thousands of missiles later,
one hostage was released. National Security Adviser Oliver North got
involved, with a way to make more money and use it to fund the
anti-Communist movement in Nicaragua. The Americans inflated the price

of U.S. arms, and the money the Iranians paid would be used to arm the contras, an anti-Communist resistance group, in Nicaragua. It's hard to tally exactly how many, if any, hostages in Lebanon were released, but one thing is clear: it was highly illegal. In subsequent investigation and trial, many heads were briefly poised under the political guillotine. Thank goodness Representative Dick Cheney muscled in: sitting on the investigating committee he helped lessen the blow from within Congress, as did George H. W. Bush, who pardoned those found guilty—namely, Elliott Abrams and John Poindexter, who along with many of the other actors became high-placed advisers and employees of the administration of George W. Bush.

THE IRAN-IRAQ WAR

A few months after Khomeini rose to power, Saddam Hussein shoved out his own boss—the Iraqi president—and began making plans. The wizened Iranian cleric was already causing problems in southern Iraq, which was dominantly Shia, and Saddam—like leaders in other countries, including Saudi Arabia and the United States—wanted the guy out. After ensuring that the United States wouldn't respond unfavorably (in fact the United States would soon offer him arms and intelligence), Saddam worked out a plan: first attack the air force (as the Israelis did to the Egyptians in 1967), then move into the oil-rich region Khuzistan, which held most of Iran's Arabs, and which had long been talking of independence; Saddam figured the Arabs would join the Iraqis in fighting the Iranian cleric. Saddam figured wrong—in every respect. The Iranian air force was protected in thick bomb-resistant hangars; even the airports weren't easily demolished. And the Arabs in Khuzistan were indeed quick to pick up arms—and fight the Iraqis. Within two weeks, Saddam was ready to call a cease-fire. But Khomeini wouldn't have it. This was just the crisis he needed to make his regime stick. The ayatollah turned it into a cause for martyrdom, encouraging would-be warriors to reenact the role of Husayn. With headbands and keys that promised immediate entry into heaven, the ayatollah inspired the people to fight back the invaders. The Revolutionary Guard teamed with the army, and the forces were bolstered by volunteers, some as young as nine, often tethered together as they were pushed out as the front line to walk across land mines, martyrs for the Iranian cause. Militarily, Saddam had the upper hand: Saudi Arabia and Kuwait were kicking in billions of dollars, and France and the United States supplied arms. Numberswise, Iran was ahead, with a population of forty-five million, triple Iraq's. Evenly matched, the two sides just kept fighting and fighting. Until finally, in 1988, when many more than a million were dead and damages were in the tens of billions, the United Nations tore them apart.

Two things truly outraged Iranians during the war: in the Tanker War, an offshoot of the war that played out in the Gulf waters, the U.S. Navy came in to escort Kuwaiti tankers. After two attacks on U.S. ships, and several U.S. attacks on Iranian oil facilities in retaliation, the war came to a climax on July 3, 1988. When a plane crossed over the Gulf, the USS Vincennes *shot it down. Alas, it was a commercial flight, Iran Air 655, and all 290 on board perished. The United States never apologized to Iran and, in fact, awarded the ship's captain with a medal. The Iranians were also outraged that when Saddam used chemical weapons there was barely a peep from the international community. In fact, within hours of the chemical attack on Iran, Donald Rumsfeld arrived in Iraq to seal the deal on the American commitment to Saddam.*

If there was a lesson to be learned for Iran, it was that the whole world was against it. Even when Iranians were gassed, the world didn't care. Widows abounded, encouraging the practice known as temporary marriages, in the hopes of keeping the baby-making machine churning. The economy was in shambles, infrastructure a wreck. And it all might have been prevented, many believed, if only Iran had a nuclear bomb. From the mid-1990s on, the plan for such a bomb was again actively pursued, until, that is, the United States moved in right next door—taking on Iraq and itching to move the playing board to the east and make a move on Iran. Within months of the invasion of Iraq, the nuclear bomb program had been shelved but the American war drums haven't ceased. And Israel, as of July 2008, is pounding them.

Fabien Dany

Tachara is part of the palace ruins at the former capital of Persepolis.

Hotshots

- -

Reza Pahlavi: He hasn't set foot in Iran since 1978, but the shah's son, now forty-eight, is still heir to the Pahlavi dynasty started by his grandfather in 1925. A fighter pilot with a degree in law from George Washington University, and a resident of Maryland, the would-have-been king is now a consultant to American politicians, whom he has begged not to invade. As for his ever returning to the peacock throne, well, he does favor a constitutional monarchy for Iran, noting in a BBC interview, "I think that the choice of future government should be left to the Iranian people to decide in a free election. What form it takes is up to them, the issue, the essential point for me is that there is no way that we can achieve the aspirations that we have as a nation unless we have the separation of church and state, and under the current regime clearly we don't have that."[23]

Mohammad Khatami: The former president started a foundation for world peace but is rallying again, along with his brother, for the Iranian-reform cause, drawing tens of thousands at rallies.

Akbar Hashemi Rafsanjani: Former president (1989–97) and involved with the Iran-Contra scheme, Rafsanjani is the ultimate insider and one of Iran's richest men. He was supposed to be a shoo-in for the 2005 presidential elections, but Ahmadinejad blew him out of the water. Rafsanjani, however, got a consolation prize and now heads the Expediency Council that rules on parliamentary decisions.

Vladimir Putin: Moscow may not now represent a superpower, but a power it is, and one increasingly active in the Middle East. This is particularly evident in Iran, where Russia is building nuclear plants (including the one at Bushehr) and negotiated a seven-hundred-million-dollar deal for surface-to-air missiles, largely to protect Iran's nuclear facilities.[24]

Library of Congress, the Matson collection, via pingnews.

Site of Husayn's tomb, Karbala, the holy city for Shia, is in Iraq. It's now a popular pilgrimage destination.

Hot Spots

The Strait of Hormuz: A seven-mile-wide squeeze in the Persian Gulf, this chokepoint through which hundreds of tankers cruise daily is a vulnerable spot in the oil industry.

Isfahan: An important sixteenth-century city, it blossomed with stunning architecture that still boggles the mind today.

Persepolis: The great ruins of the capital founded by the Persian emperor Darius are still grand: the shah held his Persian Empire celebration here.

Bushehr: Home of a future nuclear plant—and possible future bombing if Israel gets its way.

The radio waves: When in Iran, tune in to the U.S. propaganda station Radio Farda to hear the latest spin from DC; most recently, Bush asserting that Iran was building a nuclear weapon to "destroy people," despite what his own intelligence says.

Last Word

Good news: the United States may establish diplomatic relations with Iran. Bad news: an Israeli and/or U.S. strike on Iran hasn't been ruled out.

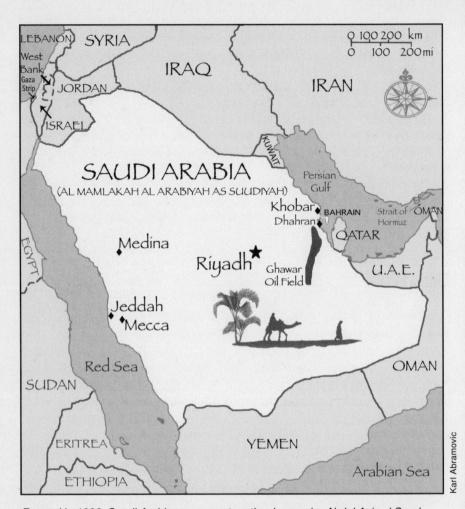

Formed in 1932, Saudi Arabia was sewn together by warrior Abdul Aziz al Saud,
who in 1902 set off with a preacher and bedouin fighters to reclaim his ancestors'
desert kingdom. He didn't know that the land he was roping together held a fourth
of the world's oil. Most petroleum fields lie in the east, also home of the country's
Shia. To the west is the Hejaz region, with holy sites Mecca and Medina and the
major port, Jeddah. The capital, Riyadh, is in the conservative central territory, the
Nejd. In the south, Asir and Najran are the poorest regions and still tied to Yemen,
from which they were captured in 1934. Saud wanted the entire Arabian Peninsula,
but Brits blocked him from lassoing the coastal sheikdoms under their watch. If they
hadn't, Saudi Arabia would now be sitting on half the world's known oil reserves.

Chapter Seven

The Kingdom of Saudi Arabia: Splitsville

S. M. Amin, courtesy of Saudi Aramco/ASC

During the hajj, the annual pilgrimage to Mecca, the city where the prophet Mohammed was born, two million Muslims partake in four days of symbolic rituals, including circling the cube-shaped Kaaba and kissing the black stone within it. The pilgrimage, required once of all able Muslims during their lifetime, sometimes turns violent: in 1979 five hundred Saudi zealots captured the Grand Mosque (shown above with the Kaaba in the background), holding it during a two-week showdown that involved the bin Ladens, killed hundreds, and nearly cost King Fahd his crown. Mahfouz bin Laden, whose family had renovated the mosque, was arrested and briefly detained. In 1990, the Sauds asked Osama to renovate it.

The Kingdom of Saudi Arabia is the world's holiest land for Muslims; for Americans it is the world's biggest gas pump. Juggling spiritual wealth and oil riches creates a split personality in this supersecretive kingdom where the austere state religion, Wahhabism, demands locking out non-Muslims and the changes they bring. For thirteen centuries, this land had remained infidel free: few non-Muslims bothered to cross the desert (or survived if they tried). Since black gold came gurgling up from the sands seventy years ago, however, a parade of Western arms pushers and developers, officials and oilmen, merchants and soldiers have sullied these sands. The fact that these infidel Westerners had been invited by the country's royal rulers was viewed by religious leaders as a betrayal of the very religion that brought the monarchy to power. Against that backdrop, Uncle Sam's most formidable enemy was born. More than the hypocrisy of leaders who said one thing, did another, and shoveled money to the religious establishment to overlook the contradictions, Osama bin Laden's biggest beef was that DC shoved him out of a war he'd wanted to fight—against Saddam.

Leader's Corner

His clan is tainted by claims of corruption, boozing, and hedonism, while his country's clerics are the world's most straightlaced. King Abdullah—known as pious, pragmatic, and clean-nosed—is a reformer, straddling the dichotomies that coexist in his land. The fifth son of Saud patriarch Abdul Aziz, he holds "national dialogues" that bring together dissidents from Shia to democracy pushers, and he called for Saudi Arabia's first-ever elections. Abdullah shredded requirements that women carry permission notes to leave home, loosened the press, clamped down on the virtue police, and has reversed controversial rulings such as one that called for prison and lashings for a vic-

Courtesy of Embassy of the Kingdom of Saudi Arabia, Washington, DC, press

King Abdullah bin Abdul Aziz brings more balance to Saudi Arabia, but it's a tough job.

tim of a gang rape. He also informed the religious establishment, which oversees schools, that the country needs to be educationally woken up, and he blocked the clerics' influence in his new science and technology university. And that's just one of King Abdullah's projects to revitalize his rapidly growing and oil-dependent kingdom.

FAST FACTS:
Al Mamlakah al Arabiyah as Suudiyah

Government:	Monarchy; the House of Saud shares power, in theory, with the religious elite
Formed:	In 1932 by Abdul Aziz al Saud (aka Ibn Saud)
Ruler:	King Abdullah ibn Abdul Aziz al Saud, since August 2005 (b. 1928)
State religion:	Wahhabism, the Salafi branch of Sunni Islam
GDP:	$376 billion (IMF, 2007)
Per capita GDP:	$15,500 (IMF, 2007)
Population:	28.2 million (5.6 million are nonnationals)
Unemployment:	12–25 percent (2004 estimate)
Literacy rate:	85 percent men, 71 percent women
Ethnicity:	90 percent Arab, 10 percent Afro-Asian
Religion:	100 percent Muslim (state religion Wahhabi/Salafi)

Population stat: half of Saudis are under age twenty-two, due to a recent population boom, during which the average woman (who may be only one of a man's four wives) bore six children. The birth rate is dropping: now the average woman has five offspring, and the typical man doesn't take four wives—they're too expensive to keep up.

WHAT MATTERS

Energy matters: Nearly a quarter of known petroleum reserves are buried here in the world's most conservative country. The most powerful OPEC member and world's largest petroleum exporter, Saudi Arabia supplied about 8 percent of the oil used in the United States in 2007, being the third-largest source of American oil.

Electricity matters: Rolling in oil and natural gas, Saudi Arabia too is signing up for nuclear, with help from France and the United States.

Arms matter: Saudi Arabia is the biggest buyer of U.S. weapons, snatching up forty billion dollars' worth during the 1990s and signing up for another twenty billion dollars in 2007. And it goes top-notch all the way: from Abrams tanks to F-15E fighter planes, and Saudi Arabia is the only non-NATO country with AWACS, the advanced surveillance aircraft.

Military/security matters: In 2003, the kingdom kicked out U.S. troops that had been hanging around for thirteen years. Reason: their infidel presence was upsetting the locals. Reality: plenty are still around, although some bases are manned by private military contractors. Lockheed Martin is now moving in to guard oil infrastructure. High-tech security walls are also going in: Saudi Arabia is erecting a high-tech barrier along its border with Iraq *and* its border with Yemen.

Religion matters: Only one religion can be practiced, Wahhabism, and Islam doesn't get any stricter than this. Saudi Arabia isn't a full-fledged theocracy, however, since it's not governed by clerics; some conservatives and militants wish that it were.

Militants matter: Outside of the occasional bedouin rebellion, militants didn't much strike here until the Grand Mosque takeover in Mecca in 1979. Al Qaeda, which is arguably an extension of that grab on the holiest place, now strikes here and is aiming where it hurts: the oil infrastructure (see p. 195).

Money matters: In 1980, with a per capita income of twenty-eight thousand dollars, Saudis were among the world's richest. The economy hit the skids in the 1990s: paying for most of Desert Storm ravaged the budget, forcing Riyadh to take out hefty loans. Between loans and low oil prices, per capita GDP dwindled to seven thousand dollars by the year 2000.

Alliances matter: Ever since FDR and Abdul Aziz al Saud met in Egypt in 1945, the Saudi-U.S. formula for success has been oil for security. Both parties have usually come through, and it typically balances out trade between the kingdom and DC. The United States usually sells the Sauds whatever they want, even when Israel objects, and DC provides protection, e.g., Desert Shield, the fall 1990 prelude to Desert Storm.

Family matters: Given that Abdul Aziz had over a hundred children, there are thousands of princes: by some estimates thirty thousand, many of whom have monthly stipends of $10,000 or more, and all of whom jet around via the royal fleet.

Gender matters: Women in Saudi Arabia have fewer rights than anyplace else in the Middle East: they can't drive or vote, can't date, and are heavily discouraged from working. Outside the home, they must be completely covered and veiled, and they can't go out alone. However, more women can read: the literacy rate soared from an estimated 2 percent to nearly 80 percent in one generation. More women than men graduate from college. After being beaten by her husband, Saudi newscaster Rania al-Baz was in a coma for days. She went public, bringing the spotlight to wife beating, one of the kingdom's darkest secrets (see p. 187).

Under the land where the prophet Mohammed once walked, in the shadows of glassy high-rises and showy sculptures, here in the world's most leave-us-alone-if-you-aren't-one-of-us country, lies the planet's biggest stash of petroleum. This treasure trove of black gold is a mixed blessing at best; some might call it a curse because of the tug-of-war and temptations it creates. The strict state reli-

Not long ago a village of adobe shacks, the Saudi capital, Riyadh, is filled with dramatic government buildings, some rising like razor blades, others seeming to hover like space ships. Much of the architecture, like the roads over which the monoliths tower, was built by American firms such as Bechtel, cashing in on the Saudi fortune. Shown in foreground, the fort where Abdul Aziz al Saud began his kingdom building in 1902.

gion, Wahhabism, demands that Saudis live like the seventh-century Prophet, while the oil industry mandates twenty-first-century modernity. And the money that petroleum brings entices royal Sauds to live lifestyles they could unabashedly indulge in anywhere but here. The push and pull between Allah and economy, devotion and luxury, make Saudi Arabia a dangerous paradox.

HISTORY IN A BOX

Mohammed bin Abd al-Wahhab wouldn't shut up. The inhabitant of central Arabia, then a disunited smattering of tribes vulnerable to attacks from roving bedouins, was furious at what had happened: Islam had been debauched. Offshoot sects—the aberrant Shia, stone worshippers, mystical Sufis who chanted poetry and spun themselves silly—had diluted the meanings revealed to the prophet Mohammed. The Koran should be translated literally, he believed; Muslims should live as starkly as in the Prophet's day. The more adamant Wahhab became, the more his tirades annoyed those around him; finally his own family ran him out. Stomping to a nearby emirate in 1744, the man with fire in his eyes found more sympathetic ears. The local emir, Mohammed al Saud, liked Wahhab's revivalist take. Together they vowed to lead Muslims back to true Islam (as interpreted by Wahhab), uniting the disparate tribes of Arabia under the rule of Saud. With the emir's fighters and the preacher's captivating words, the duo took village after village until their emirate comprised most of the peninsula. In 1819, Egyptians invaded and beat them down, but the Saud-Wahhab combo soon rose again, reclaiming lost lands. In 1891, Ottoman-backed clans ejected the rulers, who slunk over to Kuwait, where in 1902 wannabe warrior Abdul Aziz al Saud saw his destiny. With gold, guns, horses, and warriors provided by Kuwaitis and Brits, the twenty-two-year-old, along with a Wahhabi preacher, headed back to the land his ancestors had ruled and lost twice before. They began with Riyadh, where they killed twelve hundred, and over three decades the king and his mesmerizing sidekick delivered the winning one-two punch: the preacher swayed with divine words; the warrior followed with bedouin fighters, ensuring that conversion was complete. Tribe by tribe, bride by bride—Abdul Aziz plucked one from each conquered village—they stitched together the patchwork kingdom, officially united in 1932: Abdul Aziz stamped his family name on Arabia, took the seat marked monarch, and designated the holy man's clan its religious gurus. Six years later oil was discovered, and the whole kit and caboodle started unraveling.

The creation of the kingdom by sword *and* by faith gave rise to a dichotomy that has never been fully worked out: the royals, in charge of oil, business, and international relations, are forced to modernize; while the religious establishment, in charge of mosques, courts, schools, and censorship, is forced to shove modernity back—only thirty years ago the Grand Mufti maintained that the sun revolves around the earth. The royals create a physical world that requires the religion be taken with a lump of salt, while the clerics create a social climate that makes materialism and Westernization anathema. To get themselves out of any seeming hypocrisy, the royals hand the clerics bags of money to start more religious schools abroad. This dysfunctional relationship creates a dual society, a life hidden behind high walls, and breeds zealots who seek to overthrow a monarchy that isn't Wahhab enough, although King Abdullah has been adept at keeping a foot in both worlds. His religious credentials far exceed those of his predecessor, but there's tension within the royal family over how far one should step toward reform or religion.

WORDS NEEDED TO UNDERSTAND SAUDI ARABIA

Honor killing: Murder of females believed to have dishonored their family.
Infidel: A non-Muslim.
Apostasy: Abandonment of one's religious faith.

Jihad: A struggle, often shorthand for holy war.

Shariah: Law based on the Koran and teachings of the prophet Mohammed. Other countries use Shariah as a basis for law as well, but only Saudi Arabia and Iran rely solely on Islamic law, and the punishments are the most brutal.

Madrassa: Islamic religious school for the poor, now often Saudi-funded and teaching a most rigid interpretation of Islam, Wahhabism.

Wahhabi: Practitioner of the Saudi state religion, which views both conversion and jihad as duties. Wahhabism is a sect of the Salafi school, and Salafi is often used interchangeably.

Saud/Saudi: A Saud is a member of the royal family; a Saudi is anyone (including the royals) who lives in the country.

Bin/ibn: "Son of," e.g., Abdullah bin Abdul Aziz. A full name gives the family tree.

Clerics ensure that the restrictive religion is taken seriously by the masses, if not by some of the princes, by meting out gory punishments. They reinforce the faith in mosques known for their fiery imams who call true Wahhabis to reverse the path of the modernizing House of Saud. The religious establishment writes the textbooks and controls the school system, which churns out graduates well versed in the Koran and often little else. And for the day-to-day dirty work, they unleash the virtue police. Saudis who so much as laugh loudly risk tongue lashing and worse by the religious police, who roam the streets with sticks and whips they are quick to use, as though beating back the changes that surround them. But changes there are.

Deserts, once trekked by camel, are now laced with highways and rail tracks and dotted with oil rigs. Palm-fringed oases now glisten with amusement parks, and sparkling malls come complete with Dunkin' Donuts, McDonald's, and Starbucks. Wandering bedouin, once desert warriors, have hunkered down, their sporadic attacks now conducted in SUVs (see "Qatar," p. 279) and satellite TV beaming in sports games between the religious quiz shows. Mobile phones ring coast-to-coast (and call the faithful to prayer), and seventy thousand crowd into the King Fahd Stadium to watch heated soccer matches or head to the tracks for the camel races, where—wink, wink—nobody bets. Saudi men kept the red-checked kaffiyehs, but Rolexes are slipped on under dishdashas, and a man's status is shown through Mont Blanc pens and Gucci shoes. Nevertheless, the richest country in the Middle East is restricted. Neither Beatles nor Beethoven can be heard since music is banned; dancing is an activity best reserved for the devil (or those who wish to spend the afterlife with him). Nary a drop of hooch can be legally purchased in restaurant, store, or hotel, where even the minibar is dry. Saudis who don't immediately run to the mosque when the muezzin calls are shoved to the mosques by the virtue police.

THE VIRTUE POLICE

Always a drag, and frequently dangerous—they're known for beating the heck out of anyone they accuse of not living the Wahhabi way, sometimes killing them—the thousands of young male employees and volunteers of the state's Commission for the Promotion of Virtue and Prevention of Vice, aka the Mutaween, take their job seriously. Quick to demand proof of marriage if they see a male and female talking, they don't allow the giving of flowers on Valentine's Day (a pagan holiday) and whip those deemed drunk. With a force heavy on ex-cons, the virtue police became notorious in March 2002, when they shoved screaming schoolgirls back into a burning school and locked the door, blocking firemen from entering. While smoke billowed out, and the girls shrieked that their skin was burning, nearly a hundred firefighters, spectators, and even some of the girls' parents stood outside the school—nobody daring to demand that the door be unlocked and risk the wrath of the virtue police.[1] The reason the virtue police had pushed them back in: the girls had run out of their classroom without their veils. Fifteen died that day.

Wahhabism bans mingling of sexes outside the home. Segregated everywhere from buses to schools, men and women often dine separately, even at home, and the virtue police want sex-divided sidewalks too. A recent business conference where Saudi women didn't wear veils was loudly condemned by the country's religious leader, and the king ordered magazines to stop showing females, images believed to corrupt youth. A few women newscasters recently took their place in front of the cameras, wearing head scarves but their faces unveiled; until then a man could go his whole life seeing the faces of only two females, his wife and his mother, and perhaps not even then: some women *never* unveil.

Saudi marriages are usually arranged; a groom gets a quick glimpse of his bride's face just before engagement, but won't see her face again until the honeymoon; his friends will never know what his wife looks like, since the wedding is segregated and the missus will always be veiled around them.

For Saudi subjects, particularly women, the dichotomy is even more stark: the world around them looks modern, with gleaming towers and malls, filled with designer clothes and makeup they can buy but that men aren't supposed to see them wearing: women can't step out of the house unless they look like a black tent, veils concealing all but their beautiful eyes. Cars are an everyday reality, but women can't drive them, even though many husbands, sons, and brothers—sick of being chauffeurs—wish that they could. A woman can get a master's degree, but she's not supposed to work. Arranged marriages wed cousins with cousins, and a female who darkens the family name (perhaps by engaging in premarital hand-holding) risks death at the hands of her menfolk. But those are not the biggest problems, says author Jean Sasson, who lived in the kingdom for years. "The issue women most want to see addressed and changed is the abuse of women, which is simply accepted by the community," she says. "Even foreign maids are routinely raped or beaten, and the Saudi government does nothing to help them, instead blaming them for being abused."

IGNORED HOTSHOTS: WOMEN

It's difficult to get an inside glimpse of the world of women in this secretive kingdom. To get a peek behind the veil, Jean Sasson, author of *Princess*, the nonfiction story of a Saudi royal, put in a call to several acquaintances—princesses as well as women in the Saudi middle class. Sasson's report:

The good news: The widespread education of Saudi men and women is bringing a change in attitudes. Many Saudi men now seek change for the sake of their daughters, whom they confess to love. This in itself is a bit of a surprise, as only a few years ago husbands and fathers reacted adversely to the birth of a female child. The local media is writing about issues considered taboo only a few years ago, even poking fun at the clerics' primitive attitudes regarding women. Some women in the port city of Jeddah are now brave enough to refuse to veil their faces, and there is a lot of talk about allowing women to drive. Many Saudi men are pushing for this change and are allowing their women to travel in the general region—to go shopping in Dubai, for example, although a male in the family must accompany them. Women can own their own businesses and have their own bank accounts and indeed have enormous financial resources. Some families are even allowing their daughters to have a supervised visit with a young man after they are engaged. Genuine hope is breaking out that men in the highest circles are quietly pushing for restrictions against women to be loosened. Women in the royal family report their beliefs that the entire country is now on the brink of tremendous change, mostly for the good for Saudi women. Although religious clerics tend to remain backward, the royal family, now led by King Abdullah, is losing patience with these stubborn men who cling to the harshest interpretations of Muslim thought regarding women. It is said that the Saudi royal males believe the entire image of the kingdom is being damaged by restrictive Saudi laws still in place against women.

The bad news: If a man chooses to abuse the females in his family, even to the point of violence and murder, he will *not* be punished. Journalists are sometimes punished for even raising questions about the freedoms of Saudi females. The relative leniency of men toward women is not reflected in all regions; if a woman in Riyadh fails to veil, she will be punished harshly by her family and her community. The clerics are determined that women will never obtain drivers' licenses, keeping them dependent on men whenever they leave the house, and women still must seek permission from their husbands before they can travel. If a woman owns her own business, a man must "front" the business, and even if a woman has an independent income many husbands do not allow their wives to make their own decisions with these private resources. In the end, few women would be brave enough to go against their families if they are unhappy with the choice of a groom.

Court punishments are brutal: on Fridays, the holy day, the heads of hash dealers and beer smugglers go rolling in Riyadh's Deeva square, aka Chop Chop Square, the public square not far from the villas and palaces of some royals, known for blowout bashes where the champagne is free flowing, prostitutes are free, and the white powder being passed around might not be salt.[2] And should a Saudi want to dismiss hired help, the easiest way may be to call them a sorcerer or a witch: the easily convinced court rarely finds them innocent.

"Riyadh, November 2—Mustafa Ibrahim, an Egyptian, was executed here today after being convicted of practicing magic and sorcery as well as adultery and desecration of the Holy Quaran by putting it in a bathroom, said a statement released by the interior ministry."
—Statement released by Saudi Foreign Affairs office in November 2007[3]

Evidence of the pharmacist's practice of sorcery included possession of a candle, nasty-smelling herbs, and a book alleged to contain spells.[4] Religious police were first alerted to the Egyptian's misdeed when a local complained that he'd seen a copy of the Koran in the pharmacist's washroom.

A RADICALLY DIFFERENT TAKE ON ISLAM

Adherents say the Saudi state religion reflects the prophet Mohammed's teachings at their purest; others call it outdated, rigid, and problematic, particularly when it's marketed outside the kingdom. Brimstone-and-hellfire Wahhabism (aka Salafism), a revivalist take on Sunni Islam that is far more extreme than Islam practiced anywhere else in the region, is intolerant of other lifestyles, other faiths, and even of non-Wahhabis: Sufis, Shia and "moderate"

Muslims are despised as much as Israelis, Jews, Christians, Buddhists, Hindus, and Westerners. Wahhabism applauds jihad (religious war) as a means of fighting injustice *and* bringing about conversion, and harsh Shariah law is the rule of the land: burglars' hands are chopped off; adulterers are stoned; and gays, smugglers, and murderers meet the sword.[5] The sect prohibits mingling with non-Muslims or flirting with modernity and shuns wealth. So it's ironic that Saudi Arabia's lavishly decorated mosques are set in flashy, high-tech cities *and* that petrodollars fueled the spread of this faith, unknown outside of the desert kingdom thirty years ago. Billions go to madrassas that have sprung up from Sudan to Pakistan, creating the likes of Afghanistan's Taliban, which adopted the beliefs taught in Wahhabi schools. Adherents say *only* their faith is true Islam, and in Saudi Arabia teachers who teach tolerance are thrown in prison. In 2008, the government refused to sign an international petition not to trash other religions or Islamic sects. Critics, including other Muslims, contend that madrassas mold jihadists and that Wahhabism's hatred-breeding beliefs encourage groups such as al Qaeda to violently strike out at the world.[6] A fiery tool for conquering a century ago, Wahhabism, say critics, is a liability in the globalized economy, which is likewise seen as a threat. Some practitioners, such as Osama bin Laden, believe that resources from Muslim lands should be sold only to Muslims, preferably Wahhabis.

As a result of the lifestyle Wahhabism demands, Saudi Arabia is all about the hidden and the forbidden, and the foreigner rarely knows that world. Virtue police monitor all public activities; classes run by corporations for their Saudi employees are believed to hold spies. Lives of the wealthy are shielded by high walls and security guards; lives of the royals are censored by the press, coming to light only when a royal is busted internationally. The government withholds census reports; even Saudi Aramco keeps tight hold on its petroleum stats.

Despite the constraints on society, the kingdom has its bright spots. Royals and citizens are generous: they have put billions toward humanitarian causes, from tsunami relief to economic development, and the country has always picked up most of the tab for regional security (going broke after the 1991 Persian Gulf War, during which its cities were bombarded by missiles and hundreds died). The kingdom has pumped trillions of dollars into the United States economy, and with rare exception, notably the 1973 embargo, the Sauds have loyally supplied oil to the West. The Sauds have kept oil calculated in dollars, the value basis of their own currency, a hugely important move that kept the dollar the world's standard currency. Pressure is on to tie oil prices and currency values to the euro—a move that would make the crashing dollar more worthless. So far the Sauds have resisted. Abdullah is building new hospitals, modern universities, and "economic cities" to attract foreign businesses to employ locals. He's given the press new freedoms, and he released political prisoners who'd been jailed years ago for peacefully requesting a constitution. He held the country's

Courtesy of Saudi Aramco/ASC

*Dhahran used to be a dusty desert nowheresville
in the east, but after oil bubbled up in 1938, it
evolved as headquarters for Saudi Aramco. Once
foreigner-dominated, the now futuristic city is the
epicenter of the world's biggest oil corporation,
employing fifty-one thousand, and the richest.
Back when the oil biz was American-run, Aramco
used to greet new employees with the* Blue Book,
*which instructed them on how to build their own
stills to avoid having to smuggle booze into the
alcoholically arid land.*

first municipal elections (women couldn't vote, and less than half of males bothered to). He upped wages and raised the country's profile in regional affairs,
negotiating a truce between Palestine's fighting faction and floating an
Arab-Israeli peace plan. But still, he can't bridge the chasm between puritanical
religion and worldliness and wealth, the issue that's been unraveling the country
since it was formed or, rather, since Saudi Aramco, the force of modernization,
came into being.

The kingdom's oil company, Saudi Aramco, is the most progressive vehicle of
change in the kingdom. The oil company, for instance, brought electricity to the
Eastern Province and launched the first Saudi train service. Modern and PR-savvy
too—a rarity in this region—the company, now completely Saudi owned, pub-
lishes insightful magazines, such as *Saudi Aramco World*, the only English publication that continually spotlights the region's history. And Aramco was behind the
creation of the kingdom's most open school, the King Abdullah University of Science and Technology, the only public school where the curriculum is not dictated
by clerics and where the virtue police can't enter.

GLOBAL GIANT: ARAMCO

Standard Oil of California started the search for oil in Saudi Arabia in 1934. Years later, they were still drilling, this time with partner Texas Oil Company (now Texaco), blowing through millions with no success. Finally, in 1938, eureka! They hit crude at the well in the east called Damman 7. Ten years later, they hit supergiant oil field Ghawar, so big it alone provided the bulk of Saudi oil, and it's only half-dry. As more and more workers were needed, along with railways, ports, and pipelines, Dhahran swelled and the U.S. government built the country's first airport, to fly in employees. Secretly, it doubled as a military base to guard the resources. Starting as a consortium of American oil companies (the acronym Aramco was short for the Arabian-American Oil Company) that split profits fifty-fifty with the kingdom, since 1980 the corporation has been entirely a Saudi-owned affair. The Saudi Arabian Oil Company (Saudi Aramco) is a chart topper in every respect, from its muscle in OPEC to the sheer volume of exports (world's biggest), not to mention the voluminous petroleum reserves it owns (world's biggest), the sophisticated equipment it works with, and the barrels of cash it brings in. The total Saudi control makes some squeamish: entire books have been written about what some suspect may be overstated reserves, accusations Saudi Aramco loudly denies, assuring the world that it has enough oil to last almost a century at current rates of production. Whatever the reality is, one thing is usually overlooked: oil-wise, the Saudis' oil company often plays a conciliatory role with the West, keeping supply up and prices down, though that may be hard to believe in the current market. Nevertheless, Saudi Aramco is the swing producer who keeps the planet awash in oil: when Iraq's output plummeted after the U.S. invasion in 2003, for instance, Saudi Arabia produced more, as it has with every world crisis, including the Iranian revolution of 1979, and the eight-year Iran-Iraq War that followed. It's been steadfast in making sure that the United States gets its oil, with rare exception proving to be the most dependable guys on the Gulf block.

At odds with the religion, the petroleum economy mandates snuggling up with the West and foreign corporations, whose workers live in walled compounds far out of town, some with bars, and many with moonshine operations. To keep protests down to a dull roar as they welcomed in non-Muslim workers (kept isolated from Saudi society) and financially tangoed with American developers and military advisers over the past three decades, the government tossed more money at clerics and gave them more voice in running the society.

The kingdom is now a nonstop paradox. Top ministers, positions almost exclusively held by princes, demand a cut of business deals—their "commissions" factored into the final inflated price, which only screws the government that employs them. Bored Saudi youth are inspired by radical clerics to become jihadists, and they in turn strike not only in Iraq but within their own kingdom. Awash in petrodollars, Riyadh usually spends more than it brings in. Over a tenth of the GDP goes to arms, most U.S.-made, but the military isn't well-trained enough to use them, perpetuating dependency on the United States. The government is mumbling about cutting back perks to Saudi citizens, while the IMF demands that Saudis start paying income taxes.

> *Health care is currently free to all Saudis but gobbles up a tenth of the government's budget, the proportion swelling along with the growing population that has quadrupled since the mid-twentieth century when most Saudis didn't live past forty. Now there are twenty million more Saudis, and they live thirty years longer. Riyadh is pushing for private companies to provide what was never needed here before: health insurance.*

The threat of being cut off from government benefits is unsettling in the Middle East's wealthiest land, where oil revenue, which accounts for almost half of the GDP and the bulk of the federal budget, now pulls in more than ever. However, commoners are poorer now than they were two decades ago: Saudi Arabia's per capita GDP of $15,500 (IMF, 2007) is now less than Slovenia's. Even college graduates aren't trained for jobs outside the mosque, and by some estimates over a quarter of young men don't work. Men can take four wives, but most young Saudi males are so broke they can't cough up the money to buy an apartment, the minimum requirement to marry. This schizophrenia of twenty-first-century Saudi Arabia created the disturbing irony that America's supposed good buddy in the Middle East—the country that almost always comes through with the oil—produced the world's most threatening guerrilla faction specifically aiming to take Uncle Sam (and the House of Saud) down. That fifteen of the 9/11 hijackers (not to mention their hero, Osama bin Laden) were Saudi wasn't a fluke, just a reaction to the duality here, where the stark piousness demanded of commoners doesn't match the royal reality, and where the infidel is banned by the religion, but the government welcomes the West.

A STRANGE CASE[7]

Some Western journalists, including Gerald Posner,[8] have argued that some Saudi royals may have had prior knowledge of the September 11 attacks and may have helped funnel money to al Qaeda. One bizarre case involved Abu Zubaydah, an al Qaeda member captured by the CIA in 2002. The agency, hoping to frighten the Saudi, re-created a Saudi prison and brought in a Saudi interrogator, thinking that Zubaydah would spill the beans if he feared he was facing Saudi-styled torture. Instead, Zubaydah was relieved: he rattled off the phone numbers of several Saudi princes and told the interrogators to call them. The list included Prince Ahmed bin Salman, Prince Sultan bin Faisal, and Prince Fahd bin Turki. When the CIA notified the Saudi government, the Sauds denied that the princes were involved; Zubaydah recanted. Despite the denials, within a week all of the named princes were dead: Prince Ahmed died in the hospital while undergoing elective surgery; Prince Sultan died in a mysterious car accident en route to Ahmed's funeral; and, strangest of all, young Prince Fahd was discovered just outside the capital, dead in his car, apparently from dehydration.[9]

The rise of Osama bin Laden is but one sign of the deep unhappiness that's brewing in the kingdom, where poverty is hard to ignore, unemployment is high, and most rulers have pooh-poohed the admittedly contradictory wishes of the people and have sidelined the religious elite, who have long disapproved of the direction that the oil business was taking the country. The tension that has created two Saudi Arabias, the ideal one dictated by religion and the real one shaped by petroleum riches, has reared its head in the form of self-destructing youth. Unemployed and fired up by years of religious schooling, young men are dramatically entering the debate by becoming suicide bombers aiming to close down the oil industry, kick out the West, and shut down the House of Saud, which has ruled the country for over seventy-five years.

Al Qaeda in the Arabian Peninsula claims responsibility for domestic terrorist acts since 2003: now it's trying to sabotage oil infrastructure. The group says the attacks are one show of al Qaeda's "war against the Christians and Jews to stop their pillage of Muslim riches and part of the campaign to chase them out of the Arabian Peninsula."[10]

PRINCE NAIF'S FLIP-FLOP

Saudis had absolutely nothing to do with it. Clearly, it wasn't the work of *any* Muslim, not even Osama bin Laden. The September 11 attacks, you see, were actually an Israeli plot to besmirch the name of Islam and Saudi Arabia. So said Prince Naif, head of the kingdom's security, repeatedly, for six months following the 2001 attacks. All tied up with the religious elite, Naif—also minister of the Interior—didn't address the messages coming from the radical mullahs in the kingdom. Saudi cleric Ali bin al-Khudayr, for one, issued a fatwa commanding Saudis to rejoice over America's tragedy and applauded al Qaeda for the deed. But Naif soon dined on crow and stopped his denials of any Saudi involvement in 9/11. In 2003, al Qaeda unleashed its treachery on Naif's turf. The dozens of violent actions taken within the kingdom by al Qaeda in the Arabian Peninsula sullied the rep of Prince Naif, who reportedly has recently been stripped of much of his power.[11] Al Qaeda is also believed to have infiltrated Naif's security forces, possibly one reason why they are often late in responding to attacks, and the perpetrators sometimes get away.

Condemning 9/11 as an unjustifiable act in front of the Western TV cameras, within the kingdom it was another story: clerics and the government so vehemently denied that Saudis were linked to the September 11 attack that most Saudis believed that *no Arabs* were involved at all, a view still held by the majority of Muslims in 2006.[12] The country's connection to terrorism became much harder to ignore, however, after May 2003, when car bombs exploded in a housing complex, killing thirty-five, the first of a series of vicious attacks within Saudi Arabia to be claimed by al Qaeda.

> *The reason for the gruesome acts, reported the British* Sunday Times, *is that the Saudi royals had been paying off bin Laden's group not to attack within the kingdom, but under pressure from the United States recently stopped the payoffs, which over the previous few years had totaled some four hundred million dollars.*[13]

A nasty show it's been since then, with dozens of violent incidents shattering the former peace of the kingdom. Between car bombs in housing compounds, bloody shootouts with police, terror-filled twenty-four-hour murder sprees in apartment complexes, attacks on embassies and Saudi ministries, close to one thousand have died, and many of them were Saudis. The government claims to have foiled nearly two hundred other plots.[14] But recently, al Qaeda has changed tactics. Forget the blood and gore, they're now aiming at the heart of the Saudi machine: oil.

> *"One of the most important reasons that led our enemies to control our land is the theft of our oil. Do everything you can to stop the biggest plundering operation in history—the plundering of the resources of the present and future generations . . . prevent them from reaching the oil, and mount your operations accordingly, particularly in Iraq and the Gulf."*
> —Osama bin Laden on audiotape released December 16, 2004
> (BBC, December 16, 2004)

"We call on all the mujahideen to target the sources of oil which do not serve the Islamic nation but serve the enemies of the nation."
—Message posted on Internet site run by al Qaeda on the Arabian Peninsula, December 19, 2004 (Agence France-Press, December 19, 2004)

In February 2006, police foiled an attempted sabotage of Abqaiq, the world's biggest oil processing center, in a bullet-filled showdown during which four died. Following arrests of 136 Saudis for plotting attacks on oil infrastructure, security forces recently rounded up an additional 172 suspected militants, uncovering caches of weapons, five million dollars in cash, and plans to attack royals and blow up additional oil installations. In the latest busts, where seized plans showed a marked sophistication, the government discovered that many militants had been trained in Iraq, which, like Afghanistan in the 1980s, is the new hot spot for jihad. And while some of these religious warriors originally raged against the U.S. occupation, many are now battling an enemy that to Wahhabis is worse than the infidel: namely, the Shia.

FIRST JIHAD OF THE TWENTY-FIRST CENTURY

Forget the early idea instilled by the prophet Mohammed that Muslims don't kill Muslims and Arabs don't kill Arabs. Recruited by militant mullahs as part of a modern jihad, thousands of young Saudis slipped into Iraq as modern mujahideen and attacked Shia.[15] The Saudi government says they must be going through other countries, since it's illegal to enter Iraq from the kingdom. Nevertheless, it's building a fence to seal off the two countries.

In short, despite the money flooding in and a leader making a sincere stab at reform, Saudi Arabia is a mess, dangerously caught between two worlds, with unemployed, unmarried, and religiously riled-up young men—some of them fans of bin Laden—blasting into the fray. And, alas, the United States is all bound up with the ticking time bomb that is the modern kingdom, because the United States is the hand that arms it and provides Saudi security, despite the upheaval it brings.

During the Cold War, the U.S. government planted explosives near the kingdom's oil wells and refineries to destroy the resources in case of a Soviet invasion—but forgot to mention that fact to the Saudi royalty.

> *The Sauds now reportedly have their own self-destruct system: in the*
> *case of an invasion it would render their petroleum good for nothing*
> *except radioactive oil spills.*[16]

Much of Saudi Arabia's geyser of contemporary woes stems back to 1979. King Faisal sat on the throne as the 1970s began, bringing luxuries never before fathomed in the desert nation. The Arabian Peninsula was lost in a calendric black hole. Electricity hadn't shown up, transportation was four-footed, and the vast majority of its people was illiterate. Locals lived as nomads or herders, in tents and mud villages surrounding oases, amid palm gardens cultivated for dates. But the valuable muck in the ground changed all that, once Faisal got hold of the checking account.

> *"[Riyadh] in the mid-1940s was a mud-walled village of twelve thousand*
> *with only one electrical generator and a couple of telephones—one in the*
> *king's bedroom, one in his mother's."*
> —Ambassador Chas Freeman in interview with
> Association for Diplomatic Studies and Training

Long of face, sad-eyed Faisal had spent years jaunting to New York and DC as foreign minister under King Saud and representing the country at the UN, where Saudi Arabia opposed the creation of Israel in 1948 and the growing influence of Israelis in determining U.S. foreign policy.

FAISAL'S FEARS

In many ways progressive, Faisal was also an anti-Semite who believed that Jews drank the blood of Arab children and were actually Communists plotting control of the world.[17] Visitors to the kingdom were presented with *The Protocols of the Elders of Zion,* a conspiracy book debunked as a forgery, but which Faisal held up as proof of the Jews' plans for global domination. He turned Aramco, then part U.S.-owned, into his lobbying tool to sway U.S. policy toward Israel; when efforts failed, and Nixon rushed arms that helped Israel win the 1973 war, Faisal reluctantly seconded the oil embargo to the United States. As his treasury swelled in the 1970s, and Western business came a-calling, he refused to broker deals with companies with Jews on their boards and in contracts prohibited Jews from entering the kingdom. Even the U.S. government signed on the dotted discriminatory line.[18] He also fretted about

Yemen to the south, from which Abdul Aziz's forces had snatched the region of Asir in 1934; when Yemenis spilled into Saudi Arabia during that country's civil war, he lobbied JFK to send over military protection. Another woe: the Hashemites, the ruling family in Jordan. The Sauds had plucked Hejaz, containing the holy sites Mecca and Medina, from them, and Faisal worried that they wanted it back. And across the Gulf, Iran was vying to be top dog of the region, with arms purchases from the United States pumping up the shah's stature. On that point, at least, Faisal could fight back: he proceeded to load up the Saudi arsenal, occasionally with weapons that even the shah didn't have.

Faisal built hospitals, paved roads, and opened new schools—even for girls. He launched irrigation and agriculture programs, gave scholarships to study abroad, and banned slavery—a daring (if half-hearted) act that made him many enemies in the country where "no-pay servants" were common. Faisal controversially introduced TV in the 1960s; the Grand Mufti caved in to the idea after the Koran was read over the airwaves, being assured that programming would be religious. But with every change, clerics balked, issuing fatwas banning newfangled devices and cultural changes from the West. Even some royals rebelled, among them a nephew who tried to destroy a TV station. The rioting prince was killed by security guards, and Faisal would ultimately pay for that act with his life.

King Faisal, pictured here, welcomed Americans into the kingdom as part of his development projects. He rattled the religious elite, but he was nevertheless a welcome relief from his predecessor, King Saud—a sot and a money burner who did little for his people unless they were one of his hundred wives.[19]

*Egyptian president Gamal Abdel Nasser, whom the Sauds found threat-
ening, sparked Arab nationalism; King Faisal countered by reviving the
idea of a worldwide Islamic community, launching the Organization of the
Islamic Conference, still the world's foremost group of Muslim leaders.
Faisal initiated the Saudi practice of setting up madrassas, providing
Islamic education for the poor, although these schools taught the rigid
Wahhabi interpretation.*

Faisal also boosted the contents of the national piggy bank: the kingdom grew
rich in the aftermath of the 1973 embargo. That year he bought out 25 percent of
Aramco; seven years later the oil company was under full Saudi control. But
Faisal made a few dubious moves as well. Beyond strengthening the secret police, handing over land as gifts to royals, and approving the practice of "commissions" (what others might call kickbacks) to Saudi ministers when making
deals—still a common practice—he reportedly also took the first steps in launching a nuclear weapons program. According to Saudi physicist Mohammed
Khilewi, who defected in 1994, the Sauds were major financial backers of the
wizardry of A. Q. Khan, father of Islamabad's nuclear bomb.

THE SAUDI SECRET

Nobody says that Saudi Arabia has nuclear weapons yet, but a former
Saudi nuclear scientist and diplomat, Mohammed Khilewi, says it started a
program to build them back in the 1970s.[20] The impetus: Israel's nuclear
weapons, believed to have been aimed at Arab capitals during the 1973 war.
According to Khilewi, the Saudis also threw billions into a Pakistani nuclear
program to build an "Islamic bomb" that they could access, and they addition-
ally backed Iraq's nuclear ventures and earmarked about five billion of the
twenty-five billion dollars given to Saddam during the Iran-Iraq War to re-create
the Osirak nuclear project that the Israelis bombed to smithereens in 1981.[21]
The Saudi nuclear project is reportedly housed at al Kharj, a military base
some fifty miles south of Riyadh. Appearing to illustrate the country's desire to
get its hands on nuclear weapons at some point or another, according to the
Federation of Atomic Scientists, the King Khalid Military City houses nuclear
silos—still empty, presumably.

NEW-AND-IMPROVED ARABIA
BROUGHT TO YOU BY THE WEST

It had the impact of a tsunami, and appeared just as quickly. Villagers
were rattled and clerics enraged as technology arrived. Suddenly light

appeared with the flick of a switch, air was cooled with the press of a button, water gushed out of faucets, and with the arrival of the telephone one no longer had to travel for days to deliver a message. Cars roared across ribbons of highway; grocery stores arrived, filled with exotic and prepackaged food. Schools taught reading and math; doctors and hospitals wiped out ubiquitous conditions like intestinal worms. Theaters, airports, restaurants, and hotels—even military bases—appeared, as if poured out of a can. Everywhere there was yet another bold architectural statement notifying the world that Saudi Arabia had arrived in the twentieth century, approximately thirteen centuries ahead of where the shocked clerics and conservatives wanted it to be.

DC loudly applauded Faisal's development program and trillion-dollar modernization program (American firms made billions out of it), but the changes fueled the fatwa machine. This grand leap into the present was met with hand-wringing, finger wagging, and fiery shrieks by the religious establishment, which didn't like modernity and didn't like the arrival of the Western infidels, who were moving into the kingdom by the tens of thousands and even bringing the kids.

In 1975, Faisal was assassinated: when he leaned forward to greet his nephew, Prince Faisal bin Musaid, the prince pulled out a gun and shot him. The murderer was the brother of the prince killed a decade before when he'd stormed the first TV station, but revenge was dismissed as a motive. The prince had gone mad— because he'd spent time in the West, said the Saudis. Indeed, Prince Faisal had attended school in California and Colorado and was arrested for dealing LSD in 1970; charges were dropped and he skedaddled back to the Mideast. The prince had been

By the seventies, over fifty thousand Americans lived in the kingdom, mostly hidden behind walled compounds that resembled LA suburbs in the middle of the desert, complete with supermarkets, swimming pools, tennis courts, and golf courses made of sand sprayed with oil to stay in place.

T. F. Walters, Courtesy of Saudi Aramco/ASC

boozing it up the night before the assassination, while playing poker, another habit attributed to the West. And when King Faisal died, soon followed by his killer, clerics demanded more power. Their first move was to shut down the theaters and turn off the music, banning the bands that had become popular during Faisal's reign.

Faisal's successor, King Khalid, was sickly; for most of his seven-year reign Crown Prince Fahd called the shots, quietly continuing Faisal's modernization and hiring more Western firms to build the dreamworld they envisioned, including a U.S.-built military city to guard over the northeast.

The biggest military construction ever undertaken by the U.S. Army Corps of Engineers was Saudi Arabia's King Khalid Military City, one of several bases built by the U.S. government. It plunked quite a few coins into the U.S. Treasury: it's said to have cost up to thirty billion dollars to set up, the bulk paid to Uncle Sam and his arms dealers.

No matter how tightly they tried to keep the lid on what was turning into a pressure cooker, the royals couldn't prevent the hushed but harsh criticisms of the regime. More alarming in the 1970s: what was happening across the way in Iran. The rumbles of the Iranian revolution that began in 1978 provoked jangly nerves in the kingdom: Riyadh blacked out news reports of the worker strikes at Iran's oil facilities, fearing they might be mimicked by Aramco workers, many of them Shia who lived in the east. And when the shah's dynasty tumbled, and Ayatollah Khomeini returned to Iran on February 1, 1979, the Sauds were frantic.

THE GCC

The Sauds' deep distrust of Iran prompted them to do something that isn't much in their nature. In 1981, just after Iraq invaded Iran and kicked off the Iran-Iraq War, the Sauds reached out to their wealthy neighbors Kuwait, Bahrain, UAE, Qatar, and Oman and formed a club. The charter of the Gulf Cooperation Council (GCC) is filled with flowery, heart-warming language about the "deep religious and cultural ties that link the six states," their shared history, and their interwoven familial ties. On the other hand, it represented "a practical answer to the challenges of security and economic development in the area." Which was a fancy way of saying, "What the heck are we gonna do about Iran?" The first meeting stressed the need for a mutual defense club, which still has never really formed as a cohesive military unit. But the GCC did provide a forum for discussion about problems. After meeting for twenty-seven years, two significant themes emerged. One, GCC countries want to work more closely together: constructing a natural gas pipe system, "the dolphin network," from Qatar, sharing an electrical grid, and developing a shared common currency and duty-free trade. Two, somebody was always screwing the plans up, and that somebody was quite often the Sauds.

In November 1978, the Sauds became convinced an Iranian showdown of some sort was imminent. Riyadh rang up DC, pleading with President Jimmy Carter to direct fighter planes and warships to the peninsula to protect Saudi Arabia from possible attacks from Iran. Calling in the security card of the Roosevelt–Abdul Aziz handshake thirty-four years before, the Sauds wanted at least a symbolic show of force, some demonstration that even if the United States wasn't going to save the crashing government of Iran's shah, it would at least roll up its sleeves for Riyadh. They even sent over dashing Prince Saud and then oil minister Sheik Ahmed Yamani to personally lobby for the cause.

Carter was hesitant: the Gulf waters were churning; the smell of a pending military showdown between Iran and Arab countries hung in the air. Besides, the Sauds had snubbed Carter's Egyptian-Israeli Camp David peace talks. DC dithered for months, one day announcing they'd send out a naval fleet, only to nix the idea the next. Finally, in January 1979 Carter dispatched a dozen F-15s to Saudi Arabia for a "highly visible fly-in" designed to soothe the royals' "frantic concern."[22] But as the planes were streaking across the ocean, the Sauds learned the fighters weren't carrying any bombs. The Sauds were livid; even editorial boards were astounded, with the *New York Times* titling one jeremiad, "Flying to Arabia, Unarmed." The fireworks had only just begun. Khomeini, the Shia cleric now leading the Iranian nation, demanded that Shia rise up against Sunni leaders; Shia in Saudi Arabia's oil-rich Eastern Province began to rebel. But Khomeini's calls even stirred the Sunni in the kingdom: they were jealous and furious that the world's mightiest, most fiery theocracy was Shia, and Iranian no less. Clerics and conservatives in Saudi Arabia wanted a true theocracy there.

On November 4, 1979, Iranian students in Tehran stormed the U.S. embassy, taking fifty-two Americans hostage. And then the drama moved to Saudi Arabia. Five hundred militants, most of them Saudi, seized the Grand Mosque in Mecca during the hajj. What few understood at the time was that this was planting the seeds for al Qaeda.

GRAND MOSQUE

The hajj was winding up. Most of the two million pilgrims were gone, but fifty thousand Muslims stayed for final prayers. On the morning of November 20, 1979, the imam was in the middle of his services at the Grand Mosque (the world's biggest) that is the focal point of the pilgrimage to Mecca, when a group of young men appeared with rifles. One grabbed the microphone and announced that the Mahdi, the savior, had arrived. And then hundreds of militants—Saudi, Yemeni, Egyptian, and a few Americans—pulled out weapons, shot guards, and chained the gates to the mosque. Thus began a two-week showdown that killed over a thousand, and which is still a hushed-up affair today. The man who'd commandeered the microphone, Juhayman al Uteybi, was a Saudi and part of a radical Sunni group that believed the royals weren't pious enough. They blared their demands over the mosque's loudspeakers: the monarchy should be removed, a theocracy put into place, non-Muslims should be driven out, and oil supplies cut to the West. The Saudi national guard sent in fighters via helicopter; they were killed. Pakistanis were called in, and then French special forces (who had to convert to Islam before being allowed to step into Mecca, a Muslim-only city). Grenades were tossed into the mosque, and there was talk of using gas, or of flooding it. The truth and the details of what happened still aren't entirely clear. Even the numbers are debated: the Saudi government says 255 pilgrims and militants were killed, along with 127 Saudi military. Other estimates put the number of dead at closer to 4,000.[23]

Whatever happened during those two weeks in 1979, the bin Laden family was implicated. They had renovated the Grand Mosque, and someone from Bin Laden Construction or the family is believed to have given the militants detailed plans. And according to Lawrence Wright, author of *The Looming Tower*, two of the family were picked up and held several days for questioning: Mahfouz bin Laden and his half brother Osama. They were soon let go.

The event, seen as an outrageous indication that the Sauds couldn't control the country, much less Islam's revered sites, severely threatened their continued rule. As one sign that the monarchy was reasserting its control, King Fahd later changed his title, adding the reassuring mantle "Custodian of the Two Holy Places" to the royal signature.

> *Ayatollah Khomeini falsely reported that the United States had bombed Mecca. In response to that erroneous news, Pakistanis torched the U.S. embassy in Islamabad, killing two Americans.*

In December 1979, the Soviets invaded Afghanistan. But just as quickly as the great flood of problems—Iran, Saudi militants, and the Afghanistan invasion—had brewed up, the means to survive it presented themselves. The Sauds saw a way to weaken their foes, distract enemies, and simultaneously shine up their tarnished halo. They started by backing Saddam Hussein, paying him billions to further his ambitions as regional hero. His mission: take down Ayatollah Khomeini. He invaded Iran in September 1980. Then the clerics' demand for more piousness was answered in a Saudi-sponsored holy war, one that would not only quiet the clerics, but keep the radicals too busy to launch attacks in the kingdom: they'd be sent to Afghanistan as modern-day mujahideen battling the heathen Soviets.

THE BRILLIANT AFGHAN PLAN: AKA BLOWBACK MAXIMUS

The credit for the original harebrained scheme goes to Zbigniew Brzezinski, national security adviser to Jimmy Carter. On paper, the plan to give the Russians their own Vietnam looked brilliant. Reagan carried on with the program, under which the Saudi government transported young Arabs to Pakistan, where Pakistan's intelligence service, the ISI, trained them with arms supplied by DC (including the surface-to-air missile called the Stinger), while Saudi clerics molded jihadi minds. The plan was extraordinarily successful: the guerrilla fighters proved too much for the Soviets, who finally put their tanks in reverse in 1988, eight years after they'd rolled in. The war was even a factor in the crumbling of the Soviet Union in 1991. But the plan was incredibly naive: young zealous Muslims were now extremely well trained, armed, and fired up. And even when that war was over, the jihadis weren't done with their holy fighting.

The Sauds were happy to participate, not only to redeem themselves, but to boost arms sales from the United States, specifically AWACS (Airborne Warning and Control System), a sophisticated radar plane that only the United States, Britain, and France had. Carter turned down their request, and their requests to upgrade F-15s with bomb racks, without which the planes are useless for fighting. Furious, the Sauds turned to France and Britain for their arms, buying so much from London alone, some forty billion dollars' worth, that the resulting al-Yamama deal was to be declared "the biggest sale of anything to anyone by anyone,"[24] ever. But the Sauds eventually got their AWACS and anything else they wanted when President Ronald Reagan took over.

U.S. Air Force

AWACS: The Sauds wanted one. Reagan delivered it. Israel had a fit. The Airborne Warning and Control System, pictured here, has a high-tech "radar eye" on top that sweeps a wider area and can better distinguish depth. Israel didn't want the Sauds to have more sophisticated surveillance tools than it did, but Reagan pushed the sale through, endearing himself to Riyadh.

Under Reagan, the Sauds and DC got all snuggly, and all the more when King Khalid died in 1982. He was succeeded by King Fahd, never known for his accounting skills. Ignoring domestic needs, Fahd was quick to loan money to U.S. firms, and he brought in more American contractors, much to the chagrin of the clerics. Fahd kept boosting his arms arsenal and importing more Americans to man it and to train Saudi forces.

The lovefest between Riyadh and DC continued into the administration of George H. W. Bush. Even though the Saudis had to take out loans to keep the government up and running, Fahd didn't let on.

A decade later, the Saudi plan to combat the woes of 1979 appeared to have been a smashing success: the mujahideen had helped take down the Soviet Union. In 1988, Saddam was declared the winner of the Iran-Iraq War. Alas, the mujahideen came home from Afghan still wanting to fight, and Saddam was fifty billion dollars in the red. While the Saudis weren't breathing down his neck, the Kuwaitis were. And in August 1990, Saddam unveiled an unusual way to pay back the billions he owed them. He annexed Kuwait. DC was soon on the line: they had photos that indicated that Saddam would invade Saudi Arabia too.

Bin Laden offered to protect Saudi Arabia with his Stinger-toting jihadists and to run the Iraqis out of Kuwait, Muslim-to-Muslim, Arab-to-Arab. The royals nearly laughed off the offer. Instead, they offered him a contract to renovate the Grand Mosque in Mecca. To protect the oil, they brought in hundreds of thousands of U.S. servicemen, Western infidels, giving them carte blanche to wander the holy Islamic land (except for Mecca and Medina, where foreigners were not welcome to tread); to some, including bin Laden, it felt like a rerun of the Crusades, especially when troups stayed for thirteen years.

FAHD'S CALL

The other royals cautioned against it, but King Fahd insisted. Letting the U.S. military into Saudi Arabia in 1990, says former ambassador to Riyadh Chas Freeman, who accompanied Dick Cheney, then secretary of defense, and General Norman Schwarzkopf to Saudi Arabia in August 1990, was Fahd's call alone. With them they carried a satellite map prepared by the CIA, which showed Saddam's forces amassing at the border of Saudi Arabia, a map whose legitimacy some have questioned, but a map that convinced Fahd, as Schwarzkopf kneeled before him and explained it, simplifying the case in black and white, and ignoring the grays, according to Ambassador Chas Freeman. Fahd's response: "Are you prepared?" The king got a detailed plan of what would become Desert Storm, the Persian Gulf War of 1991. Impressed, the royal gave it a nod. Abdullah, then crown prince, was hesitant, but Fahd didn't want to risk going the way of Kuwait, a country he noted was now living in hotels. And to ensure that the arrival of infidels would be accepted, he nudged the Grand Mufti to write a fatwa allowing Western troops to set up in the holy land, believing they would stay only a few months.

It was a costly decision in every respect. King Fahd shucked out seventeen billion dollars to the United States for the war. He forgave loans from other Arab countries and paid them additional billions to fight with the coalition. He paid off the ulema to get the okay to allow the foreigners in. But still the fatwas condemned the move. All the more when Saudi Arabia was routinely attacked, pummeled with Scud missiles. And though it rarely made the ink of the printing presses, Riyadh itself was continually struck, with Scuds killing at least a hundred residents, according to U.S. ambassador to Saudi Arabia at the time, Chas Freeman. The workforce was so rattled that a third of the workers fled and all the Saudis who could went on a long vacation. And at war's end, the United States didn't go.

But the costliest decision of all was Fahd's dismissal of bin Laden's offer. His male ego wounded, bin Laden, once gracious, transformed into a loud badmouthing machine. So vitriolic were his diatribes against the ruling family, that in 1991 he was asked to leave the country. Even from Sudan, his antimonarchial stance was so provocative, that he was stripped of Saudi nationality in 1994. But in Sudan he regrouped, hooking up with an Egyptian member of the Muslim Brotherhood, Ayman al-Zawahiri, who, like bin Laden, had served in Afghanistan. Together they began scheming, eventually forming what became al Qaeda, with the Western world and the Saudi royals as their target.

> On June 25, 1996, a truck bomb pulled into the Khobar Towers housing complex, a U.S. Air Force living area outside of Dhahran. The explosion that left a crater where a housing tower had formerly stood, killed nineteen American servicemen. It has long been blamed on Iran, although the Sauds beheaded the militants believed responsible for it before the FBI could question them. Now many, including former secretary of defense William Perry, think it was al Qaeda. One reason: in videotapes the suicide bombers made, they hailed Osama bin Laden. It's most unlikely that an Iranian or Shia would pledge allegiance to a Sunni Arab.

Bin Laden wasn't alone, however, in condemning the royals for allowing the U.S. troops in and allowing them to stay. The clerics didn't like it at all, nor did plenty of Saudis. And from 1991 until 2003, when Abdullah forced the troops to leave, the Saud monarchy was at its weakest ever, losing not just respect but control, as terrorist acts became common in the once-peaceful kingdom and as more and more called for the overthrow of the House of Saud.

Saudi Arabia is now at a dramatic crossroads: economically unable to turn back or to slash Western ties; socially and religiously unable to ignore the calls to do so. The good news is that King Abdullah is more able than any other royal to see the country through this difficult moment: more religious than party-hearty King Fahd, he's trying to address the country's ailments and to placate the religious establishment. The bad news is that Fahd handed over a steaming heap of woes and no amount of air freshener can cover the stench. Abdullah has managed thus far to keep the place from falling apart. But the problems that rose up in 1979 still hiss from the shadows.

Hotshots

While their country is rocking with calls to change—some demanding more religion, some demanding more freedom—the al-Saud princes continue their international gallivanting, stealing the spotlight for being both heroes and hellions: Prince Waleed swoops in to save flooded villages and ailing businesses, as well as the government-funded religious schools that mold militant zealots. Abdullah personally handed over $7.2 million in 2004 for tsunami relief; other princes throw parties that cost nearly as much and are so raucous they make Paris Hilton's seem tame. The late Prince Ahmed won the world's most prestigious horse race, the Kentucky Derby, in 2002; the late King Fahd lost millions in Monte Carlo in one night, playing poker. Talking religion out of one side of the mouth, dealing oil diplomacy out of the other, the princes' reputations often have been forged on excesses, be they reports of servant beating, booze running, using diplomatic immunity to smuggle tons of cocaine,[25] or shopping sprees in Marbella, Spain, where the royal entourage racks up hundreds of thousands of dollars of sales every hour. A few of the most famous royals:

Prince Sultan bin Abdul Aziz: Crown prince and head of defense since about the time Saudi Arabia has had one, Sultan's now one of the country's richest princes, thanks in part to those hefty "commissions" plucked from every arms deal. He's built up an impressive arsenal, though few Saudis know how to use these high-tech weapons. He ruffled U.S. feathers when he cut off American military access to the state-of-the art Prince Sultan base for the U.S. invasions of Afghanistan and (theoretically) Iraq, claiming that Saudis couldn't be involved in missions that killed Muslims. Known for philanthropy, he's respected for privately building a billion-dollar hospital and funding wildlife reserves. Born in 1924, he's tapped to follow Abdullah into the power seat, but the clock's a-ticking to see if he can live long enough make it.

Prince Salman bin Abdul Aziz: Powerful mayor of Riyadh, which he runs like a fiefdom, he hired the U.S. developers that transformed what was practically a village into a sparkling metropolis (landing untold bags of money in commissions). A born-again Wahhabi in charge of a few controversial charities (as well as moving the mujahideen to Afghanistan in the 1980s), he also owns the London paper *Asharq Alawsat*, known as a whitewashing machine. Questions swirl about the untimely deaths of his sons, particularly Prince Ahmed (see p. 207).

Prince Naif: Minister of the interior, increasingly anti-Western, and accused of blocking investigations into the 1990 bombings against Americans. Naif blamed Israelis for besmirching the reputation of Arab Muslims after the 9/11 attack (see p. 193).

Prince Bandar bin Sultan: Fun-loving, hard-drinking, flirtatious Bandar— former Saudi ambassador to the United States, current national security adviser, and about the only guy in the kingdom who can actually fly the fighter planes the Sauds so love to buy. He remains an important link in U.S.-Saudi relations, so much so it's said Turki quit his job as ambassador because Bandar never really backed out. Said to be behind the "redirection," pointing al Qaeda militants toward Iraq to battle Shia, he's been instrumental in guaranteeing oil supplies to the United States. Recently slapped for allegedly taking bribes of some two billion dollars to arrange the purchase of British warplanes. Well, what would you expect—he's a Saud, and look at his pa, Prince Sultan.

Prince Waleed bin Talal bin Abdul Aziz: He stays out of politics but is well-known as the sixth-richest man in the world and the largest foreign investor in the United States. He bailed out Citibank in 1991, saved Euro Disney in 1994, and is a one-third owner of Four Seasons hotels, which are popping up all over the Middle East. His post-9/11 check for ten million dollars was tossed back by New York City mayor Rudolph Giuliani in 2001 after Alwaleed lectured that the United States should examine its Middle East posture, but he's also demanded that Saudis examine why fifteen of the nineteen hijackers came from their country.

Prince Turki bin Faisal bin Abdul Aziz: Briefly ambassador to the United States (he resigned in 2007, after eighteen months), and former ambassador to the United Kingdom, Turki was Saudi Arabia's head of intelligence for twenty-five years, suspiciously stepping down ten days before the September 11 attacks. During the 1980s, he helped fund and funnel mujahideen into Afghanistan to fight Soviets and later set up the Taliban to take over. Back before Osama bin Laden was infamous, Turki tried to persuade him to give up his guerrilla-training ways in Afghanistan and return to Saudi Arabia. Mysterious Turki seems to know lots more than he's telling.

Prince Ahmed bin Salman bin Abdul Aziz: Charismatic horse fanatic who bought the 2001 Kentucky Derby winner ten days before the race, Ahmed was also a media mogul, running dozens of publications out of London. He died in summer 2002, theoretically from a heart attack, though some say the forty-three-year-old was murdered, alleging he was linked to al Qaeda (see p. 192).

Prince Abdul Aziz bin Fahd bin Abdul Aziz: King Fahd's favorite son, he was reportedly signing the kingdom's checks during the reign of his pa. Controversially, he signed some four billion dollars' worth of them to build his new palace, definitely a bad PR move in these testy times.

Prince Talal ibn Abdul Aziz: Saudi Arabia might be a whole different place if only Talal had succeeded with his plans. In the 1950s, as finance minister to Saud during one of Saud's frequent fights with Faisal, Talal and a handful of his kin (the so-called Free Princes) convinced the king that Saudi citizens should have more rights. A constitution was drafted, but at the last minute Saud nixed the idea, saying the Koran served as the country's constitution. Talal left for Cairo, and Beirut, where he'd married the prime minister's daughter, Mouna al Solh, who had a hand in the BBC movie *Princess*. Talal recently returned to the kingdom, as feisty as ever. Now an adviser to Abdullah, he's still calling for democracy and has started up his own political party that's outlawed in the kingdom.

Rajaa Al-Sanea: Author of *Girls of Riyadh*, a novel exploring the spicy details about life behind the veil, Al-Sanea so angered the clerics there were calls for her death. King Abdullah put his foot down with a royal decree that shut the clerics right up. Amazingly, Saudis can even buy her books—in Saudi Arabia, no less.

Hot Spots

There isn't really just one kingdom of Saudi Arabia. There are at least four, all with distinctive "personalities," backgrounds, and outlooks. Namely:

Nejd: This central area, which includes Riyadh, is mostly desert and was previously inhabited by tribals and wandering bedouin. The people of the Nejd, the area from which the House of Saud originates, are typically the most hard-core Wahhabis.

The Eastern Province: This area where oil was first found is the most heavily guarded since it contains most of the oil fields, oil refineries, and military bases and is where most of Aramco's sites are located, including Dhahran, a processing center that holds about 10 percent of Saudi oil at any given time. It also is home for most of the country's Shia population, by some estimates a third of the population there or more, which makes the Sauds even more jittery about the place.

Asir: The least-developed, the poorest, and still populated by the last remaining tribes, some of whom live in grass shacks, this southern province rubs against Yemen—geographically and politically. Seized from Yemenis in 1934, its loss is still a sore point for the government of that country: it's believed that Saddam promised to give it back if Yemen supported Iraq in the 1991 Gulf War. The area where Osama bin Laden's mother was born, it's known to look unhappily at Riyadh's rule and is the region whence most of the 9/11 hijackers came.

A desert castle in Hejaz.

Dorothy Miller, Courtesy of Saudi Aramco, ASC

The Hejaz: This southwest region holds the holy sites Mecca and Medina, as well as the cosmopolitan port city of Jeddah. In some cafés and businesses in Jeddah women may even be so daring as to unveil.

Mecca: The city where Mohammed first started preaching is strictly for Muslims only and the site of the annual pilgrimage, the hajj. Nearly every year some pilgrims are killed by crushing, but in 1990 over fourteen hundred died in a mass stampede. Three years before, a hundred perished the same way when Iranian Shia, prone to turn the event into a publicity platform for praising the ayatollah, caused a riot. The 1979 siege of the Grand Mosque, however, was the most chilling pilgrimage in recent history.

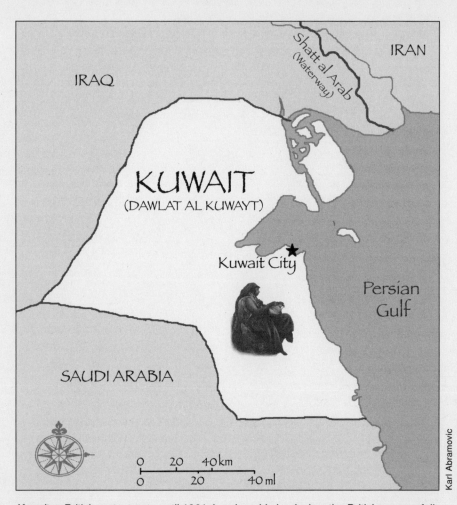

Karl Abramovic

Kuwait, a British protectorate until 1961, is vulnerable by design: the British purposefully drew its 1913 borders in such a way as to block Iraq from direct Gulf access. Making the nearby islands as well as a three-hundred-mile-long beachfront part of Kuwait while handing Iraq a forty-mile coastline of swamp unfit for development, was a move to block the German-aligned Ottomans who then controlled Iraq from moving into the British-controlled Gulf waters.[1] The British creation of Kuwait as a buffer zone virtually guaranteed the events that would finally unfold in August 1990 and redesign the geopolitical map of the whole Middle East. But Dick Cheney certainly helped.

Chapter Eight

Kuwait: Lines in the Sand

Life looks calm in Kuwait—on the surface.

A former trade stop where pearling boats docked next to mud shacks, Kuwait is now known for three things: oil, money, and Saddam—whose name westerners are more apt to connect with Kuwait than the country's longtime ruling clan, the Sabah. It was oil, specifically a disputed field, and money, in the form of a fifteen-billion-dollar Iraqi debt that the Kuwaitis called in, that brought Saddam's troops rolling into Kuwait in 1990. And it was also oil, specifically protection of vital supplies, and money, in the form of the twenty billion dollars the Kuwaitis were dangling, that brought the United States in to run the Iraqis out of Kuwait. But perhaps there's more to it—perhaps there's a reason why the United States fiercely blocked attempts to prevent what most agree now was a preventable war.[2] Perhaps since the Soviet Union—the "evil empire"—had just crumbled, the United States actually wanted a war that would serve as its entry into the Middle East. Perhaps then secretary of defense Dick Cheney needed a war to justify his nearly three-hundred-billion-dollar defense budget for pricey Stealth bombers, Patriot Missiles, and a highly conceptual antimissile defense shield.[3] As the *New York Times* reported on August 1, 1990, "In a blow to the Bush Administration, the House Armed Services Committee voted today to end production of the Stealth bomber and cut nearly $2 billion from the Pentagon's proposal for the 'Star Wars' anti-missile program."[4] The next day, Saddam—having been told by the U.S. ambassador to Kuwait that the United States had no opinion on an "Arab-Arab" war—sent his army into Kuwait. Four days later, Cheney was in Riyadh, with a satellite photo that he said showed Iraqi troops were at Saudi Arabia's border—a claim that was an overstatement,[5] perhaps an outright lie.[6] Whatever the motivations, what started in August 1990 rearranged the Middle East. In many ways, it became Cheney's playground—as secretary of defense, as vice president, and as CEO of Halliburton. And in every way, Kuwait has paid.

FAST FACTS:
Dawlat al Kuwayt

Government:	Constitutional monarchy (emir with parliament—usually)
Formed:	1961, after it cut political ties with Britain, under which it had been protectorate
Ruler:	Emir Sabah al-Ahmad al-Jaber al-Sabah
GDP 2006:	$111 billion (IMF, 2007)
Per capita GDP:	$33,000 (IMF, 2007)
Population:	2.6 million (1.3 million are nonnationals)
Unemployment:	2 percent
Literacy Rate:	94 percent men, 91 percent women
Ethnicity:	45 percent Kuwaiti, 35 percent other Arab, 9 percent S. Asian, 4 percent Iranian, 4 percent other
Religion:	85 percent Muslim (70 percent Sunni, 30 percent Shia), 15 percent other

---

Population stat: foreigners, about half of the population, make up 80 percent of the workforce.

Leader's Corner

Ruler/emir: Sheik Sabah al-Ahmad al-Jaber al-Sabah. The former prime minister Sabah wasn't slated for the ruler's seat, but he ended up in it shortly after the 2006 death of his half brother, the emir Jaber. Kuwait's parliamentarians questioned the fitness of doddering crown prince Saad al-Abdullah al-Salim al-Sabah, who was sick with cancer and believed incapable of reciting the two-line swearing-in oath. Sheik Sabah pushed in, demonstrating he had no such problem. He has others: ministerial resignations and battles with lawmakers keep shutting down the government. Kuwaitis are ticked about everything from the state of health care to the state of schools—and asking when the oil wells will run dry and how much remains in the "oil nest egg" to fund the future. The Muslim Brotherhood waits in the wings of parliament, ready to transform Kuwait into Saudi Arabia's twin (complete with Islamic law) should the Sabah dynasty give the wrong answers. Here's betting the emir won't pass on the message the international finance community keeps whispering in his ear: sooner or later, Kuwaitis—most with high-paying government positions requiring only a few hours of work daily, but demanding even better pay—are probably gonna have to get real jobs.

WHAT MATTERS

Energy matters: The oil that first bubbled up here in 1937 has brought Kuwait plenty of dough, along with twitchiness and woe over who is eyeing the black gold. Lately, the worst threats come from energy analysts. Kuwait says it holds over a hundred billion barrels, 9 percent of world oil reserves. *Petroleum Intelligence Weekly* says Kuwait is sitting on about half of what it claims.[7] The IMF predicts Kuwait's oil may be exhausted in twenty-five years.[8]

Electricity matter: Electricity demands are soaring in this air-conditioned society, and most of the plants are powered by fuel oil. The government says it'll be switching to natural gas, but we expect the nuclear salesmen should be showing up any second.

Arms matter: Kuwait's loyalty to the United States has been rewarded with its designation as a "major non-NATO ally," allowing sales of otherwise hard-to-obtain arms including Patriot antimissile systems, Stinger missiles, and a billion dollars' worth of Apache copters. Since the 1991 Gulf War, Kuwait has tossed upward of two billion dollars yearly in the direction of U.S.-made weapons.

Military matters: Having paid the United States $16 billion to chase out Saddam's soldiers in 1991, and another $4 billion for "containing Iraq," Kuwait contributed only $260 million to the 2003 Bush-led war on Iraq. Kuwait kicks in $200 million yearly (in services in kind) toward keeping Iraq stable now that Saddam's gone. However, as "supply central" for the occupation next door, Kuwait makes a pretty penny as well: convoys of trucks filled with Kuwaiti goods roar over the border, and Kuwait was hired to build the $1.3 billion U.S. embassy in Baghdad.

Religion matters: Sunni-dominant Kuwait typically embraces the one-third of Kuwaitis who are Shia, but during the 1980s there were problems, due mostly to radical Shia from other countries. There's no drinking in public places, but Islam is not harshly enforced, and workers can practice whichever religion they choose.

Money matters: The Kuwaitis are shrewd investors: their investments in the United States, Germany, Turkey, and beyond typically bring them far more than their oil. Their investment in Saddam didn't pay off: he stiffed them for fifteen billion dollars, then invaded, but the new Iraqi government has paid back the bulk of the fifty-plus billion the Kuwait government and individual Kuwaitis demanded in war reparations.

Militants matter: The first attacks in Kuwait, in the 1980s, were by Shia militants from Iraq. The most recent attacks have been by Kuwaitis—Sunni who are upset by the U.S. military presence.

Foreigners matter: Kuwait has never wanted many foreigners around, but they are needed for construction and menial labor. Kuwait allows unions and offers more protection to foreign workers than most. Palestinians, once the favored workers, were sent out after Yasir Arafat sided with Saddam in Desert Storm.

Government matters: The ruling al-Sabah family fills most top posts, but the parliament can eject them. Emirs, however, can also dissolve the parliament, which they do frequently.

Ahmad M.Y. A Al-Roomi

Kuwait City was the first Gulf capital with public schools—starting in the early twentieth century—and in this country of merchants accounting was a required subject. Kuwait was also the first country to turn on electricity and erect desalination plants. Potable water was so scarce until the 1950s that traders brought it from Iraq in camel-skin bags.

The fishing boats come in, the oil tankers go out, more money piles up in the coffers, and in this flat country of sand-colored buildings everything appears entirely laid-back and orderly. Except for the ubiquitous presence of U.S. troops and the trucks roaring off to the north, the country's tumultuous past appears to have been folded up and mothballed in some out-of-sight back drawer. Beach lovers plunge into the Gulf's warm water, snorkeling among brilliantly colored coral, boats glide by with billowing sails, and yachters hold racing events that lure the rich and famous from all corners of the map. Locals gather for parties along the waterfront, steaming up shrimp so fresh they smack of the sea.

"Think of a swan gliding across a pond. It all seems so serene—but right below the surface, the swan is actually pedaling as fast as it can just to stay on course."
　　　—An Arab diplomat describing the situation in Kuwait to former State Department adviser David Pollock[9]

ON THE ONE HAND, AND ON THE OTHER

Kuwait has traditionally been the Gulf's pioneer, the first country, for example, with a constitution and a parliament with reps voted in. Established in 1963, the National Assembly has real clout, able to veto decrees and oust ministers from office. Stressing education, Kuwait long boasted the highest literacy rates of the Arab world. There is no religious police, residents can dress as they wish and need not adopt Islam, as evidenced by the smattering of Christian churches amid the thousand-plus mosques. The Shia, sidelined in other Sunni-dominant countries, are better integrated here, represented in parliament and often in the cabinet. Workers can form labor unions, and since May 2005 women can vote. Here, unlike Saudi Arabia, those who kill their daughters are prosecuted; the constitution guarantees legal defense to all.

But headaches there are: foreign laborers, pulling down a hundred dollars a month for trash collection, sometimes go unpaid, resulting in the occasional riot. Workers, even government employees, keep going on strike. Housekeepers are so often exploited that the government set up shelters for runaway maids. The Muslim Brotherhood and other tradition-bound Islamists dominate the feisty parliament, having a fit, for instance, when education minister Nouria al-Sbeih spoke in the parliament sans head scarf; parliamentarians so often eject ministers, they trigger political crises. And when the National Assembly poses a threat, rulers simply shut it down—for years at a time.

Courtesy of Saudi Aramco

When the Kuwait Towers were unveiled in 1979, their novelty garnered international architecture awards. Now they're overshadowed by a flurry of new development. One striking example on the drawing boards is the Cobra Tower, a luxury hotel and office building shaped like an asp ready to lunge; another version envisions it as a twisting double helix of glass.

Under the country's landmark Kuwait Towers, rising like toothpicks garnished with giant blue olives, the well-planned capital is pristine as ever, glimmering with glitzy towers and ritzy stores. Shiny limos, Mercedes, and SUVs (with women behind the wheels) wind along manicured boulevards and the palm-lined corniche dotted with luxury hotels, marinas, and seafood eateries, where these days English is often heard. The theme parks are filled with laughing children, the souks beckon with their gold, the malls are hopping with women clad in everything from jeans to traditional garb as they stop in T.G.I. Friday's and Western department stores, and the *diwaniyas*—the popular meetings where men gather to discuss topics of the day—are back in full swing.

FINDING VOICE

Until 1996, only about one in twelve Kuwaitis—males from the oldest families—could vote, but that year the emir extended suffrage to all males who had held citizenship since 1976. After decades of campaigning, women finally won suffrage in May 2005 and can now run for parliament. The ruling family, which holds most top ministries, takes many of its cues, however, from diwaniyas, "citizen councils," typically open only to males. Stemming back centuries, diwaniyas are typically held in private homes and are so popular that women complain they rarely see their husbands and sons, who spend hours at the nightly power powwows. And the sentiment expressed when locals get the royals' ears, is increasingly conservative and anti-U.S.

Given that there are only one million of them, Kuwaitis (unlike Saudis, Iraqis, and Iranians) actually see the benefits of their country's oil riches. Sheik Abdullah, who reigned fifty years ago, spent his oil money modernizing: paving roads, constructing hospitals, and building houses for his subjects. Soon Kuwait was a cradle-to-grave welfare state. Life for Kuwaitis appears breezy: all health care and schooling is paid for, utilities and food are subsidized, and the government guarantees cushy jobs with three-hour workdays. The government employs 90 percent of the Kuwaitis who work, scribbling out nearly ten billion dollars in paychecks a year and spending another seven billion dollars on citizen subsidies.[10] Marriage brings financial rewards, including a multizeroed wedding gift from the emir, who sends anniversary checks too, and residents don't pay taxes. The government divvies up surplus funds and squirrels away billions in the Reserve Fund

Ahmad M.Y. A. Al-Roomi

Kuwait forbids clubs, and even public musical events are controversial. Young Kuwaitis get around the bans by throwing dance parties at home in their own private discos. Pictured: a new villa with North African influences.

for Future Generations. And as has been its wont since 1961, when the tiny, vulnerable kingdom suddenly became one of the world's wealthiest lands, Kuwait has been helpful to many neighboring countries, handing out no-interest loans that it expects to have paid back.

> Discovered in 1938, Kuwait's oil began gushing in 1946. The Kuwait Oil Company, originally a joint operation of BP and Gulf, flooded Kuwait with billions of petrodollars, but by the 1950s Kuwait was nearly bankrupt. Their "protectors," the British, had guided Kuwait's new wealth directly toward a handful of British firms, who massively overcharged and sometimes didn't deliver. The bum steer only increased the emir's desire to get rid of the Brits. In 1961, Kuwait declared independence, the first of the Gulf protectorates to do so, and by 1980 Kuwait controlled all aspects of its oil industry, from exploration to refining to oil tankers, pumping over two million barrels a day.

DINAR DIPLOMACY

Small and militarily weak, Kuwait spreads its wealth in a show not only of generosity but "dinar diplomacy," which beyond buying friendships is about preventing attacks. The Gulf country was the first to shoot to the top of the oil geyser—by 1960 Kuwait was the region's leading oil exporter and that era's richest—and the emirs knew that money talked. Sheik Abdullah quickly set up the Kuwait Arab Economic Development Fund: through grants and no-interest loans used for building schools, paving roads, erecting electric utilities, and building armies, the Sabah handed out over fourteen billion dollars (in loans alone) to leaders from Dubai to Palestine.[11] And for years those loans effectively substituted for British warships. Dinar diplomacy, for a time, even tamed Iraq, with whom newly independent Kuwait got off to a bad start: the minute the Brits shoved off in 1961, Iraq tried to lasso Kuwait, dropping the notion after being chased off by British and Arab League forces. It should not have been a surprise: for decades Iraq had repeatedly tried to annex Kuwait, using kisses, propaganda, threats, and/or political union schemes to geographically unite the land that was blocking its access to the Gulf. What was a surprise: in 1963 Iraq formalized borders with Kuwait and theoretically dropped its claim to the land, which Iraq believed belonged to it as former Ottoman territory. And Baghdad too was showered with loaned dinars, eighty-four million dollars' worth. That was just the beginning, and but a drop compared to the black hole that Iraq's war with Iran would later create. By 1990, dinar diplomacy showed it wasn't foolproof and could, in fact, provoke the very incursions it had been designed to avoid.

How long the Kuwaiti welfare state can hold up, like the question of how long its oil will last, is cause for debate: the IMF is warning that Kuwait's government expenditures need to be slashed.[12] Even the Reserve Fund looks shaky: five billion dollars recently disappeared. And Kuwaitis gripe that government services are slipping. Public hospitals, trashed during Iraq's occupation, have never returned to their former state; locals complain they're filthy, understaffed, and woefully behind the times. A brouhaha recently brewed up when the health minister spent billions sending the ill abroad for care rather than building new hospitals. Accusing him of using medical vacations to buy votes, parliamentarians (some of *them* accused of purchasing votes) booted him out of office. In response, the government briefly collapsed. Public schools, say locals, are undersupplied: Kuwaitis are ticked that their kids have to share textbooks, which themselves are a source of debate. The government is trying to delete incendiary passages that glorify jihad and insult other religions, but the Islamist lawmakers don't want to yield to pressure from the West, which they say is already influencing Kuwait too much. Demanding to know the exact oil holdings and income (figures held tightly by the oil ministry), parliamentarians blast the government for soaring expenditures on U.S. arms when warplanes are growing rusty from lack of use and few in the military can operate the super high-tech weaponry.

Such bickering only hints at the bigger problem: even with Saddam gone and U.S. bases dotting its land, Kuwait still doesn't feel safe. In fact, the presence of U.S. troops and bases only increases the anxiety in this country. Kuwait worries that Tehran, which kept "accidentally" bombing it during the Iran-Iraq War, will again make it a target if the United States should choose to drop in on that side of the Gulf. There was so much angst about the bellicose words flinging between DC and Tehran in 2007 that Kuwait's government announced in advance that if the United States battles Iran, it wanted nothing to do with it, and the war would not be conducted from here.[13] Iran is not the only concern: Kuwait's hosting of U.S. troops has reportedly garnered the kingdom the top spot on al Qaeda's regional hit list.[14] Kuwaiti militants have attacked and killed U.S. troops on several occasions, and a 2005 showdown between police and militants who were planning attacks on U.S. bases erupted into a days-long shootout in the suburbs. And that was just one more show of the dissent that is brewing up here, where Kuwaitis wonder if their bonds with DC are worth the price. Local sentiment has turned profoundly against DC; the United States is viewed more favorably in Iran.[15]

A 2006 Gallup poll showed that only 13 percent of Kuwaiti nationals held a favorable view of the United States. More alarming: the 34 percent that regards the United States very unfavorably. Factor in the foreign nationals working there and the picture is even less bright: over half of the people living and working in Kuwait see the United States in a "very unfavorable" light.[16]

The oily black smoke that hung from the skies and the fires that raged for most of 1991 are now but a memory, and the burned-out vehicles on the "Highway of Death" were long ago hauled off. The scorched and flattened buildings have been repaired, the water and electrical systems restored, the university rebuilt, and books restocked on library shelves. The thousand-plus oil wells are pumping as much as before, the museums are again filled, and ducks have returned to the waters skimmed by Jet Skis and motorboats. But despite the billions poured into restoring the capital, in exacting detail, to its state prior to August 2, 1990, when Saddam's troops blasted in, Kuwait has changed.

The Sabah are still in power, as they have been for centuries; the economy is still booming; the fish vendors still heap their offerings on beachfront stands; and the National Assembly, which had been closed from 1986 to 1991, is open and feistier than ever—but appearances belie the fact that Kuwait is scarred, divided like never before and having a panic attack in response to the violence next door. Like the land mines that, despite extensive sweeping, still lie hidden in the desert, there's a lingering sense that something might explode. Exacerbating that feeling is the transformation of the country into supply central for the war next door and the sense that you can't turn around without seeing more U.S. troops or private military contractors, who tend to be the most revved up of all.

U.S. TROOPS IN KUWAIT

The diwaniyas are buzzing with concern over increasing Westernization—the McDonald's and new Hard Rock Café are sore spots, and there's growing anxiety about U.S. troops, up to a hundred thousand of which may be around at any given time. Being the main supplier to Iraq, Kuwait is overrun with trucks heading out over the border, and an entire island is off-limits to Kuwaitis, reserved for U.S. military use; during the 2003 invasion of Iraq, over half of the country was blocked off. While most everyone is happy that the bogeyman to the north is finally dead, joy is now being replaced by resentment. And some Kuwaitis are striking out: in 2002, a U.S. marine was killed by two locals; several months later two U.S. contractors were ambushed by a traffic cop, who pulled them over and shot them. In 2005, Kuwait security rounded up a group of alleged militants, among them Kuwaiti military men. Calling themselves Lions of the Peninsula, they had plans to attack U.S. bases and American interests. The U.S. military presence and the extensive arsenal housed at the bases make some Kuwaitis fear that their country may be another terrorism target, especially if the Bush administration tries to do to Iran what it did to Iraq.

Kuwait shows all the signs of a society under stress. Divorce rates are staggering: in 2007 the Ministry of Justice released stats showing that 53 percent of Kuwaiti marriages fall apart. Drug abuse and alcoholism are quietly creeping in, even a soccer star was recently busted for drug dealing. Crime, rarely an issue

Department of Defense

When an international coalition moved into Kuwait during the ground war in February 1991, Iraqi soldiers left a farewell memento: they purposely leaked an eight-million-barrel river of petro-goop into the Gulf and torched some seven hundred oil wells that belched thick toxic smoke for the next eight months, temporarily crippling Kuwait's oil industry and causing the worst environmental debacle in the Middle East's history. Cancer rates in Kuwait have soared ever since. Then again, the depleted uranium-tip missiles and white phosphorus bombs that the United States was using may have contributed.

before, is skyrocketing, and while foreigners are behind some of it, in most serious cases they are not. Over a thousand serious incidents are reported in a typical month, and about three hundred are violent, including kidnappings and gruesome murders, from the employee who told off his boss with a machine gun to the Kuwaiti who offered an Indian woman a ride to the consulate, then raped her in the desert and killed her with a screwdriver.[17] Kuwaitis are alarmed by the appearance of youth gangs that have been known to lynch and torture foreign workers. Psychologists say the surge in crime (as well as rises in suicides and illicit drug use) is a lingering aftereffect of the 1990 Iraq invasion. By some estimates, at least a sixth of Kuwait's population is still dealing with deep depression and post-traumatic stress; even those who weren't around during the occupation aren't immune—they struggle with a form of survivor's guilt and the guilt of not defending their country.

"Before the invasion, we did not know the difference between bombs and guns and fireworks. [In the years following the invasion], we see machine guns in people's homes, antiaircraft guns on top of houses, guns in the schools."

—Fahed Nasser, an adviser to the emir[18]

> Until 2003, when Saddam was finally toppled, Kuwaitis felt like a nation under siege. Worried about when Iraq would storm in again, arms found their way into most everyone's hands: Iraqis left behind millions of AK-47s, guns, and rifles during their 1991 retreat.

In the early hours of August 2, 1990, Iraqi forces rolled over a territorial divide in a move that set off a series of events that would rattle billions of people for many years and cause a fracture in Kuwaiti society that hasn't yet healed. The events of that day had their roots in 1979. That was the year that Saddam Hussein stepped out from the shadows and took down his predecessor's regime in a bloody coup. That same year also marked the era when Kuwait's rulers began fretting about the nation's diverse population, where a third are Shia. Back then, almost half the residents were Palestinian—doctors, teachers, and laborers, even some PLO leaders—and whatever their status, you don't see very many in Kuwait anymore.

THE PLIGHT OF THE PALESTINIANS

Kuwait didn't like to get involved in the neighbors' affairs, but there was one issue they embraced: the Palestinians. The plight of the Arabs shoved out of their homes by Israel struck even the flintiest of Sabah hearts. After the Arab-Israeli war of 1967, and again after the war of 1973, the Sabah invited Palestinians into their lands, making them the preferred foreign workers. The Kuwaitis even risked international scorn and welcomed in the PLO, pressuring the West to do the same. They nearly crippled the IMF by refusing to loan money unless the PLO was given observer status. And fine thanks they got for it. When Saddam invaded Kuwait, PLO leader Yasir Arafat backed Saddam—a nod for which Palestinians in Kuwait would pay.

When Khomeini came to power in 1979, calling for Shia everywhere to topple their non-Shia leaders, the Sabah rulers had a few reasons to fret. Kuwaiti Shia had extremely close ties with Iran, having often brought in Iranian wives, making a familial bond to Tehran. Urged on by Khomeini, Shia in Kuwait began protesting. The dramatic conversion of Iran into a deeply traditional, Islamic republic, where women overnight donned scarves and the legal system was based entirely on the Koran, merely highlighted how modern and secular Kuwait had become. Fearing that they might not appear quite devout enough in an era of fiery religious fervor when even Sunnis were acting up—as evidenced in the Grand Mosque takeover in Mecca—the Sabah not only emphasized their dedication to Sunni Islam (building more mosques) but welcomed in the Muslim Brotherhood, many arriving from Egypt. Sadat's government had just signed a peace agreement with Israel, a move that every Arab country except Oman condemned. When the Muslim Brotherhood balked at the Israeli-Egyptian peace treaty, Sadat began cracking down on them, pressuring many to go underground. Some just came to Kuwait, where members of the esteemed brotherhood, whose stated goal is to make Islam a predominant part of daily life, complete with undiluted Shariah law, were provided with employment opportunities. The learned scholars became an integral part of the Kuwaiti education system, teaching in classes, devising the curriculum, and writing textbooks.

Like the Saudis, the Sabah family (also Sunni) wasn't thrilled about the shrill call of the Shia a mere falcon's flap across the Gulf. However, Kuwaitis were aloof, always maintaining strict neutrality: during the Cold War they cuddled up to neither the United States nor the Soviets, although allowing both to keep embassies in Kuwait, and they steered clear of regional feuds. But they were roped into tossing billions, then billions more, into Saddam's military pot when he took on the Iranians in September 1980; by some accounts, thuggish Saddam demanded the dough as protection money,[19] a payoff "loan" that allowed the Kuwaitis to keep their Gulf islands, which the Iraqis wanted to use, out of the Iran-Iraq War. Well, in theory at least.

Geography, however, had handed Kuwait a front-row seat to the war: it was hard to ignore when Iraqi warplanes continually ripped through the sky, creating sonic booms, and windows rattled and cabinets shook from the constant bombing twenty miles away. And before long, Kuwait itself was bombed—by Iran. Oops, claimed the Iranians, just an accident. But the accidents kept happening, so many times that between the numerous trips to Iraq to deliver war supplies, medicine, and edibles, the Kuwaitis began delivering food to Iran as well—dinar diplomacy being transformed into dinner blackmail. And still the bombing of their oil facilities and the missiles streaking toward their islands didn't cease: Iran even plucked an unarmed Kuwaiti oil boat out of international waters, demanding an apology before its release.

> *Iran blasted Kuwait for aiding Iraq with money and supplies but maintained it wasn't trying to pull Kuwait into the war. However, Tehran's calls to rebel were having an effect: during a crime wave in 1981 the government deported hordes of Iranians, and in December 1981 the emir's security rounded up seventy-three people believed to be Shia militants trained and funded by Iran, who were accused of plotting against the Kuwaiti government.*

By the early 1980s, Kuwait was blipping loudly on the American radar. The reason: the insecurity unleashed by the Iran-Iraq War prompted the Kuwaitis to invest abroad. The Sabah bought up a Hilton in Atlanta, business towers in DC, and properties from Boston to New Orleans. Now in full control of their nationalized oil industry, Kuwaitis were also expanding it, looking into setting up oil facilities from Hawaii to New Mexico and inquiring about leasing oil-rich land in the

United States, a move to which Energy secretary James Watt gave a quick nod. As the international press praised the Kuwaitis' shrewd investments, which by 1981 were yielding seven billion dollars in returns (even more than its oil), arms wheelers and dealers, from missile makers to State Department reps, began offering to bolster Kuwait's security. The Sabah turned down DC's offers of military aid: the newly formed Gulf Cooperation Council, the defense and economic coalition of the small oil-rich countries and Saudi Arabia, would be protecting the Gulf nations, or so Kuwaitis then believed.

U.S.-KUWAITI RELATIONS

The Americans liked Kuwait's money, and the Kuwaitis liked the investment opportunities in the United States, but the relationship between America and Kuwait wasn't exactly cuddly. Kuwait deplored DC's support of Israel, all the more when DC did not oppose Israel's storming into Lebanon in 1982. The late senator Daniel Patrick Moynihan, former U.S. ambassador to the UN, recalled that Kuwaitis had been "a particularly poisonous enemy of the United States."[20] *The New York Times* reported the disparaging remarks of officials who scoffed at persistent American offers to set up bases or send in U.S. armed forces, blasting the Reagan administration for having the "nerve to talk to us about security while letting the Israelis get away with murder."[21] As Iran's threatening actions grew more extreme, the Kuwaiti press even suggested that DC was putting Tehran up to it, trying to frighten the Gulf countries into cowering behind the United States and ordering U.S. arms. But the royal family was getting spooked, so much so that they put in an order for missiles—an order the Reagan administration publicly turned down but privately approved, and arms maker Raytheon was soon there in Kuwait, installing its new Patriot system designed to shoot down incoming missiles.

Saddam demanded six billion dollars in 1981 alone and kept hitting up the Kuwaitis (and the Sauds) for more.[22] In December 1982, the Kuwait Stock Exchange—a pet project of the emir that had opened earlier that year—painfully crashed: over ninety billion dollars (much of it money from other Gulf rulers) was lost in the course of a few hours, after a pyramid scheme using postdated checks collapsed. The Kuwaiti government was obliged to bail out those who were worst hit. Shaken financially, at least Kuwait had been able to prevent attacks like those in Beirut, Lebanon, where Shia radicals were blowing up U.S. facilities—including a marine barracks in an explosion that killed 241. But Kuwait was not immune. On December 12, 1983, a truck loaded with gas canisters barreled through the gate of the American embassy in Kuwait City, smashing into the main building and exploding. The blast took out most of the building and killed six. Minutes later, bombs went off all over Kuwait: at the French embassy, the Kuwait International Airport, the main refinery, the housing compound for arms maker Raytheon. Those bombs didn't properly detonate, no one was killed, and the plotters—a group of Shia radicals from Iraq called Dawa—were rounded up. By then, Kuwaitis were scared stiff, and all the more when Dawa began hijacking planes and blasting more bombs, demanding the release of the Kuwait 17, as the Dawa gang was called; but Kuwait wouldn't budge.

> *The jailed members of Dawa, an anti-Saddam group out of Iraq, finally walked out of prison in August 1990, when invading Iraqis unlocked Kuwait's prisons, perhaps not knowing they were releasing militants who loathed Hussein and who had attacked Kuwaitis because of their aid for Saddam.*

As the war dragged on, both Iran and Iraq grew more desperate: the war that was supposed to last only three weeks had already lasted three years. Then the war arena turned to the Gulf itself. Iran laid land mines in front of a Kuwaiti oil tanker off Bahrain. It was just a preview of coming attractions. In May 1985, an explosives-carrying car slammed into the motorcade of the emir, killing four; the royal was barely scratched. The next year, five bombs nearly took down Kuwait's oil facilities. Explaining that Kuwait had been "exposed to a fierce foreign conspiracy which . . . almost destroyed the wealth of the homeland,"[23] the emir shut down the parliament, where a majority of Islamists had been elected. It would not reopen for six years.

Iraq kept hitting up Kuwait for more cash, and Iran began hitting on Kuwait's oil tankers, attacking twenty-one in six months. At the next Gulf Cooperation Council meeting, Kuwait's emir brought a crucial matter before the club of oil-rich countries that had formed for mutual defense. Explaining the ongoing threats issued from Tehran, the emir did something the Kuwaitis never did: he asked his neighbors for help. He asked them to carry Kuwaiti oil under their flag. Every single head of state at the table turned down the request.

There was a reason. The Sabah family had a rep for being snots. The fact that Kuwait had always been years ahead of the others (whether in making money or investing it), the fact that Kuwaitis could perform accounting feats long before residents of the other countries could spell the word *one*, had made them both resented and rather haughty. The Sabah were infamous for their insults, which stung all the more when delivered while they turned down a loan request, as when they denied a loan to Jordan, telling the king that a poor backward country like his didn't need a university. There was another reason why the Sabah were unpopular: never known as team players, they ignored their OPEC quotas, pumping more than their allotment and weakening prices for all.

> *"When a Muslim ruler from a developing country would come to the Saudis and say, 'I need to build a new mosque . . . ,' the Saudis would hand them a bag of gold and say, 'Very good . . . please name it after King Fahd.' The Kuwaitis would say, 'Show us your project plans and we are going to send in our accountants . . .' "*
> —Ambassador Kenneth Stammerman in a July 2000 interview with the Association for Diplomatic Studies and Training

The Kuwaitis did eventually find escorts. The Soviets volunteered to transport their oil. No sooner did that news make the wire, than the phone rang with the Reagan team on the line. No need to bring in the Russians. The Americans would take it over.

ANOTHER CLOSE CALL WITH IRAN

The United States already had four frigates in the Gulf, Reagan explained to his cabinet. Escorting Kuwaiti tankers through the Gulf, he was convinced, would not take any more. Kuwait would register its ships through a corporation in Delaware, and fly the Stars and Stripes. Iran, she thought, wouldn't dare attack. But it did, in May 1987, mining the USS *Stark* off Bahrain, killing thirty-seven. Reagan put more than three dozen more warships in the Gulf. Shortly thereafter, Iran mined the *Samuel B. Roberts*; this time no Americans died. However, the United States demolished two of Tehran's ships, two oil platforms, and a half-dozen gunboats in response. On July 3, 1988, when a plane crossing the Gulf didn't identify itself, the USS *Vincennes* fired a missile, hitting the plane. It was an Iranian plane—a commercial flight. All 290 on board were killed.

That strike more or less ended the eight-year war: Iran was too tired to take on the United States, and all parties were sick of the bloody fight that by its end had killed over a million. But the fighting wasn't really over. Saddam, weakly proclaimed the victor, hadn't vanquished his fury. Especially when he, the only Arab leader who had the guts to take on Iran, had to deal with Kuwait breathing down his neck, trying to yank in fifteen billion dollars of outstanding loans when the Sabah knew he was broke. From Saddam's point of view, Kuwait was keeping him down. Kuwaitis were overproducing, lowering the price of oil, and damaging the value of Iraqi currency. They were also "slant drilling" into what he considered his part of the shared Rumaila oil field, sucking up Iraqi oil and further depleting Iraq's treasury of the money he desperately needed. The Kuwaitis, he announced, should pay him for lost oil revenue. He never did like them, and he liked them less when his intelligence agents reported a number of meetings between Kuwait and the CIA: he was convinced he was the object of a U.S.-Kuwaiti conspiracy to take him down. Given DC's defense quandary, Saddam may have been right.

DICK'S DOWNTURN

Dick Cheney knew that same feeling of frustration: the secretary of defense had been working out a new concept for revolutionizing the military with his undersecretary for defense policy Paul Wolfowitz and I. Lewis "Scooter" Libby. It called for fewer fighters, battling with space-age arms—over-the-top weapons, laser beams from outer space, stealth aircraft that eluded radar. It wasn't cheap, but his $307 billion defense budget would change the way war was fought. And it was gonna make the boys at Northrop Grumman, who'd been having a tough go of it fighting off bankruptcy, real happy that Cheney was ordering up $78 billion worth of their B-2 bombers. Not to mention the folks at Lockheed, where his wife soon sat on the board of the directors: they'd be seeing some serious work out of the billions he was requesting for global missile defense. But then, suddenly, the enemy walked out of the room. The Soviet Union was crashing down right before his eyes. The fall of the Berlin Wall was just the start: countries were demanding independence, and Russia wasn't fighting back. This turn of events seemed to negate the need for a super high-tech space-based missile defense system that could shoot down Russia's ballistic missiles before they hit the United States and for planes that couldn't be detected. Even his allies in Congress couldn't muster an iota of support. There were no immediate enemies left, and no way in hell was Congress going to fund his projects. It'd already approved twenty-five Stealth bombers—after that the program would be gone. Or at least that's how it looked on August 1, 1990.

In May 1990, Saddam made the first of his threats. If Kuwait and the UAE kept overpumping, exceeding their OPEC quota for oil production and flooding the market, he was going to take action. He made the identical threat the next month and the one after that. So it was odd that nobody seemed to see it coming. Egyptian president Hosni Mubarak had called Saddam in late July, asking about the buildup of his military at the Kuwaiti border. Just military exercises, Saddam assured him. And Mubarak believed it. Then again, maybe Saddam meant what he said when he talked to Mubarak. Because Iraqi oil officials hadn't yet met with Kuwait's crown prince. And Saddam hadn't yet heard the final insult that would prompt him to give the order to roll.

It would have been understandable if Prince Saad was in a cranky mood that day at the end of July when he walked into the Saudi palace in Jeddah. It wasn't a happy time to be a Kuwaiti, their unpopularity in the oil world now dictating their fiscal policy. First they'd been "advised," a polite way of being ordered, by Riyadh to postpone the debt collection: obviously Saddam didn't have the money on hand. Then they were "advised" to take seriously Saddam's demand for twelve billion dollars in reimbursement for lost oil income. Saudi king Fahd said he would even kick in a few billion. Thus pressured by the Arab oil producers, all of whom agreed with Saddam that indeed the Kuwaitis were overselling, Prince Saad was forced into the meeting with Iraqis in Jeddah. Negotiations had gone on for hours but had stalled over a single billion: the Kuwaitis offered to pay nine billion dollars, the Iraqis wanted at least ten. That billion turned out to be the most costly sum the Kuwaitis never paid.

Prince Saad wouldn't compromise on the point, even though Saudi king Fahd had said he'd pay the difference. Saad further infuriated the Iraqis by giving them pointers on how to lower their interest rates on debt. At that point, the Iraqi nego-tiator played the religious card. Iraqis had fought to prevent Iran from spreading into Arab countries. Couldn't the crown prince see they were in dire need? The Sabah were good Muslims—that ten billion dollars would be alms for the poor. And it was at that point that Prince Saad reportedly turned the blade. If the Iraqis were that bad off, he queried, why didn't they send their women out into the street to earn some cash? Beyond being rude, the statement hinted at the rumors of Saddam's illegitimate birth.[24]

After a bout of screaming that brought the Saudi guards running to the room and the Iraqi negotiator and the Kuwaiti crown prince a few inches from duking it out, the battle for the money was over. But the battle for "the nineteenth province of Iraq," as Kuwait was called in Iraqi schoolbooks (which never referred to it by name) was just about to begin. Barely twelve hours later, the crown prince was roused from his sleep. The Iraqis were rolling in. At news of the invasion, the en-tire Sabah family piled into cars and raced toward Saudi Arabia, followed shortly by nearly all the generals of the Kuwaiti army. The lower-class *bidun*, homeless Arabs who made up 90 percent of the army and police, stayed in Kuwait with their weapons in hand. But in the generals' haste to flee, they hadn't given the bidun orders to shoot. The soldiers were out in all corners of the city, sitting on cars, looking bored and confused.[25]

In August, the saunalike heat drives anyone who can leave out of the Mideast, turning cities into near ghost towns. A third of Kuwait's population had already left, well into the first hours of the summer getaway when the Iraqis took the capital with barely a boo. Another third, mostly foreign workers, fled. But the third that remained, those who couldn't get out and those who wouldn't get out, re-fused to give up their homeland to Saddam. And that's when the Muslim Brother-hood charged into action. While the Sabah set up a government in exile in hotels, the Muslim Brotherhood stayed, running the resistance alongside the third of the population that stayed behind. They secretly delivered food and medical supplies and ran the emergency services for which they were already well-known in Egypt.

Wheeling out territorial claims that went back to the Ottoman Empire, Hussein proclaimed Kuwait as Iraq's long-lost nineteenth province and stuck in his cousin Ali (best known for the gassing of Kurds) as president. Holding foreigners hostage, his troops cut off food supplies, snapped international phone lines, and looted everything they could find, even, according to some reports, eating the animals in the zoo. During their seven-month stay, they depleted Kuwait's banks of billions, robbed museums of their treasures, flew off with most of Kuwait Airways' fleet, and drove off with a hundred thousand cars. They ripped up the infrastructure, destroyed hospitals, shredded public records, and broke into houses and hauled off all they could find while moving into the regal abodes and torching others, along with government buildings and hotels. The sick were cut off from hospitals unless they changed to Iraqi citizenship, artists were forced to paint portraits of Saddam, and singers were forced to sing songs of praise. The Iraqis raped, they tortured, and they killed—over six hundred died at their hands.[26] And when forced out of Kuwait by the U.S.-led coalition in February 1991, they left with a vengeance, setting most of Kuwait's oil wells on fire and draining storage tanks into the Gulf. They also kidnapped hundreds of Kuwaitis, many reportedly snatched from the street. Over five hundred are still missing.

But Saddam's troops, brutal though they were, didn't rip babies from their incubators, and they didn't leave them on the cold floor to die. These were the reasons (besides, of course, oil) that the United States gave to justify the Persian Gulf War of 1991. In truth, it was a heavily propagandized affair, right down to its catchy nickname, Desert Storm. The image of sick infants tossed on the ground and left to die riled up Americans, most of whom couldn't find Kuwait on the map and didn't care much about saving a country of oil-rich sheiks. It also tipped the Senate's hand, changing the majority from opposing to supporting the war—by five votes.

THE PR HOAX THAT LED TO WAR

Only weeks before, the U.S. ambassador to Iraq, April Glaspie, had assured Saddam Hussein, when he'd asked her what she thought of Iraq invading Kuwait, that the United States had no objections to an "Arab-Arab" war. Now that Iraq had marched on Kuwait, however, the White House sure had very strong opinions. President George H. W. Bush was all for taking strident military action. But this showdown would take hundreds of thousands of troops and serious money. Bush knew he didn't have the majority he needed in the Democrat-dominated Congress to approve such a war.

And that's where a young Kuwaiti girl known only as Nayirah entered the picture. In October 1990, congressmen were called to a special Congressional Human Rights Caucus investigating the human rights abuses of Iraqi troops in Kuwait. As the hearing opened, the fifteen-year-old Nayirah took the stand, saying she'd worked as a volunteer in the al-Addan hospital in Kuwait City. A few weeks before, she told the legislators, she had been tending to premature infants in the pediatrics wing of the Kuwait City hospital. Suddenly Iraqi soldiers stormed the hospital and burst into the room. "They took the babies out of the incubators, took the incubators, and left the babies on the cold floor to die," Nayirah testified, breaking into sobs.[27] The congressmen were stunned, so was the press in attendance (others were given a media pack with notes on the testimony); Amnesty International condemned Hussein for the display of heartlessness, reporting that 312 babies had died at the hands of the Iraqi soldiers. And President Bush worked those 312 dead babies into numerous speeches selling his war. Bush ultimately won Senate approval for his war by a mere five votes. But there was one problem with Nayirah's testimony: that grim tale was a load of horse puckey. Five months after the war had been officially wrapped up, ABC reporter John Martin tried to corroborate the story in Kuwait. According to the physicians Martin interviewed, there weren't 312 incubators in all of Kuwait. The heart-wrenching testimony, it turned out, had been given by the daughter of royal family member Saud Nasir al-Sabah, the Kuwaiti ambassador to the United States. It's believed she wasn't even in Kuwait when Iraq invaded in August 1990. The hoax was the work of Hill and Knowlton, one of the world's largest PR firms, whose Washington office back then was headed by Craig Fuller, Bush's former chief of staff. As for the congressmen who'd chaired the hearing, Tom Lantos and John Edward Porter, their Congressional Human Rights Foundation received a fifty-thousand-dollar donation from the Kuwaiti royal family.[28]

U.S. Air Force via Wikipedia

The 1991 Persian Gulf War saved the defense budget of then secretary of defense Dick Cheney, which had been under serious attack by Congress until Saddam marched his troops into Kuwait. The war also gave a chance to try out some pricey new additions to the U.S. arsenal, from Stealth bombers to Patriot missiles, which supposedly intercepted a high percentage of the Scud missiles lobbed at Saudi Arabia and Israel. Later reports showed they weren't so effective at all: Israelis asserted the success rate was between zero and 20 percent.[29] Here sleek F-15s and F-16s soar over burning Kuwaiti oil wells.

The air attack raged for three weeks, but once troops entered Kuwait for a land battle, the fighting was over in four days. Before the tanks of the thirty-country coalition President Bush had assembled even pushed into Kuwait, most Iraqis were already on their way out, being called back by Saddam, who was complying with UN Resolution 660 that called for withdrawal. But few of Saddam's troops made it back to Iraq, being slaughtered en masse along a sixty-mile stretch of road the press dubbed the Highway of Death.

Sgt. Joe Coleman, Department of Defense, Desert Storm series, via Wikipedia

The details of what happened on the Highway of Death on February 26 and 27 of 1991 still aren't clear, but an estimated sixteen thousand fleeing Iraqis died[30] after being deluged with bombs. The U.S.-led coalition may have used controversial weapons, including white phosphorus bombs that burn off skin to the bone. Another questionable act the press neglected to point out: if Iraqis were indeed retreating, the coalition may have violated the Geneva Conventions with this barbarous attack, which at the very least contradicted White House spokesman Marlin Fitzwater's promise that the coalition would not attack withdrawing Iraqis.

"I visited Kuwait two or three days after its liberation, and have never seen anything like the black sky and the towering flames, something resembling the floor of Hades, on the one hand, and the so-called Road of Death north of Kuwait, in which perhaps 16,000 Iraqis were killed as they left Kuwait with their loot, in many cases killed by phosphorus bombs, which do not produce a pretty corpse."

—Ambassador Chas Freeman, one of the first
to witness what had happened in Kuwait[31]

Not all was what it appeared in Kuwait. The liberation, as captured on TV, showed Kuwaitis euphoric and waving American flags, flags that had been pressed into their hands only moments before by the U.S. government's favorite PR man, John Rendon. "If any of you either participated in the liberation of Kuwait . . . or if you watched [the liberation of Kuwait] on television, you would have seen hundreds of Kuwaitis waving small American flags," John Rendon said in his speech to the National Security Council. "Did you ever stop to wonder how the people of Kuwait City, after being held hostage for seven long and painful months, were able to get hand-held American flags? And for that matter, the flags of other coalition countries? Well, you now know the answer. That was one of my jobs."[32]

As those who had fled returned to their homeland, they were met by anger and resentment from those who stayed, and the society was quickly divided into "insiders" and "runners," distinctions that still remain. According to the "insiders" interviewed by Mary Ann Tétreault in her book *Stories of Democracy*, those who hadn't been in Kuwait during the occupation exaggerated what had happened to help sell the war to coalition members.[33]

When the emir returned in the middle of March, the once-shimmering airport where he landed was bombed out and scorched, and his palace was in ruins. Despite a small group that turned out to cheer him, the emir, who covered his face to hide his tears, had hit the lowest point in his thirteen-year rule.[34] Resuming power, he declared martial law and gagged the press, and the roundup began of those accused as collaborators; that is, the ones forced to paint portraits of Saddam or sing songs at art openings. The world press was shocked at Kuwait's kangaroo courts.

Particularly hard hit were Palestinians: since PLO leader Arafat had endorsed Saddam's occupation, Palestinians were seen as collaborators, and perhaps some of them were. But all were now in danger of being lynched by Kuwaitis or, at least, questioned by security. Some were tried before closed military tribunals, and some ended up in mass graves. Nearly all the Palestinians who could, quickly fled; their numbers in Kuwait dropped from over three hundred thousand to thirty thousand in weeks. Also condemned as traitors were the biduns who had made up the bulk of the armed forces and police; they weren't rehired, and ever since liberation there's been a push to get these "Arabs without a nation" to find a new home.

According to the *New York Times*, questioning of suspects—about how many Kuwaiti girls they had raped, and how many Kuwaiti officers they'd turned in—included torture: "They were led through what the police called the party room, barbecue room, and drinking juice room. In each, they said, at least a dozen uniformed troops tortured them: beatings with sticks and poles; electric shocks and burns with cigarettes and heated rods, and forced drinking of what smelled like sewage water."[35]

The residual insanity continued for months, and some might say Saddam's fingerprints still linger. But slowly Kuwait returned to some semblance of normality: parliament was reopened, buildings rebuilt, and the incomplete communication tower that had somehow survived the Iraqi stay was finished and named Liberation Tower. And the fears that lingered while Saddam remained a threat—on several occasions he reassembled and tried to come back—have now been slain along with the tyrant himself. And ever since the man who so rearranged their lives was last seen hanging from a noose, many Kuwaitis would like to see the force that took him down pack up and go.

Hotshots

The Sabah powerhouse: The Sabah clan has ruled here for centuries, but the succession changed over a century ago when petulant Prince Mubarak committed the only violent acts known to the family. In 1896, he fatally shot the emir, his half brother Mohammed, and his son stabbed to death the emir-in-waiting, Jarrah. Regarded as the founder of modern Kuwait, Mubarak, who proclaimed himself Mubarak the Great, aligned the country with the British, and his sons, Jaber and Salim, respectively came to rule upon his death. Their descendants, known either as the al-Jaber or al-Salim, form the two family branches, which, until recently, avoided conflict by alternating rule. That changed in 2006, when Crown Prince Saad, a Salim, was ousted from the ruling chair by Kuwait's parliament, and Sheik Sabah, a Jaber, took his place, going on to tap his brother as crown prince and installing Jabers in many top posts. The result: a royal ruckus that raised eyebrows as princes verbally duked it out, their dirty laundry flapping in the press. Animosity so poisoned the air that the emir called together two hundred royal males, telling them to shut up and also nixing a rumor that he planned to rewrite the constitution and abolish parliament. "Our constitution has no flaws," snapped the emir, "you are the flaws."[36]

The Islamic Constitution Movement: Political parties are outlawed in Kuwait, but the Muslim Brotherhood, which ran the resistance during Iraq's seven-month rule eighteen years ago, has been gaining prestige ever since. Its political arm is the Islamic Constitution Movement, whose members are the National Assembly's most numerous, conservative, and loud. Liberals say the government encourages these and other Islamists to be politically active simply to stall needed reform.

President George H. W. Bush: Struggling, like Cheney, to defend the 1990 defense budget when the Soviet threat suddenly disappeared, Bush cautioned that the United States had to worry about enemies that rose up from unexpected places. Amazingly, he uttered that warning in a speech given just hours before Saddam's forces rolled in to Kuwait.[37] Blocking moves that would have prevented a war, including offering Saddam a Kuwaiti island and halting early negotiations with Saddam, Bush ordered the war that brought the United States permanently into the Middle East. After Desert Storm, as his war was marketed, the United States negotiated security agreements with Gulf countries, sold multibillions in arms, and opened new Gulf military bases that allowed American hegemony over the region. Forgiving billions in debt to form an international coalition that included Arab countries, many of which the Sauds paid to sign up, Bush first launched Desert Shield, which controversially brought half a million troops into Saudi Arabia in 1990; this was followed by Desert Storm, which liberated Kuwait in 1991; his son finished off Saddam's regime twelve years later. In 1993, when the elder Bush stopped by Kuwait, he was greeted by flower-throwing crowds and honored with the country's highest civilian award. The celebration was marred by an attempt on Bush's life: Iraqis were blamed for the failed car bomb. Despite his crucial role in the country's recent history, there's nary a statue of the liberator or a street bearing his name.

DÉJÀ VU DICK

Lending a strange sense of déjà vu, Dick Cheney, who as defense secretary led the United States into the Middle East and Iraq in 1991, took us back under even more dubious circumstances in 2003, when he was the younger Bush's vice president. His desire for fancy armaments appears to have played a role in both wars.[38] The weapons and programs he had to fight Congress to fund in 1990, indeed became part of the arsenal, with the Stealth bomber and Patriot missile systems first put to use during the first Iraq war. The initial phase of an antimissile shield, a land- and space-based program that theoretically would shoot down incoming missiles, was also funded on his watch. Given the huge expense and poor performance of the missile defense program, it was about to be shot down again in 2001, when Cheney and Secretary of Defense Donald Rumsfeld lobbied for a new, even pricier global antimissile shield, a project estimated to cost one trillion dollars by the time it was done. Congress just could not justify it. And then September 11 provided the reason not only to put hundreds of billions into the new generation of "Star Wars" but, thanks to Cheney's knack for spin, to take down Saddam and shoot permanent roots in Iraq.

Hot Spots

Iran: Sitting just across the Gulf, Iran is one country the Kuwaitis don't want to tango with. Lately, Kuwaiti officials are quick to chime in with their support for Tehran.

Border with Iraq: The 150-mile divide between Kuwait and its former enemy is now lined with fences and electronic sensors and heavily patrolled by security. To the northwest, a stub of the finger-shaped Rumaila oil field shared with Iraq enters Kuwait.

Border with Saudi Arabia: The 137-mile map line is still contested in parts, and along it one finds "the neutral zone," where oil fields are shared between Saudis and Kuwaitis.

Gulf Cooperation Council: Independent-thinking Kuwait recently whacked the Gulf states' plan for a shared currency when it cut the dinar's peg to the plummeting dollar, which the other currencies are still tied to. However, there's increasing talk that the others might do the same.

Bubiyan Island: The largest of Kuwait's isles, Bubiyan was always a temptation for Iraq, which sits a mere three miles away. Saddam tried to convince Kuwaitis to part with it as part of the "restitution package" he demanded from them. It's likely to emerge as a sore spot in the future, all the more with plans to build the Gulf's largest container port there.

The undeveloped hinterland: Sheik Sabah's recently unveiled $9.3 billion investment-and-development package includes expanding urban areas, including creating a new Silk City to the north, to highlight Kuwait's history as a crucial stop on the legendary Silk Road. Also in the works: a new port, this one Kuwait's fourth, planned for Failaka Island, currently used as a U.S. artillery range.

U.S. military bases: Still spooked after Saddam's invasion, Kuwait initially welcomed CENTCOM's army, which set up at four bases, the most famous being Camp Doha. With ninety thousand troops stationed here at various times, and more flying in for a break from the misery in Iraq, the bases themselves are a target for terrorist attacks. To minimize potential conflicts, troops are typically kept on the bases.

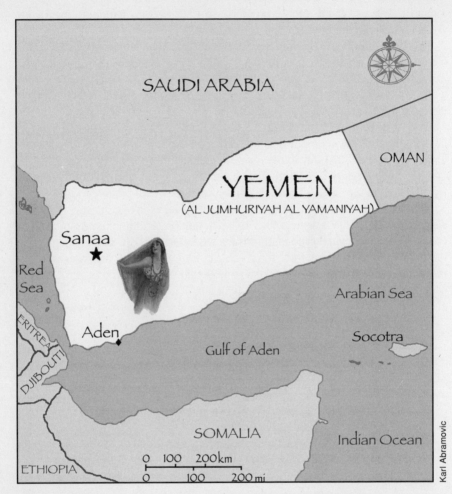

This southernmost chunk of Arabia sits in a dangerous corner. Pirates and militants threaten ships cruising near Bab el Mandeb at the mouth of the Red Sea, a hazardous chokepoint through which tankers pass to bring oil to the West. Even rinky-dink fishermen are being nabbed and held hostage. Land borders are worse: smuggling of arms, drugs, and child slaves is so rampant that Saudi Arabia is building a high-tech wall to seal the problems out. Yemen's eastern regions, once famous for frankincense, are now the lands holding oil, but these are the most lawless regions and attacks on pipelines are frequent. In the northwest, around Saada, the army has been battling a religious cult for three years but can't win despite the help of al Qaeda, now paid fighters for the government.

Chapter Nine

Yemen: In Another World

Eric Lafforgue

Soaked by monsoon rains, lush highland plains unroll against sweeping mountains. In small towns and villages, where most Yemenis live and where tribal chieftains reign, traditional garb and odd headgear abound: women herders, like those pictured here, stave off the searing sun with airy high-topped hats. Travelers adore this unusual land.

The crossroads of early trade, where dhows laden with oriental treasures pulled in and camel caravans set out loaded with frankincense and myrrh, Yemen once sparkled as the wealthiest, most sophisticated land in Arabia. Ancient Yemeni trading routes linked the Mediterranean to the South Pacific, medieval cities of towering mud buildings rose from the desert, and fifth-century engineers built massive dams and elaborate irrigation canals that kept the place brimming with food. Now the stunning architecture is *all* that remains of the land's lofty past: the wealth and knowledge of previous eras have vanished. Yemen is now the Middle East's poorest and most backward land: half the population can't read, and farmers shun food crops to grow profitable khat, a mildly narcotic shrub that's wildly popular here. Yemen is awash in arms—the government estimates there are three times more weapons than people—and five shooting deaths a day are reported, a fraction of what occurs. Tourist kidnappings and bombings of ships only hint at what's happening in this land fractured between north and south, central government and tribes, militants and sects. The reason the long-ignored country now loudly blips on the U.S. intelligence radar is that Yemen is the new headquarters for al Qaeda and friends. Beyond targeting tankers, bin Laden's boys are plotting the destruction of Saudi Arabia's oil network from here. Yemen's government appears to be helping.

FAST FACTS:
Al Jumhuriyah al Yamaniyah

Government:	Republic (in theory)
Formed:	May 22, 1990 (union of North and South Yemen)
Leader:	President Ali Abdullah Saleh (1990)
GDP 2006:	$21.6 billion (IMF, 2007)
Per capita GDP:	$972 (IMF, 2007)
Population:	23 million (July 2007 estimate)
Unemployment:	35 percent (2003)
Literacy rate:	70 percent men, 30 percent women (2003 estimate)
Ethnicity:	Mostly Arab; also Afro-Arab, S. Asian, European
Religion:	68 percent Shafii (Sunni), 30 percent Zaidi (Shia); 2 percent Jewish and Christian (all estimated)

Population stat: Yemen's population grew by a third since 1994, understandable since the typical woman bears seven children; with several wives, men frequently sire more than twenty offspring.

Leader's Corner

Despite pretenses of being a transparent democracy, Yemen's government is a one-man, one-clan, corruption-riddled show.[1,2] A land of double-speak and deception, it's a dubious ally in Bush's "war on terror." President Ali Abdullah Saleh was a hot-tempered army officer when he clamped on to the presidency in 1978, a seat that opened in North Yemen after two previous presidents were assassinated in rapid succession. When North Yemen (a military regime) merged with South Yemen (a socialist regime) in 1990, President Saleh came with the package. After the assassination of several southern political leaders, the south seceded in 1994.[3] Aided by

Courtesy of Embassy of Yemen in DC

Never can say good-bye? Thirty-year president Ali Abdullah Saleh is grooming his son Ahmed to fill his dirty shoes.

mujahideen fighters sent by bin Laden, Saleh yanked it back a few months later, fired southern soldiers, sold off southern businesses, seized southern land, and established northern hegemony with help of his kin. Saleh's son, brothers, and nephews run the armed forces, *and* his clan controls the economy, believed to be one big money-laundering machine.[4] Accused of siphoning off billions of dollars by smuggling oil, Saleh's regime tortures prisoners, intimidates the press, shoots down protesters, and turns a blind eye to the U.S.-supplied arms that keep disappearing from warehouses and heading over the border to mujahideen in Saudi Arabia.[5] Skyrocketing prices, alarming poverty, chronic malnourishment, soaring unemployment, scarcity of clean water, shortages of hospitals, lack of schools, *and* an ongoing war with a Shia cult—a showdown decimating villages, killing thousands, and boosting al Qaeda, while costing over a billion dollars to fight—are a few reasons why Yemen may again split into two. Some fear it will simply crumble. As it is, between tribes, militants, and sects all flexing muscles in this land divided by deserts and mountains, Saleh's government controls only a third of the country.

WHAT MATTERS

Energy matters: Yemen's oil is the backbone of the economy, kicking in 80 percent of the federal budget, but the black gold will be history by 2020. Lots goes missing: so much is smuggled out that gas stations in the country often go empty. Blackouts are routine in the paltry 40 percent of homes hooked to the electrical grid. Good news: natural gas, just being developed, may last decades. Bad news: the deals smack of bribery—the regime sold the rights at below market prices. Worse news: before even conducting a feasibility study, Saleh signed a whopping fifteen-billion-dollar nuclear energy contract with a Texas outfit that's never before worked in nuclear energy.[6]

Arms matter: Grenade launchers? Machine guns? Shoulder-fired antiaircraft missiles? Head to the open-air arms markets where the rat-a-tat-tats are just potential customers sampling the wares. Some are leftovers handed out by Saleh during the civil war; mujahideen bring in more.

Military matters: Some sixty-seven thousand stand under arms, and the arsenal is being upgraded with U.S.-tax-dollar giveaways. Saleh also has a personal security/intelligence agency, the Political Security Organization, in charge of everyday intimidation. The Republican Guard is headed by his son.

Money matters: Dodgy banks, an underground lending network (*hawala*), and questionable Islamic institutions create an environment ideal for washing soiled cash. When the UN mandated closing over 140 bank accounts believed to be funneling money to militants, Yemen complied—by closing one, says Yemen expert Jane Novak.

Religion matters: Yemen is devoutly Muslim, particularly in the north, an imam-led Shia theocracy ruled for a thousand years, until 1962. Shariah law is now in effect. A third of Yemenis are Zaidi, a tolerant sect of Shiism. The rest are mostly Shafii, a tolerant Sunni sect. However, incoming mujahideen are Wahhabi, the austere fundamentalist take on Islam that is spreading thanks to Saudi-funded schools and clerics.[7]

Militants matter: Yemen is brimming with a variety pack of militants, tribals to sects, but mujahideen number over fifty thousand, many loyal to bin Laden. Since 2000, al Qaeda and friends have attacked ships, killed tourists, blasted pipelines and power plants, targeted oil installations, and bombed courtrooms—for starters.

Courtesy Tourism Board of Yemen

Legend holds that Yemen's capital, Sanaa, was settled by Shem, son of the ark builder Noah. The capital's old city, pictured here, is filled with thousand-year-old buildings made of mud bricks and is just one of Yemen's touristic charms.

This strange and stunning land swings open a door to an era long gone: gingerbread towers iced with white trim rise against peaks where homes are honeycombed caves and calls to prayer tell the time. Men clad in skirts wear curved daggers in brightly colored sashes, women speak a secret language unknown to males, and roving bands of flute-playing Sufis chant poems en route to stone shrines. Necklaces of stone houses drape along narrow ridges, coffee terraces carved into mountains are stacked like green stairs to the sky in this country where colliding tectonic plates made a geological accordion of the land. Oxen plow fields, the donkey is the villager's car, and families live in earthen homes where little has changed since Mohammed's day, except perhaps the stained-glass window added a few centuries back. Stone temples hold language undeciphered, water is still pulled up from wells in many villages, and, for most, one's tribe controls all aspects of life, from job to marriage. Visitors gush that there's no place more gorgeous.

THE FLIP SIDE

Al Yaman, as the locals call it, beguiles those who drop by—tourists go nutty for the place. But it isn't so enchanting for many locals, almost half of whom live in poverty. Many suffer from intestinal worms, and polio is making a comeback. Most children aren't vaccinated and half are malnourished; one in nine dies before reaching age five. In the countryside, where 75 percent of Yemenis live and most work in farming, kids are commonly yanked out of primary school to tend fields, and hundreds of thousands are sold to mafias as slaves. Women speak their own language, never socializing with men outside of the family, and rarely even with them, since most floors of the houses are segregated by gender. They are always veiled and often entirely cloaked while in public. They can vote, drive, and run for office, but they're routinely deprived of inheritances and sometimes sold off to visiting Gulf Arabs as "weekend wives" (and then stigmatized as divorcees). In the countryside, women are often betrothed around age twelve and are responsible for cooking, cleaning, the kids, and tending the fields, while the men, like their urban counterparts, hang out for hours with their buddies while chomping on khat, an energy-giving shrub. Never a placid country of peaceniks, Yemen's ever more prone to violence given the ocean of weapons floating about: men don't leave home without an AK-47 slung at their side, clans settle disputes with shootouts, and machine guns peer down from trucks. The volatile situation has become even more deadly since al Qaeda's been thrown in the mix.

Bulging cheeks are common in Yemen. Costing about ten dollars a bunch, khat burns through the budget of those 43 percent of Yemenis who live on less than two dollars a day, although costs are shared in communal chews. Once brushed off as non-habit-forming (that idea is being reassessed), khat is favored among Yemeni men who gather in daily "chews," during which the leaves are chomped then held in the cheek for

Eric Lafforgue

hours. Farmers are switching crops to meet the demand, planting so much of the thirsty shrub that khat now sucks up a third of the water used for irrigation. Connoisseurs note that there are dozens of varieties—some for day, some for evening, some with aphrodisiac qualities—and women are taking up the habit too. Users liken its effects to drinking a pot of strong coffee.

Cities, while more modern—particularly the port city Aden—are nevertheless thick with architecture from former caliphates and ancient kingdoms, and travelers go gaga at the fishing villages with gaily painted boats, the far-flung settlements carved into canyons and connected by spindly bridges, and cliffs overgrown with wind-twisted greenery. Given the heart-stopping beauty and the billions that tourism could bring to the treasury, it's a shame that the repressive government of Ali Saleh is ruining the place—his "kleptocracy" sending poverty to new lows, his security forces ushering in an era of terror. Worse: Saleh is transforming Yemen into a homeland for Islamist militants, who are imposing their extremist views on the locals, and who see Western tourists as targets; bin Laden himself recently endorsed attacking foreigners who've come to admire the scenery although few Yemenis are heeding that call.

Over the past few years, hundreds of Western tourists have been kidnapped in Yemen, usually by members of tribes, who treated them kindly, using the hostages as leverage to negotiate with the government to build bridges, roads, or to switch on the electricity in their villages. When the government gave a nod, hostages were released. Bin Laden's boys have lethally jumped into the action recently: a suicide bomber killed six Spaniards in June 2007, and two Belgians and their drivers were shot down by an alleged al Qaeda member in January 2008.

In February 2008, bin Laden commanded his many followers to stop attacks on Saleh's government, which he praised for inviting al Qaeda warriors to fight alongside the army in a war against a Shia cult. That al Qaeda is cooperating with Yemen's army and bin Laden lauds the actions of Saleh—not long ago called "brave and wise" by CIA head George Tenet and endorsed by President George W. Bush as "an active partner in combating terror"—is one sign of how the United States is being duped. To encourage Yemen's "emerging democracy" and to lure Saleh to join up with the "war on terror," DC has continually legitimized and bolstered his crime-filled government.

> *To aid Yemen's maritime economy, the United States directed ships to its long-ignored port in Aden—the bombing of the USS* Cole *being one thanks—and launched a minesweeping program; DC has sunk two hundred million dollars into developing fisheries and millions more into programs to boost literacy, build schools, teach job skills, train midwives, promote vaccinations, fight corruption, and prevent livestock diseases.*

American dollars launched a coast guard for Yemen, and CIA-trained counterterrorism fighters were handed over hundreds of millions' worth of fancy arms,[8] all to persuade Saleh to crack down on al Qaeda and friends and to round up those perpetrating guerrilla acts.[9] Turns out that many of those special fighters the CIA was teaching the latest in antiterrorist skills were the very mujahideen whom the special fighters were being trained to attack. And those weapons keep getting ripped off by security forces, who are likewise mujahideen, and they're heading over the Saudi border to more mujahideen.

THE MUJAHIDEEN

The word *mujahideen* at its most simple means "Muslim warrior," but the term (along with Arab-Afghan) is widely used to describe the Arabs sent to Afghanistan to fight the Soviets who invaded that Muslim land in 1979. Trained as guerrilla fighters, and given weapons by the United States, mujahideen also were indoctrinated with a heavy dose of extremist Wahhabi (aka Salafi) Islam that legitimizes holy war and stamps in a hatred of infidels and Shia. Wahhabis, who demand religious governments and a return to life as it was in the time of Mohammed, believe that they are the only true Muslims and that it's acceptable to kill those who won't convert. This religious belief has made the trained killers a particularly lethal force. Many, though not all, mujahideen are linked with al Qaeda or similar militant groups.

Matthew Thistle

*Osama bin Laden's family originally hailed from Hadhramaut,
a region in the southeast, where tribes are more important
than government.*

Reigning over a land that's key to oil transport—all the more with future pipelines
that will bring oil from all over the peninsula to refineries here—and edging Saudi
Arabia, whose leaders the United States is bound to protect and al Qaeda wants to
destroy, Saleh is caught in a delicate balancing act: he's forced to bow down to DC
(after 9/11, DC threatened to attack Yemen if he didn't join up on the war on terror),
but if he helps out the United States too much, bin Laden's lackeys lash back. What
gets lost between headlines are the tit-for-tat paybacks, payoffs, threats, and erroneous assumptions. The most erroneous assumption, apparently, on the part of
the United States is that Saleh didn't want al Qaeda and the gang in the country.
He's often benefited greatly from having them around: they helped him lasso back
the runaway south in the 1994 civil war, they're believed to be hit men he uses to
down opponents,[10] and they're now fighting the Shia uprising in the north.

"Three years ago, Yemen stonewalled the investigation of the USS Cole
*bombing. Today, Yemeni authorities have moved against al Qaeda in their
own territory; hosted Army Special Forces to train and advise Yemeni
troops in counterterrorism; and increased contacts with the Defense
Department, CIA, and FBI. In November 2002, Yemeni authorities
allowed a U.S. Predator drone to kill six al Qaeda operatives in Yemen,
including senior al Qaeda leader Abu Ali al-Harithi."*
    —From the White House website: "Waging and Winning the War on
    Terror—Record of Achievement: George W. Bush"

In fact, the part of the picture that's been crucially missing in the portrayal of Yemen as a staunch ally in the war on terror, is that Saleh's government invited the mujahideen to move here in the 1990s: Saleh's half brother, General Ali Mohsen al-Ahmar, is a pal of bin Laden, who paid the general very handsomely (one payment alone was twenty million dollars) to help tens of thousands of mujahideen get cozy in Yemen during the 1990s.[11] Saleh (whom cynics might suspect got more than a free dinner out of the deal) applauded the move, hoping to make Yemen a center of Islamic revival. They came in handy during the 1994 civil war, when the socialist south seceded. For their efforts fighting for Saleh, the mujahideen were rewarded: Saleh gave them jobs in the armed forces and in the administration, even giving them seats as top officials in Yemen's government.

A CRUCIAL LINK: AL IMAM UNIVERSITY

Saleh's pal and one of bin Laden's spiritual gurus, Abdul Mejid al-Zindani, a pinched-face Wahhabi cleric living in Sanaa, has been a key player in organizing mujahideen for three decades: bin Laden hired him in the early eighties to recruit wannabe warriors to fight in the Soviet-Afghanistan War. The cleric performed his task well: Yemenis were second only to Saudis in the numbers who showed up in Afghanistan to fight. When the war ended in 1988, the mujahideen needed a place to regroup, and Zindani volunteered Yemen, offering housing and camps in which to train. Before you could say "ka-ching," Saudi money was flooding into Zindani's bank account to help him open up an Islamic institute, al-Imam University, where thousands of young men could study Islam as interpreted by Wahhabis. DC doesn't see it as a peaceful, clean-nosed operation: the Bush administration alleges that the university's students are being recruited for al Qaeda. The U.S. government also alleges that it is a money-laundering operation that provides financing for al Qaeda, and the U.S. Treasury Department has even devised a special category for Zindani: "specially designated global terrorist." Zindani denies all accusations, and Saleh frequently lobbies the United States to drop the title. The cleric, who mentored John Lindh, the "American Taliban" whom the United States rounded up in Afghanistan, is now shining up his halo with a new role: healer. He says he's found the cure for HIV—that his combo of faith and herbs makes the virus disappear.

Given his close ties with al Qaeda, it wasn't surprising that Saleh at first blocked DC's investigations into the specifics of what happened to the USS *Cole* in October 2000, when a small boat, its two occupants standing at attention and saluting as they neared the warship, exploded, blasting a twenty-foot hole in the warship and killing seventeen U.S. sailors. The source of the explosion was within the ship itself, the regime announced at the start of its disinformation campaign, which lasted for weeks. The obfuscation of facts was all the more understand-able given that Saleh's government apparently aided in the *Cole* bombing: a document introduced at a trial in 2004, considered by the court to be authentic, was written on behalf of Abd al-Rahim al-Nashiri, believed to be the mastermind of the bombing. Signed by the minister of the interior, the letter of endorsement for Nashiri directed security forces not to interfere with any of his activities, add-ing that "All security forces are instructed to cooperate with him and facilitate his missions."[12]

The USS Cole *may have been targeted because it was involved in enforcing economic sanctions on Iraq, which were much opposed in Yemen.*

The stymied investigation of the *Cole* bombing (all the details still aren't in) was helped along by the fact that the attack occurred in the twilight hours of the Clin-ton administration. But that bombing in October 2000 came back to the forefront after 9/11: the Bush administration let it be known that after dropping into Afghan-istan, the military might well stop by Yemen for a cleanup mission. Faced with the possibility of an invasion, Saleh signed up for the war on terror, making a show of rounding up hundreds of suspected al Qaeda members and flying to DC to put on a convincing act that he was on board 110 percent. The Bush administration bought it—U.S. special envoy Anthony Zinni being one to personally vouch for him. The spoon-fed media ate it right up: "Yemeni President Ali Abdullah Saleh has unambiguously chosen Washington's side in its war with al-Qaeda, arresting scores of al-Qaeda suspects," cooed *Time*, and others echoed the sentiments.[13]

Despite Saleh's widely reported crackdowns and roundups—in fact, probably because of them, since al Qaeda was seriously feeling the heat—bin Laden's boys launched another major attack in Yemen: on October 6, 2002, mirroring what happened to the *Cole*, a small rubber boat pulled alongside the French su-pertanker *Limburg* and exploded, blasting a hole in the oil-carrying vessel, which leaked ninety thousand barrels of crude into the Gulf of Aden. In response to al Qaeda's actions, Saleh gave a green light to a secret DC operation in 2002: a targeted assassination that proved the value of the neocon war toy, the drone.

A SCI-FI DEATH IN THE DESERT

The metal buzzards are stashed in U.S. military bases in Djibouti, just across the Red Sea, but the unmanned aerial vehicles began hovering over Yemen in 2002, homing in for a desert kill on the third of November. The eagle-sized drone, carrying a video camera and sensing devices, followed the movement of an SUV crossing the desert in Marib, an unruly eastern province that holds much of Yemen's oil. Inside the vehicle were six men whose movements and cellular phone conversations were being monitored by the National Security Agency in Fort Meade, Maryland. When an agent identified the voice of Abu Ali al-Harithi, alleged head of al Qaeda in Yemen, the National Security Agency gave the green light, a laser was beamed, a button was pressed, the missile was launched, and seconds later al-Harithi and companions were dead and the SUV black cinders in the sand.[14] The Bush administration was "ecstatic"[15] and confirmed that the Yemeni government was involved, although the American media hesitantly pointed out that evidence linking al-Harithi to the USS *Cole* attack was shaky and probably wouldn't have held up in court.

Yemenis were livid, asking what had happened to the notion of being tried for crimes, and irate that their government had allowed an American act of war to be committed on their soil. Saleh was furious as well: while he had known full well what the United States had in mind, the original plan had been to blame the deaths on the operatives themselves, saying a bomb they were carrying had accidentally exploded. The self-congratulatory admissions that the United States was behind it, and that Yemen's government had approved it, made Saleh look like the schemer he is.

Bombs began exploding in Sanaa in the months that followed. In December 2002, a militant broke into a Baptist-run hospital and killed three American medical workers, including a doctor, announcing that it was a payback for the murder by drone. Another militant bombed the court during the killer's trial. Government buildings became targets of bombings. Under pressure, Saleh began backpedaling big time and has been a half-assed American ally ever since: leads aren't followed, rounded-up suspects routinely escape, and he's introduced new rehab programs that are just means of letting al Qaeda members walk. Bin Laden endorsed the new moves, calling Saleh "the only Arab and Muslim leader who is not an agent for the West."[16]

Since then, Saleh's been doing the cha-cha between bin Laden and the United States, a dance step no doubt influenced by who's paying more and who's threatening more ominously that week. How his relationship is going with al Qaeda is illustrated in its attacks, or lack of them, on his turf. Starting in 2006, the United States apparently gained the upper hand: in September al Qaeda tried to bomb two oil plants, and in 2007, between hitting oil pipelines and blasting a power plant, al Qaeda began targeting tourists. Relations between Saleh and bin Laden hit a real low point after the suicide bombing that killed six Italians in June 2007: in a public speech the next month Saleh denounced al Qaeda as "agents of Zionism and colonialism."[17]

U.S. Department of Defense

The bombing of USS Cole, *now repaired and back at sea, is what started the strange relationship between the United States and Yemen. The attack on the warship, as well as that on the* Limburg *supertanker two years later—both in Aden—illustrate the increasing hazards for ships passing from the Mediterranean to the Indian Ocean, a key route in oil transport.*

Bridges between Saleh and bin Laden, however, are now apparently on the mend as noted in the latter's January 2008 message to lay off the government. Saleh's cuddliness with bin Laden's gang is making a mockery of the United States, which is quietly cutting aid. The ostensible reason for DC's sudden frostiness: the dozens of arrested terrorism suspects who keep "escaping" from high-security prisons; when a few are apprehended they "escape" again. In November 2007, when one of the "escapees," Jamal al-Badawi, suspected of planning the *Cole* bombing, turned himself in, the government let him walk after he signed an oath of loyalty. DC had a fit, and even though al-Badawi was rearrested, the damage had been done. The administration is also unhappy with Yemen's rehab programs, through which hundreds of al Qaeda suspects have been released and given jobs, money, and even wives. The rehabilitation efforts aren't very effective: 70 percent repeat their offenses.

> *Now DC is jerking Saleh around: although most prisoners at Guantánamo were released in 2008, the bulk of the hundred-plus who remain are Yemeni. Bush has coyly noted that the United States wants to make sure that those released aren't tortured upon their return, but the real concern is that they'll just be back on the streets. Besides, their release would only be another feather in Saleh's cap, and DC appears to be tiring of giving him feathers.*

Saleh's eroding relation with the United States—at the moment, at least—is only one of his woes. Yemen's economy, heavily reliant on oil—which, like water, is running out—is slipping, and his people are furious. Rare before, demonstrations

Matthew Thistle

Just one example of the serious arms that are common in Yemen, this lethal weapon was part of the arsenal used by Zaidi fighters in the ongoing war in Saada, a city now shut off to journalists and aid agencies.

are now common, as urbanites protest rising prices, lost jobs, and media censorship—protests that Saleh's private security goons break up or his army puts down. Dozens were killed by the government during the summer of 2007 alone, and outspoken journalists, frequently threatened and beaten and sometimes jailed, now face the death penalty for such crimes as criticism of Saleh, whose actions certainly warrant it. The government has cracked down so hard that few reporters dare stray from the government version of anything. This precludes them from speaking with the rebels in the ongoing Saada war, a showdown between the army and Shia rebels that is now effectively blacked out.

THE SAADA WAR

It's hard to discern what the truth is anymore given the regime's penchant for lies and the lack of access to firsthand reporting; reporters and international agencies are prevented from entering the war zone in the mountainous region, where the conflict began in 2004. But most agree it started as a protest movement led by Hussein Badr al-Houthi, a former legislator from a religious family who had rounded up a gang of teens. Called the Young Believers, they began breaking up prayer sessions in the northern mountain town Saada by loudly chanting, "Down with the U.S. Down with Israel. Long live Islam." They later threatened a small village of Jews, telling the inhabitants they had ten days to leave. The Young Believers say they want Yemen to cut relations with the United States and Israel; the government says al-Houthi was trying to reestablish the thousand-year Zaidi (Shia) theocracy that had been headquartered in Saada until 1962, when it was overthrown by the military in a coup that brought President Saleh's group to power. Starting in May 2004, first the army, and then the air force moved in, but al-Houthi's group knew the terrain far better and proved difficult to put down. Despite cease-fires, and the death of al-Houthi in 2004, the fighting has gone on ever since. Now some sixty thousand soldiers are fighting some two thousand Zaidi Shia and bombing out dozens of villages, with thousands dead on both sides. It's turned sectarian, with hard-core Sunni fighters, Wahhabis, brought in. The government is said to be shutting down Zaidi schools and all Zaidi institutions, while encouraging Wahhabism, which never caught on there before. Prayer leaders are hauled off, it's said, in the middle of prayers, and traditionalist Wahhabi preachers take their place, forcing the Shia to convert to Wahhabism or meet their maker. Some believe it's part of a plan to wipe out the Shia.

Most Zaidi don't back the Young Believer movement, and most Shafii don't back the Wahhabis, who are the least tolerant Muslims. Historically, Wahhabis killed off those who don't adopt their rigid traditionalist beliefs, a tendency that goes hand in hand with the fact that many of the incoming Wahhabis are mujahideen.

Blamed for heavy-handedness in the ongoing war, which some believe the government doesn't want to stop until the Shia have been converted or are wiped out and Wahhabism has been implanted in the North, Saleh, who is believed to have converted to Wahhabism himself,[18] has shown the same delicate touch throughout the country, particularly in Aden and the south. After the 1994 civil war, he fired all southern government employees, including all southerners in the armed forces, putting hundreds of thousands out of work. Southern businesses and southern real estate were seized by northerners, and Shariah law was imposed. The southerners are among the poorest Yemenis, and their socialist background makes them a target of Wahhabi rage. Should a showdown brew up out of these tensions, a possibility that is looking increasingly likely, you can be sure that al Qaeda troops will be sent in for fighting, as they were in the 1994 civil war.

What's mostly getting missed by the media, which still sings the "Yemen is a staunch ally in the war on terror" tune, is that Saleh's government is doing more than embracing al Qaeda as fighters and members of government. Saleh is empowering them and, through new Saudi-built schools and institutes such as

Courtesy of Yemen Tourism Board

Yemen exists in a time warp, particularly in the high-altitude mountains such as these in Amran. Only three out of every hundred people in the country have bank accounts, one in twenty has a phone, and one in a hundred has access to a computer. But the twenty-first century is charging in: satellite TV dishes and mobile phone towers are slowly appearing, oil pipelines rip through archaeological sites, modern weaponry is held by almost all, and the occasional U.S. spy drone ominously hovers overhead.

HISTORY IN A BOX: THE NORTH/SOUTH DIVIDE

Frankincense and myrrh, hauled by camel alongside pouches of spices, gold, and jewels, put Yemen on the ancient map, the hub of a complex trading system that stretched from the Mediterranean to the South Pacific. Powered by vast wealth from trade, a dozen civilizations took root here—Minean, Sabbatean, Roman, Ethiopian, and Persian among them—and early Yemenis were ruled successively by polytheists, monotheists, Jews, and Christians. As trade by ships replaced the camel caravan by the third century AD, this corner of the Arabian Peninsula, particularly the interior, became isolated, the riches once spread by camel caravans drying up. The arrival of Islam in the seventh century, however, brought new vitality and locals fervently embraced it. Northern mountain tribes, however, were at war, and in 893 a wise man was called in to settle disputes. His arrival in the walled highland town of Saada triggered a religious shift. Until then, most Yemenis were Sunni of the open-minded Shafii school, but al-Hadi Yahya bin al-Hussain bin al-Qasim, as the wise man was known, was a Shia imam of the liberal Zaidi sect, and the number of practitioners grew as the imam's religious rule stretched across the north. For the next thousand years, Zaidi imams reigned over much of Yemen, although the imamate was occasionally overthrown, as in 1539 when Ottomans claimed the territory; by 1635 they were pushed out.

A shipwreck in 1837 off the port city Aden reshaped the nation's political contour. Locals killed the crew of the British East India Company ship, and the British demanded redress. The local prince agreed to part with Aden but soon died; his son negated the promise. The British besieged the city in 1839, soon turning Aden into a thriving port and coaling station for their ships passing to and from India. A decade later, the Ottomans snatched northern coastal towns, ending the imamate in 1872. As Ottomans swept the north, the British swept the south, signing up emirates as protectorates. In 1904, the foreigners drew a map splitting the land into Ottoman and British territories, which would become North Yemen and South Yemen. The Ottomans, having lost their empire, shuffled off in 1919, and another imam restored Zaidi rule to North Yemen, while South Yemen, Aden, and its environs, remained under British control. The warrior Ibn Saud militarily clamped on to part of the imamate in 1934, making these former Yemeni tracts part of his Saudi Arabia, but the British stopped the Saud fighters from going farther.

In 1962, with an eye to the Saudis' oil-rich land, Egyptian president Nasser sponsored a coup to overthrow the imam and install a republic tied to Egypt. The angry Saudis armed royalists, Yemenis who opposed the republic; the Egyptians armed the republicans; and a civil war brewed up that lasted eight years, killing over a hundred thousand. The republicans won, ushering in a military government, but in the south another ordeal kicked up: locals ran out the British in 1967 and established a Soviet-backed socialist country. North Yemen and South Yemen went at it with border wars and assassinations, but the two sides merged in 1990, in a marriage of convenience that centered on the new wealth promised by oil discovered a few years before. But instead, Yemen, which in 1991 refused to back Desert Storm, found itself poorer than ever and shunned by most of the world. The north-south marriage has been falling apart ever since. A wave of assassinations of socialists as well as underrepresentation of southerners in government prompted the south to secede in 1994, and although pulled back into the union, it has been largely disempowered.

al-Imam University, is encouraging the spread of Wahhabism that comes as part of the mujahideen package. Enabling al Qaeda to steal and smuggle weapons to Saudi Arabia and even guiding its fighters to the border with the Saada war, Saleh's regime is only helping with bin Laden's goal to take down the monarchy in Saudi Arabia. Roundups in that country show that weapons from Yemen—rifles, bombs, missiles—are flooding in and being used in al Qaeda attacks, including the December 2004 attack on the U.S. embassy in Jeddah. What's more, recent crackdowns reveal that Yemenis loyal to al Qaeda are ringleaders in plotting bigger attacks: a bust in December 2007 brought to light a plan, headed by a Yemeni, to attack a Saudi port on the Red Sea. Perhaps Saleh's arm linking with bin Laden's boys is just a means of staying in his power seat. Then again, one might wonder if while winking at the United States he is giving a nod to a plan to make a move on Saudi Arabia in hopes, perhaps, of regaining land that once belonged to Yemen and was lost to Saudi Arabia seventy-five years ago—land that is now believed to hold oil. In any case, it's no surprise that Saudi Arabia, over the howls of Yemenis, is currently erecting a high-tech border fence.

At least some of the effects 1979 had on this country are obvious: Yemenis played a major role in organizing mujahideen to fight in the Soviet-Afghanistan War that began that year, and after it was over, provided the fighters with a new home base where they could plot more attacks. What's not so readily apparent is another link that came into play that year. Saleh, just beginning to flex his muscle as North Yemen's new president, forged a costly bond with another leader who stepped up in 1979: Saddam Hussein. The closeness between the leaders went beyond Hussein's invitation for Yemen to join his new club, the Arab Cooperation Council, an economic-political-military alliance that also included Jordan and Egypt and was a flip off to the Saudi-headed Gulf Cooperation Council. Saleh's friendship with Hussein, who provided economic aid to the country, also hurt Yemen immensely. The reason: North Yemen and South Yemen unified in May 1990, a move believed to increase prosperity. Unfortunately, three months later Saddam Hussein's army invaded Kuwait. The Yemeni government, influenced by a payoff (discount oil and promises that Saddam, if he won, would re-

Mathew Thistle

Arms aren't the only thing crossing into Saudi Arabia. Hundreds of thousands of children a year have been snuck across the porous northern border, some to sell prized Yemeni cattle to Saudi buyers or bring back supplies on donkeys, but many are sold off as slaves. A recent report showed that one out of three kids in northern Yemen is involved in illicit over-the-border work, usually led by crime rings believed to have connections to elected officials.

turn lands lost to the Saudis in 1934), refused to back the U.S.-led coalition that chased the Iraqis out of Kuwait. As a result, Saudis and Kuwaitis cut off their hefty economic aid (over two hundred million dollars a year) and DC slashed aid as well. Worse, the Saudis and Kuwaitis kicked Yemenis out of their kingdoms, firing them from jobs that had greatly bolstered the incomes of their families back home. Over seven hundred thousand Yemeni workers and their families trudged back to their corner. The sudden swelling of the workforce and the just-as-sudden dropping of aid spelled massive unemployment: crime soared as smuggling, car-jackings, and kidnappings for ransom became commonplace. The fledgling country quickly became the Middle East's poorest. And the crippled economy only set the backdrop for the 1994 civil war, from which Yemen has never fully healed.

Saleh's bond with Saddam also played out with oil: when sanctions were clamped on, Saddam's smuggled oil made its way here, part of a smuggling network that remains in place today. Although bonds with Saudi Arabia and Kuwait have been since restored—joining the war on terror didn't hurt Yemen's credit rating—Saleh's friendship with Saddam almost cost Yemen again: after Saddam was put to death by hanging, Saleh imposed a forty-day mourning, an act that so infuriated some in Kuwait there was heated talk of again cutting aid to Yemen.

Hotshots

President Ali Abdullah Saleh: (See "Leader's Corner," p. 238.)

Brigadier General Ahmed Ali Abdullah Saleh: The president's eldest son heads the elite Republican Guard and Yemen's Al-Hay car company. Likely future prez.

Prime Minister Abdul Karim al-Iryani: The prime minister, and a geneticist educated at Yale, al-Iryani vehemently denied that mujahideen had anything to do with the *Cole* bombing, although he did admit they worked for the government.[19]

Abdul al-Rahim al-Nashiri: Mastermind of the *Cole* and *Limburg* attacks, was rounded up in the UAE and ended up in Guantánamo. Said al Qaeda plans to launch more attacks on ships in the Strait of Hormuz.

Aden-Abyan Islamic Army: One of Yemen's many mujahideen groups, they claimed responsibility for the attack against the USS *Cole*, but what's for sure is their involvement in kidnapping sixteen tourists in 1998, hoping to negotiate a prisoner exchange. The government moved in and four tourists were killed in the shootout.

Yemeni Jews: There used to be about sixty thousand Jews in Yemen, but in 1948, after a Jew was accused of murdering two Muslim girls, they were widely persecuted. The United States and Britain organized a secret operation to get them out, flying most of the population to Israel as part of Operation Magic Carpet.

Jane Novak: A New Jersey–based journalist, Novak started up a blog to keep up to date with U.S. troops. Scouring world news, she ran across a case of a detained journalist in Yemen and began publicizing the case, becoming fascinated with the faraway land that few can find on the map. Before long, her blog (www.armiesofliberation.com) became a compelling roundup of Yemeni news interspersed with informed commentary and was making news in Yemen. Her site is now banned in Yemen and the government won't let her in.

Arthur Rimbaud (1854–91):   The decadent French poet who, with paramour Paul Verlaine, pioneered the Symbolist movement, Rimbaud one day torched most of his writing, left France, and after jaunts through Indonesia, Cyprus, and Ethiopia, ended up in Aden, shipping coffee.

Hot Spots

Bab el Mandeb: This seventeen-mile-wide chokepoint may soon be linked to Djibouti by a bridge built by a Dubai-based outfit: the project's head is bin Laden's half brother, Tarek. It would be the world's longest suspension bridge, and Tarek envisions that it would be crossed by car and rail, with ritzy hotel developments on either side.[20] In the meantime, piracy is rising. In 2007, twenty-five attacks were reported between the Persian Gulf and the Red Sea, most near here, and due to insurance concerns attacks are vastly underreported.[21]

ADEN

Encircling the crater of an extinct volcano, which forms a deep natural harbor, the port city of Aden, framed by bony mountains, is the most cosmopolitan, and debauched, city in Yemen, the only place where you'll (maybe) find clandestine bars and illegal prostitution, which linger despite the Shariah law put into effect thirteen years ago. Former headquarters of the British (the anniversary of their 1967 departure is still celebrated), the capital of South Yemen (dissolved when it merged with North Yemen in 1990) was the site of such brutality during the socialist rule that hundreds of thousands ran north, and it was often attacked during the 1994 civil war. Home to an aging oil refinery built by Brits, who brought oil from Persia here, Aden and its once important port had been ignored by the West since the British were chased out, but in the late 1990s the United States took the "emerging democracy" under its wing and tried to revive it by using it as a refueling stop and building up nearby fisheries. The idea that the West was trying to coax a democracy here did not play well with hard-core Muslims and the mujahideen. The Islamic Army of Aden began making bomb threats against Western targets and demanding that the Saleh government itself be overthrown and replaced with a theocracy. Ever since the bombings of the USS *Cole* and the *Limburg*, insurance rates for ships traveling here have skyrocketed, meaning that, once again, few ships pull in.

Marib: Situated in the East and the entry point into the vast Empty Quarter desert that extends into Saudi Arabia, the oil-holding Marib region was in the tenth century BC home of the Queen of Sheba, whose Moon Temple still remains, although inscriptions and assorted archaeological treasures have recently vanished. Dominated by two tribes, Marib is definitely out of government control—some might say simply out of control—one reason al Qaeda and friends like it so. They've even taken to marrying into the tribes here and elsewhere across Yemen.

Shabwa: Another oil region, Shabwa was recently the site of an oil robbery: tribes hijacked a tanker truck and filled up local gas stations, which were running dry as a result of the area's chronic oil smuggling.

Mukallah: A former center of boatbuilding and fishing, this Gulf of Aden port is turning into a major oil-export center: a refinery's going in, and a six-billion-dollar oil pipeline in the works will pump crude from all over the peninsula to here. Too bad it's in the Hadhramaut region, ancestral homeland of bin Laden, whose daddy came from here. The territory is still favored by militants.

Mocha: Made famous during the fifteenth century because of Yemen's new high-value crop, coffee, Mocha became the name given to the chocolaty Arabica beans that came out of the port city. By the seventeenth century, trade was so brisk that merchants had grown wealthy, even building lavish palaces. The imamate promptly annexed the city, and coffee fueled the theocracy's economy for centuries. When the British snagged Aden, developing it as a regional hub, business in Mocha, no longer the sole exporter of coffee, dried up, and today it's home to less than fifteen thousand.

Mystical and windswept Socotra, where medieval inhabitants practiced magic, sits away from the mainland in the Gulf of Aden. Odd flora and fauna that aren't found anywhere else flourish on the island, including the dragon's blood tree (pictured above), which bleeds red sap.

Courtesy of Yemeni Tourism Board

Chapter Ten

The United Arab Emirates: The Land of Possibilities

Novelty is a big sell in the UAE. Pictured here: Ski Dubai, where Emiratis have had their first glimpse of snow—in a mall.

Want to see the new Middle East? Look at the land that fans out along the eastern shores of the Arabian Peninsula: a mix of golden sands and glittering glass origami. Long ignored by the West, the UAE—essentially a small country made up of seven cities of varying sizes—snags headlines now for several reasons. There is serious money flying around: ten times more dough is being spent jazzing up the place than is going into Iraq. Daring architecture is being unveiled at such a dizzying pace that locals liken the landscape to an ever-changing kaleidoscope. It's a showcase for flashy engineering feats: the world's tallest building, Burj Dubai, is shooting up half a mile into the sky; the earth's first underwater hotel is being planted on the floor of the Gulf; and

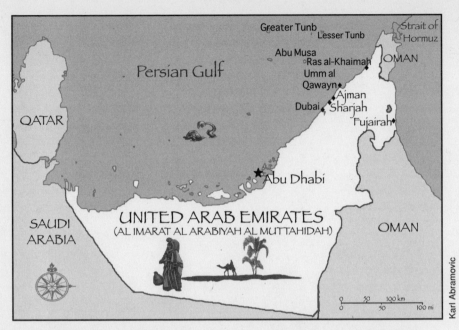

The map shows the United Arab Emirates with labels: Greater Tunb, Lesser Tunb, Abu Musa, Strait of Hormuz, Persian Gulf, Ras al-Khaimah, Umm al Qawayn, Ajman, Dubai, Sharjah, Fujairah, OMAN, QATAR, Abu Dhabi, SAUDI ARABIA, UNITED ARAB EMIRATES (AL IMARAT AL ARABIYAH AL MUTTAHIDAH), OMAN. Karl Abramovic.

Once notorious as a hotbed of piracy, these seven sheikdoms, or emirates, banded together for security after their protector, the British, pulled out in 1971. Smaller than Maine, the jointly ruled federation is dominated by Abu Dhabi, name of both the capital city and the emirate that holds most of the UAE's land and wealth. Dubai yanks the spotlight with luxury tourism, outrageous projects, and even the failed Dubai Ports deal. More affordable and superconservative, Sharjah is living quarters for much of Dubai's workforce. Oil-free emirates, such as around-the-bend Fujairah, lean on petroleum-rich Abu Dhabi for handouts. At the tip, just across from Iran, is an exclave belonging to a different country altogether, Oman—a reflection of British mapmaking in these former Trucial States, so-named after making truces with Her Majesty's men.

man-made designer islands spread out in the shape of palm fronds and Arabic poems. Emirati money is also buying up name-brand companies worldwide: recent acquisitions included Travelodge and Madame Tussaud's Wax Museums as well as the famous luxury liner the *QE2*. When a government-financed investment company in Dubai (the second-wealthiest emirate of the country's seven) bought out the British port company P&O, however, the move frosted typically warm U.S.-UAE relations. The problem: Dubai Ports World would have operated and controlled nearly two dozen East Coast ports, a thought that caused a nationwide panic in the United States. After the U.S. Senate voted to block the move, Dubai backed off from running any U.S. ports, selling those properties to an American company, but the damage was done: now the UAE is cozying up even closer with historical arms seller Paris, pouring billions into the French economy that might have gone into that of the United States. One illustration of the increasing cuddliness: the French are building a naval base there, the first non-American military base to go into the Gulf in over fifty years.

FAST FACTS:
Al Imarat al Arabiyah al Muttahidah

Government:	Federation (some powers to individual emirates)
Formed:	1971, a union of seven British protectorates once called the Trucial States
Ruler:	President/ruler of Abu Dhabi: Sheik Khalifa bin Zayed al-Nuyahhan
	PM/VP/Ruler of Dubai: Sheik Mohammad bin Rashid al-Maktoum
GDP 2006:	$192 billion (IMF, 2007)
Per capita GDP:	$43,000 (IMF, 2007)
Population:	4.5 million (of which 3.6 million are nonnationals)
Unemployment:	2.4 percent
Literacy rate:	76 percent men, 82 percent women
Ethnicity:	19 percent Emirati, 23 percent other Arab and Iranian, 50 percent South Asian, 8 percent other (1982 estimate)
Religion:	96 percent Muslim (84 percent Sunni, 16 percent Shia), 4 percent other

---

Population stat: Emiratis, a minority in their own country—which is brimming with foreign workers—are not all of equal status financially. Their wealth and potential has everything to do with which emirate their families traditionally lived in. Those in Abu Dhabi and Dubai are the wealthiest and get the most generous "wedding gifts" from their ruler—a hefty check and in Abu Dhabi at least a piece of land; real estate is getting tight in rising Dubai.

Leader's Corner

President Khalifa bin Zayed al-Nuyahhan (who is also ruler of Abu Dhabi) and the vice president/prime minister Mohammad bin Rashid al-Maktoum (who is also ruler of Dubai) have a lot in common: they're superrich, they're super-savvy, and they are both second-generation rulers of the United Arab Emirates, which their fathers stitched together in 1971. Few thought this union of rivalrous tribes could stay together, but the leader of Abu Dhabi, the late UAE president Sheik Zayed (ruled 1965–2004), along with the leader of Dubai, the late vice president Sheik Rashid (ruled 1971–1990), kept the fragile federation from fraying during stormy times of constant border disputes. Worldly, Western-educated, and aware of the hazards of relying only on petrodollars, the progeny of Zayed and Rashid display business acumen more likely to be seen in top CEOs than emirs. Perhaps that's not surprising, since they also head their government's weighty investment companies. Abu Dhabi's, throwing around one trillion dollars or so, is believed to be the biggest investment vehicle in the world. Like Abu Dhabi itself, Khalifa is more conservative and camera shy, but he appears to get along well with Mohammad, the show-stealing visionary who reshaped Dubai, the emirate his family rules. Together they are transforming the country's international profile: beyond "oil-rich," the UAE is now a financial giant known for lightning-paced development and never-before-tried projects. The transformation of the country from a sleepy backwater to a dazzling tourist mecca comes with a few price tags. One is the need for new electricity, fast. And nobody's thrilled that the Russian mob has taken a real liking to the place.

IMF

Sheik Khalifa of Abu Dhabi (not shown) is president of the UAE, but vice president Sheik Mohammad of Dubai (above) is guiding the country's direction.

WHAT MATTERS

Energy matters: The UAE holds the fifth-largest cache of oil, over 9 percent of the world oil reserves. Natural gas abounds too, but more comes in from Qatar via the new Dolphin pipeline network.

Electricity matters: Given the wild population growth and requisite air-conditioning, electricity demands already exceed supplies: blackouts are growing frequent. Natural gas powers electrical and desalination plants, but the UAE is moving into nuclear with help from its *bon ami*, the French. The U.S. is dangling nuclear ideas too.

Arms matter: Typically spending $10 billion or more a year on weaponry, the UAE topped the list of global buyers of U.S. weapons in 2000 with a $6.8 billion purchase of eighty F-16 fighter planes loaded with high-tech systems. In May 2004, the UAE signed up for $35 billion in U.S. arms[1] and more is on the way after the Condi-in-the-Gulf ordering spree of 2007. With French Mirage fighter planes, British Aerospace ground-attack aircraft, German warships, Dutch frigates, battle tanks, and refueling planes, the UAE is building a formidable force.

Military matters: The armed forces have only fifty thousand fighters, but to judge by the attention they're rating in local magazines there's a new prestige in being part of the UAE's military. Dubai's deepwater Jebel Ali port is the most common pit stop in the world for the U.S. Navy: even though the U.S. Fifth Fleet is headquartered in Bahrain, aircraft carriers can't dock in its shallow ports and instead stay here.

Money matters: A phenomenal amount of money moves around in this market. In 2007, Dubai had a whopping $365 billion worth of development under way; capital Abu Dhabi has over $200 billion earmarked for development as well. Together, that's about ten times the reconstruction budget for all of Iraq. Four letters not to string together here: BCCI, a bank that Abu Dhabi held majority assets in and that collapsed in 1991 in a multibillion-dollar scandal that involved drug-money laundering, the mujahideen in Afghanistan, the CIA, and even U.S. PR firm Hill and Knowlton.[2]

Militants/crime matter: Two of the 9/11 hijackers were Emiratis, and the initial money for the attack was wired from here, but guerrillas haven't attacked the UAE. The government says its on-the-ground intelligence is why militants don't act up; however, unsubstantiated rumor has it that payoffs are involved. Nobody mentions what sort of arm-twisting the Russian mafia, infamous for demanding "protection," might be up to, but Russians are said to be running the "night butterfly" (prostitution) business while Indians and Pakistanis are more involved with under-the-table loans and smuggling drugs and gold.[3]

Government matters: Ruling families of the seven different emirates appoint members to serve in the governing council, but it's understood that somebody from Abu Dhabi's al-Nuyahhan family will be president, and somebody from Dubai's al-Maktoum family will be prime minister. Emiratis don't vote on their leaders—the leading families have held their lands for centuries, and few are contesting their rule. A new, weak consultative council that represents the people was recently created, and a small group of VIP Emiratis was selected to vote for these reps.

Courtesy of Dubai Department of Tourism and Commerce Marketing

In the United Arab Emirates, top leaders are open-minded and business-savvy, women head government cabinets, the mood is tolerant, and dreams turn into reality: with an Aladdin-like rub of the lamp, a dazzling new landscape is sprouting up. Leading the way is Dubai, here pictured with the trademark seven-star Burj Al Arab hotel. Capital Abu Dhabi is trying to catch up.

"Does anyone ever remember the second man who landed on the moon or the second man who climbed Mount Everest?"[4]
    —Sheik Mohammad bin Rashid al-Maktoum's explanation of why his emirate, Dubai, is obsessed with being number one.

For thousands of years, life in this sandy sweep of land could be summed up in five images: the camel, the date, the falcon, the pearl, and the dhow. The camel was the main form of transportation. The date, actually the seed of palm trees that grow in scattered oases, was a source of food and a cash crop. The falcon was the trained hunter long relied on to supplement the diet with meat. The pearl brought the earliest riches to the area. And sturdy wooden dhows served not only as fishing boats but carried pearls to faraway markets. Until the 1970s, these five symbols remained the mainstays of Emirati life, a world even then largely without cars, roads, hospitals, telephones, or electricity and where most Emiratis, even the leaders, were illiterate.

HISTORY IN A BOX

Even forty years ago, the UAE was mostly sand dunes broken up by the occasional palm grove; back then it wasn't even united—just a stretch of coast ruled by seven different families. The well-being of those living there depended on one thing: trade. Dates fetched good prices, but a more valuable commodity was found underwater: glistening pearls. The opalescent beads, along with frankincense delivered here by camel caravan, showed up in far-flung corners thanks to skilled navigators and seaworthy dhows. Sailing to India and Indonesia, and returning with cinnamon, cloves, nutmeg, and pepper along with indigo, gold, and gleaming gemstones, traders grew wealthy thanks to the European market. In the 1400s, local traders began stopping by Egypt on their return and selling goods to Venetians waiting at Mediterranean ports, who in turn sold these spices and luxury items across Europe. Trade suddenly dried up in 1501, however, when the Portuguese hired an Arab guide who pointed them to India and the Gulf. When the Portuguese arrived in triple-masted warships, the Inquisition-era Catholics were so savage in their attacks that most survivors fled inland as the Europeans conquered the Gulf coasts. Wanting to control all movement of spices and pearls, the Portuguese blockaded trade. Locals could rarely sneak past the Portuguese ships or their cannons that lined the coast. Ships that entered the Gulf were heavily taxed by the Portuguese and often never left. The unemployed traders in turn raided the Portuguese vessels. The attacks on ships were so horrific that this strip became legendary as the Pirate Coast. Still the Portuguese stayed, suffocating local economies for 150 years, until the British, along with coastal tribes, ran them out in 1650. And that's how the British ended up ruling over the Gulf for more than three centuries. The Brits secured an early truce with neighboring Oman, but coastal tribes were hard to subdue, particularly the Salafi pirates from the southern emirate of Ras al-Khaimah, who wanted to keep the region free of infidels. After the British went after Ras al-Khaimah in 1819 and destroyed all its vessels, truces were easy to come by, and this strip changed names: the Pirate Coast became the Trucial Coast, and dhows hoisted special "trucial flags" to keep their vessels clear of flying British cannon balls. The emirates became British "protectorates": the British gave military protection if the tribes traded only with Brits, who settled border disputes, drawing the map of the emirates.

In fact, had not the Brits been parked off these waters, the United Arab Emirates might have a different name: Saudi Arabia. Warrior Ibn Saud, who put together the Saudi kingdom, intended to sew all parts of the peninsula into his country, but the British pushed him back. Local rulers became dependent on British protection: when the Brits shoved off in 1971, these once-warring tribes banded together to bolster their security, formally emerging as the United Arab Emirates the next year.

Two new symbols best capture modern life in the United Arab Emirates: the oil well and the construction crane. The coming of oil money in the 1960s changed everything: the country now holds the region's, and arguably the world's, most ultramodern metropolis, Dubai, and boasts world-class everything, from hotels to hospitals to universities. Now a car is a necessity, air-conditioning is a given, and a quarter of the population is online. Contemporary Emiratis are literate, many in the under-thirty crowd are also fluent in English, and everything is supermodern, including the Global Positioning System devices in every car and high-tech anti-speeding devices that annoyingly beep whenever a vehicle exceeds the speed limit. Now the United Arab Emirates is the land of the superlative, the country where anything and everything is possible. The tallest, the biggest, the first, the latest—they're all rising up in the country's ever-changing and rapidly expanding cityscapes: more cranes, it's said, are creaking in the UAE than anywhere else in the world.

Courtesy of Dubai Department of Tourism and Commerce Marketing

One of Dubai's three Palm Islands designed by UAE engineering firm Nakheel.

The UAE whirlwind is spurring change across the entire region: neighboring countries are jumping onto the luxury-tourism bandwagon that started here; impressed by the daring financial forays of the UAE's investment companies, others are revving up their investment funds too. And many are inspired by the do-gooder acts and donations coming out of the UAE. Dubai's Sheik Mohammad, for example, just put ten billion dollars toward education in the Middle East, one of the biggest humanitarian efforts ever. Like the UAE, the Gulf neighbors are also making a concerted effort to improve the lives of those in other countries, from war-lashed Lebanon to impoverished Yemen. And like the UAE, which is now opening museums dedicated to history (one is devoted entirely to the camel) along with restoring crumbling mosques, sponsoring archaeological digs, and calling for architecture that includes local motifs in designs, others are sinking billions into preserving the past.

The UAE gave one hundred million dollars to the United States in the wake of Hurricane Katrina. Along with Qatar's, it was the biggest foreign contribution to the rebuild-after-the-hurricane cause.

THE COAST WITH THE MOST

If Guinness World Records had a category for the country that tops the most categories, the title would certainly go to the UAE. Just a few projects in the works in this chart-topping land:

Saadiyat Island: Angling to become culture capital of the Middle East, Abu Dhabi is sinking twenty-four billion dollars into Saadiyat Island, planned to hold the world's largest Guggenheim museum (designed by Frank Gehry) and a flashy performing arts center and a branch of the Louvre (France was paid one billion dollars for use of the Louvre's name and shared exhibits) in what is envisioned to be the biggest art-and-culture complex ever. Yale may open an art institute there too.

Masdar: Abu Dhabi's carbonless City of the Future will have solar fields, wind turbines, and an MIT-affiliated Masdar Institute of Science and Technology to figure out how to solve tomorrow's energy woes today. Alas, nuclear is on the boards too.

Man-made islands: The Dutch perfected the process of creating new land, but the Emiratis, with help of development firm Nakheel, are turning reclaimed land into geographical designs and creating a hundred miles of new coastline: the three Palm Islands take the shape of giant fronds stretching out in the Gulf, and the designer isles known as the World Islands are in the shape of a land map, with 192 islands representing each country. They're all for sale: no takers yet for Iraq, but the island of Greece, says its new owner, will boast a luxury hotel. These island projects are rumored to have cost over three billion dollars each to create.[5]

Hydropolis: The world's first underwater hotel, with a price tag of some six hundred million dollars, will boast 220 suites, sunken gardens, a marine biology lab, and a cosmetic surgery hospital assembled in a giant submarine-like resort twenty meters under the Gulf. Guests will be transported through an underwater tunnel via a train.

Dubai Waterfront: The largest waterfront and man-made development in the world, it includes a new downtown and the world's tallest building, Burj Dubai, and will be able to house 1.5 million.

Dubailand: Twice the size of Disney World, this forty-five-thousand-acre amusement complex in the making comprises six individual theme parks, from Dinosaur World and Pharaoh World to Snow World and Motor Racing World. A few highlights of the eighty-billion-dollar project scheduled to open in 2009:

- fifty-five themed hotels with twenty-nine thousand rooms
- a snowdrome with a revolving ski mountain, skating rinks, toboggan run, and penguinarium
- a falcon-shaped city of wonders with replicas of the pyramids, Hanging Gardens of Babylon, Eiffel Tower, and a faux rain forest under a dome
- *Aqua Dunya*, the world's largest cruise ship sailing between three adventure islands
- Planetariums, art and science museums, four sports arenas, sport academies, an autodrome, and polo and equestrian club
- Golf City, featuring a golf academy, a six-star hotel, and five designer golf courses, including one dreamed up by Tiger Woods
- Beautyland, with five luxury spas, a beauty academy, a beauty institute, and beauty museum
- Arabian World, with the Mall of Arabia—twice the size of the Mall of America and featuring the world's largest Starbucks

What's triggering the development frenzy isn't simply a desire to make people figure out where the United Arab Emirates sits on the map. It's both a realization that the oil won't last forever and a means to even out the nation's wealth. The oil money that propelled the UAE into the twenty-first century isn't evenly divided among all seven emirates: Abu Dhabi's oil will last many decades, but several emirates were dealt out of the petroleum hand altogether and must lean on Abu Dhabi for help. The second-largest emirate, Dubai, used to have a fair amount of petroleum, but it's running out. Dubai's depleting oil supply prompted the construction flurry there that is now spreading across the whole region.

> *"My grandfather rode a camel, my father rode a camel, I drive a Mercedes, my son drives a Land Rover, his son will drive a Land Rover, but his son will ride a camel."*
> —Dubai's ruler Rashid bin Said al-Maktoum.[6] Sheik Rashid, who was also UAE vice president until his death in 1990, realized that with finite oil supplies, his emirate had a limited amount of time to diversify the economy.

Wanting to overhaul the economy before the barrel runs dry, Dubai's leaders took a sky's-the-limit approach that is spurring change countrywide, especially since Dubai's ruler, Mohammad bin Rashid al-Maktoum, became the country's vice president and prime minister in 2006. His goal, simply, is to make the UAE into "the most successful country in the world." Aiming to be the planet's leading transportation hub (Dubai's airline, Emirates, is the world's fastest-growing airline), the UAE will soon hold the biggest airport, and port Jebel Ali is already the world's fifth biggest. Beyond goals of becoming the planet's biggest financial market, and the country with the most audacious engineering firms, the UAE, led by the leaders of Dubai, jumped into an arena that had been overlooked there. Realizing that one flashy means to showcase the country and lure billions of dollars into the treasury is through welcoming in foreigners, Dubai created an international luxury tourism industry beginning in 1996. A decade later, drawn by luxury hotels, unique designs, and a rollicking scene, seven million dropped in; Dubai alone is planning to welcome fifteen million tourists by 2010. That trend is spilling over—much of the Gulf region is now being revamped as an over-the-top luxury paradise.

Courtesy of Park Hyatt Dubai

The UAE holds some of the world's most over-the-top hotels. Pictured here, the Dubai Park Hyatt, One&Only Royal Mirage, and Grosvenor House.

JET-SET CAPITAL

Wood-wrapped chalets that peer onto snow-blanketed ski slopes inside a mall. Desert resorts that re-create bedouin villages. Hotels threaded with canals, where guests enter the lobby via gondola, and cliff-top hotels where you arrive via parasailing. Such are a few of the luxury offerings being unveiled around Dubai, the most sizzling hotel scene in the world. Here a sleepery is more than a place to rest your head: with floors of chic outlets—wine bars and sushi bars, beachside oyster bars and leather-couched cigar bars, canopied sunset terraces and thickly chandeliered ballrooms—hotels (typically the only places where you can drink) define Dubai's frenetic nightlife, where the parties can go on until dawn, and the weekend ritual is the champagne-filled Friday brunch. Dubai alone has three hundred hotels. Nearly every luxury chain is setting up there, each competing to outdo the rest, and high-class sleeperies are sprouting up in other emirates too. Shopping is also a major to-do in the country that has the largest duty-free zone in its airports: the annual Dubai Shopping Festival in February pulls in three million shoppers, who toss a billion dollars into the retail cash registers during four weeks. Malls are designed like pyramids or old Arabian souks; the Ibn Battuta Mall is designed like the countries the fourteenth-century scribe visited; you can ski in the Mall of the Emirates, and four more megamalls are scheduled to open. Racetracks for camels and horses are a huge deal in a country where royal families spend big money buying and breeding four-footed runners. The Dubai World Cup lures in the cream of the crop, with a total purse of twenty-one million dollars, bigger winnings than anywhere else in the world: the purse for the biggest race is six million dollars. Golf courses, designed by Tiger Woods and Greg Norman, are ooh la la, and there's an abundance of water worlds and amusement park complexes being built. But the must-do event, locals cruelly insist, is the infamous Desert Safari, an adventure best undertaken by the steely stomached. Setting off into the sands in a four-wheeler, adventurers experience an hour-long roller coaster of violent plunging that makes dunes appear like high ocean waves and wraps your stomach around your neck; the adventure finishes with a camel ride, henna tattoos, and belly dancing at a bedouin camp—enjoyed by those able to rearrange their innards enough to step out of the SUV.

The country's move into tourism is profitable: in 2007 the burgeoning tourism industry kicked $250 billion into the economy, representing 23 percent of the country's GDP.[7] Lavish hotels aren't the only reason tourism is booming: the travel market has changed since the September 11 attacks. Many wealthy Arabs don't want the hassle of trying to land a tourist visa to the United States, once a top travel destination for the Middle East's well-to-do, and instead head to the UAE.

There's another reason that the UAE is a weighty name on the international scene: the government-backed investment companies of Abu Dhabi and Dubai are rearranging the global market. With $100 billion or so to throw around, Dubai's many investment vehicles—Dubai Ports, Dubai World, Dubai International Capital, and Istithmar among them—have acquired big names, from luxury clothier Barneys to German packaging company Mauser. Dubai kept Europe's Airbus—Boeing's main competitor—from folding when its Emirates Airlines placed an order for eighty-one planes in 2007, enough to keep Airbus busy for years. Also helpful: Dubai's ruling family, the Maktoum, invested $850 million in EADS, the parent company of Airbus, becoming a 3 percent stakeholder. Dubai Inc., as the investment funds are collectively known, also holds a 3 percent stake in Sony, a 2 percent stake in Daimler, and minority stakes in companies such as MGM Mirage, HSBC, Time Warner, and Standard Chartered Bank. Even weightier: the secretive Abu Dhabi Investment Authority (ADIA), which has some $1 trillion[8] to throw around. Its offshoot Mubadala holds a 7.5 percent stake in the Carlyle Group, and in late 2007 ADIA sank $7.5 billion into Citibank, becoming one of the top shareholders alongside Saudi prince Waleed.

> *Bourse Dubai (the stock exchange) may invest in NASDAQ: its share would be limited to 20 percent of the New York–based exchange.*

With all the megaprojects under way, the billions of foreign dollars flooding in, and millions of tourists swooping down—not to mention soaring oil prices—the economy is galloping. The UAE's economy, which grew 24 percent in 2006, is the fastest growing in the world. While locals recognize the potential for all emirates to dip into the tourist honeypot opened by Dubai, not everybody applauds the moves that are bringing in millions of foreign workers and foreign tourists. Some locals raise eyebrows at the cyclone of modernization that has touched down: Dubai, some believe, is a sellout. They say the emirate's brash moves have all the subtlety of a come-on from a lady of the night and frown at Dubai's catering to foreign ways, including accepting bars and clubs.

> *Most hotel restaurants serve alcohol, but most restaurants outside hotels don't, and buying hooch for home consumption is tricky: foreigners working in Dubai have to buy a special alcohol card that limits the amount purchased per month. The ceiling is based on income; most booze quotas are capped at two hundred dollars a month.*

More serious problems than booze are creeping in: the Russian mafia is moving prostitutes into Dubai, and certain streets and bars are well-known for call girls, whose business is ignored by the authorities, which really upsets some locals. So does the gay scene, which is tolerated in Dubai, even though homosexuality is illegal. In 2007, the UAE was shaken when a Swiss teen was raped by three Emirati men, one of whom was HIV positive: the incident drew international attention because the boy couldn't prosecute the rapists since there's no law against homosexual rape on the UAE books. Under-the-table money lending and smuggling is also a woe: the traditional Islamic hawala system, an international means of using shops and individuals to loan money instead of going through banks, is still practiced here despite international demands for more financial transparency. And behind closed doors, say locals, plenty of illegal drugs are being smoked and snorted. Teen crime is also on the rise, with hundreds of local delinquents, many from wealthy families, arrested over the past few years for robbery and rape. Psychologists say youth suffer from a lack of direction in the suddenly wealthy society where many don't need to work.[9]

SMUGGLING SECRETS

Historically, the boats coming in and out of the UAE weren't simply hauling off pearls or bringing in spices. The slave trade was big business in the nineteenth century and continued well into the 1960s, with many slaves actually smuggled into Saudi Arabia and sold off during the hajj. For centuries, black marketeers also moved gold, buying it in Europe and shipping it to the Indian Ocean, where smugglers met Indian traders, who slipped it into India duty free. Such smuggling through the clandestine maritime network continues today, though it includes drugs as well. And it overlaps with the informal Islamic hawala banking system, which moves money through a secret network of international merchants and makes following the money trail difficult. The UAE is a hawala center, and some of that money is believed to funnel toward guerrilla groups throughout the Middle East.

Some locals fret that Dubai is opening itself up to too much foreign ownership and that development is proceeding too rapidly, leaving the city vulnerable to even worse traffic jams, water shortages, and electrical blackouts. And ever since Dubai opened the door to the whirlwind of change, plenty are worried that the entire country is losing its heritage. Now the government at national and local levels is shoveling billions into preserving Emirati culture, with heritage villages, new construction derived from old designs, revamping centuries-old mosques, and embracing all that's left from the past, including opening camel museums to celebrate the dromedary (now seen most commonly at the racetracks).

For better or worse, the lifestyle is being irrevocably altered. Even though plenty still don traditional garb—men in white dishdashas, and some women in head scarves and form-cloaking abayas—plenty dress à la the West. Young people are now as prone to speak in English as Arabic—or a popular mix of both. With temperatures that exceed 110 degrees in the summer, air-conditioning is a necessity in a land that long relied on wind towers that caught breezes and circulated them into the home. Air-conditioning now eats up the bulk of the country's electricity. In the land where transport once meant dhow or camel, you won't get far these days without wheels, although speeds are monitored. Harder to keep under control is the legendary road rage and the thick coils of traffic in this pedestrian-unfriendly locale.

ON THE ONE HAND, AND ON THE OTHER

Life is pretty sweet for Emiratis: they don't pay taxes and can sit down for a one-on-one chat with their leaders; the government covers health care and education; food is subsidized; and marriage comes complete with a generous "wedding fund" and parcels of land. Like Kuwaitis, they're provided with jobs—most working for the government—and new universities are coming in, including a branch of New York University. Islam is the official religion, but foreigners can practice whatever they wish. There are even Hindu temples to be found. Foreign workers are paid far more than in their homelands, and you don't hear the stories about domestic abuse that are whispered about in other lands.

Western-style democracy, however, the UAE ain't. Political parties are banned, royal families fill all the posts of the Supreme Council, and normal citizens can't vote—although there's talk about extending universal suffrage for the election of the new, albeit weak, parliament. Few Emiratis are complaining. The glamour of UAE living, however, is not enjoyed by most foreign laborers—many from India, Pakistan, and Sri Lanka—who work long hours for a couple of hundred dollars a month after handing over thousands of dollars to job recruiters for visas, housing, and transport. Unionizing is banned, as are protests for more money; worker safety is jeopardized by lack of a common language. The government says about four dozen workers died in construction accidents in 2005; Human Rights Watch says the real number is over four hundred. Crowded living conditions and worker disputes with employers have led to so much labor unrest that Dubai set up a labor board, and Abu Dhabi now requires that employers pay health insurance. Another problem: trafficking. The UAE has clamped down on the kidnapping of young boys as camel jockeys and is encouraging a switch to robot riders. The record isn't so good on the Russian-mob-trafficked women who are forced to work as prostitutes, in numbers that have soared to some ten thousand a year.

When a documentary about forced sex workers from Armenia working in the UAE aired on YouTube, the UAE government quickly responded—by shutting down access to YouTube.

A final problem is one that simmers below the surface: the threat of terrorism. How is it, some wonder, that with its flashy display of modernity, embrace of consumerism, and hedonistic tendency, the UAE—particularly Western-friendly Dubai—has avoided attacks by militant Islamic groups? Perhaps potential troublemakers stay clear since many tourists are Muslims; some credit the work of the secret police for keeping the place terror-free. But some believe that groups such as al Qaeda are paid off to look the other way. In any case, the UAE has remained not only free of attacks but remarkably free of most major crime—although the Russian mob is believed to have been behind a recent hit at the seven-star Burj Al Arab hotel, apparently over a diamond deal gone bad.

The era that kicked off in 1979—a troubling one for many neighbors—has mostly suited the UAE. Even though Dubai, where many merchants are Persian and Shia, backed Iran in the Iran-Iraq War, while other emirates backed Iraq, the dispute didn't fragment the country, and the UAE actually benefited from that war: ships attacked in the Gulf were brought to the emirates for repair. Desert Storm also bolstered business in UAE ports and opened the door to friendship, and business, with the United States, with which the UAE signed a 1992 security agreement. Trade between the two countries is hearty: in 2006 the UAE was the biggest single Middle Eastern market for American goods—some twelve billion dollars' worth, from aircraft to autos, was sold to the UAE that year—a jump of 40 percent from 2005. The U.S. Chamber of Commerce, which opened a U.S.-UAE Business Council in 2007, believes that trend will continue.[10]

There have been shaky moments, however, such as the 2006 Dubai Ports debacle: the idea of Dubai managing twenty-two East Coast ports (including New York and Boston) and providing longshoremen at Texas oil ports provoked furious protests and a debate on national security until Dubai quietly dropped the idea. Although there were assurances that there were no hard feelings, the unabashed exhibition of American distrust didn't help relations. Talk of a free-trade agreement was knocked off the table (temporarily at least), and some wondered if the subsequent multibillion-dollar purchase of eight more Airbuses for Emirates Airlines and a hefty order for French arms, both on the heels of the deal, weren't a show of tit for tat. Since then, the Emiratis have only grown closer to the French, signing up for a multibillion-dollar nuclear plant deal in 2008, welcoming a French military base, engaging in war exercises with the French and Qataris (and not inviting the United States to participate).

The UAE is also asking more French universities and medical schools to open branches in the UAE: the Sorbonne is opening a branch in Abu Dhabi and the leader of emirate Sharjah wants the French to open medical schools.

Despite their rocky past, the seven emirates have stayed together as a federation, a country that few thought would pan out when it was created less than four decades ago. With its astute investment and development stunts, not to mention the trillions of dollars it's throwing around, the little land is making a very big splash.

MAJOR MOVERS

The UAE's three major airlines—Emirates, Etihad, and budget Air Arabia—are expanding their fleets so quickly that plane manufacturers, particularly Airbus, which is getting the bulk of the orders, can't keep up. The new thirty-three-billion-dollar, six-runway Dubai World Central International Airport will be the world's biggest, spreading over more land than Hong Kong. Ten-lane highways and pipelines are in the works, and a new ultraslick subway is snaking underground. Ship-wise, the Gulf's biggest port, Jebel Ali, is a magnet for containers: it's currently the fifth busiest in the world, working nonstop to load and unload seven million tons every month.

Hotshots

Sheikha Lubna: The first woman to sit on a cabinet, Sheikha Lubna Khalid Sultan al-Qasimi—from the ruling family in Sharjah—is minister of finance and planning. One of her projects: trying to hammer out a free-trade agreement with the United States.

Emaar: The UAE's real estate developer that is behind the towering Burj Dubai, Egypt's latest supermall, and Saudi Arabia's new Economic City. Armani recently hired Emaar to open thirty hotels worldwide.

Nakheel: The do-anything developer's biggest claim to fame, thus far, is the custom-made Palm Islands.

Sir Richard Branson: The Virgin mogul triggered a tsunami of PR responses when he spoke at the Leaders in Dubai Business Forum in 2007, cautioning about climate change. If global warming wasn't addressed soon, he warned, the Palm Islands would be underwater within fifty years. Developer Nakheel responded that Branson's "heart was in the right place" but his calculator wasn't. According to Nakheel, the islands won't be flooded for at least four hundred years.[11]

SHEIK SHAKHBUT AND SHEIK ZAYED

Sheik Shakhbut, who ruled Abu Dhabi beginning in 1928, led his emirate during a dismal time: the Great Depression and the Japanese invention of synthetic pearls in the 1930s, followed by World War II, all led to an era of food shortages and poverty for most Emiratis, including the royal families. The appearance of oil, first in Abu Dhabi (1958) and then Dubai (1965), drastically altered the hand-to-mouth existence. While the British succeeded in forcing Sheik Shakhbut to spread his wealth to other emirates, he refused to modernize Abu Dhabi and was rumored to keep his emirate's treasury under his bed. Preventing his own family from dipping into the coffers, Shakhbut was soon booted from power by his kin and replaced by his brother Zayed, who is considered the father of the UAE. Zayed was illiterate when he took over in 1966—a secret he soon rectified—and his wisdom, generosity, and natural diplomacy not only improved conditions for those in Abu Dhabi but helped to forge a union for what would soon become a country. What Zayed didn't know when he first took the reins was that the British, who'd protected these lands for a century and a half, were about to pull out—a thought so disturbing that the emirates (initially with Qatar and Bahrain) realized they needed to band together for mutual security. After all, there were sharks in these waters, not the least of which was Iran (which immediately made noise about taking Bahrain and soon latched on to three of the UAE's islands). Others worried that the Soviets would make a move. Years' worth of bickering, territorial dickering, debates, and power plays followed. Sharjah, which wanted to play lead fiddle, was a particular thorn, but finally an agreement was hammered out. The emirates would form a unified federation, with royal families ruling their individual sheikdoms but sitting on a Supreme Council headed by the family from Abu Dhabi, which would serve as temporary capital, a post it has never relinquished.

Sheik Zayed launched the 1973 oil embargo that created alarming gas shortages in the United States: furious that America rushed to help Israel with arms and supplies (well, Israeli prime minister Golda Meir had threatened to start a nuclear war if President Nixon didn't show up with military arms pronto), Zayed was the first to call for the all-out shutdown of oil from OPEC's Arab members to the United States and the Netherlands that led to Americans' first taste of an "energy crunch."

Hot Spots

Abu Dhabi: With the most land (87 percent) and the most oil (96 percent), Abu Dhabi is called "the richest city in the world" since per capita income of the eighty thousand nationals living in this emirate is reportedly over $275,000.[12] More cautious and traditional, it's finally coming out from under the shadow of Dubai: unveiling the $3 billion marble-wrapped Emirates Palace, said to be the priciest hotel ever built; its own flashy airline, Etihad; and a host of plans to put it on the map as a cultural hotbed and energy innovator. Unlike Dubai, it doesn't yet have a handle on public relations or tourism promotion.

Dubai: With far less oil to play with, Dubai was formed a century ago when an ancestor of the ruling Maktoum clan left Abu Dhabi, marched north, and turned Dubai creek into the Gulf's major trading port. Dubai is all about fun, flash, and dazzle; with sparkly high-rises and LA-like traffic jams, it's quickly blossomed into the most happening city in the Gulf. Dubai (where most Emiratis work and 1.5 million people live) is viewed as the world's next Manhattan and already serves as the Middle East's Las Vegas (minus the gambling but with the call girls, although they're not legal). A scene.

Sharjah: Traditional Islamic architecture abounds in souks and mosques, and Sharjah's draw is affordable rent. Culture-loving ruler Sheik Dr. Sultan ibn Muhammad al-Qasimi put on flashy major art exhibitions but his sheikdom is the most conservative; some expats call it "the Stone Age emirate."[13] Buying booze is banned and "decency laws" (thankfully) prohibit men from wearing Speedos in public; women dare not show much skin; and unless married, a local man and woman should not be left alone.[14] The reason: when Sharjah's government defaulted on five hundred million dollars in loans in the eighties, nearly pulling down commercial banks, the Sauds bailed them out but with strings attached. The Sauds routinely recognize Sharjah's sheik with million-dollar awards for being "an architect of Islam" and not getting swept away in Dubai's decadence. Best not to display anti-American sentiments here: after organizing a protest against the U.S.-led invasion of Iraq in 2003, this emirate's heir apparent was stripped of his title.[15]

Ras al-Khaimah: Ras al-Khaimah was once pirate central: tribes in this stretch were so brutal they inspired terror among European and Arab crews alike. Still an independent spirit and the last to commit to the federation (armed border disputes with Oman broke out as late as 2000), its oil reserves don't amount to much, and tourism hasn't taken root, but it's soon to be the site of an outer-space launch pad.

Fujairah: Shoved off to the south, this mountainous land settled by Phoenicians is ruled by the al-Sharqi family, and is still dotted with centuries-old forts and villages. Once called the "land of the sea giants," Fujairah's stature has shrunk due to lack of oil and the difficulty in reaching it. Despite new roads, port, and refineries (built by Abu Dhabi), Fujairah remains the UAE's poorest emirate, but with a free-trade zone and Creative City—a media complex with facilities for cinema, publishing, theater, and sound engineering that plans to broadcast ten TV channels—Fujairah is trying to rise again. The rugged coast is touted as a destination for water lovers.

Ajman: Spanning an area of one hundred square miles, this former fishing village is the micro-emirate. Ajman's touristic draw includes little except the sixteenth-century fort in the main square (it once housed the ruling family), a lovely luxury hotel full of arches, and undeveloped white sand beaches that beckon those who don't want to see and be seen. But friendly Ajman is: book in advance for twice-monthly dinners with the royal family, headed by Sheik Humayd ibn Rashid Al Nuaimi.

Umm al-Quiwain: Not much bigger than Ajman, this mangrove-fringed mini-emirate ruled by the Al Mu'alla was a maritime power and retains its fort and coral houses, and locals still make the wood dhows. Its islands are bird sanctuaries, there's a top-notch camel-racing track, and a marine club along its half-mile-wide "creek." And this emirate makes a touristic splash with Dreamland, the world's largest water park.

Stables: The royal families own tens of thousands of four-legged racers, including camels, whose genes are now studied in a camel lab. In the stables of Sheik Mohammad's horse outfit, Godolphins, many of the planet's finest stallions are kept.

Islands: In 1971, claiming historic rights, Iran sailed over and snagged several of UAE's islands: namely, Greater Tunb, Lesser Tunb, and nominally half of Abu Musa. Still a touchy point with Emiratis.

Banks: Emiratis have historically had more than their fair share of banking woes, with prominent financial institutions folding. But none collapsed with a louder thud than BCCI.

Falcons once were trained to hunt in the desert; now they're trained by clubs trying to preserve the Emirati past.

The Indian subcontinent: India and Pakistan provide the bulk of construction workers in the UAE; some states in India, such as Kerala, get the bulk of their GDP in the form of remittances from those working in the Emirates. The UAE is also thick with Indian gangsters and shysters, who get millions from investors in new businesses and then disappear.

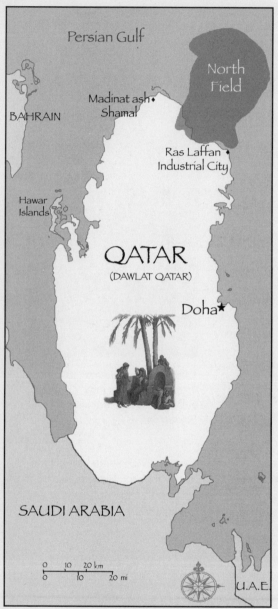

Persian Gulf

North Field

Madinat ash Shamal

BAHRAIN

Ras Laffan Industrial City

Hawar Islands

QATAR
(DAWLAT QATAR)

Doha★

SAUDI ARABIA

0   10   20 km
0   10   20 mi

U.A.E.

Karl Abramovic

A thumb of land that appears to be hitchhiking off the peninsula, Qatar is going places—big, big, big places. Recent finds of natural gas in the North Field that stretches offshore make an energy giant of this pint-sized country that could be poured into Connecticut and still wouldn't fill it up. Fueled by new wealth, it's awash with fresh ideas, novel projects, and daring plans that are already revolutionizing the Arab world. One woe: Saudi Arabia, which has always wanted this runaway digit stitched back onto the kingdom's hand, is literally at its back and (it's alleged) behind the occasional attempted overthrows.

Chapter Eleven

Qatar: Trail Blazing

The richest country in the Middle East per capita, iconoclastic Qatar is one of the few places where camels may still be used for transportation—outside cities at least. Here, a dromedary and friend wander along Qatar's inland sea.

Can an Islamic monarchy be democratic, liberal, and open to debate? Can a Middle Eastern country be on speaking terms with all the neighbors? Can innovation marry tradition? In this region known for the saying "the enemy of my enemy is my friend," can everybody just get along? Qatar's progressive emir, Sheik Hamad, apparently thinks so—he's been on a peacemaking kick, even helping to get Lebanon's fragmented government back together. He's also been showering power on the people, much to the horror of the rulers in Saudi Arabia. Even some Qataris don't like it. And the Sauds like his revolutionary TV station Al Jazeera, the CNN of the Middle East, even less.

Leader's Corner

Ballsy, brazen, and unabashed, maverick Sheik Hamad walks a tightrope with startling aplomb. The changes he's made in Qatar are radical, and his philosophy of befriending all requires political juggling: trading with Israel while bankrolling Hamas, giving the U.S. military its most important base in the Gulf, while warming up to Iran are a few actions that have set heads a-spinning. His gutsiest move: launching Al Jazeera, the provocative TV station that is as likely to harpoon Riyadh as DC and occasionally whacks Doha as well. But dissent may be brewing: Islamists in this land aren't thrilled with the disappearing veil, the women in the voting booths, and the new U.S. military bases sprouting up. Border disputes with Saudi Arabia are only one sign of the growling between the two countries.

U.S. Government Photo

Qatar's emir, Sheik Hamad bin Khalifa al-Thani, coaxes the spotlight to his tiny kingdom with high-profile events.

FAST FACTS:
Dawlat Qatar

Government:	Emirate (monarchy)
Formed:	1971, after independence from Britain, under which it had been protectorate
Ruler:	Sheik Hamad bin Khalifa al-Thani, emir since a bloodless 1995 coup ousted his pal Sheik Khalifa
GDP 2006:	$67.7 billion (IMF, 2007)
Per capita GDP:	$73,000 (IMF, 2007)
Population:	907,000 (of which about 700,000 are nonnationals)
Unemployment:	3.2 percent
Literacy rate:	89 percent men, 89 percent women
Ethnicity:	20 percent Qatari, 20 percent other Arab, 18 percent Indian, 18 percent Pakistani, 10 percent Iranian, 4 percent other
Religion:	78 percent Muslim, 9 percent Christian, 13 percent other

Population stat: vastly outnumbered by foreign workers, the two hundred thousand native Qataris are the third-wealthiest people in the world (after Luxembourgers and Norwegians) and may soon be the planet's richest.[1]

WHAT MATTERS

Energy matters: Qatar rode the petroleum geyser that shot up after World War II, but oil reserves are sputtering and will dry up in two decades. Nobody's worried though, since Qatar has the world's third-largest reserves of natural gas. Qatar's cutting-edge technology makes it easily transportable (it's the world's largest exporter of liquefied natural gas), and the United States will soon be getting loads. Neighbors want it too: Qatari gas is being piped to Gulf states as part of a multibillion-dollar network partly financed by the UAE, where much of it goes.

Electricity matters: All existing plants, including the new one Japan is building here, are fueled by natural gas, but Qatar is also going atomic, placing an order when French nuclear salesman/president Sarkozy blew into town in 2008.

Arms matter: Though Qatar previously wrestled some American arms, it was easier to get a *oui* from the French, who jetted in Mirage planes and other weapons du jour. Hamad's hospitality to U.S. troops rates him serious discounts in arms purchases, but it's unclear what boxes were checked when Condi blew through in 2007 with her arms order form. Qatar already had Stingers: Pops bought the shoulder-propped missile launchers on the black market years before; Reagan demanded them back; Pops declined.

Military matters: When Saudi Arabia booted American troops from its holy sands, Sheik Hamad invited them to resettle here. The United States Central Command Headquarters is al-Sayliyah; its air wing is at al-Udeid.[2] Giving Uncle Sam a new central home in the Gulf may risk a strike from Tehran should problems heat up but discourages a back stab from Riyadh: U.S. security has helped stave off at least two recent coups, believed to have been Saudi-backed.

Religion matters: Saudi Arabia's take on Islam, Wahhabism, took hold here, and Qataris still practice it, although theirs is a much mellower version. No religious police around here, no public beheadings, no floggings—and there is booze, at the hotels at least.

Militants matter: The few acts of recent violence—a 2005 bombing at a local theater (one Briton died), the 2004 assassination of a Chechen leader, and the killing of two Western contractors in 2001—were perpetrated by foreigners believed to be acting alone. Sheik Hamad, a peacemaker, recently ended Lebanon's political stalemate—bringing Hezbollah back into the loop.

High profile matters: Sheik Hamad is intent on making Doha a household name synonymous with *culture, sports,* and *big.* He's held WTO talks here, the Asian Games, Islamic conferences, and billions of dollars' worth of art is soon to be displayed in the country's five new museums designed by big-name architects: I. M. Pei (who designed the pyramid in front of the Louvre in Paris) came out of retirement to draw up plans for the new Islamic Arts Center, and famous Spaniard Santiago Calatrava developed the look of the photography museum. A flashy space-age library will hold a half million volumes. And Qatar Airways, one of the world's few five-star airlines, is the sheik's baby too.

Family matters: Father Khalifa and son Hamad, the former and current emirs, are at least on speaking terms these days, and there's even warmth among the once-frosty al-Khalifa cousins, the ruling family of Bahrain.

Smaller than Vermont and flatter than Iowa, this land of white sands lapped by aquamarine waters used to be even duller than Idaho: not that long ago travel-guide publisher Lonely Planet awarded resource-rich Qatar (pronounced CUHD-ter) the title of most boring place on the planet. For years, Qatar's emirs

Courtesy Sharq Village

Once a rough-and-tumble pearling village so culturally bereft that the British who kept watch over it did so from Bahrain, Qatar is booming: eye-catching architecture is rising along its corniche, lavish cultural centers are being unveiled, and Doha's Education City is a magnet for Ivy League schools, which are opening up branches here. Things are changing so fast that local VIPs wanted to capture the region's historical architecture and showcase it in the form of a hotel. The result: Sharq Village, shown here.

seemed to agree with that assessment, using the oil money to flee and rule the country from faraway posts. Granted, until recently Qatar was so lacking in excitement it could have coaxed an insomniac into a deep hibernatorial slumber. Even fifteen years ago, it didn't have the wide Parisian-style boulevards or the swanky hotels or the museums and libraries or a beachfront studded with dazzling designs and trendy restaurants. It didn't have Al Jazeera, the network that grates on every leader's nerves and triggered a social revolution. So it's understandable why leaders would want to jaunt off. Yet, as successive rulers were to learn, vacations abroad could be hazardous to their power and wealth, since they were most likely to be ousted when out of town. In 1995, the vacationing emir, Sheik Khalifa, discovered that he too was out of a job.

On a sweltering June morning that year, the crown prince Hamad bin Khalifa al-Thani, whose dark eyes are prone to light up and whose mustache runs like a woolly caterpillar across his mouth, changed the course of Qatar with one phone call and three words: "Don't come back." After he dialed up Switzerland and conveyed that message to emir Khalifa al-Thani, his father, the new self-proclaimed emir took his seat at the control board and began redesigning Qatar, the country that until then was ignored.

> *The newly unemployed emir Khalifa should not have been shocked: in 1972 he had yanked the crown off the head of his cousin Ahmed when the latter was vacationing in Lebanon, the same place where, a decade before, an unidentified assailant shot at the emir Ali—a factor, no doubt, when he abdicated to his son Ahmed shortly thereafter. Things just happened to Qatari rulers when they were away, as they so often were.*

LIKE FATHER, NOT LIKE SON

Khalifa, who'd been raising eyebrows countrywide by hitting the bottle and blowing through billions on the French Riviera, was already on dicey terms with his eldest son, Hamad, commander in chief of Qatar's armed forces since 1977 and pretty much running the show since the 1991 Persian Gulf War. Politically, they hadn't been seeing eye-to-eye for years, and much of their fighting had to do with reform. Not long before Hamad's telephone coup, forty of the country's most well-to-do citizens had politely petitioned Khalifa, requesting a constitution, parliament, and the right to vote. Khalifa responded with a royal fit. Petitioners were arrested, forced to apologize, a few were yanked off departing planes when they tried to flee. Hamad was appalled, but the crown prince was downright alarmed when he saw what his pa was doing to the country's checking account: Khalifa had drained the millions in his personal offshore account but kept writing checks from it.[3] Qatar's national treasury was zapped as the government was forced to cover the emir's multibillion-dollar bouncing checks. When Hamad confronted him, Khalifa switched loyalty and promoted another son: not long before Hamad rang up Switzerland, Khalifa had announced that Hamad's half brother Abdul Aziz would be stepping in as Qatar's prime minister. The implied message was that Hamad could start counting down his days as crown prince. So when Khalifa flew off to Europe that June, Hamad summoned most of the family and told them his plan, and then he dialed Geneva and left the three-word message; Khalifa, who'd been tipped off, would not take the "don't come back" call.[4]

Hamad might have found a better time to inform his father of the leadership change than when the erstwhile ruler was checking out the Swiss bank accounts. Khalifa took off with the contents of Qatar's piggy bank, an amount estimated at around twelve billion dollars. Qatar's credit rating and credibility instantly tumbled. Hamad did what in the world of Arab royals is unthinkable: he initiated a lawsuit to get the bucks back. Several years later, Khalifa finally coughed up the dough.

Snoozy Doha woke up the minute Sheik Hamad leapt into the emir's saddle in 1995 and began galloping down a whole new path, ushering in an era of excitement never before seen in this outpost, where wild times had been limited to wandering the souk, searching for truffles in the desert, or hanging out at the city's one hotel, the billion-dollar, pyramid-shaped Sheraton built in 1982. The shocks began the day after Hamad's coup, when the new emir actually showed up for work and continued to come in every day, something no Qatari ruler had ever done before. Among his first acts: shutting down the censorship office. Appointing ministers in their twenties and thirties, Hamad unveiled an astounding reform plan, starting with guaranteeing Qataris civil rights. He handed women the car keys and dropped the requirement that they wear the veil: his second wife, Mozah, daringly shed the head garb in public, the first Qatari woman to do so.[5] He granted Qataris over eighteen, including females, the right to vote, including Qatar's first constitution, which granted the rights of free speech and assembly and to petition the government. He founded the Qatar Foundation and pumped billions of dollars into it to start a science-and-technology center and to boost education, welcoming leading Western universities to open branches there, Georgetown and Cornell Medical School among them. He upgraded all levels of schools and rattled the Arab world not only by revamping the education system but by bringing in an American think tank to do it. Hiring the RAND Corporation, a California-based think tank, the emir allowed Westerners to introduce new teaching methods, overhaul the curriculum, and to emphasize English and science and delete messages of intolerance. When the emir's changes prompted fiery discussion of the sort that had rarely blown up there, Hamad opened up new forums for discussions in a move to bring Qataris into the creation of their future.

HOTSHOT SECOND LADY: SHEIKHA MOZAH

She's called Qatar's most powerful woman, and ebony-eyed Mozah bint Nasser al-Missned, a commoner with a sociology degree, does have a way with the emir, who is also her husband. His second wife (the other two are his cousins), Sheikha Mozah is a catalyst: she convinced her hubby to revamp education, promote better treatment of foreign workers, and give women more power. Reform may be in her blood: decades ago her father called for redistribution of the country's wealth, and Hamad's father answered by trotting the critic off to jail. Tapped by her husband to head his new Qatar Foundation for Education, Science and Community Development, where she oversees a two-billion-dollar budget, she's lured Georgetown, Carnegie Mellon, and Cornell to open branches in Qatar's new Education City. Mozah also kicked off the monthly Doha Debates, during which speakers and the audience debate heated issues, from torture to Shariah law. Overseeing a major overhaul of Qatari schools, she was appointed a special ambassador to UNESCO and launched scholarship programs, including one for higher education in Iraq. Known for speaking out about women's rights, and not wearing a veil when doing so, she's an inspiration to Qatari women and a threat to Saudi men. When a Saudi-owned tabloid in London slammed her for flexing too much muscle in Qatar—and intimated that she worked as a Qatari agent, secretly making deals with Israel—she sued for libel, donating the millions collected in damages to charity.

Carried on BBC World News and moderated by a former BBC host, the Doha Debates have taken on the region's touchiest issues, opening them up for discussion before several hundred in Doha's Qatar Foundation headquarters.[6] Among recent topics:

- *If it's time to talk with al Qaeda (audience voted yes)*
- *If torture is acceptable if performed under supervision (audience voted no)*
- *If Palestinians should drop their right to return (audience voted no)*
- *Whether the veil is a barrier to integration in the West (audience voted yes)*

> • If a new dictator in Iraq could bring it under control (audience voted no)
> • If Muslims were failing to combat extremism (audience voted yes)

But there were problems, particularly in the early days: beyond the soap opera of how to retrieve the billions that his pa snagged, there was the distinct possibility that Hamad wouldn't last—never mind what the media reported. The world news made Hamad's takeover sound as easy as pushing through a revolving door. The United States, Saudi Arabia, the UAE, and Bahrain recognized the rule of the new emir the very next day, the media reported. Behind the scenes, the coup seriously rattled regional power. The Saudis were panicked and quickly dialed DC: Hamad was a revolutionary, they informed the United States. He was, they warned, in bed with both Iraq and Iran; privately Sauds bemoaned his rep as a reformer out of fear that his changes might spread. Hamad's father, the ousted Khalifa, made furious calls to Gulf rulers: the UAE's King Zayed invited the ex-emir to Abu Dhabi, where Khalifa plunked down with his entourage, taking up entire floors of the Intercontinental Hotel. Khalifa visited his cousin, the ruler of Bahrain, who announced that Khalifa remained Qatar's true ruler. The Sauds snubbed Hamad by not showing up to the first GCC meeting he held in Doha.

More threatening than being flipped off by the neighbors were the attempts at countercoups: just months after Hamad took control, Khalifa's supporters (a group that Qatar believed also included the Sauds) slipped one hundred million dollars to the former head of secret police. He recruited over one hundred officers in Qatar's army, and hundreds more bedouin fighters, in what was a hilariously inept coup attempt. Bedouins raced across the Saudi desert in SUVs and got lost the moment they showed up in Doha. One witness, hearing a loud crash, ran out to his villa's gardens to discover that a Hummer had plowed through the villa's thick wall. Inside it: bickering bedouins, yelling into cell phones, asking directions to the palace.[7] The mercenary army hired to invade by sea somehow lost its boats.

If the neighbors, particularly the Sauds—who are also distant cousins—were initially threatened by the new emir, they became more so in 1996. That was the year Hamad staged a regionwide revolution: he unleashed Al Jazeera, the pioneering satellite news network that beamed "the Arab street" into Arab living rooms. Sauds were among the first to start hurling condemnation at the station that dared to air reports interviewing those who criticized royals. The Sauds banned Al Jazeera reporters from entry into their kingdom and became so incensed at the Doha-based station's broadcasts that they pulled out the Saudi ambassador to Qatar in 2002. He still hasn't come back.

Others too had conniptions about the station that covers the Middle East more openly than any news venue has dared before—the result being an Arabic version of CNN, with a dash of Fox News. Watched by some fifty million, Al Jazeera became the most popular news source in the Middle East, and it's shaken up the Arab world by bringing the Arab-Israeli conflict to 3-D life, in color, along with disturbing images of U.S.-led battles that often didn't air in the States and videos of al Qaeda diatribes. In fact, al Qaeda was what made it a financially viable enterprise—at least for a while. After 9/11, al Qaeda started sending in videotapes, and the Taliban regime allowed only Al Jazeera reporters into Afghanistan during the U.S.-led war there. Overnight, Al Jazeera transformed into the main Middle Eastern news dealer worldwide: major networks lined up to buy footage, doling out as much as $250,000 for a three-minute bin Laden tape.[8] That dough soon went bye-bye: the U.S. government pressured American networks to stop airing bin Laden videos, and al Qaeda itself became enraged at the station after it aired a four-minute video of Osama's right-hand man al-Zawahiri three years ago. The video, which brought the wrath of Rumsfeld for giving al Qaeda airtime, triggered the ire of al-Zawahiri since his hours of on-the-nod rambling had been reduced to four minutes.[9] Al Qaeda didn't send another video until late 2007, when Osama had the urge to rant at the United States yet again—this time about global warming.

REVOLUTION IN A MATCHBOX

Saudi Arabia created its own headache. In the mid-nineties, the Riyadh government invited BBC World News to the kingdom to launch a media coventure, and during the lead-up Arab reporters learned Western investigative skills. The project folded before one show ever aired: the BBC grew alarmed over Saudi censorship, and it looked as if hundreds of reporters would be out of a job. But Sheik Hamad got wind of it and invited them to set up in Doha in 1996, underwriting the launch of the satellite news channel, renamed Al Jazeera, "the peninsula," to the tune of $150 million. It immediately became the most talked-about news source in the Arab world. The uncensored twenty-four-hour news station knocked out every taboo, running documentaries about monarchies, reporting on prisons, airing discussions that pitted Arab secularists against theocracy-pushing Islamists, and broadcasting vivid on-the-ground reports about uprisings and wars. The no-holds-barred approach triggered discussion and change in a way no Arab media has before. Coverage of the Palestinian uprising against Israel in 2000 so shocked Arabs that they pressured their governments to do something, and footage of Israel using U.S.-made weaponry to attack Palestinians hardened Arab dislike of the arms-supplying United States. Government officials were given a new forum in which to speak out: Al Jazeera was the first Arab TV channel to put Israelis in front of the camera to explain their views, and Westerners like Condi Rice and Dick Cheney were familiar faces. The reaction from the start was one loud hissy fit. Bahrain kicked out Al Jazeera reporters, saying they favored Israel; governments from Jordan to Kuwait shut down local Al Jazeera bureaus, at least temporarily. Algeria cut electricity in cities when Al Jazeera aired a documentary about government actions after the civil war there.[10] And the videos of Osama bin Laden praising the 9/11 attacks, along with critical discussions about the role of the United States in the Middle East, caused DC leaders to join with the rest in shrieking at Sheik Hamad to pull the plug. Qatar itself is sometimes shown in an unfavorable light, being accused of subjecting prisoners to torture, for one. Some say Al Jazeera has a pro-Arab bias, rarely attacks the Qatar government that feeds it, and stirs up unrest. But the Doha-based station offers the most in-depth reporting of the Middle East, and now Americans can judge for themselves: in 2006 Al Jazeera launched a news station in English.

"All this trouble from a matchbox like this?"
—Egyptian president Hosni Mubarak upon touring
Al Jazeera's modest headquarters in Doha[11]

Despite the shrieking, Hamad wouldn't shut down Al Jazeera and still kicks in some thirty million dollars a year to keep the station on the air. But Al Jazeera war offices have gone black a few times, after being bombed by the U.S. military.

Al Jazeera had notified the U.S. military of its coordinates in Afghanistan, but the station's Kabul bureau was one of the first sites struck during the 2001 U.S. invasion. A mistake, said the DoD, whose forces hauled off reporter Sami Al-Hajj to Guantánamo. Another military "mistake": the U.S. missile strike on Al Jazeera's bureau in Baghdad on April 8, 2003, that killed a reporter and injured another.

Never mind what the neighbors think of Hamad: most of his subjects like him. For years, Qataris had whispered about the ex-emir's spending habits—the way he surrounded himself with finery while schools were mediocre; health care was free but not very modern, and industry idled. Under Khalifa, in fact, oil money was running low, and the economy was entirely dependent on that one resource. Hamad was aware of that problem even before he took over, which is why he had long been scheming about how to tap Qatar's natural gas, the resource that is now fueling Qatar's rise to the big time.

Natural gas was discovered in 1971 in Qatar's North Field, but that initial find only hinted at coming attractions. Besides, back then, natural gas was worthless. It often rests on top of petroleum deposits, and since it got in the way of tapping

Until recently, natural gas was considered a nuisance and "flared."

the crude most of it was "flared." Industry didn't use much natural gas, and transport was a nightmare: volatile and bulky, few wanted to bother shipping the flammable explosive. For decades, Hamad had been funding research into new ways to transport it, one method being liquefication, which condenses six hundred barrels of natural gas into one barrel. Smart move: natural gas is now in vogue. Cleaner burning than oil, it powers stoves and heaters, and industry adores it. After the near-meltdown at Three Mile Island, most U.S. utilities turned to natural gas for their juice, draining domestic supplies. When geologists reported that Qatar's North Field had far more natural gas than originally thought—some nine hundred million cubic feet—the largest freestanding gas reservoir in the world, with enough gas to hold out for at least a century, this oil David turned into a natural-gas Goliath. Qatar catapulted onto the radar screen of energy-hungry world powers, and with a reason. Except for Qatar, the list of the large producers of natural gas looks like the West-bashing hall of fame, with Russia, Iran, Algeria, Indonesia, and Venezuela topping the roster. The United States, rapidly increasing imports of natural gas, muscled in past longtime customers Japan and Korea and quickly drew up a multibillion-dollar deal; by 2010 nearly 8 percent of Qatar's gas will be U.S. bound.[12] Even the oil-rich neighbors are hot to tap Qatar's gold mine: the new ten-billion-dollar Dolphin Gas Project, underwritten in large part by the United Arab Emirates, is piping Qatari gas underwater to the UAE, Oman, and eventually Pakistan and India.

Hamad's knack for diplomacy first came to light in the era that began in 1979. A headache for most of the neighbors, that era unleashed a wave of events that would send Qatar to new heights. The neighbors' problems weren't mirrored there: Qatar's population didn't include many Shia and, while Wahhabi, by and large, wasn't zealous. There was little crime, thus little need to put on Shariah shows like those in Riyadh's Chop Chop Square. Back then, people were happy with Khalifa and excited about the new construction then under way on the town's first luxury hotel, the Sheraton.

"Qatar's sweet. The entire time I was ambassador there, only one person was in jail. I got him out."
— Andy Killgore, former U.S. ambassador to Qatar.[13]
The jailbird was an American, who'd lowballed construction projects and couldn't deliver.

Qatar was quick to sign up for the new Gulf Cooperation Council started by Saudi Arabia, a mutual defense club that was formed in reaction to the threat of Iran. But Hamad, along with Oman's Sultan Qaboos and leaders of the UAE, soon realized that an isolated Iran was more dangerous than one that was diplomatically engaged. Hamad in fact first initiated contact with Tehran, a move his father didn't second. And when the Iran-Iraq War ended, only to be followed by the Persian Gulf War in 1991, Hamad came even more to the forefront: unlike his father, he'd had military training, studying at Sandhurst in Britain. Hamad controversially signed on Qatar for a security agreement with the United States, thawed diplomatic relations with Iran, and opened trade with Israel, while Khalifa was hanging at his new mansion in Cannes. But Khalifa shot down any attempts at democratic reform. But those days, when Qataris were afraid to speak their minds, are now a distant memory. That era of autocratic rule and disappearing money ended that one sweltering morning in June 1995, when Prince Hamad picked up the phone to call Geneva. Qatar hasn't been the same since he left the message: "Don't come back." Lebanon, where the Qataris put the crumbling government back together in 2008, is only one country that's happy that call was made.

Hotshots

Sheik Abdul Aziz bin Khalifa: Almost Qatar's prime minister, Hamad's half brother Abdul Aziz recently blew back into Qatar with his pa. No word on how the family reunions are going.

Ex-emir Khalifa: He finally handed over the billions he owed to the government, and now comes back for the occasional visit, but his relationship is still rather frosty with the new emir.

Sheik Saud al-Thani: With a mission of buying up the pieces for Qatar's new photography museum and Islamic Arts Center, Sheik Saud al-Thani, the emir's second cousin, was the most famous Qatari in the international art world, buying up Fabergé eggs, rare photos, unusual gems, and lost Islamic art across the planet and dropping some two billion dollars in his eight years as chairman of the Qatar National Council for Culture, Arts, and Heritage. The man regarded as the biggest art collector on the planet dropped out of sight in 2005, and word had it he was stuck in Qatar—in jail. Rumored reason: he spent at least some of his art budget on whores.

Hot Spots

North Field: Stretching out to the northeast, this gas field isn't entirely Qatar's. Part of it belongs to Iran, where it's called the South Pars. Every so often, Tehran makes a crack about Qatar taking more than its fair share.

Saudi border: Still debated, this line in the sand is the site of the occasional military showdown as well as the entry point for bedouin warriors in SUVs.

Al-Udeid: The barracks are filling up as threats from DC to Iran grow louder.

The racetracks: Hamad loves his horsies and his camels too. But these days the jockeys are robots, since the jockey trade often involved kidnapped boys.

Al Jazeera offices and bureaus: In 2005, a London paper claimed that President Bush threatened to bomb the network's headquarters in Doha; the British government quashed the story[14] and, like DC, claimed the allegations absurd, even though government advisers such as Frank Gaffney had publicly advised that the U.S. government take down Al Jazeera—a militant propaganda arm, he believed—using whatever method was needed.[15]

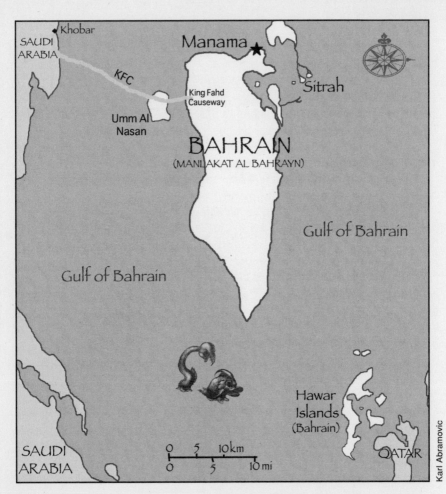

Now connected to Saudi Arabia by the King Fahd Causeway, Bahrain has histori-
cally been aligned with Iran, which is still desirously eyeing it from 240 miles to the
east. The last few decades have seen a tug-of-war, with Saudi Arabia's money (and
"borrowed voters") helping to keep the Sunni hold over the Shia majority, which Iran
is accused of putting up to attempted overthrows. With the United States' Fifth Fleet
anchoring here, some Bahrainis feel safer than ever; some feel ever more like
sitting ducks.

Chapter Twelve

Bahrain: A New Profile

Hussain Al-Baluchi

Bahrain, a major finance center already, is getting snazzier and snazzier—
opening more over-the-top luxury hotels and villas.

A speck on the world map and not much bigger on the regional one, Bahrain is known by local expats as "the Middle East lite," since everything from dress to lifestyle is pretty mellow there. A palm-fringed island kingdom that sits a date toss away from Saudi Arabia, lapped by aquamarine waters along one hundred miles of coast, the minicountry once known for the prettiest pearls is thought of as an opulent paradise. But every so often its charms are offset by uprisings: this Shia-dominant land is lorded over by the Sunni and still bears the scars of British occupation.

FAST FACTS:
Mamlakat al Bahrayn

Government:	Constitutional monarchy
Independence:	August 15, 1971 (from Britain)
Ruler:	King Hamad bin Isa al-Khalifa
GDP 2007:	$19.6 billion (exchange rate); (IMF, 2007)
Per capita GDP:	$ 25,900 (IMF, 2007)
Population:	718,000, including 236,000 nonnationals (July 2008 estimate)
Unemployment:	15 percent (2005 estimate)
Literacy rate:	89 percent men, 84 percent women
Ethnicity:	62 percent Bahraini, 38 percent non-Bahraini
Religion:	81 percent Shia and Sunni Muslim, 9 percent Christian, 10 percent other

Population stat: Some 60 percent or more of Bahrainis are Shia.

The 1999 death of its ruler Sheik Isa (he had a fatal heart attack mere minutes after making an arms deal with U.S. secretary of defense William Cohen) closed an ugly chapter in Bahrain's recent history. The succession of his son, Hamad bin Isa al-Khalifa (who soon changed Bahrain from an emirate to a monarchy) was greeted with relief by Bahrainis, particularly since he reopened the long-closed parliament, penned a constitution, reestablished the vote, gave women suffrage, ungagged the press, released political prisoners, engaged the Shia, and relieved the British head of security (torture-loving Ian Henderson) of the post he'd held for decades. Recently, Hamad has backpedaled a bit; some say his powerful uncle, the prime minister Sheik Khalifa bin Salman al-Khalifa, is stomping on Hamad's toes and embracing hard-core Sunni groups to keep the Shia down. Despite a rollicking economy, a staggering 15 percent are unemployed, many of them Shia, and human rights groups say torture has returned. Some of the freedoms that Hamad bestowed have caused headaches: now anybody with a grievance stages a sit-in in front of government buildings, and now security is rounding them up.

Courtesy Embassy of Bahrain in DC

King Hamad bin Isa al-Khalifa is on warm terms with the DC team.

WHAT MATTERS

Energy matters: None goes to the United States, but Bahrain still has a few drops of oil left, pumping about thirty thousand barrels a day (about 1 percent of Saudi Arabia's daily output). Most wells will be dry by 2020, although more oil was recently found in a field shared with Saudis. It holds a little natural gas, but these days Bahrain's mostly an oil refiner.

Arms matter: Thanks to $650 million in U.S. giveaways and a $1 billion arms shopping spree since 9/11, Bahrain is rolling in American-made weaponry, from F-16s and Blackhawk helicopters to shoulder-launched Stingers and sophisticated missile systems that the United States won't sell to any other Gulf country. Concern over the sale of these short-range ballistic missile systems led to an absurd agreement whereby the Bahrain military doesn't have the code to launch them. It's known only by U.S. military, which plans to be around if the babies are fired.

Military matters: Bahrain has only eleven thousand men in uniform, but the U.S. Fifth Fleet—from warships to minesweepers—is docked here along with NAVCENT, the navy's central command. Bahrain's bases came in handy during the Iran-Iraq War and the 1991 war to liberate Kuwait. Iraq lobbed Scuds this a-way, and some hit. More recently, the bases were integral to the U.S. invasion of Afghanistan in 2001 as well as the U.S.-led takeover of Iraq in 2003, although the government officially didn't support the latter. Five thousand U.S. military personnel mill about here, most of them navy.

Religion matters: Shia make up the majority numbers-wise, but their voice is stifled.

Legendary locale of the Garden of Eden, Bahrain started it all. An archipelago of thirty-three seamlessly connected islands (the total area is just over three times the size of Washington, DC), the minicountry was the first Arab nation where oil was struck (back in 1932), and it was also the first to scrape the bottom of the oil barrel—and thus the first to stray from the petroleum-based economy that made it wealthy. And that's only one way the country is a mirror of many issues arising in this part of the world. Once part of Persia (today's Iran), Bahrain's past left a legacy that is still playing out: some Bahrainis have kin in Iran, and Bahrain is the only Arab country outside of Iraq where the majority is Shia. Not all the Shia are thrilled at the Sunni leadership, which relegates many to second-class citizenry. What's more, as favorite headquarters for the British during those centuries when the Gulf was their closely guarded "lake," Bahrain was terribly dependent on foreigners for security.

Playground for the rich, Bahrain boasts what was for decades the Gulf's most cosmopolitan capital (until Dubai shoved it aside). Manama is where

Victor Lambourne. Courtesy Saudi Aramco, ASC

Home to Dilmun, a hopping third-millennium-BC trading center, these islands were long known for the sturdy wooden dhows in which medieval merchants with chests laden with glistening pearls set out for India, Indonesia, and beyond, returning with spices, silk, rubies, celadon, tea, and horses. The boats were also used for pearling: daring divers, weighted with stones, grabbed more than the oysters that yielded Bahrain the biggest pearls; they also filled skin bags with sweet water bubbling up from springs on the Gulf floor, a common way to get drinkable water until the 1930s.

ON THE ONE HAND AND ON THE OTHER

Headed by the al-Khalifa family (cousins of Qatar's ruling clan), Bahrain is opening up in every way, from citizens' rights to foreign investment. Thanks to King Hamad's 2002 constitution, Bahrain is a constitutional monarchy with a two-chamber parliament. Half of the parliamentarians are voted in, and women can run for seats. That's a step forward since his father, who created the National Assembly in 1973, and shut the doors two years later; they remained locked until 1999, when Hamad walked in. Parliament has limited power (most still resides with the king and his uncle, the prime minister), but it can pass laws and veto royal decrees by a two-thirds majority. Hamad also welcomed in the Internet and allowed freedom of speech and assembly as well as the right of workers to unionize and strike. He appointed five Shia men and two women to the twenty-three-member cabinet and tapped a Shia as deputy prime minister.

Offsetting his progressive moves is the parliament, where most of the seats are held by Islamists—Shia and Sunni. Conservatives—members of the Muslim Brotherhood and Wahhabi-like organizations—are moving in big time, both politically and economically. The country's laws have a distinctly conservative bent, including one that bans anyone in the national dress from entering liquor stores. And while a quarter of Bahrainis are online, many writing blogs, sites are now being blocked, including Google Earth with its satellite shots offering enhanced capabilities for users to survey Bahrain and peek into its royal palaces. With the amount of regal real estate so blatantly mapped out, critics protested that royals were hogging too much land, prompting the government to shut down access to the geography-detailing site. Security forces occasionally close down human rights groups, hamper free speech, and sometimes disrupt peaceful protests. A much-publicized meeting in 2004 to discuss the Bahraini constitution (with European legal experts flown in) was canceled by the government. The organizers were whisked behind bars (albeit briefly) and the legal experts met at the airport and escorted onto the next planes out. The people, however, have a loud fit when their rights are diluted, and protests and sit-ins routinely follow, although those are being reined in. Even though the king routinely steps in to reverse oppressive actions of the courts and overturn death sentences, Bahrainis are growing uneasy that their newly refound freedom of expression is vanishing again, as it did under his pa.

In March 2006, Bahrainis were worried sick when twenty city councilmen, many of them hard-core Muslims, disappeared after a meeting in Malaysia. The missing Bahrainis soon turned up: they lamely claimed that they had improvised a trip to nearby Thailand as part of a fact-finding mission about road systems. One might wonder what actually drove them to the land better known for its brothels than for its highways.

Westerners employed by the banks and multinational firms with regional headquarters happily while away hours on the decks of the Ritz-Carlton—overlooking sparkling waters as they down festively festooned Trader Vic's drinks. Trendy restaurants abound, and new "smart" towers are rising along the waterfront. Already an icon, the two glass sails of the Bahrain World Trade Center are connected by three giant turbines that will generate electricity for lighting, the first time wind energy has been incorporated into urban design. Bahrain is a money powerhouse, being the Gulf center for international finance and Islamic banking, and is rising as a global luxury destination that (thanks to a new $150 million state-of-the art racetrack) now hosts the Grand Prix. If Aladdin grants Saudi prince Waleed's wish, Bahrain may be the site of a future Disneyland as well. Celebs from Michael Jackson (who recently confided he was feeling "increasingly Bahraini" and wants to move here) to Shakira are swooping down to hang with the royals or live in regal style in secluded getaways, some buying condos on the new residential islands where yachts pull into the "driveways."

All-villa resort Banyan Tree Al-Areen is one of the new luxury establishments setting up in Bahrain.

LUXURIOUS MAXIMUS

Arabian-styled villas connected by canals, man-made petal islands, pro golfer–designed courses, and chalets reachable only by yacht—such are but a few of the over twelve billion dollars' worth of developments that are putting even more razzle and dazzle into Bahrain's cityscape and waterfront and helping the economy to sustain its 8-percent-a-year growth. Some four million well-heeled tourists annually drop by Bahrain, and tourism should soar even higher with the unveiling of new ultra-luxe resorts and residential communities under way, including Bahrain Bay, centered around a flashy Four Seasons Hotel, and the Al-Masra floating city. The minute the long-standing dispute with Qatar over the Hawar Islands was settled in Bahrain's favor, ritzy getaways began springing up there. Another draw for the super-wealthy: Banyan Tree Al-Areen, a desert village of sprawling villas, each with a canopied pool in the center and Jacuzzi on either side, set within private courtyards of trickling water sculptures, graceful arches, and swaying palms. Living like a sultan isn't cheap: the rate is six thousand dollars a night.

With little oil of its own, Bahrain moved into refining and has become a major producer of petroleum products (as well as cement and aluminum). Companies such as Coca-Cola, Chevron, and Citibank—even PR giant Hill and Knowlton—conduct business inside the glassy high-rises that lure tens of thousands of foreigners into the increasingly multicultural mix: foreign-born residents now make up about a third of Bahrain's 718,000 million residents, but they hold over three-quarters of jobs. Beyond its multiethnic blend, Bahrain is also home to an uneasy mix of religions, reflecting its history. Iranian workers flooded in to man the oil business in the mid-twentieth century, and now some two-thirds of the population is Shia. That bond with Iran makes the Sunni elite jittery, all the more since Iran sits only a couple of hundred miles away and has let it be known that it wants Bahrain back.

> *When the British were preparing to pull out from Bahrain, the shah of Iran was ready to pounce but was convinced by the United Nations to let the people of Bahrain decide their own fate. In the 1970 referendum, Bahrainis voted to be independent and not to merge with Iran.*

From the sixteenth century to the eighteenth, Bahrain was tugged back and forth between Portugal and Persia. Ancestors of today's royal family shoved out the Persians for the last time in 1792 and brought in the British to make sure the neighbors stayed out. Nevertheless, Tehran's shadow hangs over these islands. There's a persistent belief held by the Sunnis that the Shia want to hand Bahrain back to Iran, a claim Shia deny: they say the pictures of Ayatollah Khomeini hanging in their homes reflect a spiritual connection, not a political one. Several Shia-led attempted coups over the years (allegedly backed by Iran) have not assuaged fears. Nor did the chronic unrest in the nineties, much of it coming from Shia neighborhoods, which are poorer. Arrests were so common that, at certain points before Hamad took over, about 1 percent of the population was in jail. Iran's recent ratchetting up of its historical claims to these islands doesn't make anybody sleep easier, especially when President Ahmadinejad starts sniping about how Iran's neighbors should stop helping the United States, which Bahrain most certainly does. As for exactly how Iran would retaliate against Bahrain if the United States launched a strike, well, nobody wants to think about that, but the government is developing contingency plans, knowing that as home to U.S. Fifth Fleet they'd end up in the crosshairs.

But Iran isn't the only neighbor that makes its presence felt in these parts. Saudis pump billions into this island kingdom, giving it cut-rate prices for the Saudi crude that Bahrain refines, and until recently giving Bahrain all the proceeds from the oil-rich Abu Saafa island that both countries share. Saudis have supplied sand needed for Bahraini construction and, more important, built the King Fahd Causeway in 1986, a fifteen-mile-long bridge between the two countries. Millions of Saudi tourists haul their vacation money over that causeway, significantly boosting the local tourism chest. Saudi armed forces came to Bahrain's rescue during tense sectarian moments in the 1990s. Shia say that the causeway also turns into a voting booth: they contend that the Bahraini government extends citizenship (and voting rights) to thousands of Saudi Sunnis across the bridge, who are transported just beyond the midway point, where they vote (for Sunni Islamist candidates), turn around, and go back to Saudi Arabia, where they are actually citizens.

BANDARGATE

The Shia, who've long suspected there was funny business with the elections, were vindicated in August 2006 when a government employee, Dr. Salah al Bandar Bandar, blew the whistle on a multitentacled scam run by factions of the government to sway votes toward the Sunni. Involving gerrymandering, spying, propaganda, and media, the scam that he documented with checks, receipts, and letters included payoffs to columnists, editors, intelligence teams, and humans rights groups. Though it caused a huge flap, the government mostly just clamped a lid on the matter, hastily sending Bandar back to Britain, where he was born.

However, the long-cuddly relationship with the Saudis seems to be chilling. Suddenly Saudi Arabia is cutting oil-revenue payments to Bahrain and inexplicably dropped its export of sand, which is crucial to Bahrain's cement industry and island development. While there are rumors of Saudi disapproval over Bahrain's recent rapprochement with Qatar, home of Al Jazeera (which the Saudis detest), what's believed to be behind the chill that's breezing over from Riyadh is Bahrain's increasing chumminess with the United States, with which Bahrain signed a free-trade agreement in 2004.

Even though they are cousins, the royal families of Qatar and Bahrain have often been at each other's throats: when some of the eighteenth-century al-Khalifa sailed off to shove the Persians out of Bahrain, they believed they still owned Qatar, although the kin that remained home disagreed and wouldn't hand it back even after the al-Khalifa militarily marched in and blasted pretty much all of Qatar to pieces. For years, the two countries' ancestral tiff has centered on the Hawar Islands, geographically closer to Qatar but also claimed by Bahrain. An International Court of Justice decision handed the islands to the Bahraini branch, and with that matter behind them the rulers of both countries have more or less made up, and there's talk of building a Friendship Bridge between the two lands.

Whatever triggered the Saudis' recent cold shoulder, should Bahrain need help, they'll surely provide it: the Saudis don't want to see their getaway island turn Shia or Iranian. But while Saudis wanted to keep Bahrain Sunni dominant, Iran had other ideas: Khomeini kept calling on the oppressed to rebel. In 1981, forty Shia tried to overthrow the emir and transform Bahrain into a theocracy. Three years later, Shia militants tried to organize another coup, but their huge arms shipment from Iran was seized. Three years after that, several more were rounded up and accused of a plot to bomb oil facilities and Western banks. And throughout the eighties, the emir was loading up on arms and welcoming the U.S. Navy to run operations from his Gulf getaway. Westerners lived in fine style. The emir loved to have parties for them at his beach palace, from which his people were barred. And while Westerners had plenty of rights, his people were denied theirs.

Two decades later, quite a few Bahraini were fed up. In 1994, at the behest of Shia cleric Sheik Ali Salman, twenty-five thousand Bahrainis, both Shia and Sunni (including government employees), signed a petition demanding return of the National Assembly. This led to the cleric's imprisonment, then exile to the United Kingdom. Others were rounded up, and government employees who'd signed the petition were ejected from their posts. The emir relented, sort of, offering to create an "advisory council" of thirty Sunni. This announcement led to more protests, and even upping the number of advisers to forty had no effect. Protests turned into occasional riots, more people were tossed into prison and exiled, and anger levels kept rising. Starting in 1994, violent protests and demonstrations erupted every night—and continued for years.

When Hamad took over, he immediately loosened the iron grip. Releasing political prisoners, he promised a return of citizens' rights, including introducing the National Action Charter transforming Bahrain into a constitutional monarchy and reopening the National Assembly. In 2001, over 98 percent of Bahrain's 207,000 eligible voters gave the new emir's ideas the green light.

Hotshots

Crown prince Salman bin Hamad: He's got reform on his mind, and is intent on engaging the Shia that his uncle the prime minister is intent on shutting out.

Dissidents: Whether Shia or Sunni, unemployed youth or angry women, they now know how to make serious waves—with protests, blogs, and appeals to international organizations.

Voting booths: Dissidents accuse the government of giving Sunnis from other countries—Jordan to Saudi Arabia—the right to vote to swing the elections and disempower the Shia.

Al Wafid: The dominant Shia political organization, it won the most seats in parliament.

Michael Jackson: He snatched up an eight-million-dollar mansion in 2006 and was eyeing others, according to local media, who reported the star wanted to avoid the media spotlight,[1] but reported on his every move, including a trip to the dentist.

BLOODY IAN HENDERSON

The British officially dropped the role of protector when Bahrain became independent, but some British security and intelligence experts remained to "maintain order," ensuring that the flow of oil was unhampered and that nobody questioned what soon became a hard-knuckled autocracy headed by Sheik Isa al-Khalifa. Worried that Sheik Isa might have problems controlling his flock, the British introduced Bahrain's leader to Scotsman Ian Henderson. Later knighted by the Queen for his skill at security—a service to which he's accused of bringing torture, rape, and death—before showing up in Bahrain, Henderson had been booted from Kenya for his brutal inquisitions there. He's remembered for three decades of outrageous acts, from stringing up suspects naked and administering electric shocks to using power tools for maiming. Prodemocracy activists were rounded up; even children were reportedly apprehended—and delivered to their family's doorsteps months later in body bags. Due to Western pressure in the mid-nineties, he was demoted to security adviser and after stepping into the power seat, Hamad sent Ian Henderson and his ilk packing.

Hot Spots

Sitra: Site of Bahrain's all-important oil refinery, which produces some 270,000 barrels a day, as well as a Formula One racetrack and a power plant, the port town of Sitra sits thirty miles outside of Manama and is also home to Shia slums and outsider discontent manifested in regular confrontations between youth and security forces.

Hussain Al-Baluchi

The Al-Areen Wildlife Sanctuary, home to native gazelle and exotic fauna and flora, aims to keep nature a part of Bahrain's beauty.

King Fahd Causeway: The link between the time warp that is Saudi Arabia and the modern world, plenty of booze is smuggled into the Saudi kingdom over this bridge.

Military bases: With ports not far from downtown, the U.S. military gets VIP treatment here. Locals couldn't access a third of the island during the 2003 attack on Iraq, when Sheik Isa Air Base was also in use.

Al-Areen Wildlife Sanctuary: Home to native species like the oryx, but other animals from zebras to flamingos thrive here as well.

Mysterious mounds: Believed to be the burial spots for third-century Phoenicians, the hundred thousand mounds that pop up among the landscape have become a controversy: some want to preserve them; Islamists want to rip them up for new housing.

Chapter Thirteen

Oman: Awake at Last

With dusty northern mountains pocked with unexplored caves, lush southern hills fed by monsoons, dramatic gorges, virgin coasts, fishing villages carved into fjords, remote outposts where giant turtles amble onshore in egg-laying fests, Oman— fabled home of Sinbad the sailor—is the most alluring tourism secret of the Middle East. But for most of the twentieth century, Oman was simply a secret: foreigners couldn't get in, and locals couldn't get out of the land that was locked in time.

FAST FACTS:
Saltanat Uman

Government:	Monarchy
Formed:	1650, when the Portuguese were driven out
Ruler:	Sultan Qaboos bin Said al-Said (also prime minister)
GDP 2007:	$40 billion (IMF, 2007)
Per capita GDP:	$15,600 (IMF, 2007)
Population:	3.3 million, including 577,000 nonnationals (July 2008)
Unemployment:	15 percent
Literacy rate:	87 percent men, 74 percent women
Ethnicity:	Arab, Baluchi, S. Asian, African (no percentages available)
Religion:	75 percent Ibadhi Muslim, 25 percent other Muslim and Hindu

---

Population stat: In 1970, when Sultan Qaboos took the reins, the population was nine hundred thousand. Omanis are so thrilled with his new Oman that the birth rate is soaring: women now have six kids on average, half the population is under twenty, and 83 percent is under thirty-five. Pressure's on to create an economy that can sustain the next generation.

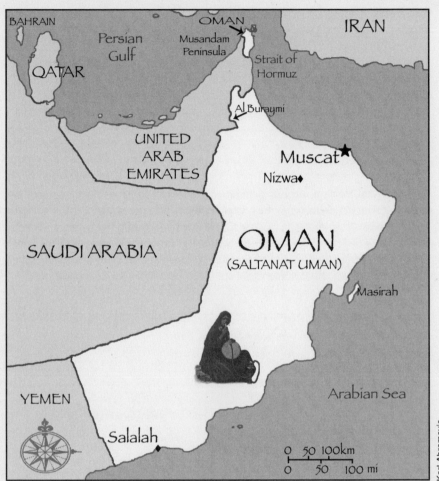

Oman borders unstable Yemen, and its exclave at the tip of the Musandam Peninsula is separated from Iran by a mere forty miles. This diplomatically minded country, which once controlled land all along the UAE coast, keeps the Gulf countries talking and bonded in the Gulf Cooperation Council.

Leader's Corner

He's got his own style: Sultan Qaboos didn't join OPEC, wouldn't ostracize Egypt's Anwar Sadat for peace with Israel, and daringly opened trade with the Israelis.[1] The first Gulf leader to allow U.S. troops on his bases, back in 1980, he doesn't play by harem rules either: Qaboos only had one wife, and they divorced long ago. Despite being unconventional, Qaboos, who booted his dad in a 1970 bloodless coup, is loved and respected by pretty much everybody. He's a peacemaker who keeps GCC members talking, opened diplomatic relations with Iran, and even got Kuwait-Iraq diplomacy thawed in hopes of defusing the 2003 U.S. invasion, which he opposed. Most of his subjects adore him: he stopped a civil war and led them out of the Dark Ages imposed by his pa. Literacy rates soared from under 5 percent in 1970 to over 80 percent; the economy blossomed, the modern world arrived, and gorgeous architecture is now unfolding in the tidy capital of Muscat. Writing a Basic Law protecting civil liberties in 1996, he created a parliament, or *majlis al shura*, which has served as more of an elected advisory board since 2003, when he granted all Omanis the right to vote. Women sat in the majlis[2] and now sit in the cabinet. Mostly he's an autocrat, but a wise and kind one who has met his people's needs. What little protest exists is mostly low key: one recent "march" consisted of an antisultan poster paraded through a village by a lone donkey.[3]

Sultan Qaboos

Courtesy of Oman Informational Ministry

WHAT MATTERS

Energy matters: Discovered in the 1960s, Oman's oil fields are smallish and scattered about and could dry up by 2020.

Arms matter: A hefty chunk of the budget goes to arms, over 11 percent in 2005, and many of them U.S.-made. Rewarding the hospitality Oman extends to U.S. troops (see below), the United States gives good deals: Sultan Qaboos scored a dozen F-16 fighter planes with full options, laser-guided bombs, and a bunch of missiles for a bit over a billion.

Military matters: The United States launched its 1980 attempt to rescue American hostages in Iran from Oman, and the air force has touched down frequently since. A few thousand U.S. armed forces were stationed here during the 2003 war on Iraq, but after a few anti-U.S. protests, most shipped out.

Religion matters: Most Omanis are Ibadhi, a Sunni sect known for being open-minded.

Family matters: Who will succeed Qaboos is the big question around here. Rumor has it that he has a son from his short-lived marriage.

Gravity matters: More meteorites are found here than anywhere outside of the North Pole.

Nik Wheeler. Courtesy of Saudi Aramco, ASC.

After being kept isolated for most of the twentieth century, Oman is now plugged into the modern world.

Limestone cliffs jut out from azure waters, thick groves of date palms and mangos fringe southern coasts, and dramatic mile-high mountains twist and tumble across the north, their towering peaks shielding the capital, Muscat, from sight. During much of the twentieth century, however, the rugged terrain wasn't the only thing that hid Muscat, which had been for centuries the center of an empire that stretched from southern Asia to East Africa. Sultan Said, the ruler of Oman who claimed power in 1932 and loomed as large as the mountains, effectively cloaked his once dynamic country, hung a Do Not Disturb sign from its neck, and made this formerly prosperous corner of Arabia disappear.

LOST ROMANCE

Land of aromatic riches and site of lost cities that lured famous explorers, Oman doesn't snag much ink now. The legends, mysteries, and the wealth, however, were recorded by early historians on papyrus and chiseled stone, and pretty much everyone who passed by, from Marco Polo to twentieth-century explorer Wilfred Thesiger, left in awe of the spectacular scenery, legends, and artifacts held in ruins and tiny fishing coves, and trapped in the sands; even today travelers may discover skeletons in forgotten caves.

The ancient cartographer Ptolemy designated it Happy Arabia, and locals had reason to be happy, thanks to a gnarly shrub that yielded frankincense, the world's leading luxury good from around 4000 BC to AD 300. The queen of Sheba met King Solomon over a frankincense deal, and Alexander the Great so coveted the fragrant resin that he hoped to capture Arabia to have a lifetime supply. The incense industry was still flourishing when Marco Polo sailed by, marveling at the local maritime trade, so advanced that Omani sailors made it to Europe long before Europeans showed up there. The adventures of Sinbad the sailor, captured in *The Thousand and One Nights*, are shrugged off as tall tales (as unlikely as the flying serpents that ancient Greeks believed lived here guarding the frankincense trees), but satellite imagery has shown that some legends may have held water: fabled Ubar, the frankincense-rich city that vanished overnight—Lawrence of Arabia (just one who tried to find it) dubbed it "the Atlantis of the sands"—may have indeed sunk into the desert. Archaeologists believe a river under Ubar dried up, swallowing the wealthy settlement in a sinkhole. And until quite recently, once-prosperous Oman itself seemed like it had gone the way of Ubar.

Oman was the first Middle Eastern country with which the United States had a treaty, dating back to 1833, an era when America was battling the piracy that plagued its ships in North African waters. Seven years later,

*New Yorkers were stunned to see a ragged and beat-up eighty-foot
wooden dhow pull into the harbor, with a dashing turbaned figure in dark
caftan hoisting a flag, and declaring that this dhow would serve as
Oman's embassy. Bearing trunks brimming with coffee, cloves, dates,
silks, carpets, ivory, and frankincense, the envoy soon sold his wares to
the government of President Martin Van Buren in exchange for three
hundred muskets complete with gunpowder, and several months later
sailed off.*[4]

Once abuzz with innovative foreigners and a haven of technological advances,
only a few decades ago Oman appeared frozen in the medieval era, shut off from
the twentieth century. Through the 1960s, each dusk a cannon thundered from
the sixteenth-century fort guarding its harbor, signaling day's end in the walled city
of Muscat, and the wooden gate was bolted shut; those wandering about in the
shadows of the unlit country were required by law to carry lanterns or risk being
shot. No radio crackled news across the land, nor was there television or newspaper or electricity to be found anywhere outside of the British consulate. Modern
books had been banned by royal decree, but then again few could read, since
Oman had only three schools. Those who studied abroad usually didn't rush back
to this backwater that lacked even indoor plumbing. Bicycles and sunglasses
were banned as too modern and cars were a rarity: the entire Kansas-sized country held five miles of paved roads, a dozen telephones, and as many hospital
beds. The sultan pooh-poohed international groups, including the UN, and
out-of-towners were rarely seen, nor was there a hotel in the land: travelers
couldn't enter without a visa personally approved by the sultan, whose rule was so
absolute that nobody could paint their house without his okay. During Said's
forty-eight-year rule, Oman was erased from the world's eye, and effectively from
the map. There was a reason: once rich, under Said's rule the country was poor,
and he was trying to dig out of the red. What's more, after decades of watching his
neighbors grow wealthy from the oil that Oman was believed not to possess, Said,
well-educated and charming when he first took power, may have gone a bit mad.

HISTORY IN A BOX

A trading powerhouse from Mesopotamian days, this land was renowned
for its navigational prowess. By the thirteenth century, Omanis had almanacs showing both the Gregorian and Islamic calendars, planetary alignments and phases of the moon, bedouin weather forecasts, and scheduled
arrivals of foreign vessels. Centuries before that they had a reputation for
charting the best maps and using the most advanced tools, including sex-

tants of knots to determine locations, and had figured out how to sail with the monsoon; fourteenth-century navigator Ahmad ibn Majid popularized and revamped the compass. In the sixteenth century, the Portuguese barreled in with their galleons and cannons and changed the nature of the warring game. Portuguese commanders invaded Oman, dropping anchor in Muscat, where they built their first forts and ruthlessly controlled most of the coastal territory for the next century and a half. Loathing Muslims and burning locals' boats, Portuguese killed Omanis' trade and monopolized the waters, ushering in economic deprivation and piracy. Gulf waters only grew more treacherous as other Europeans wandered in (en route to India), making a floating battlefield of these parts, and further killing trade. Even the powerful Ottomans, who showed up in 1550 to drive off the Portuguese, couldn't eject them.

In the mid-seventeenth century, a local imam gathered enough force to run the Portuguese out, a task completed in 1650, and his progeny became Oman's ruling family, although they were not imams, taking the title of sultan. What began in the name of liberation snowballed into regional expansion as Sultan ibn Saif oversaw the rise of Oman, which emerged as the dominant force in the Indian Ocean. Starting colonies in Mozambique, Zanzibar, Pakistan—even Bahrain and Persia's coast were briefly snagged—the Omanis ran a brisk trade in ivory, coffee, and slaves. However, rebellions have fractured the land at times, arising from conflicts between the sultan and religious leaders; during one rebellion, Oman's ruler asked Persia to come in and cool things down. Quick to help, the Persians were slow to leave: the sultan then called upon the British to pry them out. Oman benefited from the British armed forces, arms, and diplomatic ways, and Britain needed the sultan's help to battle piracy. They also wanted his land to lay telegraph wires to connect Europe with India via Morse code. The British, so helpful in battling threats to the sultanate, ended up unraveling the Omani empire. During a succession snag, they handed Zanzibar to one son and Oman to the other. They solved friction between the sultan and imam by giving the religious leader the interior and the sultan the coast. And when the Brits cracked down on the slave trade, they devastated Oman's economy, already bruised by steamships, which outraced the sturdiest dhows. By the late 1800s, Oman was a divided weakling. Sultan Faisal kept a caged lion in his palace, which served as Muscat's prison: those who survived weren't usually repeat offenders. But most weapons, including the thirty-six-gun frigate and entire fleet, had been sold off. When bedouin tribes invaded, the Omani army couldn't fight and so Faisal paid them to leave. By the time his son Taimur took power, Oman was such a mess—and facing bankruptcy—that the sultan set up in India and ruled Oman from afar. And such was the picture when Taimur's son, Said, returned to Oman, sat down in the power seat in 1932, and slammed the door. Oman was poor, backward, and boring, but at least Said put the finances in order.

In the mad search for oil, the British approached Said in the 1930s, asking to explore, but decade after decade none was found. Persia and Bahrain were gushing with petroleum, so were Saudi Arabia and Kuwait. But the oil genie ignored Oman. In the mid-1950s, the British suggested there might be some in the land ruled by the imam, and after a four-year battle Said annexed the interior to the coast that he ruled, but still none was found. Finally, prospectors struck oil in 1964. Deposits were small, scattered about, and hard to get at, but oil it was. Yet by the time there was money to show, fiscally prudent Said was afraid to use it. Oman's only hope for progress—Qaboos, the handsome crown prince who'd returned after graduation from British military school Sandhurst—was locked up in a faraway palace in southern Oman, cut off from visitors, except for his mother and the scholar who gave him lessons on the Koran. The harder the British pushed Said to put Qaboos in his shoes, the more Said panicked, until finally in 1970 the heir apparent walked out of the palace and into the throne, and Said was whisked off to London by British forces, never to see the light fully come on in the country he'd kicked back to the Dark Ages.

The country that Qaboos snagged in the 1970 ouster was not only backward and broke, it was ripped apart by a civil war that had originated six years before near Dhofar deep in the south: with Communist ideals at its roots, the war of rebels against the sultan in Muscat was funded by Russia and China and dragged on until 1975, draining most of the treasury. The war's end came about not through military action but via an illustration of the new sultan's persuasive charms: rebels gradually drifted to the sultan's side, lured by his promises for a better life (and for positions in the new government). Another factor was that the religion-loathing Communists minimized the importance of Ibadhi Islam, the country's dominant religion for centuries, and still the state religion today.

THE FIRST MUSLIM REBELS

Once largely a pagan society—moon goddesses and Bacchus were among those worshipped—the assorted peoples living in Oman converted to Islam as warriors swept in across the Empty Quarter, the vast desert that separates Oman from holy sites Mecca and Medina, the original seats of the Islamic empire. As future caliphs switched the capital first to Damascus then Baghdad, regional trade blossomed. Boats hauled goods from this corner of the empire to Iraq, but this corner was known for more than its ports. Tucked away deep in folded mountains, the settlement of Nizwa rose up as a center of Islamic scholarship, and it would soon become a magnet for the sect of Ibadhis, who are the oldest existing Islamic dissidents: shortly after the seventh-century death of the prophet Mohammed, the originators began holding clandestine meetings in caves near Basra in Iraq. Believing that Muslims should not attack fellow

Muslims first or profit from moves into Muslim lands, they objected to the militaristic campaigns of the assorted caliphs—positions that made them unpopular with the rulers. Under persecution, Ibadhi followers flocked to Nizwa, in Oman's interior, where their leaders ruled. Growing more powerful, Nizwa and environs became the seat of an imamate in the early eighth century. The existence of a rival Islamic faction raised the ire of the Islamic ruler in Damascus, who in 752 invaded Oman, killing the Ibadhi imam, though scarcely snuffing out the imamate. The effect of the caliph's occupation was divisive for centuries: never united under one flag, the interior was ruled by imams, while foreign powers—first Arab, then Persian—for centuries controlled much of the thirteen-hundred-mile coast. The division was so extreme that the territory was at points called Muscat and Oman: the sultan ruling the former and the imam the latter.

Helped along by new oil discoveries as well as natural gas, Sultan Qaboos, who was thirty when he took control, had more than a modernizing view; when the civil war finally ended, he had a budget to work with. Now in a flurry of progress, the country's lit up with more than electricity: most everyone has a mobile phone, Oman is hooked up to the Internet, most Omanis under thirty-five can read, and the government pays all the fees for those who wish to study abroad. Hotels are coming, new businesses are starting, and unlike many cities that grow up overnight, Muscat's growth and design are tightly controlled: the architecture is nearly all sand-colored or white, and all of Islamic design—which makes for a stunning effect. The capital is so tidy that drivers are ticketed for dirty cars: dusty vehicles trying to enter from the UAE are turned away.

Bringing lights, phones, roads, and modern hospitals to Oman, building thousands of schools and giving women the right to attend them (females make up over half the students attending Qaboos University), Qaboos triggered what is widely known as the Oman Renaissance. He is also pretty much an absolute (albeit benevolent) ruler, holding the post of prime minister, foreign minister, and defense minister and is even in charge of banks. Pundits point out that the "parliament" he set up lacks serious teeth, and while a free press is theoretically guaranteed by the Basic Law, it comes with a caveat that it can't run articles about defense, the royal family, or anything that would affect economic affairs; some independent agencies regard it as entirely controlled. Still, Qaboos, who makes an annual trek through his country—meeting his people one-on-one, hearing their wishes and complaints—is widely admired: his touch has been golden in the land. He put his country back on the map, signing up Oman for everything from the United Nations to the GCC and Arab League, where for decades "the hermit kingdom" had been conspicuously absent. Foreign embassies opened, and the Omani government set up embassies abroad, taking the revolutionary step of even appointing a female ambassador to the Netherlands in

1999—the first time a woman represented a Gulf country. In 2005, he appointed another woman as ambassador to the United States. In short, Oman is a gem, and the only real problem is who will fill the shoes of Qaboos: born in 1940, he is hasn't yet produced heirs, although there are rumors that he has a son hidden away somewhere.

> *The sultan has his own perfume line: retailing at over two hundred dollars a bottle, Amouage Gold, which contains frankincense, is said to be the most expensive perfume in the world. Part of the price is the bottle, which is heavy with gold.*

Hotshots

The cousins: Given that the sultan has no known heirs (beyond his rumored son), his cousins are likely to succeed. The question is, which one will it be? Haithem ibn Tariq al-Said is head of national heritage and culture and said to be building a frankincense trail to attract tourism. Some say Assad ibn Tariq, former brigadier general and unofficial foreign minister, is most likely to command the future post of sultan.[5] Well, unless that son turns up.

Imam Ghalib bin Ali: When Qaboos overthrew his father, one of his first goals was to mend fences with the imam exiled in Saudi Arabia. The imam wouldn't see him.

Hot Spots

Salalah: Oman's second-biggest city, far away in the south, is surrounded with banana plantations and coconut groves. It was the epicenter of the Dhofar rebellion that began in 1962 and snowballed into a full-scale civil war that wasn't extinguished until 1975. Salalah's developed, but its outskirts are still tribal. Some live in houses built into mountains, and many speak dialects unheard elsewhere, including a melodic "language of birds." Close to the border with Yemen, Dhofar is still a source of anxiety.

The Buraimi Oasis: Once believed to hold oil, it's long been a source of territorial debate between Saudis, Emiratis, and Omanis.

Musandam Peninsula: Site of the Khasib military base that the United States helped to revamp, this little speck of land is the closest the Arabian Peninsula comes to Iran; thousands of Iranians head across the Strait of Hormuz daily for the black-market dealing here, arriving in boats filled with goats, and leaving with boats full of booze and cigarettes.

Most of Oman's rugged beach front is still undeveloped.

Sohar: Site of Oman's biggest refinery, this city north of Muscat has a new port (built with the Port of Rotterdam Authority) and industry is booming.

Nizwa: The heartland of the Ibadhi religion and ruling post of previous imams, its stunning forts are being converted into museums, but it was recently the site of an attempted religious takeover: apparently a few want to bring back the imamate.

CHEAT SHEET 3
The Westerners

Library of Congress, Maston Collection

Petropolitics isn't what matters here in these lands that make frequent appearances in the Bible: the Arab-Israeli conflict steals center stage. Pictured: the holy city Jerusalem, which both Israelis and Palestinians claim as their capital. It is home to the holiest sites for Jews and the third-holiest site for Muslims.

Traveling west toward the Mediterranean, into rocky terrain of orange groves and wind-bent olive trees, an entirely different political landscape emerges, where neither the lifestyle nor the priorities are the same as they are in the countries that edge the Gulf. Studded with mystical ruins, these holy lands are rich in legend, but they're short on oil, unless you're talking the kind made with olives.

THE WESTERNERS: A COMPARISON CHART

Country	Religion	Population[6] (M)	GDP per capita[7]	Literacy/ women[8] (%)
Israel	77% Jewish, 16% Muslim	7.1 million	$22,500	97/96
Palestinian territories	85% Sunni 11% Jewish	4 million	$1,075 (CIA)	93/88

Country	Religion	Population[6] (M)	GDP per capita[7]	Literacy/ women[8] (%)
Jordan	92% Sunni, 6% Christian, 2% others	6.2 million	$2,800	90/85
Lebanon	60% assorted Muslim, 39% Christian	4 million	$6,600	88/83
Syria	74% Sunni, 16% other Muslim, 10% Christian	20 million	$2,000	80/74
Egypt	90% Sunni Muslim, 10% Christian	82 million	$1,800	72/60

In this region, monarchs are few: Jordan's King Abdullah is the sole royal in these parts, but republics are often dictatorships, as in Egypt and Syria, where the presidents were dubiously elected with 96 percent of the vote. Nationalism, whether Arab or Israeli, is big, and money is tight. Families tend to be large and incomes are low, most dipping deep into poverty levels; except, that is, for Israel, the national homeland for Jews that, since its birth in 1948, has been the focal point of regional politics.

Every bit as important as the discovery of oil in the Gulf states, Israel forms the backdrop of nearly every Middle Eastern conflict in this western region, including Palestinian uprisings and suicide bombers. Initially made possible by Britain, which wrote the Balfour Declaration of 1917, and now armed and supported by the United States, the creation of the Jewish state is a symbol of freedom for Jews and a symbol of Western interference in the Mideast for Muslims. The U.S. foreign policy that plays out here is rife with biblical implications for American evangelicals, particularly those known as Christian Zionists, who view the return of Jews to Israel as a necessary precursor to the return of Christ. Hard-core Muslims see both Israel and U.S. foreign policy as standing in the way of their plan to reestablish an Islamic caliphate stretching from the Mideast to Europe.

In this part of the Middle East, countries are literally defined, economically and politically, by their relationship with Israel, which in most cases is bad. Those who support Israel are treated with deference by DC; those who don't are pressured to change and sometimes punished if they don't. The United States, a staunch supporter of Israel from the start, has bent over backward to help peace happen, costly though it may be.

Library of Congress

Jesus is believed to have carried his cross up Via Dolorosa (pictured above) in Jerusalem. Although Christians are the only monotheists who aren't demanding Jerusalem as their capital, Christian Zionists believe that it will belong to Christians in the future—when Jesus returns. Christian Zionists in the United States and their affiliates, including former UN ambassador John Bolton, are turning this religious belief into a cornerstone of U.S. Middle East policy.

HISTORY IN A BOX

The problems brewing up in the region today, from suicide bombers to Arab-Israeli wars, started with a slingshot: shortly after David took down a giant with a well-aimed shot, he became ruler of Jews, says the Bible. Around 1000 BC, King David founded Jerusalem as capital of the Kingdom of Judea and Israel, which stretched from the edges of Egypt through Palestine into Lebanon, Jordan, and Syria. The kingdom of the Jews was the fulfillment of a promise God had made, says the Bible, to give a "land of milk and honey" to the descendants of Abraham, who were, according to the Old Testament, God's chosen people. David's son, King Solomon, built the first Jewish temple around 957 BC, placing in it the stone slabs that held the Ten Commandments. The temple was razed by Babylonians (from today's Iraq) in 586 BC, but Jews returned from captivity and built a new one in 516 BC. It was toppled in AD 70 by the Romans, who'd killed Jesus around AD 33 and later banished the Jews in AD 135.

Muslim rulers claimed this land in the seventh century, building a gold-capped shrine, the Dome of the Rock, in 688, just where the Jewish temple had stood. These lands remained part of the Islamic caliphate until 1099. That year, Christian Crusaders claimed the holy city of Jerusalem and remained until Kurdish warrior Saladin pushed them out in 1187. The Ottomans, Muslim Turks, ruled here from the sixteenth century until World War I, when Britain and France moved in, rearranging the region politically and religiously. The French created the first Christian-dominant country when they sliced off Lebanon from Syria; the British had a more profound effect: when lobbied by the head of the World Zionist Organization, they agreed to establish a homeland for Jews in Palestine.

Since the 1880s, Zionists had been moving to the area and buying up land through an international trust to purchase a homeland, and their arrival was at first not alarming to the Arab farmers, the Palestinians, who lived there. However, when the British announced the homeland plan in the 1917 Balfour Declaration, locals balked, since the idea of "a land without people for a people without a land," as the Jewish national homeland was billed, overlooked reality: there were already plenty of people in this land—the Arabs had farms and olive groves all over the place. Protests turned into revolts. Jews and Arabs who once traded now fought, particularly as more Jews moved in after escaping the Nazis. The British couldn't control the ensuing chaos. When they stopped immigration, the Zionists took aim at them, and so, in 1947, they finally tossed the problem at the United Nations, which divided Palestine into a land for Jews (55 percent), with the leftover patches going to the Palestinians, and Jerusalem to be shared by both. The Arabs said no; the Jews said yes anyway and proclaimed their new country on May 14, 1948. Fighting began the next day and has continued in one form or another ever since. Israel ultimately took Jerusalem, expanded its holdings to 78 percent, and occupied the rest. In the process, over a million Palestinians were run out of their homes. Those wounds have never been dressed and are now horribly festering.

The right of Palestinians to return to their land, mandated by UN Security Council Resolution 242, but ignored by Israel and global policeman the United States, is one of several problems that plagues Middle East peace.

It appeared that the Arab-Israeli wars would finally end with the signing of the 1979 Israeli-Egyptian peace treaty. Some credit the history-rearranging treaty for relative peace after three decades of fighting and others blame it for the unhealthy

Sa'ar Ya'acov, Israel National Archives

The world's most expensive handshake. When Egyptian president Anwar Sadat and Israel's prime minister Menachem Begin signed a treaty in 1979, it cost the United States a pretty penny. American taxpayers have so far shelled out over $150 billion for these two countries to get along. It's ironic that most of the U.S.-given money spent to keep peace goes for arms.

power arrangement that seems to breed violence. It changed the alliance system in the Middle East, since without Egypt's army no Arab country could challenge Israel. By signing the agreement, Anwar Sadat, some felt, had also kissed off the rights of the Palestinians, leaving them to fend for themselves.

THE 1979 ISRAELI-EGYPTIAN PEACE TREATY

This groundbreaking, earth-shaking peace treaty between Egypt's Anwar Sadat and Israel's Menachem Begin, negotiated by President Jimmy Carter, was signed in 1979. The agreement called for Israel to return the Sinai Peninsula (taken during the 1967 Arab-Israeli war) to Egypt in exchange for Egypt recognizing Israel's "right to exist." The agreement also included provisions to address Palestinian refugees, but that clause has been forgotten. The Israeli-Egyptian peace treaty was revolutionary because it marked the first time that an Arab country had formally acknowledged Israel as a legitimate nation, and Sadat and Begin shared a 1978 Nobel Peace Prize for their work. An added incentive: the United States offered to pay some three billion dollars annually to the two countries if they continued to get along, most of it in the form of U.S.-made weapons. On paper they still do, but their rapport is dicey: outside of the gas Egypt pipes over to Israel, trade doesn't amount to much, and 97 percent of Egyptians still regard Israel as an enemy. When Israel gave up the Sinai, it lost the only land that held oil, but the United States signed an understanding with Israel that it would be responsible for providing oil should Israel have difficulty obtaining it.

The leaders paid heavily for the peace: Sadat was shunned by the Arab world (which cut all financial aid and kicked Egypt out of the powerful Arab League) and was killed by a still-simmering dissident two years later. Menachem Begin was later gunned down by a radical Jew.

Not only is the peace chilly, there have been two unintentional results of the treaty. The first is that Israel has become far more aggressive: invading Lebanon a number of times, striking at Syria, and tightening its hold over the remaining Palestinian territories through military operations, targeted assassinations, and economic strangulation. One means Israelis use to pen Palestinians in and simultaneously expand Israeli territory is to build settlements. The settlers, many motivated by biblical promises and the coming of the Jewish Messiah, are staking land outside the recognized borders. They become an extension of the military, literally creating forts. Some four hundred thousand Israeli settlers are now living in Palestinian territory and Syria with financial backing from the Israeli government and top leaders, who arm them and waive taxes. Groups once considered radical, such as Gush Emunim, which believes that the acquisition of "Greater Israel" is required before the Messiah arrives, now run the government housing ministry. Many are wondering how far they're going to take it. Some of the biblical revisionists, who formed the basis of the Likud Party in Israel, say Greater Israel should extend into Jordan; some groups think Lebanon and even part of Iraq should be included. And since the creation of Israel in 1948, Arab nationalists, including Saudi king Faisal, have been obsessed with the notion that Israel intends to expand far beyond that. These fears are still played up by militants, including Osama bin Laden.

"We must remember that Iraqi oil fields too are located on Jewish land."
—Rabbi Avrom Shmulevic, leader of the "for the homeland" movement Bead Artzein in September 2001, as reported in *Novosty Nedely*, a Russian-language Israeli newspaper

The second result of the peace treaty is that since countries can't overtly fight Israel, independent actors have taken over: militias now fight Israel, whether with rockets or suicide missions. Some are started by the Muslim Brotherhood, and some are funded by Iran and/or wealthy Muslims. And they're winding up youth to fight on the streets. Palestinians are now taking on Israelis in intifadas, uprisings in which they've killed hundreds with human nail bombs. Those acts have triggered violent responses from Israel, which is killing members of militant

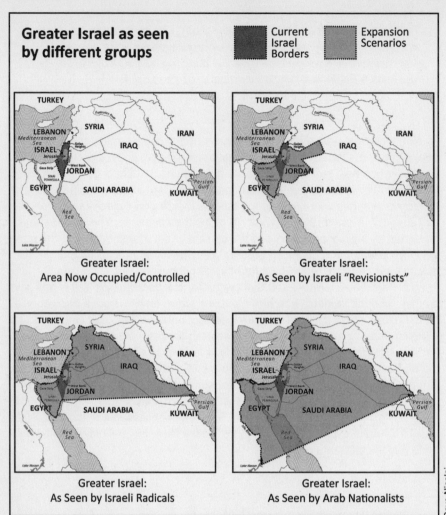

Greater Israel as seen by different groups

Current Israel Borders — Expansion Scenarios

Greater Israel:
Area Now Occupied/Controlled

Greater Israel:
As Seen by Israeli "Revisionists"

Greater Israel:
As Seen by Israeli Radicals

Greater Israel:
As Seen by Arab Nationalists

Dave Nicolai

groups. Forget the idea of lumping guerrillas into one "terrorist" pot: usually they're competing with one another and trying to set each other up. What is missed by the Western media is that if one group makes an agreement with Israel, their rival tries to screw it up.

MILITANTS

PLO: Started in 1964 by the Arab League to protect rights of Palestinians displaced by the 1948 war, the Palestinian Liberation Organization quickly became a guerrilla group that was never terribly effective except in creating violence wherever it set foot. Broken into factions, the assorted Palestinian groups that started under the PLO banner became infamous for bloody raids into Israel, hijackings, kidnapping OPEC ministers, killing ambassadors, and murdering eleven Israeli athletes at the 1972 Munich Olympics. Run out of Jordan in 1970 for criminal activities and violence, the PLO became even more militant in Lebanon, where Arafat tried to start a revolution and helped kick off that country's civil war. The PLO was shipped out of Lebanon in 1982. With Saudi Arabia and Kuwait throwing their oil weight around to get more recognition for Palestinians, the PLO was internationally acknowledged in 1984 as voice of the Palestinian people, and Arafat mellowed a bit. When he backed Saddam in the 1991 Persian Gulf War, he lost his multibillion-dollar backing from Kuwait and Saudi Arabia and was forced to make peace with the Israelis. The result: the 1993 Oslo Accords, which created the first interim government for Palestinians, the Palestinian Authority—alas, with Arafat as its leader.

Fatah: The largest branch of the PLO, and the one Arafat headed, it's now led by Palestinian president Mahmoud Abbas, who is at least slightly sharper than Arafat. Despite its previous atrocities and former avowal to take down Israel, Fatah has lightened up and is not labeled as a terrorist group by the United States or Israel anymore; now both want Fatah alone to represent the Palestinians. Hamas begs to differ.

Hamas: Started in 1987 by the Palestinian branch of the Muslim Brotherhood, Hamas wants to take down Israel and start an Islamic government. The group runs clinics, ambulances, and social services much needed by Palestinians. It is also known for its well-trained, gung-ho militants and for being the main force behind suicide bombings before winning the Palestinian elections in 2005, which caused it to clean up its act for a while. In 2008, however, it sent more suicide bombers to Israel—shocking not only because Hamas reverted to this frightening means of making a point, but because the bombers got in. Not only does Hamas hate Israel, it also despises Fatah. When Fatah makes a promise to halt violence against Israel, Hamas has two reasons to break it.

Islamic Jihad: Also started by the Muslim Brotherhood, Islamic Jihad has the same goals as Hamas, including a belief that all land from the Jordan River to the Mediterranean was given by God to Palestinians. Islamic Jihad wants to be top dog in Gaza, where Hamas is trying to run the show without them. When Hamas makes a promise to halt violence against Israel, Islamic Jihad has two reasons to break it.

Hezbollah: Working out of Lebanon, Hezbollah is *not* Palestinian, and Hezbollah *is* Shia, unlike the rest. Hezbollah provides social services and has entered politics, until recently holding two cabinet seats and fourteen seats in Lebanon's parliament; the ruin of Israel is a stated goal. Formed in 1982 to push Israel out of Lebanon, it is headed by Hassan Nasrallah, a hero to Arabs for militarily standing up to Israel during a devastating attack on Lebanon in 2006.

As part of a "two-state" solution—one country for Jews, another for Palestinians—the 1993 Oslo Accords between Israel and the PLO laid the foundations for a future Palestinian state. The accords granted Palestinians control of some cities, while Israel controlled the countryside. Controversial from the start, since the intifada (Palestinian uprising) that began in 2000, and Israel's attacks on Palestinian territories, the agreement is so shaky that it's no longer much in effect.

There's only one bright spot in this very dark picture. Guerrillas *can* change: many of yesterday's terrorists are today's peacemakers, among them the former head of Irgun, a Zionist guerrilla group that blew up the King David Hotel in 1946, killing ninety-one. Namely, former Israeli prime minister Menachem Begin, who went on to sign up for Israeli-Egyptian peace. It would be great to see Hassan Nasrallah, Hamas leaders, and the rest go the same way.

PLO chairman Yasir Arafat and Israeli leaders Shimon Peres and Yitzhak Rabin won the Nobel Prize for the 1993 Oslo Accords, which set the framework for a Palestinian state. It marked the first breakthrough in Palestinian-Israeli relations since Israel's creation—an event regarded by Arabs as the Naqba, or holocaust.

Last Word

Egypt's president Hosni Mubarak shoved Israel and Hamas into a (weak) truce in summer 2008. Turkey got Israel to finally take Syria seriously. Qatar got Lebanon's political factions talking—and after nineteen months without a head, the Lebanese elected Michel Suleiman as president in May 2008. The UN pushed Israel and Hezbollah to exchange prisoners. All of these are precarious agreements that may not hold. But that outside agents, most of them leaders of Middle Eastern countries, have extracted them is remarkable—and a promising sign that the Middle East can take care of itself without the United States getting involved. And that behooves all of us.

Chapter Fourteen

Israel: Fulfilling Prophecies

Library of Congress

In this mystical patch of holy stones and olive trees, petroleum doesn't dictate politics. Biblical promises and ancient prophecies do.

Desert sweeps across two-thirds of this thirsty country prone to drought and tight on arable land. Biblical plagues, such as swarming locusts, still descend; earthquakes rattle frequently and seismologists predict a major tumbler around the bend. A Realtor's nightmare elsewhere is a gold mine here, where land is too much in demand: Jews arrive from afar to work on collective farms and stake new claims in the Holy Land, evangelical Christians from the United States buy front-row-view housing for the "last days," and Palestinians want to

Karl Abramovic

The map of Israel has vastly changed since the UN first drew it in 1947, allocating 55 percent of Palestine (outside of Jerusalem, which was to be international territory) as a homeland for Jews in the wake of their persecution during World War II when millions died in concentration camps. After the Arab-Israeli war of 1948, Israel expanded its territory to cover 78 percent of Palestine. After 1967, it occupied all of it, and controversially annexed Jerusalem as its eternal capital too. Occasionally, there are plans (such as the 1993 Oslo Accords and the "road map to peace") to create a Palestinian state in the West Bank and Gaza, where many Palestinians live after the expansions took their land. As of 2008, these plans appear to be crashing. This area is tiny, however it's partitioned: all of Israel and the Palestinian territories would fit into Maryland.

reclaim their orchards now lost on the other side of Israel's byways and security wall. The thorniest of the Middle East's problems sprouts up around here on the soil where Jesus walked, prophets talked, temples rose, and Mohammed ascended. This is the national homeland for Jews, whose ancestors prospered here in a powerful ancient kingdom three thousand years ago but were driven out by Romans in AD 135, creating the diaspora, which formally gathered together as a nation again on this land in 1948. But Israelis remain under threat: Israeli borders, which tend to expand, are marked by constant conflicts. The underlying issue (besides water) is that many Israelis, even those who are not devout, believe that this is land promised to Jews by God.[1] The Arabs who previously lived on this land disagree; some believe that Allah gave it to them.[2]

FAST FACTS:
Medinat Yisra'el

Government:	Parliamentary democracy
Formed:	May 14, 1948 (from British Mandate)
Leaders:	Prime Minister Ehud Olmert, President Shimon Peres
GDP 2006:	$161 billion (IMF, 2007)
Per capita GDP:	$ 22,000 (IMF, 2007)
Population:	7.2 million, including over 460,000 settlers[3] occupying lands in West Bank, East Jerusalem, and Golan Heights (July 2008 estimate)
Unemployment:	8 percent
Literacy rate:	99 percent men, 96 percent women
Ethnicity:	76 percent Jewish, 24 percent non-Jewish (mostly Arab)
Religion:	76 percent Jewish, 16 percent Muslim, 2 percent Christian, 2 percent Druze, 4 percent unspecified

Population stat: the 1950 Law of Return invites Jews from around the world to relocate in Israel, where they all speak Hebrew, the national language. The aliyah, or wave of arrivals, of over a million Jews from Russia and former Soviet states since 1989 has boosted the population dramatically, being the largest wave since Israel was formed.

Leader's Corner

Israeli prime minister Ehud Olmert of the Kadima Party inherited the premier's seat in 2006, when Ariel Sharon fell into a coma. Olmert is aggressive and controversial: his government is building a security wall that snakes into Palestinian territory and has sealed off Gaza entirely. Israel often cuts electricity to Gaza and at points has blocked all emergency goods into that Palestinian territory. Olmert has also launched a number of hard-hitting military operations. In June 2006, when militants snuck out from under the wall that surrounds Gaza, killing three border guards and kidnapping a soldier, he responded by pounding the twenty-five-mile-long strip with bombs, killing hundreds during attacks that lasted months. In July 2006, when Lebanese militia (and U.S.-designated terrorist organization) Hezbollah captured two Israeli soldiers, he sent out the military to pummel Lebanon for over a month, causing billions in damage and killing a thousand civilians. His disproportionate responses and refusal to accept calls for a cease-fire were loudly condemned by the world (except the United States). Israel's investigating commission called the war rash, poorly planned, and ineffective. When Gazan militants continued to shoot thousands of rockets over the wall, killing an Israeli in March 2008, Olmert's deputy defense minister promised a "holocaust" for Gazans in response,[4] and Olmert launched another attack that killed over a hundred within three days. His term has been plagued by scandals: he's being investigated for fraud, and his president, Moshe Katsav, resigned facing allegations of rape. The United States pushed Olmert into peace talks, but he doesn't appear sincere. Lately, however, he's been on a diplomatic whirlwind— making truces with Hamas, negotiating with Hezbollah, thawing toward Syria (see "Last Word," p. 339).

WHAT MATTERS

Petroleum matters: There's barely enough oil here to power the war machine,[5] but there's some natural gas offshore. More natural gas comes in from Egypt via pipeline.

Electricity matters: Israel lessens electrical demand by using more solar power per person than anyplace else: sun-powered water heaters dot roofs countrywide, and the Negev Desert may soon be transformed into a vast field of ray-concentrating cells.[6] The country is also considering investing in nuclear energy.

Arms matter: Famous for Uzis and Arrow missiles, Israel is the world's fourth-biggest arms seller (India is the biggest customer) but snags some two billion dollars' worth of free U.S.-made weaponry a year—F-16s, Apache helicopters, snazzy laser-defense systems—as part of the Israeli-Egyptian peace deal brokered by the United States in 1979. Among the gifts: controversial weapons such as cluster bombs and white phosphate bombs. The United States and Israel are also jointly developing weapons systems as part of the Star Wars II missile shield. Although it doesn't admit it, Israel possesses at least two hundred nukes.[7]

Military matters: At age seventeen, almost every Jewish Israeli, male or female, is drafted into the armed forces; men serve three years, women two. Ultraorthodox Jews, however, are exempt from service; the Druze, a sect in the north, are the only Muslims/Arabs allowed to serve. Military service shapes Israelis' national identity, and the Israel Defense Forces are Israel's most trusted and important institution. Armed and paid by the government, settlers are also used for strategic matters, pushing Israel's boundaries further into the West Bank and Syria as they set up housing settlements that simultaneously serve as defensive fronts and help to gain water, often being built over springs and aquifers.

Demographics matter: Israel is worried that Palestinians in the occupied territories (about 4.5 million) will outnumber Jews, which is why the ultraorthodox are encouraged to have large families (see below). A quarter of Israelis are not Jewish; various right-wing factions want non-Jews, most of them Arab Muslims, out of the country; Arab Muslim settlements within Israel pay taxes but don't get full municipal services, such as trash pickup, and some aren't fully electrified.

Religion matters: In Israel there is no constitution, since some Israelis protest that it would interfere with Jewish law; marriages and funerals can only be conducted by rabbis, and airlines don't fly on the holy day, Saturday. Not all Israelis practice Judaism or practice the same form of Judaism, and almost half don't regularly attend synagogue services. Increasingly powerful ultraorthodox Jews, about 8 percent of Israel's Jewish population, pray three times daily, don't watch TV, dress modestly, eat only kosher food, demand gender segregation on their buses, and refrain from work on Saturday. Among the ultraorthodox, 60 percent don't work, couples usually have six children or more, 50 percent of families require government subsidies, and they're known to clash with secular Israelis over matters such as dress.[8] About 12 percent of Israelis are orthodox, practicing most of the strict traditions but more amenable to engaging with modernity. Another 35 percent of Israelis are traditional, observing many Jewish customs and holidays, while about 44 percent say they are secular.[9] They dress in more modern ways and may drive on the holy day, but most are not atheist and many hold Jewish beliefs: most, for instance, eat only kosher food and partake in holidays. Secular Israelis typically want to keep religion out of politics, but this is increasingly difficult as more parliament seats are taken by religious parties: ultraorthodox parties now hold 20 of the Knesset's 120 seats.

Money matters: Lots of funny money floating around here—one illustration that organized crime is alive and well in Israel, alas.

You can sense it everywhere from the Western Wall, its cracks stuffed with notes to God, to the hilltop collective farms amid flowering orange groves: in Israel—the most developed democracy in the Middle East and by far the most literate and economically diverse—joy, relief, entitlement, and worry intermingle in all corners at all hours. You can feel it as the sunset drapes down over the glittering port city Haifa, as dawn's seagulls swarm along the beach bars at Tel Aviv, as the sun's rays catch on the gleaming gold dome that rises over Jerusalem's walled Old City. The country first envisioned by late nineteenth-century Zionists came to fruition in 1948 when prime minister David Ben-Gurion and Zionist president Chaim Weizmann declared the birth of Israel. Created for Jews and by Jews, Israel is a homeland where they live freely without the persecution they'd long suffered, most horribly during World War II

Israeli Tourism Board

The Old City in East Jerusalem is home to the holiest sites for Jews. Shown here is the favored place of prayer, the Western Wall, with the Muslims' Dome of the Rock looming over it.

when Nazis sent most to concentration camps, and six million died. With the motto "Never again!" Jews from all corners arrived to create this small, strong, and self-made country where riches don't come from petroleum: cooperation and innovation are what fuel the place.

A NATION, A SYMBOL, A WAY OF THOUGHT

Israel isn't merely a country: it's a state of mind. Here, Jews—persecuted for centuries—can live with fellow Jews on the land where over three thousand years ago their ancestors lived under King David. Here in Palestine is their most sacred site, the Holy of Holies, a small room from their first temple—now buried under the Old City of Jerusalem—that once held the tablets of the Ten Commandments and to which Jews direct their prayers. In Israel they can make good on the prayer recited for thousands of years at the end of every Passover seder: "Next year—in Jerusalem." Here they can embrace the rituals and culture that were kept alive in the Diaspora after Jews were kicked out of this land in the second century AD. And here they can fulfill biblical promises from God to Abraham recorded in the Old Testament thousands of years ago, that they should live and prosper on this land, which would be taken from them, and returned.

"Behold, I will take the sons of Israel from among the nations where they have gone and I will gather them from every side and bring them into their own land. I will make them one nation in the land, on the mountains of Israel." Ezekiel 37:21–22

"They will rebuild the ruined cities and live in them, they will plant vine-yards and drink their wine and make gardens and eat their fruit." Amos 9:14–15

Solar panels are spreading across the desert, diamond companies cut and polish gems to a high gleam, kibbutzim have made Israel the world's top grower of organic produce, and so many software and electronic firms have sprung up in the desert that it's called Silicon Wadi. Scoring high on quality-of-life charts, the country that edges the Mediterranean is diverse: an hour's drive takes one from the cafés and clubs of hopping Tel Aviv to groves of thousand-year-old olive trees, from ski resorts to old stone cities that haven't changed much since Jesus was stomping around. But even though a calmness and happiness pervades, even though the beauty of the ancient architecture overwhelms and museums filled with treasures such as the Dead Sea Scrolls (found in caves) can astound, even though this little country has made itself a world player and has fought off enemies even when it was

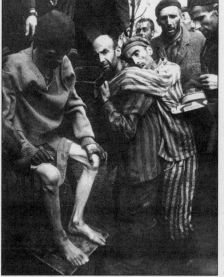

Pvt. Ralph Forney, Department of Defense

The treatment of Jews during World War II was hushed up and denied. Many Americans didn't know about concentration camps until the last years of the war, when U.S. forces and other Allies liberated them, encountering thousands of starved Jews at work camps such as Wobbelin (pictured above). By then, millions had died. The unofficial motto of Israel reflects that grim time: "Never again!"

outnumbered three to one, even though Israel has proved it's not going away, the country still lives in a shadow. The threats to Israel's existence never fade and the Israel Defense Forces are everywhere: near the Western Wall, on the buses, at the borders, even toting their machine guns to the beach as they snatch up some rays (the women fighters wear them like a fashion accessory as they go shopping). Under siege since the day it was born, Israel was first attacked by Arab countries but more recently by Palestinian suicide bombers who with one yank of a cord send exploding nails flying, the shrapnel often killing dozens at a time. And the threats just don't disappear, no matter how many walls are built, checkpoints erected, and travelers are strip-searched to ensure they're not carrying bombs. But the problem is no longer persecution of Jews, the issue that prompted the creation of this country. The problem is now anger at Israel coming from all corners—an anger that has rarely been addressed, an ire now burning like an acid and that appears likely to spill into yet another regional war. What could spark it: an Israeli strike on Iran.

WHERE JEWS SHINE

Theodr Herzl, one imagines, would be perplexed. The Hungarian journalist who launched the Zionist movement in 1898 was alarmed and fed up with the treatment of Jews in Europe. Russians had killed hundreds of Jews in pogroms already—thousands more would die—and the Dreyfus Affair, when a French officer who was Jewish was falsely convicted of treason, had led to riots calling for the death of all Jews. For millennia, Jews had been persecuted: blamed for bringing the Black Death to Europe, blamed by Christians for killing Christ (an act in fact perpetrated by Romans), and long before World War II, when Jews were stripped of all rights and killed by the millions, Herzl believed that such discrimination would always continue if Jews were forced to live in non-Jewish society. Zionism, the search for a Jewish national homeland, became his solution to the problem, although Herzl was initially considering sites from Uganda to Alaska. As the movement grew, others decided the new homeland should arise in Palestine, the traditional Jewish homeland. Were Herzl to visit the planet now, he might be shocked to see how Jews have flourished in genteel settings, particularly in the United States. From Albert Einstein to Robert Oppenheimer, Woody Allen to Jerry Seinfeld, Saul Bellow to Neil Simon, Rod Serling to Rodgers and Hammerstein, Mel Brooks to Gilda Radner, Susan Sontag to Gloria Steinem, Bob Dylan to the Coen brothers, Dr. Katz to Carl Bernstein, David Mamet to Arthur Miller, Howard Stern to Jon Stewart, David Halberstam to River Phoenix, Mike Wallace to Barbara Walters—not to mention the hundreds of Nobel Prize winners—Jews are among the most influential, celebrated, adored, and respected Americans. In the United States, they have thrived. Famous Israelis—Ariel Sharon, Golda

Meir, Moshe Dayan, and Shimon Peres among them—are typically famous for wars or the treaties they've negotiated. The country itself has flourished, but unlike the Jews in America, who shine in every arena from arts to science, the brilliance of Israelis most famously shows up on the battlefield or in stellar intelligence maneuvers. In Israel, the name of the game has been to survive in a hostile environment, an endeavor that drains and consumes and has arguably held Israelis back from becoming the guiding lights of their American counterparts—although they too are beginning to shine in fields from medicine to biotechnology.

A little more than half of the world's thirteen million Jews live in the United States; a little less than half live in Israel.

Arab neighbors won't point them out, but Israel has many applause-worthy qualities and achievements to its name. This is a land of entrepreneurs and engineers, where the Pentium MMX chip was designed as well as the first micro–video camera to scope out internal disorders. New treatments for everything from diabetes to Parkinson's have been invented here, and Israel may be on the verge of curing cancer with mini-missiles that cause cells to commit suicide. Israelis have developed new earthquake sensors and ways for the deaf to talk on the phone. Using innovative farming methods, developing new seed strains and eco-friendly pesticides (such as spiders that eat strawberry mites), collective villages have not only made the desert bloom but have made Israel food-independent with plenty left over to export. New techniques for irrigation, including recycling, are cutting down on water needs. The government flies in physicians from Africa to teach them the latest in HIV treatments. Israelis are beginning to rate headlines with poignant films such as *The Band's Visit,* about an Egyptian military band that gets lost in the desert. The list goes on.

And there is an infectious Israeli humor: "Let me tell you something that we Israelis have against Moses," noted Prime Minister Golda Meir. "Moses dragged us for forty years through the desert to bring us to the one place in the Middle East where there was no oil." Or as another saw goes, "Put two Israelis together and you'll have three political parties." Even some intelligence maneuvers are so audacious as to be almost comical: when Palestinians hijacked an Air France plane, landing it in Uganda and holding 105 Israeli passengers hostage, Mossad flew a Mercedes Benz limo like the one driven by Idi Amin to Uganda. Guards, believing it was Amin, let the limo drive to the hijacking site in the airport, where the hostages were rescued in a brilliant operation. In 1967, Israel destroyed Egypt's new air force while it was sitting on the ground, and despite being outnumbered 3 to 1 took all the Palestinian territories plus part of Egypt and Syria. During the 1960s, a Mossad spy infiltrated so high in the Syrian government that he was in line to replace the president.

Of course, such stories aren't found amusing by Arab neighbors, who see Israel as an aggressive and dangerous enemy. Whether through wars or settlements or annexations, Israel's expansion pushed out over a million Palestinian refugees over the decades. During Israel's eighteen-year occupation of southern Lebanon that began in 1982, some eighteen thousand Lebanese and Palestinians died. When Israel pulled out of Lebanon in 2000, the move was applauded but news stories didn't mention the million land mines left behind, which have killed hundreds of farmers and children. The pullout from the 2006 invasion left behind hundreds of thousands of unexploded cluster bombs. Targeted assassinations and attacks have killed thousands of civilians in neighboring countries and Palestinian territories during Olmert's reign alone. Now the enemies are militants who fight in crude and cruel ways, such as bombs exploded by suicide bombers on buses. And Israel has responded aggressively—walling Palestinians out, annexing more of their territories, moving more Israeli settlers in, and frequently attacking the territories, where the bulldozer is a weapon and in the name of clearing out militants they kill just as many civilians.

The neighboring countries that once threatened Israel (four Arab-Israeli wars blew up between 1948 and 1973) have been subdued, either by signing peace treaties or by military alliances that were shredded as the result of the treaties. The most recent threat to the existence of Israel has been Palestinian uprisings, the intifadas (see p. 354). The first intifada began in 1987 and lasted six years, killing over 1,200 (1,100 Palestinians and 160 Israelis).[10] The hostilities ended with a hopeful turn: in 1993 PLO chairman Yasir Arafat, Israel's prime minister Yitzhak Rabin, and its foreign minister Shimon Peres signed a peace agreement that was so promising it landed them the Nobel Peace Prize the next year. The Oslo Accords, the first concrete step toward setting up a Palestinian state, created the Palestinian Authority as a temporary government. As part of the deal, Israel would hem in the settlers and relinquish military control in some Palestinian cities, and the Palestinians would rein in the militants.

That idea went haywire in the autumn of 2000, when Ariel Sharon triggered a second intifada by appearing at a Muslim holy place with a thousand guards. Protests turned into riots: Palestinians demonstrated, Israeli soldiers killed demonstrators, then Israeli police were killed, and the suicide bombs began exploding—everywhere. On buses, in malls, at nightclubs, during wedding parties. Israel blocked Palestinian entry into Israel, launched bombing raids on the West Bank and Gaza, and began building a security wall. Armed Israeli settlers meanwhile continued moving into Palestinian territories. By early 2008, suicide bombers and bombing raids had killed over 5,000: 1,143 Israelis[11] and over 4,400 Palestinians, most on both sides civilians.

THE WALL

Israel is literally gaining new ground with the contours of its controversial "security fence," a 436-mile-long wall of concrete, barbed wire, and electronic sensors. At points it reaches thirty feet high as it snakes across Palestinian territories, straying from internationally recognized boundaries and in the process annexing new land. Israel erected the wall to keep suicide bombers from attacking its civilians. Ruled illegal by the International Court of Justice, the wall has reduced the number of suicide bombing attacks: in 2007 there was only one attack, killing three. But the wall also cuts off Palestinian villages from one another, preventing free movement even within the Palestinian territories. The Israeli government shows few signs of stopping even with a steady trumpeting of demands from Israelis themselves, along with international calls, court judgments, and UN resolutions to do so.

To many in the Middle East, these acts are made possible by the United States, which not only supports Israel but arms it, heavily, with freebies. Understandably security obsessed, Israel has even more strongly teamed up with the United States, which is now Israel's main arms supplier, strategic planner, and partner in war. Even when the United States doesn't fight, it's often involved in the planning and always supplies many of the weapons used. The friendship raises eyebrows. It's costly: Israel gets a fifth of U.S. foreign aid, totaling some $120 billion over the years, much of it for arms. And the relationship is riddled with paranoia and spies. Israel even bugged the U.S. embassy there—planting a device in the decorative eagle.

A FEW NOTABLE MOMENTS IN THE U.S.-ISRAELI FRIENDSHIP

1956: President Eisenhower demands that Israel, Britain, and France pull out of Egypt during the Suez Crisis.

1962: President Kennedy, fearing that Israel has a nuclear weapons program, pushes for inspections of its nuclear reactors; Israel balks.

1967: During the Six Days' War in June, Israel attacks the USS *Liberty* in international waters, killing thirty-four. The ship's crew says it wasn't an accident. An Israeli pilot who flew on the mission agrees, and the whole thing was strangely hushed up. The secretary of defense says that President Johnson wasn't about to "embarrass an American ally over a few sailors." Even though a brief investigation found it was a mistake, the attack "couldn't be anything else but deliberate," the National Security Agency director. Lt. Gen. Marshall Carter would later tell Congress.

1969: Henry Kissinger advises President Nixon of Israel's nuclear program and warns that Israel is most likely to actually use nuclear weapons.

1970: Senate aide Richard Perle, future deputy assistant secretary of defense, is accused by FBI of leaking classified information to Israel.

1973: Nixon, fearing that Israel will use nukes, rushes $2.2 billion to help Israel win the 1973 Arab-Israeli war. Arabs put an embargo on oil to the United States in response.

1978: Paul Wolfowitz, working in the State Department, is investigated for passing classified information to Israel.[12]

1979: President Carter negotiates Israeli-Egyptian peace, with the promise of annual giveaways of multibillion dollars' worth of U.S. arms to both.

1981: The United States condemns Israel for destroying Iraq's budding nuclear program by bombing the Osirak reactor.

1982: After Israel pounds Lebanon with weapons given by the United States, Reagan suspends sales of cluster bombs for six years. Douglas Feith reportedly loses his job at the National Security Council for passing classified information to Israel.

1986: Jonathan Pollard, a U.S. Navy intelligence officer and a paid Israeli spy, is—along with his wife—found guilty of conspiracy for passing classified national defense information to Israel about Iraq's missiles and U.S. global surveillance. He was given a life sentence, though his wife got only five years.

1991: The United States keeps Israel out of the Gulf War and restrains it from responding to Iraq's missiles by setting up Patriot missile defense systems.

1995: American neocons Douglas Feith and Richard Perle coauthor a report for Israel's Likud leadership. Called "A Clean Break," it recommends halting "land for peace" treaties with Arabs, becoming more militarily aggressive, toppling Saddam Hussein, and reordering the power structure of the Middle East. The authors put many of their ideas into motion with the election of George W. Bush, when Feith is hired by the U.S. Defense Department and Perle becomes a top-level adviser.

2002: President George W. Bush condemns Israeli prime minister Ariel Sharon for building a wall; U.S. evangelicals swamp the White House in protest, and the issue isn't raised by Bush again.

2003: The United States, UN, European Union, and Russia—the so-called quartet—propose a "road map," calling for Israel to stop building settlements and for Palestinian territories to rein in the militants; Bush later announces that it's okay to expand on existing settlements.

2004: Lawrence Franklin, working for Wolfowitz and Feith in the Department of Defense, is arrested (and later sentenced to thirteen years) for passing state secrets about Iran to the American-Israel Public Affairs Committee; two of AIPAC's top dogs are indicted on spying charges.

2006: The United States controversially backs the Israeli invasion of Lebanon, and U.S. ambassador to the UN John Bolton, dubbed "Israel's man at the United Nations,"[13] blocks UN calls for a cease-fire.

2007: At the Annapolis peace summit, Israeli prime minister Olmert agrees to stop settlements in occupied territories; within forty-eight hours Israel approves additional settlements in the West Bank.

Nobody has done more than the United States to promote peace between Israel and its neighbors. The United States brought Egypt and Israel together for the 1979 peace treaty. And although the secret negotiations known as the Oslo Accords started in Norway, with a proposal from a political science class in Oslo, the United States jumped into that as well, not to mention the next year's peace treaty with Jordan.

Whether through arming Israel, backing its military moves, vetoing resolutions at Israel's urging, negotiating peace treaties, or battling those who are more enemies of Israel than of the United States, American support for Israel is unflagging, questionable, and even hypocritical. Israel has transformed from victim to bully, pulling stunts that wouldn't be condoned if they were done by anyone else.

Helped along by weighty lobbies such as AIPAC, the American-Israeli alliance has been cemented by U.S. officials who are neocons, Paul Wolfowitz, John Bolton, Douglas Feith, and Richard Perle among them. The Zionist Organization of America conferred its Defender of Israel Award on U.S. ambassador to the UN John Bolton in 2005, and the Jewish Institute for National Security Affairs awarded Paul Wolfowitz (described by the Jewish press as "hawkishly pro Israel") its Distinguished Service Award in 2003, the same year he was toasted as Man of the Year by the *Jerusalem Post*. Even some in Jerusalem find it strange—a *Haaretz* columnist noted that prominent neocons were "walking a fine line between their loyalty to American government . . . and Israeli interests."[14]

Even the Bush doctrine—"Either you are with us or you are with the terrorists"—was a rewrite of early Israeli policy: "Either you are for or against us" was the Israeli government line employed in the earliest days of the state.[15]

Indeed, neocon war plans often appeared to address Israel's fears and priorities above those of the United States. As the fruitless search for WMDs illustrated, Saddam didn't pose a threat to the United States, but he did to Israel: in 2002 he was paying fifteen thousand dollars to the family of every Palestinian suicide bomber who blew himself up killing Israelis. The most recent case in point is Iran, which poses little physical threat to the United States but threatens to obliterate Israel, which unlike Iran *does* have nuclear weapons. Israel is the only Middle Eastern country with nuclear weapons, a fact that the Bush administration forgot to bring up when lambasting Iran's nuclear facilities. Then again, DC can't mention Israel's two hundred or so nukes, since the United States isn't supposed to give aid to a country with nuclear weapons that aren't subject to international inspections.

THE ICING ON THE YELLOWCAKE

It's hard to forget President Bush's 2003 State of the Union address, when he falsely accused Saddam Hussein of acquiring yellowcake in Africa to build nuclear weapons. As Ambassador Joseph Wilson pointed out, in what would soon blow into Plamegate, that claim was bogus—if it was pinned on Saddam. It was Israel that bought uranium for weapons from Africa, acquiring it from South Africa, with help from the French, starting in the late 1950s as well as from Argentina and Belgium.[16] That was all part of a hush-hush nuclear program that came out of Israel's 1950s alliance with France. The Gauls provided Israel with arms, fought with Israel in the 1956 invasion of Egypt, and swapped intelligence from Israel for nuclear know-how. In the 1960s, the United States learned of the Dimona nuclear reactor in the desert and over the years pressured Israel to stop producing nuclear weapons—only to be given the runaround and finally to receive the promise that Israel would not be the first country in the Middle East to use nuclear weapons. However, that may be a wavering promise: in 1973 Defense Secretary Moshe Dayan, panicked that Egypt would win the war, reportedly wanted to unleash those very weapons.

Starting in 2005, the neocon gang begin building the case for an invasion of Iran. Cheney publicly supported an Israeli strike on Tehran and appeared to egg Israel on when he matter-of-factly observed that "Israel might well decide to act first" and "let the rest of the world worry about cleaning up the diplomatic mess afterwards."[17] The Israeli secretary of defense suggested that the United States lead the way. In 2007, with Cheney's appearance on a warship near the Strait of Hormuz, painting the threat of Iran in the gravest of colors, the United States appeared to be heading that way. But in December that year, U.S. intelligence took the Bush administration aback by releasing a report that stuffed a cork in that plan: Iran had frozen its nuclear program in 2003, the National Intelligence Estimate reported. That news elicited an irate response in Israel, with editorials and reports bemoaning how the United States was abandoning the Jews and condemning the intel as hogwash.[18]

Increasingly, and controversially (they receive a lot of flak for doing so), academics and pundits are pointing out the influence of Israel's lobby, which funnels millions into the political-funding system and is believed to have the power to take politicians down. Former State Department employees note that their attitudes toward Israel influenced their standing; those who questioned the actions of Tel Aviv or the United States' unwavering support for Israel believed those views influenced their transfer to unglamorous posts or even dismissal.[19]

But while some are questioning the ties to Israel, and what's behind them, growing ever louder is the forceful voice of the American Christian Zionists who believe that U.S. policy should *create* the situations forecasted by biblical prophets: many evangelical Americans don't want to see Palestinians get a state, for example, because Israel was prophesied to have *all* the land; and they urge the removal of the mosque in old Jerusalem, which they fear is impeding the return of Christ. Christian Zionists and those associated with them could be found throughout the Bush administration, including UN ambassador John Bolton. The late senator and chairman of the Senate Foreign Relations Committee, fundamentalist Jesse Helms once described Bolton as being "the kind of man with whom I would want to stand at Armageddon." And the most common means for Israel to expand into all of the Palestinian territories—a move the evangelicals support—is to erect new settlements.

According to a 2006 poll conducted by the Pew Forum on Religion and Public Life, 42 percent of Americans believe that Israel was given by God to the Jews, and 35 percent of Americans believe that the creation of Israel fulfills the prophecy of the Second Coming.[20]

THE LORD'S WORD, THE GOVERNMENT'S DIME

Founded on the belief that this was "the promised land," an idea embraced even by secular Zionists during the formation of the country, Israel is now divided by interpretations of religious prophecy. Some Israelis believe that Jews have the right (by God's covenant with Abraham) to claim *all* Palestinian territories, and some say the swatch should include Jordan too. Some translate the biblical promise of land from the river in Egypt to the Euphrates to mean that Jews are entitled to the land from the Sinai through Lebanon, Syria, and into Iraq. And many of those who translate the Bible most literally, have moved into the occupied territories in the West Bank (in Palestine) and Golan Heights (in Syria) to set up homes and battle for the control of this holy, blood-soaked land. The settlements, now numbering 226 in the West Bank (including 105 illegal outposts), began in 1967 after Israel stunned the world in a victory against Egypt, Syria, and Jordan before a week was out. Some rabbis, particularly Moshe Levinger and Tzui Yehuda Kook, called it a miracle. Indeed, they preached, the Messiah would soon be arriving—as soon as Israelis claimed all of the land that they'd been promised: a strip, according to Levinger and Kook, that includes the West Bank and beyond. While the religious leaders called the faithful, military strategists such as Ariel Sharon, who headed the housing ministry in the mid-1970s, encouraged the move, seeing it as a means to fortify boundaries and extend farther into lands that held water, from the West Bank to the Golan Heights. The 460,000 Israeli settlers tend to be evenly split between those drawn by biblical prophecy and those drawn by the economic payoff. The Israel government makes it a worthwhile investment, offering tax cuts and reduced rents and military protection among other bennies. According to the newspaper *Haaretz*, the Israeli government has spent over five billion dollars (not including the military sent in to guard them) since the settler movement took off in the 1970s.

Settlers are only one wheel in the security machine: the green-uniformed Israel Defense Forces have become as much of a symbol of Israel as the Star of David. But Israel's military and defensive strategies, once so crucial for holding on to turf, have recently become so aggressive that the protection of Israel sometimes appears to be what most threatens Israel's existence.

The Israeli government's aggressive behavior of late is exactly what Arab leaders warned would happen back in 1979. It's why they were so mad at Egyptian president Anwar Sadat that they booted Egypt out of the Arab League. When Sadat signed a peace agreement with Israel stating that Egypt would recognize Israel's right to exist if Israel handed back the Sinai Peninsula, he took Egypt's army out of any Arab wartime equation. Without the threat of a multicountry war, Arab leaders feared that Israel would not be contained.

Clearly Israel *is* surrounded by enemies, but many—even within Israel—are now criticizing the Israeli government for creating foes. B'Tselem, the Israeli Information Center for Human Rights in the Occupied Territories, has issued reports that show Israel's response to suicide bombers: killing roughly four Palestinians for every Israeli killed, caging in Palestinians behind a security wall, bombing refugee camps, cutting off electricity, strangling trade, closing off transportation, as well as the targeted assassinations of Palestinians suspected of being militants (and those unfortunates nearby). Plenty of Israelis, including the group Peace Now, decry their government's actions as well as the de facto annexations by settlers. Israel's actions are not an effective way to solve the problem. But nobody is sure what the next step should be.

Being surrounded by enemies does, however, have one payoff: it keeps society more cohesive. As a homeland for Jews from across the world, Israel is actually a divided society, which makes its high productivity and low violence all the more remarkable. Politically, it holds doves and hawks, traditionally symbolized by the Labor and Likud parties, as well as parties that represent different takes on Judaism. Religiously, it's divided into secular Jews, orthodox, ultraorthodox (see "Religion Matters," p. 327), ranging from those who aren't devout to those who spend hours in prayer; many ultraorthodox believe that the state of Israel should not have been created until the Messiah appeared, while others believe that by claiming lands that were part of the old Kingdom of Israel, from Sinai to the Euphrates, they are creating the conditions necessary for the Messiah's arrival. And while most Israelis consider themselves ethnically Jews, they come from countries as diverse as Yemen and France, Ethiopia and the Ukraine. And those divisions do play out in society: Jews from Asia and Africa—the Mizrahi—say they are discriminated against by the Ashkenazi Jews from Eastern Europe. But while there are huge ranges of opinion on issues from settlements to war to biblical prophecies, many are bonded in fear. Yet despite all the problems, Israelis' drive to survive keeps the country chugging away.

Last Word

For all the bad news in this neck of the woods, good news began blowing through in summer 2008. For one thing, the UN brokered a deal between Israel and Hezbollah for a prisoner exchange. Moderated through Turkey, Israeli talks with Syria became a little more serious and hopeful. Israel is considering pulling out of Shebaa Farms and perhaps even Golan Heights in Syria, lands it has occupied for decades. Egypt negotiated a truce between Israel and Hamas that at least briefly opened borders and stopped rockets from flying from Gaza—although that truce looks unlikely to hold up long. What's behind all this peacemaking, alas, may be plans to hit Iran; all of the above parties are Iran's friends, who may well come to Tehran's aid if it's struck by Israel, an option that may still be on the table, all the more in the twilight of the Bush administration. Whether warming up with these groups would actually prevent them from partaking in a counter-attack is anyone's guess, but it certainly makes Israel appear more diplomatic (and once again willing to yield land for peace) than it has for a decade.

Hotshots

Ehud Olmert: (See "Leader's Corner," p. 326.)

Shimon Peres: The current president, who was prime minister thrice and foreign minister under Ariel Sharon (November 2001–October 2002), Peres shared the 1994 Nobel Peace Prize with Israeli prime minister Yitzhak Rabin and PLO chairman Yasir Arafat for his work on the Oslo Accords the year before. A needed voice of moderation in this hawkish government, he's said Israel can live with Gaza's rockets, which rarely hit victims, and has publicly fretted that the Olmert government will be tried for war crimes. The longest-serving member of the parliament, he ditched his former Labor Party and joined Kadima.

Ehud Barak: Labor prime minister in 2000, he couldn't cut a deal with Arafat, and the former dove turned bitter. Now head of the defense ministry, he's made a number of questionable calls, including ordering that fuel and emergency supplies to Gaza, where 1.5 million are trapped behind walls, be cut off. A disappointment.

Ariel Sharon: Israeli prime minister from 2001 until 2006, when he suffered severe strokes and slipped into a coma, the former general with a history of bullying and disregarding orders, caught hell back in 1982 for standing by and allowing the Lebanese massacre at Sabra and Shatila to take place. Hot-tempered, aggressive, and blamed by Palestinians for triggering the last intifada when he strolled across the grounds of the Temple Mount with a thousand soldiers and guards at his side, he responded to waves of suicide bombers by unleashing tanks into Palestinian communities and holding Arafat personally responsible, trapping him in Ramallah and putting him under house arrest. He pulled back settlers from Gaza in 2005, a surprising and controversial move that caused members of his own party, Likud, to walk out, forcing Sharon to form his own party, Kadima. The disengagement, which has now turned into a slow strangulation, seems like part of a wider plan to push Palestinians out.

Sa'ar Ya'acov, Israel National Archives

Benjamin Netanyahu: Hours after 9/11, the former Israeli prime minister (1996–99) was on a flight to DC, where he presented a moving speech about Arab guerrillas and the need to fight terror—a brilliant PR move that linked Israel and the United States even closer. Now heading the Likud Party, hard-line Netanyahu supports Israeli settlements in the West Bank and is opposed to the creation of an official Palestinian state. Could fly as prime minister again. Yikes.

INFLUENTIAL PARTIES AND GROUPS

Likud (Consolidation): An offshoot of the religious Herut Party, which believed Jews should take all of Palestine, Likud changed the dynamics when it took a majority in the parliament in 1977. Politicians began saying that "Jordan *is* Palestine" and discussing means to get Palestinians to move there. Although Likud leader Begin made peace with Egypt, the era of Likud rule launched more militarisitic operations, such as the 1982 invasion of Lebanon, which led to an eighteen-year stay and an expansion of settlements.

Kadima (Forward, as in a battle charge): Sharon created this supposedly centrist party in 2005, and it's now headed by Olmert. The 2006 invasion of Lebanon, frequent incursions into Palestinian territory, and the ever-tightening wall make it a near mirror of Likud; it was supposed to be moderate.

Yesha Council: Linked to the National Religion Party, this powerful group oversees the settler developments.

Yisrael Beiteinu (Israel, Our Home): A party that addresses the new Russian and Eastern European immigrants, it's headed by controversial Avidgor Lieberman, who wants to administer loyalty tests and drown Arab prisoners in the Dead Sea. He has a real problem with the few Arab parliamentarians and took his party out of the ruling coalition over peace talks with Palestinians. His shows pay off: he may be future prime minister.

Menachem Begin (1913–92): The first prime minister of the Likud Party when he took over in 1977, the former head of the guerrilla group Irgun showed his diplomatic side when he signed the Israeli-Egyptian peace treaty of 1979, which earned him a Nobel Prize along with Anwar Sadat. He was still a tough cookie, however: he bolstered the settlement program and bombed Iraq's Osirak reactor in 1981.

Yitzhak Rabin (1922–95): A two-time prime minister (1974–77 and 1992–95), Rabin softened over the years and okayed the secret negotiations between Yasir Arafat and Shimon Peres that resulted in the Oslo Accords. Some say that the plan for Palestinian independence wouldn't have crumbled if he hadn't been assassinated in 1995, by a radical Jew who was a follower of rabbi Kahane.

Rabbi Meir Kahane (1932–90): First famous as a Brooklyn rabbi, Kahane was charismatic and his style brought to mind 1950s comedians, but his racist messages were deadly. For starters, Kahane wanted Palestinians out of Israel *and* the Palestinian territories, which he believed belonged to Jews. A hard-line right-winger and an influential force for settlers, he founded the murderous Jewish Defense League (JDL) in the United States—considered a terrorist group by the State Department for attacks on Russian embassies among other things—and Kach, an ultraconservative party in Israel, which he formed after moving to Israel and being voted to the parliament. His speeches fired up Dr. Baruch Goldstein, also a former Brooklynite and member of JDL, who in 1994 shot down 29

Golda Meir (1898–1978) threatened to unleash Israel's nuclear bombs if the United States didn't deliver arms promptly during the 1973 war.

Cohen Fritz, Israel National Archives

Muslims praying at a holy spot in Hebron, and wounded 150 more. Kahane was soon barred from the parliament and was gunned down by an Egyptian after giving yet another fiery speech in New York.

Hot Spots

Jerusalem: This symbolic piece of real estate is the number-one holiest spot for Jews, is the number-three holiest spot for Muslims, and Christians claim plenty of history there too. The UN thought it could be shared, but Jordan took the east half during the 1948 war and Israel took the west half the same year. For the next nineteen years, Jerusalem was divided by barbed wire, with Jews unable to enter, not even to pray at the Western Wall. In a victory that seemed to some to be prophecy coming true before their eyes, Israel took East Jerusalem in 1967, moving the parliament there to controversially underscore the idea that Jerusalem was now its capital. The Muslim holy sites, such as the Al-Aqsa Mosque, while controlled by Israel, are maintained by Palestinians. However, most Palestinians are pushed into small neighborhoods of East Jerusalem and don't see many services—there are also few streetlights, no trash pickup, and the streets don't have formal names. Then again, Palestinians refuse to vote in city elections, believing it legitimizes Israel's occupation of the city.

Psychologists say some who enter the city develop "Jerusalem Syndrome," which causes religious delusions.

Temple Mount / Haram al-Sharif: Thirty-five acres sacred to both Jews and Muslims, this Jerusalem compound contains the Al-Aqsa Mosque, the third-holiest place for Muslims, and the Dome of the Rock, where Mohammed is believed to have ascended. Jews say the Temple Mount was the site of their first two temples, razed and buried underneath along with the sanctuary called the Holy of Holies; fundamentalists believe this is where ascension will occur when the Messiah arrives. The Western Wall of the compound is believed to be the only remains of the second Jewish temple.

The Church of the Holy Sepulchre: A few miles west of the Temple Mount is the site where Christ is believed to have risen. Constantine's mother had a vision that it was so several centuries after Jesus stomped around here.

Tel Aviv: The historical capital on the Mediterranean is still the economic capital: lined with cafés and filled with computer geeks and business sorts by day, at night restaurants and clubs rock out.

Checkpoints: Dotting the outskirts of Israel, they clog up traffic for hours and tempers rage at these dangerous crossings known for suicide bombs. Now Palestinians can't enter without special permits.

Lebanon: It's been a sore spot for Israel ever since the PLO ran over to the south in the 1970s and used it as a launchpad for attacks, prompting Israeli invasions, including one in 1982 that led to an eighteen-year occupation and over eighteen thousand deaths. But while Israel helped to run the PLO out of Lebanon, the resentment toward Israel there led to the rise of the militant Shia group Hezbollah, which took over where the PLO left off (see "Lebanon," p. 365.)

Golan Heights: After the cease-fire that ended the 1967 war, Israel claimed this fertile land in Syria, which holds the water resources it needs, and shoved out most of those who lived there. One exception: the Druze, an Islamic sect, who live mostly as farmers in mountain villages and are known as fine fighters; they are the only non-Jews who are drafted into Israel's military. Putting most of this forty-square-mile area under military control, Israel is now luring settlers there with the usual promises of tax cuts and low-cost luxury housing. The Druze protested over a telephone tower, linking it to high cancer rates, a fear some studies support. When their concerns were ignored, they burned the phone tower down. The Israel Defense Forces entered the zone, two days of riots broke out, and several were killed—fueling more anti-Israeli sentiment.

Iran: Still a good chance Israel will strike Iran.

Syria: Still a good chance Israel will strike Syria—as part of an attack on Iran.

Courtesy of Israeli Tourism Board

The lovely Sea of Galilee provides much of Israel's water.

Separated by fifty miles and shrunken by Israeli expansion, the West Bank and Gaza Strip are all that's left of the land allocated to Palestinians by the UN in 1947. Israel occupies much of the West Bank with illegal settlements, walls, and Israeli-only highways that prevent Palestinians from getting out of their towns. Israel walled off Gaza and controls what gets in or out—and little does, including food. The international community— except for DC, which helped create this mess—is outraged, screaming that Gaza is a prison.

Karl Abramovic

Chapter Fifteen

Disappearing Act: The Palestinian Territories—the West Bank and Gaza

Palestinians, such as these early peasant farmers in Ramallah, have always lived close to the land. Two-thirds of Palestinians still live in rural areas.

Before Westerners began chopping it up, Palestine, the land between the Mediterranean sea and the Jordan River,[1] was home to Arab farmers who swapped goods in village markets. Shepherding, spinning yarn, making soap, and tending their valuable groves of olives and oranges, Palestinians lived on the same tracts of land for generations. Loosely under Ottoman rule until 1919, they had little use for land titles for properties divvied up centuries before. Most saw little threat in the late nineteenth-century arrival of Europeans, many of them Jewish. Feelings changed as hundreds of thousands more arrived and a plan for a Jewish national homeland emerged in 1917; Palestinian-Israeli violence began shortly thereafter. Over a million Palestinians lost their land first with the 1948 creation of Israel from 55 percent of the Palestinian territory, and then in the wars that followed, during which Israel claimed 78 percent of Palestine and illegally occupied the rest. Now descendants of Palestinians, four million squeezed into the West Bank and Gaza, have little but olive branches to show for land lost. As Israel pushes into the last corners of their territory, erecting settlements and walls, Palestinians unleash suicide bombers, and Israel answers with bombs. The longest-lasting headache in the Middle East, the Israeli-Palestinian problem has worsened with the recent walling off and strangulation of Gaza, partly a response to the 2006 election of anti-Israel militants Hamas. Now everybody from the International Red Cross to Osama bin Laden is bellowing that despite the rockets Gazans fire over the walls, which result in perhaps three Israeli deaths a year, Israel's blocking off of Gaza isn't fair. Few agree on a solution, but nobody disputes that with Israel cutting off electricity, food, fuel, and goods from getting in, the situation grows more volatile daily.

FAST FACTS:
Palestinian territories: West Bank and Gaza

Government:	Interim government with parliament (West Bank only)
Formed:	Not a country; UN divided Palestine in 1947 (see p. 354)
Leaders:	President Mahmoud Abbas (West Bank), ex–Prime Minister Ismail Haniya (Gaza, but not recognized outside Gaza)
GDP 2007:	$4 billion (exchange rate)
Per capita GDP:	$1,100 (IMF, 2007)
Population:	4.1 million total; 2.6 million West Bank, 1.5 million Gaza
Unemployment:	40 percent[2] (44–70 percent in Gaza)[3,4]
Literacy rate:	97 percent men, 88 percent women
Ethnicity:	83 percent Palestinian Arab, 17 percent Jewish
Religion:	West Bank: 75 percent Muslim, 17 percent Jewish, 8 percent Christian and other. Gaza: 99 percent Sunni Muslim

---

Population stat: 85 percent of Gazans live in poverty;[5] in the West Bank 46 percent live in poverty. Many Palestinians no longer live in this area: some became citizens of Jordan, where over four million are originally Palestinian; some seven hundred thousand live in Lebanon in refugee camps. Another million or more are working in other Arab countries.

Leaders' Corner

There has never been effective leadership in the Palestinian territories, and it's worse now than ever: the West Bank and Gaza are no longer really united, given a recent power struggle that pits what has historically been the leading party, Fatah, against Hamas, a militant group that is Islamist and anti-Israel. There are now effectively two different leaders for the two territories. Palestinian Authority president Mahmoud Abbas, recognized by the United States and Israel, really only speaks for the West Bank. In Gaza, most recognize the rule of Hamas, which won the 2006 parliamentary elections that DC had demanded take place. After Hamas won the elections, Hamas leader Ismail Haniya was made the prime minister of the Palestinian Authority. However, Israel and the United States freaked: Hamas, the masked militia in green, runs clinics and schools but is better known for organizing suicide missions to Israel. Under pressure from the United States and Israel, Palestinian president Abbas ultimately kicked Hamas out of the Palestinian government, and Hamas took over the western territory, Gaza, and refused to recognize the legitimacy of the Palestinian Authority. To isolate Hamas, Israel has taken a number of aggressive steps: even though Gaza was already walled off, Israel suffocated it further by restricting the flow of goods in and out and frequently bombing it. Israel says it's responding to aggression, sometimes saying the cause is the rockets blindly shot over the wall. In June 2006, it pummeled Gaza after militants kidnapped an Israeli soldier. In the meantime, the United States and Israel heap recognition and rewards on Abbas, but even to those in the West Bank, which he rules, he looks like a sellout, because until 2008 he ignored what was happening to Gazans. Shunning Hamas, the United States keeps trying to hammer out a peace treaty between Israel and Abbas. This is a ridiculous endeavor because (a) Israel doesn't appear to want peace with Palestinians at the moment, and (b) Abbas doesn't really speak for all of them anymore. The upshot is this: the Palestinians have less control than ever, they are broker than ever, and the idea of any future Palestinian state is looking more and more like a cruel joke. The self-rule experiment started in 1993 by the Oslo Accords peace treaty between the PLO and Israel has failed fabulously, and the Palestinian Authority's clout is greatly weakened. In both the West Bank and Gaza, Israel mostly calls the shots—literally, since it keeps sending the Israeli armed forces in.

WHAT MATTERS

Energy matters: Gas fields lie offshore of Gaza, and Israel once promised the revenue to Gazans. That is unlikely to happen now that Gaza is run by Hamas. Hoping to spur an ouster of Hamas, Israel has cut down on the fuel it allows into Gaza.

Electricity matters: Palestinians in Gaza and the West Bank are mostly dependent on Israel for electricity, because Israel has made a point of targeting their power plants. Now Israel cuts off electricity to the territories, particularly to Gaza, as punishment for rockets that Gazans shoot over the wall.

Arms matter: Most Palestinian arms are smuggled in, some through tunnels from Egypt. There aren't many, as evidenced whenever Israel attacks Gaza, and there are few if any casualties among Israeli soldiers. Militias, particularly in Gaza, make rockets and shoot thousands over the wall: they rarely hit anything, though one Israeli was killed in 2007. In a show of support for the leadership of Abbas in the West Bank, the Bush administration began arming Abbas's security forces.

Military/militants matter: The Palestinian Authority has no standing army per se, but there are plenty of militias, Hamas topping the list. Its rival Islamic Jihad is the one that regularly sends homemade Qassam rockets over Gaza's Israeli-built security wall into Israel—just one example of turf wars that play out here. Both the West Bank and Gaza are also overrun by tribal gangs that kidnap people and hold them for ransom. Security is so bad in the West Bank that many politicians hire their own paramilitaries as guards.

Money matters: The Palestinian territories were never well-to-do, but the "Israeli closures" as the walls and checkpoints that surround Palestinian areas are called, have throttled business and trade. It's *hard* for goods to come in or go out of the West Bank. Since June 2007, when Hamas took over, it's been *impossible* for them to enter or leave Gaza, where Israel imposed a ban on imports and exports. In both territories, economies are tanking: 90 percent of Gaza factories are shut down.[6] In the West Bank, nearly half the population is unemployed.

Truce matters: In June 2008, Egypt negotiated a truce between Hamas and Israel, but it is fragile and Gaza is still mostly cut off.

Religion matters: Most Palestinians are Sunni, although some are Christian or Jewish. Most of the militias, including Hamas and Islamic Jihad, were formed by the Muslim Brotherhood and want to install an Islamic government. However, many of the Palestinians themselves, largely a literate and well-educated group, are moderate, and the majority of them are secular. The reason they voted for Hamas had little to do with their religious agenda—it was a vote expressing disgust with the Palestinian Authority under Fatah.

Land and resources matter: This is the crux of the issue: the Palestinians never supported the creation of Israel in 1948; nevertheless they were run out of their homes, losing their farms, when the United Nations gave Israel 55 percent of Palestine to create a national homeland for Jews. That land shrunk further: Israel now spreads over 78 percent of what was once Palestine and occupies most of the rest. Palestinians are being squeezed: for forty years illegal Israeli settlements have encroached on their remaining patches, settlers and the army often uprooting their olive trees.[7] Most of the water from Palestinian aquifers and springs goes to Israelis,[8] and Israel controls the Palestinians' electricity, fuel deliveries, and movement. The Palestinians are hemmed in, and typically dozens of times a year, sometimes dozens of times a month, Israel brings out the air force and bombs cities and refugee camps—sometimes as targeted assassinations, sometimes in response to rockets shot over the walls. Other times, Israel sends out demolition teams to raze houses. Israel says such acts are needed to control Palestinian suicide bombers who've killed a thousand Israelis since 2000, although there have been few suicide bombings since 2003. Israel has killed thousands in response and has crushed the economies. Many believe what is happening is an attempt to push the Palestinians out of these last remaining corners.[9]

The Palestinian territories are dying. In the southwest corner of what used to be Palestine, beyond the thirty-foot-high walls that Israel built around Gaza, a twenty-five-mile stretch of coast, buzzing spy drones hover over bombed-out buildings and refugee camps, which are short on food and lit mostly by candle. Clothing and furniture factories have folded since the clothes and furniture can't get out; across Gaza, businesses are shutting down because they can't get the supplies needed to survive, and nearly four out of five Gazans are now unemployed. While isolation and strangulation are the techniques Israel is using to control Gaza, a different technique is put to use in the West Bank. There Israel has turned the territory into geographical Swiss cheese, dividing town from town and people from stores by erecting walls, no-go zones, settlements, and

Dick Doughty, Courtesy Saudi Aramco, ASC

Outdoor markets have been a way of life in Palestine for thousands of years, but they're being shut down. Building "buffer strips" that Palestinians can't tread, even in Palestinian towns, Israel prevents locals in cities such as Hebron from getting to the markets and restricts movement through checkpoints that block goods from getting in.

Israeli-only highways that crisscross the land. Take for example the city of He-bron, until recently the commercial center for the whole West Bank: it is now be-ing cleared of Palestinians, who are being driven out by Israeli settlers. The once bustling fruit market and stores have shut down since Israel won't allow Palestin-ians on the road to get to them. Across the West Bank, transportation is a night-mare: hundreds of checkpoints block entry into Palestinian areas; walls cut deeply into Palestinian territory; roads that can be used only by Israelis snake around Palestinian towns severing one from the other. Even though this is the last remaining bit of Palestinian land, Palestinians can't easily move in it. What used to be a fifteen-minute drive from one Palestinian town to another now takes hours, if you can get through at all.

Besides controlling imports and exports into the territories, Israel also controls most of the electricity, and all the more since 2006. In June of that year, Hamas fighters tunneled out from under the wall surrounding Gaza and kidnapped a soldier from an Israeli checkpoint. Israel responded with a brutal attack on Gaza, killing dozens of civilians. Targets included beaches, cars, bridges, and the local power station, which now runs at one-third capacity when it runs at all. In 2007, Israel began cutting off fuel as well as electricity, and Gaza is frequently in a blackout. The cutoffs wreak havoc on hospitals and factories, and stop water from pumping, leading to chronic water shortages and sewage backups. In 2007, Pales-tinians killed 13 Israelis; Israel killed 373 Palestinians—290 in Gaza.

THE INTERNATIONAL COMMUNITY

Although everyone recognizes that Palestinians pose a risk to Israel, the international community is getting very upset at Israel's actions, particularly those in Gaza, where it has tried to shut down Hamas by choking the popula-tion. As the International Crisis Group, a respected group of powerful diplo-mats in Brussels, noted in March 2008: "The policy of isolating Hamas and sanctioning Gaza is bankrupt and, by all conceivable measures, has back-fired. Violence is rising, harming both Gazans and Israelis. Economic condi-tions are ruinous, generating anger and despair . . . The peace process is at a standstill . . . Gaza's export harvest rots in containers at crossing points . . . Because manufacturing, construction, and transport all have been devastated, dozens of businesses have relocated to the West Bank, Jordan, or elsewhere. By late 2007, all but 35,000 of Gaza's 110,000 private sector workers had been laid off . . . Poverty and unemployment rates have skyrocketed. The siege has been accompanied by Israeli military moves . . . Observers rou-tinely wonder when Israel will re-enter Gaza, but to a large extent it already is there . . . [By] November 2007, 17 percent of Gaza—and 35 percent of its agricultural land—was inside [Israel's off-limits to Palestinians] buffer zone."[10]

The International Red Cross summed up the situation in its November 2007 report *Dignity Denied*: "While the Gaza Strip is sealed off, the conflict between militants and Israel continues inexorably. Palestinian militants are launching rockets towards Israel almost every day. The Israeli army regularly carries out incursions deep into the Strip, air strikes and attacks from the sea. The civilian population remains trapped, with no escape possible . . . Gazans are getting increasingly anxious as shelves in grocery shops begin to empty because of the closure. Prices have skyrocketed, and the little that comes in to Gaza is virtually unaffordable. The prices of many foodstuffs, such as chicken, have at least doubled in the past four months, as stocks dwindle without resupply . . . 80,000 Gazans have lost their jobs since June 2007 . . . Many local industries had to shut down and fire their personnel, as 95% of local production depends on imports of raw materials from Israel. Israel has restricted imports to what it deems 'basic goods'—mostly staple food products—while other essential items needed to keep industry running or repair infrastructure cannot enter the Strip. Gaza farmers remember how green and fertile their land was in the recent past. Rich harvests from their citrus and olive trees were exported to the West Bank and Israel. Today, a large part of their land has been leveled and their trees uprooted during the frequent military incursions. Some 5,000 farmers who rely on exporting tomatoes, strawberries and carnations to support their families are about to suffer a 100% drop in sales."[11]

United Nations special rapporteur on human rights John Dugard put it more simply: "Gaza is a prison and Israel seems to have thrown away the key.[12]

Israel insists that such extreme measures are necessary to keep Israelis safe from suicide bombers, even though the threat is now minimal (numbers have dwindled substantially since 2003). But Israel says the drop is due to its security measures, including the hundreds of checkpoints and the security wall. Palestinians say *they* are the ones who are not safe, since Israel invades their territories, bombs them, and conducts frequent targeted assassinations of suspect militants with missiles that kill civilians as well. Palestinians, most of whom didn't even support the intifada by 2002, say Israel is terrorizing *them* and killing Palestinians at a rate four times higher than Palestinians kill Israelis. Palestinians say the violence is the result of Israel's moves into their land, the bombings, and the asphyxiation of their economy. But in this chicken-or-egg situation, one thing is clear: it's just getting worse.

As of February 2008, the ongoing Israeli-Palestinian violence that started in September 2000 had resulted in the deaths of 4,604 Palestinians and 1,033 Israelis, most victims on both sides being civilians.[13]

GEOGRAPHICAL BRIEFING: PALESTINE, ISRAEL, AND THE PALESTINIAN TERRITORIES

Palestine: Palestine was the name previously given to the land that runs from the Jordan River to the Mediterranean Sea. This chunk of land was seized from the Ottomans by the British, which controlled it from 1920 until 1948. The Brits hacked off part as Transjordan (today's Jordan). In 1947, the United Nations divided what remained of Palestine: 55 percent became a homeland for Jews and the rest Palestinian territories, with Jerusalem designated an international city to be controlled by the UN. The Zionists (Israelis) agreed to the plan; Palestine's Arabs did not.

Israel: Proclaimed in May 1948, the homeland for Jews has elected leaders, a high GDP, well-trained military, probing intelligence, a sophisticated media, and a belief held by many—even secular Jews—that, whether due to security concerns, water resources, or God's promises to Abraham thousands of years ago, Israel should take *all* of Palestine. Initially the underdog, Israel is now organized and the government has become more aggressive, grabbing up Palestinian territory (with battles, bulldozers, and Jewish settlers) as well as water-rich parts of Syria and Lebanon.

Palestinian territories: Divided into the West Bank and Gaza, the Palestinian territories—disorganized, disunited, and poor—are a patchwork of enclaves that house millions of Palestinians made homeless as a result of Israeli expansion. Beginning in the mid-1990s, the Palestinian Authority governed about 40 percent of these Israeli-occupied territories until the government fractured in 2007. Then Hamas took the Gaza Strip and was thrown out of the government. Israeli armed forces frequently drop in for house raids, targeted assassinations, and bombing attacks. Palestinians' rights are severely restricted.

West Bank: The larger of the two Palestinian territories, and sitting over an aquifer, the West Bank, like Gaza, was originally land given to Palestinians by the UN's 1947 partition. During the Arab-Israel war of 1948, most of it was taken by Jordan and the rest by Israel. In 1967, Israel took it all and occupied it with military and settlements. After the 1993 Oslo Accords, Israel gave Palestinians some control of the cities here but still controls most of it. The name reflects this territory's location relative to the Jordan River, which it lies west of, but it is called Judea and Samaria by Israelis, at least a third of whom claim it as part of their biblical "promised land."

Gaza: A twenty-five-mile-long strip of dusty white houses, palm-lined beachfront, and refugee camps, Gaza was the land where David slew Goliath some three thousand years ago. Now it is miserable and militant, with Hamas taking up torturing those who don't accept its rule and Islamic Jihad launching rockets at Israel. Domestic abuse is running high and honor killing never went away in these parts. It's now being overrun with hard-core Islamists who burn down Christian stores and threaten women—including newscasters—who don't don the veil.

The population of Israeli settlers in the West Bank grew 5 percent during 2007, reaching over 282,000 by the end of the year.[14]

There is no black and white in this situation. Palestinians have acted violently and so have Israelis, who definitely have the upper hand. But the situation in the Palestinian territories is the source of problems across the Middle East: it's used as a political tool and raised by militants in their calls to destroy Israel. It remains a huge, festering wound, and even when middle-of-the-road groups start to wave red flags, nothing is done to alleviate the problem—mostly

Library of Congress

Beginning in 1917, when the Balfour Declaration announced that the British favored the creation of a Jewish national homeland in Palestine, Arabs who lived there organized to show their disapproval of an idea that would take away the land where they lived. Their shows of protest were ultimately ignored.

because DC, under the Bush administration, refused to recognize it as a crisis. While DC has made stabs at negotiating Arab-Israeli peace, it absurdly does so without recognition of Gaza, and with little attention to Israeli aggression there. DC has mostly backed Israel in its actions, and the U.S. media has mostly ignored the calls of humanitarian and human rights groups, from the United Nations to the Red Cross, that have been screaming since 2007 that the situation has gone from bad to a full-on crisis. That message rarely reached Americans, many of whom were shocked to learn in 2008 that Gazans had broken down a wall into Egypt that had kept them jailed in—most Americans didn't even know that the Gazans were walled in by the Israelis. The American media is far more prone to connect the word *Palestinian* with *suicide bomber*, which since the fall of 2000 is exactly how Israelis have come to view the people whose land they had been taking. The intifada that began in 2000 gave Israel every reason to go at the territories full throttle and gave Ariel Sharon and others every reason to shred peace agreements and to push in militarily and to build Israeli-only highways and "The Wall."

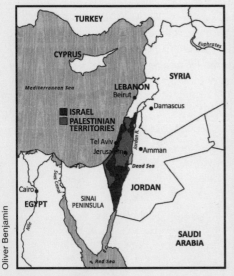 

Palestine/Israel: 1947.   Palestine/Israel: today.

In 1947, the UN split Palestine into a Jewish state (Israel) and Palestinian territories, with the city of Jerusalem to remain neutral and owned by neither. Today, thanks to wars and annexations, the Palestinian territories have shrunk, and they are almost entirely controlled by Israel, which has made a maze of the land with walls, checkpoints, Israeli-only highways, and Israeli settlements restricting movement within the territories. Over 282,000 Israeli settlers are illegally living in the West Bank, ignoring international orders to get out. Israel also annexed Jerusalem, where an additional 190,000 or so Israeli settlers live.

THE BACKGROUND TO THE SUICIDE BOMBINGS

Since Palestinians don't have a country, they don't have an army, but militias have blossomed as a result of popular uprisings. Hamas, for one, changed from a religious youth group that grew out of the Muslim Brotherhood to a militia during the first revolt against Israel in 1987. It started that December, when an Israeli army truck slammed into several cars carrying Palestinian workers, killing four. The accident, Palestinian rumor had it, wasn't accidental, and when a protest kicked up the next day, the crowd threw rocks at Israeli soldiers who in turn fired into the crowd, killing a teenage boy. At his funeral, another riot broke out, and more were killed by Israeli soldiers, prompting more riots, where the soldiers fired at the crowd. Within a week, Israeli soldiers had killed twenty-three. From then on, it snowballed: the Palestinians called work strikes at Israeli factories, they protested in angry demonstrations, and they burned tires and threw rocks. Children by the thousands became rock-throwing brigades, seeking out soldiers to pummel. In response, Israeli soldiers broke their arms: over thirty thousand Palestinian children were treated for broken arms between 1987 and 1989, one-third of them under age ten, said the Swedish branch of the well-known international children's rights organization Save the Children.[15] That tactic caused global outrage in 1988 when CBS aired footage of Israeli soldiers breaking children's arms, but other acts weren't well reported. The Israelis imposed curfews, closed schools for the next year, and began demolishing the homes of suspected rabble-rousers. Fifty thousand were arrested, thirteen thousand put in prison, and in response to the rock-throwing incidents the Israeli armed forces uprooted nineteen thousand olive trees.[16] And when Palestinians protested by not paying taxes to Israel—an amount that came to over $150 million a year—the Israeli army began to lock up Palestinian businesses, literally fusing them shut. As the intifada continued, by the end of five years Israelis had killed 1,034 Palestinians and 38,000 Palestinians had been injured. Palestinians had killed Israelis too: forty soldiers and fifty civilians, injuring an additional twenty-five hundred. The dynamics of the war changed in 1993 when Hamas unleashed a weapon more effective than rocks, one that cost less than $150 to assemble. In April of that year, they sent out the first suicide bomber. Islamic Jihad soon followed with suicide bombers of their own. Between 1993 and 1997, when a cease-fire was called, the two groups sent out a total of thirty-seven bombers, killing nearly 300. In fall 2000, when the second intifada began, they started winding up the self-exploders again. Hamas and Islamic Jihad are responsible for almost all of the suicide bombings in Israel.

> *Suicide bombing missions are not random affairs. Martyrs for Hamas are interviewed extensively: they must be devout, committed, and any that are married are disqualified. Only the tip of the pyramid of volunteers is accepted. According to Israeli human rights group B'Tselem, between September 2000 and June 2008 Palestinians killed 1,056 Israelis,[17] striking shopping malls, discos, buses, and wedding parties. Israel has retaliated by killing 4,857 Palestinians, nearly 3,000 of whom were not involved in any hostilities,[18] and many of whom had opposed Palestinian violence against Israel—at least initially.*

In 1993, the situation suddenly looked more hopeful—as an indirect result of Desert Storm. Then PLO chairman Yasir Arafat infuriated Kuwait and Saudi Arabia by backing Saddam Hussein in Desert Storm. They'd been his main funding source for years, and when they cut him off, Arafat was forced to seek Western backing. To do so, he signed the 1993 Oslo Accords, a peace treaty with Israel. In return for recognizing Israel's right to exist, which Arafat never got around to making official, the agreement created a temporary, limited Palestinian self-government in the West Bank and Gaza Strip, both of which had until then been occupied by Israel, complete with military presence and settlers. The peace treaty was significant, being the first step toward an independent Palestinian state: the Palestinian Authority (PA), as the accords-created government was called, governed most Palestinian cities, while Israel continued to control the outlying 40 percent of the land, where Israelis continued to build settlements and construct Israeli-only roads. The Oslo agreement had opponents on both sides: in the Palestinian territories, Hamas didn't want to recognize Israel's right to exist; in Israel, hard-core factions did not want to give up the Palestinian land, considering it part of Greater Israel (see, p. 320). Another problem: the Palestinian Authority has at best been a corrupt and ineffective government. Criminal gangs run Palestinian cities and towns, the black market powers the economy, and police work for individual officials, not for the government.[19] Together, these problems helped bring the Oslo agreement to its knees—most dramatically with the intifada that started in 2000 after Ariel Sharon (the father of Israeli settlements) took a stroll with a thousand guards at Islam's third-holiest site, the Haram al-Sharif complex in Jerusalem, a hill that's known as the Temple Mount to Jews.

The second intifada began on September 26, 2000, in Jerusalem—the city that most Palestinians claim as their capital, although few have been there. And now, without a special ID issued by Israel they couldn't get in if they tried. Located in East Jerusalem, the sacred hill in the Old City is a touchy issue for Muslims and Jews: they both claim it as a holy spot. For Jews, this number-one sacred spot is the site of their first temple, a room called the Holy of Holies that once held the Ten Commandments. Muslims' third-holiest place, the Al-Aqsa

Mosque, and the Dome of the Rock, sit directly above the Holy of Holies. That fact alone causes considerable ire, and several Israelis (as well as hard-core Christians) have plotted to bomb the Muslim holy sites, including radical fundamentalists who follow Rabbi Kahane.

But there's another reason the Old City is prickly. From 1948, when Jordan captured East Jerusalem, to 1967, when Israel claimed it during that year's Six Days' War, Jews had been barred from entering the Old City at all. When Israel took it in 1967, and annexed it as their capital the next year, they were careful about allowing the local Islamic authorities to retain responsibility for the care of the mosque and the Dome on the Rock, both of which sit on the mount. This too has become an issue: both Muslims and Jews claim the other is tunneling and desecrating the holy spot. A final issue is the one that indirectly prompted the second intifada: Jews frequently prayed at the Western Wall under the mount, but for centuries the mount itself has been closed off to Jews—*not* by Muslims, but by rabbis, who claimed the area was too holy for mere mortals to tread.

Israel Tsvika, Israel National Archives

Hamas made a martyr of Mohammad Al-Durrah, displaying his photo on posters calling for Palestinians to rise up against Israel in what became known as the Al-Aqsa intifada, after the mosque where Sharon's appearance kicked it off.

Some suspect that the rabbinical law is meant to prevent violence between Jews and Muslims, but whatever the reason it rankles many Jews. And Israel's former defense minister Ariel Sharon, who in the autumn of 2000 was campaigning and hoping to become prime minister, was determined to test this prohibition, believing that Jews should be allowed to climb the sacred mount. As a campaign publicity stunt for the hawkish Likud Party, on September 28, 2000, Sharon lumbered up to the Temple Mount/Haram al-Sharif simply to cause a stir. Never mind that Sharon had received an okay to enter the area from Yasir Arafat: his appearance, with one thousand security guards, at the Muslim site was seen as an act of aggression. The fear was that Sharon planned to take it from Palestinians too—just as he'd sent settlers by the hundreds of thousands to illegally occupy land. The next day, when Muslims protested, at first peacefully, Israeli police and the IDF entered into the picture; it turned into a riot, and thirteen Arabs were killed. And that, along with two images etched into brains by the media—one of a dead boy and one of bloody hands—was the beginning of the second intifada.

SYMBOLS TO FIGHT FOR

On September 30, 2000, Arab TV began airing the tragedy that befell Mohammad Al-Durrah, a fifth-grader who'd walked across a checkpoint from Israel to Gaza with his father. A gun battle between Gaza police and the Israeli Defense Forces broke out, and Mohammad cowered behind his father, screaming, "Daddy, protect me!" Minutes later, the child lay dead on the ground. French TV reported that the IDF shot the fatal bullets; that assertion has since been questioned. The boy became the poster child of the uprising: Dubai's leader wrote a poem in his memory, Kuwait named a foundation after him, and Osama bin Laden invoked his name as a reminder to Arabs and a warning to the West. Two weeks later, when two Israeli soldiers made a wrong turn and accidentally entered Ramallah in the West Bank, they were arrested by the Palestinian Authority. A mob stormed the police station and lynched both. The image of one Palestinian killer's bloody hands raised to the cheering crowd in joyous victory over their deaths was for Israelis every bit as chilling and symbolic as Al-Durrah's death was to Arabs. The second intifada, a crude war of sheer hatred, had begun.

The first explosion of nails in October 2000 was followed by more flying nails—the human bombs virtually assuring the election of no-nonsense Ariel Sharon as prime minister. Sharon's response sent the Palestinian territories into a tailspin from which it may be impossible to recover. The military was unleashed: bulldozers demolished homes, tanks blasted factories, planes bombed refugee camps, killing hundreds. The Israeli Defense Forces struck cisterns and water towers, electrical plants, and other key infrastructure, forcing dependence on Israel for the most basic needs. Special forces targeted militia leaders, including those in Hamas, while psy-ops programs made the Israeli military seem all the more ominous, with the chronic buzzing of the unmanned, all-seeing spy drones and the sonic booms created when planes streaked low across Gaza.[20] In 2002, Sharon began building the high-tech security walls and more highways in the Palestinian territories that Palestinians could not use. He created buffer zones out of former farms and olive groves, where no Palestinians could tread: even children who wandered into them were shot at, and at least one twelve-year-old was killed.

Sharon also reinforced the group that he'd empowered decades before as minister of housing, when he was dubbed the "father of the settlements." The settlers he'd encouraged to set up in Palestinian territories in the 1980s were so grateful for his funding of their outposts that they named a West Bank settlement for him: Ariel. He wasn't just being generous; Sharon viewed the settlements as military fortifications that allowed Israel to stretch its boundaries. They became de facto annexations of land. During his reign as prime minister, even more were encouraged to stake out new claims—preferably near aquifers and springs.

This physical asphyxiation of Palestinian land was bolstered by more checkpoints and new ID cards. Most Palestinians suddenly found themselves unable to travel between Gaza and the West Bank, since it requires traversing fifty miles of Israel. Even travel within the West Bank itself became troublesome: checkpoints slowed traffic for hours and between the weavings of the wall and the roads, driving from Bethlehem to Jerusalem (once a quick hop) suddenly required going via Israel because the roads that connected Palestinian cities were now blocked. Most Palestinians didn't have permits to enter Israel, and thus were cut off. So while the security program was meant to keep Palestinians away from Israelis, it also separated Palestinian from Palestinian and subdivided Palestinian land. And the wall strayed from the Green Line that determined the 1949 borders between Israel and the West Bank: the barrier itself turned into another means of annexation.

The infamous wall

Milner Moshe, Israel National Archives

> *"If Mr. Sharon pulls it off, about 50 percent of the West Bank will be annexed to Israel and the Palestinian 'state' will be made up of a number of districts that are not contiguous. In apartheid-era South Africa, such regions were called bantustans."*
> —Neve Gordon, political science instructor at Ben-Gurion University, 2004[21]

In 2005, however, Sharon did something that at first seemed befuddling: while encouraging more settlers to move to the West Bank, he controversially yanked the settlers out of Gaza—including two settlements that he had personally established. Settlers felt betrayed when their former hero pulled them out of Gaza in 2005. It took the IDF to drag some out, but the government compensated them handsomely for the change of residence, forking over between two hundred thousand dollars and five hundred thousand dollars to each household that was abandoned. The move had several payoffs: it made Sharon look like a peacemaker to the international community—particularly Bush, who gave a silent nod to the continued existence of those dozens of settlements in the West Bank that already existed. But it also allowed the isolation of Gaza, the strip where most suicide bombers came from and the territory best known for Hamas—a group that Israel particularly loathes, because Israel helped create it.

HAMAS

Wheelchair-bound and nearly blind, Sheik Ahmed Yassin of the Palestinian Muslim Brotherhood must have seemed a harmless do-gooder when he petitioned Israel to start a new group in 1987, a group that would promote the understanding of true Islam and serve as an antidote to the violence unleashed by Arafat and the PLO. Israel not only gave it a nod, it initially funded the study group. And indeed it turned out to be an antidote to Arafat and the PLO, which Hamas hated. It also hated Israel, the destruction of which was soon a charter goal, as was the creation of an Islamic state across the land held by Israel and the territories. Yassin's boys put down their books and picked up their weapons beginning with the intifada of 1987, when Hamas pioneered suicide bombings, becoming the most active in the new field. And it sent out more when the next intifada kicked up in 2000. According to the IDF, Hamas alone killed 377 Israelis in the first four years of the intifada in over four hundred attacks, and Israel paid back Yassin with a bomb that crashed on his house in 2004. Fighting isn't Hamas's only activity, however: by some accounts, at least 90 percent of its projects are nonviolent—running soup kitchens, opening libraries, and keeping the kids entertained with eye-opening TV shows on Al-Aqsa, essentially the broadcast wing of Hamas. In April 2007, a Mickey Mouse–like puppet named Farfour appeared on kiddy show *Tomorrow's Pioneers*, slamming Jews and planting ideas for the return of an Islamic caliphate that spanned East and West. Farfour's religious brainwashing triggered worldwide outrage, and his career was short-lived. In his final appearance that June, Farfour was killed by an Israeli settler who'd demanded that Farfour sell his land. With his last words he called the Israeli a "terrorist." At least he didn't self-explode.

By walling off the troublesome strip, Sharon was in the position to turn the knobs and suffocate it. But before trade to and from Gaza had been completely strangled, he suffered a stroke in January 2006 and slipped into a coma. Three weeks later, Hamas was elected to a ruling majority in a parliamentary election, fair and square. The United States quickly stepped in alongside Israel to help smother its power. Hamas, which had already called a cease-fire with the Gaza pullout, was making offers it had never made before, including recognizing Israel's right to exist if Israel pulled back to the 1967 borders and allowed the Palestinians to return to their lost land. But it didn't matter: Israel and DC were in no mood to deal.

WHEN DEMOCRACY DOESN'T COUNT

Nobody could have foreseen what would happen in January 2006. So claimed Secretary of State Condoleezza Rice when the Palestinian parliamentary elections gave Hamas more than half the seats in parliament and made it the party that would fill the prime minister's seat. Never mind that the Jordanians, known for their street-level intelligence, had indeed been warning DC—which demanded the election as a show of true democracy—that Hamas would win if the elections were held then. Running on an anticorruption campaign, Hamas's victory reflected disgust with Fatah, the PLO arm headed by Arafat, as much as belief in the militia. Fatah was so dirty that ten ministers were on the lam, accused of stealing some seven hundred million dollars and funneling it into nonexistent factories. Although Hamas was fairly voted in, the United States and Israel did everything they could to undermine them: cutting off promised aid, freezing accounts held in Jordan, withholding money due, making reform impossible, and launching an international campaign bad-mouthing Hamas, which in fact had called for a halt to attacks on Israelis. But Hamas's history of organizing suicide missions in Israel had gotten it on the terrorist list, and the group had in the past refused to acknowledge Israel's right to exist. So the United States and Israel refused to recognize Hamas or its leadership and made it impossible for the government to function. The government broke down, and Fatah and Hamas began fighting, killing hundreds in their intra-Palestinian battles. The Saudis intervened and helped to stitch the government back together, but the United States kept pressuring Abbas, who ultimately dissolved the government and refused to recognize Hamas. In June, Hamas took over the Gaza Strip, and Israel went on to completely wall it off, ultimately blocking all trade and traffic.

Now Palestinian Authority president Abbas, who was prime minister under Arafat, is recognized by the international community as the leader of the Palestinian territories, even though that's a fallacy. Only Abbas was invited to the Bush 2007 peace summit in Annapolis. The Bush team promised arms and training to Abbas's security forces and funding was restored to the Palestinian Authority. Thus the West Bank is doing somewhat better while Gaza is still being strangled. Moves to steamroll Hamas have backfired: the group gained even more popular support in January 2008 when they knocked down the wall on the Egyptian side of Gaza and Palestinians ran out with their carts and their donkeys, loading up on food and escaping their pen for a few days at least. The wall was mended—Hamas helped—and the Gazans are still penned in, but the rule of Hamas isn't much questioned locally.

At the much ballyhooed 2007 Annapolis peace summit, Israeli prime minister Olmert met with Abbas and agreed to stop settlements in occupied territories. Within forty-eight hours of his return, however, Israel approved additional settlements in the West Bank. Since that conference in December, Israel has set up more checkpoints in the Palestinian territories, their number increasing from 521 to 562, and the number of monthly Israeli attacks on Palestinian territories is up as well.

It's hard to escape the conclusion that Israel simply wants the Palestinian land—without the Palestinians. According to the "biblical literalists," who are powerful in the Knesset, where they hold about one-third of the seats, Israel must occupy all of Palestine (by some definitions including Jordan) and both East and West Jerusalem before the Jewish Messiah will drop in. Military strategists want the land for security. Resource planners want it for the aquifers that run underneath it. Jewish purists want Muslims run out of the former Israeli kingdom. If the true goal of these recent exercises is not (as marketed) battling terrorism in the territories but to get the Palestinians to leave, then they are working. Since the al-Aqsa intifada started, over two hundred thousand have moved to Jordan.

"We will destroy them. We won't kill them all. But we will destroy their ability to think as a nation."
                        —Benzi Lieberman, chairman of Israel's Council
                        of Settlements, in 2004[22]

"We will have to kill them all."
                        —Effir Eitam, former housing minister, in a 2004 interview
                        with the *New Yorker* on how to deal with the problems
                        of Palestinians in land deemed to be Greater Israel[23]

Indeed, without land and without bright economic prospects, many Palestinians have moved elsewhere—to Jordan, Lebanon, Egypt, or anywhere else they might raise their families with dignity, even if they aren't given residency anywhere but Jordan. Those who have stayed behind often live in permanent refugee camps, many without water or bathrooms, and these unhappy slums have become even unhappier recently now that they are cut off from reaching their jobs in Israel. Screwed by Israel, and screwed by crappy leaders like Yasir Arafat, whose government frittered most of its money away, Palestinians are rightly angry. The question of their future at this point hinges on strong leadership more than on rockets and guns, but the strong leader who can nonviolently march Palestine out of its current woes hasn't been found.

Israel is holding some ten thousand Palestinians in its prisons, many in tents in the desert. Hundreds of Palestinians are held without being charged.

Hotshots

Dr. Mustafa Barghouti: A physician and democracy activist, Barghouti came in second in the 2005 elections and has been making an international ruckus, meeting with Western leaders about what is happening in the Palestinian territories and presenting ideas for economic revival. Could be a future leader.

Dr. Hanan Ashrawi: Controversial for defending the right of Hamas and Hezbollah to exist, Ashrawi is a scholar who has championed human rights, peace, and democracy by starting up Miftah, the Palestinian Initiative for the Promotion of Global Dialogue and Democracy. Her attempts to get parties to the table have won her acclaim. She was awarded the Sydney Peace Prize.

Matson Collection, Library of Congress, via pingnews

Hot Spots

Hebron: Abraham and his kin are buried in a cave in Hebron, and King David was anointed there. The first site populated by settlers in their move to reclaim Palestine, Hebron has suffered heinous violence, including American Baruch Goldstein's machine gun massacre at the caves that killed twenty-nine. Settlers celebrated his at-

The birthplace of Jesus and long a pilgrimage site, Bethlehem, now in the West Bank, still has a Christian community. Christians typically make up a third of the thirty thousand people living in the territories. Israeli-Palestinian violence, however, is driving them out too—thousands have left over the past few years.

tack. Now the settlers have more to celebrate: the Palestinians, cut off from their businesses, are leaving.

Ramallah: A hotbed of crime and a depressing symbol of Arafat's impotence. Sharon trapped him in his compound here in 2002.

Last Word

As of July 2008, a shaky truce is in effect between Israel and Hamas, which controls Gaza. While violence levels have dropped, the truce is dicey not only because of troubled relations between Israel and Hamas, but because enemies of Hamas are trying to weaken it. Meanwhile, Israel is choking funding to Hamas and trying to shut down Hamas's propaganda-heavy TV channel, which encourages violence against Israelis.

A strip of mountainous coast that was previously Syria's front door to the sea, and
holding water that Israel would like for itself, Lebanon has spent most of the past
four decades occupied by one or both of its neighbors. Trouble spots include the
Shia-dominant south, where the militia Hezbollah is currently entrenched, and from
which it sometimes shoots rockets into Israel and targets Shebaa Farms, a
fifteen-square-mile Israeli-occupied pocket in Syria. UN peacekeepers now guard
that border as well as the one between Lebanon and Israel. Another dodgy area:
the fertile Bekaa Valley in the northeast, where militants train and fields of
poppies grow.

Chapter Sixteen

Lebanon: The Cedar Devolution

Andrew McLoughlin

In the fifties and sixties, lovely Lebanon was a playground of the rich, and it still is—in between devastating wars. Thanks to outside interference, including that of the United States, this recently rebuilt country is once again falling apart.

A land of tumbling green mountains, palm-studded coasts, and stunning ruins, Lebanon is often rollicking fun. Powdery snow draws skiers, seaside getaways beckon yachters, Beirut's zesty nightlife lures jet-setters, and vacationers plunk billions in the national piggy bank—during good years, that is. The last couple of years, however, haven't been good; they've been horrifying—for tourism and everything else. Unknown assassins keep silencing top leaders, and the government is falling apart. Lebanon is still pulling itself together after Israel's punishing 2006 attack that left a country of bomb-gutted homes and broken bridges. The economy's tanking, Hezbollah's rising, refugee camps are guerrilla breeding grounds, and the capital erupts in citywide protests and crippling strikes. Only a few years ago, Lebanon was being feted for its dazzling renaissance after a fifteen-year civil war. Lebanon is shattered again, and civil war looms. What triggered this chaos? The 2005 assassination of Rafiq Hariri (see p. 375). And among the deeper problems: weak Lebanon serves as battlefield in the Arab-Israeli conflict and is currently the stage in an ongoing power struggle over who calls the shots in "the new Middle East" that pits Syria and Iran against Israel and the United States. One indication of the importance of this turf: as of 2008, the USS *Cole* is conspicuously parked off its shore.

"Lebanon can serve as a great example for what is possible in the broader Middle East."
> —President George W. Bush in April 2006.[1] Weeks later, he called it the third front of his war on terror.

FAST FACTS:
Al Jumhuriyah al Lubnaniyah

Government: Republic
Formed: November 22, 1943 (from French Mandate)
Leader: President Michel Suleyman; Prime Minister Fouad Siniora since 2005
GDP 2007: $24.6 billion (IMF, 2007)
Per capita GDP: $6,600 (IMF, 2007)
Population: 4 million, includes 410,000 noncitizen Palestinians (July 2008 estimate)
Unemployment: 20 percent[2] (2006)
Literacy rate: 93 percent men, 82 percent women (2003 estimate)
Ethnicity: 95 percent Arab and Phoenician,[3] 4 percent Armenian, 1 percent other
Religion: 60 percent Muslim,[4] 39 percent Christian;[5] specifically:[6] 34 percent Shia, 20 percent Sunni, 19 percent Maronite Christian, 8 percent Druze (a Muslim offshoot),[7] 6 percent Greek Orthodox, 6 percent Armenian Christian, 5 percent Greek Catholic, 2 percent other

---

Population stat: The 410,000 Palestinians in Lebanon, most of whom are Sunni, occupy the lowest rung on the social totem pole. They aren't citizens, they have no rights, they aren't allowed to buy property, and they can take only menial jobs. Special Palestinian-only buses shuttle them to work. They are encouraged to stay put in the dozen permanent refugee camps built over the past sixty years, which are mostly overcrowded slums housing 15,000 or more. The United States is pushing the Lebanese government to grant them citizenship, but to do so would offset the power balance in this country where religion is more than simply faith (see, p. 368).

Leaders' Corner: Nasrallah versus Siniora

It's a toss-up who's running Lebanon, now a frail country whose strings are so fiercely yanked by outside forces that it may unravel. Prime Minister Fouad Siniora, cheered on by DC, led an unhinged government. From November 2007 to May 2008, the president's seat was empty, and parliament didn't convene. Thanks to Qatar, which negotiated an agreement, Lebanon has a president again. But Lebanon's instability makes it a conducive stage for tug-of-war contests between foreign countries such as the United States and Syria. Mostly a war of cold words between Damascus and DC, and heavy on the cold shoulders, the U.S.-Syria struggle has triggered a fiery wave of assassinations: sixteen pro-U.S./anti-Syria politicians and pundits have been blown up or shot down since 2005; anti-U.S./pro-Syria militants have been killed as well. That the government can't determine who's behind the ongoing killing spree (or stop it) illustrates its impotent rule. The government's biggest thorn: Hezbollah, the Shia militia that controls southern Lebanon and is pro-Syria since Damascus smuggles in its arms. Hezbollah is also a social agency, a political party, and is listed as a terrorist group, although *only* by the United States, Israel, and Britain. Headed by Hassan Nasrallah, the group formed during the Lebanese civil war is a classic "yes, but"

Andrew McLoughlin

International Monetary Fund

Hassan Nasrallah (left) doesn't hold a government post, but as leader of the Shia militia Hezbollah, which is armed by Iran and backed by Syria, he is more powerful than the prime minister, Fouad Siniora (right). A "messianic figure" for some, Nasrallah is the most popular person in the Middle East,[8] even among Sunni.

organization, lately with an emphasis on the "but." Yes, Hezbollah helps out poor Shia, opening schools, clinics, and running soup kitchens, but it sometimes shoots rockets at Israel. Yes, Hezbollah is a political party with elected parliamentarians, but it is an ally of Syria and Iran, causing endless grief to Siniora—most recently by trying to take power in Beirut and toss Siniora's government, after Siniora tried to clamp down on Hezbollah. In July 2006, Hezbollah kidnapped two Israeli soldiers, triggering the Israeli reprisal that devastated Lebanon, but making the members of Hezbollah look like heroes since they emerged barely scratched. That fall, Nasrallah unplugged the mostly pro-U.S. government by pulling back Hezbollah representatives from the parliament. The reason: Hezbollah wanted to derail a bill calling for a UN investigation into the assassination of Rafiq Hariri, since any trial looked likely to nail Syria. Nasrallah's callback prevented the bill's passage *and* a presidential appointment: the Shia speaker of the parliament wouldn't convene the legislature since without Shia parliamentarians there weren't enough votes to make it valid. DC and Tel Aviv want Hezbollah out—but the group keeps getting more powerful. Hezbollah got Shia more representation in parliament—and veto power—in the 2008 Qatar-negotiated deal.

WHAT MATTERS

Energy matters: Lebanon was dealt out of the energy hand; it possesses neither oil nor natural gas.

Electricity matters: The country often experiences electrical blackouts due to Israel's strikes at power plants.

Military matters: Historically weak (especially after they splintered during the civil war), Lebanon's armed forces (currently around seventy thousand troops) are getting beefed up. In 2007, they successfully battled the newly arriving militia Fatah-al-Islam in Tripoli.

Arms matter: Weapons are flooding in: the United States is loading up the military, and militias and individuals are stocking up on assault rifles.

Militants matter: Most of the militias that fought during the civil war (1975–90) remained disarmed for over a decade, but they are forming again, alas. Most formidable: never-disarmed Hezbollah, now with over five thousand fighters. New kid Fatah-al-Islam, a group of Sunni foreigners inspired by al Qaeda and trained in Iraq, showed up in 2007.

Religion matters: Religion defines power in government, chances for wealth, even where one lives, but nobody knows the exact breakdown. Formed as a country where Maronites (Catholic-affiliated Christians) would be top dog, Lebanon hasn't taken a census since 1932, when Maronites were the majority. The reason: a new census would rearrange the National Pact, a government power-sharing agreement hammered out long ago based on that 1932 census. The agreement puts a Maronite as head of government with the presidency. A Sunni takes the number-two spot, the prime minister's seat. A

Shia takes the number-three spot, as speaker of parliament; the parliament is half-Christian and half-Muslim. The problem: the pact doesn't reflect today's realities. The Shia now are most populous, being about a third of the population, while Maronites are less than a fifth. Also politically influential: the Druze, whose religion is a Shia offshoot.

Money matters: Lebanon is a hotbed of dirty money and black market dealings, with tainted money tidied up in banks and real estate acquisitions.

Foreigners matter: Syria and Israel are both obsessed with Lebanon: Syria needs its economy, Israel wants its water. Both moved in as occupiers during the civil war—Syria staying from 1976 to 2005; Israel from 1982 to 2000—occasionally battling (Israel took out most of Syria's air force in 1982) and trying to screw each other all the while. Other players are also involved: the United States wants to protect ally Israel but sees Lebanon as a strategic base, perhaps to guard future oil and gas pipelines and Russia's moves into the Middle East. Iran, which has an alliance with Syria and Hezbollah, uses the latter as a defensive protection: if the United States and/or Israel hit Iran, Hezbollah will strike Israel. That the USS *Cole* moved off Lebanon's coast in early 2008 may be an indication that the United States still plans to take on Iran—and wants to mitigate Hezbollah's response.

Lubnan, as it's known locally, is a melting pot right down to the architecture, a dramatic mosaic that blends Arabic with French colonial, glassy modern with ancient Roman, ooh-la-la luxe with broken-roofed poverty. There's not a millimeter of desert in this folded land where thousand-year-old cedar trees, monasteries, and Ottoman fortresses peer down from mountains, valleys burst with red flowers, narrow roads twist past roadside Madonnas, and hilltop towns pour down to the sea. Along with Israel, Lebanon is the most liberal, open, and Westernized country of the Middle East. The openness is particularly evident in trendy Beirut, where unmarried couples live together, chichi bars and underground clubs abound, and daring designer fashions are in vogue. Freedom of expression is a well-flexed right: the lively media broadcasts a variety of views in this country, the only one in the Middle East where Christians play a dominant role in

International Monetary Fund

A fusion of cultures, flashy Beirut was a cosmopolitan star where cultural fairs unfolded amid ruins, the arts flourished, and one could find everything from ritzy bars and yachting clubs to designer boutiques and French restaurants famous for garlicky snails. It's now trying to bounce back after the 2006 attack.

government. And the reason Christians, particularly Maronite Christians, hold so much power here has to do with the French—and a partridge.

HISTORY IN A BOX

Until the partridge incident, the Maronites and the Druze were chummy as mountain clans go. Persecuted for their religions—one Christian, the other a Shia sect—both ended up on densely forested Mount Lebanon, where tunnels and caves served as natural defenses from foes. Under the Ottoman Empire, starting in 1516, the region was an autonomous Druze emirate. Still, the two groups peacefully coexisted until foreigners changed the dynamic starting in 1831. Egyptians invaded and ran out the Druze. In their absence, Maronites drifted into Druze land. French missionaries then arrived, opened French schools, sold the Maronites arms, and ran out the Egyptians. The Druze returned to find armed Maronites on their lands and in turn bought equally fancy arms from the British. In 1841, a Maronite shot a partridge—on Druze land, said the Druze. The ensuing battle killed three hundred; relations went downhill from there. Two decades later, a fight between two boys—one Druze, one Maronite—led to more deaths, mostly Druze. In response, the Druze massacred twelve thousand Maronites in a week; many Maronites fled to Beirut, until then dominated by Sunni. The French stopped the rampage and negotiated terms: the Druze moved farther south, in turn pushing the Shia who lived there farther south still. From then on, the Maronites snuggled closer to their French protectors. In 1919, when the fate of Ottoman lands was being decided in France, the privileged Maronites requested their own country. The European map makers gave them more land than they'd even wanted, creating a country that stitched together land held by Christians, Sunni, Shia, and Druze. But the Maronites, who according to a 1932 census had the largest population, would be kingpins.

The Middle East's most diverse country faith-wise, Lebanon is home to seventeen religious sects, and the population is a mix of Arab and Phoenician, Armenian, Greek, and Kurd. Cohesive it's not: Sunnis and Maronites and urban Druze are the bankers and business-owning upper crust, Shia are often poor farmers, and Palestinians are mostly isolated. Religion divides the land into a geographical patchwork: well-heeled Sunnis live in coast-hugging West Beirut; Maronites perch in the posh hills of East Beirut; many Druze live in the mountains; Shia are found in the so-called Misery Belt of Beirut's southern suburbs and the Hezbollah-controlled south, which is nearly a separate country. Palestinians live in the same ratty refugee camps they'd been sent to since they began arriving six decades ago. Not welcomed to begin with, the Palestinians' fate only worsened in 1970 when the PLO was chased out of Jordan and ran over here, Lebanon having been chosen by Egypt's president Nasser and PLO leader Yasir Arafat as the new PLO home. Acting like outlaws, pushing Shia out of the south, and creating "a state within a state" where Lebanon's rules didn't apply, the PLO kidnapped Lebanese, raped, and murdered. Arafat's gangs were so threatening that some Lebanese, particularly powerful and wealthy Christians, began forming private militias for protection. It all came to a head one Sunday in April 1975, when a car raced by a church, spraying bullets into the crowd where one powerful Christian, Pierre Gemayel, was stepping out of the service. Three died in what Gemayel believed was an attack directed at him, and he sent his militia out to avenge it, starting a war that would last fifteen years and bring the country to its knees.

LEBANON'S CIVIL WAR (1975-90)

What began in 1975 as a showdown between a Christian militia, which slit the throats of thirty innocent Palestinian workers on a bus, and the gangsterish PLO, which avenged their deaths, led to a bizarre kaleidoscope of ever-changing alliances between sects and militias. The Druze, who'd been cut out of the government-ruling triad and wanted a change, jumped in and aligned with left-ists against the Christian militias; the Sunni fought along with the PLO, which split into competing factions; the Lebanese army cracked up and soldiers began fighting against former comrades. The Syrians jumped in, first fighting on the Palestinian side, then backing the Christians. PLO raids over the border briefly brought Israel into the fray in 1978, and it returned in 1982 and teamed up with a Christian faction of the former army, the Southern Lebanon Army, which ran torture camps. The Shia, initially not fighting, greeted the Israelis with flowers, thinking they could return to the homes that the PLO had taken, but Israel welcomed only Christians back to the south, which they proceeded to occupy for eighteen years, and during which their armed forces killed 18,000. The Shia formed a militia, Amal, but hard-core types within it decided it wasn't militant enough and formed Hezbollah. Lebanon's confusing and convoluted civil war, which turned the country into rubble and killed over 150,000, had a mind-boggling number of effects. Syria kept stirring up and prolonging the conflict by arming different sides and creating new militias; by war's end in 1990 Syria was running the country through its ever-present military and security forces. The Israeli occupation led to the creation of Hezbollah, thereby bringing in Iran, which armed and trained the Shia militia. The civil war had but two positive effects: (1) the PLO finally shipped out in 1982, sailing off to Tunisia; and (2) a construction mogul named Rafiq Hariri rushed in and briefly saved Lebanon from its self-destructive tendencies.

*Among the most gruesome acts of that brutal civil war was the 1982 Sabra
and Shatila massacre, named after the two Palestinian refugee camps in
West Beirut where the travesty unfolded. The PLO, which had been
"protecting" the Palestinians, had by then been shipped out; the U.S. envoy
who'd arranged their voyage, Philip Habib, extracted promises from Israel
that Palestinians would not be harmed. That September, Israeli forces stood
guard outside the camps, blocking Palestinians from leaving as the Phalangists, the Christian militia that started the civil war, entered the camps
with knives, machetes, and guns—raping, stabbing, chopping, and shooting
the trapped Palestinians in a "cleanup operation" that killed between eight
hundred and four thousand, including many women and children, over three
days. Israel's defense minister Ariel Sharon, who'd sent the Phalangists in,
was later found indirectly responsible for their deaths. The resulting scandal,
which evoked huge protests in Israel, forced him to resign. In 2002, the
Christian leader of the massacre, Elie Hobeinka (then a parliamentarian)
announced he had further revelations about Sharon's involvement. Days
before he was scheduled to testify about Sharon (then Israel's prime
minister) before a war crimes tribunal in Brussels, Hobeinka was killed in a
car bomb explosion in Beirut. The Lebanese government blamed Israel for
the death, but as usual around these parts nobody knows for sure.*

Lebanon's tendency to fragment makes it vulnerable—the army, out of commission during the civil war, still isn't well-muscled, one reason why Hezbollah insists
its militia is needed to defend Lebanon from Israel, which like Syria just can't
seem to stay out of the place.

DRIVING DESIRES: DRUGS AND DRINKING

Syria's looming shadow and Israel's frequent invasions—nine as of
2006—are often cast solely in terms of political desires and responses to security threats. Syria resents that Lebanon was hacked off from Greater Syria in
1920; Israel responds to rockets and raids from southern Lebanon, most recently from Hezbollah. Root causes go deeper: Syria's lackluster economy
gets a needed boost from crops flourishing in the rich soils of the Bekaa Valley,
where poppies and cannabis grow unabated (though the crops are no longer
as big as they once were), and heroin labs dot the land. With operations supervised by the Syrian army through the 1990s, the drug industry cultivated by
Damascus kicks billions into the Syrian economy, with the proceeds laundered
in Beirut's banks (see p. 374). Israel, which uses three times more water than
any Middle Eastern country, mostly for agriculture, longs for the 100-mile-long
Litani River, which is just a few miles over Lebanon's border. As early as 1919,

Zionists asked that the Litani River be part of the Jewish national homeland, and leaders, starting with David Ben-Gurion, have been preoccupied with it. During Israel's eighteen-year occupation of southern Lebanon (1982–2000) it controlled the river. Israel denies any desire to annex southern Lebanon or to divert the Litani's waters, but its frequent forays into the area suggest otherwise.[9] Rumors abound that during the occupation the army built tunnels to draw water south.

For all its loveliness—striking ruins, seaside coves, and urban hotspots nudging the Mediterranean—danger once again lurks here, as Lebanon slides into one of its infamous black holes. Politicians now hide in thickly walled, heavily guarded compounds out of fear for their lives, car bombings make not-long-ago-classy Beirut sound like a gangland, and the place is a militant magnet. In early 2007, Palestinians in Tripoli's refugee camp complained to the police that a guerrilla group had moved in and was recruiting teens, but nobody took much notice—until May when the police cornered Fatah-al-Islam after a bank robbery. The showdown with that radical Sunni Islamist group, which apparently moved over to Lebanon after fighting in Iraq, led to an urban war with the army that lasted months and killed hundreds. The army declared victory, but the group hasn't gone away. Leader Shaker al-Absi escaped, and it's believed Fatah-al-Islam is behind a recently discovered car bomb factory and the recent bombing aimed at a U.S. embassy vehicle, which killed three. In early 2008, Fatah-al-Islam shot rockets into Israel and killed UN peacekeepers on the border—risky moves that threaten to bring Israel rolling back in and that threaten repercussions from Hezbollah, whose turf they were launching from. How Fatah-al-Islam is funded, nobody knows, but there are rumors that money's been funneled their way from Saudis, from the United States, even from Rafiq Hariri's son Saad, and that the guerrilla group was formed to take down Hezbollah.[10] Predictably, such rumors are denied by all.

Embraced as a touristic hotspot after the Second World War, Lebanon nevertheless had a seamy side not suitable for tales in the travel magazines and a history of romancing the underworld: during the Cold War it was teeming with spies, and money in this land isn't necessarily clean. A key financial link between East and West, Lebanon has a preponderance of banks, where transactions have long been shrouded by banking secrecy laws. With no controls on money laundering until recently, Lebanese banks were blacklisted in June 2000, and they are still notoriously corrupt. The black market thrives, turning Lebanon into a sort of lost-and-found department: U.S. weapons meant for Iraqi police, but somehow lost, are showing up here,[11] and so is missing Iraqi money—millions were found on a plane, sent to Lebanon by an Iraqi official. And this shadowy world is the source of many of Lebanon's impossible-to-ignore problems: the smuggling and money laundering do more than attract criminal sorts and provide funding for militias—they are believed to be the source of the payoff money for whoever killed Rafiq Hariri, an event that sent the country into a tailspin, launching what appears to be another civil war that is sure to bring all the neighbors on in and, who knows, perhaps the United States too.

DIRTY DOUGH

Finance mags hail Lebanon's banking sector as "robust," but *fishy* is another word that might apply to Beirut's al-Madina bank, which quietly collapsed in 2003 when over one billion dollars went missing: some say it was a deliberate cover-up of a hard-churning money-laundering machine.[12] Saddam's "black" oil money, dough from Russian mobsters, earnings from drug networks ended up here, where investment funds laundered it in yachts, fancy cars, and art.[13] A bank employee made six-figure payments to groups such as Hezbollah and to Syria's head of security Rustum Ghazali.[14] Other deals involved buying real estate from Lebanese "friends," forking over ten million dollars for the villa of defense minister Elias Murr (son-in-law of former president Émile Lahoud), which was valued at under three million.[15] The bank is at the center of the UN tribunal's investigation into Hariri's assassination, since it may have caused his death, twice: not only funding it but being what triggered it—Hariri may have been planning to launch an investigation of al-Madina.[16]

The unsolved murder of Rafiq Hariri (pictured above) is the mystery of the Middle East. Some say Syria, others blame Hezbollah, and Hezbollah points at Israel.

Getty Images

During the 1990s, it seemed unlikely that Lebanon might again descend into a civil war like the last, when a Green Line split the Christian and Sunni zones and to cross it was to risk being gunned down, and buildings on both sides were so bombed-out and bullet-pocked they looked like Swiss cheese. The country had dusted itself off and pulled itself together. The snipers, car bombs, hijackings, and massacres that were daily events in the eighties faded into the background, as cranes replaced tanks, AK-47s were swapped for hammers, and the world the Lebanese had once loved rose again at least in Beirut. The capital city so dazzled twenty-first-century jet-setters that it appeared in travel mags' top-ten "must go" lists. The force behind the resurgence, the man driving the reconstruction, the leader who sewed back together the pieces of the Lebanese crazy quilt was tycoon/peacemaker/prime minister Rafiq Hariri.

REMEMBERING RAFIQ

Lebanese-born Rafiq Hariri, with his silver hair combed back in an S-shaped wave, thick mustache neatly trimmed, and dramatic caterpillar-like eyebrows, made his mountain of money in Saudi Arabia as a real estate developer to the royals. Named Saudi king Fahd's special envoy, he returned to Lebanon in 1982, hoping to end the civil war. Forging cease-fires and paying workers to mend bomb-ravaged roads, he engineered the 1989 Taif Agreement that terminated the fighting. The face of a fresh era, Hariri jumped into politics. As prime minister (1992–98 and 2000–2004) he unified a fractious society, rebuilt a war-blasted country, and rejuvenated Lebanon. The changes he put in place, most would say, were for the better, not the least of which was Beirut's sparkling downtown, which he restored to its previous grandeur. Squeaky clean he wasn't, starting with bribing his way into office.[17] But that's how politics went in Lebanon, where voters cast ballots for parliamentarians who select the president, who taps the prime minister, and where top selections until recently were preapproved by Damascus.

Hariri built a mansion for Syria's president Hafez al-Asad and gave Syria's top official in Beirut, Abdul Halim Khaddam, a villa. And he donated a palace to Lebanon's president Elias Hrawi, who three months later tapped Hariri as prime minister. The resurrection of Beirut barreled along; Hariri owned 10 percent of the reconstruction company. He bought a TV station and a newspaper, which painted him as economic savior. He took out thirty-five billion dollars in international loans, making Lebanon the world's most indebted country per capita. His development largely ignored the south, home of the Shia, Lebanon's poorest group. Nevertheless, Hariri was a miracle worker and to many a true hero.

His golden years ended in 1998 when Bashar al-Asad, the son of Syria's president, took over "the Lebanon portfolio." Bashar didn't like Hariri's independence or his international ties, including those to French president Jacques Chirac, whose campaigns may have benefited from Hariri money. And Bashar *did* like army man Émile Lahoud, tapping him as president and applauding as Lahoud steamrolled Hariri's pet projects. One morning Hariri heard, via radio, that Lahoud had accepted his resignation, which he hadn't given. Two years later, Hariri swept parliamentary elections; Lahoud was forced to name Hariri prime minister but again smashed his plans. Once tolerant of Syrian interference, once willing to kowtow and pay whatever was needed, Hariri was fed up. All the more when Bashar, by then Syria's president, announced in 2004 that he wanted Lahoud's presidential term extended three more years, which would require a constitutional amendment that Hariri was to push through.

Hariri called Chirac, who called Bush, the result being UN Security Council Resolution 1559 that demanded Syria pry itself out of Lebanon. Bashar called Hariri to Damascus. According to Hariri's friends, including Druze parliamentarian Walid Jumblatt, the message conveyed that day was that if Chirac and Hariri tried to smash him, Bashar would smash Lebanon.[18]

When shortly thereafter he turned up in parliament to urge passage of the amendment, his arm bandaged in a sling, Hariri explained that he'd taken a fall. Not long after that, on October 20, 2004, Hariri again stepped down as prime minister.

On Valentine's Day 2005, Rafiq Hariri, dressed as usual in an expensive suit, slipped behind the wheel of his black Mercedes, accompanied by his motorcade, and headed for a meeting in downtown Beirut's Central District. Only a few years before, these waterfront blocks had been a toxic wasteland of scorched building shells occupied by rats, wild dogs, and snipers. The motorcade eased past tree-lined sidewalk cafés and French restaurants, past balconied apartments and the clock tower rising from the Place d'Étoile, and veered left toward the water, where sailboats bobbed in the afternoon breeze. As the Mercedes neared the promenade and drove past the St. Georges Hotel, a white van blew up in a fiery explosion that that sent body parts flying, crumbled buildings, blasted out windows for blocks, and shook the ground miles away.

The massive bomb killed Hariri and twenty-one others, injuring over a hundred more, and ripped the country in two. Within hours a line had been painted, as divisive as the Green Line that had once cleaved Beirut during the civil war. This newly painted line divided opinion about Syria: within days most of the country had stepped on one side or the other—blaming Syria for Hariri's death or believing Damascus was victim of a frame-up.

INNOCENT UNTIL PROVEN SYRIA

"U.S. Seems Sure of Hand of Syria," announced the *New York Times* headline the day after the bomb exploded. "U.S. recalls its envoy in Syria, linking nation to Beirut blast," blared another. "Mr. Hariri's assassination may frighten Lebanese critics of Damascus into temporary silence," advised the *Times* editorial board, "but its long-term effect should be a renewed push for Syria to get out of Lebanon."[19] The White House was no less subtle in linking the assassination to Damascus. "We condemn this brutal attack," said White House spokesman Scott McClellan, calling it "a terrible reminder that the Lebanese people must be able to pursue their aspirations and determine their own political future free from violence and intimidation and free from Syrian occupation." Syrian president Bashar Asad denounced the murder as "a horrible terrorist act" and denied involvement. Few questioned that Syria was capable of offing its enemies, few doubted that Lebanon would be better off without Syria bossing it around—or any other country for that matter. But some had to wonder if the timing was just a little too perfect. That Syria would set itself up for that fall seemed to many surprisingly stupid. It was already under the gun from the United States, which had recently clamped on economic sanctions, had frequently lambasted it, and had, with Chirac, pushed through the UN resolution that demanded Syria get out. *Time* noted that "if Syria was involved," the move would represent "uncharacteristically brazen recklessness" from a regime marked by self-preservation and caution.[20]

As plumes of black smoke rose from the death scene, as fire engulfed the ripped cars causing secondary explosions, as the news spread through Beirut, a few hundred protesters took to the streets holding photos of the late prime minister. Hariri's enemy, President Lahoud, declared that the dead man was "a martyr for an independent Lebanon," put his loyalists in charge of the investigation, and prohibited public gatherings. Powerful Druze parliamentarian Walid Jumblatt was the first to officially point the finger at Damascus and the Damascus-supported regime. Jumblatt led the march out of parliament as thousands—given orange and white scarves that had suddenly materialized as symbols of outrage—protested in the streets, chanting "Syria out!" Organizers handed out "freedom bracelets" and laminated "Independence in 2005" cards. Tens of thousands of Lebanese were demanding that Syria leave, reported the Western media. With widescreen video monitors, flags waving, and production assistants milling about, the protests seemed "stage-managed"—like the set of a TV show.[21]

Not everyone was against Syria, however. Some had benefited from the secret flow of money: Hezbollah, the sole civil war militia that wasn't disarmed, didn't have to worry about being shut down as long as Syria ruled. Some believed Syria's military presence ensured that Israel wouldn't launch a major attack. And there were some who thought Hariri's death was perhaps the work of the United States or Israel, and that Damascus was being falsely pinned. On March 8, Hezbollah's Hassan Nasrallah called a rally of his own. Half a million turned up to show their support of Syria and to denounce the United States, which Nasrallah claimed was manipulating the murder as part of the American-Israeli agenda to control Lebanon. He said any actions taken by Syria had nothing to do with the demands of UN Security Council Resolution 1559, which also called for Hezbollah to be disarmed, and which he denounced to the wild cheers of his followers. "Isn't this Western democracy?" he asked. "The majority is rejecting Resolution 1559!"[22]

Six days later, a million anti-Syria demonstrators crowded into Beirut's Martyrs' Square to chant "Enough! The truth! Syria out!" while waving the red and

Michael Totten

Druze parliamentarian Walid Jumblatt, whose family has led the Druze community for generations, is a political chameleon. In 2003, he snidely lamented that a mortar that blasted the Baghdad hotel where Paul Wolfowitz was staying had missed its neocon target; not long thereafter Jumblatt was a featured speaker at neocon think tanks. During a visit in March 2007, he secured hefty checks for Lebanon from DC, announcing: "I am here to seek U.S. help to combat the totalitarian regimes of Syria and Iran, which seek to dominate my country through their Hezbollah agents." He's now chummy with State Department reps Elliott Abrams and David Welch.

white flag with the outline of the country's beloved cedar. In speech after speech, including those of Hariri's son Saad and parliamentarian Walid Jumblatt, the deceased Hariri was hailed as a martyr, thereafter part of his official title. The event crystallized into a new "March 14 coalition" that brought together most Christians, Sunni, and Druze in a united attempt to wash Syria out of Lebanese politics. And the protests had an effect: the government shut down and called for new elections. And Syria rolled out the troops that had rolled in twenty-nine years before.

The Lebanese called the March 14 protests the Independence Intifada, but the term was touched up by Paula Dobriansky of the U.S. State Department, who dubbed it the Cedar Revolution.

Saad Hariri's party, Future Movement, part of the March 14 bloc, won a majority in the spring election, qualifying Saad for the prime minister's seat. Having little understanding of politics or Lebanon—he'd grown up in Saudi Arabia—he tapped finance minister Fouad Siniora, former chief financial officer of his father's banking concerns. Now that Syria was out of the picture, however, few seemed sure how to proceed, beyond renaming the airport Martyr Rafiq Hariri International and trying to pass a law demanding an international investigation into Hariri's death. Even that bill couldn't pass, requiring that the UN Security Council launch the investigation on its own. The problem: actions of the anti-Syria bloc (the pro-U.S. March 14 coalition) kept being blocked by the pro-Syria faction (Hezbollah and the Shia party Amal), which had been well-treated by the Syrians.

> *Hezbollah and Amal's determination to block the UN investigation was fishy, particularly if Syria was innocent. However, they did raise two valid points: (1) the political system doesn't duly represent Shia, now the largest bloc; and (2) the United States was nosing in to "call the shots," including demanding that Hezbollah turn in weapons.*

Despite the deadlock, President Bush was delighted to meet with Prime Minister Siniora when he stopped by DC in April 2006 to hit up the United States for cash. During their joint press conference, the name Hezbollah didn't come up. "The United States strongly supports a free and independent and sovereign Lebanon," announced Bush, applauding the creation of a Lebanese "government that is free, truly free." Siniora echoed, "I am really convinced that President Bush and the United States will stand beside Lebanon to have Lebanon stay as a free, democratic, united, and sovereign state." But Bush didn't tell Siniora, as they strolled around the White House lawn, the president's arm slung around the prime minister's shoulder, about a plan cooking up in Israel—a plan the White House knew about and that the State Department's own Elliott Abrams reportedly finessed.[23] It was a plan that very much contradicted the idea of a "free, truly free" and sovereign Lebanon, a plan that would shred the Siniora government and make even the pro-U.S. faction wonder if the United States was friend or foe. The plan had been in the works for over a year and was just waiting for a catalyst to set it off—a catalyst that Hezbollah provided.

> *As U.S.-designated terrorists go, Hezbollah is usually mellow with regards to Israel. Unlike caged-in Gazans, who blindly shoot thousands of rockets a year over their wall into Israel (though about one in two thousand hits anything), Hezbollah typically confines its rocket attacks to the military installation at Israeli-occupied Shebaa Farms—and even those aren't all that frequent. Until 2006, Hezbollah rockets had been launched into northern Israel for a few days in 1993, sporadically during 1995 and 1996, and for a week during November 2005. Hezbollah rarely conducts*

> raids; it doesn't send out its own suicide bombers. It's mostly involved
> with border defense, and when it acts there's usually a reason. In 2006,
> the reason was that Hezbollah wanted the release of Samir Kantar, who'd
> broken into an Israeli apartment in 1979, killed a toddler by cracking open
> her head, then shot her father, and had been in Israeli prison ever since.

What Hezbollah did that Wednesday morning of July 12, 2006, was indeed provocative. One might wonder if, under pressure to disarm, Hezbollah was trying to
legitimize its existence. While firing several rockets on the northern Israeli town
Haifa as a diversion, Hezbollah fighters crossed into Israel, shot at two Humvees
driven by Israeli soldiers, and abducted two. The idea, Hezbollah said (and which
was supported by phone intercepts Israel had picked up in May), was to negotiate a prisoner exchange. Nasrallah thought Israeli prime minister Olmert was
weak and perhaps wouldn't respond militarily at all. That's a strange assumption
given that in June Hamas had kidnapped one soldier and weeks later Israel was
still pounding Gaza. But few could have predicted that Israel would respond as
vindictively as it did.

> The aim of Operation Just Reward, said Israeli lieutenant general Dan
> Halutz, who headed the armed forces, was to "turn back the clock in
> Lebanon by twenty years." In terms of that goal, it succeeded. As for the
> other goals of decimating Hezbollah or getting back the kidnapped
> soldiers, Israel failed miserably.

At the news, Israel announced that the capture was "an act of war" and put a
previously developed plan into action.[24] "This morning's events were not a terrorist attack," announced Israel's prime minister Ehud Olmert, "but the action of
a sovereign state that attacked Israel for no reason and without provocation. The
Lebanese government, of which Hezbollah is a member, is trying to undermine
regional stability. Lebanon is responsible and Lebanon will bear the consequences of its actions."[25] Siniora responded that the government hadn't known
of the plans, didn't endorse them, and wasn't responsible. But no matter: the
war—if that term can be used to describe this unmatched encounter that pitted
thirty thousand Israelis armed with high-tech weaponry against perhaps five
thousand Hezbollah militants armed with rockets, automatic rifles, and a hundred missiles—was on.

Israeli forces knocked out Hezbollah's TV station al-Manar in South Beirut
and its radio station in the Bekaa Valley, bombed runways at the international
airport, and then a power plant's fuel storage tank, which oozed fifteen thousand
tons of fuel oil into the sea. By the time they were done, 150 bridges and another

dozen power plants had been demolished. Dropping leaflets over southern towns warning residents to evacuate, Israel attacked the civilian-carrying convoys as they left, which before long couldn't get far, since all the bridges over the Litani River had been destroyed. "Nowhere is safe," said Israel's General Halutz, "it's as simple as that."[26] Within a few days there was no gasoline and little food, and Israel attacked emergency aid teams as well. Blocking all sea and air traffic, Israeli forces bombed the Shia slums and villages in the south and then the chichi Central District of Beirut. The Israeli army's radio station reported that Halutz had a formula: the Israeli forces would take down ten multistory buildings for every rocket Hezbollah fired.[27] And Hezbollah was firing a hundred or more rockets daily.

Starting the first day, Nasrallah announced that Hezbollah didn't want to fight. It only wanted to exchange prisoners, and military bombardment would not prompt their release. Siniora called DC, Riyadh, the UN, begging for a cease-fire. The State Department steadfastly backed Israel—DC rushed shipments of laser-guided five-thousand-pound bombs to Israel to help out. As bombs pummeled the land, Siniora devised a withdrawal plan. He wrote op-eds for the *Washington Post* and the *Guardian*: "We in Lebanon call upon the international community and citizens everywhere to . . . end this folly now."[28] Israel was creating "a humanitarian and environmental disaster . . . [H]omes, factories and warehouses have been destroyed; roads severed, bridges smashed and airports disabled."[29] Hundreds of civilians were dying. But the UN resolution for a cease-fire was blocked by U.S. ambassador John Bolton, who admitted he wanted to give Israel more time to demolish Hezbollah.

The international community was screaming, and DC looked callous. "What we're seeing here," Condoleezza Rice explained, "[are] the birth pangs of a new Middle East."[30] On July 27, after Israel bombed a UN observer post, killing four, the UN's secretary general Kofi Annan said he was "shocked and distressed at the apparently deliberate targeting" of the observer station, and again called for a cessation of the fighting. Condoleezza Rice was by then on her way to the Middle East. The Israelis halted most bombing of Beirut the day she met with Siniora, but what she saw caused her to ditch Bolton's and the other neocons' plan. She flew to Jerusalem pushing a cease-fire.

NO CEASING THE FIRE

In the middle of Secretary of State Rice's meeting with the Israeli defense minister Amir Peretz, she received an urgent e-mail from her underling David Welch in Beirut. The Israelis had hit Qana, a village in the south, the night before, where a building collapsed on civilians hiding in the basement, including babies and old women, one in a wheelchair. Fifty were believed dead. The village was already a sore spot from the last time Israel had hit it in 1996, killing over one hundred refugees in a UN shelter. Qana was such a vitriolic symbol that it was mentioned in every fiery speech, including those of bin Laden. The Lebanese were livid. They mobbed the UN in Beirut, smashing windows. They chanted "Down with the U.S." and to destroy Tel Aviv. Beirut disinvited Rice from returning—nobody wanted to meet with her. "We are working very hard to try to stop the violence," a shaken Rice announced at that day's press conference in Jerusalem. "Too many innocent people—Lebanese and Israeli—have suffered. Too many people have lost their lives; too many families are homeless and too many children have been killed, injured, are living in fear for their lives," she said. "I think it's time to get a cease-fire."[31]

The Israelis and the neocons in DC wanted two weeks more. Rice finally convinced Israel to stop attacks for two days and allow humanitarian aid teams to tend to the injured. But before her plane reached DC, Prime Minister Olmert reversed that decision. "No cease-fire, no cease-fire," he told the press. And the bombs kept raining on Lebanon for another two weeks.

On August 11, after thirty-four days of Israel's nonstop pummeling, UN representative John Bolton gave in. The United States backed the UN cease-fire. Hezbollah agreed to disarm. Israel agreed to withdraw. But just before Israel pulled back, its U.S.-made planes showered southern Lebanon with a million U.S.-made cluster bombs, which in the next months killed dozens as they tried to plow their fields. Parts of the south are still uninhabitable.

> During the war, Hezbollah fired four thousand rockets and killed 44 Israeli civilians and 119 Israeli fighters. Israel ran over thirty-six hundred sorties and killed over eleven hundred civilians and perhaps five hundred Hezbollah fighters.

According to the *New Yorker's* Seymour Hersh, the 2006 war, which wracked up some seven billion dollars in damages, had little to do with Hezbollah: it was actually a test run for an attack on Iran. DC and Tel Aviv knew that Iran, like Hezbollah, had hardened, subterranean targets. Another goal: DC and Tel Aviv had hoped Hezbollah would not only crumble but that Lebanon would turn against them for triggering the war. It didn't turn out that way at all. Israel had demolished Lebanon but hadn't come close to destroying the militia, which emerged strong and celebrated the Israeli pullback as a Hezbollah victory.

"Hezbollah Wins!" headlines around the world announced; even the *Economist* proclaimed Nasrallah as the victor, if only because Hezbollah held up despite the relentless attack. The militia, pundits concluded, is fiercer, better organized, and better fortified than anyone thought. Hezbollah celebrated with fireworks and parties countrywide; children waved banners, rejoicing in the "Divine Victory."

Even Lebanese who didn't like Hezbollah sided with Nasrallah's team: everyone was furious at Israel and at the United States for arming and not stopping it. Hezbollah stuck signs in the piles of rubble: "Made in the U.S.A." Hezbollah handed out thick bundles of cash: twelve thousand dollars for each displaced family to rent an apartment. Hezbollah teams and Iranian firms—along with workers from the UAE, Qatar, and Kuwait—began fixing bridges and roads, houses, clinics, and schools. The United States sent in a group from the private sector, and they held some meetings. The United States pledged over three hundred million dollars for reconstruction. But mostly, the United States appeared to sit on its hands while Hezbollah and Iran made a show of getting the place back to order—making a PR victory out of the mess.

The war was a PR fiasco for the United States, which was seen worldwide as the outside party most responsible for the war.[32] A Gallup poll taken in November 2006, showed that 64 percent of the Lebanese said their opinions of the United States had worsened as a result of the Israeli War, and 59 percent held an unfavorable view toward the United States.[33]

Physical rebuilding was under way, but politically and psychologically the country was devastated. Nasrallah, emboldened by his successes—and polls that showed that he was the Middle East's most popular man—started pushing power buttons. He saw an easy way to permanently block the bill calling for a UN investigation into the Hariri murder. He directed Hezbollah's thirteen parliamentarians to demand veto power for the Shia; Siniora wouldn't allow it, and Hezbollah reps walked, along with the Shia party Amal. Hezbollah kicked up a fiery antigovernment movement, calling Siniora's government illegitimate and even setting up a tent city of protesters not far from his office; by preventing a quorum on a presidential appointment and leaving the government headless, Nasrallah made Siniora look like a wuss for the next year and a half.

Hezbollah, Amal, and Christian leader Michel Aoun began talking about starting a government of their own. President George W. Bush—faulting Iran, Syria, and their proxy fighter Hezbollah for the state of the country—proclaimed Lebanon the third front in his war on terror. Given the state of his other two fronts, Afghanistan and Iraq, that announcement had a most ominous ring, portending more attacks from Israel, proxy fighter for the United States. Indeed such may be the case: the 2008 assassination of Hezbollah military strategist Imad Mugniyah—his car blew up in Syria—had Nasrallah vowing revenge. Assuming that Israel was behind it, a logical guess, Nasrallah promised to take the battle to the world stage. And the next week, the USS *Cole* pulled up off Lebanon's coast.

In May, it was discovered that Hezbollah had snuck cameras into the Beirut airport and was monitoring runways. The Siniora government flipped and started cracking down to disarm it. Hezbollah lashed back militarily and took West Beirut. And just when it appeared civil war was imminent, Qatar saved the day.

In a remarkable turn, the Qatari foreign minister yanked all parties back to the table and got the government working again. In the Doha Agreement hammered out in May, the Shia were given one-third representation in the government—effectively giving them veto power. Hezbollah and Amal were compelled to allow a president to finally be elected after nineteen months of blocking it. General Michel Suleyman, who headed the military, was voted in as president in May 2008. Another small miracle: the UN stepped in and negotiated a prisoner exchange between Hezbollah and Israel—which is what had prompted Hezbollah's 2006 kidnapping in the first place. And tourists are coming back.

However, Sunni militants are acting up in Tripoli again; the army began battling them in July. The country is still rickety—and one's stance toward Hezbollah is now a defining sword that could lead to a new civil war, this one between Shia and Sunni. And despite the prisoner exchange, should Israel strike Iran, Hezbollah will probably strike back at Israel.

The events that kicked up in the 1970s had an obvious hand in Lebanon's current shaky state. The most dramatic event was the fifteen-year civil war, the longest in the twentieth century. It scarred the country in every way, even rearranging geography. Southern Lebanon, once a peaceful, if poor, Shia and Christian farm belt, was transformed into a base for the PLO and thus a strategic threat to Israel that also happened to hold the tempting Litani River. It's been embroiled in fighting ever since—whether occupied by Israel or controlled by Hezbollah.

When Israel occupied the southern belt, beginning in 1982, Hezbollah ran attacks there, trying to push Israel out. When Israel pulled out in 2000, Hezbollah moved in.

The civil war also transformed the country into an international playing field as other countries jumped into the action. Occupiers Syria and Israel played the most obvious roles, but Iran got involved too: Tehran trained the Shia militants who would form Hezbollah. And the United States and France also entered the fray: while trying to help out, they both became targets in what was the biggest terrorist attack until 9/11: the Marine barracks bombings of October 1983.

THE UNITED STATES IN THE CIVIL WAR

The situation was already very messy—even President Reagan couldn't figure out what was up with the Lebanese civil war. When Israel invaded Lebanon in 1982, he thought the United States could just tell it to pull out. But the preplanned operation, under the direction of defense minister Ariel Sharon, was just looking for a reason to happen. When Palestinian Abu Nidal tried to kill the Israeli ambassador in London in 1982, Sharon saw an excuse to invade Lebanon. The Israeli assault was ferocious, blasting into southern Lebanon and flattening much of Beirut. Surrounding the parliament with tanks, Israel dictated the winner of the ongoing election: Bashir Gemayel. When he was killed, Sharon okayed his older brother Amine as replacement.

When Sharon announced that Israelis would go door-to-door to find every last PLO member, an operation guaranteed to be a bloodbath, the United States stepped in. Reagan sent U.S. envoy Philip Habib to negotiate a deal to ship the PLO out. A peacekeeping team of U.S. Marines and French paratroopers moved in to oversee the effort. Habib also forced Sharon to promise not to harm Palestinians now that the PLO was no longer there to protect them. Sharon broke the promises, allowing a Christian militia to enter two refugee camps while Israeli forces guarded the exits, blocking any Palestinians from escaping. The resulting Sabra and Shatila massacre (see p. 372) was so shocking, Reagan sent in twelve hundred more Marines to keep an eye on the situation and keep Israel from repeating that move. Italy and Britain also joined the multinational force in Lebanon. The United States didn't appear to be a white hat to militants, however: many believed that Habib had allowed, even encouraged, Israel to undertake the Sabra and Shatila massacre, an assumption that appears to be false.

On April 23, 1983, militants bombed the U.S. embassy in Beirut, killing sixty-three. And the multinational force, theoretically peacekeepers, kept getting involved in fighting, mostly against Shia and Druze militants. On October 23, a yellow truck rumbled into the barracks where fifteen hundred U.S. Marines were stationed and exploded with such force that it blasted the four-story structure off the ground for several seconds before the building crashed in on itself in a fireball, killing 241 Marines and the Lebanese groundskeeper and injuring hundreds more. The French force, stationed a few miles away, hearing the explosion and seeing the smoke, ran to the terraces of its eight-floor building. Several minutes later, they met the same fate, when another truck bomb exploded, killing fifty-eight French and four Lebanese. Four months later, the multinational forces pulled out. The violence wasn't yet over for Americans, however: the U.S. embassy annex was bombed in September 1984, killing twenty-four. And CIA bureau chief William Buckley was kidnapped by Shia militants, and within the next ten years a total of thirty Americans would be abducted.

Several groups, including Islamic Jihad, claimed responsibility for the 1983 barracks bombings. U.S. intelligence believed that both Iran and Syria were involved. Hezbollah, in its nascent stages at least, and Iran are now usually blamed for the barracks bombings and the U.S. embassy bombings. And Hezbollah, or at least Imad Mugniyah (the military planner believed to have been involved in its creation), is usually fingered in the kidnappings of CIA station chief William Buckley and others that would ultimately result in the sale of arms to Iran in the Iran-Contra affair. The Shia group Dawa isn't typically mentioned in connection with the bombings of the U.S. forces in Lebanon. And that's odd: not only did the group introduce the use of truck bombs as a guerrilla technique, it was responsible for the bombing of the Iraqi embassy in Beirut in December 1981 as well as the U.S. embassy in Kuwait two months after the Marine barracks bombings. And the man who organized Dawa's foreign operations in that era, the guy who may have some insight into who was really behind the Marine barracks bombing, is currently in Iraq: Prime Minister Nouri al-Maliki.

Hotshots

Hezbollah: Hezbollah, which announced its existence in 1985, is the group that most vividly illustrates the effect of foreign hands in shaping Lebanon. Armed and funded by Iran, supported by Syria, and loathed by Israel and the United States, this group mixes up everything. Alternating between being a helpful social service agency, belligerent militia, dissenting political party, and dangerous rebel, Hezbollah casts itself as defender of an independent country that won't bend to the pressures of "the Zionists" or the United States. It also runs a sophisticated media network, including TV station al-Manar, which is propagandistic and hateful, calling Israelis "dogs" and running programs that "show" Jews killing children because they want their blood for the Passover feasts—a pervasive Arab myth. Hezbollah's 1985 manifesto called for the United States and other colonial forces to leave Lebanon, the ruination of Israel, and the creation of an Islamic state in Lebanon, although the last goal has since been dropped. One thing's for sure: Hezbollah is a surprisingly formidable foe.

Sayyid Hassan Nasrallah: To many Arabs he is a shining star, leader of the only force able to send Israel packing, and lots are naming their kids after him. Some of his criticisms are valid, but Nasrallah, a simple-living husband of one and father of three who has the potential to be a problem solver and one of the great leaders of the Middle East, is mostly just a well-spoken pain in the ass. The camera-lovin' secretary general of Hezbollah since 1992 is supersmart, charismatic, and extremely powerful—able to gather five hundred thousand for a demonstration at the drop of a hat. Some of his gripes, such as more representation for Shia, are legit; demands that Shia have veto power look like they are coming through. He complains that the United States is too powerful in Lebanese government, but he supports Syria and Iran, which aren't exactly clean-nosed and out to help Lebanon either. More a divisive force than a unifying one, Nasrallah has the clout to lead Lebanon into a civil war—or keep it out of one. Calling for militia action on Beirut in May 2008, he seems to be gunning for the former.

March 14 coalition: Named after the 2005 demonstration that brought out a quarter of the country to protest against the killing of Rafiq Hariri, this political bloc fingers Syria as the culprit and prompted Damascus to march its troops out of the country. Uniting diverse parties and sects, and holding a majority in parliament, the coalition has been weakened by assassinations: with six already dead, it will lose its majority if another five are killed.

Saad Hariri: Elected to parliament in a 2005 landslide in response to his father's death, telecom mogul Saad is supported by DC and Riyadh. His Future Movement party, part of the anti-Syria March 14 coalition, wants to negotiate disarming Hezbollah—a difficult task.

Michel Aoun: During the civil war this Maronite leader holed up in the presidential palace and refused to leave. He

Courtesy of Otrakji Family Collection on mideastimage.com

Traditionally, fashion indicated religious affiliation. Maronite men wore billowy trousers that stopped above the ankle, while accessories worn by Druze women broadcast faith and marital status. The Druze headgear shown here, the tantur, conveyed, "Sorry fellas, I'm taken," and could double as a weapon to make the point.

was finally forced out by Syria in 1990. Vehemently anti-Syria, the exile set up in France, blasting Syria's every move for fifteen years. He returned in 2005 and shut up about Syria, instead bonding with Hezbollah. Now heading the Free Patriotic Movement, he wants to move back into the presidential palace—this time as president.

Maronites: Headed by patriarch Cardinal Sfeir, the Maronites are the Christian sect whose bond with the French was behind the idea that Christians would head the Lebanese government. They are now divided into factions with different views on Syria and the United States. Famous Maronites include the Gemayel family, which created the deadly Phalangists.

The Druze: This intermarrying sect (believers aren't allowed to leave, and no newcomers are allowed in) still lives in the Chouf Mountains and is as secretive as ever. They're so guarded about their religion, which holds that a long-ago Egyptian ruler was the reincarnation of God, that the vast majority of Druze are barred from even looking at their holy books.

The Phoenicians: The wealthy fifth-century BC traders who lived along these shores, Phoenicians set out in ships made of cedar, and often filled with cedar, and along their routes they popularized letters and numbers. They also

Studded with fabulous ruins (the Jupiter temple at Baalbek, above) and home to Lebanese vineyards, the Bekaa Valley is now synonymous with drug crops and Hezbollah training camps.

invented the color purple as a dye, from boiling snails, a product that made them so famous it's the source of their name in Greek.

Hot Spots

The Syrian border: The border with Syria is still not officially demarcated, and who knows what's rolling over it. Israel says one frequent shipment is arms—bound for Hezbollah.

Shebaa Farms: It's only ten square miles, but Shebaa Farms has become a symbol of the Israeli-Hezbollah conflict. Even though Israel pulled out of the south in May 2000—granted, leaving the ground studded with a million land mines—it won't pull out here, and Hezbollah won't shut up about it. Formerly a frequent destination of Hezbollah rockets.

The Israeli border: A UN international peacekeeping force now patrols it, but all hell could break loose if Israel attacks Iran.

Chapter Seventeen

Syria: Crumbling Support

Syria is littered with mementos of its former stature. These are found in Palmyra.

Eric Lafforgue

There are two Syrias. One is the touristic Syria: gorgeous, culturally vibrant, and brimming with meandering souks, stunning ruins, creaking waterwheels, and crumbling Crusader castles. The other is political Syria and its secretive Baathist government. Headed by the Asad family, this mafia-like dictatorship militarily clamped on to Lebanon and for three decades sucked its economy dry, turned it into a drug-smuggling operation, and ran dirty money through its

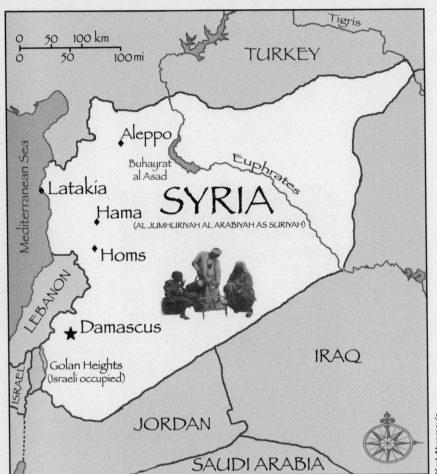

Syria is now a wisp of its former self, thanks to the French, who barged in after World War I and hacked it up, giving away a third of the land to the neighbors. The most painful loss: Syria's former beachfront, which in 1920 the French re-created as an independent country, Lebanon. Syria treats Lebanon like a runaway child and panted down Beirut's neck during a thirty-year occupation that only theoretically ended in 2005. Another geographical sore spot: the Golan Heights, occupied by Israel, which snatched this water-rich and strategic perch from Syria in 1967 and is filling it with Jewish settlers. Syria sorely wants it back too.

banks. Syria's thuggish security men in Beirut decided who ruled Lebanon and what laws parliament passed. Allied with the Lebanese militia Hezbollah, Syria's presence in Lebanon lingers, despite officially being shoved out in 2005 during protests after the Lebanese prime minister was killed, an act blamed on Syria. Damascus denies it but tried to prevent a UN tribunal from holding hearings to investigate the death. Syria flirts with Iran and sneaks arms to Hezbollah; other anti-Israel militias, from Hamas to Islamic Jihad, have offices here. Syria doesn't like Israel: they fought three wars, and Israel occupies Syria's Golan Heights and often swoops into Syria for pinpoint attacks.[1] One thing is clear, however: Syria's substantial help to the United States is ignored, and peace offers to Israel elicit yawns. Post-9/11, Syrian intelligence prevented several major attacks on U.S. targets; Syria took in millions of refugees from the 2003 Iraq War it opposed; Syria tries to negotiate with Israel and the United States on matters from peace to border security. Nevertheless, neocons have Syria in their crosshairs: it is under sanctions, derided, accused of having WMDs by Israel and the United States, and neocons are still gunning for an attack. If the corroded regime falls, however, the real winner may just be the Muslim Brotherhood, years ago run out in a river of blood. And the bros would love to transform Syria into an Islamic theocracy.

FAST FACTS:
Al Jumhuriyah al Arabiyah as Suriyah

Government: Republic (a militarily enforced dictatorship)
Formed: April 17, 1946 (from French Mandate)
Ruler: President Bashar al-Asad[2]
GDP 2007: $37.8 billion (IMF, 2007)
Per capita GDP: $1,900 (IMF, 2007)
Population: 19.7 million (July 2008 estimate)
Unemployment: 20 percent[3]
Literacy rate: 86 percent men, 74 percent women
Ethnicity: 90 percent Arab, 10 percent Kurds, Armenians, and others
Religion: 74 percent Sunni, 10 percent Alawite/Shia,[4] 6 percent Druze and other Islam, 10 percent Christian

---

Population stat: One illustration that Syria's economy is kaput is that a quarter of Syrians live below poverty level. This explains why Syria sunk its talons into Lebanon: there aren't enough jobs in Syria, so the government poured Syrian workers into the Lebanese system, who sent back remittances. It's also a reason Syria delves into "black" economies and smuggling—its above-the-board economy sputters. Refugees are also a big deal here—two million have poured in recently: Iraqis who fled Bush's war in 2003 were later joined by Lebanese refugees who arrived during Israel's 2006 bombardment of Lebanon, which was backed by the United States. According to Refugees International, of all the nearby countries Syria has done the best job absorbing them, providing free medical care and setting up additional clinics and schools. Since Syria is on the State Department rogue list, the United States hasn't directly handed over a penny to help.[5]

"The price of this [Iraqi refugee] disaster is being paid mainly by the refugees themselves and by two countries: Syria and Jordan. The international community can't let [them] bear this burden alone."
    —António Guterres, the UN high commissioner for refugees[6]

Leader's Corner

With a gorgeous wife, an opthalmology degree, and a fondness for Phil Collins, Bashar al-Asad hadn't planned on leading Syria, the country long dictated by his dad, President Hafez al-Asad. Syria calls itself a republic but is actually a hereditary dictatorship. Bashar's older brother, Basil, had been next in line, but his death in a 1994 car crash changed the plan: Bashar was yanked away from his vision charts in London to be the successor.[7] When Hafez died in 2000, Bashar was "elected" with 97 percent of the vote, since nobody could run against him. Bashar, then thirty-four, promised a more open Syria and began releasing prisoners, switching on mobile phone networks, hooking up the Internet, and opening new universities. Activists demanded multiparty elections—demands that previously would have gotten them killed—and the press opened up. Bashar even secretly aided DC: after the 9/11 attacks his men handed over thick files on Sunni extremists (also a problem here), helping U.S. agents unravel the trail. The CIA dropped off terror suspects for "interviews" with Syria's security team,[8] and Bashar relayed info that prevented attacks on the U.S. Navy headquarters in Bahrain and the U.S. embassy in Lebanon. In 2002, however, Bashar muzzled the press, tossed activists behind bars, rounded up released prisoners, and intel from Damascus dried up. One reason: DC put Syria on the second "axis of evil." Announced by the State Department's John Bolton at a Heritage Foundation speech that year, the second axis included Syria, Cuba, and Libya: "rogue states intent on acquiring" WMDs. That was one clue that Syria was the next neocon target. Now Asad's peace proposals to Israel are pooh-poohed by Tel Aviv and DC, both of which are tightening the screws on his regime: Israel bombs Syrian sites, with no right to do so, while the United States is funding the UN tribunal investigating the assassination of Lebanese prime minister Rafiq Hariri—hearings that could send the Asad regime crashing. And both allege that Syria is toying with nukes.

WHAT MATTERS

Energy matters: There's oil here—it kicks in a quarter of the government's revenue but will be gone by 2020 or so. Previously, Saddam's black market oil was smuggled through a pipeline to Syria: the neocons loudly condemned Syria's role in the crooked deals, forgetting to mention that U.S. oil companies were pulling in to load up their tankers with the ill-gotten oil.[9]

Arms matter: Noticing it's in the neocon crosshairs, Syria's been madly buying Russian weapons. Putin recently forgave some thirteen billion dollars in arms debt, perhaps for allowing Russia to set up bases here. Former U.S. ambassador to the UN John Bolton repeatedly accused Syria of having bio-chemical WMDs and of trying to develop nuclear weapons; the CIA disagreed and told Bolton to shut up. Israel claimed that Saddam sent his WMDs for hiding here, but, like rumors of nuclear activities, that was never proven.[10]

Military matters: With over 215,000 soldiers and as many reserves, more than a tenth of this wobbly economy goes for military upkeep. Russia's building a naval base on Syria's Mediterranean coast; the United States is rumored to be setting up a naval base twenty miles away on Lebanon's shores.

Religion matters: The socialist Baath Party that dominates the government is (theoretically) secular: Arab nationalism is the key and religion is unimportant. Nevertheless, the Asad family leans toward the Shia: the ruling echelon and military elite are mostly Alawite, a sect that marries Shiism with astrology, making it an eyebrow-raiser for hard-core Sunni. Most Syrians *are* Sunni: in Damascus religion isn't a huge deal, but it is more important in the north where the Muslim Brotherhood tried to overthrow the regime in 1982. Some twenty thousand were killed in that year's showdown in Hama. The brotherhood was run out, but many trickled underground. A tenth of the population is Christian, often living in villages where the apostles once lived.

Militants matter: Syria has homegrown militants: members of hard-core Sunni Jund al-Sham attacked the U.S. embassy in 2006, but Syrian security forces killed them. However, the Asads welcome in some militants: the head of Hamas lives here; so did Hezbollah militant Imad Mugniyah until his mysterious assassination in February 2008, which is widely blamed on the Israeli intelligence agency Mossad. Syrian hospitality to those considered terrorists by the United States is another reason Syria sits on DC's rogue list.

Alliances matter: Syria has few friends: Iran, Russia, and Hezbollah are the main three. The United States was chummier with the government of Hafez al-Asad, at least when he signed up to fight in Desert Storm; after that the United States let Syria do whatever it wanted in Lebanon. Asad's son Bashar was snubbed by the neocons, and his peace proposals to Israel fall on deaf ears. With help from the United States, Syria was run out of Lebanon by the Lebanese.

Money matters: This is the crux of Syria's problem: outside of state-controlled oil and manufacturing companies, the government has been so obsessed with Lebanon, Israel, and keeping itself in power that it hasn't much developed its economy. Syria didn't even have much of a banking system until recently. Its tentacles were instead coiled in Lebanon's dirty banks, where the Syrian head of security stuffed his wallet directly from bank vaults and it tidied up drug money earned from poppies grown under Syrian direction in Lebanese fields. Being recently cut off from Lebanon hurts this lame economy, and U.S. sanctions don't help. Russia is silently moving in.

Creative Syria

Courtyards were once a common feature in Damascene homes: they offered women sunlight and fresh air without having to leave. Now they serve as sites of many of the capital's favorite restaurants. In modern Syria, women work and hold top-level positions, including attorney general and vice president.

For ages, Syria was in the middle of everything. Final stop on the Silk Road from China and home of several apostles, Damascus was capital of the seventh-century Islamic caliphate headed by the Umayyad dynasty during one of Islam's most sparkling architectural eras. Known for merchants' mansions with elaborate murals and courtyards in their center, Damascus was also the heart of nineteenth-century intellectual movements that led to the first active parliament in the Arab world. That stellar past is still evident around every corner in this mysterious country that holds the world's longest-inhabited cities but is now thick in contradictions. Among them, the fact that Syria wants to promote tourism, but the government makes it difficult for American tourists to enter—one reflection of the unhappy relations between the two countries.

CONTRADICTIONS ON THE TOURIST TRAIL

The streets of the Old City in Damascus are sunless, but light streams into fountain-adorned courtyards hidden inside eighteenth-century buildings. These inside-out enclaves are filled with lime trees and all the greenery missing on the street. Swanky nightclubs and elegant restaurants are regularly packed in this capital city, the daring speak their minds in blogs, an art scene is springing up, and most women don't wear head scarves. Even those who do may be seen puffing on cigs—a move that defies the traditional Islam the head scarves represent. Rooftop satellite dishes rise against minarets to surreally define the skyscape; popular rooftop eateries are filled with laughing partiers singing and dancing against the backdrop of the Umayyad Mosque, symbol of Islam's once overbearing importance in Damascus. Computer literacy is emphasized in schools, but donkeys are still the main transport in tiny hilltop villages that wind around thousand-year-old Crusader castles and old Roman ruins; serpentine alleys weave through souks thick with shops selling brocades and wooden mosaics. In this Arab country, the countryside is sprouting with Christian churches—this being the land where part of the Bible was written—and around every corner dramatic monuments left by the Romans give a hint at the mighty past.

Tourists probably won't see it, but there's another side to Syria that's not so alluring—one that illustrates how Syria *still* appears to be in the middle of everything in the Middle East: whenever a regional showdown brews up, DC blames Damascus. Whether the issue is Hezbollah shooting rockets at Israel, suicide bombing in Tel Aviv, insurgents in Iraq, or even why Gulf states should stock up on U.S. arms, fingers point here. Syria's culpability is even underscored in the Syrian Accountability Act, a neocon-pushed law passed by Congress in 2003 that could be referred as the Blame Syria for Everything Act.

Jeremy and Bridget Palmer

Hilltop churches of Malula, a pilgrimage site where many
locals are Arab Christian and the tongue is ancient
Aramaic, the three-thousand-year-old language of Jesus
that's now spoken only here.

HISTORY IN A BOX

The past century helps explain what's eating Syria, once a wealthy Mid-east star, now a shady drifter. Early twentieth-century Damascus was brimming with merchants and intellectuals and had evolved far beyond the Ottoman Empire that ruled it. Promised independence by the British, in 1916 Syrians took arms alongside Europeans and Arabs to break the long lasting Ottoman yoke. Instead of freedom, Syria was handed to the French colonizers, whom most Syrians loathed.[11] That era of foreign rule, called the French Mandate (1920–46), is what ruined Greater Syria, many say. Killing tens of thousands to wrest control, the French refused to recognize the order Syrians had established: they ejected King Faisal, who'd been voted in as Syria's ruler in 1919; they shredded the Syrian constitution; closed parliament, which kept proclaiming French rule illegal; and shut down the press. France divided Syria by religion, chopping off the prettiest coastal strip to become Lebanon, a country to be dominated by Christians,[12] and giving Lebanon preferential treatment and greater autonomy than Damascus. Despite agreements to move out in 1936, the French wouldn't bid adieu, and when World War II blew up and France was taken by the Nazis, suddenly Syria was part of the Axis, which gave the Allies reason to invade it. After numerous bloody uprisings, the French finally left in 1946, leaving the economy devastated, the political system a mess, and the territory shrunken.

Shattered by coup after coup, with a dozen overthrows in two decades and numerous rewrites of the constitution, in 1958 Syria even hooked up with Nasser's Egypt in the United Arab Republic, a jointly ruled experiment in Arab nationalism that failed after three years. In 1967, Israel snatched Syria's mountainous Golan Heights in the Six Days' War, a devastating blow. Finally in 1970, Defense Minister Hafez al-Asad of the secular Baath Party, which was originally conceived here, took over and never let go. Hafez created a repressive security state, massacred Islamists, and supported militias such as Hezbollah to drive Israel out of *his* Lebanon. Hafez's secret security forces ran the country, specializing in nefarious activities.[13] Hafez never got Syria's economy off the ground and never opened his country politically. And when he died in 2000, all eyes turned to Bashar, hoping for a reformer but getting a juggler who lately seems to be dropping his balls.

Syria is scarcely lily-white: it's known for smuggling oil, arms, and drugs, and its relationship with Lebanon is sick and incestuous at best. Nevertheless, the demonization of Syria and chilling of U.S.-Syrian relations reflects an overzealous neocon campaign that's not entirely based in fact. Neocons call for regime change, seeing Syria as a threat to Israel, and have stated that Syria possesses WMDs, even though the intelligence community disagrees, believing the case made by neocons, particularly UN ambassador John Bolton, has been overstated.[14] DC and Damascus had a cordial relationship not long ago; now relations between the two countries are so icy that the State Department yanked back the U.S. ambassador in 2005, after the assassination of Lebanon's premier Hariri, for which Syria was immediately blamed. There's still no U.S. ambassador in Damascus.

Calling back the ambassador from Syria was one recommendation of a plan spelled out by Daniel Pipes and signed by neocons in a report for the Middle East Forum, a neocon think tank noted for its links with Israel's Likud Party.[15] The report was released in 2000, five years before Hariri died. Titled "Ending Syria's Occupation in Lebanon: the U.S. Role," the report recommends ending U.S. trade with Syria (mission accomplished), condemnations from Congress (mission accomplished), official economic sanctions (mission accomplished), and declaring war on Syria over supposed WMDs (mission not yet accomplished). Signed in 2000 by Douglas Feith (the Department of Defense's number three), David Wurmser (Cheney's Middle East adviser), Paula Dobriansky (State Department undersecretary), and Elliott Abrams (Deputy National Security Adviser for Global Democracy Strategy), it's no big surprise that

> *the report's plans were put into motion when this gang began filling the Bush administration's desks. Even suggestions calling for the use of military force were considered and looked at, points likely to be a plan of action: troops serving in Iraq in 2003 were put on notice that they might soon be heading to Syria.*

The orchestrated "smear Syria" campaign officially began in 2002 when State Department undersecretary John Bolton listed Syria on the axis of evil part two, alleging Syria had sarin gas and was acquiring more WMDs. Like Bolton's speech, the anti-Syria campaign has been full of exaggerated allegations: when Bolton was scheduled to testify about Syria's supposed development of nuclear weapons in 2003, the CIA wrote a thirty-five-page memo to Congress warning that his claims were not supported. From the economic sanctions the United States slapped on Syria in 2004 to the United Nations resolution pressuring Syria to get out of Lebanon, these moves were pushed by neocons who assail Syria for being allied to Hezbollah and for its friendship with Iran.

> *"If Syria does not ally itself with Iran, what country in the neighborhood is an alternative? The Syrians, at daggers end with the U.S. since 2003, are surrounded by a pro-American regime in Jordan, an anti-Syrian regime in Lebanon, an American regime in Iraq, and Israel. With such a neighborhood, Syria naturally sides with the Iranians."*
> —Syrian analyst Sami Moubayed, writing in 2006[16]

BREAKING UP IS HARD TO DO

The relationship between Syria and Lebanon reveals Syria's many faults. One is sheer jealousy. Favored by the French, Lebanon always managed to stay ahead of Syria. While Syria's government kept collapsing in the fifties and sixties, Lebanon was gelling, and the fetching land that was formerly Syria's became *the* place to visit—its dazzling ruins and gorgeous beachfront were cooed about in travel magazines that ignored Syria. The Syrian economy was a mess, but Lebanon's was soaring, and it was amassing wealth as a banking center, albeit a shady one. When a major to-do brewed up in Lebanon—the PLO and Christians began a civil war in 1975—Syria figured out how to recapture the land that had escaped. In 1976, it rolled in as "peacekeeper." Creating new militias, arming and fighting on both sides of the war, Syria can be credited for helping to keep the Lebanese civil war going until 1990. That was also the year that Hafez al-Asad signed up to fight alongside the United States in what would become Desert Storm. After that, Hafez had a green light from the

United States: Syria had free rein to do as it pleased in Lebanon. Pumping Syrian workers into the Lebanese economy, Syria made all the decisions—right down to who would head the government and what bills the parliament would pass. To back up those calls, Syria parked thirty-five thousand troops in Lebanon and sent in its fearsome security men, notorious for white-knuckled brutality. Beyond deciding who would work and what consumers could buy (Lebanese stores were brimming with Syrian-made goods), Syria also made Lebanon more of a crime hotbed than it already was: using its soldiers, Syria transformed Lebanon's lush Bekaa Valley into a rolling pot and poppy field, setting up heroin-making labs and organizing smuggling operations.[17] Syria also controlled finance, turning Lebanese banks into money-laundering investment companies and personal stash machines. It moved money from illegal Iraqi oil deals and drugs through Beirut's al-Madina bank, where Syrian security chiefs filled their wallets with hundreds of millions. Syria printed billions of counterfeit hundred-dollar bills that were so good the Federal Reserve machines couldn't tell they were faux.[18] Syria's musclemen demanded huge kickbacks for every big project, sucking up such a large portion of the billions allocated to build power plants, for example, that many were never completed. And whenever anybody—including the press—pointed out that Syria's drug running, money laundering, counterfeiting, and graft were devastating the Lebanese economy, somebody shut them up or permanently silenced them; fifteen lawmakers and media people who espoused anti-Syrian views have been murdered since the death of Hariri in February 2005. Syria says it's not involved.

Despite the pullout in 2005, Syria apparently still sways Lebanese politics. Its cause is helped along by NBN, a pro-Syrian TV station owned by the pro-Syrian speaker of Lebanon's parliament. An NBN newscaster caused a brouhaha in June 2007 when, after reporting on the assassination of an anti-Syrian minister, she predicted—thinking the mic was turned off—that the sports minister would be next and noted that, while "not gloating," she was counting how many anti-Syrian voices had been silenced. The cameraman speculated that they needed to hit another "four, five" more.[19]

The growing dislike of Syria culminated with the car bomb that killed Lebanon's premier Hariri in 2005. The ensuing Cedar Revolution that drove Syria out was embraced by neocons as well. The assassination gave neocons exactly what they needed for international condemnation. The United States, which doesn't recognize international jurisdiction in the UN-affiliated International Criminal Court, is now hypocritically footing much of the bill for the UN tribunal that is holding hearings about the assassination—hearings that could bring the Asad government down if it's found guilty. But one question remains: did Syria really do it? The massaged neocon messages and the political lynching that has turned Syria from dangerous thug into horned evildoer are stinky enough to make one wonder if Syria is telling the truth. Damascus maintains that it wasn't behind the February 2005 car bomb that killed Hariri and twenty-two others, insisting it's been set up by enemies. The only problem is that Syria is stinky too, and while maintaining its innocence, its attempts to throw off the investigation, along with the mysterious suicide of the former head of military intelligence, only appear to implicate it further. One thing is crystal clear: Syria is worried. It's so antsy about the UN tribunal that it's believed to have dismantled Lebanon's government simply to prevent it.

IF THE FRAME FITS, WEAR IT

The case surrounding the February 2005 assassination of Lebanese prime minister Rafiq Hariri doesn't look good for Syria. If it's a frame-up—some point at Israel's secret service Mossad, which is infamous for assassinations by car bomb—it's a good one. Some say that Syria's government, already under the gun, wouldn't be so stupid as to openly assassinate Lebanon's most beloved man, but others say that Bashar isn't the sharp cookie that his father was, and they point to potential involvement of his powerful brother-in-law, Asif Shawkat, who was promoted to head of military intelligence the very day Hariri was shot down. The Syrian security men sent to work in Lebanon were heavy-handed. Gangsterish Rustum Ghazali, accused of lifting thirty-five million dollars from one of Lebanon's money-laundering banks, was known to show up at parties of parliamentarians, toying with his gun and predicting how they would vote. President Bashar al-Asad himself had threatened Lebanese prime minister Hariri when the latter grew upset over Syria's continuing interference in Lebanese politics. When Hariri was killed, and Syria was widely blamed, Lebanese protests were so fiery that Bashar yanked back his twenty thousand troops from Lebanon and didn't interfere with the subsequent elections. However, Syria probably had something to do with what happened next: when the Lebanese government pushed holding an international investigation into the premier's death, Syrian ally Hezbollah walked out of the Lebanese government, effectively crashing it. A president can't be elected without Hezbollah back in parliament, and so the presidential seat was empty for eight months, meaning the whole government wasn't fully functioning. Syria has been directly accused of engineering the holdup. There's more fishy behavior than that: while initially cooperating with the UN investigation when initial findings pointed at Damascus, the Syrian government aired a program with a witness who claimed he'd faked testimony just to throw the investigation off track.

And just before the first UN findings were released in October 2005, the former head of Syria's military security Ghazi Kenaan showed up dead, by his own gun—a death that some call assisted suicide. Also hurting Asad's credibility: his former vice president, Abdul Halim Khaddam, who was booted from the regime after Hariri's death in 2005, maintains that just after the death Bashar "addressed the Parliament, and said mistakes were made in Lebanon."[20] He's stopped just a hair short of saying it was Asad's fault, but the UN tribunal may go further.

These days, Syria can't do anything right; what's more, it apparently has no rights. Tel Aviv not only ignores Bashar's calls for a peace treaty, the Israeli air force keeps bombing Syria—hitting an alleged militant training camp in 2003, buzzing the president's palace in 2006, and bombing a mystery facility the next year. These *are* violations of airspace and provocative acts that in some countries—say, the United States or Israel—would lead to war. But nobody condemns them: "Yeah, whatever" seems to be the word from DC, which all but laughs at Syria's indignation, while neocon columnists such as Charles Krauthammer whisper that Syria was trying to build a nuclear plant—more rumors that haven't been proven, and in fact have mostly been dispelled. Nevertheless, in its twilight hours the Bush administration recycled them—leading some to wonder if a move on Syria, Iran, and Hezbollah is still on the boards.

Not only is Syria's fingerprint seen in every regional misdeed, the United States and Israel appear to be egging Bashar to put up his dukes and join a regional war. Israel's 2006 attack on Lebanon was aiming to get Bashar into the fighting, say many, including area specialist Meyrav Wurmser, whose hubby David was Cheney's Mideast expert; she says there were plans to cross over Syria's border, and the cease-fire was stalled by UN "rep" John Bolton[21] for a month to give additional time for that part of the operation. Other reports have it that Israel did cross into Syrian airspace, but Bashar wasn't game—at least then. Another showdown between Israel and Hezbollah appears to be looming, and Damascus was right in the middle of it: in early 2008, a car bomb blew up Hezbollah hero Imad Mugniyah in Syria's capital.

Saudi King Abdullah, who was friends with Hariri, apparently wants Bashar out: not only did Abdullah read Bashar the riot act after Hariri's assassination (some say the telling off was more influential than the Lebanese protests in getting Bashar to pull out of Lebanon), the Sauds are busy interviewing for Bashar's replacement. Bashar's hated uncle Rifaat stopped by Riyadh for a chat, but gamblers might put their money behind Brillo-haired and weary-eyed former vice president Abdul Halim Khaddam. Now exiled in Paris, he formed a party with the head of the exiled Syrian Muslim Brotherhood, the National Salvation Front. The Sauds have apparently given Khaddam and the party a nod, reportedly funding the National Salvation Front, which has set up in DC, where it met with members of the Bush team.

And that's pushing Bashar's panic button: the Syrian Muslim Brotherhood is to the Asads what al Qaeda is to the United States. But to understand why the Syrian Muslim Brotherhood is so important to Bashar, one has to travel to the north and to look back at the rule of his father, Hafez. In the north, Syria is a stunning 3-D museum of architectural history. Beyond the ruins of Palmyra, thick with columns rising like the skeleton of that forgotten caravan city, the northern stretch from the ancient waterwheels of Hama to the overhanging balconies and centuries-old souk of Aleppo, is far more conservative. There, Islam is taken far more seriously than in largely secular Damascus, and something is bubbling up to the surface. When women don head scarves, thick abayas, and gloves to go out in the sun on a 110-degree July day, it's a political statement. The message: hard-core Islam is making a comeback—if for no other reason, to avenge the deaths of thirty thousand. This was the turf where Sunni Islamists rose up to try to push Hafez out and paid for it with one of the most brutal massacres in the history of the modern Middle East (see box, p. 403).

The problems that the northern half of Syria, particularly that Hama-to-Aleppo stretch, posed to the Asad regime became clear to President Hafez al-Asad in 1979. That year, several events wove together to change Syria's role and alliances in the region. The first was that Hafez inadvertently caused the rise of Saddam Hussein. In 1979, Hafez and Iraqi president Ahmed Hassan al-Bakr startled the world by announcing that Syria and Iraq would merge. The two countries would share oil resources, armed forces, and even a united leadership. This merger was prompted by the Egyptian-Israeli peace treaty: Egypt made peace with Israel before the Golan Heights was returned to Syria. And that was reason enough for the Syrian-Iraqi political alliance: united they might be able to fight Israel; alone, forget it.

However, the idea didn't play well in Iraq. The power-sharing move between Syria and Iraq put Vice President Saddam, at best, in the number-three role; some say he was cut out of the power pyramid altogether. The Syria-Iraq union never took place. Instead, Saddam shoved out Bakr, and nixed the alliance; the Baath Party in Syria and Iraq irrevocably split. Before long, both Hafez and Saddam were accusing each other of trying to start uprisings, and they would soon take opposing sides in the upcoming regional war. Namely, the eight-year war that Saddam kicked off with Iran, where Ayatollah Khomeini had just launched his Islamic Shia government.

When Hafez backed Iran in the Iran-Iraq War, he may have done so simply because by then he hated Saddam. But the move wasn't approved by hard-core Sunni in Syria, who were opposed to backing the Shia. And by linking himself to Iran, Hafez underscored a fact that he didn't go out of his way to publicize in the Sunni-dominant country he ruled: he was Shia, of the Alawite sect. And so were the heads of his government.

In the spring of 1979, when the first hit men began targeting Syria's Alawites and throwing hand grenades at their cars, some of Hafez al-Asad's intelligence team suspected Saddam was behind it. But as the shootings and bombings increased, killing two or three Alawites every day, the trail led elsewhere: radical Sunnis. In mid-June, a bomb went off in a military school reserved for Alawites, killing over fifty cadets. Hafez rounded up two hundred Sunnis and hanged fourteen, found guilty of murder. They were members of the Muslim Brotherhood, and they announced their plan to topple the Alawite leadership and install a Sunni theocracy. The daily bombings didn't stop, nor did the retaliatory measures. Strikes and riots were common in the north; and in March 1980, when the military killed hundreds during a riot in Aleppo, thousands were arrested. When a thousand members of the Muslim Brotherhood were later released from prison in Palmyra, the government shot them down as they left the building. Rifaat al-Asad, brother of Hafez and in charge of the military, announced that the army would kill a million Syrians if necessary to root out enemies of the state. That brutality was answered with a Muslim Brotherhood assassination attempt on Hafez in June, after which Hafez outlawed the organization: belonging to the Islamist group became a crime punishable by death. Some members turned themselves in, taking advantage of an amnesty offer; others began to quietly organize a rebellion. On February 2, 1982, the message that echoed from minarets across the town of Hama wasn't the typical "God is great." That day the muezzin called out that all good Muslims should rise up in a jihad against the Alawite regime of Hafez al-Asad.

THE REEMERGENCE OF THE SYRIAN MUSLIM BROTHERHOOD

The Syrian government's version was that the Muslim Brotherhood launched a pogrom against Alawites, killing men in their beds, dragging mutilated corpses of women and children through the street, and attacking them even in the mosques; other reports say it started when the army discovered a stash of arms in Hama, a city best known for ancient waterwheels, and the Muslim Brotherhood killed ninety soldiers. However it began, by early February 1982 bombs were raining down on the city, compliments of the Syrian air force. The army encircled the city, shelling nonstop for twenty-two days; Amnesty International believed it also used poison gas to drive those in hiding from their homes. By the end of that barrage, between ten thousand and forty thousand were dead, and a third of the city was demolished. Neither Asad's anger nor his absolute control was ever questioned again, although it was actually his brother Rifaat who was calling the military shots. Residents who had survived left in droves, moving to towns that weren't graveyards. The remaining Muslim Brotherhood fled, and the problem of Islamists was considered settled. The Muslim Brotherhood, however, had simply regrouped elsewhere: in Jordan, in London, in France. And they were waiting for a chance to pounce. Regrouping as the National Salvation Front, they may have their day.

Jeremy and Bridget Palmer

Hama's peaceful waterwheels, from the thirteenth century, belie the city's tragic history.

However you slice it, Bashar al-Asad may not last long in the driver's seat. Whether found guilty by the UN tribunal or overthrown by remnants of the Muslim Brotherhood, the question becomes, what happens next? The Asad regime *is* corrupt. Despite new schools, higher literacy, and more opportunities for women, it hasn't done much to help its people, who are still subjected to ridiculous faux elections and who don't have many job options. The Syrian economy still lags, and Syrians are still the poorest of the region, save for Yemenis. But the replacement of this dictatorship with a party largely made up of the Muslim Brotherhood may just open up another can of worms—namely a theocracy.

Hotshots

Baath Party: Never mind religion, specific ethnicity, or geographical location. All Arabs everywhere were to be united by this political movement started in the 1940s by a Christian and a Muslim. The socialist-leaning party soon split, and some banded in Iraq, where they brought Saddam Hussein to power. The Iraqi and Syrian branches usually don't get along, which is one reason Asad was happy to join the 1991 U.S. coalition against Saddam Hussein.

Hafez al-Asad: Syrian "president-dictator" from 1970 to 2000, this smart but brutal despot, whose hate list included Yasir Arafat, Saddam Hussein, the Muslim Brotherhood, and Israel, marched Syria into Lebanon and was obsessed with the return of the Golan Heights, lost during his watch as defense minister. He nearly got it back in 2000 but died in the midst of negotiations.

Rifaat al-Asad: When Hafez al-Asad suffered a heart attack in 1983, his brother, military leader Rifaat, stepped into his sib's shoes. When Hafez recovered, he was so livid that their mother had to be called in to sort it out. Rifaat, named vice president, was essentially exiled. Stripped of all titles in 1998, he has been verbally bashing Bashar since Hafez's death and should be showing up shortly to stage a comeback.

Basil al-Asad: Daddy's decided favorite, dashing, daring Basil was groomed to fill Hafez al-Asad's seat but screwed up plans in 1994 when, racing to the airport, his car careened out of control, killing him. Like they wouldn't have held the plane.

Farouq al-Sharaa: Syria's powerful vice president and former foreign minister, al-Sharaa snags more ink than Bashar. Last seen assuring the Lebanese that Syria's military and security would never be back, he foresees a warm future in their continuing special friendship.

Hezbollah: Headman Nasrallah led huge protests—by some estimates rallies attracted five hundred thousand—when Syria was booted from Lebanon in 2005, saying Syria was the best thing that had happened to Lebanon. Syria is said to be an integral link in getting Nasrallah his arms from Iran, though most proof of this comes from Israel.

Islamists: Syria doesn't much like them on its turf, to judge by the slaughter of the Muslim Brotherhood. However, Hezbollah itself is an Islamist group, as is Hamas, which Syria also allegedly funds. In Hezbollah's case, however, they're Shia. (See "Lebanon," chapter 16.)

The Druze: Don't mess around with these mountain folk who have their own Islamic sect and are fierce fighters. They took down Shukri al-Quwatli, father of Syria, when he sicced his military on them; now the most powerful Druze in Lebanon is screaming to topple Bashar.

Kurds: Kurds are an ethnic group indigenous to a region often referred to as Kurdistan, an area that includes adjacent parts of Iran, Iraq, Syria, and Turkey. In 2004, a football game in Aleppo turned into a multiday, multicity riot when Kurds were harassed by Syria's Arabs; twenty-five died. Kurds have on the whole been mellower here: most say they want to stay part of Syria, though Turkey pulled up at Syria's border in 1994, demanding that Syria hand over any members of the Kurdish guerrilla group PKK.

Dr. Imad Moustapha: Sharp and charismatic ambassador to DC who says the United States keeps rebuffing Syria's offers.

Shukri al-Quwatli: A nationalist who's considered by some the father of the country, he was president during the first days of the Syrian republic. Tossed in a coup, he returned in another one ten years later. Ruling unruly Syria was so rough that he finally handed it over to Egypt's president Gamal Nasser in the union called the United Arab Republic. Warned Quwatli, "You have just become a leader of a people all of whom think they are politicians, half of whom think they are national leaders, one quarter that they are prophets, and one tenth that they are gods."[22] Al-Quwatli died from a massive stroke upon hearing the results of the 1967 June war, which Israel definitively won in six days.

Hot Spots

Iraqi border: At 375 miles long, it's not impermeable but it's far less porous than it was at the beginning of Bush's war. Syria readily cops to having allowed jihadists to cross over in 2003 but says it's been trying its hardest to seal the holes for the past four years. Nevertheless, the Bush administration and assorted politicians keep recycling the idea that insurgents cross over from Syria. U.S. border patrol and intelligence reports support the Syrian claims that few jihadists are coming through.

Lebanon: Syria's shadow still looms large in Lebanon, and the border between the two countries still isn't clearly delineated.

Shebaa Farms: Syria says it's Syria's. Lebanon calls it Lebanese. Hezbollah likes it. And Israel occupies much of it.

Golan Heights: Ten miles wide and forty miles long, this plateau that rises up in Syria's southwest is one of the most hotly contested bits of Middle East real estate. Lassoed by Israel shortly *after* the cease-fire of the 1967 Arab-Israeli war had been announced, it was ordered returned to Syria in UN Resolution 242, which Israel doesn't abide by. Syria snatched a bit back in 1973, and its strategic military placement and abundant water resources make it coveted by both sides. Syria won't make peace without it and wants every last inch. In the meantime, daily communication between families caught on one side or the other is kept up with bullhorns as they scream back and forth across the Valley of the Shouts.

The Euphrates: The Turks dammed the heck out of it. Downstream, Syria is damning the Turks.

A church in the Golan Heights still surrounded by rubble left from the wars fought over the land.

The Blogosphere: Since getting into Syria can be tough (save yourself a headache and get a visa through your hotel), and reportage about Syria often comes through the lens of Tel Aviv, the Internet is proving to be the best way to figure out what gives in the secretive country. A few of the most insightful sites:

- Creative Syria: Think tank, debate, photos, arts, links to the best Syrian blogs in and out of the country and raves from everyone who's checked it out: www.creativesyria.org
- Sami Moubayed: Damascene businessman, Middle East analyst, author, and columnist. Always has a keen sense of what's really going on. His blog: www.samimoubayed.com
- Syria Comment: All the latest news, covering a wide range of views collected by Professor Joshua Landis of the Peace Studies program at University of Oklahoma: http://www.joshualandis.com/blog/
- Weblog of a Syrian Diplomat in America: Ambassador Imad Moustapha's personal journal includes current affairs and politics, book reviews, artworks, and jabs at his "famously annoying brother-in-law": http://imad_moustapha.blogs.com/

Jeremy and Bridget Palmer

Palmyra: northwest of Damascus, it was a major caravan trading spot in Mesopotamian days, but its ruins and tombs still astound today.

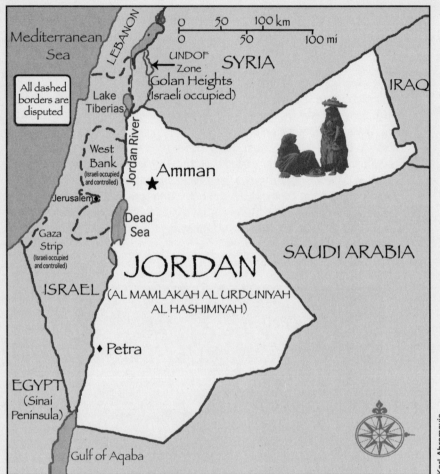

The size of Indiana—and the setting for Indiana Jones and the Last Crusade—
Jordan expanded during the 1948 war, clamping on to the Palestinian land dubbed
the West Bank since it lies west of the Jordan River. Israel then snatched back the
West Bank during the 1967 war, but Jordanians, many of them originally Palestinian,
remain emotionally attached to it because their kin still live there. It's hard to see
them, though. Israel's checkpoints and security wall block traffic and curtail the
billion-dollar trade that once existed between Jordan and the West Bank, part of
which Israel occupies and most of which Israel controls.

Chapter Eighteen

Jordan: Stuck in the Middle

Melissa Rossi

The ancient city of Petra was home to Nabateans, wealthy traders of gold, spices, and incense who chiseled tombs and amphitheaters into the canyon's pink sandstone around the sixth century BC. They disappeared in the fourth century AD, leaving little record of their history. Petra fell off the map, but medieval Crusaders and poets kept tales of the vanished city alive. In 1812, European adventurer Johann Ludwig Burckhardt, trekking through a gorge and rounding a bend, caught the first glimpse in centuries of the legendary rose-colored city.

Take a stunning land of Roman ruins, biblical artifacts, and geological wonders. Deprive it of water and oil. Stick it in the middle of the world's two hottest
flash points, fill it with unhappy refugees from every Middle Eastern war in the
past sixty years, pump unemployment to the 30 percent mark, make it dependent on the whims of foreigners, and there you have it: Jordan—the right
place in a bizarre time.

FAST FACTS:
Al Mamlakah al Urduniyah al Hashimiyah

Government:	Constitutional monarchy
Formed:	May 25, 1946 (from British mandate)
Leader:	King Abdullah II (1999)
GDP 2006:	$16 billion (exchange rate); (IMF, 2007)
Per capita GDP:	$ 2,800 (IMF, 2007)
Population:	6.2 million (July 2008 estimate)
Unemployment:	15–30 percent (2005)
Literacy rate:	95 percent men, 85 percent women (2003 estimate)
Ethnicity:	98 percent Arab (70 percent Palestinian), 1 percent Circassian, 1 percent Armenian
Religion:	92 percent Sunni, 6 percent Christian, 2 percent Druze and Shia sects

---

*Population stat: Two-thirds of Jordanians were originally Palestinians, and
Jordan is the only country that has ever given Palestinian refugees
citizenship. The other third of Jordanians, many of whom belong to the
country's elite, are called East Bankers: they are descended from the
bedouins who rode in with the Hashemite prince Abdullah in 1921 or from
the Circassians, Armenians, and Druze who escaped Ottoman persecution by running to this nowheresville in the early 1900s.*

Leader's Corner

The fourth ruler of Jordan from the Hashemite clan—descendants of the
prophet Mohammed—Western-educated King Abdullah II took the throne
upon the 1999 death of his father, the widely revered King Hussein. Now, like
his pa, he juggles the demands of his people, the economic needs of his

resource-poor country, the nudging of Arab neighbors, the dictates of a treaty with Israel, *and* the manipulations of DC, which dangles money that Jordan desperately needs. A devoted diplomat—nobody lobbies harder for regional peace—he's seen as a sellout by some. He all but begged Bush not to invade Iraq; when the United States did anyway, Abdullah quietly provided support for military missions. What's more, his interrogators took on jobs from the United States, torturing suspected militants dropped off in Jordan by the CIA for questioning.[1] DC rewarded Jordan's help with a handsome $1.1 billion grant in 2003 and over $500 million in yearly aid since, about a third in military grants. Abu Musab al-Zarqawi, a native Jorda-

Courtesy of Jordanian Embassy in DC

King Abdullah II of the Hashemite Kingdom of Jordan

nian, didn't applaud the king's moves: in 2005 his men exploded bombs in three hotels, killing sixty—a shock in a country where security and intelligence agencies are famous for foiling plots.

WHAT MATTERS

Energy matters: Jordan has some natural gas, but Egypt pipes over more, which fuels electrical plants.

Electricity matters: The king is following the dubious advice of U.S. energy secretary Samuel Bodman, who recommended nuclear energy.

Arms matter: U.S. tax dollars are buying Jordan gifts of Patriot missile systems, Blackhawk helicopters, and upgrades for F-16s.

Military matters: Armed forces (numbering eighty-eight thousand) are well-trained, but the United States helps man the Patriot missile systems and runs supplies to Iraq from bases here.

Money matters: Foreign aid props up the economy; the IMF, to which Jordan owes billions, pushes privatization. Topping the donor list, the United States uses aid as a political lever. Jordan is the fourth-largest recipient of U.S. aid, after Israel, Egypt, and Iraq.

Militants matter: Even though Zarqawi is dead, militant sorts are still found near his hometown of Zarqa, and refugee camps are fertile recruiting grounds.

Courtesy of Jordanian Tourism Board

An eye-pleasing assemblage of sun-bleached houses stacked upon seven hills, Jordan's capital, Amman, where high fashion meets burkas, is built upon ancient civilizations: centuries before the birth of Christ, Jewish king David fought the Hittites here; Babylonians battled Persians to claim this city; and the Romans called it Philadelphia after the regional leader Philadelphus. Ignored during Ottoman rule, a century ago Amman was barely inhabited.

Library of Congress

This desert camp, where an Arabian prince, the Hashemite emir Abdullah, was preparing to charge into battle against the French in 1920, instead became the foundation of his new country, Transjordan.

Urdan, as Jordan is locally known, is the strange and beguiling Oz of the Middle East. From the glistening boulders surrounding the Dead Sea (so salty it's fish-free) to the thick corals and neon-colored fish of the Red Sea, Jordan is beautiful and enchantingly bizarre. Moses trekked the land, secretive traders stashed riches here, and Romans made it the main crossroads of their Middle Eastern territories, their streets still visible today. Studded with cultural and archaeological jewels—ancient mosaics envelop the floors of early holy spots, and the ground is still laden with prehistoric pottery—the country annually draws over five million visitors, who drop billions of much-needed cash into the coffers. Jordan's lack of cash and paucity of resources is forever putting the royalty in the position of begging for dough—a kneeling position that creates dangerous problems.

HISTORY IN A BOX: BRITISH CREATIONS

The creation of Jordan, from its odd shape to awkward location, was the brainchild of Winston Churchill, who drew the rigid borders himself. Churchill whacked the uncurving territory from Palestine in 1921 and gave it the unpoetic name of Transjordan. His cartographical handiwork was promptly translated into reality and forked over as a gift to the Hashemites, a royal clan that ruled Arabia's holy cities and had rounded up Arab fighters to battle with the British against the Ottoman Empire in the First World War. The territory served as partial fulfillment of the British promise that lured the Hashemites into entering the war: in reward for their service, said the Brits, the clan could rule over the whole Middle East. The offer was made with an eye to petroleum: if the Hashemite princes were dropped into power by the British (who would economically maintain the monarchs and militarily protect their kingdoms), the Hashemites, Brits believed, would happily part with the oil in their lands.

The postwar plan went awry. Hashemite prince Faisal, voted in as king of Syria by the Syrian parliament, was nevertheless run out by the French when they took control of Damascus in 1920. The British whisked Faisal to another country they'd thrown together, an oil-rich land they called Iraq. That switcheroo, however, put Hashemite prince Abdullah, previously promised Iraq, out of a throne. As consolation prize, and a diversion to prevent Abdullah from battling the French to regain the throne in Syria, Churchill drew up Transjordan and installed Abdullah as ruler.

The move wasn't applauded: Zionists were ticked that they'd lost holy territory they wanted in their soon-to-be-created homeland for Jews. Locals were ticked that they were ruled over by a foreigner installed by the British. The Hashemites were ticked that the Brits kept pulling strings; besides, the small, parched, undeveloped country boasted little but roving bandits. The dud of the Hashemites' real estate hand, Jordan nonetheless turned out to be a valuable property. The Hashemite monarchy in Baghdad was violently toppled in

1958, nearly taking Jordan's king with it. The Hashemites never did regain rule in Syria; even their Arabian kingdom, which held cash cows Mecca and Medina, was snatched away by the Sauds in 1925. Now Jordan is the entire Hashemite "portfolio" and all that's left of the British promise.

Courtesy of Jordanian Tourism Board

Arty Amman is filled with swanky designs, groovy bookstores, chic restaurants, and trendy clubs. Here, the popular Blue Fig, a multicultural restaurant showcasing local art and music.

At first glance, Amman appears to be the Soho of the Mideast: hipsters hang out in bookstores, puff hookahs at rooftop bars, write e-mail on laptops, organize art shows, and design solar-powered hotels. King Abdullah revamped education and is pushing high tech: students study information technology and English starting in the first grade; adults

Courtesy of Jordanian Embassy in DC

learn computer skills in government-funded night schools. Jordanian women work—a half-dozen parliamentary seats are reserved for females; royally backed foundations embrace progressive projects, bringing together Jordanian, Israeli, and Palestinian scientists on water-conservation projects, for instance, even broaching taboo topics such as birth control. Jordanian leaders are lauded in the West for their levelheadedness: King Abdullah and Jordan's religious establishment loudly issued the Amman Message in 2004, calling on Muslims everywhere to embrace moderation; the gov-

Queen Rania heads a royal foundation started by her hubby that's big on "microfinance," giving start-up loans of perhaps fifty dollars to kick-start small businesses, whether an at-home textile-making operation or falafel-selling street stalls. U.S. aid helped, donating seventy-three million dollars for this and other microfinance ventures in Jordan.[2]

ernment hosts peace powwows, and Jordan became the second Arab country to recognize Israel's right to exist when King Hussein signed the Jordanian-Israeli peace treaty in 1994.

The pretty and promising side of Jordan is, alas, only half the story. Take, for instance, the U.S.-Jordanian Free Trade Agreement that King Abdullah signed in 2000: slashing economic barriers, it made the United States the top destination for Jordanian goods, creating fifty-five thousand new jobs and a new textile industry; dozens of factories rose up. However, few Jordanians, one out of three of whom are unemployed, work in them, although wealthy Jordanians own them: the low pay and on-site dorms draw mostly Indian and Sri Lankan workers, and a 2006 report from an American human rights group slammed them, saying twenty-eight of one hundred were sweatshops.[3]

> The free-trade agreement dovetails with the 1994 Jordan-Israel peace treaty: garments from Jordan, made in special "qualifying industrial zones," enter the United States duty free if 8 percent of the materials came from Israel.

Not far away from the heady discussions in Amman bookstores, editors slash newspaper stories—deleting all criticisms of government as part of a new law package the king recently wrote up when parliament was not in session. Not far from the Israeli embassy, professional societies (on par with unions) organize boycotts of Israeli goods and circulate "blacklists" of Tel Aviv–friendly businesses. Ever since the Palestinian uprising began in fall 2000, Jordanians have been banned from demonstrating unless protests are preapproved by the government, and most aren't. And the government ignores loud calls to amend the peace treaty with Israel; given the ongoing problems between Israelis and Palestinians, many Jordanians simply want to torch it.

> The al-Aqsa intifada, the Palestinian uprising against Israel that began in 2000, echoed loudly in Jordan, particularly when Israeli prime minister Ariel Sharon, responding to Palestinian suicide bombers who killed hundreds of Israelis, sent out his armed forces to kill thousands of Palestinians. By 2002, when the assaults on Palestinian towns heated up, Jordanians' protests became more fiery, some turning into riots. One demonstration headed toward the Israeli embassy, aiming to forcibly shut it down, until security blocked the way. During another protest that year, ten thousand marchers tried to cross a bridge to the West Bank during a March of Return, a reference to the Palestinian "right to return" to land seized by Israelis.[4] They too were blocked by Jordan's military.

HASHEMITE-ISRAELI BONDS

Jordan and Israel didn't sign a formal peace treaty until October 1994, but despite occasional Israeli plots to conquer Jordan or send all Palestinians fleeing there, leaders of the two nations were closer than headlines reveal: according to historian Avi Shlaim, Jordanian rulers secretly met with Israeli leaders dozens of times,[5] even colluding to divide Palestinian land,[6] which both Israel and Jordan seized in the 1948 war, smashing the idea of a Palestinian state for a while. Jordan, however, nabbed the Old City in East Jerusalem, site of Judaism's holiest sites: the subsequent barbed wire division of Jerusalem into east and west, and the barring of Jews from the Old City, pretty much guaranteed that arrangement wouldn't last.

Israel took the Old City and all of Jordan's Palestinian territory during the 1967 war, which Jordan was pulled into reluctantly. The king gave up the properties without much fuss, and the Jordanian-Israeli relationship soon strengthened since the leaders shared common enemies: Palestinian guerrillas threatened King Hussein's rule as well as the security of Israel. Lambasted by Arabs for not helping Palestinians regain land in Israeli-occupied territories, Hussein was forced to tolerate Palestinian militants, such as the PLO, setting up in Jordan beginning in 1964. However, by 1970 the militants' violence, mafia-like ways, and hijackings compelled King Hussein to run them out in a river of blood.

The U.S.-led war to push Iraqi forces out of Kuwait in 1991 changed dynamics: the PLO, which backed Saddam Hussein in Desert Storm, was cut off financially from Arab benefactors who'd supported the U.S.-led coalition. Broke and needing to garner funds from the West, the PLO's Yasir Arafat signed a peace treaty with Israel in 1993, thus opening the door to Hussein, also financially suffering from siding with Saddam. He signed the Jordanian-Israeli peace treaty in 1994. The treaty, it was hoped, would boost trade, tourism, diplomacy, and ensure fair water distribution, but unlike the 1979 treaty between Egypt and Israel, which rewarded both parties with billions in free U.S. arms every year, Jordan didn't get much: Israel guaranteed access to only a third of the river water that Jordan wanted, the United States forgave over seven hundred million dollars in debts, and several European countries dropped their debts as well.

Jordanians were livid. The most contentious issue for many was simply that Jordan, like the PLO, had recognized Israel's right to exist. With that recognition, many felt, the king gave up Palestinians' right to ever return to their land, now occupied by Israel.

Most locals still think of themselves as Palestinian and feel intrinsically connected to the plight of the West Bank and Gaza. They're mad that their relatives are living poorly; they're mad when Israeli raids kill civilians; they're angry that it's a major ordeal to drive twenty miles and get into the West Bank to see them and that even then, after hours of waiting in checkpoints, many can't make it through. And they're also mad that their homes were taken away, forcing them to flee to Jordan.

An affluent elite lives in contemporary comfort in Amman, but just outside three hundred thousand live in refugee slums built to house the uprooted Palestinians who came over five decades ago. Fashion plates rove the city in SUVs and designer threads, but their shopping pals in the front seat may be in traditional *hijab*, and in outlying towns, where traditionally garbed women don't work, "honor killings" of women are common. Jordanian women can now end marriages, but they lose financial support if they do and are forced to return all gifts, right down to the gold earrings. Conservatives don't like the Westernization of education: private Islamic schools, which stress the Koran, are in vogue. The government is turning more autocratic: the prime minister is weak; the parliament anemic; and after a number of militant attacks—a few successful—the king, previously moving toward a more open society, has done an about-face; civil rights are being shredded. The situation is multifaceted, but the two biggest problems for the king are Palestinian rights groups and hard-core Islamists, particularly Jordan's mujahideen, which returned in the early 1990s, riled up from the war in Afghanistan and wanting to install an Islamic government. The man who had a huge hand in all that was Jordanian Abu Musab al-Zarqawi, who would become most famous for leading al Qaeda in Iraq.

HOMEGROWN HEADACHE: ABU MUSAB AL-ZARQAWI

Born into a poor beduoin family in Zarqa, the town he would later highlight by changing his name to Zarqawi, the young Ahmed Fadeel was a high school dropout and flunkee working at a video store, unable to hold a job even as clerk. A young hood—he reportedly pimped and was charged with sexual assault—his world changed when he went to Afghanistan in 1988, becoming a born-again Muslim with a zeal for taking out Jordan's king and installing Islamic governments everywhere. Although the United States linked him to al Qaeda, he and bin Laden hated each other. Zarqawi refused to take an oath of allegiance to bin Laden until the year before he died. His first major attack in Iraq was blowing up the Jordanian embassy in 2003, and he was also behind that year's bombing of the UN offices in Iraq as well as the 2005 suicide bombings in Jordan. All told, Zarqawi et al., were responsible for the deaths of over three thousand. Too bad the video clerk job didn't pan out.

Simultaneously worried about Palestinian violence, the rise of Islamist extremists, and the appearance of antimonarchial jihadists, the king slammed through new laws. Now the press can't publish news that might stir violence, and it's illegal to publicly condemn the government—one parliamentary candidate was tossed in jail for lambasting Amman's car insurance program—and political parties are forced to display a portrait of the king on the wall of their headquarters. After Hamas, a group that blends Palestinian rights with Islamist desires to install a religious government, swept the 2006 election in the Palestinian territories, the monarchy flipped out, fearing that Islamists could win in Jordan too. The government is accused of redrawing voting districts and paying voters to minimize votes for the Muslim Brotherhood's party, the Islamic Action Front, which typically wins eighteen or so of the parliament's 110 seats. Despite what appears to be a rise in its popularity, in the most recent election the party won only six seats—a downturn it blames on gerrymandering and high jinks. What's more, several of its reps were recently tossed behind bars after they publicly lamented the death of Zarqawi.

"Expressing condolences to the family of a dead man, however murderous he might be, is not a crime . . . and shouldn't be grounds for prosecution."
—Human Rights Watch Middle East director Sarah Leah Whitson, on the roundup of Jordanian parliamentarians[7]

A FEW TUMULTUOUS YEARS

1980s: Jordanian youth head to Afghanistan for jihad against Soviets; many are swayed by fundamentalist Wahhabi preachers while there.

1991: King Hussein won't back the U.S.-led coalition in Desert Storm: Saudis cut off oil to Jordan. Kuwait expels Palestinian workers—250,000 move to Jordan. The industrial town Zarqa becomes a hotbed for Islamic radicals, who bomb cinemas showing porn films and stores selling booze; Zarqawi involved.

1994: Intelligence unveils a plot to overthrow the monarchy; Zarqawi imprisoned not long before Jordan and Israel sign peace treaty.

1995: Parliamentary elections bring in Islamists, who take a fourth of seats, as they will continue to do in most upcoming elections.

1999: King Hussein dies; King Abdullah II releases prisoners, including Zarqawi. A plot to bomb a hotel is thwarted. Zarqawi is blamed. Hamas pushed out of Jordan.

2000: Palestinian intifada unleashes anti-Israel protests, which continue for years.

2001: Jordan signs up for Bush "war on terror."

2002: A plot to bomb the American and Israeli embassies is thwarted. U.S. diplomat Lawrence Foley is fatally shot in November; Zarqawi blamed. Thousands of U.S. fighters enter Jordan in lead-up to the Iraq invasion; the monarchy denies their activities.

2003: King Abdullah allows the United States to use bases for logistics and forays into Iraq. The Jordanian embassy in Iraq is bombed in August; eleven killed. Zarqawi blamed.

2004: Plot to use chemical weapons in attacks against intelligence headquarters and Western embassies foiled; Zarqawi blamed.

2005: Two rockets fired in September by Jordanian militants narrowly miss two U.S. warships in Aqaba; Zarqawi blamed. Explosives detonated in November by three suicide bombers rock three Western chain hotels in Amman; sixty die; Zarqawi blamed.

2006: Zarqawi killed in June; government won't allow corpse to enter Jordan.

There are valid reasons for the sudden turnaround in Jordan, away from its heralded march toward democratic reform. The monarchy wants to avoid the kind of showdowns that have embroiled the neighbors—whether the Palestinian uprisings to the west or the Islamist guerrillas who've stirred up violence in Iraq to the east. The king's feeling heat from Palestinian citizens who want him to oust the Israeli ambassador, close the embassy, and stop doing business with Israel; he's also under threat from radicals, such as the group that Zarqawi led. Meanwhile, he needs money to boost his sputtering economy, which was hurt when trade collapsed with the country's two biggest markets, Iraq and the West Bank. But his domestic situation is worsened by his arm-linking with the United States, which suffers a particularly bad rep in these parts.

VIEWING DC FROM AMMAN

You won't see it as a tourist in Jordan, a friendly land where most everyone can speak at least four words in English: "Welcome to my country!" But some harbor ill feelings toward DC thanks to the Bush administration's toxic effect on Iraq, a Jordanian ally and supplier of discount oil for decades. Jordanians, who did not support Bush's 2003 invasion of Iraq, hold the United States responsible for the refugee crisis it caused. The effects are felt acutely in Jordan, where Iraqi refugees make up about one-sixth of the population. They were also furious that the United States and Britain wouldn't lift sanctions on Iraq until 2003 and squelched other countries' calls to ease them. As neighbors, business partners, and friends, Jordanians saw the disastrous effects of wars and sanctions on Iraqis. They also witnessed the official death of trade between the two countries, although some was pushed into the black market—like the clandestine oil deliveries that kept coming even when sanctions were clamped on.

Iraq isn't the only issue that makes some Jordanians boycott American goods. That Americans don't seem to understand the Palestinian situation is incomprehensible to them. More bewildering and upsetting are DC's annual arms gifts to Israel—freebies used to pummel Palestinian cities and towns believed to harbor terrorists and known to house tens of thousands of non-militant Palestinians. Many Jordanians don't like DC's unfaltering support of Israel. Even more, some are aghast at the hoops the king is jumping through to get DC's money.

According to polls by the Pew Global Attitudes Project, 15 percent of Jordanians held a favorable view of the United States in 2006. At least that was up from 2003, when only 1 percent viewed the United States favorably.[8] Zero percent of Jordanians held a favorable view of Jews.[9]

Indeed, some wonder if the American cash that is now flooding into the country is swaying the monarch's positions. At the behest of the United States, which once envisioned Ahmed Chalabi as the founding father of a new Iraq, the Jordanian government pardoned Chalabi, who'd been sentenced in absentia to twenty-two years in jail for fraud after his bank in Amman collapsed in 1989. At least ten suspected terrorists kidnapped by the CIA have been tortured here in controversial secret renditions. In 2006, when the United States ordered Jordan to freeze Hamas assets in Jordanian banks, the king complied. And when President Bush peddled nuclear energy as the energy panacea (reactors are now an important U.S. export) the king gave nuclear a nod. "Take a look at the price of oil," he explained, even though oil has little to do with electricity in his country, where most plants are powered with natural gas.[10]

Both the United States and France are snatching up contracts across the Middle East for nuclear energy, also dubiously hawked as a cheap source for water desalination. Jordan, Egypt, Israel, Qatar, and the UAE are among the many countries embracing nuclear.

The monarch's recent utterances sometimes resemble DC-inspired propaganda: King Abdullah's alarm ringing in December 2004 about the deadly "Shia crescent" that arched from Tehran to Beirut smacked to some of a thinly disguised device to further demonize Iran—part of a prelude, some feared, to a U.S.-led attack on Tehran. The king himself had to backpedal after his "Shia crescent" pronouncement, when fiery imams in Jordan began preaching about the evils of the Shia, and passport guards began routinely asking if those trying to get in from Iraq were Sunni or Shia, barring entry to the latter.

The real threat of the "Shia crescent" to a Sunni country like Jordan isn't simply that the Shia, who run Iran and now Iraq, are gaining more power. A bigger fear is that what happened to the shah of Iran, who was ousted during the Iranian revolution of 1979 when the monarchy was replaced by an Islamic government, could happen here. Indeed militants in Jordan as well as in Egypt and Saudi Arabia, where leaders backed the Jordanian king on his "Shia crescent" warning, have been plotting overthrows, with plans to install theocracies along the lines of the one in Iran. But these militants are not Shia but Sunni, many of them former mujahideen that these same governments sent off to fight the holy war in Afghanistan.

The king's knee-jerk condemnation of Hezbollah for prompting Israel's punishing 2006 attack was, along with the "Shia crescent" alarm, echoed in chorus by Egypt and Saudi Arabia. But all three had to switch their messages soon

Courtesy of Saudi Aramco

Temporary refugee camps, like this one set up during Desert Storm, are a common sight in Jordan. However, most Palestinian refugee camps, which started out as tent camps, are now permanent ghettos of cheap construction.

enough, demanding a cease-fire as the monthlong destruction of Lebanon was broadcast on TV screens across the Middle East, deeply angering their people. In Jordan especially, the televised images of destruction and refugees stirred up an ugly sense of déjà vu.

REFUGEE MAGNET—AGAIN AND AGAIN AND AGAIN

Whenever there's a war, refugees barrel into Jordan, putting a huge strain on the country with a population of around six million—most of whom were originally refugees. Saddam Hussein's invasion of Kuwait in 1990, and the subsequent Desert Storm, brought hundreds of thousands of foreign workers from Kuwait; after the war was over Kuwait booted out the Palestinians (since the PLO had sided with Saddam), and 250,000 came to Jordan. The U.S.-led invasion of Iraq in 2003 unleashed another wave of refugees, this time Iraqis fleeing the violence next door—over 700,000, though some estimates put the number at a million. Upper-crust Iraqis who moved here to weather the storm are buying up villas and running businesses; the middle class is holed up in apartments, plowing through savings; the poor are in tent camps. Plenty of Iraqis who came here plan to remain: some reports state that only one out of five, if that many, plans to go back.[11]

"We do not want to be a dumping ground for refugees. At the same time, we have a humanitarian obligation; we can't really close the borders and turn back people who are in need. It's very difficult to strike the right balance."
               —King Abdullah, in an interview with the German magazine
                    Der Spiegel in late 2007[12]

The presence of so many refugees would make any country a pressure cooker of discontent, but it's even more true in Jordan, where the economy is seriously ailing, especially lately.

Jordan's current woes smack up against the ever-looming "Palestinian question" that's gone unanswered for too long. Do Palestinians who were run off their lands have the right to return to their homes? Or shouldn't they at least be compensated for their loss? The debate's gone on since 1948, and what appears to be Jordan's solution—that Palestinians in Jordan should just forget the past and be happy as Jordanian citizens—doesn't suffice.

The peace plan that King Abdullah II is now pushing, along with Egyptian and

Saudi leaders, is the same that's been peddled for decades: if Israel pulls back to its borders before the 1967 war, Arab countries will recognize the right of Israel to exist and involve it in the regional economy. However, besides the fact that Israel doesn't want to pull back to those pre-1967 borders—to do so would entail losing access to water resources as well as the Old City of Jerusalem, for starters—it's unlikely that radical militants or many Palestinians would accept the plan, since it does not fully address the right to return for those who lost their land in 1948.

Previous solutions, such as creating the PLO and making it the agent responsible for Palestinian rights, were no better: Arafat and associates made a gangland of the Middle East, beginning in Jordan. And it all culminated in September 1970.

BLACK SEPTEMBER

Throughout the 1960s, Jordan was crawling with armed Palestinian groups, over a dozen of them, many firing up the residents of refugee camps with calls for Palestinian revolution that would end Israel and return lost lands. King Hussein never wanted the militants around, but the Arab League that created the Palestine Liberation Organization in 1964 pressured him, not only to tolerate their activities, but to give them training areas. Jordanians paid the price for every Palestinian raid into Israel: Israel responded with brutal attacks on Jordan, including the refugee tent camps, where residents dug holes for protection. The PLO and other Palestinian militants kept extorting Jordanians, forcing them to cough up protection money, as well as setting up their own armed checkpoints and battling Jordanian security. And their stunts grew more outrageous, from kidnapping VIPs to hijacking planes. Hussein tried to negotiate, then issued a ten-point edict; they tried to kill him in response.

The most outrageous terrorist act prior to 9/11 took place in 1970. On September 6 of that year, five days after assassination attempts on the king, the Popular Front for the Liberation of Palestine simultaneously hijacked four planes bound for New York, taking hundreds of hostages. One plane landed in Cairo and two in Dawson's Field near Zarqa, Jordan; the fourth attempt was unsuccessful. After several days, most hostages were released, though dozens were kept as political prisoners. The evacuated planes were blasted sky high by the militants. In response, Hussein unleashed the military to run out the militants, many of whom hid in refugee camps. Over the next few weeks, more than seven thousand were killed on both sides, including many civilians. Finally the PLO agreed to leave—and were driven to Lebanon. The bloody ordeal nearly evolved into a civil war. Many Jordanian soldiers actually sided with the Palestinians they were fighting, and Jordanians were furious at the civilian deaths. But Hussein endured, amazingly, and so did the PLO.

> *The Muslim Brotherhood, which supported Hussein's actions, was rewarded by being given greater participation in government. Some members, however, were opposed to backing Hussein and split off, becoming a more radical group.*

Decades-old simmering started to come to a boil thanks to the events kicked off in 1979. That was the year Egypt made peace with Israel, thereby nixing its involvement in future wars and yanking back support for the Palestinian right to return, a move loudly booed by Palestinians in Jordan. That same year, Saddam Hussein grabbed the reins in Iraq—and Jordan's monarchy bonded with him, backing his battle against the Shia who had knocked out the shah and put in a theocracy in Iran. Also that year, the Soviets invaded Afghanistan, and as part of a CIA plot to weaken them young Jordanian militants were shipped off with other Arabs to be trained in guerrilla warfare. Among them: Zarqawi. These elements would all come together in the 1990s, creating a force that would snowball through that decade and be felt even more violently today.

A NEXUS OF WOE[13]

Pieces of the "terrorist puzzle" snapped together in Jordan. Among the Palestinians arriving in the 1967 refugee wave was scholar Abdullah Azzam, who joined the Muslim Brotherhood, was active in PLO incursions, and taught at the University of Jordan until 1980, when his political extremism got him canned. Moving to Saudi Arabia, the charismatic professor worked with Saudi royals and Osama bin Laden, becoming the key figure for recruiting jihadists to fight Soviets in Afghanistan and running the welcoming center in Pakistan for incoming Arabs. Abu Musab al-Zarqawi was among the recruits, though he arrived too late for the fighting—or to meet Azzam, who had been killed when his car exploded a few weeks before.

Surviving the explosion that killed Azzam and two of his sons was a third son, Huthaifa, who met Zarqawi at the Peshawar airport in 1989.[14] There he introduced him to Palestinian cleric Abu Muhammad al-Maqdisi, who preached the puritanical Wahhabi take on Islam. His words deeply influenced Zarqawi, previously a porn-crazed thug. Zarqawi returned to Jordan, intent on over-throwing the monarchy and putting in a religious government. Maqdisi showed up soon, part of the wave of Palestinians who fled to Jordan in 1991 when they were run out of Kuwait. The group reassembled in Zarqa, home to a sprawling refugee camp and to Zarqawi, who was not Palestinian but empathized with their cause.

Targeting Jordan's porn theaters and stores that sold booze, their first bomb attacks didn't do much except get most of the group arrested in 1994.

Tellingly, they were thrown into prison just months before King Hussein signed Jordan's peace treaty with Israel. During their five years in prison, Zarqawi and Maqdisi recruited followers and indoctrinated them with their militant take on Sunni Islam. And their ideas congealed—from setting up guerrilla training camps to a long-term plan for how to restore the Islamic caliphate that had once ruled from India to Portugal (see Fouad Hussein, p. 426). When King Hussein died in 1999, his son Abdullah granted general amnesty, and Zarqawi flew to Pakistan and set up his training camp. By 2003, he was in Iraq awaiting the upcoming American invasion. Maqdisi helped recruit members but even more of a help, at least initially, was Huthaifa Azzam, who set up a base in Fallujah and trained insurgents. Zarqawi and his militants, later known as al Qaeda in Iraq, soon ticked off both Azzam (alienated by Zarqawi's attacks on Shia) and Maqdisi (who denounced his attack on Jordanian hotels in 2005). But by then it didn't matter: Zarqawi—whom Colin Powell and the Bush administration had linked to al Qaeda long before he was officially affiliated with them—had made his mark. By the time he was killed in June 2006, Zarqawi and his followers had killed at least three thousand, among them dozens of Jordanians, in the attacks that he organized in Iraq and Jordan.

Zarqawi is dead. Maqdisi is back in jail, after calling for the king's overthrow on Al Jazeera. Azzam was last seen selling mobile phones and working on his PhD. But the call to turn Jordan into an Islamist state hasn't gone away, which is one reason why the place is crawling with spies. Also not resolved: the problems between Israel and the Palestinians that created the situation that now bedevils Jordan. Well, at least things are going well for Petra, which was recently voted one of the seven wonders of the modern world.

Hotshots

King Abdullah II: (See p. 409.)

Queen Rania: Jordanian queen since 1999, the Kuwait-born Palestinian is known to lead pro-Palestinian demonstrations—hers are government-sanctioned. She also pushes programs promoting everything from vaccinations to small businesses for women.

King Hussein: Jordanian king from 1952 to 1999. At age sixteen, Prince Hussein was entering Jerusalem's al-Aqsa Mosque, with his grandfather, King Abdullah I, when a Palestinian radical fatally shot Abdullah. Hussein was a target as well, but the bullet that nearly pierced his chest was eerily deflected by a decorative pin. Abdullah had given it to Hussein only the night before—or so the legend goes. Taking the throne as a scrawny teenager in 1953—photos show Egyptian president Nasser looking at him with an expression like "Why am I talking with this kid?"—Hussein survived dozens of assassination attempts in his forty-six years of rule, finally succumbing to cancer. Regarded as the Middle East's finest diplomat, he was also on the CIA payroll—but nobody seems clear on what he did to merit the pay.

> To the dismay of the United States and Saudi Arabia, King Hussein wouldn't back the U.S.-led Desert Storm coalition in 1991, officially remaining neutral. He was forced into it: his people sided with Iraq, which supplied Jordan's discount oil. The Saudis and the United States cut off most aid to Jordan after 1991, but when Hussein died, the funeral was attended by nearly every head of state on the planet.

The former queen Noor: King Hussein's fourth wife, the American-born urban planner Lisa Halaby, who converted to Islam and changed her name to Noor, hangs out mostly in DC these days but recently persuaded Jordan to get rid of its arsenal of land mines.

Prince Hassan: Rumors abound on why Hussein's crown prince was canned at the last minute. Some say his supporters slandered Queen Noor, some say the CIA didn't like him, but it's rather a shame that he didn't get a hand in running the place, as he's wise and not afraid to speak his mind. Hassan says the sources of the biggest problems in the Middle East—which, he told *Time* in 2007, was turning into a "black hole"—were extremists, both radical Islamists and American Zionists, and too many arms being thrown into the pot.[15]

Muslim Brotherhood: Welcomed into Jordan in its earliest days, the Muslim Brotherhood provided social services desperately needed in the struggling country. A gentleman's agreement was worked out—it would support the monarchy, and the monarchy would let the Brotherhood do as it pleased, even using it on occasion to run subversive operations, such as the 1980 Muslim Brotherhood uprising in Syria to overthrow the Asad regime. Lately, the agreement looks shaky: the group's political party, the Islamic Action Front, says the government is pulling tricks to keep it out of parliament. It just doesn't have the power it once did under King Hussein.

Lawrence Foley: It's still unclear exactly who was behind the 2002 assassination of the head of USAID in Jordan or what exactly prompted it; although a group called the Nobles of Jordan confessed, it was pinned on Zarqawi and al Qaeda. Some say the killers were actually Palestinians upset about Foley's efforts to revamp Jordanian finances and security.[16]

Fouad Hussein: A Jordanian journalist who met Zarqawi in 1996 (they were in the same prison), Hussein wrote a book capturing what he says is al Qaeda's long-term strategy. In *Al-Zarqawi: The Second Generation of Al Qaeda*, he says 9/11 was merely a step to get the U.S. in the Middle East and al Qaeda on the

Library of Congress

A Hashemite who thought he would rule over Iraq, King Abdullah I, third from the right, instead got oil-free Jordan—a present from Churchill. The famous spy-adventurer Lawrence of Arabia, the hard-hatted chap to the far left, hooked up the Hashemites with the British.

media map. Through different stages, he says, al Qaeda plans to target Israel and secular governments in the Middle East, ultimately becoming an ally with China and fighting against infidels in a global war that will end with a worldwide caliphate restored sometime around 2020.

Khaled Mashaal: Planner for the military arm of Hamas, he was nearly killed by Israeli intelligence in Jordan. In 1997, two Mossad agents grabbed him in Amman and injected a deadly poison into his left ear. His bodyguard nabbed the "shooters," Mashaal was hospitalized, and King Hussein called Israeli prime minister Netanyahu—who'd ordered the hit—demanding the antidote. If he didn't send it, Hussein said he'd publicize the plot and behead the agents.[17] The antidote arrived and Mashaal survived. King Abdullah whisked Hamas out of the country during a 1999 kingdom cleaning, sending Mashaal to Qatar, although he's now in Syria.

Hot Spots

Border problems: These days the doors are pretty much shut to the West Bank, thanks to Israel's security wall and checkpoints. The same is true for Iraqi refugees trying to enter Jordan.

Israel: The leaders stay in contact, but neither tourism nor trade between the countries has flourished, despite the 1994 treaty. Although there haven't been any wars since then, many Jordanians believe Israel still has a few plots up its sleeve. Early Israeli leaders, such as David Ben-Gurion, considered conquering all of Jordan, land they believed was promised to them before the British chopped it off. However, given Jordan's moderate rulers, who warned Israeli leaders about upcoming attacks, many decided that Jordan was most useful as a buffer zone, blocking advances from Iraq, for example. For decades, Israeli leaders warned that if any country invaded Jordan and toppled the Israeli-friendly king, Israel would attack.

Nevertheless, some Israeli military planners pushed the idea of a forced transfer of all Palestinians to Jordan, and some right-wing Israelis still abide by the slogan that "Jordan *is* Palestine," implying that Palestinians should leave their remaining land and head toward Amman. Not long ago, King Abdullah voiced his fear that Israel is trying to run the four million Palestinians currently in the West Bank and Gaza over to Jordan.

The Jordan River: The sacred river, where John the Baptist is believed to have dunked Jesus in a baptism ritual, is much lower than it used to be: Israel and Jordan heavily tap the river and tributaries. The Jordan River was indirectly responsible for World War I—after Karl Ludwig, heir to the Hapsburg throne, sipped from it, as pilgrims did in that day, he croaked. His death led to the appointment

Strangely twisted giant rocks fill the deserts of Wadi
Rum—once a riverbed—where camels now roam the sands
and tourists camp with bedouins.

of a new heir, Archduke Franz Ferdinand, whose assassination kicked off the war.

Zarqa: Home of a refinery and lots of unhappy refugees. The Muslim Brotherhood's social services are needed here, but militants remain popular.

Maan: Impoverished town in Jordan's south, known for Islamist radicals, and home of fundamentalist cleric Mohammed Shalabi. Some fear it could be the site of rebellion and a government clamp down. The government is trying to round up weapons.

Both Jordanians and Israelis zip around in motorboats and glass-bottom cruisers on the Red Sea. Thick with coral and sea life, it's a snorkeler's dream. Shown here: Aqaba, Jordan's only port and a booming tourist hot spot.

The Dead Sea is the lowest place on the planet, and the emerald water is so mineral-rich that it's prescribed for skin ailments. Hard to drown here: it's so salty, everyone floats. The sea, alas, is drying up, but Jordan and Israel signed a 2002 agreement to pump whatever research and money it takes into keeping this natural wonder from sinking further.

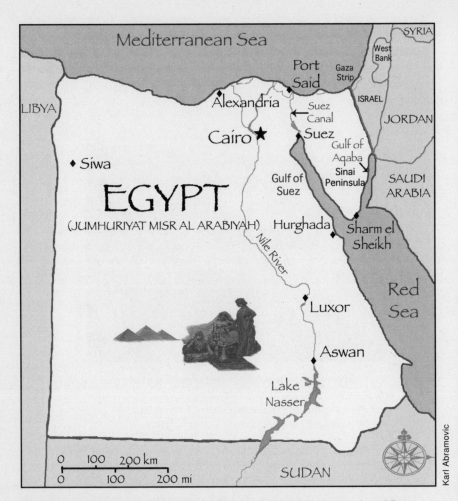

Only 5 percent of the Arab Republic of Egypt is inhabitable, the rest is swirling Saharan sands. Most Egyptians live along the Nile, where mysterious civilizations rose along the fertile banks five thousand years ago. Two other legendary places: the oil-holding Sinai Peninsula, which was traded for Egyptian-Israeli peace in 1979, and the Suez Canal, which connects the Red Sea to the Mediterranean and is crucial for oil transport. An engineering marvel when it opened in 1869, the 120-mile canal trimmed six thousand miles off many journeys by negating the need to circumnavigate Africa. Also key to oil transport: the Sumed pipeline, which pumps oil from ships on the Red Sea to a Mediterranean port.

Chapter Nineteen

Egypt: Secret Society

The guardian of hidden knowledge, the Great Sphinx at Giza, carved nearly five thousand years ago, is itself something of an enigma. Nobody's sure what happened to its nose. Some say Napoléon, frustrated that Egyptians weren't giving in to his rule, shot it off with a cannonball in 1801; others say an angry Sufi blasted it off centuries before or that windstorms simply wore down the pug. Like the Sphinx, Egypt keeps close tabs on its secrets, including influential clandestine societies.

It's easy to fall in love with Egypt. Travelers to this country once known as *Umm Dunya*, "Mother of the World," have been swooning since the time of the ancient Greeks. No place better immortalizes the civilization of early humans—their history, beliefs, and lifestyles captured in hieroglyphics that detail everything from ancient trades to the multiple stages that unfold in the afterlife. The secrets and magic of the land still beckon Egyptologists, mystics, and scientists, and the mysteries of how these ancient builders did what they did still have not been solved.

The gorgeous sun-baked land that's been known for eons as a hotbed of scholarship, from Greek to Islamic, has a distinctive aura: Arab and African mix against an ancient pharaonic backdrop, with European architecture threaded into the tapestry. Despite hopping Cairo, the country still feels lost in time. Beckoned by its history and versatility—here you can hang with desert bedouins, scuba dive in the Red Sea, tap the utmost in modern luxury, and explore ancient mysteries—Egypt lures millions of foreigners a year. Its tourist industry is the biggest in the Middle East. There's another side to Egypt—one missed by travelers, that's shooed away and kept underground, although it keeps popping up in other countries. And that's the world of the secret societies, particularly the Muslim Brotherhood, which was born here eighty years ago as a reaction to the foreigners who couldn't seem to stay out of this place and insisted on running the political machine. Even though an Egyptian now leads, he's too Western for the Bros.

FAST FACTS:
Jumhuriyat Misr al Arabiyah

Government:	Republic (in theory)
Formed:	September 9, 1922 (theoretical independence from Britain; a coup by the Free Officers ended the monarchy in July 1952)
Leader:	President Hosni Mubarak (1981); Prime Minister Ahmed Nazif (2005)
GDP 2007:	$127 billion (IMF, 2007)
Per capita GDP:	$1,700 (IMF, 2007)
Population:	82 million (July 2008 estimate)
Unemployment:	10–25 percent (2007)
Literacy rate:	83 percent men, 60 percent women (2005 estimate)
Ethnicity:	98 percent Egyptian; 1 percent Berber, Nubian, bedouin; 1 percent European
Religion:	90 percent Muslim (mostly Sunni), 9 percent Coptic Christian, 1 percent other

Population stat: 40 percent of Egyptians live at or below the poverty line of two dollars a day.

Leaders' Corner

Since becoming a republic in 1953, Egypt has known only three leaders: the first revered; the second revolutionary in his effects; and the third, Mubarak, a survivor, ducking bullets now for nearly three decades. President Gamal Abdel Nasser

(1956–70) ended the corrupt monarchy and snatched back the Suez Canal from the British, who had controlled it and took the revenue. His daring acts inspired nationalism across the Middle East, and Arabs elsewhere rebelled against their leaders, wanting to hook their country to his shooting star. When he fell on his face during the humbling 1967 Six Days' War, he took Arab pride with him (see chapter 4). President Anwar Sadat (1970–81) restored face by trying to regain lost land with a 1973 attack against Israel, a war that initially Egypt looked likely to win (schoolbooks in Egypt teach that it did). Armed by the United States, however, Israel reversed most of Egypt's territorial gains. When Sadat later signed a peace treaty, a ground-breaking move applauded in the West and decried in the Mideast, he brought the country to its nadir: Egypt was kicked out of the Arab League, the political forum it had started.

Lifetime president Hosni Mubarak: dollars from DC buy his loyalty and military, in one form or another.

President Hosni Mubarak, neither as powerful as Nasser nor as controversial as Sadat, has managed twenty-seven years of continuous rule, regaining respect for Egypt, while keeping cold peace with Israel, *and* running the biggest regional army, without unleashing it—except when directed to by the United States. He doesn't perform all the tricks DC demands, but his loyalty to a foreign power is a glaring black mark. Granted, his government (along with charities) keeps people fed, mafia out, and crime rates low, but the misleading show of his popularity in "elections," where he usually takes 97 percent of the vote, reflect only the fact that until recently nobody could challenge him. In 2005, he opened up the race to other candidates, that year taking only 89 percent of the vote. Tellingly, his main rival, human rights activist Ayman Nour, who won 8 percent, was in jail—where most who openly oppose the regime end up, especially during elections.

WHAT MATTERS

Energy matters: Egypt has a smidgen of oil (0.3 percent of world reserves), but along with natural gas (1 percent of world reserves) piped to Israel and Jordan, it's a top export.

Electricity matters: Electricity comes from hydro- and gas-fired plants, which Bechtel and Shell built. Egypt is shopping for nuclear reactors too.

Arms matter: It pays to play nicey-nice with Israel—to the tune of $1.3 billion in free war toys from the United States every year.

Military matters: With nearly half a million under arms, the Arab world's largest military force is ever-present and the key to the Mubarak's government's long-lasting reign: it's also the country's biggest employer.

Religion matters: A center of Sunni thought thanks to Al-Azhar, the world's oldest Islamic university, Egypt was the original hotbed for the Islamist movement, being the birthplace of the extremely powerful Muslim Brotherhood, which shows its muscle mostly in other countries. Coptic Christians are powerful too: many of the richest Egyptians are Copts.

Militants matter: Most name-brand troublemakers are dead or permanently vacationing out of the country.

Marriage matters: In Egypt, men can't get married unless they have an apartment to offer the bride. Since many are broke, many aren't getting married—and increasing numbers, it's feared, are becoming Islamic extremists.

Melissa Rossi

Cairo is a modern, bustling, Westernized metropolis—the cityscape sliced by the Nile and broken up by lush gardens.

You may not notice it in the coiled, horn-blasting traffic of Cairo, where a green light means "go" and a red light means "go faster," or in the spice markets' cinnamon breeze or in thick smoke-clouded cafés where turban-wrapped men play dominoes around bubbling hookahs. You might miss it sailing down the

THE EGYPTIAN PARADOX

The Middle East's most populous country, where fiery regional movements—from Arab nationalism to militant Islam—always seem to brew up, Egypt is a paradox. Pyramids, mummies, and obelisks have awed everybody who's stopped in for thousands of years, but Egypt's highest religious leader, the Grand Mufti, recently declared statues such as the Great Sphinx immoral and un-Islamic, since he considers them to be animal forms and Islam forbids representations of living beings in art. His views are not shared by the government, which bends over backward to stimulate tourism. Officially a republic with an elected president and parliament, Egypt is actually a militarily enforced dictatorship where elections are rigged; lawmakers don't initiate laws, they rubber-stamp those passed down from the president. The modernizing administration, working on novel plans to bring computers to every home (low monthly payments are added to phone bills), doesn't have municipal garbage collection—a job left to ragpickers. And while the government subsidizes food prices, it often overlooks housing: the problems of thousands so poor they live in tombs are "solved" by hooking up electricity to the graveyards. Mandating that religion be noted on identity cards, the bureaucracy won't issue IDs to those who aren't Muslim, Christian, or Jew, and while Egypt's constitution says Shariah is the main basis of law, this secular government tries civilians in military courts (if it gets around to charging them), and hard-core Islam is stomped out. Still important—and a peacemaker—Egypt was once the Arab world's leader; its regional power is diluted by its relationship to DC, which showers it with billions in aid. And this co-option by the West spawns powerful secret societies and a brand of Islamic militants conspiring to put a theocracy in place, although their muscle is most often flexed elsewhere.

Nile in a graceful felucca or descending into subterranean tombs that were pharaohs' launchpads to the netherworld. But Egypt, or *Misr* as it's known around here, is changing, despite efforts of the government to keep Egyptians complacent.

You can see the changes on college campuses, where professors are being arrested for demanding an end to police monitoring of their classes, where topics such as politics, sex, and the Koran are taboo; you can see it at the mall, where young women don the veils that their mothers ripped off. It's evident in the workers' strikes, when everyone from teacher to tax collector demands pay hikes. Protests are illegal in Egypt, but people demonstrate anyway—against Israel, the United States and the "emergency law" imposed after President Sadat's 1981 assassination and still in place, which strips civil rights. Proud Egyptians are sick of their faux republic and false democracy, where the administration is kept in place by the military and where international calls to open up only result in freedoms being further shut down. Which way Egypt is turning, whether it will become more democratic or more Islamic, isn't clear. Case in point: the parliamentary elections of 2005, the year Bush inflicted democratic ideals on Egyptian politics with disastrous results.

After DC cracked the democracy whip—Condi Rice canceled a meeting when Mubarak tossed reform activist Nour behind bars, alleging signature fraud on his party application forms—the 2005 elections were a novelty: it was the

EGYPT AND THE UNITED STATES

It's fitting that the pyramid that made Egypt famous sits on the back of the dollar bill (a design choice credited to FDR's VP Henry A. Wallace, a Freemason), since plenty are flapping this way—sixty billion dollars since 1978, making Egypt the largest recipient of U.S. aid except Israel. Twenty-five billion landed as economic and food aid, but more went to Egypt's military, which is well trained and well armed thanks to that billion-plus a year in arms giveaways. Implied in the billions was DC's right to wind up the Egyptian army and march it over to whatever wars the United States might be embroiled in that week. Lately, the formula isn't working: lured by twenty billion dollars in debt forgiveness, Mubarak sent thirty thousand to fight in 1991 in Desert Storm, but he declined sending fighters to Afghanistan and Iraq after 9/11. In fact, Mubarak opposed the 2003 war against Saddam, correctly prophesizing that it would "create one hundred bin Ladens." Egyptians supported him on that move at least: the country was filled with anti-American protests when the United States attacked Iraq. In response to Mubarak's refusal to back the war in Iraq, Congress threatened to drop the military aid that's kept his militarily enforced government comfortably propped up since 1981. Lately, Congress threatens to cut him off rather frequently, for everything from allegedly allowing arms smuggling to Gaza or for yanking his ambassador back from Israel. Truth be known, however, Mubarak's military and security forces help the United States—they have a rep for "roughing up" the terror suspects the CIA drops off.

The press is heavily censored in Egypt: many knowledgeable Egyptians will insist that their country receives only economic aid from the United States, when in fact Egypt has long been the second-largest recipient of military gifts from the United States—arms that keep the dictatorship in place. Even economic aid, however, is a sore point, since the United States is linked so closely with Israel, and Egyptians are furious about Israel's treatment of Palestinians. Mubarak forged a truce between Israel and Hamas in mid-2008.

first time a variety pack of political parties was allowed to field candidates, including the new Tomorrow Party that promoted government reform and human
rights. The election that September was "irregular": vote-buying was rampant,
as was intimidation. Violence broke out when the army took aim at protesters:
thirteen were killed and thirteen hundred arrested. Mubarak's National Democratic Party kept a majority; the Tomorrow Party won one measly seat of the
National Assembly's 454, but 88 seats were taken by the technically outlawed
Muslim Brotherhood, to which Mubarak has long turned a blind eye. Campaigning as independents with the slogan "Islam is the solution," the Muslim Brotherhood wants to ban booze, keep women and Coptic Christians from top positions,
and transform Egypt into a religious government ruled over by Islamic clerics—for
starters.

*A woman's place: in Egypt women drive—fast—and many don't wear
head scarves; in fact, since the 1950s, the government has encouraged
them not to. However, many young women are covering up, including
wearing gloves in the blazing sun, perhaps as a political statement about
their faith, perhaps bowing to pressure from their menfolk, or perhaps to
avoid being harassed. Women rarely live alone, and the new trend is for
brides to make their future hubbies sign a prenuptial agreement that if he
takes a second wife a good share of the riches—and the house—goes to
her. Women make sacrifices too: many undergo clitoral "circumcision,"—a
time-honored Egyptian custom that's become controversial.*

The success of the Muslim Brotherhood at the polls is just one sign of how
Egypt is changing. The wealthy and intellectual may lean toward the liberal left,
but the middle class and the poor are shifting toward the tradition-hugging Islamic
right: the Muslim Brotherhood is Egypt's most popular organization, one that marries social services with religion and politics. There's a reason so many Egyptians
respect the group: the Muslim Brotherhood often helps out those in need—with
loans, housing, food, clinics, and schools. And few forget what happened in Cairo
on a Thursday evening in October 1992—just after government offices had shut
down for the weekend and when Mubarak was out of town.

SHAKING LOYALTIES

The ground rocked in a violent earthquake measuring 5.9 on the Richter
scale, which collapsed hundreds of flimsy buildings, killing 550, injuring

6,000, and leaving 100,000 homeless. Who blasted into action, sending crews to dig out those trapped under the rubble? Who set up clinic tents and tended the wounded? Who found housing for the homeless and handed out food, water, and blankets within hours? It wasn't the government workers—they didn't get around to tending to the disaster for nearly two days. Heading the physicians' professional society and the union of engineers, the Muslim Brotherhood mobilized and coordinated efforts—winning lifelong supporters in the process. Even during economic shocks, like when the currency was sharply devalued in 2005 and prices soared overnight by nearly half, the Muslim Brotherhood was out in the poor neighborhoods the next day, handing out loaves of bread. This charity work brings it deep loyalty.

But while the Muslim Brotherhood's do-gooder streak runs wide, it's all part of its plan—along with running schools and study groups for youth—to promote its agenda: namely, to bring back Islamic rule and reestablish the caliphate that once ran from India to Portugal, a goal the government doesn't support in the slightest. Ever since that 2005 vote, when the Muslim Brotherhood took 20 percent of the seats in one chamber of Egypt's weak parliament, Mubarak has been running it underground. Shortly after the election, Mubarak's government changed the constitution, barring all parties with religious affiliations, and began rounding up members of the Brotherhood, accusing some of inciting terrorism, holding many with no charge. Over three thousand were rounded up; hundreds are now facing military trials. In short, Mubarak is repeating the actions of presidents Nasser and Sadat before him and trying to stomp out the Muslim Brotherhood, long the biggest threat to the government.

THE BROTHERLY CONUNDRUM

The Muslim Brotherhood, whose members are often physicians, teachers, and lawyers, takes numerous forms. Part secret society, charity, political party, it's an Islamist movement that uses whatever means necessary to win support. The group was formed in 1928, against a backdrop of fierce anticolonial sentiment. The British, who barged into Egypt in the late 1800s to control the Suez Canal, had theoretically granted Egypt independence in 1922, but wouldn't leave and were running the Egyptian government, then a monarchy, from offstage. Cairo was becoming Westernized as Europeans launched businesses, and while the British and French lived regally, they treated their Egyptian workers shabbily. The king was out to lunch, and Islam appeared to be taking a nap. The religion that had once defined Egypt was so out of vogue, there was talk of knocking down mosques in a wave of renovations. A soft-spoken twenty-two-year-old teacher named Hassan al-Banna found the events disturbing: believing Egypt's identity *was* Islam, he started a secret society hoping to revive the religion, complete with an Islamic government, and offering study groups for teens to rekindle interest in the dying religion. His movement enveloped Egyptians who were sick of the lingering British presence and furious about colonial expansion through the region—from Baghdad to Damascus, Jerusalem to Aden. Although al-Banna officially encouraged only peaceful moves, as membership quickly rose to half a million, militant wings sprouted: in the 1930s the Brotherhood bombed movie theaters and European-owned stores, and in 1948 it assassinated Egypt's prime minister.

Among its members were rebellious officers who wanted Egyptians in power: even King Farouk, of Albanian stock, was a foreigner. Linking up with the Free Officers, a secret society of Egypt's military elite, the Brotherhood helped to topple the king in 1952. When it aided in the coup, the Brotherhood thought all parties shared the same vision for establishing a religious government in Egypt. The man who stepped into power after the coup, President Gamal Abdel Nasser (elected in 1956), didn't want Islam to be the determining force in the government. While he wanted to cut British interference in Egyptian affairs, it wasn't because the Brits weren't Muslim but because they were foreign. Nasser's bent was Arab nationalism. When he refused to establish a religion-based government, the Brotherhood felt betrayed. When Nasser leaned toward atheistic Communists—buying arms from the Soviets—the Brotherhood took aim for his head. For that assassination attempt, they were banned in 1954: some were executed, and some four thousand were marched to prisons and concentration camps in the sand.

Outlawed by Nasser in 1954, the Muslim Brotherhood led a shadowy existence in the years that followed. Those members who escaped execution and prison crept underground, forming hundreds of secret chapters and subgroups. They infiltrated Egypt's military, schools, and labor unions—subtly pushing their agenda to rid the country of Western influence and install religious rule. Some left to become teachers in Saudi Arabia; some headed for Jordan, Syria, and Kuwait to spread the word there—aiming to control education and write the curriculum in countries far and wide. Extremely influential, the Brotherhood evolved into the most powerful international force for spreading Islamist thought and is linked to militant groups from Hamas to Islamic Jihad. During the 1970s, when released from prison by Nasser's successor, President Anwar Sadat, members of the Muslim Brotherhood moved into social services, setting up low-cost clinics, unemployment centers, and ambulance services—all of which actively illustrated the Muslim goal of charity and were compelling instruments of PR.

The Aswan High Dam (pictured here) isn't pretty, but Nasser regarded this dam on the Nile River as so important to modernizing Egypt that he seized the Suez Canal from the British to get the funding to build it. Providing irrigation water and hydroelectricity, it now supplies about a sixth of Egypt's power.

However, there were problems: when Sadat, despite promises, did not institute Shariah law and then did the unimaginable by making peace with Israel in 1979, his days were numbered. Two years later, he was gunned down by Egyptian al-Jihad, one of the Brotherhood's younger offshoots. Again, Islamists were rounded up by the thousands—this time by President Hosni Mubarak. And among those thrown into prison and tortured (ripping out fingernails was an Egyptian specialty) was Ayman al-Zawahiri, leader of Egyptian al-Jihad, who'd been following in the footsteps of the Muslim Brotherhood since he was a teen, being particularly influenced by a member named Sayyid Qutb.

BROTHER QUTB: ADDING A MILITANT ELEMENT

With sad almond-shaped eyes, thin Brillo hair, and a bristly mustache to match, Sayyid Qutb never had a wife or a girlfriend, being too chaste and pure minded to be tempted by carnal pleasures. A writer and literary critic, the Egyptian wasn't a cleric, holding instead a government post in Cairo's education department. Had he not been sent to the United States in the 1950s to study the American school system, today's world might be a little safer. On his first trip abroad, Qutb focused less on classes and more on decadent American society and its temptations and aberrations: the bobby-soxers with tight sweaters and skirts that exposed their ankles, the sock hops where teens held hands when they danced, the pom-pom-waving cheerleaders jumping and doing splits, the stands filled with fans cheering at thuggish sports, the garish neon-lit bars, the smoky back rooms where jazz bands played. All disgusted him, and by the time he set foot on the steamer ship back to Cairo he was a changed, and even more pious and repressed, man.

A member of the Muslim Brotherhood, he was accused of conspiring in an assassination attempt on Nasser and was imprisoned in 1954. The torture inflicted on him made him like Egypt's secular government even less. Muslims had fallen into a state of ignorance, having lost the true traditional practice of Islam, he would later write, and the only way to address the state of affairs was conversion of the straying masses and jihad against those rulers more concerned with money and power than with the Koran. Writing his theories on how to elevate Egypt and the Arab world, Qutb's second book, *Milestones*, published shortly after his release from prison in 1964, struck a chord in Cairo, with old and young alike, including a thoughtful fourteen-year-old named Ayman al-Zawahiri, who was the son of a prominent Cairo physician. The book, which called for overthrowing the government, also got Qutb killed: Nasser's government hanged the subversive—an act that only made Qutb holier, a martyr in the eyes of his fans. Al-Zawahiri, who had never met Qutb, vowed to carry on the mission that Qutb hadn't completed: to rid the Muslim world of the West and to oust those leaders who were, by Qutb's standards, apostates. Al-Zawahiri later cofounded al Qaeda.

"The American girl is well-acquainted with her body's seductive capacity," Qutb wrote in his article *"The America I Saw"* for an Egyptian publication. *"She knows it lies in the face, and in expressive eyes, and in thirsty lips. She knows seductiveness lies in the round breasts, the full buttocks, and in the shapely thighs, sleek legs—and she knows this and does not hide it."*[1] Given that his writings were extremely influential for al Qaeda and the most radical Muslim militants, it's odd to note that at least one reason behind the fall of the Twin Towers on September 11, one factor in why the United States was condemned, is apparently that Qutb, who died a bachelor, thought American females were sexy. Apparently, he didn't score with them during his visit.

Prison only instilled more fervor in Ayman al-Zawahiri. When released in 1984, he headed for the jihad in Afghanistan, returning to Egypt in the early nineties to help organize and unleash an Islamic uprising. Beginning in 1992, Zawahiri and other Muslim militants, including fighters returned from Afghanistan, attacked Christian Copts, opened fire on tourists, battled police, tried to assassinate Mubarak, blew up the Egyptian embassy in Pakistan, and made the first attempt to topple the World Trade Center, in 1993. By the end of their rampage, in 1997, over twelve hundred had died, and by then al-Zawahiri was in Sudan, where he was plotting with a wealthy Saudi who'd been run out of Saudi Arabia after continually slamming the monarchy for allowing Westerners to come in and fight Desert Storm. Abandoning al-Jihad, Zawahiri hooked arms with Osama bin Laden to set up the World Islamic Front, which issued a statement in February 1998 calling all good Muslims to fight pagans and Westerners, a fatwa of sorts called "Jihad Against Jews and Crusaders." That message marked the beginning of al Qaeda.

A FEW OTHER EGYPTIAN MILITANTS

Many of the best-known Islamic guerrillas cut their teeth in Cairo, where they embraced the Muslim Brotherhood—considered the ideological mother of most Muslim extremist movements—particularly the teachings of Sayyid Qutb. A few standouts:

Takfir wal-Hijra: Started in 1971 by Egyptian Brotherhood member Shukri Mustafa (a colleague of Qutb), this fundamentalist Muslim movement wants to return Islam to the way it was when Mohammed was alive. It denounces most modern Muslims as fakes: followers adopt Western garb and behavior (such as drinking) to make themselves inconspicuous as they conspire to overthrow those preventing a return to "pure" Islam.

Mohammed Atta (1968–2001): Influenced by Qutb and part of Takfir wal-Hijra, Cairo-born engineer Atta led the 9/11 attacks.

Omar Abdel-Rahman (the Blind Sheik): A devotee of Qutb, the cleric issued a fatwa calling for the death of Sadat after he signed the peace treaty with Israel and subsequently served time in an Egyptian prison, where he was allegedly tortured. Upon release, he founded Gamaat Islamiyya, best known for its 1997 attack at Luxor, which killed fifty-seven tourists. By then, however, Abdel-Rahman was in New York: he'd entered in 1990 and was preaching at local mosques, issuing fatwas against the United States and Jews. After the 1993 bombings of the World Trade Center, he promoted a plan to simultaneously blow up the UN, FBI headquarters, and tunnels and bridges into New York. Convicted of sedition in 1995, he's serving a life sentence in the U.S. penal system.

Abu Hamza Al-Masri: Born in Alexandria, a devotee of Qutb and fighter in Afghanistan, he was a fiery imam at the Finsbury Park mosque in London and organized attacks in Yemen. Tied to a bombing attempt in Oregon, he was extradited to the United States.

Not all Egyptians rally behind the Brotherhood. By some estimates, fewer than 10 percent of Egyptians endorse the Muslim Brotherhood, which in itself is not militant, although it inspires those who are. But many Egyptians do feel frustrated that a once mighty civilization has lost its way. Support for the group blossomed after Egypt's defeat in the 1967 war against Israel, which to some bore out the idea that Muslims were being punished for having strayed from the Islamic path as envisioned by thinkers such as Qutb. In general, many Egyptians are sick of foreign influences, whether directly imposed or evident in manipulations such as those of the United States, which they see as a threat to Egypt's nascent independence. Until Nasser's Free Officers booted the king in 1952, the country had been run by foreigners for millennia. And the reason it had been dominated by foreigners for so long goes back to the ancients' fondness for cats, which were once worshipped as deities—or so the legend goes.

HISTORY IN A BOX

Ten thousand years ago, tribes first settled along the Nile River banks, where annual floods fertilized soil with nutrient-rich silt, but the most dramatic marks on the landscape were those made by the pharaohs who lived around 2500 BC. Their monuments, such as the pyramids, attest to remarkable engineering skills. Papyrus scrolls covered in hieroglyphics reveal a finely honed understanding of the stars—the flood cycle of the Nile formed the basis of early calendars. Early Egyptians practiced medicine and dentistry: their understanding of anatomy and embalming is evidenced in the herb-and-frankincense-sealed royal mummies that have survived to this day.

Sun-worshipping pagans, they revered animals from dogs to crocodiles, but none more than felines, whose likeness was captured in the form of the sphinx: cats were so adored that the death of the family cat was deeply mourned for months—the grieving shaved their eyebrows and mummified the kitty corpse. When the Persians invaded in 525 BC, they threatened to kill off the creatures if the Egyptians did not surrender. Faced with the local extinction of the animals regarded as gods, the kingdom was handed over to the invaders, or so legend has it. However they took it, the Persians stitched the country into their empire, allowing Egyptians to rule only in name. The last local ruler, Pharaoh Nectanebo, lost Egypt again in 332 BC, when Greeks snagged it, erecting marvels of their own. Among them was the Great Library at Alexandria, which held wisdom accumulated from all corners of the known world; its destruction is widely blamed on the Romans, who took over in AD 30. Romans ruled until the march of Islam spread to these corners six centuries later, and a procession of Sunni, Shia, even Kurds and royal guards, reigned over the land until 1517, when it was lost to the Turks, becoming part of the Ottoman Empire.

Napoléon showed up in 1798, wanting to snag this strategic piece of property that lies along the British trade route back from India: he was obsessed with the notion that the flags of his empire would wave from the pyramids and believed his rule would be welcomed. Wanting to understand the local secrets, Napoléon arrived, not only with thirty-eight thousand soldiers, but also with hundreds of scientists, linguists, painters, and poets, whose mission was to study and capture the little-known and mysterious land: their works are immortalized in what is still the most thorough examination of Egypt of that era, the twenty-two-volume *Description de L'Egypte*. His fighters easily took down the ruling Mamluks, but Egyptians didn't want him around, and neither did the British: they sank his fleet anchored off of Alexandria. Napoléon persisted in his idea of ruling Egypt and the Middle East for three years, but in 1801 the British finally blasted him out, and the frustrated Frenchmen loaded up ships with antiquities, including obelisks and the Rosetta Stone, and shoved off. The Ottomans returned to reclaim the land, but one of their officers, an Albanian named Mohammed Ali—considered the father of modern Egypt—had ideas of his own. As ruler, he weakened ties with the Ottoman Empire, developed the country, planting the cotton that would make Egypt rich and annexing Sudan to the South. His son Ismail took the ruler's seat when the cotton was even more valuable, after the American Civil War had devastated world supplies. Setting up hospitals and thousands of schools, Ismail was advised by Europeans and built numerous lavish palaces in the European style.

A Frenchman, Ferdinand-Marie de Lesseps, talked Ismail into building the Suez Canal, and Europeans loaned money at ridiculous rates. Ismail blew through the dough, building more palaces and gardens in the French style, and held a lavish ceremony in 1869, bringing in VIPs from across the world to witness the opening of the canal that many had deemed an impossible task. The project, which killed hundreds of thousands of Egyptian construction workers, had gone vastly over budget, and when cotton prices tumbled, Egypt went bankrupt. Unpaid soldiers mutinied, and the Brits sailed into the picture in 1882, to put out the fire. Taking control of Egypt and Sudan, the British took the revenue accrued from the Suez Canal, closed schools and hospitals, and supposedly funneled the money into paying off Egypt's debt. Over the decades, Egyptians rebelled against them in huge uprisings, and in 1922 the British allowed them independence, at least in name. Finally, in 1952, the military ejected the British-backed King Farouk and Egyptians again ruled their own country, for the first time in centuries— and also set Sudan free. But new president Nasser refused to install the religious government he'd promised to the Muslim Brotherhood that helped bring him to power.

Courtesy of Saudi Aramco

The Great Pyramid of Giza, built in the third millennium BC, illustrates engineering know-how: each block weighed over 1.5 tons.

Egypt may be independent, but it isn't free of foreign influence. It is now divided between those who want a secular modern country and those who want a country that is more Islamic. As the headquarters of Al-Azhar University and Mosque, Egypt finds itself even more torn. The university issues fatwas at a mind-boggling rate and is stirring up what has become a religious revival. And most of the religious-minded have a big problem with the piece of paper Anwar Sadat signed in 1979. The Camp David Agreement, the first peace treaty between an Arab country and Israel, recognized the Jewish nation's right to exist in exchange for the return of the Sinai Peninsula, which Israel had seized in 1967. Brokered by the United States, the agreement brought both countries a vast supply of U.S. arms. But it was also a source of outrage from other Arab leaders: by negotiating peace Sadat had signed off the use of his army for further wars against Israel. It prompted fiery riots and a slew of criticism from the Muslim Brotherhood, which Sadat, who'd earlier released them from prison, began once again rounding up and shutting down. In 1981, Sadat was gunned down by Egyptian al-Jihad, one of the Brotherhood's militant offshoots. When Mubarak stepped up, he continued the steamrolling of the Brotherhood. By the 1990s, however, he allowed them to slowly creep back into society. Their relatively moderate behavior—of the sort endorsed by founder Hassan al-Banna—was seen as an antidote to the militancy of newer groups, such as those of those of Ayman al-Zawahiri. Given the show of their popularity in the 2005 elections, Mubarak is once again pushing them down, rounding them up, whisking them off to prison, and trying to relegate them to the shadows. This time, however, they have stronger backing: if Mubarak pushes too hard, he may risk an explosion.

With upward of ten million stopping by to take in these majestic sights each year, tourism kicks in over 12 percent of Egypt's GDP, being one of the country's top five money makers. The others are money sent home from workers abroad, revenue from the Suez Canal, gas and oil sales, and economic aid.

Hotshots

Hosni Mubarak: Egyptian president since 1981, Sadat's former vice president took the power seat during chaos and has dodged bullets, cracked down on militants with a heavy hand, and tried to openly support the United States despite a public that is more and more anti-American. But he's had to contend with an increasingly conservative populace: Islamic courts now operate alongside civil ones; many of his people want to send the Egyptian-Israeli peace agreement to the recycling bin; and were it not for his beloved army, Mubarak might not be in power.

Gamal Abdel Nasser: Egyptian president from 1956 to 1970, Nasser brought Egypt to the tip of the Arab power pyramid: he told the West to shove off when he nationalized Egypt's Suez Canal (causing an attack from Israel, Britain, and France in the process) and got chummy with the Soviets; he tried to unite the Arab world, and in 1958 created the United Arab Republic with Syria (four hundred miles away), which lasted three years; he initiated the 1967 war against Israel and was sorely defeated—and promptly resigned. He stepped back into power a few hours later.

Anwar Sadat: Egyptian president from 1970 to 1981, Nasser's vice president took the reins upon his death and became a study in reversals: he started off buddy-buddy with Communist Russia then cut those ties; he alternately released, then jailed, members of the Muslim Brotherhood and other Islamists; he tried to restore Egyptian pride by ordering a 1973 attack on Israel; then he made peace with the former foe, for which he paid dearly. After he signed the Camp David Agreement in 1979, Egypt was shunned by the Arab world (which cut off all financial aid), and Sadat was killed by a still-simmering dissident two years later.

Gamal Mubarak: The president's business-savvy son is believed to be a likely successor. In his forties, and now heading the National Democratic Party, he is more worldly and flexible than his pa, and even some of his father's opponents may give him the thumbs-up; his foes call him corrupt.

The Muslim Brotherhood (aka Al-Ikhwan): The group's original members are gone or have gone batty, but its influence carries on—molding the thoughts of twenty-first-century Islamists across the Muslim world. Still simmering over a broken political promise to make Egypt an Islamic, not secular, state, the group has quietly worked against the government it helped install five decades ago. This is the godfather of nearly all Islamist movements in the Middle East, with a reach that extends from Malaysia to New Jersey.

Al-Jihad: A younger, more violence-prone group that likes to work stealthily: like a social virus, it infiltrates the organizations it hopes to bring down. Allegedly behind the assassination of Anwar Sadat, it has also assassinated diplomats and blown up the Egyptian embassy in Pakistan. Once headed by al Qaeda power boy Ayman al-Zawahiri.

Gamaat Islamiyya: Mostly country boys, these guys were behind the 1997 Luxor attacks that killed fifty-nine tourists. Their leader is now advocating peace, from his prison cell, and has penned a book, *The Initiative of Stopping Violence.* Hasn't hit the bestseller list.

Coptic Christians: Headed by patriarch Pope Shenouda III, this group descended from the earliest Christians is sometimes targeted by Islamists who try to convert members, and militants who take aim at the Copts' gold store. Although less than 10 percent of Egyptians, they hold sway in society—many of them being quite wealthy from the gold trade they monopolize. Oddly, many are also among Egypt's poorest: the ragpickers who collect the trash are often Copts. They haul it back to their homes and comb through it, serving as recyclers as well. The Copts are not well-represented in government, although Mubarak recently appointed several to parliament.

Melissa Rossi

The Nile, here shown in Aswan, was the cradle of Egypt's early civilization and even determined its calendar. Black obelisks once ran alongside it: they were real estate markers, since the flooding Nile washed most other land markers away. The river is now a mainstay of Egyptian tourism, with hundreds of ships cruising along from the ruins at Aswan and Luxor.

Hot Spots

Al-Azhar University and Mosque: Islam's most esteemed place to study and headquarters of Egypt's most powerful religious circles; now under close government scrutiny, the university alumni include the blind sheik Omar Abdel-Rahman. Recent fatwas issued by Grand Mufti Ali Gomaa allow surgery to reconstruct the hymen but prohibit full nudity during sex.

THE BORDER WITH THE GAZA STRIP

Home to Palestinians, who have been walled in by Israel, the Gaza Strip poses difficult problems for Egypt. For many Egyptians, the fact that their leader had teamed up with Israel in "jailing" Palestinians within the Gaza Strip symbolizes the hypocrite that Egypt has become. Until the 1979 peace treaty, Egypt had fought Israel in four wars over its territorial advances, essentially protecting the Palestinians; the plight of the Palestinians was forgotten once Egypt, through the treaty, got the Sinai territory back. In 2005, after Hamas—a group founded by the Muslim Brotherhood—took over the Gaza Strip, Israel sealed Palestinians into the Gaza Strip with high walls, including walls on the southern border with Egypt. Tunnels have been the source of arms smuggling from Egypt to Gaza but on a small scale along the heavily patrolled border. In early 2008, Hamas knocked down the southern walls, and hundreds of thousands spilled into Egypt. Mubarak allowed them to go shopping for a few days—they spent some thirty million dollars stuffing suitcases with food and medicine, loading bags of flour on donkey carts, and carrying back mattresses on their backs—but eleven days later the wall was rebuilt and the Gazans were sent back to live in their pen. Egyptians have protested against Israel's actions against the Palestinians for years, but the incident triggered yet more calls to torch the Egyptian-Israeli peace treaty. Instead, Mubarak got both parties to call a truce.

Alexandria: The port city along the Mediterranean, which inspired Lawrence Durrell's famous Alexandria Quartet, was hugely important for millennia, serving as capital for the Greeks who ruled here, the Ptolemies, Cleopatra among them. The Great Library of Alexandria, where parchment scrolls held much of the world's collected knowledge, was also an early think tank, where Eratosthenes, head librarian in the third century BC, calculated the circumference of the earth within fifty miles. Containing eight hundred thousand scrolls, the library was torched around 48 BC, but a new twenty-first-century model is now aiming to become the world's largest repository of knowledge. Among the groovy projects: putting a million books online.

A popular resort town on the Red Sea, Sharm El Sheikh is a favorite meeting spot for Middle East summits. Pictured here, the festive beach at the Ritz-Carlton.

Erected in 270 BC on an island just off Alexandria, the Pharos Lighthouse was the first maritime beacon, guiding sailors to this popular port, which into the fourteenth century was a distribution point for Europe-bound spices. Actually a grandiose torch, its flame made brighter with mirrors that also made it shine during the day, the lighthouse was one of the Seven Wonders of the ancient world, another being Egypt's pyramids, which served as tombs for the kings awaiting their boat trip to the next life.

Notes

--- --- --- --- --- --- --- --- --- --- --- --- --- --- --- --- --- ---

Chapter 1. Misunderstanding the Middle East
1. World Health Organization estimate of civilian deaths as of July 2006; the World Health Organization study, which relied on interviews with Iraqi families, showed with a 95 percent degree of statistical certainty that between 104,000 and 223,000 Iraqi civilians had died since the United States invaded in 2003. The estimate of 151,000 deaths is based on that range.
2. It's unclear if Saddam had directly invited Zarqawi, although the Jordanian guerrilla was planning operations from Iraq's north by early 2003.
3. When Alan Greenspan wrote in his 2007 book, *The Age of Turbulence,* that the Iraq invasion was motivated by oil—a sentiment echoed by Henry Kissinger—the Bush administration dismissed the idea.
4. Harald Frederiksen, "Return Palestinian Water If Not Land: A Proposal," *Middle East Policy*, Spring 2005. Frederiksen is a water consultant who works with the World Bank.
5. How much water was diverted isn't clear because Israel refused observers access to the sites. Mostafa Dolatyer, "Water Diplomacy in the Middle East," in *The Middle East Environment*, ed. Eric Watins (Cambridge: St Malo Press, 1995).
6. Seymour Hersh, "The Redirection," *New Yorker*, March 5, 2007.
7. "Egypt's Budding Nuclear Program," *The Risk Report* (Wisconsin Project on Nuclear Arms Control), Sept.–Oct. 1996. "Saudis Consider Nuclear Bomb," *Guardian*, September 18, 2003. "Saudi Arabia Working on Secret Nuclear Program with Pakistan Help," *Forbes/AFX*, March 28, 2006: http://www.forbes.com/home/feeds/afx/2006/03/28/afx2629000.html.
8. "Egypt's Budding Nuclear Program," The Risk Report (Wisconsin Project on Nuclear Arms control), Sept.–Oct. 1996.
9. "U.S. Foreign Aid to Israel," Congressional Research Service, January 2, 2008.
10. "U.S. Arms Sales: Agreements and Deliveries to Major Clients 1997–2004," Congressional Research Service, December 29, 2005.

Chapter 2. Jogging Through the Millennia
1. Astronomers in the third millennium BC decided that the year had 360 days, like the degrees they'd assigned to the circle. Samuel Noah Kramer, *History Begins at Sumer* (New York: Doubleday, 1959).
2. Leonard Cottrell, *Lost Cities* (London: Pan Books Ltd., 1961), p. 32.
3. Juliet Highet, *Frankincense: Oman's Gift to the World* (New York: Prestel Publishing, 2006).

4. Genesis 17:7.
5. There's debate over exactly when Zoroaster lived, but one dominant school of thought has it that he helped Cyrus II build the empire, which began in 550 BC.
6. As noted by Sandra Mackey in *The Iranians* (New York: Plume, 1998).
7. According to some accounts, Zoroaster would have already been dead by this time.
8. Justin Pollard and Howard Reid, *The Rise and Fall of Alexandria: Birthplace of the Modern Mind* (New York: Viking, 2006).

Chapter 3. Pulling the Pieces Together

1. Karen Armstrong, *Islam* (London: Phoenix Press, 2001).
2. Among those who theorize that Mohammed was having seizures is Alford T. Welch, a professor of religious studies at Michigan State University.
3. Armstrong, *Islam*.
4. Hugh Kennedy, *The Great Arab Conquests* (Cambridge, MA: Da Capo, 2007).
5. Wikipedia, "Uthman."
6. S. Brock, "North Mesopotamia in the Late Seventh Century: Book XV of *Rise Melle* by John Bar Penkaye," as noted in Kennedy, *Arab Conquests*.
7. Hugh Kennedy, *When Baghdad Ruled the Muslim World* (Cambridge, MA: Da Capo, 2006).
8. Kennedy, *When Baghdad Ruled the World*.
9. Thomas Asbridge, *The First Crusade: A New History* (London: Free Press / Simon & Schuster, 2005).
10. Elias Antar, "Story of a Hero," *Saudi Aramco World*, May/June 1970.

Chapter 4. European Designs: Hacking Up the Middle East

1. Chaim Weizmann was actually born in Motol, Poland, when it was part of Russia, and he is widely referred to as Russian.
2. Alain Gresh and Dominique Vidal, *The New A–Z of the Middle East* (London: I. B. Tauris, 2004), 346
3. The Alhambra in Granada being one such example.
4. Max Rodenbeck, *Cairo* (New York: Vintage, 1999).
5. Ibid.
6. Sandra Mackey, *The Iranians* (New York: Plume, 1998).
7. Robert Ruby, "A Six-Day War: Its Aftermath in American Public Opinion," *Pew Forum on Religion and Public Life*, May 30, 2007: http://pewresearch.org/pubs/491/six-day-war.
8. McMahon later tried to modify the agreement, saying that the Hashemites couldn't have the land west of Syria—which would be Lebanon—but it turned out that McMahon meant Palestine.
9. Many figures for deaths during World War I include only Europeans, of which there were about twenty million, almost equally divided between military and civilians.
10. Daniel Yergin, *The Prize* (New York: Free Press, 1992).
11. Two exceptions: the Maronite Christians welcomed the French when they arrived in Syria; the rest of the inhabitants rioted. And initially the Zionists in Palestine were happy to see the British, whom they believed were about to grant them a homeland.
12. Shibley Telhami et al., "Does Saudi Arabia Still Matter?" *Foreign Affairs*, Nov./Dec. 2002.
13. Ibid.
14. Said Aburish, *Nasser: The Last Arab* (New York: St. Martin's Press, 2004).

15. Polish Record of Meeting of Soviet Bloc Leaders (and Tito) in Budapest, July 11, 1967, "Virtual Archive, Cold War International History Project, Woodrow Wilson Center: www.wilsoncenter.org.
16. Washington Special Actions Group Meeting, October 17, 1973, White House Situation Room, National Archives: http://www.gwu.edu/~nsarchiv/NSAEBB/NSAEBB98/octwar-36a.pdf.
17. *CIA World Factbook*, 2007.
18. Ibid.
19. Ibid.
20. Economist Intelligence Unit, Assorted Country Profiles, 2007: http://www.eiu.com.
21. *CIA World Factbook*, 2007.
22. Ibid. July 2007 estimate; figure includes 5.6 million nonnationals.
23. Ibid. July 2007 estimate; figure includes 1.3 million nonnationals.
24. Ibid.
25. Ibid. July 2007 estimate; figure includes 578,000 nonnationals.
26. As noted in "U.S. Foreign Assistance to the Middle East: Historical Background, Recent Trends and the FY2006 Request," in *U.S. Agency for International Developments, Overseas Loans and Grants, Obligations and Loan Authorizations, July 1, 1945–September 30, 2001*, Congressional Research Service, June 13, 2005.
27. Ibid.
28. Ibid.

Chapter 5. Iraq: Pardon Our Mess

1. If pumped at 2.2 million barrels a day.
2. Although this Islamization of society is happening throughout Iraq, Basra is particularly dangerous for women; at least 133 were killed in 2007 for "un-Islamic behavior," and the numbers are rising since the British pulled out. See Arwa Damon, "Violations of Islamic Teachings Take Deadly Toll on Iraqi Women," CNN, February 8, 2008: http://edition.cnn.com/2008/WORLD/meast/02/08/iraq.women "Tossed from a Car and Shot in Cold Blood," *Sunday Times* (London), December 12, 2007: http://www.timesonline.co.uk/tol/news/world/iraq/article3056693.ece; Solomon Moore, "Ominous Signs Remain in City Run by Iraqis," *New York Times*, February 23, 2008.
3. See Letter from Project for the New American Center to President Bill Clinton, January 26, 1998: www.newamericancentury.org.
4. Frankly, it appears they have always been wrong in their assumptions, but we will give them the benefit of the doubt that maybe they have been correct about something. See my book *What Every American Should Know about Who Is Running the World* for more information, including about "Plan B."
5. "Iraqis Say They Were Better Off Under Hussein," *Angus Reid Global Monitor*, January 3, 2007; Based on polling by the Iraq Centre for Research and Strategic Studies / Gulf Research Center.
6. Should you have any doubt that a propaganda campaign was waged in the United States to sell the 2003 attack on Iraq, here are a few eye-opening reads: Douglas McCollam, "Ahmed Chalabi's List of Suckers," *Columbia Journalism Review*, July 12, 2004: http://www.alternet.org/mediaculture/19210/?page=entire; Craig Unger, "The War They Wanted, the Lies They Needed," *Vanity Fair*, July 2006; Deputy Inspector General for Intelligence, U.S. Department of Defense, "Review of the Pre-Iraqi War Activities of the Office of the Undersecretary of Defense for Policy," Report No. 07-INTEL-04, U.S. Inspector General, Feb. 2007: http://www.gwu.edu/~nsarchiv/NSAEBB/NSAEBB219/iraq_media_03.pdf; Joyce Battle "Iraq: The

Media War," National Security Archives, George Washington University: http://
www.gwu.edu/~nsarchiv/NSAEBB/NSAEBB219/index.htm

7. "Shiites Chose Nominee," *USA Today*, April 21, 2006. "Working for a United Iraq,"
Gulf News, December 30, 2006: http://archive.gulfnews.com/articles/06/12/29/
10092923.html.

8. Current legislator Jamal Jaafar Muhammad, until recently a fellow member of
Dawa, the party that Maliki now heads, was convicted of the U.S. embassy bomb-
ing in Kuwait. See Qassim Abdul-Zahra, "U.S. Probes Embassy's Bombing in
Kuwait," *Washington Post*, February 6, 2007.

9. As he agreed to do in the Friendship Treaty signed with the United States in
November 2007.

10. Guy Raz, "Nouri al Maliki's Rise to Leadership," NPR, July 27, 2006.

11. Richard A. Oppel Jr. "U.S. to Halt Payment to Iraqi Group Headed by a One-time
Pentagon Favorite," *New York Times*, May 18, 2004.

12. "Iraq: Energy Data, Statistics, Analysis—Country Analysis Brief," Energy Information Administration, U.S. Dept. of Energy, Aug. 2007.

13. Source: Energy Information Administration.

14. So estimates Nobel Prize–winning economist Joseph Stiglitz. See Diane Francis,
"It's the Bush Iraq Recession, Stupid," *Financial Post*, March 24, 2008: http://
network.nationalpost.com/np/blogs/francis/archive/2008/03/24/wall-street-and
-the-dalai-lama.aspx.

15. Charles Lewis and Mark Reading-Smith, "Study: Bushies Lied 935 Times to Sell
Iraq Invasion," Center for Public Integrity, January 24, 2008: http://www.alternet.
org/waroniraq/74715.

16. Poll conducted by Oxford Research International, released March 2007.

17. "Those Missing Guns in Iraq," editorial, *New York Times,* August 7, 2007.

18. The guerrilla attacks on barbers are only one illustration of the street-level theocracy. See: Sudarsan Raghaven, "Iraq's Barbers Under Threat," *Washington Post*,
October 6, 2006; Robert F. Worth, "A Haircut in Iraq Can Be the Death of the Bar-
ber," *New York Times*, March 18, 2005.

19. UNHCR figures for January 2008.

20. Iraq body-count figures for 2007 estimate that between 25,700 and 27,500 civilians were killed, although these figures are considered conservative.

21. UN figures for civilian deaths in 2006 were 35,000, as noted in "Country Report:
Iraq," Economist Intelligence Unit, 2007: http://www.eiu.com.

22. Peter W. Singer, "Warriors for hire in Iraq," *Salon*, April 15, 2004.

23. Jim Krane, "Audit: US-led Occupation Squandered Aid," AP, January 29, 2006.

24. James Glanz, "Rebuilding of Iraqi Pipeline is Disaster Waiting to Happen," *New York
Times*, April 25, 2006. "Al Fatah Pipe River Crossing," *SIGRI Report*, March 7, 2006.

25. Robert Dreyfuss, "Tinker, Binker, Neocon, Spy," *American Prospect*, Nov. 2002:
http://www.prospect.org/cs/articles?articleId=6614.

26. Ibid.

27. James Paul and Celine Nahory, "War and Occupation in Iraq," *Global Policy Forum*, June 2007; This 117-page reports compiles information from government
audits, government agencies, and government watchdog groups.

28. John Chapman, "The Real Reasons Bush Went to War," *Guardian*, July 28, 2004.

29. Callum MacRae and Ali Fadhil, "Iraq Was Awash in Cash," *Guardian*, March 20,
2006.

30. "U.S. Lost Track of $9 Billion in Iraq Funds," CNN, January 31, 2005: http://edition
.cnn.com/2005/WORLD/meast/01/30/iraq.audit/.

31. SIGIR audit, April 2005; See Farah Stockman, "U.S. Firms Suspected of Bilking Iraq Funds," *Boston Globe*, April 16, 2006.

32. James Glanz, "Congress Tells Auditor in Iraq to Close Office," *New York Times*, November 3, 2006.

33. According to author Rajiv Chandrasekaran. See "The Lost Year in Iraq," *Frontline*, October 17, 2006: http://www.pbs.org/wgbh/pages/frontline/yeariniraq/.

Chapter 6. Iran: Isn't the Party Over *Yet*?

1. "Persian Gulf Analysis Brief," U.S. Energy Information Administration, 2007: http://www.eia.doe.gov/cabs/Iran/Full.html.

2. For an easy-to-understand, comprehensive account of the deteriorating relations, see *Frontline*'s "Showdown with Iran," which aired October 23, 2007: http://www.pbs.org/wgbh/pages/frontline/showdown/.

3. Neil MacFarquhar, "With Iran Population Boom, Vasectomy Receives Blessing," *New York Times*, September 8, 1996.

4. Canada holds the second-biggest reserves if one includes unconventional sources of oil, such as tar sands.

5. See "Iran: Country Briefing," U.S. Dept. of Energy, EIA, 2007: http://www.eia.doe.gov/cabs/Iran/Full.html.

6. Figures from the IMF and Energy Information Administration of U.S. Department of Energy; Iran subsidizes more than any other country. See: "Carrots and Sticks: Taxing and Subsidies," EIA, January 17, 2006: http://www.iea.org/textbase/papers/2006/oil_subsidies.pdf; and "Iran: Country Briefing," U.S. Dept of Energy, EIA, 2007: http://www.eia.doe.gov/cabs/Iran/Full.html.

7. See Greg Bruno, "Iran's Revolutionary Guards," *Backgrounder*, CFR: http://www.cfr.org/publication/14324/.

8. See "Sadjapour: Revolutionary Guards have Financial Interest in Keeping Iran Isolated," Gwertzman interviews the experts, Council on Foreign Relations, May 29, 2007: http://www.cfr.org/publication/13466/sadjadpour.html.

9. Mehdi Khalaji, "Iran's Revolutionary Guards Corps, Inc." *Policy Watch* 1273 (Washington Institute for Near East Policy), August 17, 2007: http://www.washingtoninstitute.org/templateC05.php?CID=2649.

10. As noted by photographer Fabien Dany, a frequent visitor to Iran.

11. Source: *Christian Science Monitor*

12. Scott Peterson, "Waiting for the Rapture," *Christian Science Monitor*, December 21, 2005.

13. "Showdown with Iran," *Frontline*, October 23, 2007, www.pbs.org/wgbh/pages/frontline/showdown/view/main/html.

14. David Sanger, "Bush Aides Say Tough Tone Puts Foes on Notice," *New York Times*, January 31, 2002.

15. "Showdown with Iran," *Frontline*.

16. Document can be found at: http://www.nytimes.com/packages/pdf/opinion/20070429_iran-memo-expurgated.pdf.

17. Kenneth Katzman, "Iran: U.S. Concerns and Policy Responses," August 6, 2007.

18. Ed Blanche, "Iran takes on the US, but at what cost," *Middle East*, March 2006.

19. Author interview with Ambassador Andrew Killgore, October 2007.

20. For a detailed account of the events and others leading up to them, see Charles Kurzman, "The Qum Protests and the Coming of the Iranian Revolution, 1975 and 1978," *Social Science History*, Fall 2003.

21.   D. Park Teter, "Iran Between East and West," *Congressional Quarterly Researcher*, January 26, 1979.
22.   Robert Parry, "Bush Sr.'s Iran-Iraq Secrets," consortiumnews.com, May 24, 2004.
23.   "Interview with Reza Pahlavi," *Breakfast with Frost*, BBC, January 2002: http://news.bbc.co.uk/1/hi/programmes/breakfast_with_frost/1771714.stm.
24.   Thomas Land, "Putin Visit Exposes Deep Divisions in Tehran," *Middle East*, December 2007.

Chapter 7. The Kingdom of Saudi Arabia: Splitsville
1.   Lawrence Wright, "Kingdom of Silence," *New Yorker*, January 15, 2004.
2.   In 1999, for instance, a Saudi prince was busted for hauling in two tons of cocaine when his 747 made a pit stop in France. See Brian Ross and Jill Rackmill, "Secrets of the Saudi Royal Family," *ABC News*, October 15, 2004.
3.   See http://www.mofa.gov.sa/Detail.asp?InSectionID=3982&InNewsItemID=71006.
4.   "Saudi Executes Egyptian for Practicing 'Witchcraft'," Reuters, November 2, 2007: http://africa.reuters.com/wire/news/usnL02434180.html.
5.   There were reportedly over one hundred public decapitations in 2007.
6.   See "Saudi Time Bomb?" *Frontline* with *New York Times*, November 2001: http://www.pbs.org/wgbh/pages/frontline/shows/saudi/, and http://www.pbs.org/wgbh/pages/frontline/shows/saudi/analyses/wahhabism.html.
7.   See Gerald Posner, *Secrets of the Kingdom* (New York: Random House, 2005), pp. 3–7, from which much of this account is drawn.
8.   Ibid.
9.   Ibid.
10.   Simon Henderson, "Al-Qaeda Attack on Abqaiq," Washington Institute, February 28, 2006: http://www.washingtoninstitute.org/templateC05.php?CID=2446.
11.   Ibid.
12.   "The Great Divide," *Pew Global Research*, June 22, 2006: http://pewglobal.org/reports/display.php?ReportID=253.
13.   Nick Fielding, "Saudis Paid bin Laden 200 Million," *Sunday Times*, August 25, 2002.
14.   Ian Black, "Huge Saudi Force to Defend Oil Field from al Qaida," *Guardian*, August 28, 2007: http://www.guardian.co.uk/print/0,,330637492-110491,00.html.
15.   John R. Bradley, "Al Qaeda and the House of Saud: Eternal Enemies or secret Bedfellows?" *The Washington Quarterly*, Autumn 2005.
16.   Posner, *Secrets*.
17.   Ibid.
18.   Ibid.
19.   Charles Stuart Kennedy, "Interview with Ambassador Talcott W. Seelye," The Foreign Affairs Oral History Collection of the Association for Diplomatic Studies and Training, Library of Congress, September 15, 1993.
20.   Marie Colvin, "How an Insider Lifted the Veil on Saudi Plot for 'Islamic Bomb'," *Sunday Times*, July 4, 1994. See also "Saudi Arabia Country Profile," SIPRI, June 2004, http://www.sipri.org/contents/expcon/cnsc2sau.html and Ewen Askill and Ian Traynor, "Saudis Consider Nuclear Bomb," *Guardian*, September 13, 2003.
21.   "Saudi Arabia Country Profile," *SIPRI*, June 2004: http://www.sipri.org/contents/expcon/cnsc2sau.html. This report by the well-respected international arms watchdog cites reports from Saudi nuclear physicist and former Saudi diplomat Mohommed Khilewi, who defected to the United States in 1994, as well as reports from former CIA agent Robert Baer.
22.   "Flying to Arabia, Unarmed," *New York Times*, January 14, 1979.

23. Lawrence Wright, *The Looming Tower: al-Qaeda and the Road to 9/11*, (London: Penguin, 2007). See also "The Event That Inspired Al Qaeda" an interview with author Yaroslav Trofimov, November 22, 2007: Rediff.com.

24. Will Self, "Addicted to Arms," BBC, April 28, 2002: http://news.bbc.co.uk/2/hi/ programmes/correspondent/1939250.stm.

25. In 2002, Prince Nayef bin Sultan bin Fawwaz al-Shaalan was charged with using diplomatic immunity to smuggle two tons of coke into France on a Saudi royal plane.

Chapter 8. Kuwait: Lines in the Sand

1. Habibur Rahman, "Kuwaiti Ownership of Warba and Burbiyan Islands," *Middle Eastern Studies*, April 1, 1993.

2. The Saudis suggested that Kuwait give or lease Saddam one of their islands that he'd previously wanted to lease, but the United States shot down that idea. Jordan's King Hussein wanted to negotiate with Saddam, but Bush wouldn't give him his requested forty-eight hours. The Soviets tried to negotiate, but the United States wasn't listening.

3. Cheney had threatened to have President G. H. W. Bush veto the defense bill if funding for the Stealth bomber and defense shield wasn't provided, using Scud missiles fired at Israel during Desert Storm as a reason the space-based missile defense system was needed. See "Cheney Opposes a Budget without Stealth," AP report, *New York Times*, May 19, 1991.

4. Eric Schmitt, "House Panel Votes to Cut Off Bomber," *New York Times*, August 1, 1990.

5. Ambassador Chas Freeman, present at that meeting, admits that, in trying to simplify the situation for King Fahd, Cheney gave a black-and-white pitch for something that was actually many shades of gray. See Charles Stuart Kennedy, "Interview with Ambassador Chas W. Freeman," The Foreign Affairs Oral History Collection of the Association for Diplomatic Studies and Training, Library of Congress, April 14, 1995.

6. See Maggie O'Kane, "No casus belli? Invent one!" *Guardian Unlimited*, February 5, 2003.

7. Jamie Etheridge, "Why Kuwait Should Keep Its Oil Reserves Secret," *Kuwait Times*, July 11, 2007: http://www.kuwaittimes.net.

8. Yasmine El-Rashidi, "Easy Money: In Kuwait, Gush of Oil Wealth Dulls Economic Change," *Wall Street Journal*, November 4, 2005.

9. David Pollock, "Kuwait: Keystone of U.S. Gulf Policy," Washington Institute for Near East Policy, November 2007: http://www.washingtoninstitute.org/templateC04.php?CID=283.

10. El-Rashidi, "Easy Money," *Wall Street Journal*, November 4, 2005.

11. According to the Kuwait Fund for Arab Economic Development, the total amount loaned as of August 18, 2007, was 3,882,254,315 Kuwaiti dinar; the $14 billion figure reflects the exchange rate as of that date and does not account for inflation and fluctuations in currency values and exchange rates since 1961. See: http://www.kuwait-fund.org/e/about.asp.

12. See: El-Rashidi, "Easy Money," and Etheridge, "Why Kuwait Should Keep."

13. "Kuwait Says It Won't Be Launchpad for Strike in Iran," Reuters, June 11, 2007.

14. "Kuwait on Top of Al Qaeda Hit List," *Kuwait Times*, February 26, 2007; "Group Targets East Arabs," *Arab Times*, February 27, 2007; W. Andrew Terrill, "Kuwaiti National Security and the US-Kuwaiti Strategic Relationship after Saddam," *Strategic Studies Institute*, September 2007: http://www.strategicstudiesinstitute.army.mil/pdffiles/pub788.pdf.

15. Richard Burkholder, "Sixteen Years after Gulf War, Kuwaitis Cool Towards US," summary of Gallup poll conducted fall 2006, Gallup, February 27, 2007: http://www.gallup.com/poll/26713/Sixteen-Years-After-Gulf-War-Kuwaitis-Cool-Toward-US.aspx.

16. Ibid.

17. Fouad al-Obaid, "Crime and Punishment," *Kuwait Times*, October 8, 2006. Crime stats released by Ministry of Justice showed over three thousand crimes from March to May 2006.

18. Howard Schneider, "Kuwaitis Seek Role 10 Years after Invasion," *Washington Post*, July 31, 2000.

19. Henry Tanner, "Kuwait Searches for a Gulf Peace," *New York Times*, March 28, 1982.

20. Theodore H. Draper, "The True History of the Gulf War," *New York Review of Books*, January 20, 1992.

21. Tanner, "Kuwait Searches."

22. Ibid.

23. John Kifner, "Kuwait Dissolves Its Parliament," *New York Times*, July 4, 1986.

24. Stewart Ross, *Teach Yourself the Middle East Since 1995* (New York: McGraw-Hill, 2004).

25. Mary Ann Tétreault, *Stories of Democracy: Politics and Society in Contemporary Kuwait* (New York: Columbia University Press, 2000).

26. Estimate of Kuwait Information Ministry.

27. John R. MacArthur, *Second Front: Censorship and Propaganda in the Gulf War*, (Berkeley, CA: University of California Press, 1992).

28. Sources include, John R. MacArthur, "Remember Nayirah, Witness for Kuwait," *Seattle Post-Intelligencer*, January 12, 1992; John Stauber and Sheldon Rampton, *Toxic Sludge is Good for You* (London: Robinson, 2004). See also: http://www.prwatch.org/books/tsigfy10.html.

29. Eric Schmitt, "Israel Plays Down Effectiveness of Patriot Missiles," *New York Times*, October 31, 1991.

30. Estimate of former U.S. ambassador to Saudi Arabia Chas Freeman, who worked closely with General Norman Schwarzkopf during the 1991 Gulf War and was one of the first to survey the scene in Kuwait.

31. Interview with Ambassador Chas Freeman by Charles Stuart Kennedy, The Foreign Affairs Oral History Collection of the Association for Diplomatic Studies and Training, Library of Congress, April 14, 1995.

32. "The Pentagon's Information Warrior: Rendon to the Rescue," *PR Watch* (Center for Media and Democracy), Fourth Quarter 2001: http://www.prwatch.org/prwissues/2001Q4/rendon.html.

33. Tétreault, *Stories of Democracy*.

34. Youssef Ibrahim, ""Kuwaiti Emir, Tired and Tearful, Returns to His Devastated Land," *New York Times*, March 14, 1991.

35. Kenneth Roth, "Mass Graves in Kuwait," *New York Times*, June 11, 1991.

36. "Kuwait: Country Report," Economist Intelligence Unit, May 2007.

37. David Armstrong, "Dick Cheney's Song of America," *Harpers*, October 2002.

38. You can get the full scope of Cheney's far-out defense budget trail by doing a search for "Cheney" in the 1990 and 1991 *New York Times*. See also: Armstrong, "Dick Cheney's Song," and Eric Schmitt, "House Panel Votes to Cut Off Bomber," *New York Times*, August 1, 1990.

Chapter 9. Yemen: In Another World

1. In 2007, Transparency International's Corruption Perception Index, which ranks the cleanest countries at the top of the list, knocked Yemen down 20 spots to 111 out of 131 countries rated.
2. The high degree of corruption is noted by numerous international agencies. See "Country Evaluation: Yemen," United Nations Development Programme, 2005.
3. Fred Halliday, "The Third Inter-Yemeni War and Its Consequences," lecture to the British-Yemeni Society, London, October 11, 1994.
4. "U.S. critical of Yemen Money Laundering," *Al Sahwar*, July 14, 2007; "U.S. Report on Money Laundering Inaccurate," Al-Motomat.net, July 14, 2007: http://www.almotamar.net/en/3021.htm.
5. Jane Novak, "Journalism in Yemen: A Battle for Truth in the Age of Terror," Worldpress.org, September 7, 2005: http://www.worldpress.org/Mideast/2144.cfm.
6. Raidan Al-Saggat, "Yemen's Big Time Nuclear Fraud," *Yemen Times*, October 4, 2007.
7. To simplify complicated matters, here Wahhabi is used interchangeably with salafi, the umbrella term for fundamentalist Sunni.
8. Patrick Tyler, "Yemen, an Uneasy Ally Playing Off Old Rivalries," *New York Times*, December 19, 2002.
9. Ibid.
10. Jane Novak, "Al Qaeda Escape in Yemen," Worldpress.org, February 16, 2006: http://www.worldpress.org/Mideast/2267.cfm.
11. See roundup of articles on this period at "Context of May 21–July 7, 1994: North Yemen, Backed by U.S. and Bin Laden, Win Yemen War," Cooperative Research History Commons: http://www.cooperativeresearch.org/context.jsp?item=a052194yemencivilwar.
12. Ahmed al-Haj, "Lawyer for Accused *Cole* Plotters Presents Document Implicating Government," AP, August 25, 2004.
13. Tony Karon, "Yemen Strike Opens New Chapter in War on Terror," *Time*, November 5, 2002: http://www.time.com/time/world/article/0,8599,387571,00.html.
14. James Bamford, "He's in the Backseat!" *Atlantic*, April, 2006.
15. David Johnston and David Sanger, "Fatal Strike in Yemen Was Based on Rules Set Out by Bush," *New York Times*, November 6, 2002.
16. Novak, "Al Qaeda Escape in Yemen."
17. "Ali Saleh: Al Qaeda—Zionists," *al-Hayat*, July 12, 2007; See: http://armiesofliberation.com/archives/category/yemen/aexternal/other-countries/.
18. Jane Novak, author interview, January 2008.
19. John E. Burns, "Yemen Links to bin Laden Gnaw at FBI in *Cole* Inquiry," *New York Times*, November 26, 2000.
20. John Follain, "Biggest Bridge in the World . . ." *Sunday Times*, July 22, 2007.
21. "Piracy and Armed Robbery against Ships: Annual Report 2007," ICC International Maritime Bureau, January 2008.

Chapter 10. The United Arab Emirates: The Land of Possibilities

1. According to the Center for Strategic and International Studies (CSIS). See Anthony H. Cordesman and Khalid R. Al-Rodhan, "The Gulf Military Forces in an Era of Asymmetrical War: The United Arab Emirates," CSIS, June 28, 2006.
2. Sen. John Kerry and Sen. Hank Brown, "The BCCI Affair: A Report to the Committee on Foreign Relations," U.S. Senate, December 1992.

3. The *Economist's* 2008 "City Guide Dubai" notes the Russia-prostitution link and the Indian loan racket; others, including Ajai Sanni writing for the Asia Pacific Initiative, mention the Pakistan link.
4. Roula Khalif, "Dubai's Ruler Has Big Ideas for His Little City-State," *Financial Times*, May 4, 2007.
5. "Country Profile: The United Arab Emirates," Economist Intelligence Unit, 2006.
6. "Rashid bin Saeed Al Maktoum," Wikipedia.org.
7. "Tourism adds 22.6% to UAE Economy," *Gulf News*, March 9, 2008.
8. "Abu Dhabi Fund Attracts Attention on Wall Street," *International Herald Tribune*, February 27, 2008.
9. Lina Abdul Rahman, "Juvenile Crimes on the Rise," *Khaleej Times*, September 23, 2005.
10. See www.usuaebusiness.org.
11. "Nakheel Dismisses Branson Warning," *7 Days*, November 22, 2007.
12. Christopher Davidson, "The Emirates of Abu Dhabi and Dubai: Contrasting Roles in the International System," *Asian Affairs*, March 2007.
13. See blog "Secret Dubai": http://secretdubai.blogspot.com.
14. Bassma Al Jandely, "Sharjah Decency Law Takes Effect Today," *Gulf News*, September 26, 2001: http://archive.gulfnews.com/articles/01/09/26/27418.html.
15. Kenneth Katzman, "The United Arab Emirates (UAE): Issues for U.S. Policy," Congressional Research Service, May 9, 2005.

Chapter 11. Qatar: Trail Blazing

1. As reflected in terms of per capita GDP.
2. Hassan M. Fattah, "Arab States Wary of Iran, Add to Their Arsenal, but Still Lean on U.S.," *New York Times,* February 23, 2007.
3. John Mason, "Qatar to Pursue Case Against Ex-Emir," *Financial Times*, September 24, 1996.
4. Mary Anne Weaver, "Revolution from the Top Down," *National Geographic*, March 1, 2003.
5. So report Doha locals.
6. See: www.thedohadebates.com.
7. Weaver, "Revolution."
8. Rick Zednick, "Inside al Jazeera," *Columbia Journalism Review*, March/April 2002.
9. During the broadcast, Ayman al-Zawahiri (Osama bin Laden's right-hand man) continually closed his eyes, nodding off in a manner similar to those on heroin. His performance in that video leads one to wonder if reports were true that al Qaeda had developed a superstrong type of heroin.
10. Davan Maharaj, "How Tiny Qatar Jars Arab Media," *Los Angeles Times*, May 7, 2001.
11. David Hirst, "Backwater TV Station Rattles Arab World," *San Francisco Chronicle*, June 19, 2000.
12. EIU Country Report, Qatar, 2005.
13. Interview with author, November 2007.
14. "Gagging for the Truth," *Guardian*, November 24, 2005: http://www.guardian.co.uk/leaders/story/0,3604,1649144,00.html.
15. "Take Out al-Jazeera," *Fox News*, September 29, 2003: http://www.foxnews.com/story/0,2933,98621,00.html.

Chapter 12. Bahrain: A New Profile
1. Habib Tourmi, *Gulf News*, January 23, 2006.

Chapter 13. Oman: Awake at Last
1. Trade was mostly cut off after the 2000 Palestinian intifada triggered by Israeli Ariel Sharon.
2. Two women were elected to the majlis al shura in 2003; in the next election, no women were voted in.
3. Mark N. Katz, "Assessing the Political Stability of Oman," *Middle East Report*, September 2004. Dale F. Eickelman, "Kings and People: Information and Authority in Oman, Qatar, and the Persian Gulf," in *Iran, Iraq, and the Arab Gulf States*, ed. Joseph A. Kechichian (New York: Palgrave, 2001).
4. Joseph Fitchett, "Oman: Embassy Ahoy," *Saudi Aramco World*, May/June 1993: http://www.saudiaramcoworld.com/issue/198303/oman-the.terrain.htm.
5. "Country Profile: Oman," Economist Intelligence Unit, 2007.
6. *CIA World Factbook*.
7. Assorted country profiles, Economist Intelligence Unit, 2007.
8. *CIA World Factbook*.

Chapter 14. Israel: Fulfilling Prophecies
1. When Prime Minister David Ben-Gurion pronounced the creation of Israel in 1948, he noted that in accordance with the UN, the state was created "in virtue of the natural and historic right of the Jewish people," reflecting the biblical promise made between God and Abraham. Even though about half of Jews are secular according to a 2006 survey by the Dahat Institute—they adopt the culture but are not devout—the majority of secular Jews do hold religious beliefs. And even though Zionism (named after the mount in Jerusalem that symbolized the promised land) was in itself not a religious movement initially, it incorporated the belief that the historic home of Jews was the promised land. "As the joke goes," note Alain Gresh and Dominique Vidal in *The New A-Z of the Middle East*, "even atheist Israelis are forced to believe that God promised them the Holy Land" (p. 159).
2. Hamas, which controls Gaza, holds that Palestine was Allah's gift, to Arabs.
3. This figure is from *Palestine Monitor* and includes Israeli government-approved settlements and illegal outposts. According to the Israeli interior ministry, Israeli settlements in the West Bank alone grew by over 5 percent in 2007, to 282,000. See "Numbers of Settlers Rises by 5% in 2007," *Ynet*, January 20, 2008. The CIA estimated in July 2007 that 177,000 settlers lived in East Jerusalem.
4. "Israeli Minister Warns of Holocaust for Gaza if Violence Continues," *Guardian*, March 1, 2008: http://www.guardian.co.uk/world/2008/mar/01/israelandthepalestinians1. Deputy defense minister Matan Vilnai used the word "shoah," typically used only for the Holocaust during World War II.
5. About one hundred thousand barrels of oil per day are pumped.
6. "Solar Energy in Negev for Half of Israel," June 14, 2006: http://solar.rain-barrel.net/solar-israel/.
7. Warner D. Farr, LTC, U.S. Army, "The Third Temple's Holy of Holies: Israel's Nuclear Weapons," in *The Counterproliferation Papers*, Future Warfare Series No. 2, USAF Counterproliferation Center, Air War College, Air University, Maxwell Air Force Base, Alabama, September 1999: http://www.fas.org/nuke/guide/israel/nuke/farr.htm.
8. Steven Erlanger, "Israeli Ultra-Orthodox Drive a Thriving Kosher Economy," *International Herald Tribune*, November 2, 2007.

9. Benjamin Beit-Hallahmi, "The Secular Israeli Jewish Identity," *Religion in the News*, Spring 2003.
10. Paul Morro, "The Palestinian Territories," CRS, July 5, 2007.
11. Israeli Figures from Israel Ministry of Foreign Affairs
12. Jim Lobe, "Spy Probe Scans Neocons," Inter Press Service, September 1, 2004: www.commondreams.org/headlines04/0901-20.htm); Stephen Green, "Serving Two Flags," *Counterpunch*, February 28, 2004.
13. Tom Barry, "Israel's Man at the United Nations," International Relations Center, July 26, 2006.
14. As noted by John Mersheimer and Stephen Walt in "The Israeli Lobby," *London Review of Books*, March 10, 2006.
15. This statement, "You are either for or against us," made attempts at objectivity difficult for those of the United Nations Truce Supervisory Organization, as noted by General Carl Von Horn in Colin Chapman, *Whose Promised Land*? (Oxford: Lion Publishing, 2002). 183–4.
16. Farr, "The Third Temple's Holy of Holies: Israel's Nuclear Weapons."
17. Cheney was interviewed on MSNBC in January 2005. See Jim VandeHei, "Cheney Warns of Iran as Nuclear Threat," *Washington Post* January 21, 2005: http://www.washingtonpost.com/ac2/wp-dyn/A24677-2005Jan20?language=printer.
18. Caroline Glick, "The Abandonment of the Jews," *The Jerusalem Post*, December 6, 2007.
19. Interview with Ambassador Andrew Killgore, November 2007. And see Chris Hedges, "It's Time for a Declaration of Independence from Israel," *Alternet*, July 6, 2007.
20. "Many Americans Uneasy with Mix of Religion and Politics," Pew Forum on Religion and Public Life, August 22, 2006: http://pewforum.org/publications/surveys/religion-politics-06.pdf.

Chapter 15. Disappearing Act: The Palestinian Territories—the West Bank and Gaza

1. Under the British Mandate drawn in 1920, the original Palestine included the tract from the Mediterranean Sea to the Jordan River and beyond—originally including today's Jordan. However, the land that would become Jordan was sparsely populated—most Arab farmers lived between the sea and the river.
2. UNICEF figure, cited in Toni O'Loughlin, "International Blockades Threaten Palestinian Schools," UNICEF, August 29, 2006.
3. According to *Palestine Monitor*, in 2007 unemployment rates in Gaza were 44 percent. "Palestine Red Crescent: Working and Living under Siege in Gaza," *Palestine Monitor*, February 2, 2008. Other sources put the figure higher.
4. The higher figure was reported by Zaki Chehab, "Gaza: The Jailed State," *New Statesman*, May 2007.
5. "Children in Palestine," *Palestine Monitor*, August 4, 2007.
6. "The Closure of the Gaza Strip: The Economic and Humanitarian Consequences," United Nations Office for the Coordination of Humanitarian Affairs (OCHA), December 13, 2007: http://domino.un.org/pdfs/GSclosure.pdf.
7. Uprooting olive trees has been going on for decades. Extremist settlers, often followers of Rabbi Kahane, frequently attack groves, and the defense forces routinely uprooted them during the first intifada, which started in 1987, but road construction and the erection of the wall is making it worse: some eighty-three thousand trees have been uprooted because of the wall alone. See: "Settlement

Time Line, Settlement Report," Foundation for Middle East Peace, Nov.–Dec. 2007: http://www.fmep.org/reports/vol17/no6/04_settlement_timeline.html; "Country Profile: Palestinian Territories, 2006," Economist Intelligence Unit, July 2007; "The Intifada: An Overview: The First Two Years," Jerusalem Media and Communications Center, December 1989.

8. According to British military and security think tank Janes Information Group, Israeli settlers use three to five times as much water as the Palestinians, and Palestinians are forbidden from drilling wells; *Palestine Monitor* notes that many settlements are built directly over aquifers and springs. See: "Security, Gaza and West Bank," *Jane's Sentinel* (Jane's Information Group), December 28, 2008; "Israeli Settlements: Fact Sheet," *Palestine Monitor*, 2007.

9. Among those who believe the Israeli aggressions of the last few years are meant to run Palestinians out is King Abdullah of Jordan. This is a stated goal of many settler groups as well as the popular Rabbi Kahane, who launched a movement.

10. "Ruling Palestine I: Gaza Under Hamas," The International Crisis Group, March 19, 2008.

11. "Dignity Denied: In the Occupied Palestinian Territories," International Committee of the Red Cross, Nov. 2007; http://www.icrc.org/eng/palestine-report

12. United Nations special rapporteur on human rights John Dugard, as reported by *Palestine Monitor*, "Fact Sheet: The Gaza Strip," February 2008.

13. Figures reported by, B'TSelem: http://www.btselem.org/english/statistics/Casualties.asp.

14. "Number of Settlers Rises by 5% in 2007," *Ynet*, January 20, 2008.

15. "The Intifada: An Overview" Jerusalem Media and Communications Center.

16. Ibid.

17. B'Tselem, "Statistics: Fatalities," showing totals as of December 15, 2007.

18. Ibid.

19. "Security, Gaza and West Bank," *Jane's Sentinel*.

20. Darryl Li, "Disengagement and the Frontiers of Zionism," *Middle East Report*, February 16, 2008.

21. Neve Gordon, "The Militarist and Messiahnic Ideologies," *Middle East Report*, July 16, 2004.

22. Jeffrey Goldberg, "Among the Settlers," *New Yorker*, May 31, 2004.

23. Ibid.

Chapter 16. Lebanon: The Cedar Devolution

1. "President Bush Welcomes Prime Minister Siniora of Lebanon to the White House," White House press release, April 18, 2006

2. It's hard to calculate the exact job loss since Israel's 2006 attack, which caused businesses to close and hundreds of thousands to flee; some say actual unemploymentts is closer to 50 percent.

3. Many Maronite Christians consider themselves descendents of Phoenicians.

4. Muslim includes Shia, Sunni, Druze, Ismail, Alawite, and Nusayr.

5. Christians include Maronite, Greek Orthodox, Melkite Christian, Armenian Orthodox, Syrian Catholic, Syrian Orthodox, Chaldean, Assyrian, and Copt.

6. See Alfred B. Prados, *Lebanon*, Congressional Research Service, November 28, 2006; this report cites the religious estimates based on the work of Colbert C. Held, *Middle East Patterns* (New York: Westview Press, 2000).

7. CIA estimates.

8.   This finding has been confirmed in numerous polls since fall 2006. See also: Dan Murphy, "New Hero Emerge in Arab World," *Christian Science Monitor*, August 29, 2006; "Arab, Muslim World: President Bush Most Hated, Nasrallah Most Popular," *Israel Insider*, February 20, 2007.

9.   See: Kaveh L. Afrasiabi, "It's About Annexation, Stupid," *Asia Times*, August 15, 2006: http://www.atimes.com/atimes/Middle_East/HH05Ak01.html.

10. Seymour Hersh, "The Redirection," *New Yorker*.

11. Robert Fisk, "Secret Armies Pose New Threat to Lebanon," *Independent*, October 19, 2007.

12. Mitchell Prothero, "Beirut Bombshell," *Fortune*, May 15, 2006.

13. Gary C. Gambill, Ziad K. Abdelnour, "The Al-Madina Bank Scandal," *Middle East Intelligence Bulletin*, January 2004.

14. Edward J. Pound, "Following the Old Money Trail," *US News & World Report*, March 27, 2005.

15. Ibid.

16. Prothero, "Beirut Bombshell." See also Mitchell Prothero, "The Money Scandal Behind the Hariri Scandal," *Time*, October 27, 2005.

17. See: Max Rodenbeck, "Lebanon's Agony," *New York Review of Books*, June 28, 2007: http://www.nybooks.com/articles/20311.

18. Neil MacFarquhar, "Behind Lebanon's Upheaval, Two Men's Fateful Clash," *New York Times*, March 20, 2005.

19. "Hit Job in Beirut," *New York Times*, February 15, 2005.

20. Tony Karon, "Why Syria Feels the Heat From a Beirut Bombing," *Time*, February 15, 2005: http://www.time.com/time/world/article/0,8599,1028217,00.html.

21. Mary Wakefield, "A Revolution for TV," *Spectator*, March 12, 2005.

22. "Hezbollah Rallies Lebanese to Support Syria," CNN, March 9, 2005: http://www.cnn.com/2005/WORLD/meast/03/08/lebanon.syria/index.html.

23. Seymour Hersh, "Watching Lebanon," *New Yorker*, August 21, 2006.

24. Ibid.

25. "Israel: Lebanon Responsible for 'Act of War'," *Israel News Agency*, July 12, 2006: http://www.israelnewsagency.com/lebanonisraelhezbollahislamterrorismwar 77480713.html.

26. Chris McGeal, "Capture of Soldiers Was 'Act of War,' Says Israel," *Guardian*, July 13, 2006.

27. "More Aid Pledged to Lebanon as UN Calls Hezbollah Cowards," July 25, 2006.

28. Ibid.

29. Fouad Siniora, "End This Tragedy Now," *Washington Post*, August 9, 2006: http://www.washingtonpost.com/wp-dyn/content/article/2006/08/08/AR2006080800990 .html.

30. "Special Briefing on Travel to the Middle East and Europe," State Department transcript of press briefing by Secretary of State Condoleezza Rice, July 21, 2006; http://www.state.gov/secretary/rm/2006/69331.htm

31. "Briefing on Efforts to Stop Violence in Lebanon," transcript of press briefing in Jerusalem, July 30, 2006: http://www.state.gov/secretary/rm/2006/69720. htm.

32. Over a third of those interviewed considered that "besides Israel and Hezbollah, the U.S. is also involved either directly or indirectly in the war." Source: "Israel/ Lebanon Poll," Gallup International press release, August 28, 2006.

33. "Poll: 64% of Lebanese Say Opinion of U.S. Worsened After War," AP/*Haaretz*, November 14, 2006: http://www.haaretz.com/hasen/spages/787931.html.

Chapter 17. Syria: Crumbling Support

1. Seymour Hersh, "A Strike in the Dark," *New Yorker*, February 11, 2008.
2. Asad is sometimes spelled Assad.
3. "Country Report: Syria," Economist Intelligence Unit, 2006.
4. Estimated.
5. Author interview with Jake Kurtzer, spokesman for Refugees International, November 2007.
6. Andrew Lee Butters, "Syria," *Time*, March 1, 2007: http://www.time.com/time/magazine/article/0,9171,1595251,00.html?iid=sphere-inline-sidebar.
7. To distinguish between current president Bashar al-Asad, former president Hafez al-Asad, and former heir-apparent Basil al-Asad, this chapter refers to the Asads by their first names.
8. Among those questioned there: Syrian-born Canadian Maher Arar, who was never proven to have done anything questionable but was erroneously identified by the Canadian government as a suspected terrorist. The CIA picked him up in 2002 at JFK airport in New York and flew him on a CIA rendition for questioning in Syria, where he was kept for ten months and beaten frequently. See Alan Feuer, "Federal Judge Calls Rendition Process Outsourcing," *New York Times*, November 10, 2007: http://www.nytimes.com/2007/11/10/world/americas/10arar.html.
9. The pipeline was an "open secret" in the oil industry. Neela Banerjee with Felicity Barringer, "Iraq Pipeline to Syria No Big Secret, Experts Say," *New York Times*, April 17, 2003.
10. Tufts University history professor Gary Leupp notes this in "John Bolton: The Undiplomatic Diplomat," *Counterpunch*, April 25, 2005.
11. The Syrians would have much preferred American rule or, best yet, no foreign rule at all, found the King-Crane Commission, which traipsed through on a 1919 fact-finding mission for President Woodrow Wilson.
12. A Maronite always holds the position of president, a Sunni is premier, a Shia heads parliament in a ridiculously complex French-designed system that rarely works.
13. Gary C. Gambill, "Hooked on Lebanon," *Middle East Quarterly*, Fall 2005.
14. Douglas Jehl, "Ex-Officials Say Bolton Inflated Syrian Danger," *New York Times*, August 26, 2005.
15. Jim Lobe refers to it as a "pro-Likud group" in "Attack on Syria Has Neocon Fingerprings," October 13, 2003, which details one of several Israeli attacks on Syria.
16. Sami Moubayed, "Syria's One True Friend—Iran," *Asia Times*, July 12, 2006: http://www.atimes.com/atimes/Middle_East/HG12Ak01.html.
17. Gambill, "Hooked on Lebanon," *Middle East Quarterly*.
18. Ibid.
19. "Lebanese Minister Sues TV Anchor Over On-Air Gaffe," Reuters, June 15, 2007: http://www.reuters.com/article/oddlyEnoughNews/idUSL1577206020070615?feedType=RSS.
20. "Former Syrian Vice President Abd al Harim Khaddam: Syrian President Bashar al-Assad Threatened to Crush Rafiq al-Hariri," MEMRI TV transcript, December 31, 2005.
21. Jonathan Cook, "Why Did Israel Attack Syria?" *Counterpunch*, September 27, 2007.
22. "Syrian Ambassador to the U.S. Discusses Pressure to Withdraw from Syria," NewsHour Online, April 2, 2005: http://www.pbs.org/newshour/bb/middle_east/jan-june05/syria_3-02.html.

Chapter 18. Jordan: Stuck in the Middle

1. Alfred Prados, "Jordan: U.S. Relations and Bilateral Issues," Congressional report to Congress, Congressional Research Service, January 25, 2007. As noted here, according to Amnesty International ten suspects brought by the CIA to Jordan had been tortured, and others were subjected to extreme aggression while being questioned.
2. "USAID: Jordan—Summary of Achievements 1951–2004," *USAID Report*, August 2004. According to the report, USAID has dispersed grants of $2.3 billion between 1951 and 2004, including for water treatment and family planning campaigns.
3. Prados, "Jordan: U.S. Relations and Bilateral Issues," Congressional report.
4. Joseph Nevo, "Jordan, the Palestinians and the Al-Aqsa Intifada," *Civil War*, Autumn 2003.
5. Avi Shlaim "From the Desert He Rose," *Economist*, November 22, 2007.
6. Avi Shlaim, *The Politics of Partition* (Oxford: Oxford University Press, 1990).
7. Prados, "Jordan: U.S. Relations and Bilateral Issues," Congressional report.
8. "America's Image Slips, but Allies Share U.S. Concern Over Iran, Hamas," National Pew Global Attitudes Survey, June 13, 2006.
9. Jordanian attitude survey 2005. See also "Conflicting Views in a Divided World, 2006," *Pew Global Attitudes Project* (Pew Research Center), Fall 2006.
10. "Yes, We Do Have a Nuclear Program." Interview with King Abdullah II of Jordan," *Spiegel International*, November 19, 2007: http://www.spiegel.de/international/world/0,1518,518131,00.html.
11. Stephen Glain, "Exodus," *Nation*, June 11, 2007.
12. "Interview with King Abdullah II of Jordan," *Spiegel International*.
13. This box draws on a number of sources, including Nir Rosen, "Iraq's Jordanian Jihadis," *New York Times*, February 19, 2006; Mary Anne Weaver, "The Short Violent Life of Abu Musab Zarqawi," *Atlantic*, July/August 2006: http://www.theatlantic.com/doc/200607/zarqawi; Lawrence Wright, *The Looming Towers* (New York: Penguin, 2007).
14. Weaver, "The Short Violent Life of Abu Musab Zarqawi." Wright, *The Looming Towers*.
15. Scott McLeod, "Conversations: Jordan's Prince El Hassan Warns Against Taking Another Go at Iran," *Time*, September 17, 2007: http://time-blog.com/middle_east/2007/09/conversations_el_hassan_warns.html#comments.
16. So speculates Israeli site DEBKAfile. See "U.S. Diplomat Foley's Killers Were Palestinian," DEBKAfile, December 15, 2002.
17. Although not widely publicized in the United States, the event was reported in the Israeli press. See: Jonathan Broder, "Bibi the Bunglar," *Salon*, October 7, 1997: http://www.salon.com/news/1997/10/07news.html; P. R. Kumaraswamy, "Israel, Jordan and the Masha'al Affair," *Israel Affairs*, January 21, 2003: Greg Myre, "Leader of Hamas Killed by Israel in Missile Attack," *New York Times*, April 18, 2004.

Chapter 19. Egypt: Secret Society

1. As noted in "Sayyid Qutb," Wikipedia.org. "Amrika allati Ra'aytu" (America that I Saw) as quoted in Sayyid Qutb's *Milestones,* note 16.

Bibliography and Online Resources

Bibliography

Aburish, Said. *Nasser: The Last Arab.* New York: St. Martins, 2004.

———. *The Rise, Corruption and Coming Fall of the House of Saud.* London: Bloomsbury, 1994.

Adkins, Lesley and Roy. *The Keys of Egypt: The Race to Read the Hieroglyphs.* London: HarperCollins, 2001.

Al-Radi, Nuha. *Baghdad Diaries: A Woman's Chronicle of War and Exile.* New York: Vintage, 2003.

Al-Rasheed, Madawi. *A History of Saudi Arabia.* Cambridge: Cambridge University Press, 2002.

Amery, Hussein A. and Aaron T. Wolf. *Water in the Middle East.* Austin: University of Texas Press, 2000.

Andrew, Christopher. *For the President's Eyes Only: Secret Intelligence and the American Presidency from Washington to Bush.* London: HarperCollins, 1996.

Armstrong, Karen. *Islam: A Short History.* London: Phoenix, 2004.

———. *Jerusalem: One City, Three Faiths.* New York: Ballantine, 2005.

Asbridge, Thomas. *The First Crusade: A New History.* London: Simon and Schuster, 2005.

Bell, Gertrude. *The Desert and The Sown.* Boston: Beacon Press, 1987.

Bennis, Phyllis. *Before & After: U.S. Foreign Policy and the War on Terrorism.* Gloucestershire: Arris, 2003.

Bowden, Mark. *Guests of the Ayatollah: The First Battle in America's War with Militant Islam.* New York: Atlantic Monthly Press, 2006.

Brown, L. Carl, ed. *Diplomacy in the Middle East.* London: I. B. Tauris, 2004.

Chapman, Colin. *Whose Holy City? Jerusalem and the Israeli-Palestinian Conflict.* Oxford: Lion Books, 2004.

Cottrell, Leonard. *Lost Cities.* London: Pan, 1961.

———. *Wonders of Antiquity.* London: Pan, 1959.

Duncan, David Ewing, *The Calendar.* London: Fourth Estate, 1998.

Fernea, Elizabeth Warnock and Robert A., *The Arab World: Personal Encounters.* New York: Anchor Books, 1987.

Gerner, Deborah J. *Understanding the Contemporary Middle East.* London: Lynne Rienner, 2000.

Gettleman, Marvin E. and Stuart Schaar, eds. *The Middle East and Islamic World Reader.* New York: Grove Press, 2005.

Gies, Frances and Joseph. *Cathedral, Forge and Waterwheel: Technology and Invention in the Middle Ages.* New York: HarperPerennial, 1995.

Goldschmidt, Arthur. *A Concise History of the Middle East.* Cairo: The American University in Cairo Press, 2004.

Gresh, Alain and Dominique Vidal. *The New A-Z of the Middle East.* London: I. B. Tauris, 2004.

Harris, David. *The Crisis: The President, the Prophet and the Shah—1979 and the Coming of Militant Islam.* New York: Little, Brown, 2004.

Herodotus. *Snakes with Wings and Gold-digging Ants.* London: Penguin, 2007.

Highet, Juliet. *Frankincense: Oman's Gift to the World.* Munich: Prestel, 2007.

Hourani, Albert. *A History of the Arab People.* Cambridge: Belknap Press / Harvard, 1991.

Juhasz, Antonia. *The Bush Agenda.* New York: ReganBooks, 2006.

Karabell, Zachary. *Parting the Desert: The Creation of the Suez Canal.* New York: Random House 2003.

Kennedy, Hugh. *The Great Arab Conquests: How the Spread of Islam Changed the World We Live In.* Philadelphia: Da Capo Press, 2007.

———. *When Baghdad Ruled the Muslim World: The Rise and Fall of Islam's Greatest Dynasty.* Cambridge, MA: Da Capo Press, 2006.

Lamb, David. *The Arabs: Journeys Beyond the Mirage.* New York: Vintage, 1988.

Laqueur, Walter and Barry Rubin, eds. *The Arab-Israeli Reader.* New York: Penguin, 2001.

Leick, Gwendolyn. *Mesopotamia: The Invention of the City.* London: Penguin, 2001.

Mackey, Sandra. *The Iranians: Persia, Islam and the Soul of a Nation.* New York: Plume, 1998.

MacLeod, Roy. *The Library of Alexandria.* Cairo: The American University in Cairo Press, 2002.

Mansfield, Peter. *A History of the Middle East.* New York: Penguin, 2004.

Morgan, Michael Hamilton. *Lost History: The Enduring Legacy of Muslim Scientists, Thinkers and Artists.* Washington, D.C.: National Geographic Society, 2007.

Mostyn, Trevor. *Egypt's Belle Epoque.* London: Tauris Parke Paperbacks, 2006.

Nasr, Vali. *The Shia Revival.* New York: Norton, 2007.

Owen, Roger and Sevket Pamuk. *Middle East Economies in the Twentieth Century.* London: I. B. Tauris, 1998.

Palmer, Alan. *The Decline and Fall of the Ottoman Empire.* London: John Murray, 1995.

Pappe, Ilan. *The Modern Middle East.* London: Routledge, 2007.

Pax, Salam. *The Baghdad Blog.* London: Atlantic Books, 2003.

Phillips, Jonathan. *The Fourth Crusade and the Sack of Constantinople.* New York: Penguin, 2004.

Polk, William R. *Understanding Iraq.* New York: HarperCollins, 2006.

Pollard, Justin and Howard Reid. *The Rise and Fall of Alexandria: Birthplace of the Modern Mind.* New York: Viking, 2006.

Posner, Gerald. *Secrets of the Kingdom.* New York: Random House, 2005.

Qumsiyeh, Mazin B. *Sharing the Land of Canaan: Human Rights and the Israeli-Palestinian Struggle.* London: Pluto Press, 2004.

Riddell, Peter G. and Peter Cotterell. *Islam in Conflict.* London: InterVarsity Press, 2003.

Rodenbeck, Max. *Cairo: The City Victorious.* New York: Vintage, 1999.

Roux, Georges. *Ancient Iraq.* Middlesex: Penguin, 1972.

Sim, Katharine. *Desert Traveller: The Life of Jean Louis Burckhardt.* London: Phoenix Press, 2000.

Stark, Freya. *The Southern Gates of Arabia.* New York: The Modern Library, 2001.

Takeyh, Ray. *Hidden Iran.* New York: Henry Holt, 2006.

Thesiger, Wilfred. *Across the Empty Quarter.* London: Penguin, 2007.

————. *The Marsh Arabs.* London: Penguin, 1967.

Wallach, Janet. *Desert Queen.* New York: Anchor, 2005.

Wheatcroft, Andrew. *The Ottomans: Dissolving Images.* London: Penguin, 1995.

Woodward, Bob. *State of Denial.* London: Pocket Books, 2007.

Wright, Lawrence. *The Looming Tower: Al-Qaeda's Road to 9/11.* London: Penguin, 2007.

Yergin, Daniel. *The Prize.* New York: Free Press, 2003.

Online Resources

Alternet.org: Insightful alterna-press.

American ambassador interviews: Conducted by the Association for Diplomatic Studies and Training, these interviews are part of the American Memory series of the Library of Congress. Type a country name in the search engine and take a fascinating behind-the-scenes tour of American diplomacy. http://memory.loc.gov/ammem/collections/diplomacy/index.html.

B'Tselem: The Israeli Information Center for Human Rights in the Occupied Territories. http://www.btselem.org.

CIA—The World Factbook: This mini encyclopedia of countries gives reason to applaud the CIA. https://www.cia.gov/library/publications/the-world-factbook.

Columbia University's Middle East Internet resources: http://www.columbia.edu/cu/lweb/indiv/mideast/cuvlm.

Commondreams.org: A roundup of interesting articles from the alternative, mainstream, and/or foreign press.

Congressional Research Service reports: American tax dollars pay for these information-packed reports to Congress, but it's hard for taxpayers to find some reports about arms sales and foreign policy. The nonprofit organization Open CRS, http://opencrs.com, links to sites that post them, such as the Federation of American Scientists, http://www.fas.org/sgp/crs/index.html.

Cooperative Research History Commons: Tracks history via press reports. http://www.cooperativeresearch.org.

The Doha Debates: Qatar sponsors public debates on heated issues. http://www.thedohadebates.com.

Economist.com: Learn about the world painlessly; some articles are free.

Frontline: Watch shows, read transcripts, and get detailed info in posted interviews. http://www.pbs.org/wgbh/pages/frontline.

Guardian.co.uk: A stellar paper from London.

Israel Ministry of Foreign Affairs: http://www.mfa.gov.il/MFA.

The Middle East: The definitive source for the region's news. http://www.africasia.com/themiddleeast.

Mideastimage.com: Lots to ponder at this lovely site.

The New Library of Alexandria: The Bibliotheca Alexandrina looks like a spaceship and is putting a million books online with help from the United States and China. http://www.bibalex.org/English/index.aspx.

The New York Times: Archives go back to 1852, giving great context for deciphering history. http://www.nytimes.com.

Project Gutenberg: Read history from accounts written at the time they were created, from Mark Twain to Herodotus. http://www.gutenberg.org.

Saudi Aramco World: A fabulous magazine that keeps Middle Eastern history in the spotlight. http://www.saudiaramcoworld.com.

Special Inspector General for Iraq Reconstruction (SIGIR): Congress created it, but Bush, et al., tried to shut it down for tracking missing bucks. http://www.sigir.mil.

UNHCR: The UN Refugee Agency. Read it and weep. http://www.unhcr.org.

United States Department of State: http://www.state.gov. See "Issues and Press" and "Daily Press Briefings." http://www.state.gov/r/pa/prs/dpb/2008.

Index